At the Dawn of Modernity

At the Dawn of Modernity

Biology, Culture, and Material Life in Europe after the Year 1000

DAVID LEVINE

University of California Press

BERKELEY   LOS ANGELES   LONDON

University of California Press
Berkeley and Los Angeles, California

University of California Press, Ltd.
London, England

© 2001 by the Regents of the University of California

Library of Congress Cataloging-in-Publication Data

Levine, David, 1946–
    At the dawn of modernity : biology, culture, and material life in
Europe after the year 1000 / David Levine.
        p.   cm.
    Includes bibliographical references and index.
    ISBN 0-520-22058-7 (cloth : alk. paper)
        1. Civilization, Medieval.   2. Europe—Church history—
    600–1500.   3. Social history—Medieval, 500–1500.
        4. Human body—Social aspects—History.   I. Title.
CB351.L44   2001
940.1—dc21   00-034384

Printed in the United States of America

9 8 7 6 5 4 3 2 1

Contents

Preface

At the Dawn of Modernity got its inspiration from my aging mother's absolute confusion in trying to grasp the implications of twentieth-century social changes for the way that she lived during her last years. The writing of this social history got its energy from my desire to make my understanding of those "implications of social change" intelligible for Matthew and Rachel, to whom this work is lovingly dedicated.

I should also like to thank my eclectic network of academic colleagues—Donna Andrew, Ernest Benz, Stan Engerman, Chad Gaffield, John Gillis, Stan Holwitz, Ed Hundert, Catherina Lis, Kate Lynch, Angus McLaren, Hans Medick, Pavla Miller, Leslie Moch, David Sabean, Roger Schofield, Wally Seccombe, Ned Shorter, Hugo Soly, Louise Tilly, Keith Wrightson, and Zvi Razi—each in his or her own way, none in the same way; their intellectual comradeship has been invaluable over the years. I remember Andy Appleby fondly; his encouragement and the generous confidence he showed in my abilities still buoy my spirits. Charles Tilly stands *primum inter pares;* my academic godfather has always made himself available to me while being generous with his time, his criticisms, and his immense intellectual gifts.

Cathy Lace, Ron Silvers, and Hesh Troper stood by me during some crazy times while this book was written. Above all, Jennifer has had to listen to my stories about the ups and downs and the fits of exasperated frustration that any author endures. She has been patient, steadfast, confident, and ironically detached from it all. Who could ask for more?

Considering the Subject

The roots of the modern world can be located in the new kind of society that emerged after the year 1000—distinct from its ancient predecessors and its modern successors. This transition may have been provoked by changes in the network of social relations that were due to population growth and technical change, but once the transition was under way, both population growth and technical change became at least partly endogenous. Technical developments and, in particular, the division of labor were partly a response to the new climatic trends, spatial expansion, and deepening of market relations, but they were also partly a consequence of investment in improved equipment and superior management technologies.

Another way of conceiving of these interactions is by describing them as a positive feedback process—an autocatalytic cycle in which population grew partly in response to improved peasant prosperity, which it, in turn, enhanced. Material forces thus interacted with biological and cultural factors to frame the ways in which participants understood their actions. Indeed, many novel processes—religious and spiritual, legal and constitutional, social and economic, technological and demographic—recombined to create a social mutation. Together, these changes "played a decisive role in the emergence of the modern world."[1] For, as Jacques Le Goff writes, "In the history of civilizations, as in that of individuals, childhood is decisive. Much, if not everything, is then at stake."[2] To highlight the lineages of this

1. Judith Herrin, *The Formation of Christendom* (Princeton, 1987), 480. For a similar suggestion see R. I. Moore, "Duby's Eleventh Century," *History* 69 (1984): 36–49.

2. *Medieval Civilization 400–1500* (Oxford, 1988), 113. In another essay, Jacques Le Goff suggests a chronology that is quite similar to the one I am advancing; Le Goff, "For an Extended Middle Ages," in *The Medieval Imagination* (Chicago, 1988), 18–23.

mutation, I have avoided the normal periodization of European history by seeking the roots of *early modernization* in what is usually considered to be the high Middle Ages. This is an explicitly teleological procedure—assigning purpose and design to processes that were not conducted according to any kind of master plan. Indeed, it is good to recognize at the outset that "historical thinking is always teleological"[3] because, as E. H. Carr writes, "History properly so-called can be written only by those who find and accept a sense of direction in history itself. The belief that we have come from somewhere is closely linked with the belief that we are going somewhere. A society that has lost belief in its capacity to progress in the future will quickly cease to concern itself with its progress in the past."[4] In following this line of reasoning, I have discovered the origins of the world we have made one thousand years ago, in the reorganization of an earlier European world. The year 1000 ushered in an extended "historical moment" involving a lengthy and protracted process in which a new social formation took shape.

1.

At the Dawn of Modernity describes the first phase of early modernization, the protracted transition away from antiquity and toward the creation of a novel social formation. What is at issue in describing early modernization is not a factor-chain approach but rather a form of network analysis that pictures society as an interdependent whole. To construct this picture we need to concentrate on "the relations between the parts, rather than on the parts themselves. Instead of a causal chain we have a network of mutually dependent relationships; and these relationships are such that a change in any one of them will have clearly determinable effects upon the others."[5]

Social reproduction is ultimately based on a family system producing human capital and providing the substructure of all social relations.[6] *At the*

---

3. Johan Huizinga, quoted in E. H. Carr, *What Is History?* (Harmondsworth, 1961), 108.

4. Carr, *What Is History?*, 132. Carr seems to be predicting that our lack of confidence in the present would lead to intellectual fascinations with post-modernism, new historicism, and the end of history that have been so dominant since the social democratic vision disintegrated.

5. Edward J. Nell, "Economic Relationships in the Decline of Feudalism: An Examination of Economic Interdependence and Social Change," *History and Theory* 6 (1967): 313–350.

6. I would be remiss not to mention that my own earlier studies on the demographic history of English industrialization provided the starting point for the way I would frame the argument by directing my attention to those parts of the past

Dawn of Modernity turns on a vision of historical experience in which demographic relations structure daily life. The key intersection between social formations and family formations occurs at the points of reproduction: demographic, cultural, social, and political. Marriage is the key demographic event; it is the moment at which families are divided and recombined anew.

Families have always been in a strategic balance between the centrifugal push of individual members—resulting from the contradictory requirements of their age-graded and gendered roles—and the centripetal pull of the primary domestic unit's role as the ultimate guarantor of both physical security and personal identity. Various elements are combined and recombined during the process of reproduction. Inevitably, mutations occur. In nature, mutations occur constantly, and it is only after the fact—in the struggle for survival and the descent of species—that we can determine their success or failure. Social formations and state formations—just like family formations—also mutate. Societies, states, and families divide and recombine. The mere existence of mutation, however, is not by itself sufficient to explain change; mutations are only the necessary precondition for change. The context in which mutations occur and develop is crucial.

The reproduction of families took place in relation to control over and access to material resources while being conditioned by cultural expectations that played a crucial part in the way in which individuals understood the timing of marriage to be related to age, gender, birth order, and the resources made accessible to the young couple by the parental generation. The creation of a new family thus hinged on the availability of resources that made it possible to create another niche in the social order. In demographic statistics we capture the outward signs of immense social movements because the transformation of reproductive patterns was part of a massive shift in the nature of social relations.[7]

---

that led to my own period. My main area of specialization has been the history of England, which probably accounts for the fact that I emphasize its history more than that of other countries.

7. Social evolution was the product of selective adaptation to local circumstances—creative mutations—which flourished in the relative freedom of peripheral frontier zones where both regulation and custom were more flexible. The very ways in which societies change have their own logical structures. Because diversity depends less on the isolation of various groups than on the relations between them, the process of modernization is reproduced as local diversity; Marshall Sahlins, "Goodbye to *Tristes Tropes:* Ethnography in the Context of Modern World History," *Journal of Modern History* 65 (1993): 1–25. At this point in the argument it is perhaps useful to quote "Darwin's Bulldog," Thomas Henry Huxley, to the effect

Demographic statistics are like the sea foam, not the deeper historical currents. When we stand on the shoreline amid the crashing waves it is hard not to be impressed by the surf, but as we go out further and the shoreline recedes beyond the horizon, the surface is calmer even though the tidal flows still course deep below the spume. To chart transformations of human social life it is necessary to probe these ocean depths. The fact that the demographic transition has taken place on the dry land of modern history no more precludes an understanding of its submarine origins than does the paleontologist's study of the origin of life on earth narrow that field of study to terrestrial creatures. In both instances, extended moments of change punctuated states of equilibrium to bring about fundamental evolutionary developments. In both instances, what went on below the ocean surface is crucial to understanding those extended moments during which the helical strands first separated and then recombined anew.[8]

---

that "The more we learn of the nature of things, the more evident is it that what we call rest is only unperceived activity; that seeming peace is silent but strenuous battle. In every part, at every moment, the state of the cosmos is the expression of a transitory adjustment of contending forces; a scene of strife, in which all the combatants fall in turn. What is true of each part, is true of the whole"; quoted in Jonathan Weiner, *The Beak of the Finch* (New York, 1994), 83.

8. Successful mutations can have dramatic—revolutionary—results, although the evolutionary success of each mutation depends on the context in which it occurs. Stephen Jay Gould has popularized the term "punctuated equilibrium" to propose that while there is a constant rate of molecular reproduction at the cellular level, mutations are infrequent occurrences. Rather than a smoothly gradual model of change, the theory of punctuated equilibrium suggests a jerky and episodic model of change, like stepping up a flight of stairs rather than rolling up an inclined plane. On this point regarding the historically contingent construction of biological evolution, see Stephen Jay Gould, *Wonderful Life: The Burgess Shale and the Nature of History* (New York, 1989). In addition, see the original formulation of the theory of punctuated equilibrium in the essay which Gould coauthored with Niles Eldredge, "Punctuated Equilibria: An Alternative to Phyletic Gradualism," in T. J. M. Schopf (ed.), *Models in Paleobiology* (San Francisco, 1972), 82–115. It is interesting to note that the same language was used by Henri Pirenne in 1914: "History does not present itself to the eye of the observer under the guise of an inclined plane; it resembles rather a staircase, every step of which rises abruptly above that which precedes it. We do not find ourselves in the presence of a gentle and regular ascent, but of a series of lifts"; "Stages in the Social History of Capitalism," *American Historical Review* 19 (1914): 495. Mutations develop successfully only when conditions will allow; we cannot begin to predict the path of change, but we can describe it. The reproduction of social order takes place both temporally and spatially. Drawing on Gould's concept of punctuated equilibrium, Robert Dodgshon has argued that social systems are more likely to mutate in peripheral regions where constraints are less rigid or in conditions where the prior restraints have broken down. The geographer's spatial grid thus provides a necessary complement to the chrono-

2.

State formation and class formation have been identified as two of the key master-processes of social development in the modern era.[9] Three others—mastery of the material world, the invention of the privatized family, and the technology of knowledge—cannot be ignored from a social history of modernization. Modernization was an extended process that took place in three phases—first, breaking with antiquity to establish the foundations of a new kind of society; second, extending European capitalism and its system of state formation from the core across the face of the globe; and third, the most recent stage of industrialization and mass modernization, which has dominated the past century. This book focuses on the first of these stages to give depth—and diachronic emphasis—to the way that modernization took place in the context of early modern European history. Throughout the text, I will be emphasizing the year 1000 as a shorthand way of designating the onset of an extended historical moment; in fact, the year 1000 was at the cusp of a lengthy and protracted process of transition in which a new social formation took shape.

At the Dawn of Modernity ends with the cataclysm unleashed by the Black Death in 1348. In the aftermath of the social earthquake triggered by the Eurasian epidemic, a revised social landscape was fashioned. Fernand Braudel writes cogently on this point:

> the disasters of the Black Death and the awe-inspiring recession of the mid-fourteenth century . . . [were] a spectacle of this disintegration, this headlong tumble into darkness—the greatest drama ever registered in European history. More catastrophic tragedies have indeed occurred in the course of the world's long existence. . . . But nowhere else did a disaster of such magnitude engender such a recovery; that uninterrupted

---

logical progression of the historian—an "epigenetic paradigm of social evolution." Combining these two ways of seeing provides a perspective on European social change, a scheme in which "the early stages of social evolution can be seen in terms of whole systems leap-frogging each other towards greater complexity"; the complexity of this "multiple acephalous federation" provided the context in which changes within—and between—the system's competing parts created a different dynamic; Dodgshon, *The European Past: Spatial Evolution and Spatial Order* (London, 1987), 361. On the characterization of European society as a "multiple acephalous federation," see Michael Mann, *A History of Power from the Beginning to A.D. 1760*, vol. 1, *The Sources of Social Power* (Cambridge, 1986), chaps. 12–14. For a provocative discussion of some ways in which the interaction of center and periphery creates turbulence and thereby leads to social change and mutation, see Patrick L. Baker, "Chaos, Order, and Sociological Theory," *Sociological Inquiry* 63 (1993): 123–49.

9. Charles Tilly, *As Sociology Meets History* (New York, 1981), 212.

movement which began in the mid-fifteenth century and led eventually to the industrial revolution and the economy of the modern state.[10]

After the Black Death, Europe entered a new historical epoch. In a nutshell, "Here was the turning point, not in the history of Europe (that happened around 1000) but in the history of the world, from which Dante's heirs went out to conquer new continents over the next four centuries."[11]

Beginning in the late eighteenth century, a third change in social organization ushered in the age of mass modernization. Insofar as one can write this history in purely technological terms, its most impressive characteristic is the almost complete predominance of English innovations in the crucial sectors of energy substitution and, particularly, the transformation of that energy into motion. Human mastery over the material world was "as great a human exploit as Athens."[12] If the English experience of early modernization was the pacemaker directing Western historical development, its influence peaked after three generations of industrialization when it had

10. Fernand Braudel, *The Perspective of the World* (New York, 1984), 314–15. I wonder what Braudel had in mind when he wrote that "More catastrophic tragedies have indeed occurred in the course of the world's long existence." In terms of human lives lost, I think the only other tragedy that was comparable in magnitude to the Black Death was the post-Columbian invasion of the Americas. No European historian can fully appreciate this impact without reading Alfred Crosby, *The Columbian Exchange: Biological Consequences of 1492* (Westport, 1972) and its companion *Ecological Imperialism: The Biological Expansion of Europe, 900–1900* (Cambridge, 1986).

11. Robert Fossier (ed.), "Introduction," in *The Cambridge Illustrated History of the Middle Ages, 1250–1520* (Cambridge, 1987). While we may still marvel at the audacity and hubris of these early modern Europeans, it is crucial to bear in mind that "It would take a vastly superior European technology, and a capacity for the control of space far beyond sixteenth-century logistical possibilities, for a united world to become even superficially a European world. Insofar as this was achieved at all, it would be achieved only in the nineteenth century"; J. H. Elliott, "The World after Columbus," *New York Review of Books*, October 10, 1991, 13.

12. Benjamin Disraeli, *Coningsby*, book IV, chap. 1; quoted in Stephen Marcus, *Engels, Manchester and the Working Class* (New York, 1974), 38. Although, as Daniel Chirot has written,

> to consider England in isolation, simply because it industrialized first, and for about a century led European technological and economic progress is to miss the point of the long period of Western advances which preceded the eighteenth and nineteenth centuries. . . . Later industrialization could not have occurred had markets of all sorts not achieved such a high state of development in pre-industrial Europe: capital markets; land markets; labor markets; commodities markets; and even, by analogy, a kind of intellectual market for new ideas, important thinkers and artists, and technological innovations. . . . [W]ithout the preceding millennial rise of the West, the story of England's industrial revolution would have been entirely unthinkable. ("The Rise of the West," *American Sociological Review* 50 (1985): 181–95).

created a revolutionary solution to the population/resources squeeze that had been so characteristic of the pre-modern world. In the succeeding period of full-scale mass modernization, the historical record is one of social convergence; in that context the particularities of the English become rather less important historically, if no less important in terms of lived experience.[13]

3.

My own way into the subject started with the paradox that the experience of the past two centuries has disproved Edmund Burke's gloomy foreboding that "the labouring people are only poor because they are numerous. Numbers in their nature imply poverty. In a fair distribution among a vast multitude, none can have much."[14] If anything, the opposite has been true. Joseph Livesay was born in 1795, the year that Burke penned his tendentious prognostications regarding the impossibility of plebeian social advancement. Livesay's autobiography reveals the lie in Burke's claims, noting that when he was growing up there were "no National Schools, no Sunday schools, no mechanics institutes, no cheap newspapers, no free libraries, no penny postage, no temperance societies, no tea parties, no Young Men's Christian Associations, no people's parks, no railways, no gas, no anything in fact that distinguishes the present time [c. 1870] in favour of the improvement and enjoyment of the masses."[15] Of course, when Livesay died there were no central heating systems, no light bulbs, almost no indoor plumbing or clean water or toilet paper, no radios, no movies, no automobiles, no airplanes, no cheap and reliable birth control, no painkillers, no sulfa drugs, no public medical insurance, no unemployment insurance, no statutory holidays, no sick days, no adult suffrage, no free schooling, and most assuredly no computers or Coca-Cola—"no anything in fact that distinguishes the present time in favour of the improvement and enjoyment of the masses." Such lists, which could be endlessly ex-

13. On this point I take issue with my good friend Susan Watkins, who has suggested that the role of the modern state is the primary force distinguishing citizens of Germany, say, from those of Italy. I am not unconvinced that Germans and Italians display differences, but rather I am more impressed that these differences are so much smaller than would have been the case in the nineteenth century, or before. See Watkins, *From Provinces to Nations*, (Princeton, 1990).

14. Edmund Burke, *Details on Scarcity* (1795; reprint, London, Henry G. Bohm, 1855), 634; quoted by Donna T. Andrew, *Philanthropy and Police: London Charity in the Eighteenth Century* (Princeton, 1989), 182.

15. Joseph Livesay, *Autobiography of Joseph Livesay* (London, National Temperance League Publications, c. 1870), 5–6.

tended, have a limited value, yet they underline the point that the last two centuries have been a time of spectacular material advance and remarkable increases in the very experience of living.

People born in 1750 had a life expectation at birth of around thirty-five years. Of one hundred children born alive, almost one-half either died before marrying or never married. Survivors spent most of their adult lives with little children underfoot so that the typical woman was usually either pregnant or nursing a child from marriage right through menopause. People born in 1750 would expect to die about twelve years before the birth of their first grandchild; we usually live twenty-five years after the birth of our last grandchild. The pre-modern life-cycle was thus compressed by the sheer weight of reproductive imperatives. For women, in particular, these changes in life expectation have radically altered the contours of lived experience—now, two-thirds of women's adult years will be spent without children in the household, and possibly half to two-thirds without a husband.[16]

The dominant explanatory paradigm employed by social scientists to explain the unexpected and somewhat paradoxical evolution of modernity turns on a definition of modernization which is constructed of polarized antinomies—public/personal, traditional/modern, pre-industrial/industrial, rural/urban, popular culture/rationality. These schematic dichotomies are deployed to distinguish the modern world from its traditional precursor. For the social historian modernization theories are problematic because schematic dichotomies tend to telescope the past, to flatten its narrative structure, and to lose sight of its contingent contextualization. Furthermore, recent historical scholarship has drawn our attention away from public struggles and toward the reproduction of daily life, away from the political and toward the personal. It is thus relevant to note that the transformation of reproduction patterns was part of a massive shift in the nature of social relations—just like the Industrial Revolution, urbanization, the doubling of life expectation, the institutionalization of mass society, the politicization of war, and the militarization of the world economy, all of which took place contemporaneously with it.

Modernization theory has been half right in assessing the benefits of massive historical change, but it has been half wrong in ignoring its costs.

16. Michael Anderson, "The Emergence of the Modern Life Cycle in Britain," *Social History* 10 (1985): esp. 72 ff.; Kingsely Davis and Pietronella van den Oever, "Demographic Foundations of New Sex Roles," *Population and Development Review* 8 (1982): 508; see also Susan Cotts Watkins, Jane Menken, and John Bongaarts, "Demographic Foundations of Family Change," *American Sociological Review* 52 (1987): 346–58.

These costs were not incurred once and for all but have been a persistent feature of modern society, which may have succeeded in making it possible for some people, some of the time, to rise from want but has yet to exert any effort in making it possible for all to enjoy the full benefits of modernization all the time. Moreover, capital accumulation was as much a cultural process as it was a method of fiscal extraction. It was, in fact, a "long arduous process of education"[17] transforming nobles and peasants into capitalists and proletarians while recasting the personalities of everyone into citizens and consumers.

There is a vast literature on "modernization theory." I prefer to keep the term while finding Marc Raeff's definition most useful because of its emphasis on human capital formation:

> modernization is that attitude of mind and that form of conduct that aim at maximizing and making full use of the potential resources of a society for an ongoing increase (whether it be considered an improvement or not) of its material and cultural creativity, promoted both for the benefit of its members and for the creativity's own sake.[18]

For William Greg, who lived in the midst of these changes, social life was coming to be experienced in terms of high pressure involving "an amount and continued severity of exertion of which our grandfathers knew little." In the words of this contemporary witness, "the most salient characteristic of life in the latter portion of the 19th century is its SPEED."[19]

Modernization theory captures something of this change, but it is politically compromised, neglectful of agency, and lacking in depth in its account of the making of modern history. As well, the theory of modernization is in bad odor because it smells of both the social engineer and the cold warrior. Yet, there is a decided similarity in the way in which both marxists and modernizers have construed the problematic: how has economic growth/modern industrial capitalism fundamentally changed social relations? Modernizers have privileged its benefits; marxists have been quick

17. Max Weber, *The Protestant Ethic and the Spirit of Capitalism* (New York, 1968), 62.

18. Marc Raeff, *The Well-Ordered Police State: Social and Institutional Change through Law in the Germanies and Russia, 1600–1800* (New Haven, 1983), 120 n. 150.

19. William Greg, quoted in Walter Houghton, *The Victorian Frame of Mind* (New Haven, 1957), 7. Greg wrote in 1875, when these changes were only just beginning to take hold. An endless mountain of citations could be proffered to corroborate his view that contemporaries were aware of, and disturbed by, the massive shift in social relations that was occurring in their lives.

to point out its costs.[20] Moreover, both schools of thought have tended to look at social change from a top-down perspective, privileging structural relationships and systemic forces at the expense of historical experience. For a social historian, this top-down perspective is problematic.

Social change was experienced by thinking people who reflected on it and changed their behavior with regard to it. Of course, causal arrows also flowed in the other direction: changing forms of behavior modified social systems. Whether or not we prefer "systematic history," the play of circumstances gives shape and motion to the systematic structures.[21] One cannot study the one without the other. The best that historians can hope to do is to specify the various combinations in which the individual and the social confront one another. The key point is that the historian is concerned with both the diachronic and the synchronic character of historical experience, always aware of the essential point that History itself is a "variable."[22] Seeing things in this way enables us to apprehend "the crucial ambivalence of our human presence in our own history, part subjects, part objects, the voluntary agents of our involuntary determinations."[23] The social construction of decision making connects the private behavior of individuals to the wider networks of intersecting and overlapping relationships in which everyone is enmeshed. Yet individual experience is intractably problematic—no readable history can be simply the regurgitation of one damn thing after another; history is something more than "the essence of innumerable Biographies."[24] Or, as Richard Cobb put it, "Nothing could be further from my intentions than to drill the *petit peuple* into tight formation, march them up the hill, and march them down again."[25]

20.   Ian Roxborough, "Modernization Theory Revisited," *Comparative Studies in Society and History* 30 (1988): 753–61. Michael Mann similarly suggests that the supposed opposition between neo-classical theories of modernization and marxist theories of social change is rather more rhetorical than real; *The Sources of Social Power*, 410. For a similar line of argument, see also Theda Skocpol, *States and Social Revolutions: A Comparative Analysis of France, Russia, and China* (Cambridge, Mass., 1979), esp. 3–43.

21.   Emmanuel Le Roy Ladurie, *The French Peasantry, 1450–1660* (Berkeley and Los Angeles, 1987), 118.

22.   Royden Harrison, "Introduction," *Independent Collier: The Coal Miner as Archetypal Proletarian Reconsidered* (Hassocks, Sussex, 1978), 14.

23.   E. P. Thompson, "The Poverty of Theory: Or an Orrery of Errors," in *The Poverty of Theory and Other Essays* (London, 1978), 280.

24.   Thomas Carlyle, quoted by George A. Reisch, "Chaos, History, and Narrative," *History and Theory* 30 (1991): 7 n. 13.

25.   Richard Cobb, *The Police and the People: French Popular Protest 1789–1820* (Oxford, 1970), xvii. Cobb goes on to write that "My subject is chaotic, and I may well have written about it chaotically!" I can only hope to be able to present such a chaotic argument in what will follow.

4.

In contrast to Burke's bleak prediction and the dismal science of Malthusian political economy, modern society is distinguished from its predecessor by its potential democratization of both its wealth and its political process. This state of affairs—with its attendant individual freedoms and responsibilities—is of very recent origin, although that is not to say that equality prevails in modern societies; rather, there is today quite simply nothing like the inequalities that prevailed in the past.[26] Furthermore, our modern society is premised on its ideology of equality whereas earlier social formations were not only unequal but also explicitly patriarchal, in the sense that they were organized by the Fourth Commandment's injunction to honor fathers (and mothers). This massive shift in social relations dominated the lives of the last generations of the nineteenth century and the first generations of the twentieth century. To my way of thinking, it is mistaken to concentrate on only the most recent—and most visible—manifestations of modernization. Here, I think, it is relevant to refer to Fernand Braudel's comment that

> The almost complete elimination from our vocabulary of the word *progress* is to be regretted in this context. It had almost the same meaning as development, and a convenient distinction could be made (convenient that is to historians) between *neutral* progress (that is without alteration to existing structures) and *non-neutral* progress—which broke down the framework within which it had developed.[27]

At the Dawn of Modernity takes it for granted that there was a known way forward from antiquity, through the long transitional stage of early modernization, culminating in modernity. Of course, that "known way forward" is known to us—we are fortunate to be living on the sunlit plains of late modernity—but it was quite obviously unknown (and unknowable) to those who lived in the express train shuttling through the unredeemed time of early modernization.[28]

---

26. It is my firm opinion that we live in a more democratic world than did our ancestors. This is not to say that our world is without inequalities but rather that these contemporary inequalities are different in both kind and number from those specters which haunted past generations. It is probably more likely that a revolution in rising expectations has made the remaining inequalities seem the more unnecessary and, so, distasteful.

27. Braudel, *The Perspective of the World*, 304.

28. In this sentence I have borrowed language and phraseology from E. P. Thompson, "The Peculiarities of the English," in *The Poverty of Theory and Other Essays*, 86.

Historical writing is an attempt to stop a moving process and to give it shape. Historical writing is therefore a reflection of the author's understanding of the present and the way that it emerged. No two accounts are going to be the same. Moreover, and much more important, in attempting to give shape to the past we condense and therefore we simplify. This is inevitable. Historical processes are the construction of historians; history proceeds along a rather different set of tracks in which one damn thing led to another in a continuously mutating condition of self-adjustment.

> The texted Past is always beached in Presents that always re-invent it. It is never absolutely within the time of one culture: there is a joining as well as a division between Past and Present. But be wary of those who claim to understand this double helix of now and then.
> Texting the Past—and that by making History—is always one-sided and selective. . . . The Past is never likely to recognize itself in History, any more than natives are likely to recognize themselves in ethnography.[29]

Historians do not usually confront the totality of the past—every period has its champions, every system has its students, every hero has her or his advocates, and every group has its partisans. In this way, historians reduce the multiplicity of events into order.

Acknowledging this difference in perspective between the historian and the subjects of historical study is a necessary cost that must be absorbed to enjoy the benefit of employing a bifocal optic which keeps in view both the context of social experience and the end-product of social change. This dualistic approach highlights not only what is relevant but also what is important. This optic distinguishes the social experience of those who lived in the period of early modernization from both their ancient predecessors and their modern descendants.

5.

The argument of *At the Dawn of Modernity* has been subdivided into five main sections.

First, in "Lineages of Early Modernization," I focus on the social upheaval of the year 1000 which transformed not only the organization of power and dependency in the lives of their plebeian subjects but also the relationship between the aristocratic rulers of the state and the church. "The Feudal Revolution" is a top-down discussion of the violent imposi-

---

29. Greg Dening, *The Death of William Gooch: A History's Anthropology* (Honolulu, 1995), 24.

tion of a new system of control that caught the rural population in its empire of subjugation. Furthermore, the feudal revolution was based on an unequal contract between lords and peasants; this inequality looked backward to the slave models that had given ancient society its flavor while the contractual elements looked forward to modern legal relations. The organization of social power in early modern society, then, was a hybrid which blended its inheritance of subjugation with its promise of future liberation. The Gregorian Reformation, too, combined discordant elements—the act of "Re-forming Christendom" looked back to ancient models of apostolic purity while looking forward to the time when interpretation of the Christian gospels would be freed from clerical controls. At the same time, the Gregorian Reformation made Christianity the religious framework of everyday life by imbricating its routines into the daily rhythms of the population. If Christianity was not completely successful in creating a flock of believers, it was not for lack of trying. The missionary zeal of the Gregorian Reformation brought early modern Christianity into the lives of Europeans in a way that was totally novel, distinguishing its thrust from the monastic spirituality that dominated the age of late antiquity.

Second, "Shards of Modernity" considers the ways that political and cultural early modernization interacted with the material world. The first part of this chapter, "Technologies of Power," looks at state formation practices—the organized monopoly of violence pursued by secular and papal governments—as well as administrative innovations sparked by the introduction of literacy and bureaucratic routines. The second part, "Sailing on the Tide of History," considers the ways that urbanization and commercial relations acted as a solvent on the rural society envisioned by feudalism. "Positive Feedbacks," the third part of the second chapter, is concerned with the interplay among population growth, land clearance, and modes of production that combined to transform the relationship between the ancient Mediterranean core and the northwestern periphery. In the dozen generations that lived between the year 1000 and the Black Death, the spatial balance in Europe shifted northward and westward. By the fourteenth century, Europe had evolved into a bipolar social system: the Mediterranean nucleus was now counterbalanced by a northwestern counterpart. This spatial reorganization had enormous implications for the internal structure of European society as well as setting the stage for the globalism that would take place when recovery from the Black Death got under way in the fifteenth century.

Third, "Living in the Material World" is concerned with the social conditions in which the rural majority of the population lived. "The Seigneurial Mesh" is a bottom-up discussion of the imposition of servitude resulting from the feudal revolution of the year 1000. I then move on to consider the gradations of servitude which developed over time. In addition, the changing character of social relations is examined in relation to such issues as the incidence and costs of personal unfreedom, the profitability of servitude, the enforcement of discipline, and the resistance to it. "Degrees of Unfreedom" analyzes the relationship between labor services and wage work, with particular reference to the English experience because the survival of its manorial documents is exceptional. Additionally, the inflections caused by geographical factors, cropping systems, and local patterns of lordship and domination are taken into account to explain the differentiation among the peasantry by comparing the idealized peasant farmer with the historical record. The pressures of downward social mobility are then discussed in relation to diminishing returns brought about by land hunger, population pressure, and changing climatic conditions that came to a head around 1300, two generations before the Black Death.

Fourth, "Reproducing Feudalism" reviews the interaction between the formation of early modern social relations of production and the family formations of the peasantry. "Thinking with Demography," the first part of this chapter, sets forth an explanation for the emergence of the European marriage pattern that was characterized by late ages at first marriage for women. This system of reproduction was a unique feature of social life in the northwestern region of Europe, and its contextualized explication is a major goal of this essay. The next section, "Strong Stems/Weak Branches," provides a framework for understanding the reproduction of the peasant family in feudal society and, in particular, the forces that led to population growth after the year 1000. Here again, the survival of documentary evidence from manorial court rolls is the reason why this section is largely, though not exclusively, concentrated on English experience. "The Limits of Patriarchy" next turns our attention to the inner dynamics of family formation. It begins with a discussion of peasant housing and then considers the tension between the ideals of patriarchal domination and the reality of marriage strategies. This chapter also talks about the way that gender was constructed—and contested—within the peasant family as well as considering the exercise of domestic power, with special reference to the role of violence in everyday interpersonal relations.

Fifth, "Negative Feedbacks" is concerned with the reorganization that took place in the wake of the Black Death. "The Bacteriological Holocaust" provides a discussion of the initial impact and demographic implications of the recurrent visitations of the plague. "Luxuriant Despair" describes how the generations living in the shadow of the Black Death reworked the early modern discourse on holiness. Internalized feelings of guilt and anxiety about the Church's promise of salvation were combined with its macabre anthropology of original sin to create an explosive atmosphere in which heresy and witchcraft would become the focus of inquisitorial surveillance. Martin Luther's spiritual progress is recounted to explicate the first trend, while Joan of Arc's experience embodies the second tendency. "The Social Earthquake" next reviews the literature about the implications of changing population levels for the demise of feudalism in England where this mode of exploitation had been most firmly rooted.

In my final chapter, "Recombinant Mutations," I summarize the note-worthy characteristics of the first stage of early modernization after the year 1000 as well as considering the role of the Black Death in changing its course. *At the Dawn of Modernity* concludes with some final thoughts ("After-words") about my method in writing a social history.

1 Lineages of Early Modernization

THE FEUDAL REVOLUTION

Antiquity had imagined the Centaur; the early Middle Ages made
him the master of Europe.

> Lynn White, Jr., *Medieval Technology*
> *and Social Change*

In the year 1000 the organization of political power was still fundamen-
tally ancient. Power in ancient society was imposed from above—based on
the unlimited exercise of potestas. In the aftermath of "The Feudal Revo-
lution," the exercise of power was re-organized around rituals of reciproc-
ity so that social relations would come to be mediated by contractual obli-
gations which were still unequal but essentially unlike what had existed in
late antiquity. The cornerstone of feudal society was the revolution in
combat technology. This transformation in the means of violence had
made mounted knights the rulers of others. Partly because of the critical
requirement to feed their war-horses, feudalism developed most com-
pletely in the Seine and Thames basins, which were the centers of the
French and Anglo-Norman monarchies. In contrast, its development in
Germany took an essentially different course which will be discussed at
length. That difference is good to think with in understanding the variety
of ways in which early modernization led to the creation of novel systems
of political power and new modes of family formation.[1]

1. This chapter provides a top-down discussion of the reorganization of power
and social control; a bottom-up explication of these processes is to be found in the
third chapter of this book. "Living in the Material World" examines the living conditions of the rural majority of the population and explains how the character of social relations changed in the wake of the feudal revolution of the year 1000. While

1.

After the passing of the Justinian pandemic and Charles Martel's victory at the Battle of Poitiers, which halted the Moslems' advance in 732, a new society began to take shape in the northwestern region of Europe. This was a confused and contradictory process; it may have begun in the eighth century, but it was only around the year 1000 that historians can speak of a definitive turning point.[2] In the interim, the Viking and Magyar invasions had acted as "the solvent of Carolingian society," while Arab Moslems continued to nibble at Europe's southern flank.[3] The end of this external threat was a necessary—but not sufficient—aspect of the reassertion of authority. The new style of warfare had initially contributed to the expansion of the Carolingians' dominion, but feudalism would later create the seeds of insuperable contradiction which led to their demise.

Feudalism developed from a military revolution. The new warfare was based on the mounted horseman's massive advantage over the foot soldier. Unorganized ground troops were smashed by the cavalry's shock force. The stirrup enabled the horseman to concentrate the combined force of weight and speed at the point of impact, at the end of his lance, radically enhancing his advantage.[4] A key indicator of the military Centaur's advantage over the foot soldier was provided by his massive iron toolkit: first and

the technological and economic aspects of the feudal revolution have been treated in separate chapters, it needs to be understood that they are two sides of the same coin.

2. Even this turning point, the year 1000 in the shorthand version I will employ, is under siege: see Dominique Barthélemy and Stephen D. White, "Debate: The 'Feudal Revolution,' " *Past and Present* 152 (1996): 196–223. This article was written in response to T. N. Bisson, "The 'Feudal Revolution,' " *Past and Present* 142 (1994): 6–42. I will try to keep these contending positions in view in the following discussion, although I cannot pretend to give more than my own summary of these arguments and others which I have taken into account.

3. This sense of change and continuity is neatly captured in Geoffrey Barraclough, *The Crucible of Europe: The Ninth and Tenth Centuries in European History* (Berkeley and Los Angeles, 1976), 13–21, 166. Why did the Viking invasions commence around 800? Lynn White suggests that the arrival of the moldboard plow in Scandinavia created a huge agricultural surplus which led to population growth and expansionary pressures (*Medieval Technology and Social Change*, 54).

4. Maurice Keen suggests that the triumph of the new mode of warfare—"the charge of heavy cavalrymen holding their lances in the 'couched' position (tucked firmly under the right armpit and levelled at the enemy)"—took place "after the year 1000"; *Chivalry* (New Haven, 1984), 23–24; see also Bernard S. Bachrach, "Mounted Shock Combat, the Stirrup, and Feudalism," *Studies in Medieval and Renaissance History* 7 (1970): 49–75. Allowing this technical point, it still seems rather obvious that an armed horseman had a massive advantage over a foot soldier even when they both fought with freehand weapons. So, we might accommodate Keen's revision by suggesting a protracted, two-stage process in which the armed

foremost was his heavy coat of mail armor which weighed as much as thirty pounds, while his sword, helmet, spurs, and lance-head together with his mount's horseshoes, stirrup, bit, and bridle added another twenty pounds.[5] All this iron represented a massive capital investment.

War-horses were even more expensive than the specialized armor of the knightly cavalryman. The state-of-the-art man of war needed a veritable herd of his own—a couple of huge war-horses, which were trained to gallop into battle carrying the knight, his armor, and the horse's armor, as well as some pack horses to move the properly outfitted fighting equipage around the countryside. Feeding these war-horses put pressure on available agricultural practices because these animals were fed on a bulk commodity whose conveyance strained the resources of primitive transport technology. Because of communication inelasticities, their bulky feed could not be moved any significant distance. In effect, this meant that the only way that herds of horses could be maintained efficiently was by relocating them to the source of supply and by distributing them throughout the innumerable agricultural communities that dotted the northwest European countryside:

> the limited agricultural capacity of the Mediterranean littoral . . . [meant that] it had not been practical to extend the role of horses above their ceremonial function in the ancient world. Charles Martel's cavalry, therefore, depended as much on the development of a new source of provisions as on the introduction of the stirrup. Just at this moment . . . a new, heavy plow capable of handling the deep, wet soils, made its appearance in northern Gaul.[6]

The heartland of feudalism was prized open for exploitation by the new plow and, in a positive reciprocating feedback, the new mode of warfare found its material base in the deep, rich soils of the valleys of the Seine and the Thames. Even today these alluvial lands produce higher yields per acre than land almost anywhere else in the world.

Thus the Carolingian revolution was based on two complementary transformations in the material relations of society—the stirrup gave the mounted rider an enormous advantage, while the means to feed an unprecedented number of war-horses enabled a class of knights to be sustained. It is conventionally estimated that the knight's basic outfit—a horse, a sword, a lance, a shield, and his kit of armor—were worth the eighth-century equivalent of twenty oxen, or the plow teams of ten of the wealthiest peasant fam-

---

rider fighting with a sword was only slowly supplanted by the Centaur—man and horse configured into a coordinated fighting machine.

5. Robert Bartlett, *The Making of Europe* (Princeton, 1993), 61 n. 328.

6. Edward Whiting Fox, *History in Geographic Perspective* (New York, 1971), 43.

ilies.[7] The *benefice,* land and appurtenances granted to warriors in exchange for their services, was originally designed to provide a knight with the necessary income to supply these new means of violence. In essence, this contract exchanged royal land for knightly service. At the outset, it was a conditional exchange that was subject to the satisfaction of the royal partner. As time passed, the original size and shape of the *benefice* mutated; its original purpose also was lost.

This technological revolution in the means of violence created conditions ripe for the formation of a new class. The pace of this development was, in terms of our recent assumptions about cultural change in human history, glacially slow. The Frankish expectation that all free men had the right and the duty to bear arms was eventually rendered obsolete by the new means of warfare. A vast gulf came to separate those who could afford to meet the requirements for mounted shock combat from the rest of the population: "Those economically unable to fight on horseback suffered from a social infirmity which shortly became a legal inferiority." This social revolution found expression in a kind of cultural exclusivity because "to learn to fight like a knight one must start at puberty." The characteristic features of the knightly caste—aggression, physical prowess, bravery, loyalty, solidarity, self-consciousness, specialized education, tournaments, ceremonies, rituals, and armorial devices—slowly fused to form the lineaments of a chivalrous society. Its members understood themselves to be warriors and, incidentally, to be the rulers of others.[8]

These patrimonial relationships—which established a ritual bond of fraternity between the two parties while maintaining their juridical inequality—were at the heart of feudalism. They were, as Max Weber writes,

> regulated by a code of honour and by obligations which were loaded with tensions. In its most developed form, the fief relation forced together, in highly peculiar fashion, components which stood in obvious opposition to one another: on the one hand strongly personal relations of fealty, on the other the establishment through contract of rights and obligations. In turn, these were objectified by connecting them with a concrete source of rents, with the security—ultimately transmissible through inheritance—of certain relationships of possession.[9]

The early Carolingians benefited from these new military techniques and quickly amassed a huge territory. For as long as the Franks' imperial power

7. White, *Medieval Technology and Social Change,* 29.
8. White, *Medieval Technology and Social Change,* 29–33.
9. Quoted in Gianfranco Poggi, "Max Weber's Conceptual Portrait of Feudalism," *British Journal of Sociology* 39 (1988): 220.

was hegemonic, they resisted the demand to make their vassals' benefices hereditary. Not for the last time were the spoils of victory used to put off the day of reckoning. By the declining years of Charlemagne's reign, however, Viking raiders had appeared on the northern horizon; they not only closed that frontier but soon threatened the Frankish heartland.

The impact of these Viking invasions was compounded by the weakness of Charlemagne's successors and the sheer improbability of keeping such a huge territory under the authority of a single sovereign. The polarities of the field of political forces swung violently against central command. Civil war first broke out in 829, and the precarious balance between the crown and its vassals inexorably disintegrated. In this regard, historians have noted that the Meersen capitulary (847) and the later capitulary of Quierzy-sur-Oise (877) were milestones. The first ordered all free men to choose a lord, while the second granted hereditary succession to vassals.[10] With these acts the Carolingians formally recognized the changing balance of power. In explicitly recognizing the decline in royal authority, they sought to use the feudal system as a means of maintaining their hold on power itself. The center would not hold.[11]

The Viking raids from the north—and those of the Magyars in the east—had unleashed forces which dissolved Carolingian power in the ninth and tenth centuries. The response to these incursions was widely variable. Overall, the impact of these invasions broke apart the fragile unity imposed over most of the mainland of northwestern Europe by the Carolingians.[12] The disintegration of the Carolingians' imperial power shattered the ancient system of authority within whose discursive framework Charles Martel and his family had deployed their power. In its place, the forces of a "multiple acephalous federation" were subtly transformed, over the course of the next centuries, into the more familiar geopolitical balance of power within a system of competitive states.[13]

10. Barraclough, *The Crucible of Europe*, 90.

11. Fox, *History in Geographic Perspective*, 44–45.

12. Of course, this disintegration was the experience of west Francia—the heartland of the Carolingian Empire in the West. In the German lands a completely different dynamic took place. The Saxon kings took control over these new means of warfare to create a trajectory toward greater centralization from the early tenth through the late eleventh centuries—that is, at the same time that the old structures in the western empire dissolved. There was, therefore, nothing determinative about the transformation in the means of warfare since, in these two different contexts, its deployment led to two different outcomes.

13. On the characterization of European society as a "multiple acephalous federation," see Michael Mann, *A History of Power from the Beginning to A.D. 1760* vol. 1, *The Sources of Social Power* (Cambridge, 1986), chaps. 12–14. The Magyars

The "first feudal age," from the mid-eighth century to around about the year 1000, has been described as "feudalism without feudal law."[14] Marc Bloch's "first feudal age" is now questioned by historians who contend that before the eleventh century, the household, the *familia*, was much more important than the fief or vassalage. Bloch's first period is not, therefore, regarded as properly feudal.

> What is feudal about it is its ending: the time when the judicial
> seigneury was established and when, in correlation with this, the use of
> what our texts call "fiefs" and "homage" became common among a
> wide stratum of people with origins in the peasantry. In many regions
> this happened in the space of a few generations. These crucial decades
> were indeed clearly feudal, but they do not constitute a period. These
> years represent the crisis during which the new relationships were
> crystallized and established, when the structures were formed that were
> to govern, or claim to govern, society in the following centuries. In this
> sense there was no first feudal period.[15]

Whatever we choose to call the ninth and tenth centuries, they were characterized by lawlessness. Warfare was constant in an almost capricious struggle for mastery in which bravery and brawn, charisma and cunning, all counted for more than either right or legitimacy. Out of these confrontations, members of the knightly class gained both jurisdictional and administrative immunities (also called liberties), thereby limiting the lord's control over them and their benefices. The knight's relationship to his lord came to be based not on overt command but rather on a contractual basis within a larger system of mutual obligations. Indeed, many commentators have argued that the feudal contract represented a novel stage in political development which marked a decisive break with ancient, despotic forms of power.[16]

---

established their own state in Hungary in this period after having had their advance stopped at the Battle of Lech, near modern-day Augsburg, on August 10, 955. The Saxons also defeated the Slavs in 955 on the edge of the Recknitz. The domestication of these invaders was substantially aided when they were incorporated into the orbit of Christianity. Latin Christian states grew up in Denmark (950), Poland (966), Hungary (986), Norway (995), and Sweden (1000); at about the same time (988) the Ukrainian Church was established, which marked the beginning of the Christianization of Russia.

14. Marc Bloch, *Feudal Society* (Chicago, 1961), 60. See also Harold J. Berman, *Law and Revolution: The Formation of the Western Legal Tradition* (Cambridge, Mass., 1983), 297.

15. Jean-Pierre Poly and Eric Bournazel, *The Feudal Transformation 900–1200* (New York, 1991), 354.

16. For a recent restatement of this point of view—often associated with Max Weber—see Orlando Patterson, *Freedom in the Making of Western Culture* (New York, 1991), esp. 347–75.

It is crucial to recognize, as does Bloch, that "feudal Europe was not all feudalized in the same degree or according to the same rhythm and, above all, that it was nowhere feudalized completely." Indeed, as he goes on to write, "No doubt it is the fate of every system of human institutions never to be more than imperfectly realized."[17] Bloch's point is seconded by Jean-Pierre Poly and Eric Bournazel in their recent synthesis of research in the field:

> Instead of trying to eliminate contradictions through yet further detailed research, by explaining them as exceptions to an ideal schema or as "impurities," we should use them as our starting point. Then the gravitational center of our analysis is shifted; amid the extreme variety of concrete expressions there emerges a single and profound movement.[18]

One might also extend this line of argument by noting that every system of human institutions is constructed in history. This elementary point must be related to the fact that all are hybrids, the products of numerous mutations which have occurred both temporally and spatially.[19]

17. *Feudal Society,* 445. This is, to say the least, an important point. The blend of change and continuity that characterizes historical relationships is less clear than the "ideal type" which is our referent. Do we therefore dismiss generalizations? Theorizing about feudalism has its limits if such theories are consistently contradicted by the historical record. One should be uneasy about such activity, yet one should be equally uneasy about the indiscriminate fetishism of mere facts that is often paraded forth as the sensible alternative. This seemingly commonsense approach makes for a flaccid history which excludes a conceptual approach to the political economy of social change. It marginalizes the role of power by denying its systematic deployment; or, finding a hybrid system, it declares that this mutation somehow disables our ideal type. For an example of this kind of academic point-scoring, see Elizabeth A. R. Brown, "The Tyranny of a Construct: Feudalism and Historians of Medieval Europe," *American Historical Review* 79 (1974): 1063–88. For a most valuable corrective to Brown's kind of historiographical nominalism, see Bisson, "The 'Feudal Revolution.' " There is another line of criticism against this so-called commonsense alternative: terms like "feudalism" (or "capitalism" or "industrialism" or "the family") have a plasticity about them. Does this mean that we must forswear using them or use them only by rigorously defining them in such a way that we have made them into caricatures? I find this counsel of perfection to be intellectually vapid. It denies the systemic complexity of social relationships by focusing on the ambivalence of our language. But, surely, our terminological ambiguity is itself a reflection of that complexity. I will not, therefore, enact self-denying ordinances that obscure more than they reveal.

18. *The Feudal Transformation,* 352.

19. For this reason, the societies of the tenth-century Franks and thirteenth-century England were both "feudal" in that both insisted on the primacy of personal bonds of loyalty to a uniquely constituted sovereign whose power was created in ties of obedience and protection. These ties may have been more "real" (i.e.,

Might was usually right. This was not a recipe for stability so much as
the rule of the strongest. Feudalism was "a social order or, if one prefers, an

---

closer to the ideal type) for the tenth-century Frank than for the thirteenth-
century Englishman because in the intervening centuries their form had mutated
and the ideal had fossilized. In addition, the variable of history meant that feudalism in thirteenth-century England had its own developmental path, which was different in all kinds of ways from that of tenth-century Germany. A nominalist concern with specificity—of events, time, and place—might therefore counsel us to
deny the efficacy of the paradigm of "feudalism," but to do so is to deny "the dual
task of discovering the few significant facts and turning them into *facts of history*,
and of discarding the many insignificant facts as unhistorical"; E. H. Carr, *What
Is History?* (Harmondsworth, 1961), 14–15 (my emphasis). It is worth quoting
Carr further as he immediately goes on to write: "This is the very converse of the
nineteenth-century heresy that history consists of the compilation of a maximum
number of irrefutable and objective facts" (14). Earlier, Carr stated: "The belief in
a hard core of historical facts existing objectively and independently of the interpretation of the historian is a preposterous fallacy, but one which is very hard to
eradicate" (12). Carr continues.

> Anyone who succumbs to this heresy will either have to give up history as a
> bad job, and take to stamp-collecting or some other form of antiquarianism, or
> end up in a madhouse. It is this heresy which during the past hundred years has
> had such devastating effects on the modern historian, producing in Germany, in
> Great Britain, and in the United States, a vast and growing mass of dry-as-dust
> factual histories, of minutely-specialized monographs of would-be historians
> knowing more and more about less and less, sunk without trace in an ocean of
> facts." (15)

Determining these *facts of history* requires us to employ a comparative method
to establish broad processes which take shape not only in relation to some ideal
type but also in comparison with other broad processes that precede and follow
them. Historical specificity, then, exists in the contingent relationship between
these broad processes (or other *facts of history*). Historical reality is a historian's
construct; it is a jerry-built order based on interpretation. It is a fallacy to regard it
as anything else; we simplify in order to comprehend. I might profitably digress a
bit more by referring to the way in which complexity is understood in another discipline: Thus, "The few really big steps in evolution clearly required the acquisition
of new information. But specialization and diversification took place by using differently the same structural information." So, "What makes a chicken wing and a
human arm different is not so much the material out of which both are made, as the
instructions specifying the way one or the other is built. Small changes modifying
in time and space the distribution of the same structures are sufficient to affect
deeply the form, function, and behavior of the final product: the human animal";
François Jacob, *The Possible and the Actual* (New York, 1982), 41. We know what a
human is by comparing it with a chicken, not with other humans, and most certainly not by looking for some essential "humanity" which makes some of us more
"human" than others. Similarly, we know what "feudalism" was by comparing it
with antiquity or modernity, not with an exclusive concern with the various hybrid
forms it took. It must be mentioned that this is the essence of Bloch's comparative
method: he writes "The simplest way will be to begin by saying what feudal society was not"; *Feudal Society*, 443.

established disorder."[20] This "profound social revolution" developed furthest in France, which, by the year 1000, had been divided into fifty-five separate territories whose ties with the monarchy were limited, conditional, and contractual.[21] The "parcelization of sovereignty" was peculiar to feudalism. It was, in fact, its most characteristic feature. French feudalism was a system of reciprocal social, economic, and military functions built from the ground up, not imposed from the top down.[22] Feudalism was not, therefore, the source of anarchy; rather, it was a reaction against anarchy.

Built from the ground up, in multiple tiers, France was the classic case of "subinfeudation." The Paris basin was its heartland. We cannot establish the exact moment of feudalism's birth since local conditions were so crucial and so variable. Nevertheless, as late as 987 protection was afforded by a written document supplied by the king. Then, suddenly, respect for ancient legitimacy vanished.[23] The Carolingian Empire had been based on local structures of governance that predated it and were to survive after its fall.[24] The ancient social system was weakened when its roots in the countryside were cut so that taxes no longer rose to the cities. The supersession of the state's functions created a breathing space in which new solutions were found to the problem of governance. The state had been the keystone of the ancient system of urban domination, and its decline led to the ruralization of society. Towns withered. Trade shrank through the contraction of urban demand and the diminished circulation of money. Relaxing the fiscal vise that had characterized ancient state formations was a key factor contributing to rural growth.

The new society that began to emerge at the end of the tenth century developed from processes of reconstitution within the lower levels of the social structure.[25] The domination of the locality by the first layer of the aristocracy previously had been sustained by its possession of slaves to work the land, but in the new conditions of the late tenth century, these men, too, were being squeezed. The decline of the state apparatus had con-

---

20. Poly and Bournazel, *The Feudal Transformation*, 5.
21. Geoffrey Barraclough, "The Origins of Modern Germany," in G. Barraclough (ed.), *Medieval Germany 911–1250: Essays by German Historians* (Oxford, 1962), 17; Barraclough, *The Crucible of Europe*, 95–96, 90. The English response to the Viking invasions was radically different; I shall turn to the implications of this difference shortly.
22. Perry Anderson, *Passages from Antiquity to Feudalism* (London, 1974), 193.
23. Poly and Bournazel, *The Feudal Transformation*, 11, 15.
24. Poly and Bournazel, *The Feudal Transformation*, 11.
25. These implications are dealt with more fully below, in "The Seigneurial Mesh" (chap. 3).

demned this stratum to extinction. Some families would resurface as knightly lineages; the rest went down with the old order. This realignment occurred because the field of recruitment for fighting men was narrowed to those who could afford to join the mounted militia:

> The vast majority of these henchmen, these "fist men," were born of the decomposition, the "kulakization," of ancient country society. In order to be "higher" than the others, they agreed to serve, thus making possible the final victory of the warrior households over the peasant neighborhoods. Once the fundamental character of this movement was determined, there was little room for chronological fluctuations: by the decades around the year 1000 the Western European world had fundamentally changed.[26]

In the words of Raoul Glaber, a contemporary monk and chronicler, "It was said that the whole world, with one accord, shook off the tatters of antiquity."[27]

In the space of two or three decades, the countryside was divided vertically into a series of territorial units based on a castle or a great monastery. Free men in the countryside who had managed to avoid servitude or dependence suddenly lost the main center of their collective social life. "A more effective and also more grasping power forced them to bow their heads, a narrower framework restricted them. The castles ceased to be refuges and became threats. The rule of the *bannum*, until then more or less justified by collective necessity, now became a legitimized and daily servitude at the disposal of the lord."[28]

The disintegration of Carolingian authority had led, in the first place, to the anarchy of the war of all against all. But, in the second place, disorder and discord were resolved in a novel way:

> For the old principles of government, which had perished, it substituted a new principle: the subordination of man to man, in a long hierarchy, through vassalage; a society based not on equality of all under the state and a direct connection between each individual and the government, but on class and class-gradation, a hierarchical society.[29]

26. Poly and Bournazel, *The Feudal Transformation*, 353. "Kulaks" is a term that was popularized in Stalinist Russia, denoting the rich peasants who were driven by their selfish greed instead of socialist solidarity. The word—and derivatives like "kulakization" used by Poly and Bournazel—has seeped into the language of historians of the peasantry.

27. Quoted in Guy Bois, *The Transformation of the Year 1000: The Village of Lournand from Antiquity to Feudalism* (Manchester, 1992), 35.

28. Poly and Bournazel, *The Feudal Transformation*, 25.

29. Barraclough, *The Crucible of Europe*, 97.

As late as 802, Charlemagne had required all free men to bind themselves by an oath of fealty to the king. In contrast, feudal society was cemented by a multiplicity of oaths of homage.

Rather than working through a system of centralized authority, the king's only contact with the free population was through a long chain of oaths of homage, owed by one man to another, and on to the next and to the next, and only finally to the king. The ranks of "free men" radically narrowed to include only those knights who were able to bear arms. The ruler's contact with his subjects was mediated by these "free men." The Franks' free/unfree distinction was replaced by the knight/non-knight distinction as the main criterion of social rank.[30] The dominance of the new mode of warfare was instrumental in shifting the center of gravity northward in western Europe, to the "land of plains and open spaces where . . . breakneck gallops could be deployed."[31] First in France and then across the length and breadth of the feudalized core of northwestern Europe, local protection sprang up against both the pagan invader and the armed rider.

2.

At the very outset of the process of early modernization, France was slowly reassembled by the Capetians. Similarly, England's distinctive process of state formation can be traced back to its deep traditions of central organization that had first emerged in the Anglo-Saxon resistance to Norse invaders and were later accentuated by the Norman conquerors. By way of contrast, Germany became not so much a nation as a decentered federation. In this next section it will be instructive to dwell at length on Germany's historical path. Its divergence from that of the more familiar French and English examples is important not only in its own right but also in comparative perspective.[32]

Matters played out in Germany to create a distinctive configuration: a federated state formation in which bundles of rights, privileges, and liberties were combined in different ways, for different people, in different places, at different times. This complex of jurisdictions was constructed in history as the product of historical contingencies, which accounts for the multidimensional, labyrinthine layering of its political organization. Moreover, these

30. O. Hintze, "The Nature of Feudalism," in F. L. Cheyette (ed.), *Lordship and Community in Medieval Europe* (New York, 1968), 22–31.
31. Jacques Le Goff, *Medieval Civilization 400–1500* (Oxford, 1988), 55.
32. There is some rich irony here—an observer in the year 1000 would have been much more impressed with the Germans' chances for achieving a coherent national state than the chances of either the French or English.

jurisdictions were only imperfectly congruent with social, economic, and cultural regions so that Germany's inherently asymmetrical federalism was given yet other twists by the peculiarities of its history. The contingency of early modern German polity was, thus, its most salient characteristic. The very idea of Germany was—and still is—good to think with.

The Carolingians—through dint of sheer force, inherited military skill, new war technologies, and luck—had been able to vault the Frankish tribes from their ancestral lands straddling the Rhine to imperial status in the eighth century. Yet, within a matter of two generations, their sacred kingship was in tatters. The Treaty of Verdun (843) terminated the Frankish empire and divided it into three independent kingdoms. The western realm formed the heartland of historic West Francia; the middle kingdom stretched through present-day Lombardy, Savoy, Switzerland, and Alsace-Lorraine into the Netherlands; and the eastern lands of the empire, East Francia, were the historic embryo from which early modern Germany would develop. After the dissolution of the Carolingian empire, all three parts staggered under the hammer blows of invading Vikings and Magyars.

The German peoples were themselves subdivided into a variety of tribal associations. The Saxons' military standing in the ninth century had been one of subordination to the Franks. Ninth-century Saxons grappled on even terms with the Slavs and the Danes, although they were largely defenseless against the Magyar horsed fighters. The tenth-century Saxons' assertion of mastery over the eastern regions of this military disaster area enabled them to gain preeminence. Henry I, who founded the Saxon dynasty, developed his military skill by providing leadership to a large and motley crew of free nobles. What gave the Saxon nobility a particularly malleable shape was its practice of partible inheritance, which meant that

> large kins of agnates and cognates had expectations or interests in an estate, [but] even massive accumulations of landed wealth could crumble or shift relatively swiftly within or between family-groups. The *nobilis pauper* was no rarity and even in a rich and important *stirps* [kin group] there was scarcely room for more than two or three of its members to cut a great figure in the world in any one generation. The rest had to seek service. . . . [and for] those who belonged to an obscure and less wealthy family . . . [prospects were] worse.[33]

The primary effect of this system of downward mobility, engendered by the bimodal dynamics of Saxon family formation, was that it threw out many

33. K. J. Leyser, "Henry I and the Beginnings of the Saxon Empire," in *Medieval Germany and Its Neighbours 900–1250* (London, 1982), 11–42 (quotation on 41).

men who sought to recapture fame and fortune. They wanted to become successful warriors, to recapture the status to which they had been born.

Political society in East Francia had revolved around large, interrelated family groups that contested for places and honors close to their kings. These fluctuating familial relationships—kindred alliances as well as fictive kinships revolving around *amicitia* (loving friendship)—held together a patrimonial society at whose center was the shining sun of the king's household. Around it orbited a number of lesser planets that were headed by the great nobles of the realm. The politics of these times thus dissolve into family history. For this reason many recent historical studies have been prosopographies (collective biographies) of the upper classes—their members are the only people for whom information has survived. For them, disaster always loomed when an inheritance was to be divided. The best way to appease the disinherited was to create new zones of exploitation through conquest and expansion. Then, the king could be generous in rewarding the loyalty and service of followers so that the success of the whole would reverberate in the individual fortunes of its main parts.

One thousand years ago, German kings ruled by virtue of their ability to lead men in combat, not as a result of their ability to command them in peacetime. This is a crucial point. The German kings, insofar as they were interested in confronting this dilemma, encountered a two-faced problem in changing the very character of their sovereignty from leadership in battle to the management of everyday life: first, they had to improve their administrative organization and to staff it with reliable servants; and second, they needed to develop reliable and independent sources of revenue. The stakes were very high because if they could do these two things then they could effectively extend their domination over the locally based aristocracies. If they could not, they would have to distribute sovereignty to their subordinates, thereby relinquishing an essential attribute of royal power. It is not too much to say that this dilemma was the hinge on which German state formation swung between 919 and 1272.[34] It might be even more correct to say that this dilemma was a field of forces within which German state-formation strategies oscillated, since the trajectory was inherently unpredictable as a result of the essentially unstable balance of power between the contending parties.

German kingship was conditional, based on a knot of countervailing constraints. German kings claimed a hereditary basis for their dynasty, but

34. Indeed, one might almost want to argue that this was the quintessential dilemma of early modern state formation.

the upper aristocracy would not endorse a blank check. German kings' abilities to enforce their hereditary, dynastic claims were subject to the vagaries of adult male succession. Their ability to enforce these claims was also threatened by the practice of partible inheritance, so they had to chart a perilous course between the Scylla of no heirs and the Charybdis of too many. German kings wanted to establish their preeminence, but their power was almost always restricted by their itineraries—where the king was not seen, he was less likely to be obeyed, because his writ ran no farther than his presence. German kings tried to establish sovereignty over subordinates, but the aristocracy never acknowledged that its actions were constrained by royal command. This meant that German kings could not delegate power to subordinates in the expectation that these men would obey their commands without sweetening the pot. There was thus no inherent regal authority, nor was there an infrastructure of royal administrators drawn from the free nobility.

The use of *ministeriales* (armed, servile followers) came about because German princes (and clerics) found that the loyalty of their free vassals was unreliable. In a society in which the feud was endemic, the nobility was held to be justified in launching attacks in defense of its rights and advancing its claims which could not be settled by agreement, blackmail, or some other method of negotiating. Not only were German retinues larger than those employed in other European countries, but the German king never established the hegemony of royal justice and so never organized a monopoly over the means of violence. Nobility thus needed an armed retinue to help it in feuds and to serve in its *familia* as household administrators in the four traditional offices—marshal, chamberlain, butler, and seneschal.[35]

The Ottonian kings' sacral aura was enhanced by their military victories and abetted by their control of the rich veins of silver which were discovered in the Harz Mountains of Saxony just before the year 1000. Sacral kingship had to be seen to be effective, but the Ottonians' journeys rarely

35. Benjamin Arnold, *German Knighthood 1050–1300* (Oxford, 1985), 14, 29, 184. See also Karl Bosl, " 'Noble Unfreedom': The Rise of the *Ministeriales* in Germany," in Timothy Reuter (ed.), *The Medieval Nobility* (Amsterdam, 1979), 291–311. I benefited enormously from reading a series of articles by John B. Freed: "The Origins of the European Nobility: The Problem of the Ministerials," *Viator* 7 (1976): 211–41; "The Formation of the Salzburg Ministerialage in the Tenth and Eleventh Centuries: An Example of Upward Social Mobility in the Early Middle Ages," *Viator* 9 (1978): 67–102; "Reflections on the Medieval German Nobility," *American Historical Review* 91 (1986): 553–75; "Nobles, Ministerials, and Knights in the Archdiocese of Salzburg," *Speculum* 62 (1987): 575–611; and "The Crisis of the Salzburg Ministerialage, 1270–1343," *Studies in Medieval and Renaissance History*, new ser., 11 (1989): 111–71.

took them outside their home and native land. This meant that the pressure of Ottonian government bore down most heavily in Saxony, since it was there that the kings were most frequently feasted and hospitality was most often extended to their moving court. The Saxon nobility's wealth was at the itinerant court's disposal, but it was not under the crown's control. This is a critical point. The nobility maintained its "allodial independence," which meant that it had control over its *Eigen* (proprietary lands). These 300 widely ramified family networks kept all governmental rights in their possession through their control of all countships and dukedoms,[36] and their accumulations of land endured for centuries. The point that this land was essentially private property, free from royal control, was one of the fundamental facts of German medieval history. The complex relationship between the kings' imperial reach and their often-tenuous grasp leads us directly to a consideration of the character of German state formation.[37] This relationship is of crucial significance because it set Germany on its own unique path of early modernization, what its historians have called *Der Deutsche Sonderweg* (the special German pathway).

German kings therefore ruled by personal authority, which constantly abutted upon the independent sphere of action claimed by the other members of the free nobility. German kings claimed extensive powers and control over material resources, but they were frustrated by the traditional expectation that the king's role was to protect the peace, liberty, and property of his subjects. Finally, German kings were also rulers of an empire of which Germany itself was only a single constituent part. One thing is clear: the German kings may have held many face cards, but they had few trumps in their hands. Nonetheless, the German conditional monarchy was not without its own resources. The first and most important was the sacral powers of kingship. Second, the king held power and wealth so far superior to that possessed by any other member of the free nobility that he could routinely master the great game of divide and rule. Third, he could expand the frontiers of the realm. Fourth, he could devise an administration that was free from dependence on aristocratic goodwill. But with two exceptions—the discovery of silver and the chartering of towns—the German kings were unable to devise intensive strategies of colonizing new forms of wealth to press ahead with a program of state formation. They

36. Theodor Mayer, "The Historical Foundations of the German Constitution," in G. Barraclough (ed.), *Medieval Germany 911–1250: Essays by German Historians* (Oxford, 1962), 16.

37. John Gillingham, *The Kingdom of Germany in the High Middle Ages (900–1200)* (London, 1971).

were thus limited in their ability to tap their subjects' wealth, which was why the attraction of "Empire" was so strong—it promised not only secure German borders but also a lucrative source of revenue that was free from the control or supervision of the nobility. The imperial card created immense complications, and it was ultimately to become the Achilles' heel of the German monarchy. The other method of expanding royal influence throughout this period—creating a staff of dependent retainers—was also fraught with difficulty. Although the tenth-century Saxon kings were successful in employing clerical administrators, this tactic backfired on the eleventh-century Salian rulers during the Investiture Crisis that developed when the papacy inserted itself between the monarchy and its administrators.

If early modern Germany was to become a "delayed nation," we might seek the reason for retardation in the growth of parceled sovereignty and the constitutional principle of "mediatized authority"—the king was the overlord of his vassals but not the overlord of their vassals.[38] Around the year 1000 the statecraft of the German king consisted in his ability to keep the equivalent possibilities of power, authority, self-defense, self-help, and justice in equilibrium. Exercising the principle of association, which was immanent in the governing process, constituted the way in which the whole ruling class participated in royal rule. Lordship and association interacted dialectically in the same force field. Although power was decisive, it was a subjectively defined right. Norms were evident before they were publicly expressed in law. The social formulation of the law, then, consolidated what had already been there in traditions, ethical values, and religious prescriptions. "Law was not given but found, pointed out. Therein lay a fair portion of individual power. Self-help, feud, the legitimate use of force, so-called 'private' execution were the inheritance of earlier times, were the 'givens' of society and culture." Moreover, when the king made political decisions he was expected to act together with the people. Although in the course of time "the people" changed, they were always there.[39]

The contrasting trajectories of German and French state formation are germane to this point: in Germany, the ability of the Saxon and Salian monarchs to lead and to manage their nobility meant that feudalism did not become politically sovereign in the aftermath of the Carolingian dissolution, whereas in France the center had not held. Then, from the eleventh

---

38. H. Fuhrmann, *Germany in the High Middle Ages c. 1050–1200* (Cambridge, 1986), 157–76 (the phrase "delayed nation" is quoted on 167).

39. Karl Bosl, "Ruler and Ruled in the German Empire from the Tenth to the Twelfth Century," in Cheyette (ed.), *Lordship and Community*, 357–75; quotation from p. 360.

century onward, a contrary set of trajectories resulted in the emergence of sovereign feudal principalities in Germany, whereas in France the growth of royal power reassembled a central authority by depriving the feudality of its independent power bases and by gradually reducing its powers so that the French nobles became a social caste.[40]

The key moment in the development of early modernization in Germany took place in the 1070s. It resulted from the "stubborn, tenacious, and unyielding" conjunction of secular and ecclesiastical rebellion against the Ottonian and Salian system of kingship.[41] The spark which fired this conflagration occurred in the summer of 1073 when a number of East Saxon and Thuringian nobles rose up against Henry IV in response to what they perceived to be his policy of overly aggressive kingship.[42] Their grievances concerned two issues: first, the royal policy of castle building and policing the countryside with armed *ministeriales* seemed to strike directly against their local powers; and second, the Salian king's energetic reappropriation of the lands which had been distributed among them during his minority seemed to threaten their independence. The rebel nobles of 1073 represented an articulate and mature secular cause whose persistent political rhetoric spoke to their struggle for the *patriae leges*—their struggle for their own control over their own lands and their own ability to pass on their own inheritances to their own heirs. In this sense, they had struck at the contradictory heart of the royal policies of state formation that had been pursued since 919 by the Ottonians and the Salians.

40. J. W. Thompson, "German Feudalism," *American Historical Review* 28 (1923), 447–48.

41. Karl Leyser, "The Crisis of Medieval Germany," *Proceedings of the British Academy* 69 (1983): 409–43; also Barraclough, *The Origins of Modern Germany*, 72–134. This argument is contested by Gillingham, who situates the "real decline" a century later, between 1198 and 1215, during the Welf-Hohenstaufen struggle for the crown (*The Kingdom of Germany in the High Middle Ages*, 5). While Gillingham's criticisms are cogent, they do not seem to me to undermine the standard interpretation, which locates a crucial transformation in the course of development in the crisis of the 1070s.

42. At exactly this same time, the Normans were establishing their control over England while the French monarchy was gradually extending its power outward from its base in the Île de France. "This first attempt of the German monarchy to stabilize its position, both territorially and economically, only became a really important factor in determining the actual course of constitutional development when it came face to face with the opposition of the Saxon folk . . ."; Paul Joachimsen, "The Investiture Contest and the German Constitution," in Barraclough (ed.), *Medieval Germany, 911–1250*, 111. Note that the "Saxon folk" referred to in the previous sentence actually denotes a small slice of the total population—the politically active nobles. The rest of the "Saxon folk" were spectators—or, what was worse, unwilling accomplices in their own subjugation.

The trouble between the Saxons and their Salian kings pivoted on the discretionary powers that the kings claimed over their gifts. These lands, which had been granted by earlier kings to their followers *in proprietatem*, were now claimed by Henry IV as part of his *regalia*, but they were regarded by his followers as their own private property. Each side had dug in its heels over conserving invented traditions and improvised rights. Conflicts tended to involve breaches of honor, trust, or rank. Nobles rebelled against the king not to overthrow him but rather because he had somehow offended their *dignitas*. Such conflicts played out "a certain ritual of escalation, which proceeded step by step and which gave each party opportunities to seek out satisfactory compromises. At each level of escalation friends and relatives intervened until finally a *consensus omnium* ending the conflict was achieved, at which time the king was expected to demonstrate the cardinal virtues, *clementia* and *misericordia*, by pardoning the noble offenders."[43] What was unusual in this case was that from 1073 until 1122 Germany was engaged in more-or-less continuous civil warfare. By 1106, after the death of Henry IV, "German rulers did not possess powers equal to levelling off the princes into subjects and satellites of the court." The result was that "the political future of the Medieval German Empire remained in the regions, in a complex geographical structure of diverse legal custom, local economies, and small-scale aristocratic, ecclesiastical, and urban jurisdictions."[44]

These civil wars lasted so long because Pope Gregory VII "threw a flaming brand into Germany" which "not only sowed dissension among his supporters but also prolonged the social upheavals and thus added to the horrors of a bitter civil war."[45] Papal intervention came when it seemed that Henry IV was on the verge of a historic success which would have enabled him to abolish the duchy of Saxony, to govern it through royal officials, and to make it, with Goslar as capital, the keystone of the strong monarchy he was intent on creating. The Investiture Conflict which began in 1075 pitted the pope against the German king/emperor. The Gregorian papacy found secular allies among sections of the German ruling class which would benefit from the permanent weakening of Salian power—the Saxon nobility and south German dukes as well as the Tuscan nobles and Normans in southern Italy.

43. Charles R. Bowlus, "The Early *Kaiserreich* in Recent German Historiography," *Central European History* 23 (1990): 359.

44. Benjamin Arnold, *Princes and Territories in Medieval Germany* (Cambridge, 1991), 59–60.

45. Barraclough, *The Origins of Modern Germany*, 116.

Gregory VII attacked the ideas of imperial legitimacy, divine right, and paramount overlordship. In so doing, he attacked the imperial theories of theocracy that reached back to Charlemagne's coronation by the pope in 800. Deploying secular power in the administration of the church ran up against the spirit of clerical reform that was championed by the "holy Satan," who knew no gray areas.[46] Gregory was a revolutionary who attacked the traditional Gelasian "two-sword" division between the secular and spiritual. There was a striking element of "political Manichaeism" in his political thought: "All who professed to be Christians and still refused to obey the Roman See joined the body of the Devil, for they had fallen into the sin of idolatry, into heresy, into paganism, and could no longer be numbered among the true believers."[47]

The response of the German monarch, however, was intemperate. Henry IV is reported to have said: "You have dared to touch me, who although unworthy have been singled out by unction to rule, and whom, according to the traditions of the Holy Fathers, God alone can judge."[48] Henry was speaking in accordance with the traditional discourse of sacred kingship which the Ottonians had used to legitimize their supremacy. Yet he ruled a theocracy that was administered through the offices of clerical administrators. The king's position as the supreme "advocate" over the church in Germany rested on his *Mundeburdium* (protective powers) and on the system of *Eigenkirche,* which empowered him to make discretionary use of church property while maintaining his authority to designate his own men—nobles who were, at one and the same time, his relatives, friends, and vassals—to clerical positions.[49]

Henry IV had more legions than the pope but was forced to seek papal absolution at Canossa in 1077 in order to thwart the princes' election and advancement of a counter-king. "The intervention of Gregory VII, reviving all the old animosities and tearing open the old wounds before they had time to heal, was a turning-point not only in the reign of Henry IV but also in the whole history of Germany."[50] Although both the princes and the papacy were opposed to the Salian conception of kingship, their common an-

---

46. Peter Damian, quoted in Uta-Renate Blumenthal, *The Investiture Controversy: Church and Monarchy from the Ninth to the Twelfth Century* (Philadelphia, 1988), 116.

47. Karl F. Morrison, "Canossa: A Revision," *Traditio* 18 (1962): 121–48.

48. Barraclough, *The Origins of Modern Germany,* 97, 113, 114.

49. Joachimsen, "The Investiture Contest and the German Constitution," 99–100.

50. Barraclough, *The Origins of Modern Germany,* 96–97.

tagonism to Henry IV did not signify that they shared a common attitude toward secular power.

The three-sided nature of the struggle made it immensely complicated to resolve the issues that divided the contestants for power and earthly dominion.[51] That is why, in the end, a compromise was devised that ended the fighting but never really tried to settle the basic differences between the three parties. The Concordat of Worms of 1122 brought the fifty-year civil wars in Germany to an end. The German monarchy lost the symbolic signs of independence for which it had fought when "Henry [V] agreed to renounce the traditional investiture with ring and staff—a form of investiture which through age-old tradition implied conferment of the ecclesiastical office—but in exchange the pope recognized his right to confer the *regalia* by investiture with the sceptre. This latter investiture was to take place before consecration, thus ensuring that the elected prelate should not enter into his duties until he had sworn homage and fealty to the king."[52] It was a *modus vivendi*.

The princes were the real winners in the Investiture Crisis. The elections of new kings in 1125 and 1138 revealed that the principle of hereditary succession was not a dead letter, but it only just breathed life. Furthermore, the end of the Ottonian/Salian dynasty created an uncertain situation with regard to the material foundations of the monarchy. With the recognition of the established rights of individual feudatories, the crown renounced both monarchical rights to property and the policy of state formation based on a strong, independent, and centralized administration. "The structure of German government and administration, as the Investiture Contest left it, was—like the structure of German society—feudal, and the particularism which now became a dominant factor was feudal particularism. The Investiture Contest set the princes in the saddle."[53] In promoting an elective monarchy—"a kind of legalized antikingship"[54]—the Concordat of Worms signaled a radical change in the balance of power not only in Germany but also in Italy because, there too, the imperial mandate was effective only when the emperor and his army were present.

Even a successful monarch like Frederick Barbarossa (1122–90) was the head man of a feudal household first, the emperor second, and king of Germany third. Frederick's actions were in tune with his times in trying to

51. I. S. Robinson, "Pope Gregory VII, the Princes and the *Pactum* 1077–1080," *English Historical Review* 94 (1979): 721–56.
52. Barraclough, *The Origins of Modern Germany*, 154.
53. Barraclough, *The Origins of Modern Germany*, 159–60, 163.
54. Fuhrmann, *Germany in the High Middle Ages*, 96–97.

maximize his family's powers and properties within the constraints imposed on an elected German king by the Concordat of Worms. Frederick, then, was a dynast in charge of a "composite monarchy" whose loose associations allowed for a high level of local proactivity when it was simply not feasible for a monarch to control outlying provinces. A German king's success depended upon his ability to guarantee the local elites' existing privileges. His failure resulted from his inability to strike the right balance between the centrifugal forces of particularism and the centripetal forces of federal state formation.[55]

The late eleventh century had thus witnessed a social revolution that transformed German society and the German state. From a loosely organized alliance of kindreds, tracing their descent through both women and men and fragmenting their wealth whenever an inheritance was transmitted, it became possible "to base dynasties permanently on the possession of great offices, counties, advocacies, not to mention duchies, landgraviates and margraviates." The territorialization of power thus eluded the grasp of the monarchy; "what the princes gained, the crown lost."[56] These principalities were based on "agglomerations of manorial, comital, advocatial, and forest jurisdictions extended by further valuable rights of dominion. These were prerogatives over towns, markets and mints, over roads, bridges, and tolls, and over castles, other fortifications, and their knightly garrisons."[57] The German civil wars that broke out alongside the Investiture Controversy were the crucial formative period in the making of the German princes. Before the Investiture Crisis, private warfare had been unusual and was quickly squashed.

What the Hohenstaufen Reich lacked was not communication between the emperor and the intermediate holders of rank, authority, and power, but uniformity. There was a teeming welter of developing princely and aristocratic lordships, lay and clerical, as well as a bewildering variety of substructures like counties, advocacies, immunities, burgraviates, *banns,* and *mundeburdia.* Unlike the English shires, these substructures did not possess any common underlying grid of shared uniformities. In the Capetian heartland of the Île de France, such a grid—of rough and elemental

55. J. H. Elliott, "A Europe of Composite Monarchies," *Past and Present* 137 (1992): 48–71. Elliott's concern is with the sixteenth and seventeenth centuries, but his ideas are relevant in considering the activities of the German kings of an earlier period. See also D. J. A. Matthew, "Reflections on the Medieval Roman Empire," *History* 77 (1992): 363–90, esp. 373 ff.
56. Barraclough, *The Origins of Modern Germany,* 139.
57. Arnold, *Princes and Territories in Medieval Germany,* 169–70.

samenesses—was to emerge with the *bailliages* and *sénéchaussées*, and in an admittedly more limited area, *prévôtés* had made their appearance a good deal earlier.

Twelfth-century German aristocratic possessions were made up of patrimonies: allods, fiefs, advocacies deemed to be fiefs, and *honores*, comital and higher office together with their *banni*. Frederick Barbarossa wanted to define these diverse possessions as being held of the Reich and bestowed by the emperor. But this was a shadowy region where conflicting claims and aspirations mingled—and memories of the two-generation civil war were still very much alive, which suggested that the king had to be cautious in trying to rewrite the provisions of independence won by the princes in the Concordat of Worms.

What ends were served by Barbarossa's vast accumulations of inheritances, allods, lordships, advocacies, and ecclesiastical fiefs? The answer must be, first and foremost, to endow the king's family of four sons in lay estates. The chroniclers, whether close to the Hohenstaufens or indifferent to the fortunes of the emperor, are quite explicit. Otto of Saint Blasien is the best guide. Having recited all the inheritances and acquisitions, he continued: "The lands of all these and others which came into the emperor's right (*in jus*), and all the fiefs which they held by homage of ecclesiastical princes, bishops, and abbots, he caused to be given to his sons and possessed by them *potestative*," which suggests that the sons held them in law, but for the moment Barbarossa controlled them. By giving his sons so much, Frederick sought to make sure that all these lands, rights, fiefs, castles, and *ministeriales* would become Hohenstaufen house possessions, and not imperial demesnes which would revert should the Hohenstaufen at any time be passed over and not elected to the kingship. They would thus fight a future civil war from a position of strength.[58]

What was the long-term impact of all this acquisitiveness on the Hohenstaufen polity? The massive buildup of the Hohenstaufen fortune in Germany weakened rather than strengthened common bonds and did not further the growth of a superregional political society. It brought about dissonances and rifts which undermined rather than fostered solidarity. The princes, their houses, and their ambitions expressed the coming of age of regional cultures and power structures without a single preponderant core, which the Hohenstaufen had been unable and unwilling to nurture.

---

58. This paragraph and the next are based on Karl Leyser, "Frederick Barbarossa and the Hohenstaufen Polity," 157, 160, 167, 170, 172, 174. Otto of Saint Blasien is quoted on p. 170.

In Karl Leyser's revisionist view, Frederick Barbarossa was, first and foremost, one of these princes.

Political organization began to center on the lords' castles, and "Under the stress of the times the weaker freemen, in particular the peasantry, went down to serfdom, while the stronger freemen became knights or *ministeriales* and were bound to higher lords by ties of vassalage and homage. The disintegrating effects of the civil wars drove small nobles to larger ones for protection, while others, owing to the collapse of royal authority, lost their direct relationship with and protection by the crown, and were reduced to dependence by the strong." Feudalism in Germany undercut the older Saxon and Salian forms of kingship, which had been based on an extensive class of freemen who owed direct loyalty to the monarchy. In the civil wars accompanying the Investiture Conflict, new forms of dependence "spread in a sudden wave from below [but] stopped short at the crown." The great nobles enforced feudal subjection on those below them while denying their submission to the crown by insisting on their ancient freedoms and liberties.[59] Legal security lay in the special standing of not only every individual but also every piece of land. "Instead of a systematic legal order, to which all were equally subjected, there was a series of personal relationships, and each person and thing had an individual place in the legal order."[60]

German princes were possessive of their legal standing. After the year 1000, and particularly in response to the perceived aggression of the Salians under Henry IV, these inherited rights were transmuted into territorial lordship.[61] The contrast with England is striking. After 1066, the English state was based on the territorial domination of the whole country by its liege lord. In fact, even before that time, there had been a long tradition of both local government and effective centralized authority. Germany was never transformed from a federated, tribal monarchy into a territorial state with central lines of command. In part, this difference reflects radical scalar differences confronting a German king, but mostly it stands as a testimony to independent state-formation practices of the princes.

Furthermore, the near doubling of German territory took place in the face of royal indifference or even outright opposition. The princes directed the expansion of Germany's eastern borders. As early as 1180 this shift was

59. Barraclough, *The Origins of Modern Germany*, 219.

60. Freiherr von Dungern, "Constitutional Reorganization and Reform under the Hohenstaufen," in G. Barraclough (ed.), *Medieval Germany 911–1250, Essays by German Historians* (Oxford, 1962), 219.

61. Arnold, *Princes and Territories in Medieval Germany*, 280–83.

evident: half of the sixteen lay princes drew their titles from lands east of the German boundaries of 919. The Elbe, which had been Germany's eastern frontier, replaced the Rhine as its main artery. The princes were granted hereditary fiefs, complete powers of jurisdiction, a veto on royal castle building and taxation, and control of the German towns. These rights were enshrined in the constitution of 1232, *Statutum in favorem principum,* which has been called the Magna Carta of princely liberties. The contemporaneous *Riechsspruch* (imperial decision) referred to princes as *domini terrae,* and it was ordered that these powerful men were not to enact constitutional novelties in their territories without the consent of the *meliores et maiores terrae* (the privileged upper classes who composed the political nation of the *Länd,* of which there were several hundred, each with its own character).

Royal authority had disintegrated in Germany; the state's internal equilibrium could not be balanced. Germany imploded; its nationhood was "delayed." German destiny "passed out of the hands of the monarchy into the control of a princely aristocracy, whose horizons rarely extended beyond the boundaries of their own territories." The patchwork state had shredded into the thousand tiny threads with which the once-mighty German kings had held down their challengers. The princes secured their victory over the Staufers by electing Rudolph, count of Habsburg, to be their nominal leader in 1273. His election was a recognition of the spatial reorganization of Germany. The old kingdom had ceased to exist in all but name; "Lands and power in the east were a prerequisite of kingship." Germany became a confederation of princes who elected one of their own on the understanding that this "king/emperor" would have no effective royal authority. The centrifugal forces of princely power won the day in Germany.[62] The German core remained decentered.

If Germany was without a preponderant core, then it is important to recognize that each of the smaller satellites was itself engaged in a process of state formation that was as completely frenzied as that which engaged the largest prince. It was a war of all against all. This not only makes generalization almost impossible but also gave the process a chaotic dynamic

62.   Barraclough, *The Origins of Modern Germany,* 242, 233, 250–51, 236, 240, 280 (quotations in this paragraph and ideas in the preceding one); M. M. Fryde, "Studies in the History of Public Credit of German Principalities and Towns in the Middle Ages," *Studies in Medieval and Renaissance History* 1 (1964): 224–25; O. Brunner, *Land and Lordship: Structures of Governance in Medieval Austria* (Philadelphia, 1991).

so that some grew quickly but could not stay the course. Others grew rich feeding on their corpses. A small number of exceptional dynasties had quite incredible staying powers: the Habsburgs first entered the historical record in 1028 as the holders of a fortress called *Habrichtsburg* (the hawk's castle), which had been built by the bishop of Strassburg; the Württembergs appeared in the archival record for the first time in the eleventh century when they erected a castle on a mountainous peak near Stuttgart; and the Wittelsbachs—who rose from the ranks of the castle-building nobility and were able to maintain their line and to rule Bavaria right down to November 1918—appear for the first time in the early twelfth century. The Hohenstaufens, too, had risen from the elite of the Swabian nobility. The earliest known progenitor of the line was Frederick, count of Büren (d. 1094), whose son—yet another Frederick—had built a castle at Staufen (or Hohenstaufen) and called his line by this name. Through a quite spectacular marital coup, this second Frederick married Agnes, the daughter of Henry IV—apparently a mark of appreciation for his support in the civil wars of the late eleventh century.[63] Obviously these were men on the make who made the best of the turbulent conditions of their times. Others were not so fortunate.

For most of the Germanic peoples, culture and politics occurred in the transition from tribalism to early modernization. This has led some historians to a reductive model—"generated out of the masturbatory Germanistic mystique that seemed intensely 'relevant' in the 1930s"—that tried to create an "autogenic" rather than historical model of explanation. This led to the glorification of the German *Volk* and focused on its tribal inheritance and essentially ethnic characteristics.[64] Much of the older literature gives me a profound sense of unease since, in the light of later developments, it

63. I have drawn the genealogical information on the Habsburgs, Hohenstaufens, Württemberg, and Wittelsbachs from the *Encyclopaedia Brittanica*. It should be noted that the prevalence of partible inheritance among these great families was a continuing problem which led to some curious twists and turns. For example, among the Wittelsbach connection the question of legitimacy was resolved only with the Treaty of Pavia in 1329, which established the older line in the Rhineland and the younger line in Bavaria. Nearly three hundred years later, when the tide turned against the Protestant Palatines in the early days of the Thirty Years' War (1618–48), a deal was cooked within the family so that titles—the most important of which was the Electorship—and key parcels of land were transferred to the Catholic, Bavarian side of the family, whose status and wealth thereby rose dramatically.

64. Howard Kaminsky and James Van Horn Melton, "Translator's Introduction," in Brunner, *Land and Lordship*, xxxii.

smacks of ethno-racist overtones.[65] Yet one needs to keep hold of this baby while throwing out its filthy bathwater.

If state formation in France was characterized by the slow reassembling of royal authority, and if state formation in England was developed within the framework of royal law courts and county administration, then it is not farfetched to suggest that in Germany the practice of state formation was linguistic. The centrifugal forces of particularism were balanced by the centripetal forces that created a society through its common language. Of course, the German language covers a multitude of local variations, yet the *Annolied* (c. 1090) has been called the "birth certificate of the German language" because it gave currency to the concept of *Deutsche Sprache*. For much of its history this German language was the tongue of a cultured elite, and the language itself underwent substantial change.[66] In fact, there was "no Old High German word for 'Germany.' . . . It was only from the sixteenth century that the word *Deutschland*, 'Germany,' became widely used." Of course, many words and phrases were used to describe the German peoples, but that is a different matter from the nationalist fusion of a people and their state. Marc Bloch suggests that the term *Diutischin Lant* was known far earlier, as there is evidence from the ninth century onward that the German peoples were identified by their language: *Diutischiu Liute*. In the Latin of the documents, however, they were generally called *Teutonici*.[67]

In 1123 the "linguistic frontier" separating Germans and Slavs was still where it had been in the reign of Charlemagne. In the following two centuries, the aboriginal people in some of these eastern lands were integrated into the new society, in which " 'economic Germanization' was frequently followed by the linguistic"; but in other places they were first dispossessed

---

65. Thus, in the concluding sentences to an otherwise outstanding essay, Theodor Mayer writes (in 1935!) that

> What was necessary was a synthesis of the institutional state which came into existence in the later centuries of the middle ages with the old Germanic state, the ancient folk-community; and this the modern German state has achieved. Personal loyalty and the will to serve have again become vital elements in the life of the community, and have given both state and folk that moral foundation without which they cannot exist. As at the beginning so at the end of fifteen centuries of political development, state and folk are one. ("The State of the Dukes of Zähringen," in Barraclough (ed.), *Medieval Germany 911–1250*, 202.

66. F. R. H. Du Boulay, *Germany in the Later Middle Ages* (London, 1983), 2, 4, 114, 219.

67. Fuhrmann, *Germany in the High Middle Ages*, 19; Bloch, "The Empire and the Idea of Empire under the Hohenstaufen," in *Land and Work in Medieval Europe* (New York, 1967), 2.

and then driven from their land. The German migrants, who were expert in new forms of agricultural exploitation, took possession of the river marshes and tablelands which the native Slavs had not populated. Germanization was driven by the process of Christianization; acculturation meant the Germanization of the Slavs.[68]

The transition from tribalism to early modernization was forged in the crucible of warfare—directed inward against competitors for power and directed outward against the threats from the Magyars and Norsemen. In the vastness of Europe east of the Rhine, we witness a slow accretion of both jurisdictions and labor power. Material life was essentially located somewhere between the unsettled vagaries of migratory freedom and the demanding certitudes of manorial serfdom. The reproduction of these social relations took place in deep time, and we can only dimly understand their outlines from a historical geography which privileges place names, field names, and settlement sites over and against the human actors in this process. German history is viewed from the top down—there is no equivalent to the English manorial studies, the French analyses of the social geography of human settlement, or the Italian study of the Florentine *catasto*.

German social life was largely experienced from the bottom up, in communities. While the peasantry's rights were limited to specific freedoms or liberties, the very fact that negotiation took place speaks to the essentially contractual Germanic legacy to which the peasantry, too, was heir. These documents were created by the lords, who were in the process of establishing an empire of subjugation within which they could appropriate surplus value from the peasantry. Self-regulation grew slowly, but it had its roots in the reorganization of agricultural systems that accompanied feudalization and the territorialization of the land. This meant, above all, that it became important to develop agreements on planting, harvesting, and pasturing livestock. The social interaction displayed in speech acts between lords and peasants is most revealing; it is worth discussing in some detail.[69]

---

68. Fuhrmann, *Germany in the High Middle Ages,* 11 (quote on 123), 7, 124; Barraclough, *The Origins of Modern Germany,* 257–58, 273, 42; H. Aubin, "Medieval Agrarian Society in Its Prime: The Lands East of the Elbe and German Colonization Eastwards," in M. M. Postan (ed.), *The Cambridge Economic History of Europe,* vol. 1 (Cambridge, 1966), 449–86; Friedrich Lotter, "The Crusading Idea and the Conquest of the Region East of the Elbe," in Robert Bartlett and Angus MacKay (eds.), *Medieval Frontier Societies* (Oxford, 1989), 303–5; F. L. Carsten, "The Slavs in North-Eastern Germany," *Economic History Review,* 2d ser., 11 (1941): 61–76.

69. The following discussion paraphrases the arguments put forward in Michael Toch, "Asking the Way and Telling the Law: Speech in Medieval Germany,"

In the first examples, which come from literary sources, the lord initiates contact while the male peasant deferentially waits for his superior to speak. The lord addresses the peasant by the vocative personal pronoun "du" while the peasant underscores the public transcript of subordination by acknowledging both social distance and power asymmetry by addressing the lord as "Herr," or "Dominus," or some other respectful term of homage. In these early texts, lords gave orders while peasants cringed obediently.

The next examples come from the twelfth century, after the massive feudalization of the German countryside. These communications are different in that they no longer take place between two individuals but rather involve a lord and a peasant-community.

Collective peasant speech aimed at achieving concrete goals in relation to the newly constituted village communities, which were disassociated spatially, socially, and economically from the lord while being bound together in a legal relationship. Personal, continuous intercourse between lord and serf was not a feature of most estates in the medieval German countryside. Lordships were usually scattered holdings comprising lands and people; most were administered by estate officers. In this context, communications were institutionalized. The key document was a *Weistüm* which wrote down the "telling" of the law. Oral recitation took place several times a year. These collective ceremonies constituted the operational definition of legitimate rule. Historical consciousness emerged from the continual forming and re-forming of the dialectic between arbitrariness and legitimacy. This meant that there was a continuous redefinition of needs and rights. For the lords, this blended acknowledgment of their powers with the ritualized submission of their peasants. For the peasants, this activity provided the opportunity to assert rights with the aim of limiting the lords' appropriations. The peasantry, then, played an active—but subordinate—role in defining the political organization of local life. These rituals involved the whole community in making and remarking its laws.

The first *Weistümer* survive from western parts closest to France—Alsace and the Lower Rhine. The eastern regions, and particularly small lordships there, generated them later. The impact of these lawmaking protocols was modified by the progress of territorial state formation. In the southwest, for example, where there were numerous dwarf states carved out of the disintegration of the Hohenstaufen dynasty, these *Gemeinde* were the

Journal of Interdisciplinary History 16 (1986): *passim*. I have also employed some ideas put forward by David Sabean with regard to the practise of *herrschaft*; *Power in the Blood* (Cambridge, 1984), 20–27.

vehicle with which local society balanced the contradictory ambitions of both lordly domination and peasant self-government. Peasants were thus formed into a corporate presence in which they were able to act as a collectivity of equals. This equality spoke to their potential for mediating the divergent interests of the different strata within the peasantry and inhibited the private appropriation of common resources. In Bavaria, by way of contrast, the precocious emergence of a territorial state under the ægis of the Wittelsbach dynasty overrode these local systems of lordship and replaced them with *ämter* (administrative districts) under ducal jurisdiction. In Bavaria, then, the peasantry did not achieve effective corporate representation, but it did gain protection from the territorial government against the private exercise of domination—"intermediary lordship"—by local lords.[70]

Overall, the weakness of the empire meant that the powers of executive government devolved upon the territorial governments, and it was in the largest of them—the electorate and duchy of Saxony; the duchies of Bavaria, Württemberg, Brunswick, Austria, and Carinthia; the Palatine electorate; the Landgraviate of Hessen; the county of Tyrol; the prince-bishoprics of Münster, Bamberg, Magdeburg, Trier, and Würzburg; and the wealthiest city-states like Augsburg, Cologne, Frankfurt, Nuremberg, Strasbourg, and Ulm—that the new methods of top-down governance most completely supplanted the older forms. These large jurisdictions contained the vast majority of the German population, yet it is appropriate to remember that the German territories should not be considered on an equal level with the French and English states. "In a garment that fits a giant a dwarf must necessarily suffocate, and if the dwarf grows and the old garment becomes too constricting he is smart enough to get another one."[71] The German wardrobe was ill-fitting.

The empire remained a general court of legal complaint, constitutional arbitration, and political appeal. It was a forum where territorial rulers could negotiate with each other and where even territorial subjects could at times take their own worst grievances, if they dared to do so and provided they could afford it.[72] This is not to deny the decentered character of early modernization in the German territorial states; rather, it is to keep sight of the fact that this process was contingent in the sense that no single state

70. Heide Wunder, "Serfdom in Later Medieval and Early Modern Germany," in T. H. Ashton, P. R. Coss, Christopher Dyer, and Joan Thirsk (eds.), *Social Relations and Ideas* (Cambridge, 1983), 260–63, 269–70.

71. Elisabeth Bamberger, quoted in Fryde, "Studies in the History of Public Credit of German Principalities and Towns in the Middle Ages," 227.

72. G. Benecke, *Society and Politics in Germany 1500–1750* (London, 1974), 31.

was an independent entity which could control its own destiny. The key problem for territorial princes was "mediatized authority." Public functions that would later be identified with the sovereign powers of the state were subject to private agreements. This dispersal of control was the hallmark of feudal society. Complex obligations, legal rights, military service, feudal dues, and forced labor services were knotted together. This was a result of subinfeudation working through generations of contractual exchanges. If the larger territorial states had won the upward battle to secure their rights against the German king's imperial pretensions, they also had to fight the war downward to secure their rights to appropriate the surplus wealth of their subjects. In a certain sense, this was the royal predicament writ small.

Money spoke a language that all rulers understood. So, how was the state apparatus financed? In the first place, there was a general expectation that rulers would be able to cover their own expenses from their own treasuries, and this was not unreasonable as long as the expense of warfare was under control.[73] Even allowing for the cost and upkeep of castles, the maintenance of a crew of *ministeriales,* and the extraordinary purchases of mercenary services, it seems that princely incomes were more or less sufficient to finance the military undertakings until the later part of the fourteenth century. After this time, however, princes found themselves simultaneously confronting a fall in income (as their tenantry melted away in the aftermath of the Black Death) and steeply rising costs (as gunpowder began to change the face of war). This scissors was a general, pan-European phenomenon that forced a decisive moment of truth upon territorial rulers who had to find new sources of revenue or else pledge their lands to financiers.

Feudal Germany in the period between the thirteenth-century collapse of the Hohenstaufens' kingship and the Reformation was characterized by a bewildering dynastic roulette. Those lineages which were able to combine demographic good fortune with fiscal prudence and military aggression were able to survive and to amass vast financial resources. Those who were impotent, profligate, or pusillanimous were ground to pieces. The Hohenstaufens were, of course, the most prominent case of dynastic failure. Their example was emulated by the Ascanians and the Welphs (Guelphs) in the fourteenth century. The Habsburgs, the Hohenzollerns, and the Wittelsbachs were among the most prominent cases of dynastic success.

---

73. By the fifteenth century there was no independent imperial demesne (or estate); the emperor's wealth was his own rather than being a perquisite of the office.

The subterranean pressures of the age manifested themselves in the conflictual relationship between the territorial lord and his subjects. They needed each other for protection in the ongoing wars of all against all. It would be misleading to underemphasize the extent to which the territorial prince garnered new power by being the biggest bully in the neighborhood in an age of the robber baron and his "straggling band of proletarian knights."[74] In effect, he was able to collect protection money from his subjects, who were as afraid of him as they were endangered by his enemies. Together, the local ruler and his henchmen extracted wealth from the peasantry to finance the state apparatus. The key seems to have been found in financing the system of castle, *ministeriales*, and feudal levies while employing mercenaries as circumstances demanded and revenues permitted. Establishing the prince's rights as the *Ländesfurst* was his ability to collect this protection money in an age of incessant warfare.

In Germany, as everywhere, money provided the sinews of power. The territorial princes' problem was to find ways of gaining access to their subjects' resources in exchange for providing them public services, the foremost of which was the maintenance of public peace. Each local dynasty faced a congerie of lesser powers—knights, cities, and corporations—which contested attempts to centralize power. In this regard, German history was in the mainstream of the western tradition of "multiple acephalous federation" and its constant power struggles.

3.

The making of feudal society paralleled the spread of castles. The Anglo-Saxon practice of constructing defensive strongholds anticipates the wider process of establishing counterweights to the armed knight. Indeed, Georges Duby has written that the period between 1030 and 1180 was "less an age of fiefs than an age of castles." These castles were not all the huge masonry structures of our imaginations; rather, these two-roomed wooden fortifications were built on raised mounds (*mottes*).[75] These new local units of power were quite literally built from the ground up. The most familiar form was the moated castle, which was usually situated on an optimal natural location but sometimes required substantial labor to re-

---

74. Gerald Strauss, *Nuremberg in the Sixteenth Century* (Bloomington, 1976), 53.

75. For a brief discussion of this chronology, see Robert Fossier, *Peasant Life in the Medieval West* (Oxford, 1988), 54–55, 127–28. Duby's words are from his thesis *La société aux xi et xii siècles dans la région mâconnaise,* quoted in R. I. Moore, "Duby's Eleventh Century," *History* 69 (1984): 46.

create the defensive advantages afforded by rising ground. These first-generation castles had a small footprint, but they were tall enough to raise their fighting force into the sky so that it could rain down destruction on besiegers. The castles' towers, walls, and moats visibly dominated the surrounding countryside. Administrative controls and military hegemony, located in these castles, were the means and symbol of noble power. In the words of one contemporary:

> The men of great fortune and noble birth spent most of their time fighting and making war. . . . In order to shield themselves from their enemies, vanquish their equals, and oppress the weak, it is their wont to throw up earthworks as high as possible, and to dig a broad, deep ditch all about them. Around the top run ramparts made of tree trunks, squared and sturdily put together.[76]

It was a time when "every rich man built his castles. They cruelly oppressed the wretched men of the land with castle-works; and when the castles were made they filled them with devils and evil men."[77] Encastellation proceeded together with a knot of allied technologies: siegecraft, the development of ballistic weapons thrown by trebuchets, and the crossbow, whose bolts could be fired with enough force to pierce a knight's iron mail. Taken together, the military technology of armored cavalry, castles, siege machines, and crossbowmen formed an integrated system of warfare that coalesced in the heartland of feudal society and then slowly spread outward from the northwestern core.[78]

While the material foundations of the fighting class were the lands and appurtenances attached to a knight's benefice, not all knights became extralocal powers. Most found themselves subordinated to the local hero. Indeed, the lesser knight's inability to establish himself as independent of a patron was the other side of the coin of the royal power vacuum. Two social institutions were truly stable in the early stages of the feudal revolution: the dukes and their castle garrisons, the *caballarii casati*. The whole structure depended on the coexistence of "the holdings of the *casati*, which were grouped around the castle, and the great fiefs of the powerful lords that stretched along the borders of his territory. The fealty of the first group consisted of active dependence, that of the second group tended to be

---

76. Quoted in Georges Duby, *The Age of Cathedrals* (Chicago, 1981), 34.
77. This quotation from the Anglo-Saxon Chronicle dates from the early twelfth century; quoted in N. J. G. Pounds, *An Historical Geography of Europe 450 BC–AD 1330* (Cambridge, 1973), 261.
78. Bartlett, *The Making of Europe*, 60–84.

reduced to a pact of nonaggression."[79] The feudal system was part of a world of violence in which only the fittest survived. Yet, curiously, this world of violence was orchestrated by acts of homage and submission. These linkages proved to be very tangled. This complexity was not a sign of the structure's decadence but rather its essential condition, extant from the outset. In fact, obedience to a public authority could be established only through feudal bonds. Therefore, these chains were greatly multiplied so that every man and every piece of land was enmeshed in them.[80]

If the use of armed horsemen anticipated the creation of a knighthood, then the building of castles would come to be predicated upon control of the state's financial apparatus. Not all parts of France were decentralized. In some counties, like Anjou and Normandy, the ruler's central power involved significant control over both the economy and public life.[81] The activities of Fulk Nerra, count of Anjou, are relevant here: between 992 and 1039 he ordered the building of at least thirty-five fortresses.[82] The concentration of political power into royal hands was accompanied by the consolidation of ownership of castles.

In France, where sovereignty was only slowly reassembled by the Capetians and the monopolization of violence was therefore uncertain, some 10,000 castles were built after the year 1000. Even before this date, however, there had been almost two centuries of defensive building in reaction to both post-Carolingian political breakdown and Norse invasions. In England, around 1100, there were 500 castles which had been built in the previous two generations by the Norman conquerors. After the civil wars of the second quarter of the twelfth century, the crown tightened its control over the castle building of its underlings.[83] In 1154 the king of England had 49 castles and his barons had 225; in 1214, royal fortifications had nearly doubled (93) while the baronial strongholds had declined in number (179). Moreover, many of the fortresses held by the English barons were held at the king's "pleasure," and most were situated in border regions.

79. Poly and Bournazel, *The Feudal Transformation,* 73, 71, 76.

80. Poly and Bournazel, *The Feudal Transformation,* 202. A few pages later they write that "The renaissance of royal power in the twelfth century, far from opposing the feudalization that had led in the previous century to the setting up of banal lordship, existed only through it. It completed the process by controlling it" (210).

81. Bernard S. Bachrach, "The Angevin Economy, 960–1060: Ancient or Feudal?," *Studies in Medieval and Renaissance History,* new ser., 10 (1988): 3–55.

82. Bernard S. Bachrach, "The Angevin Strategy of Castle Building in the Reign of Fulk Nerra, 987–1040," *American Historical Review* 88 (1983): 533–60.

83. Sidney Painter, "English Castles in the Early Middle Ages: Their Numbers, Location, and Legal Position," *Speculum* 10 (1935): 321–32.

In addition, of course, the king of England held other castles in his French domain. In Germany, by way of contrast, nobles were at first limited in their ability to build their own independent fortifications, and such structures were regarded as "adulterine" in the eyes of the Saxon and Salian kings, who destroyed them or else appropriated them for their own use. After the onset of the Investiture Crisis, when Germany descended into two generations of civil war, an estimated 20,000 castles were constructed by the nobility, which was freed from royal supervision and control.[84] In late eleventh-century Germany, castles were "to be found all over the land as if raised by an enchanter's wand."[85] Before this time, private warfare had been unusual and was quickly squashed. Thus, the trajectory of castle building in Germany was precisely opposite to the English example.

What did it cost to build a castle? The tenth- and eleventh-century *mottes* were comparatively both quick and cheap to build, whereas the later stone castles were slow and expensive. Building the massive Norman stronghold of Château-Gaillard, "a turning point in the history of western fortifications," provides us with an example of the enormity of these undertakings. This fortress, which "rose on the rock above Andeli [on the Seine, between Rouen and Paris] with the unhurried speed and confidence of some magical creation," was inspired by Richard the Lionheart's first-hand experiences at the siege of Acre during the Third Crusade. Fortunately, fragments of the documentary record survive; these suggest that £21,203 was spent during 1197–98 on castle building, out of a total defense budget of nearly £50,000. Labor was the main item in the budget, accounting for almost 83 percent of all costs. This sum has been calculated to represent a staggering 2,544,436 working days at the prevailing rates of pay for unskilled labor. Perhaps as many as 10,000 men would have been employed in the construction of Château-Gaillard, each working an average of 250 days, in the year covered by this account.[86] One can only wonder where so many workers would have been found at such short notice, but

84. Thompson, "German Feudalism," 450–51; Arnold, *German Knighthood 1050–1300*, 201.

85. Thompson, "German Feudalism," 452, 457. Notice that Thompson takes for granted that labor to haul the building materials and erect the castles was not only available but also forthcoming. One of the evasions of medieval historiography is its neglect of the labor process—in terms of both the supply of labor and the conditions of work. Not all studies are negligent, but a great many do not concern themselves with these issues. One can be sure, however, that the subjects of these studies did not take the supply of labor for granted.

86. Maurice Powicke, *The Loss of Normandy* (Manchester, 1961), 190–96, 204–6; Philippe Contamine, *War in the Middle Ages* (Oxford, 1984), 109–11. Despite its seemingly impregnable command over the surrounding countryside,

the sources are silent on such concerns. It is hardly surprising that a historian of this episode imagines the king surrounded by a "hive of soldiers and workmen." Angevin castle building during Fulk Nerra's reign required the employment of 1.6 million worker-days over a period of forty-three years.[87] Expenditures on this scale precluded the participation of all but the very richest warriors in the great game of siege warfare.

The millennial generation experienced a "crisis of fidelity" as neither the king nor princes were any longer regarded as guarantors of social order.

> This may be likened to a revolution (as well as a revelation) because it confirmed, rewarded and institutionalized the subversive inroads of lordship on public power, while sanctioning patrimonial claims to service, fidelity and dependence. . . . The reorienting of fidelities coincided with discussions of tenurial right whence arose customary law in many regions. . . . Everywhere there was defiance of royal or princely authority, not in principle, but on the definition of peace: that is, on the control of castles.[88]

In its purest form, this "feudal revolution" meant that power could not be delegated because there was no guarantee that dependents would act as agents rather than aggressive lords on the make. "The greater domains were not only hard to control by traditional means of trust, they were also vulnerable to the demands of a numerous class of petty lords and knights (and would-be lords) who were creating and inflicting their own lordship without any accounting at all." This was not a classic class struggle but rather a deadly form of internecine warfare: "The crisis of the millenium was one of power, which (as always) survived; what collapsed was govern-

---

Château-Gaillard was taken by cunning mercenaries in the pay of Philip Augustus who surprised its defenders by creeping like rats through its latrine shafts. "Contemporaries found it particularly shocking, because this form of attack was totally devoid of prowess, operating at a distance and then striking without warning, like the plague"; Georges Duby, *France in the Middle Ages, 987–1460* (Oxford, 1991), 159. A note with regard to the deployment of labor: on the other side of the world (and several centuries later), the reconstruction of the Nikko Tōshō-gū mausoleum complex in the mid-1630s required 4.5 million days of labor to complete; William H. Coaldrake, *The Way of the Carpenter: Tools and Japanese Architecture* (New York, 1990), 138. When labor was readily available at near-subsistence wages, it was deployed without much concern for cost management in monumental, gigantic projects that were built to glorify secular rulers and to underscore their supernatural ties.

87. Bachrach, "The Angevin Economy," 21–22.

88. Bisson, "The 'Feudal Revolution,' " 27–29, 39, 42. To my way of thinking, this is the crux of Bisson's argument, and the criticisms of Barthélemy and White do not really concern themselves with the political economy of "violence" so much as its rhetoric and discourse.

ment. . . . One might hope to evade one's lord's violence, one expected him to demand and constrain. Few expected him to govern."[89] The breakup of the tenth-century principalities and the establishment of banal lordships are two faces of the same social transformation, which can be called feudal because it introduced new social relationships into the countryside: the knight's *casamentum*, the lord's castle, the territorial principality, and sometimes even the peasant's holdings were all fiefs. A new balance was established in which these relationships were central to social life.

Violence was deflected from external aggression and expansion, and it was turned against the dependent population. Moreover,

> Violence was nurtured in the economy and sociability of castles. . . .
> Armed, pretentious and poor, the knights clung to their stoned-off
> space, talking of weapons and deeds, of strikes, of demands; of lucrative
> stratagems more than management or incomes. . . . All indifferently
> were capable of: violating churches or the sanctuaries about them (on
> excuse of protecting them); attacking unarmed priests, monks or pil-
> grims, or seizing their horses and property; plundering domestic ani-
> mals; seizing, robbing or ransoming villagers (male and female) or
> merchants; seizing crops at harvest; destroying mills or confiscating
> grain from them; beating villagers' animals; attacking "noble women
> without their husbands" or widows or nuns.

The violence of the castellans and their patrols of thugs was a method of lordship. "It was unconstructive; it had neither political nor administrative character, for it was based on the capricious manipulation of powerless people."[90] A "cacophony of symmetrical evidence"—self-justifying and arbitrary habits of lordship as well as the series of councils from 989 to 1014 in which the Peace of God was proclaimed—led to a new vocabulary of power and lordship.[91]

89. Poly and Bournazel, *The Feudal Transformation,* 238.
90. Bisson, "The 'Feudal Revolution,' " 17–19. Both Barthélemy and White are critical of this aspect of Bisson's argument. They suggest that he has taken the monastic and ecclesiastical writers at face value and not provided any evidence that the scale of "violence" at the turn of the millennium was any worse—or, indeed, any different—than it was in the preceding or following century. In essence, Barthélemy and White suggest that the sources are themselves flawed (i.e., written by interested parties) and that this bias makes them problematic. This seems to be a point well taken, but it also seems to be somewhat beside the main point that, whatever the scale of "violence" might have been, there was a significant change in the social relations between the different subsets within the upper class and the rest of society. I remain unconvinced that this revisionist criticism does much to upset the "mutationist" theory of social change around the year 1000.
91. Bisson, "The 'Feudal Revolution,' " 22.

By the second and third generation of this social landslide—toward the end of the eleventh century—the imbrication of violent lordship in everyday life was more or less taken for granted. All societies are ultimately—in the last instance—based on violence. Feudal violence existed in the the first instance, as it were. This is really what was revolutionary about the "feudal revolution."

4.

Early castles were crude edifices built for military reasons, not comfort or pleasure. This world of violence was a hard anvil on which the construction of domesticity was only slowly forged. Inside the castle, private life took place in public. While the fief and/or vassalage were crucial, they too were subordinated to living at the side of the master, what was called the *convivium*.[92] The history of housing was thus a reflection of the history of power. At the center of each local cell was a single dominant couple who sat by day and slept by night in the same space. "Fertile marriage was the bedrock of social order. There was no house without marriage, no marriage without a house. At the center of every household was a single married couple." Indeed, betrothal and the marriage ceremony itself were followed by the final ritual of the marital process: the couple was witnessed together in bed and blessed by the priest. Gradually, the central hall was replaced by a new organization— "a nucleus surrounded by its satellites [which was] . . . unquestionably the atom of private life in the feudal era."[93] This nucleation was not a matter of constructing new rooms so much as using tapestries to create partitions to divide and to compartmentalize space.

Within the fortresses of the knightly class, the spatial organization of private life took place on both class and gender lines. As long as the vacuum of royal power left the local heroes in control of the countryside, the lesser knights were forced to find places for themselves within the households of the mighty warriors. "We see the male and female sections of the household staring at one another in fascination and fright, occasionally joining together or furtively communicating and interpenetrating." Paradoxically,

92. Poly and Bournazel, *The Feudal Transformation*, 353. See also chap. 2, "Honorable Dependence," 46–85. This argument is drawn from Georges Duby's many works; references to them stud this section and have played a major role in the development of my understanding of this historical epoch.

93. Georges Duby, "The Aristocratic Households of Feudal France: Communal Living," in Georges Duby (ed.), *A History of Private Life*, vol. 2, *Revelations of the Medieval World* (Cambridge, Mass., 1988), 56. See also Dominique Barthélemy, "The Aristocratic Households of Feudal France: Kinship," in Duby (ed.), *Revelations of the Medieval World*, 132–33.

the distinction between male and female domains became harder and faster as women lost power within marriage.[94] Women with connections to the Carolingian nobility had previously played an essential role in transmitting an aura of legitimacy "to new men without any doubt ever being cast on their pedigree."[95] This older system of family relationships came under great stress during the feudal crisis, between 1020 and 1060, and it was in reaction to these tensions that the assertion of social dominance by the nobility resonated in the private life of its fortified houses and in its family formation strategies.[96]

The key aspect of knightly survival was a new form of inheritance that limited descent to the eldest male heir. Patrimonies were thereby maintained intact rather than being divided and subdivided, as had been the case before the year 1000.[97] The conjugal family was only a single cell of a larger organism, the lineage. The shift from clan to lineage—from extended to dynastic family—was a relatively gradual process of change. The Norman Conquest of England in 1066 captures this transition in a snapshot; it "must be seen as involving not simply the replacement of one aristocracy by another but also the replacement of one set of family relationships by another, a change not merely in personnel, not merely in all those external relations of the aristocracy . . . , but a change in internal organization, in familial structure, in assumptions about property." Before the Normans, English surnames were neither hereditary nor toponymic. After the Battle of Hastings it became possible to identify individual families—their history and their fortunes—by their property.

The whirlwind of military energy that flung the Normans across the length and breadth of Europe in a few generations satisfied the ambitions of brothers and younger sons through the establishment of colonial lineages in their vanquished territories. Thereafter, "the most ancient tenure which might be claimed [at law] was tenure 'a conquestu.' " In this way the Normans hoped to establish military institutions which could descend unimpaired and unfragmented in order to guarantee the permanence of their army of occupation. Of course, matters did not work out this way, and

94. Barthélemy, "Civilizing the Fortress," in Duby (ed.), *Revelations of the Medieval World*, 416–23. For a demonstration of the organization of space in these "Tower Houses," see Margaret Wood, *The English Medieval House* (London, 1965), 166–176.

95. Poly and Bournazal, *The Feudal Transformation*, 91–92, 107–8.

96. T. N. Bisson, "Nobility and Family in Medieval France: A Review Essay," *French Historical Studies* 16 (1990): 597–613.

97. Georges Duby, *The Knight, the Lady, and the Priest: The Making of Modern Marriage in Medieval France* (New York, 1983), 94.

the stewardship of these knight's fees took on a life of their own. Behind the fictions of lineal descent, most members of this new upper strata were "men raised from the dust" whose primary characteristics had been their loyalty to the Crown and their luck in staying onside through all the twists and turns of the maelstrom of civil war, attempted parricide, and fratricide. Those who were disobedient lost everything—at the time of Magna Carta, only four of the twenty-one family heads among the Twenty-five Barons could trace their lineage back to the Conquest, 150 years earlier. Of course, many lineages simply did not reproduce themselves in the male line. Indeed, only one family lineage which had been prominent in pre-Conquest Normandy was still influential in early thirteenth-century England.[98]

We can gain a much more subtle insight into the workings of this system of restricted marriage, and the organization of feudal society, from the career of William Marshal, the greatest knight of the later twelfth century.[99] William, the second son of an Anglo-Norman nobleman's second marriage, was sent away from his paternal home at puberty when he was apprenticed to his cousin in Normandy to undergo the arduous training which would teach him to become a warrior, a knight errant. He was the wonder of the day: making his fortune at tournaments; gaining the eye of Eleanor of Aquitaine, Henry II's queen; becoming responsible for training

98. The quotations in these two paragraphs come from J. C. Holt, "Feudal Society and the Family in Early Medieval England: I. The Revolution of 1066," *Transactions of the Royal Historical Society*, 5th ser., 32 (1982): 199–200, 207, 208. In three further essays, Holt suggests that the richness of English evidence—and its secular character—moderates Duby's strong theories by introducing a more nuanced sense of change to the shift from kin to lineage. In particular, Holt allows more leeway for royal intervention and situational arrangements. See "Feudal Society and the Family in Early Medieval England: II. Notions of Patrimony," *Transactions of the Royal Historical Society*, 5th ser., 33 (1983): 193–220; "Feudal Society and the Family in Early Medieval England: III. Patronage and Politics," *Transactions of the Royal Historical Society*, 5th ser., 34 (1984): 1–25; "Feudal Society and the Family in Early Medieval England: IV. The Heiress and the Alien," *Transactions of the Royal Historical Society*, 5th ser., 35 (1985): 1–28. The upper classes developed family names before 1200, and the free and servile peasantry followed suit in the thirteenth century; David Postles, "Notions of the Family, Lordship and the Evolution of Naming Processes in Medieval English Rural Society: A Regional Example," *Continuity and Change* 10 (1995): 169–98.

99. Our knowledge of Marshal's life is derived from the *Histoire de Guillaume le Mareschal*, a Middle French poem of 19,214 lines in rhyming couplets which was written by a member of his household a few years after the great man's death in 1219. It is the only contemporary surviving source for a biography of someone who was neither royal nor saintly. By and large, my account follows the explication provided by Georges Duby (*William Marshal: The Flower of Chivalry* [New York, 1985]), although I have supplemented Duby's text with the biographies written by David Crouch and Sidney Painter, which will be footnoted when appropriate.

the royal couple's young son; and later discharging that royal student's un-fulfilled vow to crusade in the Holy Land.

A man on the make, William was able to translate his military prowess into a political career of the greatest magnitude. On a personal level, his ca-reer culminated in an extraordinarily advantageous marriage to a rich heiress whose dowry included a Welsh estate and claims to vast stretches of Ireland. On his marriage, William Marshal became a magnate; he was ruler of one of the flatter, and therefore richer, lordships in the Welsh Marches. He was the lord of two powerful stone fortresses (Chepstow and Usk) and the overlord of other lesser castles; in addition, he was patron of Tintern Abbey as well as the priories of Chepstow and Usk.[100] "On that day, his wedding day, a warrior crossed the decisive threshold; he entered the much narrower circle of those who really ruled." William Marshal was forty-seven; his wife, Isabel de Clare, was still a teenager. His marriage meant "a change of class"; he had arrived.[101]

The change in status that took place at marriage was also connected with a shift in the male's sexual economy. Because the purpose of marriage was procreation, the act of impregnation required not only "pure women" but also "adult men" whose seed was devoted to reproducing the lineage. The wedding was a "cultic ritual of generation" in which clerics circled the nup-tial bed and sprinkled holy water over the newlyweds. The father of the groom likewise beseeches God to bless his children who are "joined to-gether by a holy copulation and by the rites of marriage." While the Church was able to gain control over the institution of marriage, the wed-ding itself remained an essentially domestic rite designed to promote fer-tility. This concern with sexuality within marriage did not preclude extra-

100. David Crouch, *William Marshal: Court, Career and Chivalry in the Angevin Empire 1147–1219* (London, 1990), 63–64.

101. Duby, *William Marshal*, 131. William Marshal became a magnate upon his marriage, but he was not immediately transformed into a great magnate, as his earlier biographer Sidney Painter has claimed. Crouch notes that "in England he held precious little other than the potential to make money that the services of sixty-five and a half knights' fees gave him. The fat demesne manors of Weston in Hertfordshire and Parndon and Chesterford in Essex that were part of his honor were, until she died, in the hands of his mother-in-law." Furthermore, it was only during Richard's absence from England that William Marshal was raised to the level of co-justiciar. William Marshal's powers in the Welsh Marches increased rad-ically in 1199–1200 when, as one of the late King Richard's main men, he paved the way for John, the dead king's brother, to gain the crown. The flower of chivalry was amply rewarded with lands and a new title—earl of Pembroke. It was in this capac-ity that William Marshal went to Ireland in 1200–1 to firm up his land claims and receive homage; Crouch, *William Marshal*, 77–79.

marital promiscuity. But, unlike the "youths," the adult man's seed was not spilled outside the confines of the house. There was, as Georges Duby notes, an endogamous circuit of illegitimate sexuality that provided the lineage with a constant supply of "beautiful," "noble" women. Duby cites the example of Count Baldwin II, whose funeral was attended by his ten legitimate children and his twenty-three bastards of both sexes.[102]

William Marshal enhanced his newfound position by marrying off his children to cement friendships.[103] These alliances underscore the centrality of inheritance strategies in the organization of feudal family formations. Though they married when he was middle-aged, William and Isabel were prolific. In 1219, when William died, they had ten surviving children.[104] Three of his five daughters were by then already established in the families of his fellow earls, the fourth was married off to a lower-grade nobleman (the vassal of one of his new friends), and the fifth was still a little child at the time of William's death in 1219. She was showered with loose cash for her dowry and trousseau so that her eldest brother could marry her off as soon and as well as possible. William Marshal's five sons were more problematic: of course, the eldest (William) inherited the patrimony, but what about the other four? Richard, the second son, had thrown in his lot with Philip Augustus to protect his Norman fiefs, but the old warrior still granted him yet another Norman seigneury in the hope that he would neither envy nor torment the heir. Gilbert, the third son, was already established in the Church with a rich clerical position. The fourth son, Walter, was granted a scrap—a small manor, not taken from the family patrimony but bought expressly to settle his inheritance. Anselm, the fifth son, was just a toddler. It was Anselm who was to recapitulate his father's career: in his last words the old warrior granted his little boy an annual pension of £140, a staggering

102. Duby, *Medieval Marriage: Two Models from Twelfth-Century France* (Baltimore, 1978), 90–94. Crouch notes that bastards were "great assets": girls were used to cement alliances with lesser families while boys were made knights, clerks, and/or stewards whose loyalty to their fathers and legitimate older brothers had to be total since they had nothing else; *William Marshal*, 62.

103. Duby, *William Marshal*, 131, 132.

104. In his "prolific power," William Marshal was very much his father's son. In one of the more famous incidents of the feudal period, little William Marshal had been held hostage by King Stephen, his father's enemy; when John Marshal was threatened with the death of his five-year-old son, "he told the king's messenger that he cared little if William were hanged, for he had the anvil and the hammers with which to forge still better sons." In the event, of course, little William survived at least in part because the little boy seems to have charmed his captor; Sidney Painter, *William Marshal, Knight-Errant, Baron, and Regent of England* (Baltimore, 1971), 14.

sum of money from which he was to be apprenticed—"to become a knight, he must ride errant till he win honor; then he will find someone who will cherish him and do him great honor, more than any other."[105]

As astonishing as William Marshal's irresistible rise had been, his later life was even more amazing. The tenacity and strategic intelligence which characterized his military actions served him well in the snake pit of dynastic politics. Service to his lord was William Marshal's natural habitat: "he was as happy in the royal presence as nowhere else, unless it were behind the king's banner in the field." His own banner had the royal red lion rampant on a half-green, half-yellow field.[106] He served three English kings as a trusted counselor, yet he was also able to remain a loyal vassal of Philip Augustus, from whom he held lands in Normandy. In his final years, when the great warrior was over seventy years old, he became the regent to the nine-year-old boy-king Henry III. The estwhile knight errant had become king of England in all but name: *rector regis et regni Angliae*. With his characteristic unquenchable thirst for honor, William set himself on "a sea without bottom or bank." With his characteristic shrewd calculation, William was convinced to do this duty only after seeking and receiving a plenary indulgence for a lifetime of sins from the papal legate.[107] Finally, it was in these last fateful years that William achieved his greatest glory: on May 20, 1217, he commanded the English forces at the Battle of Lincoln, driving the French army from England and thereby ensuring an English succession to the English throne.[108]

In his very last days William Marshal forsook both his family and the secular world and entered the order of the Templars. He "died with his eyes fixed on the cross. He had met an enemy whom he could not defeat." On May 16, 1219, he was buried in London at the Temple church in silken winding sheets he had brought back from the Holy Land in the 1180s when, so long ago, he had been a crusader.[109] A giant of a man, William Marshal quite literally bestrode his world: he had "more honor than any other knight for prowess, wisdom, and loyalty."[110] In his career one can see

105. The information regarding these inheritances is found in Duby, *William Marshal*, 7–10.

106. Crouch, *William Marshal*, 74, 44.

107. Painter, *William Marshal*, 196.

108. In the previous millennium, England had been overrun by a series of foreign invaders. The Battle of Lincoln would be the last time that a foreign power would do battle on English soil, excepting, of course, incursions by Scottish and Welsh borderers and the German aerial attacks in World War II.

109. Painter, *William Marshal*, 289.

110. These words are reported to have been spoken to Marshal on his deathbed by the Master of the Temple; quoted in Painter, *William Marshal*, 284–85.

both the flowering of chivalry and its inexorable subordination to the demands of money, the church, and the state, as well as the interplay between feudalism and family life.

By 1245, William Marshal's line was finished. Nothing, not even prudent marital alliances, could protect such men and their families from the vicissitudes and turbulence of the times. The best-laid plans frequently do not work out. So it was with William Marshal's testament: his sons died without heirs. "Young William perished only twelve years after his father, in 1231; Richard, three years later; Gilbert, who was a cleric, then left the ecclesiastical state, buckled on the sword, assumed the titles, and died of a fall from his horse in 1241 without having begotten a legitimate heir. There then remained only Anselm, the youngest—whom the earl, as he lay dying, had abandoned to his fate, judging that he had no chance whatever of inheriting; upon him fell the succession. His fortune was brief; by 1245 he was dead." Failure in the male line was common at this time among the higher nobility. Usually, however, it was the result of "excessively prudent measures" which forbade the younger sons to marry and thereby put all the lineage's eggs in one basket, as it were.[111]

In Germany, the social dislocation caused by the downward social mobility of so many of the younger sons of aristocrats found its expression in *Minnesang* (courtly love poetry). Herbert Moller's argument is worth detailing because it explains the intersection between state formation, social formation, and family formation. The continual rise of new men and the existence of numerous aspirants to knighthood created an extremely high sex ratio in the secular upper classes. Every castle had its "bachelor" knights, boys of fourteen to twenty-one years of age who were training for knight's service as well as older men belonging to the lowest rank of the knights. From the latter half of the eleventh century to the early thirteenth century these *baccalarii, simple chevaliers, Knappen,* and others were extremely numerous. Many unattached young men on the make migrated to southern Germany, where the high sex ratio among the regional ruling classes became magnified, with some specific implications for marriage, status, and property.

Marriage was not only dangerous but also desirable for these men—for them, as for William Marshal, marriage would mean a change in status, but the unbalanced sex ratio meant that there was a contrived shortage of marriageable, upper-class women. It was imperative for a nobleman, or a knight, or even a young aspirant to the knighthood to avoid a misalliance. A false

111. Duby, *William Marshal*, 30–31.

step in the process of family formation jeopardized both his status and his chances for promotion as well as the status and inheritance of his children. This circumstance also affected the old nobility because public opinion and usage insisted that marriage to a woman of lower social status necessarily depressed the status of the issue from this union. A nobleman's right of inheritance could be dependent on his mother's being a *nobilis*.

The *ministeriales,* for their part, were also as a rule extremely careful to avoid hypogamy (marriage downward). Their social position was precarious. They were a rising social class, but their dignity and privileges were juridically poorly defined. These social climbers schemed to marry women of a social status superior to their own, and they often succeeded in doing so. In Germany, despite its emphasis on neat class labels, such marriages were not infrequent. Indeed, there is no noble family tree without these marriages. Such alliances did not affect the legal status of the daughter's parental house and were often economically advantageous for it.[112] The surplus of men in the secular upper classes of the twelfth and thirteenth centuries, which was due to upward social mobility and to migration, was aggravated by the preference of males for hypergamy (marriage upward) and avoidance of hypogamy.

The imbalance of the sex ratio, in combination with the desire for social ascent through marriage and the dread of losing status through hypogamy, produced a situation which explains certain semirealistic features of troubadour poetry. In the light of our knowledge of the feudal marriage market, it can be taken for granted that some of the wailing about the one-sidedness and hopelessness of love was not so much an expression of

112. The tendency of men to marry upward was a particular characteristic of this period. The great interest of the *ministeriales* in alliances with families of unquestionable nobility was sometimes shared by their lords, who wished to establish them as a recognized professional class or to root them in a new territory. Despite the frequency of intermarriage there was still a deep gulf between a *ministerialis* and the free nobility in the twelfth and thirteenth centuries. As a consequence, a strange discrepancy resulted in that women could easily marry beneath their status, while men, as a rule, could approach only daughters of their peers or superiors with the intention of marriage. Because servile status was handed down through the female line, a marriage between a male *ministerialis* and a free woman was desirable. Moreover, there is considerable evidence that many lords were particularly sensitive to "extrinsic marriages" so as to ensure that their retinues would not be weakened nor their fiefs lost. But since it was almost impossible for the lords to ban such extrinsic marriages, they insisted upon consultation, permission, and other safeguards such as specifying which other retinues would qualify, or supervising the devolution of inheritances, or dividing the ownership of progeny with the lord of the other retinue. This gave lords the expectation that their losses could be balanced by their gains when their *ministeriales* entered the marriage market.

amorous sentiments as an oblique way of verbalizing disappointments over failure to secure a desirable match. When the *Minnesingers* expatiated upon their "true love" of a great lady, they created a twilight zone between fantasy and reality in which the process of symbolization became operative. Here the hopes, strivings, and insecurities of contemporary reality evoked images connected with deeper, more elementary needs of proving oneself worthy of being loved and being singled out for a special share of approval. The poems verbalized anxieties of rejection and at the same time helped to allay these anxieties. What would have been painful to discuss as personal problems could be worked through in a communal fantasy centering on the image of a woman who was able to grant acceptance in privileged society, self-assurance, and a feeling of personal worth in a world of changing values.[113]

Of course, the dynasts, the knights, and even the lovelorn *ministeriales* formed only the thinnest upper crust—in 1300, for example, there appear to have been rather more than ten thousand knights in a German population that totaled perhaps ten million[114]—yet the top-down perspective that has for so long dominated historiographical tradition has given this minority an importance out of all proportion to its social numbers.

RE-FORMING CHRISTENDOM

Religious life in late antiquity was only incompletely dominated by Christianity, which still retained its monastic character in the year 1000. The Gregorian Reformation of the eleventh century spearheaded a religious revival: the Crusades were the proverbial tip of an iceberg of religious transformation which took place under clerical direction. Christianity entered the social world when concern with outer, worldly signs of impurity and pollution came to be as important as the late antique attention to inner, spiritual virtuosity. The Church began its earnest engagement with the social world by first controlling clerical sexuality; this soon spread to the regulation of all Christians' worldly comportment as the inquisitorial Church imposed its mission on the common people. The Gregorian project of social purification represented a new direction in spiritual life which sought to enmesh all social relations in its web of surveillance. The super-

113. These three paragraphs paraphrase selected sections from Herbert Moller, "The Social Causation of the Courtly Love Complex," *Comparative Studies in Society and History* 1 (1959): 137–63. I have also supplemented Moller's account by consulting Arnold's chapter on "*Ministeriales* and Marriage" (*German Knighthood 1050–1300*, 162–83), especially with regard to "extrinsic marriages" (163–66).

114. Du Boulay, *Germany in the Later Middle Ages*, 69.

vision of everyday life redrew the boundary between the sacred and profane and, in so doing, the post-Gregorian Church was "Re-forming Christendom."

The history of the Christianization of Europe, as distinct from a history merely of the growth of the Christian Church in Europe, remains to be written.

> Before the conversion of Constantine and for centuries after, the Church should never be seen (as it is so often presented in maps) as a single wash of color spreading evenly and inexorably across the *orbis terrarum:* it was an archipelago of little islands of centrality scattered across an "unsown sea" of almost total indifference.

Early Christendom was a deeply underclericalized society. The holy man or saint who bore Christ in his person could stand for a little drop of the "central value system" of Christianity oozing tremulously to the surface.[115] The premier historian of the world of late antiquity has summarized this position as follows:

> For St. Augustine, this *saeculum* is a profoundly sinister thing. It is a penal existence, marked by extremes of misery and suffering, by suicide, madness, by "more diseases than any book of medicine can include," and by the inexplicable torments of small children. It is also marked by a disquietening inanity. Like a top out of balance, it wobbles up and down without rhyme or reason. . . . There are no verbs of historical movement in the City of God, no sense of progress to aims that may be achieved in history. The Christians are members of a far country . . . they are registered aliens, existing, on sufferance, *in hoc maligno saeculo.*[116]

The new Christian communities of the Dark Ages were primarily monastic. Romanesque Christianity spread throughout northwestern Europe under the influence of the Irish missionaries of the sixth and seventh centuries. Romanesque Christianity was also pervasively liturgical. For those who were not part of the spiritual elite, then, Romanesque Christianity was a vicarious and essentially passive experience. The house of God was richly decorated with shining, reflective objects to provide a fascinating visual stimulation to people for whom gleam and glitter were al-

---

115. Peter Brown, "The Saint as Exemplar in Late Antiquity," *Representations* 2 (1983): 9–10.
116. Peter Brown, "Saint Augustine," in Beryl Smalley (ed.), *Trends in Medieval Political Thought* (Oxford, 1965), 11.

most entirely absent in everyday life.[117] On at least one occasion related in contemporary Books of Miracles, monks were horrified when the rustic pilgrims disturbed the solemnity of the sacred vigils with their *ferales reisticorum vociferationes* ("savage vociferations") that produced an inappropriate tumult of *incompositas cantationes* ("uncomposed songs"). There was thus a complete opposition between—and mutual incomprehension of—the monks' learned culture and the peasants' living folklore.[118]

Within the monasteries, incessant prayers and recitations were constructed according to strict formulations and infused with Old Testament vocabulary, imagery, and thought patterns. Not only did monks and nuns have a better chance of achieving salvation, but the laity also were kept doctrinally and linguistically ignorant. They were also kept physically separate within the church. Lay people believed that they could influence their salvation "and the decision of the 'Judge,' not through direct intervention but by propitiary generosity toward those who, at two levels, could intervene on their behalf: the saints and the monks."[119] This gives us an insight into a critical reason why the Christianization of the countryside was such a protracted process: the only places of worship conveniently accessible to the rural population were the private churches built by great landowners. These buildings were erected on slave-estates, and one expects that they would have had little attraction for the free peasantry, who were numerous but perhaps not the majority everywhere.[120]

The Franks under Charlemagne tried to standardize monastic life by impregnating it with their own culture of sacred kingship. Paul Johnson remarks that "If Christianity had been 'imperialized' in the fourth century, it was to some extent 'barbarianized' in the West, during the three centuries beginning about 500." In his view, the role of Charlemagne was influential because "Despite the charisma of things Roman, in northern Christendom at least, the Church was Germanized, rather than the society Roman-

117. Heinrich Fichtenau, *Living in the Tenth Century: Mentalities and Social Orders* (Chicago, 1991), 76.

118. Pierre Bonnassie, "From One Servitude to Another: The Peasantry of the Frankish Kingdom at the Time of Hugh Capet and Robert the Pious (987–1031)," in *From Slavery to Feudalism in South-western Europe* (Cambridge, 1991), 301–2.

119. Lester K. Little, "Romanesque Christianity in Germanic Europe," *Journal of Interdisciplinary History* 23 (1992): 456–57.

120. Pierre Bonnassie, "The Survival and Extinction of the Slave System in the Early Medieval West (Fourth to Eleventh Centuries)," in *From Slavery to Feudalism in South-western Europe*, 31 n. 122. On this point, however, see the comments of William Jordan, "Book Review of *From Slavery to Feudalism in South-western Europe*," in *Slavery and Abolition: A Journal of Comparative Studies* 13 (1992): 97–102.

ized."[121] But Charlemagne's influence was also limited because, prior to the Gregorian reforms of the eleventh century, the Christian's relationship with her or his social environment was fundamentally ancient. Not only was the infraculture of western Christianity revolutionized after the year 1000, but its relationship with society also underwent a fundamental mutation. The Papal Revolution transformed Augustine's vision of the relationship between the City of God and the City of Man.

> the pope had assumed a new power of intervention and direction in both spiritual and secular affairs, the Benedictine Rule had lost its monopoly in the religious life, an entirely new impulse had been given to law and theology, and several important steps had been taken towards understanding and even controlling the physical world. The secular odyssey in quest of salvation was located in a more ample social space generated by broader human concerns that could be realized in historical time. Christianity entered the world. The expansion of Europe had begun in earnest. That all this should have happened in so short a time is the most remarkable fact in medieval history.[122]

1.

The apostolic bankruptcy of the pre-Reformation Church reflected its desperate financial straits. In the Carolingian period it would seem that "the shadow of the saint fell ever more widely across the fields of Europe." At the end of the ninth century the Church owned as much as one-third of the land of Europe. The trend thereafter was downward. Clerical lands were being secularized while at the same time the Church played a relatively small part in the colonization movements which extended the total land mass in the following centuries.[123] Certainly, the thrust of contemporary behavior and commentary leaves little doubt that Church wealth was being asset-stripped by nobles who were using the disintegration of central authority to enrich themselves at the clergy's expense. In particular, the Roman nobility treated the papacy as little more than a satrapy.

The Holy Roman Emperor and German king, Henry III, threw his influence behind the Cluniac reform movement, which had identified the critical necessity of staunching these hemorrhaging losses. The policy spearheaded by Hildebrand, who later became Pope Gregory VII, was five-

---

121. *A History of Christianity* (Harmondsworth, 1976), 161, 176.

122. R. W. Southern, *Western Society and the Church in the Middle Ages* (Harmondsworth, 1970), 34. See also Little, "Romanesque Christianity in Germanic Europe," 472–73.

123. David Herlihy, "Church Property on the European Continent, 701–1200," *Speculum* 36 (1961): 91, 87.

fold: first, the gold and silver hoards—often in the form of artworks—were either melted down or bartered for land; second, a new organizational structure was devised to oversee the administration of clerical property; third, a vast legislative program was aimed at regularizing practice and defining property rights; fourth, ecclesiastical property was to be controlled by clerics without secular intervention; and fifth, the clergy was to be celibate and therefore without heirs.[124] To a significant extent, the Gregorian Reform's material success in containing property losses provided the capital on which a new kind of religious community would be built.

It is not farfetched to see the "heirship strategies" of the great feudal lords mirrored in those of the clerical population. In both instances, the incumbent was merely granted *usufruct* rights by the greater lineage to which he belonged and, in both instances, a form of restricted inheritance was developed around the year 1000 in order to preserve the patrimony. Similar heirship strategies were also evident in Italian cities, where "patrician consorteries begin to appear in our sources from the late tenth and eleventh centuries. Typical of the constitution of these consorteries, if not its very basis, was the ownership of land in common." Finally, there are "shreds of evidence" that the reformed Church's interest in preserving the integrity and efficiency of its landed estates led it to make an effort to impose the practice of primogeniture upon its leaseholders.[125]

The social life of the post-Gregorian Church—its devotion, theology, liturgy, architecture, finances, social structure, and institutions—was established on the absolute obligation to procure the release of souls in purgatory that fell upon their living friends and relations. This responsibility was accomplished with the intercession of the clergy, who performed masses which bound together the living and the dead in a Christian community.[126] These changes in the practice of everyday Christianity represented nothing less than a cultural revolution. Reaching out to the general population, the post-Gregorian Church departed from its ancient inheritance of monastic spirituality by athletes-in-Christ. Church power was both broadened and deepened in this missionary practice.

124. David Herlihy, "Treasure Hoards in the Italian Economy, 960–1139," *Economic History Review,* 2d ser., 10 (1957): 1–14; D. B. Zema, "Reform Legislation in the Eleventh Century and Its Economic Import," *Catholic Historical Review* 27 (1941): 16–38; Zema, "Economic Reorganization of the Roman See During the Gregorian Reform," *Studi Gregoriani* 1 (1947): 137–68.

125. David Herlihy, "Agrarian Revolution in Southern France and Italy, 801–1150," *Speculum* 33 (1958): 33, 32.

126. John Bossy, "The Mass as a Social Institution, 1200–1700," *Past and Present* 100 (1983): 42.

Focusing on the supply of Christianity looks at only one side of the equation. The demand side can be encapsulated in the following question: Why did the general population adopt the Church's views? Leaving aside the clerical establishment's ability to make life unbearable for dissidents, an answer to this question lies in the novel revolutionary ideology of secularized Christianity in which there emerged a "mapped area of security" to keep the forces of social "chaos at bay."[127] A whole battery of rituals was created in response to uncertainty, anxiety, impotence, and disorder. Their repetitive character provided symbolic predictability, which in turn imparted a basic sense of ordered certainty to frightened people: "ritual connects past, present, and future, abrogating history and time. Ritual always links participants one to another and often beyond, to wider collectivities that may be absent, even to the ancestors and those yet unborn."[128]

The turbulence of feudal social relations was profoundly unsettling for the clerical order. The ecclesiastical program of "normative pacification"[129] took place in three stages. First, there was an attempt at limited disarmament; second, the warriors' violence was redirected outward, against new enemies defined by the Church; and third, the Church tried to regain control over its own resources. The Benedictine spirituality of patient humility, propagated by the Cluniac monks, provided one example of opposition to the endemic violence of the ninth and tenth centuries. In reaction to knights' feuds and their assumption of royal control over church appointments, clerics organized resistance movements. The most momentous form of protest found expression in the Peace of God in the last quarter of the tenth century and the Truce of God in the early eleventh century.[130]

These mass campaigns were important for a number of reasons. First, they established moral counterweights to knightly feuds and violence; second, protection was afforded to those who were most susceptible to violence—not only clerics but also women, merchants, pilgrims, and the poor, who were impotent against the knightly ruffians; third, they created a model for the behavior of the military classes *within* the framework of a

127. Victor Turner, "Metaphors of Anti-Structure in Religious Culture," in *Dramas, Fields and Metaphors: Symbolic Action in Human Society* (Ithaca, 1974), 297; see also Janet L. Nelson, "Society, Theodicy and the Origins of Heresy: Towards a Reassessment of the Evidence," in Derek Baker (ed.), *Schism, Heresy and Social Protest* (Cambridge, 1972), 65–77.

128. Barbara Myerhoff, "Rites and Signs of Ripening: The Intertwining of Ritual, Time, and Growing Older," in David Kertzer and Jennie Keith (eds.), *Age and Anthropological Theory* (Ithaca, 1984), 305–6.

129. Mann, *The Sources of Social Power*, 377.

130. Poly and Bournazel, *The Feudal Transformation*, 141–62.

Christian community, and in so doing they provided a model of justice which was particularly apposite for secular authorities who also wanted to find ways to monopolize violence in their own hands; fourth, they organized the religious fervor of the times and sought to direct it for their own ends; fifth, they laid the groundwork for the later mobilization of crusading energies in the hands of the papacy; and, most significantly, clerics began to create their own independent, worldly ecclesiastical polity, which would soon find its expression in the massive expansion in the powers of the Church in the age of the Gregorian Reformation.[131]

The eleventh-century spiritual revival sought to encompass all social groups within its rule. Even the knightly classes were enjoined to give up their arms, renounce their random violence, and take on the posture of the penitent. This provided the way in which the knights were to be Christianized, their violence was to be subdued, and their energies were to be channeled into appropriate pursuits. Knights, eager to appease the wrath of God, almost destroyed their wealth in showering alms on the Church. They dedicated their bodies to the glory of asceticism by making pilgrimages to holy sites as far off as Jerusalem and Santiago de Compostela in northwestern Spain.

Crusading adventures—in Spain and in the Baltic as well as in the Levant—played a crucial role in the domestication of the warrior class. First planned by Pope Gregory VII and later undertaken by Pope Urban II in 1095, the Crusades became "a great chivalrous adventure, in which the service of God and the quest for earthly renown and reward . . . [were] so interlaced that it is no longer practical to seek to unravel the strands."[132] This reciprocity between the militarization of sanctity and the sanctification of military life was captured in the contemporary comments of Guibert of Nogent, who wrote "In our own time God has instituted a holy war, so that the order of knights and the unstable multitude, who used to engage in mutual slaughter in the manner of ancient paganism, might find a

---

131. Georges Duby, "Laity and the Peace of God," in *The Chivalrous Society*, (Berkeley and Los Angeles, 1977), 123–33; H. E. J. Cowdrey, "The Peace and the Truce of God in the Eleventh Century," *Past and Present* 46 (1970): 42–67. It should be noted that Cowdrey makes it clear that the "educational value" of the Peace movement was much stronger "in the old Carolingian lands and particularly southern France—where the disarray of feudal social relations was most prevalent—and practically unknown in England until after the Norman Conquest of 1066 because of the remarkable strength of Anglo-Saxon royal administration and of the local organization of shires and hundreds [which were] . . . admirable alternative means of peace-keeping" (66).

132. Duby, "Laity and the Peace of God," 131–133; Keen, *Chivalry,* 55.

new way of gaining salvation."[133] Indeed, the same forces drove forward the First Crusade and the founding of the Cistercian Order as well as the fighting monks, the Knights Templar.[134]

Creating a defensible border was part of the reason for the Germans' drive to the east. As a cleric wrote in 1108: "The [Slav] heathens are the worst men, but their land is the best of all with meat, honey, flour, when it is cultivated! Here, you Saxons, Franks, Lotharingians, Flemings, most famous conquerors of the world, you can save your souls and, if you want to, you will acquire the best land to live in!" Planned colonization turned non–revenue-producing resources into veritable fountains of bread-corn and silver. Thus, those who took part in crushing the heathens by taking part in the Eastern Crusades for liberating the Church from oppression were promised not only the remission of all sins but also fertile land to settle. This dual promise made it possible to transfer the crusading ideal to the Elbe frontier; Christian settlement in the former pagan lands had proved to be the only way to advance Christianization.[135] More generally, racist ideologies had an insubstantial quality in the cultural heartlands but not on the cultural frontiers. On the frontiers, there was a "biological identity of lineage and race [which] bound human beings past, present, and future into unchanging mental structures." On Europe's frontiers, the distinction between insiders and outsiders had an altogether more sinister intent.[136]

2.

Is it coincidental that the Gregorian reform movement should have begun at precisely the time of the final separation between the eastern and western branches of Christianity? Basing his authority on the Donation of Constantine, which was forged around 760, Pope Leo IX launched an attack against the intransigent patriarch of the Eastern Church. This same line of argument was taken up by his understudy, Gregory VII, against those in the Latin Church who were either lukewarm supporters or outright oppo-

---

133. Quoted in I. S. Robinson, "Gregory VII and the Soldiers of Christ," *History* 58 (1973): 191.

134. Lionel Rothkrug, "Religious Practices and Collective Perceptions," *Historical Reflexions* 7 (1980): 15–36.

135. Friedrich Lotter, "The Crusading Idea and the Conquest of the Region East of the Elbe," in Bartlett and MacKay (eds.), *Medieval Frontier Societies*, 267–306; Bartlett, *The Making of Europe*, 152.

136. Richard C. Hoffmann, "Outsiders by Birth and Blood: Racist Ideologies and Realities around the Periphery of Medieval European Culture," *Studies in Medieval and Renaissance History*, new ser., 6 (1983): 3–34. See also Bartlett, *The Making of Europe*, 197–242.

nents of Roman domination.[137] To be sure, the Gregorian reformers' aim was avowedly otherworldly even if their methods were entirely secular. When it was combined with a novel theology of judgment, the mixture was explosive. In its quest for absolute power, the Papal Revolution created the modern system of bureaucratic government and legal process.

As Marc Bloch writes, "the Gregorian reform proclaimed both the unique character and the supreme importance of the spiritual mission with which the church was entrusted; it strove to set the priest apart from and above the ordinary believer."[138] This occurred even if that ordinary believer was the Holy Roman Emperor—as Henry IV discovered in January 1077, when he was humbled at the Italian city of Canossa. Gregory VII forced him to wait three days, barefoot in the snow, before being admitted to the papal presence to make his penance. In an age when symbolic representations of power were as important as their material demonstration, Gregory's actions manifestly demonstrated religious authority over civil rulers. In consciously inverting the very act by which a vassal subjected himself to his lord, the pope audaciously turned the imagery of feudal society against itself. Worldly power was thus seen by all to have been symbolically subordinated to the overlordship and domination of God's representative.

In the next century, this exemplary lesson was again played out on the stage of high politics at the expense of both the Capetian king of France and the Plantagenet king of England. When Philip I was accused of bigamy and incest, he placated his ecclesiastical critics by appearing barefoot, in the clothes of a penitent, at the abbey church of St. Germain-des-Prés near Paris in 1105.[139] Henry Plantagenet's later attempt to wrest control of legal processes from ecclesiastical courts precipitated the king's rift with Archbishop Thomas Becket, "an unreconstructed Gregorian." Henry II might have been the king of England, the overlord of the counties of Normandy, Maine, Brittany, Anjou, Touraine, Poitou, Auvergne, Aquitaine, and Gascony, as well as a claimant to the throne of France itself, but he, too, was nonetheless required to walk barefoot to do penance at Canterbury in

137. Ian Stuart Robinson, " 'Periculosus Homo': Pope Gregory VII and Episcopal Authority," *Viator* 9 (1978): 103–31.
138. Bloch, *Feudal Society,* 107.
139. Duby, *France in the Middle Ages, 987–1460,* 114. In point of fact, Philip was able to keep his wife and maintain his sinful marriage because the papacy was more concerned with his ritual submission than anything else. Part of the papacy's concern was motivated by its desire to get the French king onside in its battles with the emperor in the Investiture Crisis, which was then tearing apart both Germany and Italy.

1170. Two years later, he submitted to the papal legate on the heights of Avranches, overlooking Mont St. Michel in Normandy, where he received absolution and renounced his anti-papal Constitutions of Clarendon.[140]

When Henry II's son refused to accept the papal nominee to the bishopric of Canterbury, the pope (Innocent III) responded in 1208 by excommunicating King John, closing all churches, and threatening to throw his weight behind Philip Augustus, the Capetian king of France, who wanted to extend his claims to the throne of England. "England groaned under the interdict" and King John was forced to back down. The first provision of the Magna Carta (1215) guaranteed the freedom of the English Church: *quod ecclesia Anglicana libera sit.*

These were only the most spectacular events among a series of skirmishes between an aggressive papal party and its secular opponents. "The Papal Revolution was like an atomic explosion that split Germanic Christendom into two parts: the church, viewed as an independent, visible, corporate, legal structure; and the secular order, viewed as divided among various polities."[141]

3.

The newly acquired powers of the papal state radically changed the social organization of western society. In this regard it is perhaps apposite to underline a point made by Pierre Bourdieu:

> The struggle over classifications is a fundamental dimension of class struggle. The power to impose and to inculcate a vision of divisions, that is, the power to make visible and explicit social divisions that are implicit, is political power par excellence. It is the power to make groups, to manipulate the objective structure of society. As with constellations [of shared symbolic meanings], the performative power of designation, or naming, brings into existence in an instituted, constituted form . . . what existed up until then only as a *collectio personarium plurium*, a collection of varied persons, a purely additive series of merely juxtaposed individuals.[142]

Whether the Church was able to carry out its programmatic ambitions to its own satisfaction is rather beside the point that the Papal Revolution created the justification for, and the methods of, clerical supervision of daily life.

140. Sidney Packard, *Twelfth Century Europe: An Interpretive Essay* (Amherst, Mass., 1973), 286.
141. Berman, *Law and Revolution*, 262–63, 531.
142. "Social Space and Symbolic Power," *Sociological Theory* 7 (1989): 23.

Family formation pivots on the ceremony of marriage, and it is of the highest importance that marriage was subjected to ecclesiastical control *and* definition. At the Council of Rome in 1069 "the leaders of the Church, while expelling marriage from its own fold, began to aim at trapping the whole of the laity in a net in which each mesh was a duly consecrated marriage."[143] Clerical celibacy and the indissolubility of marriage were enforced by the Church court's exclusive jurisdiction on matrimonial issues. How successful was the Church's campaign to abolish clerical marriage? Christopher Brooke's evidence, derived from a study of the secular canons of St. Paul's cathedral in London, suggests that these lowly clerics only slowly conformed to their new role. Even those prebendaries who had given up their wives still maintained concubines; such women were often wives in all but name (and legal status).[144]

Clerical intervention followed a few decades after the secular ruling class had radically shifted its marriage strategies through the exercise of strict control of the lineal patriarch over his sons and daughters. The new system of primogeniture effectively reduced the possibility of dividing the patrimony and thereby played a crucial role in the invention of family traditions.[145] At the same time, however, the Gregorian Church's fear of incest was based on the unrealistic view that consanguineous marriages occurred among kin related to the seventh degree. This was an awkward and essentially unenforceable rule—who was not someone else's sixth cousin among the aristocracy? Jean-Louis Flandrin has computed that someone who followed these rules would have had at least 2,731 cousins of his or her own generation with whom marriage would have been forbidden.[146] It was

---

143. Duby, *The Knight, the Lady, and the Priest*, 118.

144. *The Medieval Idea of Marriage* (Oxford, 1989), 78–89.

145. Duby, *The Knight, the Lady, and the Priest*, 94. However, in the south of France—the Languedoc and Provence, where Catharism was strongest—a rather different tradition prevailed. Here, women were able to inherit in their own right, and it was only the Albigensian Crusades (1209–13)—and especially during their aftermath, when the South was colonized and subjugated by the North—that independent women like Eleanor of Aquitaine became part of the silenced past. The violent subjugation of southern France, in the wake of Simon de Montfort's scorched-earth warfare, was the proving ground of the Inquisition. One of the crucial points that exercised the inquisitors was the southerners' free-and-easy sexuality and marital arrangements. On this last point, see Emmanuel Le Roy Ladurie, *Montaillou: Cathars and Catholics in a French Village 1294–1334* (London, 1978), esp. 139–203.

146. This is a minimum number because, in his calculations, Jean-Louis Flandrin supposed that "in each generation each couple had brought up and given in marriage one boy and one girl—which was lower than the real average, taking into account the increase of population in the eleventh and twelfth centuries"; *Families in Former Times: Kinship, Household and Sexuality* (Cambridge, 1979), 24.

therefore expedient for noble husbands to discover they were living in sin and to demand a divorce or annulment. The historical record is full of such discoveries, which usually occurred—fortuitously, no doubt—when the marriage was without children or when political realities swiftly changed in an unexpected fashion. In 1215, at Lateran IV, the ruling on incest was amended so that marriages outside the fourth degree of kin were ruled non-consanguineous. Bringing canon law into line with social reality created a much greater chance that marriage could be made indissoluble. At the very least, a spurious divorce would be more difficult to obtain for the rich and powerful.

The insistence on clerical celibacy prevented the creation of a hereditary caste of priestly scholars.[147] In each generation, the clergy was sustained by the donation of *oblates* to holy orders. This had two very significant implications: first, literacy was not confined to a self-perpetuating caste but was widely dispersed among the children of the whole population from whom the clergy was recruited; and second, it brought the clerical aristocracy and the secular aristocracy to a common ground. William Marshal was not alone in giving one of his sons to the Church; such donations were inspired partly by piety and partly as form of familial insurance.

By the end of the twelfth century there was a shared bond of common interest between landlords, who sought an orderly system of inheritance, and the clerics, who were trying to enforce Christian monogamy. For most purposes, aristocrats were prepared to be subject to clerical control—"not only in fits of penitence, but actually when making marriage treaties affecting their inheritances and standing in the world. This was largely because legitimate monogamy had come to be the heart of the system of inheritance, as it was to be the heart of the Church's idea of marriage as an institution."[148]

While much attention inevitably devolves upon the marital alliances and strategies of the upper class, it would seem that the post-Gregorian Church's new marriage policies had a significant resonance for the lower orders. In establishing the centrality of consent in the making of a Christian marriage, the canon law of marriage made the marital union easy to create, endowed it with serious consequences, and made divorce difficult.

---

147. M. T. Clanchy, *From Memory to Written Record* (Cambridge, Mass., 1979), 195.

148. Brooke, *The Medieval Idea of Marriage*, 154. See also Constance B. Bouchard, "Consanguinity and Noble Marriages in the Tenth and Eleventh Centuries," *Speculum* 56 (1981): 268–87.

This was exactly the opposite of the situation prevailing in both Roman and barbarian law. The Christian desire to evangelize the servile population, by drawing it into the cultural domain of the Church, was founded on a remarkably democratic principle: all men and women—no matter whether free or servile—were considered to be morally responsible agents whose sins were an abomination in the sight of God. Is it merely coincidental that the creation of a radically new system of marriage occurred at exactly the same time that the last vestiges of slavery were disappearing from northern Europe? The post-Gregorian Church's marriage policies were deliberately fashioned to help the lower orders avoid the sins of concupiscence and adultery, at the cost of abridging the rights of feudal lords to control the intimate lives of their dependent, servile population.[149] Is it, therefore, difficult to understand why the popular classes could seek their own liberation under the sheltering cover of the Church's theology?

We should be careful to avoid telescoping this process, which may have begun with the Gregorian attack on married clerics but was hardly completed by Lateran IV's attempt to strengthen the Church's hold over secular marriages by demanding that banns be read and weddings be publicly celebrated. Equally, we must give some attention to the ideological skirmishes which wove the Virgin Mary into the fabric of patriarchal politics, since it was during these decades that Mariolatry was spread by the Cistercians throughout Europe.

St. Bernard of Clairvaux's ecstatic strain of piety fused asceticism, Mariolatry, and marriage in a novel mixture. As Marina Warner writes:

> By continuing the traditional cult of Mary's virginity and purity, by coupling it with a constant emphasis on the feminine virtues of humility, obedience, modesty, and self-effacement, the menace contained in the idea of *regina angelorum* could be wiped out. Above all, by contrasting human women with the sublime perfection of the Virgin, earthly love could be discredited and men's eyes turned once again heavenwards.[150]

The point that Warner is making in the first sentence refers to the struggle with Catharism and courtly love that had scarred southern France at the end of the twelfth and beginning of the thirteenth century. She deftly makes the point by comparing and contrasting the sexual politics of

149. M. M. Sheehan, "Theory and Practice: Marriage of the Unfree and the Poor in Medieval Society," *Mediaeval Studies* 50 (1988): 457–87.
150. *Alone of All Her Sex* (London, 1976), 147–48.

Eleanor of Aquitaine (1122–1204) with those of her granddaughter Blanche of Castile (d. 1252), Saint Louis's mother, who sublimated her sexuality by focusing her ardor on the Virgin.[151]

It is important to note that, while the intent of the Gregorian reform's project was sacramentalizing the act of marriage, it was much less interested in the internal dynamics of family life except insofar as the Holy Family was rendered in sermons, in images, and, finally, in print as the ideal against which all others could be measured. If the Christianity of the first millennium was Christ-centered, after the year 1000 the Virgin Mary and then, after about 1350, Joseph were also celebrated. These celebrations depicted an obedient, well-regulated little family. In one of the many Christian appropriations of pagan worship, barren women appealed to the Virgin because she was regarded as an interested patroness.

In promoting a domestic ideal through the image of the Holy Family, the post-Gregorian Church accommodated itself to the reality of daily life in a way that distinguished its activities from the ancient model of religiosity. Domestic idealism was a curious fusion of two of the dominant tendencies of post-1000 Christianity: first, the triumph of the spirit in the world which wove the religious ethic into the social fabric; and second, the call to evangelize and rescue the souls of the whole population, which drove the Church out of the monastery, onto the roads and into the marketplaces.

The simultaneous rise of confraternities suggests that while the Church was concerned with regularizing entry into marriage, it was also interested in sponsoring fictive kinship among believers, especially adult males whose intimate bonds were shared with other men residing outside the household's walls. These all-male institutions must have been detrimental to the promotion of domestic values and, in particular, the emotional primacy of the nuclear-family unit. Women, by way of contrast, were rarely involved in confraternal organizations. Indeed, the very word suggests the reason for their exclusion from this gendered model of piety. The spread of *beguinages* in the thirteenth century suggests that some women were able to break free, but it needs to be kept in mind that relatively few women abandoned their families, and rejected maternity, to pursue a life as a bride of Christ.

Churchmen's suspicion of carnal pleasures had its roots in Augustine's theory of the sexual transmission of original sin. Their concern with concupiscence led them to opine that no sexual activity could take place without

151. *Alone of All Her Sex,* 147.

its corrupting effect—without passion and unruly desire.[152] Clerical regulation was not solely negative; alongside the social control of marriage the Church developed its carefully enunciated code of sexual behavior, which was transmitted to the general population through its hierarchical command structure. This code looked with conditional favor toward marital sexuality and family life. In this way it differed radically from the earlier penitentials, which were written in an age of monasticism and exhibited a much more negative attitude toward sexual sins and their correction.[153] "The newly converted peoples of western Europe seem to have had a strong attachment to a more open, diversified, and freely expressed sexuality than could be countenanced by the Christian ethic."[154]

The regulation and control of sexual activity gave rise to anxieties among the Church Fathers. A massive prescriptive literature of penitential manuals for confessors, originally aimed for a clerical audience, developed in the Irish monasteries. The earliest surviving examples date from A.D. 591. These injunctions were to be the principal agent in the formation and transmission of a Christian code of sexual morality. The penitentials were not superseded until after the age of Gregorian Reform, when they were replaced by a new type of literature, the *summae confessorum*, which reflected the achievement of the new canon law and a modification of the penitentials' rigor.[155]

Irregular sexual relations had constituted the single most important classification of sinful behavior which exercised clerics: from a representative sample of seven penitentials, up to the eleventh century, 33 percent of all offenses were concerned with sexual deviance.[156] Yet, as Pierre Payer notes, "the medievals did not speak about sex as such," and for this reason there were no Latin counterparts for "*aphrodisiac, bestiality, contracep-*

---

152. On the ancient Church and sexuality, see Peter Brown, *The Body and Society: Men, Women, and Sexual Renunciation in Early Christianity* (New York, 1988); and Elaine Pagels, *Adam, Eve, and the Serpent* (New York, 1988).

153. Sheehan, "Marriage of the Unfree and the Poor," 485. See also J. Murray, "The Perceptions of Sexuality, Marriage, and Family in Early English Pastoral Manuals," unpublished Ph.D. dissertation, University of Toronto, 1987.

154. Pierre Payer, *Sex and the Penitentials* (Toronto, 1984), 121. This process of conversion took place as a result of long centuries of missionary activity by the clergy. For a fascinating glimpse of this cultural mutation in one of the peripheral, dark corners of Christendom, where it was implanted much later than in the core, see Jenny M. Jochens, "The Church and Sexuality in Medieval Iceland," *Journal of Medieval History* 6 (1980): 377–92.

155. Pierre Payer, "The Humanism of the Penitentials and the Continuity of the Penitential Tradition," *Mediaeval Studies* 46 (1984): 340–54.

156. Payer, *Sex and the Penitentials*, 52–53.

tion, *fornication* (in the strict sense of heterosexual relations between two unmarried people), *homosexuality, lesbianism, masturbation*. The practice of the penitentials is to employ a general-duty verb such as *fornicare* (literally, to fornicate) in conjunction with a word or phrase which usually succeeds in identifying the act."[157] Seen in this way,

> mediaeval discourses on sex were largely legal, theological, and penitential, focussing on *acts* and institutions. The theory of marriage which determined it as the exclusive domain for legitimate sexual behaviour controlled the content, character, and direction of the discourses. The conceptual locus for discourses on sex was provided by the theory of the moral virtue of temperance with its divisions, subdivisions, and opposing vices.[158]

The sexual economy of the Gregorian reform movement was thus Janus-faced: it looked back to older traditions—Jewish, Christian, and Stoic—in setting its horror of bodily defilement and the narrowly construed reproductive function of sexual relations over and against the dynastic politics of the family, while it looked forward to the sacralization of marriage. One of the results of the Gregorian Reformation was to channel these anxieties toward a concern with both acts *and* intentions. Another result was to specify in minute detail what was acceptable in regular sexual relations. What is most striking about this prescriptive literature is the high value it places on marriage and reproduction within marriage. This represents a continuity with ancient systems in which marriage was a form of social necessity required for social reproduction between unequal partners. But it represented a deviation from antiquity in terms of the esteem with which marriage was held in comparison with any other intimate relationship.[159]

---

157. *Sex and the Penitentials*, 14. It should also be pointed out that for almost all those who wrote on the subject, only the so-called missionary position ("women supine below, men prone above") was considered permissible. Deviations from this posture were regarded as sinful because they were either evidence of a quest for pleasure/gratification or else were too much like homosexual behavior in the case of rear-entry heterosexual intercourse; James A. Brundage, "Let Me Count the Ways: Canonists and Theologians Contemplate Coital Positions," *Journal of Medieval History* 10 (1984): 81–93.

158. Pierre Payer, "Foucault on Penance and the Shaping of Sexuality," *Studies in Religion* 14 (1985): 318.

159. The most valuable treatment of this theme is to be found in Michel Foucault's posthumously published volumes *The Care of the Self* (New York, 1986) and *The Uses of Pleasure* (New York, 1986). See also James A. Brundage, *Law, Sex and Christian Society in Medieval Europe* (Chicago, 1987), esp. chaps. 5–8.

If sexuality was the problem, then, for most men and women, marriage was to be the solution. "Virginity is preferred, but intercourse in marriage, for procreation only, is permissible."[160] Most clerical regulation was concerned with the form and especially the frequency of marital sexual relations. In theory, this meant that many times during the year were to be marked by sexual abstinence. In particular, communicants were urged to avoid sexual relations when they were planning to receive the eucharist. The elaborate theological discussions would, if followed by the faithful, have proscribed sexual relations on about half the days of the year.[161] This last point speaks directly to a long-standing inability to reconcile sex and the sacred. Sex was viewed as something unholy and unclean, and therefore inconsistent with the more elevated spirituality demanded of the Christian life.[162] Theoretical writing was disassociated from the laity's everyday life. There is a substantial body of evidence that clerical injunctions to practice sexual relations only in connection with reproduction did not strike deep roots among the laity—indeed, quite the opposite. In addition, there is very little evidence that many imbibed the theological instructions that sex was sinful and that lay persons should therefore strictly control their passions—again, quite the opposite.[163]

Concern with the sinfulness of human sexuality put theologians in a corner. But because the decretalists saw carnal pleasures as distinct from—and lower than—human rational capacities, they developed a two-tiered approach. The clergy were to be sexually abstinent and thereby both elevated and purified, while the lay population's inability to resist its passions was indulged as venial sin and the passion itself was channeled into procreative intercourse. The "conjugal debt" was, however, owed to both partners, which was a striking recognition of the sexual equality of men and women.[164] In addition, the clerical insistence on monogamy not only ended concubinage but also legitimated the clerically sanctioned lineage at the ex-

160. J. T. Noonan, *Contraception: A History of Its Treatment by the Catholic Theologians and Canonists* (Cambridge, Mass., 1958), 58.

161. P. Riché, "Problèmes de démographie historique du haut moyen âge (V^e–VIIIe siècles)," *Annales de Démographie Historique* (1966): 44.

162. Pierre J. Payer, "Early Medieval Regulations Concerning Marital Sexual Relations," *Journal of Medieval History* 6 (1980): 353–76.

163. Jean-Louis Flandrin, "Contraception, Marriage, and Sexual Relations in the Christian West," in R. Forster and O. Ranum (eds.), *Biology of Man in History* (Baltimore, 1975), 23–47.

164. Elizabeth M. Makowski, "The Conjugal Debt and the Medieval Canon Law," *Journal of Medieval History* 3 (1977): 99–114.

pense of all offspring.[165] Ending concubinage and creating clerically sanctioned marriages did not end the sexual exploitation of women, but henceforth such mistreatment became a matter of abusive power rather than accepted as a matter of course.

It is not surprising that the reforming Church turned its administrative
machinery toward regulating entry into marriage by clarifying the meaning and intention of consent. This emphasis on consent informed by marital affection stood over and against the fundamental law of the Roman empire that a slave lacked civil capacity to depose of his or her body and,
therefore, to freely marry. In the eyes of the Church, there was neither
slave nor free man in Jesus Christ, just as there was neither male nor female.[166] The Church policed marital relations by demanding that its parish
clergy report notorious adulterers and fornicators to the proper courts. Ap-
prehension was directed inward toward an examination of one's conscience
in the confessional and outward in that "sedulous quest for intellectual
uniformity and corporatism" which led to a search for scapegoats whose
impure thoughts and actions explained misfortune.[167]

In considering this prescriptive material, which translucently refracts
the practice of everyday life, we have to read it against its grain—that is, we
have to accept that these writers inform us about something more than
their own hysterical fantasies. Their desire both to classify sins and to create hierarchies of depravity within these categories provides us with an opportunity to consider their observations from our vantage point. For example, fornication was considered less sinful than adultery. Contraceptive
intercourse was less sinful than homosexual relations but much more serious than solitary masturbation. The "sin of Onan" became more problematic in the later fourteenth and fifteenth centuries, however, when population levels plummeted.

Were sexual relations an act of violence carried out by other means?
Were medieval sexual relations nasty, brutish, and short? Were women
only victims? We might first begin to answer this question with a consideration of Héloise's remonstrations to Abelard:

> so delectable were the lovers' joys which we sought together, that
> they still cannot seem displeasing to me, nor can I yet forget them.

165. Margaret Clunies Ross, "Concubinage in Anglo-Saxon England," *Past and Present* 108 (1985): 3–34.

166. John T. Noonan, Jr., "Power to Choose," *Viator* 4 (1974): 419–34.

167. John Boswell, *Christianity, Social Tolerance, and Homosexuality* (Chicago, 1980), 270. See also Jeffrey Richards, *Sex, Dissidence and Damnation: Minority Groups in the Middle Ages* (London, 1991).

Whichever way I turn, I always see them calling to me, luring me. They do not even spare my dreams at night. Even in the celebration of the Mass, when prayer should be wholly pure, the obscene phantoms of those pleasures thus utterly encompass my wretched soul, that my time is spent more in such wicked thoughts than in prayer. It is not only the actions, but places and times when we enjoyed each other are so instilled in my mind's eye that I go over them again and again even in my sleep.[168]

Like a beam of light issuing from a dead star which ceased to exist nearly a millennium ago, Héloise's words continue to illuminate the existential dilemma that fully charged sexual desires posed for her. The veil of prescriptive obfuscation which would patronize the sexuality of people in past time cannot obscure Héloise's erotic delight from our view. Nor should it conceal from our view the fact that her reproach toward Abelard was based on the prior understanding that their love was mutual, an expression of companionship. In rescuing her full humanity from the arrogance of late modernity, it is crucial to recognize that some aspects of the human condition cannot be reduced to historical relativism. But, in so doing, there should be an equal recognition that Héloise's example is exceptional—not only in her frankness but also in our access to it.

Héloise's recollections of her erotic satisfactions provide a counterweight to simpleminded reductionism which would see individual experience as some kind of residue derived from patriarchal norms and values. The prevalence and toleration of misogynistic violence does not provide the whole story of marital relations. Comparable evidence of direct personal testimony comes from Christine de Pisan's description of her husband's consideration, respect, and tenderness: "On the first night of marriage I immediately experienced his great goodness, even without committing outrage towards me, nor hurting me. But, before it was time to awake, he kissed me a hundred times, so I maintain, without seeking any other villainy, most certainly my sweet loves me truly."

168. Quoted in Brooke, *The Medieval Idea of Marriage*, 114. In contrast to his lover's memories, Abelard's recollection was that "I gratified in you my wretched desires and this was all that I loved"; quoted in M. T. Clanchy, *Abelard: A Medieval Life* (Oxford, 1997), 151. His biographer suggests that the trauma of castration may have not only disgusted him with sexuality but also distorted his memories of his pleasure. Be that as it may have been, it is also germane to note that after he was castrated by Héloise's irate uncle's henchmen, Abelard essentially renounced their sexual relationship, and he got her to a nunnery. Yet, they still met on occasion and continued to write to one another until the end of his life. By the standards of the day, this was a most peculiar relationship.

Despite a disparity in their ages at marriage—she was fifteen and he was twenty-four—this was a compassionate and companionate marriage cut short by her husband's early death, so that she was widowed at twenty-five, with three small children. Christine never remarried. In the wake of this sudden and terrible loss, "I was so confused with grief that I became like a recluse, dull, sad, alone and weary." Christine de Pisan was born in Venice, the daughter of a member of the Venetian Council who became royal astrologer to the French king. Her husband, Étienne de Castel, was also a royal councilor—notary and secretary. It is not likely that one can generalize from this example to lives of plebeian women, but her story is the only evidence I know in which a married woman describes her marriage in her own words.[169]

At the same time that both popular culture and the canon law sanctioned violence within marriage in order to buttress familial discipline, the clerical vision of marriage enunciated by St. Thomas Aquinas and San Bernardino of Siena emphasized companionship and loving consideration. While the Church was successfully advancing its vision of sacralized marriage, the sacrament was one which the two partners could administer in their exchange of consent. Clerical intervention was not required to legalize consensual unions. A commitment to marry was sufficient to initiate sexual relations, particularly when this agreement was public knowledge.[170] Other churchmen wrote powerfully about the sentimental side of marriage. Thomas of Chobham wrote "In contracting marriage a man gives a woman his body, and she hers; apart from the soul, nothing under the sky is more precious." William of Pagula wrote that when the priest solemnized marriage, he should instruct the man to place the ring on his wife's fourth finger because "in that finger there is a vein which leads right up to the heart, and likewise the man and woman ought to be of one heart."[171]

The processes of early modernization sought to control the popular urge for apostolic purity. They preserved the mystery of the clerical relationship with secular society by circumscribing the puzzling ambivalences of human sexuality and wrapping them inside the enigmatic state of

169. *Oeuvres Poétiques de Christine de Pisan*, edited by M. Roy (Paris, 1886), I:237; Patricia Bonin Eargle, "An Edition of Christine de Pisan's *Livre du chemin de lonc estude*," lines 119–21, unpublished Ph.D. dissertation, University of Georgia, 1973, 30 (my translation). I was directed to this source by Shulamith Shahar, *The Fourth Estate* (London, 1983), 73.

170. Flandrin, *Families in Former Times*, 131.

171. Quoted in P. P. A. Biller, "Marriage Patterns and Women's Lives: A Sketch of a Pastoral Geography," in P. J. P. Goldberg (ed.), *"Woman Is a Worthy Wight": Women in English Society c. 1200–1500* (Stroud, 1992), 70.

sacralized marriage. While we will never be able to probe very deeply into the character of affective ties between wives and their husbands, we know that the Church's interest in controlling marriage brought its inquisitorial process into contact with the intimacy of everyday life. In allowing for a marriage to be initiated by the informed consent of the two partners, the Church kept the whole population under surveillance to monitor the legality of all unions. In the fifty years after Lateran IV (1215), the English Church promulgated regulations to implement "general church law with the detail that was only possible on the local level and that, to a considerable extent, instructed the parish clergy in the theology that lay behind the rules they were expected to enforce."[172]

Ecclesiastical law was enforced by the rural chapter, which met monthly. Rural deans brought offending parties to the chapter's attention. The Achilles' heel of the system was its grassroots organization.[173] The Church was not able to exert a totalitarian hegemony over either the minds or the bodies of the population. Rather, it tried to police those individuals and groups who ignored, abused, or ridiculed its edicts. "The rural chapters fined or flogged men and women guilty of fornication or adultery. The church's theology, its pastoral functions, its very marital theory, were remote from the peasants. But the archdeacon's rod was not. They could either take the beating or pay."[174] Through this policy of external supervision, most members of the village community were drawn into the Church's sphere of influence.

Administrative discipline was both energetic and diligent. Church courts of the later fourteenth century spent about a quarter of their time dealing with martial disputes. While we can never be sure about the representativeness of these English courts' business, it is nonetheless germane to note that they reveal "an astonishingly individualistic attitude to marriage and its problems. Familial and seignorial decisions as to the time of betrothal and the choice of spouse, practices that are always associated with medieval society, are simply not found in the register."[175] In contrast to the

172. M. M. Sheehan, "Marriage Theory and Practice in the Conciliar Legislation and Diocesan Statutes of Medieval England," *Mediaeval Studies* 40 (1978): 412.

173. Tim North, "Legerwite in the Thirteenth and Fourteenth Centuries," *Past and Present* 111 (1986): 5.

174. Jean Scammell, "Freedom and Marriage in Medieval England," *Economic History Review*, 2d ser., 27 (1974): 535. See also Scammell, "The Rural Chapter in England," *English Historical Review*, 86 (1971): 1–21.

175. M. M. Sheehan, "The Formation and Stability of Marriage in Fourteenth-Century England: Evidence of an Ely Register," *Mediaeval Studies* 33 (1971): 263.

freedom from parental control enjoyed by English men and women, it seems that French parents played a more active role in their children's process of family formation.[176]

Family formation was thus drawn into the process of early modernization by the Church's novel attitude to the ebb and flow of the acculturation of a nominally Christian population. The Church was forced to compromise with worldly realities and accept the lesser evils of consensual marriage and conjugality at the expense of what were perceived to be the greater evils of promiscuity and female vulnerability. A sensitive indicator of the Church's ability to reach into the private lives of families in Christendom is suggested by naming practices in Tuscany after 1200. Not only was there a radical reduction in the number of listed names, but the prevalence of celestial sponsorship grew. In 1219 50 percent of the population were designated by 109 leading names, whereas in 1427 one-half of the male househeads were accounted for by eleven names. Of the fifteen leading names in *quattrocento* Tuscany, thirteen were those of saints. Moreover, this movement toward nominal homogeneity included both men and women, upper and lower classes, and urban and rural residents. The desire for powerful spiritual protectors was part and parcel of a single cultural sentiment that found expression among all Tuscans. These names may be "only whispers from the past," but they were in the process of becoming "a lecture, given to the young" which paradoxically "emphasized individuality by giving the person not only firm identity in the present but ties with the past and prospects for the future." The fact that this reorientation in religious psychology took place under the Church's aegis suggests the Church's ability to enter into the processes of family formation and reconfigure them in its own image. In choosing to name themselves after the popular saints, whose legends had been publicized by the mendicant preachers and were thus venerated in current teachings, Tuscans were signifying their allegiance with their triumph over pain and suffering through their solidarity in Christ.[177]

176. Charles Donahue, "The Canon Law on the Formation of Marriage and Social Practice in the Later Middle Ages," *Journal of Family History* 8 (1983): 144–58. For a view which dissents from Donahue's emphasis on the primacy of intrafamily dynamics—parental versus individual consent—see A. J. Finch, "Parental Authority and the Problem of Clandestine Marriage in the Later Middle Ages," *Law and History Review* 8 (1990): 189–204.

177. David Herlihy, "Tuscan Names, 1200–1530," *Renaissance Quarterly* 41 (1988): 561–82. For further evidence of the plethora of vernacular names in the thirteenth century and the relative absence of names with a religious connotation, see Pamela Waley, "Personal Names in Siena, 1285," in Peter Denley and Caroline Elam (eds.), *Florence and Italy* (London, 1988), 187–91.

4.

This project of social purification was abetted by the astonishing rise of new ascetic orders—both those which remained true to the monastic traditions and the newer groups who reached out to spread their message in secular society. The reformers of the twelfth century "split the single traditional vision of the monastic life into twenty different divisions, as it were the colours of the spectrum, each realizing a potentiality implicit in the monastic life but neglected by most contemporary manifestations," thus meeting a more complex and articulated social demand.[178] The absolute number of people involved in the spiritual project was quite astonishing. Between 1066 and 1300, when the wave of enthusiasm for monasticism had peaked, the English population rose threefold while the religious population grew twenty times. Men were predominant; there were an estimated 2,000 nuns and 33,500 men in holy orders in 1377, at which time the religious and secular clergy accounted for roughly 3 percent of the male population.[179]

Among the regular monks were the revived order of Augustinians ("black canons"), which has been promoted by Gregory VII, the Carmelites, the Carthusians, the Templars, the Premonstratensians ("white canons"), and a number of smaller orders including all-female ones like the Poor Clares, whose foundation paralleled that of the Franciscans in the early thirteenth century. Above all, there were the Cistercians, whose immense popularity led the original establishment at Cîteaux to divide and subdivide itself into 350 monasteries between 1098 and 1145. Under Saint Bernard's direction, the second generation "mother-house" of Clairvaux was responsible for sixty-eight offspring in a period of some thirty-five years. The growth of the Cistercians, and the other new orders, was to some extent balanced by the decline in the reformed order of Benedictines, which had reached its absolute zenith in 1109, when there were some 1,450 communities living under the rule of the abbot-primate of Cluny.

In addition, a census of these monastic orders should include the bewildering variety of lay communities devoted to ascetic piety that emerged alongside the officially recognized religious life. Of particular interest, one

178. David Knowles, *From Pachomius to Ignatius: A Study in the Constitutional History of the Religious Orders*, quoted in Giles Constable, "The Diversity of Religious Life and Acceptance of Social Pluralism in the Twelfth Century," in Derek Beales and Geoffrey Best (eds.), *History, Society and the Churches* (Cambridge, 1985), 29–47.

179. J. C. Russell, "The Clerical Population of Medieval England," *Traditio* 2 (1944): 177–212.

must mention the mushrooming growth of noncloistered religious females—among whom the Belgian *béguines* were the most noteworthy. It
is striking that religious women were disproportionately drawn from the
most economically advanced sections of the population. These women,
who represented a distinctly feminine expression of popular spirituality,
could trace their origins to the same wellspring of apostolic piety that led
to the creation of the reformed monastic orders—particularly the Cistercians and the Premonstratensians, although at the end of the twelfth century, these two orders tried (and failed) to eliminate their female branches.
The nuns'—and especially the Premonstratensian lay sisters'—lives stood
as a model to a new generation of women who articulated their lives of lay
devotion as *béguines.* Like the men who would become friars, for them living the life of apostolic poverty in the world was more relevant than following the monastic rule by withdrawing from the world. These women's
groups were characterized by chastity and extraregular status that left
them free from governance by a monastic rule. They were thus known by
their separation from males, both as bodily mates and as spiritual fathers.

The most renowned of the Belgian *béguines* was Mary of Oignies. She
was made famous through her friendship with James of Vitry, who had
hoped that her example would be valuable to the orthodox Church in its
struggle with heretics, especially the Cathars, whose attraction to females
was a legend in its own time. Mary of Oignies exhibited a heightened ascetic impulse which was connected with her rejection of sexuality. Even
though she had been married off at the age of fourteen, she never consummated her marriage and, indeed, converted her husband to a life of devotion,
chastity, and charity. She abused her body, never wearing warm clothes and
clinching her waist with a rough rope girdle that chafed her skin so that it
bled constantly. Like many other saintly women of this period, Mary of
Oignies ate little and was subject to divine mystical visitations.[180]

Mary of Oignies was also characteristic of a distinctly feminine brand of
piety in her devotion to the Eucharist and her extreme self-denial. Recent
historical writing has made it clear that in the period after 1000, women
who were canonized or revered were significantly more likely than their
male contemporaries to have lived in extreme austerity. Interestingly, extended food abstinence had been almost exclusively a male phenomenon in
early Christianity, but it became a female behavior after the year 1000.
Women who submitted to a regimen of extensive fasting were much more

180. Carol Neel, "The Origins of the Beguines," *Signs* 14 (1989): 321–41; John
B. Freed, "Urban Development and the 'Curia Monialium' in Thirteenth-Century
Germany," *Viator* 3 (1972): 311–27.

likely to have experienced Eucharistic visions and miracles as well as being subject to miraculous bodily changes. Because they connected food abstinence with chastity, and greed with sexual desire, such women seem to have been not only controlling themselves in relation to their social world but also explicitly controlling their sexuality. In these ways, a very small number of female athletes-in-Christ discovered an alternative to their expected roles as wives and mothers.[181]

These new groups emerged not only as a rebuke to the worldliness of the Cluniacs but also as a reaction against the logical dialectic of the university scholars who had the temerity to analyze the revealed word of the Bible by subjecting it to the new intellectual technology of dialectical reasoning. The preaching friars—Dominicans and Franciscans, as well as a number of smaller orders, and the ancillary lay organizations—represented a new thrust in western Christianity: a battle for the minds as well as the bodies of the whole population. In this way, they represented a definitive break with the Christianity of late antiquity: "They brought the desert communities to the mob. A map of the Franciscan and Dominican houses at the end of the thirteenth century is a map of urban Christian Europe."[182] In 1300 there were about 600 Dominican convents, with 12,000 friars, and about 1,400 Franciscan houses with a complement of 28,000.[183] These new orders sprang from the same evangelical concerns that gave birth to the Peace and the Truce of God. Together, they produced a powerful elixir.

5.

If the Benedictine monasteries had their fingers on the spiritual pulse of the early Christian world, and if the holiness of the Cistercian monks was the measure of the age of Gregorian Reform after the year 1000, then the immense popularity of the mendicant orders was attuned to the developing complexities of early modernization. Their rise coincided with the emergence of a people's religion: the friars were popularizers, "mass emotionalists . . . plucking the heartstrings . . . [with] inexhaustible eloquence." Their preaching "formed part of a show or popular festivities and was surrounded by painted or carved symbols in good view, accompanied by sung processions and interspersed with theatrical performances." The liturgical drama was turned into a personal exercise of faith in which inner aware-

---

181. Caroline Walker Bynum, "Fast, Feast, and Flesh: The Religious Significance of Food to Medieval Women," *Representations* 11 (1985): 1–25.
182. Le Goff, *Medieval Civilization*, 87.
183. Johnson, *A History of Christianity*, 235.

ness was confirmed in collective celebrations.[184] Nowhere, perhaps, was this confrontation between the fundamentally ancient Christianity of monastic life and the fundamentally early modern piety of the burgher more acute than in the urban centers of commerce.

The friars' missionary project provides us with a valuable insight into the embedded folk beliefs that existed alongside and sometimes in opposition to the ordered religion of learned culture. What, then, was the character of popular religion? Our sources almost exclusively view popular religion from a top-down perspective.[185] This is unfortunate because the syncretic character of popular belief—a patchwork of ideas and interests—is contrasted to the intellectual rigor of orthodox dogma. "The [tenth-century] population lived in a plurality of cult units, similar to those of the pagan period, with the difference that there was now a sort of head unit, Christendom. In popular understanding, this larger concept played a minor role by comparison with local loyalties."[186] So it is probably not unjust to note that folk piety was most probably experienced as *bricolage*—continuously and chaotically recycling materials derived from the high culture of formal philosophy and theology as well as other materials emanating from the little traditions of indigenous folklore, oral communication, and material pragmatism.[187]

184. Duby, *The Age of Cathedrals,* 223–25; C.N.L. Brooke similarly argues that one of the unforeseen consequences of the spiritual intensification of the year 1000 had been the close association between the lower orders of the clergy and the general population and that the institutionalization of reform in the later twelfth century was achieved at the cost of separating these groups. St. Francis's mission, then, was an attempt to recapture this association—leadership by example and quiet faith, as opposed to St. Dominic's more activist method of evangelism by preaching; "The Missionary at Home: The Church in the Towns, 1000–1250," in G. J. Cuming (ed.), *The Mission of the Church and the Propagation of the Faith* (Cambridge, 1970), 59–83.

185. There is a vast literature on this subject. I found the following articles to be particularly helpful: John Van Engen, "The Christian Middle Ages as an Historiographical Problem," *American Historical Review* 91 (1986): 519–52; Natalie Zemon Davis, "Some Tasks and Themes in the Study of Popular Religion," in C. Trinkhaus and H. Oberman (eds.), *The Pursuit of Holiness in Late Medieval and Renaissance Religion* (Leiden, 1974), 307–36; Davis, "From 'Popular Religion' to Religious Cultures," in S. Ozment (ed.), *Reformation Europe: A Guide to Research* (St. Louis, 1982), 321–41; Thomas Tentler, "Seventeen Authors in Search of Two Religious Cultures," *Catholic Historical Review* 71 (1985): 248–57; and Lionel Rothkrug, "Religious Practices and Collective Perceptions."

186. Fichtenau, *Living in the Tenth Century,* 325.

187. Robert Scribner, "Symbolising Boundaries: Defining Social Space in the Daily Life of Early Modern Germany," in G. Haschitz, H. Hundsbichler, G. Jaritz, and E. Vavra (eds.), *Symbole des Alltags* (Graz, 1992), 821–41.

The veneration of saints and relics lay at the heart of this religious project, creating the incentive for large numbers of people to make pilgrimages to myriad local shrines as well as the three major international holy sites—Jerusalem, Rome, and Santiago de Compostela in Spain. An economic geography of holiness sprouted in rural Europe. The Perigord in southwestern France, for example, was crisscrossed by pilgrimage routes. The *chemin de Paris* and the *chemin de Vézelay* brought the faithful from the north and funneled them toward the Spanish frontier, where they joined others who had traveled toward Santiago de Compostela along the *chemin du Puy* and the *chemin d'Arles*. Along country roads there was an almost constant demand for hospitality—food and lodging. This brought the vitality of early modernization into obscure villages by commercializing economic relations as well as drawing countrymen and countrywomen into the currents of religiosity.

The "improper worship of the true God" drew the clergy's attention as paganism receded. Superstitions, the degraded and perverted forms of religion practiced by the illiterate masses, were particularly dangerous because the hegemony of the clerical discourse was incomplete. Local amalgams were in a state of flux in comparison with the uniform doctrines of trained scholars. Recently, historians have sought to rehabilitate these religious cultures by reading the outpourings of this great tradition against its own grain. In this way they have tried to recover the spiritual sufferings and satisfactions of those who were condemned to silence by their illiteracy.[188]

Because it lacked the firm discipline of an authoritative text, popular religion seems to have been awkwardly connected with the great tradition of biblical exegesis. In common with other societies in which literacy was confined to a specialized group, the content of the authoritative text was communicated by the literate clerisy to nonliterates. "The teacher expounds, the audience responds or memorizes. . . . 'Traditional' societies are marked not so much by the absence of reflective thinking as by the absence of the proper tools for constructive rumination." The reproduction of oral knowledge is therefore a series of discrete events because in oral societies, the author's "individual signature is always getting rubbed out in the process of generative transmission." Changes in the mode of communication have enormous implications for content; thus, writing sharpens the outlines of categories and encourages "the hierarchisation of the classificatory system." The systematization of knowledge is the result of a technology of the

---

188. Jean-Claude Schmitt, *The Holy Greyhound: Guinefort, Healer of Children since the Thirteenth Century* (Cambridge, 1984), esp. 14–24, 39 ff.

intellect—a gradual process of accumulating, writing down, assessing, and augmenting a body of knowledge in the process of which spontaneity is not just restricted but also suspected by the knowledge workers.[189]

What especially troubled contemporary commentators about popular religion was its potential for engendering unconventional beliefs, which were often nothing more than deviations from the increasingly ossified formulae derived from their literate religion of the book. Oral culture, by its very nature, was reflexive and mutable; popular religion, which was largely the product of illiterates, was characteristically volatile and unstable. In contrast to the intellectual moral seriousness which characterized the official culture of the book, situational strategies for coping with the exigencies of daily life were spontaneous, vital, and exuberantly effervescent. Popular manners were shot through with a primitive materialism. Birth and death, eating and drinking, sex and sociability, laughter and forgetting—these human pursuits all undercut the perfectionism demanded by the athletes-in-Christ who were committed to the domestication of the savage mind.[190] A dialectical tension between the centripetal imperatives of the corporate Church and the centrifugal force of their own eclectic search for piety pulled the masses away from the institutionalized, centralizing tendencies of the Church at the same time that Christianity (however understood) became the measure of religious sentiments.

The mendicants' preaching mission reached out to an illiterate population. In this sense, the friars were the shock troops of the Church. They would evangelize the uninformed and lead them in the paths of righteousness. Some were obdurately unwilling to compromise with the vulgarity of the masses, but most started from the proposition that "there are those in the Church who are less able, who cannot identify or distinguish the articles of the Creed; yet they believe what is contained in the Creed, for they believe what they do not know." This "implicit faith" was held to characterize the unlearned quest for spiritual piety. It was obviously the role of the learned, whose literate knowledge enabled them to gain explicit knowledge, to lead this mission.[191] For those in charge of the pastoral care of the common people, an easygoing exchange between the rigors of the dogma and harmless, folkloric beliefs and practices meant that the adherents of many religious cultures could be brought within the orthodox fold, accul-

189. Jack Goody, *The Domestication of the Savage Mind* (Cambridge, 1977), 151, 44, 27, 102, 144–45.
190. Michel Despland, "How Close Are We to Having a Full History of Christianity?," *Religious Studies Review* 9 (1983): 24–33.
191. Peter Lombard, quoted in Van Engen, "The Christian Middle Ages," 545.

tured, and thereby Christianized. The rhythms of their lives would henceforth be contained within the Church's house of many mansions.

The emotional agenda of the people would be encapsulated in the Church's calendar so that their time would be reckoned according to the liturgical year described by its preaching, confession, penance, masses, communions, holy days, cults of the saints, relics, fasts, vigils, miracles, and harvest festivals. Space would be imagined in relation to holy ground and shrines; it would be traversed by processions and pilgrimages. Rites of passage—birth, naming, coming of age, betrothal, marriage, childbearing, and death—would be conducted without reference to other traditions. Although the people were ignorant of the niceties of doctrinal orthodoxy, their faith would be kept pure and simple as long as it was based on the regurgitation of simple prayer formulas like the Pater Noster, Ave Maria, and Creed. These ritual observances were to be realized in daily life by close observance of the Ten Commandments and resistance to the Seven Deadly Sins.[192]

A key aspect of this process can be seen from another angle in the policy of Germanization in the Slavic, East Elbian region. This was an explicitly Christian missionary project which oriented the reproduction of everyday life through the enforcement of new ecclesiastical patterns and new definitions of the family. A new system of spiritual kinship was introduced with impediments to consanguineous marriage and polygamy which might have had small demographic consequences but immense domestic ones. In addition, female infanticide was outlawed. The calendar and festive year were also reorganized—"the ashes of the old temporal rhythm were scattered [to prevent] the flame of pagan worship" from being sparked again.[193] However, one must not telescope the process of cultural homogenization. The human geography of settlement dappled the landscape as these different ethnocultural groups lived cheek by jowl and slowly merged—the last woman to speak the Wendish dialect died only in 1404. The peasants in sixteenth-century Prussia repeatedly gathered for the sacrificial feasts honoring their ancient "goat divinity," while as late as the

192. Alexander Murray, "Piety and Impiety in Thirteenth-Century Italy," *Studies in Church History* 8 (1972): 83–106; "Religion among the Poor in Thirteenth-Century France: The Testimony of Humbert de Romans," *Traditio* 30 (1974): 285–324; "Confession as a Historical Source in the Thirteenth Century," in R. H. C. Davis and J. M. Wallace-Hadrill (eds.), *The Writing of History in the Middle Ages* (Oxford, 1981), 275–322.

193. Robert Bartlett, "The Conversion of a Pagan Society in the Middle Ages," *History* 70 (1985): 185–201.

eighteenth century, near Berlin and Leipzig, sermons were still being preached in the Slavonic languages of the peasantry.[194]

Submission to the authority of God's representatives here on Earth meant that people would willingly pay their tithes and gladly contribute alms. This project was utopian; it was also double-edged. It presumed that the clergy would lead and the laity would follow. It hoped that observance would be internalized in the process of making a Christian society. Success itself set in train other forces which can be measured in the dynamic whereby members of the laity sought to acquire for themselves active membership in the priestly sacred culture. This was problematic for those who wished to retain a monopoly on spiritual virtue because the scholastic formulation of Church doctrine was that each person had dignity as a rational human being. The ambivalent relationship between oral culture and literate culture also speaks to this point. The mendicant orders were able to tap this spontaneity, which accounted for their phenomenal success. But as their relationship with the common people became more formal and developed its own conventions, this immediacy became attenuated.

The success of the Gregorian Reformation implanted Christian spirituality into the marrow of daily life in Western Europe. The spiritual flowering of early modernization was only partially answered by the rise of the mendicant orders. The organization of the parochial system created a spatially regulated grid of surveillance and education which acculturated the religious ardor of the folk and steered it into orthodox channels. Twelfth-century canon lawyers hammered out a new territorial system of parochial life. Christians were henceforth required to attend mass, to baptize their children, and to be buried in their local parish. In return, Christians owed tithes to their parish to support its priest and its church fabric.[195] Another spiritual response was the massive proliferation of nonprofessional groups which sought to follow an apostolic life according to the pure light of the gospel—heretics, hermits, and spiritualists on the fringes of orthodoxy represent one end of this spectrum; confraternities like the Brethren of the Common Life or Corpus Christi guilds represent the other end. In order to co-opt the more advanced laity, who were eager to emerge from a passive

194. Walther Hubatsch, "Albert of Brandenburg-Ansbach, Grand Master of the Order of Teutonic Knights and Duke in Prussia, 1490–1568," in Henry J. Cohn (ed.), *Government in Reformation Europe 1520–1560* (London, 1971), 172–73; M. M. Postan, "Economic Relations between Eastern and Western Europe," in Geoffrey Barraclough (ed.), *Eastern and Western Europe in the Middle Ages* (London, 1971), 144.

195. Brooke, "The Missionary at Home," 68–69.

faith and attracted to heretical doctrines, the Church revised its approach to worship. It threw its weight behind confraternities, guilds, mutual aid associations, trade societies, district and parish corporations, and hospital and charity organizations, as well as groups of penitents who were committed to an apostolic way of life. In this way, the Gregorian Reformation was institutionalized and imbricated into the infraculture of everyday life.

Riding the crest of a wave of popular spirituality which had focused initially on the millennium of Christ's birth and then on the millennium of the Passion in 1033, "Heresy—radical, disruptive, appearing shortly after the year 1000 [w]as one sign, perhaps the most convincing sign, of that tumultuous vitality that impelled Western civilization forward in its sudden advance."[196] Heresy was an ongoing problem of doctrinal and institutional deviance of a kind that was unknown before the year 1000. Heresy turned on questions of obedience to constituted authority rather more than on doctrinal issues. It was the result of obstinate, public persistence in wrong belief that was compounded after that error had been identified. Heresy was thus indistinguishable from disobedience. Heretics did not just make mistakes, nor were they simply ignorant of dogma; rather, they arrogated the magic, mystery, and authority of the clergy to themselves. In the eyes of the clergy, heretics were guilty of overweening pride—and, of course, pride goeth before the Fall. The main thrust of anticlerical criticism turned on the "impurity" of simoniacal and, especially, married priests.[197] To remedy this danger, the reformers "dismissed the idea of a pontifical king . . . [and] replaced it by the regal pontiff, thus turning the old imperial theory of government upside down." The imperial papacy dispensed its form of justice, combining superior efficiency with the charisma attached to the Church's religio-magical authority.[198]

Having opened Pandora's Box, the Church tried to control its contents; the recognition that the orthodox faith had only a tenuous hold upon the mass of the population particularly concerned the clerical bureaucracy in

---

196. Georges Duby, *The Three Orders: Feudal Society Imagined* (Chicago, 1980), 31. Cowdrey suggests that another factor which impelled the search for peace was the agony of *ignis sacer* (ergotism, a disease resulting from eating tainted rye-flour), whose "mental and bodily torments came and went with a suddenness for which eleventh-century men knew neither natural explanation nor human remedy"; "The Peace and the Truce of God," 48.

197. Ideas of "pollution" and "impurity" are intimately connected with these historical changes by R. I. Moore. See *The Origins of European Dissent* (London, 1977); "Family, Community and Cult on the Eve of the Gregorian Reform," *Transactions of the Royal Historical Society*, 5th ser., 30 (1980): 49–69.

198. Johnson, *A History of Christianity*, 196.

its policing of belief. A new emphasis on the social competition for achieved status began to take place alongside the older system of ascribed roles. In this way, it was accompanied by new lifestyles and a frantic search for social communion. The older religious beliefs and practices had provided no meaningful social patterning to newly felt demands.[199] In place of the dichotomous eternities of heaven and hell, the evolving vision of purgatory introduced a new vision of time management into daily life.[200] The Church was successful insofar as it appropriated many of the erstwhile heretics' goals that sought nothing less than a return to the purity and simplicity of the apostolic life.[201] A little knowledge was indeed a dangerous thing; verifying its orthodoxy was a Sisyphean task to which the Church devoted a massive amount of energy and resources. After all, life after death hung in the balance.

Success was not just a matter of direction from above, by the agents of the Church; the friars' preaching met a real, felt need, which sometimes sought its satisfaction outside the ritual of the Church yet desired to reform the Church itself. At its heart was "a new self-awareness that called for the simultaneous cultivation of the individual conscience and an internalization of Christian morality. The very conception of sin itself changed by shifting attention from the external act to the inner intention."[202] As Abelard told Héloise: "The crime lies in the intending, not in the doing."[203] Early modern society was convulsed with a series of reforming movements which aimed at endowing the laity with some of the trappings of priestly sacred culture. Ironically, most of the energy powering these convulsions

---

199. Nelson, "Society, Theodicy and the Origins of Heresy," 65–77.

200. Berman, *Law and Revolution*, 166–81. The dating of the "birth of purgatory" is a matter of dispute: Jacques Le Goff would date its appearance in the later twelfth century, while Aron J. Gurevich suggests that this was only the moment of scholastic recognition, and purgatory had already had a long life. See Le Goff, *The Birth of Purgatory* (Chicago, 1984), 135–65; Gurevich, "Popular and Scholarly Medieval Cultural Traditions: Notes in the Margin of Jacques Le Goff's Book," *Journal of Medieval History* 9 (1983): 71–90. See also Gurevich, *Medieval Popular Culture: Problems of Belief and Perception* (Cambridge, 1988), 175. In addition, John Bossy supports a less formalized birthdate of purgatory; "The Mass as a Social Institution," 37.

201. H. Focillon, *The Year 1000* (New York, 1970); for the continuing reciprocity between popular religion and elite religion, see also Brenda Bolton, "Innocent III's Treatment of the *Humiliati*," in G. J. Cuming and Derek Baker (eds.), *Popular Belief and Practice* (Cambridge, 1972), 73–82.

202. Barbara H. Rosenwein and Lester K. Little, "Social Meaning in the Monastic and Mendicant Spiritualities," *Past and Present* 63 (1974): 19.

203. Quoted in Duby, *The Age of Cathedrals*, 117.

was to be found within the contradictions of priestly sacred culture. Thus, the young schoolmen of Abelard's generation invented the word "modern," at the beginning of the twelfth century.[204]

6.

Lateran IV marks a new phase in Church history, a willingness to proselytize the laity. This Council defined the sacraments and limited their number to seven, thereby fashioning the Christian's life on earth from birth to death. From this time, the explicit corporate policy of the Church was that all Christians were expected to be like the monks of the early Middle Ages who "lived the life of the angels." The Fourth Lateran Council entrenched the Church's commitment "to legislate for the Christian life as lived by layfolk." This was not a one-shot affair; rather, it was built into the fabric of the secularization of Christianity and the acculturation of the whole population in an apostolic way of life.[205]

Lateran IV sought to give shape to the community of the faithful by defining the conditions of membership as well as the expectations of a revitalized clerical mission. This explains the novel requirement that at least once a year all adults, of both sexes, must confess and were required to perform penance on penalty of being deprived of Christian burial in death. Michel Foucault draws our attention to the wonder of it all: ·

> The confession is a ritual of discourse in which the speaking subject is also the subject of the statement; it is also a ritual that unfolds within a power relationship, for one does not confess without the presence (or virtual presence) of a partner who is not simply the interlocutor but the authority who requires the confession, prescribes and appreciates it, and intervenes in order to judge, punish, forgive, console, and reconcile; a ritual in which the truth is corroborated by the obstacles and resistances it has had to surmount in order to be formulated; and finally, a ritual in which the expression alone, independently of its external consequences, produces intrinsic modifications in the person who articu-

204. Indeed, Abelard thought of himself as a modern man in that he did not want to destroy the legacy of his predecessors but rather to surpass it. It was this overweening pride in his own intellectual capacity that twice plunged Peter Abelard into deep trouble with the clerical establishment. He was brought to trial in 1121 at Sens and again in 1140 in Soissons; both cases were so important that papal intervention was forthcoming in each instance; Clanchy, *Abelard*, 17; for his trials, see chap. 13.

205. Peter Brown, "Society and the Supernatural: A Medieval Change," *Daedalus* 104 (1975); see also David Knowles, *The Christian Centuries* (London, 1969), 219.

lates it: it exonerates, redeems, and purifies him; it unburdens him of his wrongs, liberates him, and promises him salvation.[206]

It is important to recognize that sex took a proportionally diminished place in the confessional manuals, not a greater place. But if the methods of confession and penance became less rigorous, they also became part of a system of surveillance which aimed to scrutinize the whole population. One doesn't want to paint this picture in overly dramatic tones: in late medieval Flanders, for example, all the members of the parish were never gathered together for Sunday Mass, and the demand for annual confession was poorly observed. It is estimated that half the urban population failed to fulfill its Easter duties–10 percent never communicated, 40 percent did so irregularly, another 40 percent did so regularly, and just 10 percent went beyond the prescribed minimum of annual confession at Easter.[207]

The practice of penitence was not in itself new. Rather, eleventh-century religiosity extended the widespread desire to purify the social world which had found expression in the Peace of God. In understanding the interaction of religious revival and social relations, it is useful to refer here to Mary Douglas's explanation of the relationship between concerns for purity and disorder. She writes: "The whole universe is harnessed in man's attempts to force one another into good citizenship. Thus we find certain moral values are upheld and certain social rules defined by beliefs in dangerous contagion," and "ideas about separating, purifying, demarcating and punishing transgressions have as their main function to impose system on an inherently untidy experience. [Purification] thus represents a positive effort to organise the environment."[208]

206. *The History of Sexuality*, vol. 1, *An Introduction* (New York, 1978), 61–2. This book's original French title, *La volonté de savoir* (The will for knowledge), better captures the remarkable insight of Foucault's brilliant argument.

207. Roger Chartier, *The Cultural Origins of the French Revolution* (Durham, N.C., 1991), 93–94, quoting the findings of Jacques Toussaert, *Le Sentiment religieux en Flandre à la fin du Moyen-Age*, esp. 122–204.

208. Mary Douglas, *Purity and Danger* (London, 1984), 2–4. It is, perhaps, germane at this point to mention that Hildebrand/Gregory VII was a member of the Peirleone clan of Rome. Scholarly opinion reflects the uncertainty of the sources, but it is thought that Hildebrand/Gregory was the the descendant of a Jewish moneyer who converted in 1030. Doubts remain, however, about the "Jewish blood in him, despite his allegedly Semitic looks"; D. B. Zema, "The Houses of Tuscany and of Pierleone in the Crisis of Rome in the Eleventh Century," *Traditio* 2 (1944): 170–71. This article summarizes a scholarly controversy of an earlier generation; for a more recent evaluation of this evidence, see Joachim Prinz, *Popes from the Ghetto* (New York, 1966). My reason for drawing attention to this issue is the congruence between Hildebrand/Gregory's political policies and his evident fear of *pollution*—which seems both sexual and religious and may have had its roots in his family's ex-

Augustine's contribution to Christian thought is crucial at this point. The Augustinian inheritance stitched together Jewish theism and Platonic philosophy of understanding the universe as an external realization of a rational order.[209] Concern with the pervasiveness of sin—the overwhelming sense of oneself as being both depraved and powerless—led to an obsession with self-examination. The pain of eternal damnation resulting from original sin was ameliorated with a new system of penitential atonement. A few centuries after Augustine's death, and from the farthest shore of European Christendom, Irish monasteries in the Dark Ages developed an elaborate system of accounting to weigh individual sins and to prescribe appropriate penalties. These calendars of depravity spoke to a tiny audience of spiritual professionals; it is unlikely that the Irish penitentials made any impact whatsoever on popular behavior.

After the year 1000, a new technology of the self began to locate itself within the infraculture of Western society. It was built upon an inward shift of moral governance. The key element of this religious mutation, however, was not intellectual but practical. Among the laity, a stable configuration of shared activities emerged that can be understood as being peculiarly Christian. As Charles Taylor would have it, this practice was vague and general—a pattern of do's and don'ts that took place at all levels of social life: family, village, and larger community. Ideas were, in an important sense, secondary because Christian practices were based on these patterns that were inculcated from childhood. Articulations—intellectual justification—came later.[210]

Taylor's formulation of this issue is stimulating, although it begs rather more questions than it answers. In particular, one would like to know when and how these practices penetrated daily life. Historians of everyday religion speak to this issue in many tongues. As I noted in the previous section, the Christianization of the general population did not take place simultaneously, nor did this process result in a homogenized laity. Rather, Christianization was experienced as acculturation—another long, arduous process of education.[211] Popular religion was syncretic, and we should

---

perience of rejecting Judaism and embracing Christianity. Saying this, however, is not intended to label Hildebrand/Gregory as an anti-Semitic Jew so much as to make sense of his profound desire to be more Catholic than the unreformed popes who had held office in the Rome of his boyhood and youth. Or, as Mary Douglas would have it, purifying the papacy was "a positive effort to organise the environment" in order "to impose system on an inherently untidy experience."

209. Charles Taylor, *Sources of the Self* (Cambridge, Mass., 1989), 128.

210. *Sources of the Self,* 204.

211. I will return to this point, and discuss it in more detail, in the "Luxuriant Despair" section of chap. 5, which considers popular religious behavior in the

never lose sight of the primordial fact that the syncretizers had a large say in what was accepted and incorporated into their lives.[212] While we know too little about religious practices, we are on much firmer ground when it comes to the history of religious thought, which tends to be concerned with the ideas of great men.

In a highly developed form, it was Abelard (1079–1142) who shifted the focus of penitence from external sanction to internal contrition.[213] Richard Southern has suggested that Abelard's reinterpretation of redemption was one of the great new ideas of the time. "It left out the whole idea of compensation to God for human sin, and threw the whole emphasis of the Incarnation on its capacity to revive man's love for God."[214] This new line of thinking led to the novel idea that salvation had to be earned by an effort of self-transformation, not simply acquired by sheeplike participation in religious rites. As Peter Brown has written, "Gifted men could find leisure, incentive and personal resources to tackle more strictly delimited tasks. The laity also, though technically made inferior to the clergy, came to enjoy the freedom that came from a vast unpretentiousness. . . . Throughout society, the disengagement of the sacred from the profane opened up a whole middle distance of conflicting opportunities for the deployment of talent."[215] This exploration of conscience in turn privileged the private individual who adopted an attitude toward the sacred similar to that which previously had been limited to the clergy. Systematic theology and legal

---

shadow of the Black Death. To be sure, there were important discontinuities after the bacteriological holocaust, but the historiographical importance of the Reformation has led generations of scholars to research this topic more deeply for the fifteenth century than for the period before 1348. The main point at issue is not seriously affected by this chronological displacement since the gap between the orthodox religiosity of the educated elite and the syncretic beliefs of the plebeian masses persisted for centuries. Indeed, one of the very best studies on this subject I have read relates to the beliefs and practices of Lincolnshire Victorians—James Obelkevich, *Religion and Rural Society: South Lindsey, 1825–1875* (Oxford, 1976), esp. chap. 6.

212. In a similiar vein, Richard Hoggart's autobiographical memory of English working-class life notes that this "is not simply a power of passive resistance, but something which, though not articulate, is positive. The working-classes have a strong natural ability to survive change by adapting or assimilating what they want in the new and ignoring the rest"; *The Uses of Literacy* (Harmondsworth, 1957), 32.

213. J. Le Goff, "Merchant's Time and Church's Time," in *Time, Work, and Culture in the Middle Ages* (Chicago, 1980), 39.

214. Quoted in Clanchy, *Abelard*, 287.

215. "Society and the Supernatural," 134.

science came to be understood as proper strategies of regulating the community of sinners on earth.[216]

The Fourth Lateran Council thus marked the culmination of a long tradition in the Church's history of private penance which had begun seven centuries earlier with the Irish penitentials.[217] While we must be careful to distinguish between the claims of innovators and the reality of social experience, it is quite clear that the confessional—a technology of the soul—represented a keystone which held up the great arch of early modernization. In the words of one contemporary: "The seed is sown in preaching; the fruit is harvested in penance." That "fruit" was not simply the promise of cash payments to redeem one's failings but a form of preaching directed to the laity "which had as its goal an inner conversion of the individual listener to a deeper involvement in the faith that he already professed."[218]

The new preaching orders of friars, who spearheaded the implementation of the new injunction linking the office of preaching, the hearing of confession, and the administration of penance, were themselves drawn disproportionately from the most commercially advanced social groups. Not only was their practice suffused with a desire to persuade, but that persuasion was itself negotiated. Such penitential debts were bargained in the currency of monetary exchange—"indulgences" were transactions with the church's Treasury of Merits. To be sure, this was frequently rather more a matter of style than of substance, but the foundations were laid for a distinctively western and Christian *volonté de savoir*. It incorporated a distinctively non-ancient pattern of faith and worship into the everyday life of the population. Peter Brown's remarks are germane here: "the development of a confessional literature is one of the spearheads of self-awareness in the twelfth century. The intimate shame of self-revelation came to be considered expiation enough. The role of shame was all the more relevant to an age whose sense of professional achievement had created a particularly brittle façade in knights and clerics alike. . . . Now it was possible to canalize these bitter feelings into an intimate, non-communal relationship to a father-confessor."[219]

It was a system of confession and penitence which spared no one, as William Marshal discovered: on his deathbed this great warrior and states-

216. Georges Duby, "The Emergence of the Individual. Solitude: Eleventh to Thirteenth Century," in Duby (ed.), *Revelations of the Medieval World*, 513, 529–33.
217. Payer, "Foucault on Penance and the Shaping of Sexuality," 317.
218. Rosenwein and Little, "Social Meaning," 22.
219. "Society and the Supernatural," 145.

man lucidly put his own spin on the teaching of the Church and its role in mediating his relationship with his God.

> The clerks are too hard on us. They shave us too closely. I have captured five hundred knights and have appropriated their arms, horses and their entire equipment. If for this reason the kingdom of God is closed to me, I can do nothing about it, for I cannot return my booty. I can do no more for God than to give myself to him, repenting all my sins. Unless the clergy desire my damnation, they must ask no more. But their teaching is false—else no one could be saved.[220]

The dying knight feared God but distrusted the clergy. His skeptical piety is instructive; we must recognize that systematic surveillance was more ominous in its implications than in its daily operation. Confessors were instructed to be prudent, cautious, humane, and tolerant; many were also lax or ignorant.[221]

Not coincidentally, the same Church Council which created and staffed the Inquisition was also active in transforming the boundary between the sacred and profane in daily life. The same way of thinking lay behind Lateran IV's prohibition against clerical participation in trials by ordeal while sanctioning a new doctrine of the Eucharistic transubstantiation in which bread and wine were transformed into the body and blood of Christ. In the older, Carolingian notion of the Church, the Eucharist was conceived in terms of a relic and had "its doctrinal counterpart in the insistence that the Incarnation, the at-one-ment with God, deified human nature. Christ's appearance as a supernatural person resident in heaven, emphasizing His Ascension, introduced the notion that the Passion, that is, God's merciful humanization, caused man to participate in the divine." This new theory was part of a "radical upwards displacement of supernatural ascription, occurring as it did concomitantly across the entire spectrum of religious life and thought, [which] necessarily expanded the idea of the Church or society beyond the limits of mere personifiable representation." This new idea of incommensurability—embodied in Saint Anselm's "ontological definition" of God as "that than which nothing greater can be conceived"—both introduced the notion of discontinuity between divine and human law and developed the idea of Christendom as a universal society.[222]

---

220. Painter, *William Marshal*, 285–86.
221. For an assessment of the confessors' attitude to the penitent, see Lawrence G. Duggan, "Fear and Confession on the Eve of the Reformation," *Archive for Reformation History* 75 (1984): 153–75.
222. Rothkrug, "Religious Practices and Collective Perceptions," 28–29.

The priesthood—unmarried males who were undefiled by sexual pollution—gained from its ritual performance of sacramental purification. This
was not merely an academic matter: Lothar of Segni, who would become Pope
Innocent III, climbed the long ladder of ecclesiastical officeholding by writing
an influential treatise which connected scholarly reflections on transubstantiation with the needs for institutional uniformity. Thus, "every priest, in
every parish, at every altar, during every mass, should encapsulate the
church's message of mediation, in a way that was recognisable, uniform, and
supportive of sacramental claims." With a fine sense of theater, the church reformers focused the ritual so that the elevation of the host came to mark the
moment of consecration when the bread and wine were turned into the body
and blood of Christ. There is some suggestion that the designers of the ritual
were responding to popular demands to see God; thereby, they were also undermining the popular appeal of heretics against the priestly estate. This
seems credible in view of the way that all the senses were called into play—
"Bells pealed, incense was burnt, candles were lit, hands were clasped, suppli-
cations were mouthed."[223] The magical powers of the priesthood were in this
way made evident, for all to see. In fact, there can be no question about the
way in which the image of the elevation of the host became central to the representation of both clerical authority and the community of the faithful.

The new ritual of Eucharistic transubstantiation was therefore of crucial
importance in buttressing the massive expansion of the powers that the
Church claimed and wielded in everyday life in the wake of the Gregorian
Reformation. Indeed, it was in no small part the culmination of that sea
change in the relationship between church and state. Needless to say, these
novelties deepened the gulf separating the clergy from the laity. In particular, the new dogma of the Eucharist enhanced the sanctity of the host and
its official intermediaries by raising fears that the body and blood of Christ
would be polluted by profane participation.

The changed relationship between clergy and laity provoked a spatial
reorganization of the celebration of the Mass. The altar had been a solid
structure, lavish in materials and workmanship housing relics, but after
1200 the position of the celebrant began to be reversed—to the near side of
the altar, with his back to the congregation. The far side of the sacred plat-
form, which faced both the celebrant and the congregation, was now to become a decorated altarpiece, the focus for ornament, splendor, and im-

223. Miri Rubin, *Corpus Christi: The Eucharist in Late Medieval Culture*
(Cambridge, 1991), 52–53, 57–58. It is germane to note that the first sustained debate on the Eucharist took place around the year 1000 (16–19).

agery.[224] It was crucial that the faithful see the Host and witness its transformation in the magical act of transubstantiation. "The eucharist was the hinge on which the symbolic world turned."[225] Clerical control over that symbolic power was prized in the same way that feudalism pivoted over its control of arms and men. A whole series of strategies was deployed to that end—theatrical techniques, liturgical actions, sermons, and, of course, bodily deportment.

The mass was the central public rite of the Latin Church. It amalgated the tradition of public worship practiced by whole communities with the domestic cult which took place in the privacy of the family. Originally a prayer for the sacrificing congregation, the mass became a commemorative prayer for the souls in purgatory, whose piety was offered as a model to those present. In this way, "the quick and the dead [were ritually joined] as two distinct, contrasted and, in some respects, opposed articulations of a single social whole." Venerating the ritual murder of Christ in the ceremony of consecrated sacrifice purified social relations through the *Pax* (Kiss of Peace), which enabled feuding rivals to displace violence in a communal act of solidarity.[226] Establishing harmony within the community of the faithful was one side of this process; its other side was the establishment of a boundary which demarcated the faithful from the faithless. For these reasons, we can understand why the practice of confession was intimately linked with the Eucharistic ritual, which promised salvation through physical incorporation with Christ. In this way, the clergy acted as brokers between the mass of humans born into original sin and the grace offered to them by God by the crucifixion of His only begotten son. In contrast to ancient practices—of holy men/women, saints, and relics—the early modernization of Latin Christendom immersed the whole population in sacramental routines that channeled—and thereby controlled—Christian life on earth through the offices of the clergy.

7.

The rise in absolutist governments—in both the clerical and secular realms—was characterized by "a sedulous quest for intellectual unifor-

224. Nicholas Penny, "Bidding for Favours," *London Review of Books,* December 19, 1991, 18. It is relevant that in Eastern Christendom the mass is celebrated behind a screen, hidden from the laity; Rubin, *Corpus Christi,* 360.

225. Rubin, *Corpus Christi,* 353.

226. Bossy, "The Mass as a Social Institution 1200–1700," 50–53. For another example of conflict resolution through ritual purification, see Bossy, "Blood and Baptism: Kinship, Community and Christianity in Western Europe from the Fourteenth to the Seventeenth Centuries," *Studies in Church History* 9 (1973), 129–43.

mity and corporatism" which was accomplished by strengthening regulatory technologies administered by systematic, comprehensive, and standardized bureaucratic machineries.[227] The crusading energies which had accompanied the chialiastic calls for worldly reformation were not only turned inward but also displaced against social groups who were deemed to be deviant and dangerous. The presence of alien elements could not be allowed to pollute the larger social formation. Toward the end of the twelfth century there was a change from toleration to surveillance and persecution which was paralleled in the Church's attitude toward gays, heretics, infidels, lepers, prostitutes, usurers, and witches. Lepers shook their rattles to warn others of their presence, Jews were ordered to wear yellow stars, penitent heretics wore yellow crosses, false witnesses wore red tongues, prostitutes wore red cords (*l'aiguillette*), and perjurers were likewise separated from the multitude by additional marking stitched to their clothing; the civil rights of these stigmatized peoples were fiercely abridged.

Lepers are an interesting case since, according to a twelfth-century "Codex of Sins," "Everyone in a state of mortal sin is a spiritual leper."[228] These unfortunates' rotting bodies were thus thought to be the objective, material expression of their diseased souls. The sickness of their spirits, according to the humoral theories of the time, expressed itself in fits of anguish and melancholy. Lepers were thought to be temperamental and capricious, and in particular, they were unable to resist their carnal desires, with the result that their sexual appetites were supposed to be insatiable. Lepers were, of course, the quintessential "other" in this period, so it is not altogether unexpected to find that contemporary conflation of impurity and social danger targeted them. It is thus particularly telling that their sexuality was so closely connected with the social peril they posed for others.

Anathematizing heresy and heretics was a method of constructing ecclesiastical power and reserving the judgment of Truth to a cadre of professionals.

> Every time a Christian suspect is tried by the inquisitorial process, and sentenced, or cleared (for most suspects were cleared), the authority of

227. Boswell, *Christianity, Social Tolerance, and Homosexuality,* 270. See also R. I. Moore, *The Formation of a Persecuting Society* (Oxford, 1987); J. B. Russell, *Dissent and Reform in the Early Middle Ages* (Berkeley and Los Angeles, 1965); N. Cohn, *The Pursuit of the Millennium* (Oxford, 1970); Jacques Le Goff, *Your Money or Your Life: Economy and Religion in the Middle Ages* (New York, 1988).

228. Quoted in Arlette Farge and Jacques Revel, *The Vanishing Children of Paris: Rumor and Politics before the French Revolution* (Cambridge, Mass., 1991), 110. Concerning the association of leprosy with social banishment, see Michel Foucault, *Madness and Civilization* (New York, 1965), 3–7.

the Church is affirmed. Every time heretical beliefs and practices are defined or identified as error, the single Truth is maintained. Every time the Church establishes a new rule, elaborates an existing doctrine or allocates a fresh responsibility, the forms and consequences of transgression are multiplied. Every time a transgression is properly dealt with, a danger is successfully overcome and the authority of the Church confirmed. These institutional processes are not to be explained by the experience of individuals, whether heretics or orthodox Christians.[229]

This was an asymmetrical power relationship in which one partner quite literally lorded its power over the other.

The springtime of early modernization thus contained the seeds of its own negation; in the course of the twelfth century there began a reaction that was both nasty and brutish, but not short. Cruelty, technical progress, and the creation of a skilled body of interrogators increased the fear of the law and enhanced the power of its administrators. The spread of Roman law was accompanied by the use of torture, which slowly came to be a central part of the judicial procedure.[230] The Inquisition was created to look into men's and women's souls and to ferret out heretics, deviants, and freethinkers. The Fourth Lateran Council threw the weight of the papacy behind the Dominican order—the so-called *domini canes* (hounds of God)—which was charged with witch hunting and repressing diversity in the name of orthodoxy. The Black Friars had proven their value during the Albigensian Crusade when thousands of heretics were randomly slaughtered in the southern French town of Béziers in the belief that "God will know his own."[231]

A look at the techniques of detection is most revealing, since it connects macro processes of state formation with micro processes of family formation. Starting with deviant individuals, the inquisitors attacked the network of Cathar households to discover if the cancerous poison of heresy

229. Talal Asad, "Medieval Heresy: An Anthropological View," *Social History* 11 (1986): 354–57.

230. Torture was most usually directed against the lower classes. The Inquisition was not allowed to operate in England. But, when the established order was threatened by the many-headed monster of popular revolt and religious heterodoxy in the later fourteenth century, other systems of surveillance were empowered with protecting the status quo; Margaret Aston, "Lollardy and Sedition, 1381–1431," *Past and Present* 17 (1960): 1–44. This repression was so thoroughgoing that the Bible was not translated into English before the Reformation, and even translating the Pater Noster was viewed with suspicion; Aston, "Lollardy and Literacy," in *Lollards and Reformers* (London, 1984), 193–217.

231. Sidney Painter and Brian Tierney, *Western Europe in the Middle Ages, 300–1475* (New York, 1970), 293.

had traveled along the channels of kinship. What was at issue was not merely criminal behavior but something far more threatening: the transmission of monstrosity.[232] Inquisitors conceptualized the communication of this pollution in a way similar to that proposed by Augustine when he sought to explain the genealogical transmission of original sin, which, he claimed, passed by means of human semen from generation to generation, from Adam to all living contemporaries. Heresy was, then, insidious because it could spread to infect other parts of the body of the Church. It required drastic measures from the new shock troops of God. They perfected their inquisitorial procedures in ferreting out heretics from among the defeated population through the use of novel methods of judicial procedure—keeping dossiers and, particularly, incarcerating suspects for long periods of time: "the inquisitors delimit[ed] a space in which they could isolate individuals from the outer world and subject them without interruptions to an enforced and forcible persuasion . . . for what we would label behavior modification."[233] The inquisition's carceral strategy and its crossexamining techniques represented a milestone in the social history of power in Europe.

The secular pretensions of the Church raised expectations of its behavior by claiming preeminence for the clerical calling in worldly affairs. Having let loose a series of calls for spiritual reformation, the Church and its cadres found their daily behaviors viewed in the glare of their own spotlight. Clerics had to be like Caesar's wife: above suspicion. Many were not. The stigma of hypocrisy is hard to expunge. The Church's insatiable monetary demands focused another spotlight on the double standard of clerical morality. The practice of granting plenary indulgences, guaranteeing passage through purgatory, not only debased the Church's spiritual coinage but also became hard to distinguish from a money-making racket. Beset on one side by demands for apostolic purity stemming from the spiritual demands of the time while being squeezed from the other side by its own secular and fiscal politics, the papacy and its clerical cadres had become hostages to their own good fortune.[234] In so doing, the visible Church had become a gigantic engine dedicated to the transmutation of income into prayer.[235]

232. Ivan Illich, *Gender* (New York, 1982), 152.

233. James Given, "The Inquisitors of Languedoc and the Medieval Technology of Power," *American Historical Review* 94 (1989): 346–47.

234. G. Leff, "Heresy and the Decline of the Medieval Church," *Past and Present* 20 (1961), 36–51.

235. A. R. Bridbury, "The Hundred Years' War: Costs and Benefits," in *The English Economy from Bede to the Reformation* (London, 1992), 222.

The fiscal requirements of the papal empire seemed insatiable even though, in fact, much of the money it collected was plowed back into social works—cathedrals, churches, schools, alms, and so on—which proclaimed the greater glory of the ecclesiastical project. The gift was an important manifestation of lordship. Largesse was a striking continuity with the ancient world's practice of *euergetism*—a complex system of unequal and incommensurable exchanges which were an essential activity for the noble political man whose magnificence was emphasized in his public displays of generosity, gift-giving, and social works. Indeed, the Church's accumulation of wealth was rather less an end in itself and rather more a means to another end—the "focalization effect" that resulted from concentrating a fraction of the whole social wealth on a particular objective. Yet, as Paul Veyne notes,

> This gigantism is misleading. It is much less costly to build what archaeologists and tourists call a high culture, rich in monuments, than to feed a population more or less adequately. Everything depends on the possessing class, which controls the surplus and decides what is to be done with it. The mere splendour of the monuments arouses suspicion. Even the buildings intended for everyday purposes have an imperishable look that points to their irrationality. Everything has been built to last for ever, which means that everything is too solid for its purpose.[236]

Monastic communities, which were among the largest and most efficient manorialists, spent lavishly on construction projects for the glorification of God. The Cistercian order, which was progressive in its farming practices, disbursed huge sums building in stone to replace its original wooden structures.

Masonry churches, cathedrals, and monasteries sprouted up across the length and breadth of Europe after the year 1000. More stone was quarried in France between 1050 and 1350 than was used in the entire history of ancient Egypt.[237] We can gain added understanding of the magnitude of this collective effort by considering the volume of construction in England, where, in addition to twenty-six cathedrals, we should also consider the building of 563 religious houses—191 could be termed "large" and 372 "small"—as well as 8,838 parish churches, 110 hospitals, and 2,374 guild, chantry, and free chapels. Over and above this basic construction, we should take account of clerical offices, accommodations—palaces, resi-

236. *Bread and Circuses: Historical Sociology and Political Pluralism* (Harmondsworth, 1990), 56.
237. Jean Gimpel, *The Cathedral Builders* (New York, 1961), 5.

dences, and dormitories—libraries, kitchens, cellars, stables, gates, cloisters, stained-glass decoration, statues, tombs, stallworks, screens, altars, and shrines which constituted the fabric of these ecclesiastical structures. This building campaign involved huge amounts of labor and capital. It has been estimated that the twenty-six English cathedrals could be considered to be the equivalent of between two and three million cubic yards of "building product." To raise them would have required the efforts of at least 590 fully employed, adult males per year; most likely, however, twice that number would have been seasonally employed, year after year, for centuries. If we add the labor and capital required to build and to furnish all the other ecclesiastical foundations, we can begin to grasp the colossal amount of surplus wealth that was channeled into erecting the material infrastructure of Christian society in Europe after the year 1000.[238]

However we quantify these efforts, we must note that they created linkage effects—fairs, markets, demand for both materials and labor, and human capital formation.[239] Yet it is absolutely crucial to bear in mind that,

238. In addition, of course, we have to make allowance for equal amounts of labor inputs to account for the transportation of raw materials from the quarries where the stone was cut and the forests where the timber was felled. Similar amounts of labor and capital were requisitioned by the state—when Edward I was engaged in the pacification of Wales, the building of Beaumaris Castle in Anglesey entailed the assembly of a "labour force of 400 masons, 2000 minor workmen, 200 quarrymen and 30 smiths and carpenters, together with a supply organization of 100 carts, 60 wagons and 30 boats bringing stone and sea-coal to the site" in 1296; A. J. Taylor, "Master James of St. George," *English Historical Review* 65 (1950): 448. For a rather low estimate of the labor requirements of ecclesiastical works, see H. Thomas Johnson, "Cathedral Building and the Medieval Economy," *Explorations in Economic History*, 2d ser., 4 (1967): 191–210; for a higher estimate—double that of Johnson—see B. W. E. Alford and M. Q. Smith, "The Economic Effects of Cathedral and Church Building in Medieval England: A Reply," *Explorations in Economic History*, 2d ser., 6 (1969): 158–69. Building a cathedral (or any other stone building) was an "essentially capitalist" undertaking, like that of administering a factory: "experts in the difficult business of directing the contemporaneous labours of large numbers of men were necessary; . . . piecework was by no means unfamiliar; and, last but not least, . . . the craftsmen employed approximated more nearly than did other mediæval artificers to modern workmen, being mere wage-earners, paid for working on raw material owned by their employer, and with very little prospect of rising above this condition." According to the classic account of medieval stone building by Douglas Knoop and G. P. Jones, the "impressment" of workers was commonplace in building projects, although most masons were usually temporary or "short servicemen"; Douglas Knoop and G. P. Jones, *The Mediæval Mason* (Manchester, 1933), 4, 3, 89, 140.

239. For a general discussion of the labor deployment in English stone building, see Knoop and Jones, *The Mediæval Mason*. On the rather narrower subject of skill development and coordination, see L. R. Shelby, "The Role of the Master

in these centuries, surplus wealth was diverted from agricultural investment for the glorification of God, not the reproduction of capital. In this
way, the Church symbolically destroyed—or, at least, consumed—its
working capital.

Mason in Mediaeval English Building," *Speculum* 39 (1964): 387–403, and "The
Education of Medieval English Master Masons," *Mediaeval Studies* 32 (1970):
1–26.

2   Shards of Modernity

TECHNOLOGIES OF POWER

[T]he dust of history, micro-history . . . [is made up of] little facts which . . . by indefinite repetition, add up to form linked chains. Each of them represents the thousands of others that have crossed the silent depths of time and *endured*. It is with such chains, such "series," and with history in the "long term" . . . [that we] provide the horizons and the vanishing-points of all the landscapes in the past. They introduce a kind of order, indicate a balance, and reveal to our eyes the permanent features, the things that in this apparent disorder *can* be explained. . . . For civilizations do indeed create bonds, that is to say an order, bringing together thousands of cultural possessions effectively different from, and at first sight even foreign to, each other—goods that range from those of the spirit and the intellect to the tools and objects of everyday life.

> Fernand Braudel, *The Structures of Everyday Life*

The idea of the State belongs to all ages, but it only matters when it takes over the armed forces, taxation, justice, gets involved with the guilds, controls the finances and the regulations of groups in which men thought they were safe; the communes, guilds, and fraternities. The emergence of this single ruling body necessarily annuls all the functions, which have devolved on one or another order of society.

> Robert Fossier, "Europe's Second Wind,"
> in *The Middle Ages*

Power in early modern Europe radiated both upward and downward, in contrast to ancient society, which was organized according to orders from its governing class. New "Technologies of Power" brought together the centrifugal forces of decentralization and the centripetal forces of consolidation. The papacy was the most innovative early modern state formation; it not only imposed law and order but also revolutionized the methods of domination. Administrative literacy was a novel method of social control, pioneered by the Church. The clerical monopoly of learning gave the Church a head start in deploying both the artificial memory of the written record and the legal science of normative pacification. But the papacy's influence was limited to moral persuasion because it had no legions of its own. Warfare initially was dominated by armed horsemen and fortified castles, yet feudal hosts were not always the only source of fighting men. Mercenaries were commonly deployed, which made control over the supply of money a key factor in the centralization of power. It was only toward the end of our period—in the mid-fourteenth century—that siege warfare was threatened by new explosive weapons.

1.

Perhaps the most important result of the Papal Revolution was the entrenchment of a pluralistic system of government. It was in response to this explosion that a new form of royal law emerged to offset the secular rulers' loss of their sacral character. It is probably not coincidental that the kings of England and France discovered their thaumaturgic powers at the same time that the Church was stripping the monarchy of its sacral character.[1] Deprived of their role as supreme rulers of the Church, secular rulers were reduced to the status of temporal monarchs, although their power was enhanced by the Church's support of a new territorial concept of kingship. This backing helped to transform clan chiefs and feudal overlords into supreme rulers of a defined geographical area.

In the early Middle Ages, kings had usually governed their magnates, wise men, and tenants-in-chief directly; it was through them that kings governed local and tribal leaders, subvassals, and plebeian subjects. The older method of peacemaking through seeking consensus became one strategy among many. New state-formation initiatives created royal officers who were delegated to perform more-or-less specific roles, such as the royal judges and tax officials. The royal law was used to set this novel system of secular government in motion.[2] This system had an inherent bias

1. Marc Bloch, *The Royal Touch: Monarchy and Miracles in France and England* (New York, 1989).

2. Harold J. Berman, *Law and Revolution: The Formation of the Western Legal Tradition* (Cambridge, Mass., 1983), 534–35.

toward absolutist rule, by which I mean a centralization of power and authority in the hands of the ruler and his agents. Absolutist rule stood in opposition to the contractual reciprocities that distinguished feudal bonds between rulers and vassals.

The legal infraculture of the state imposed law and order: "The gallows could speak for itself without mystification." At the heart of this state-formation initiative was the exercise of reason, the belief that the social world possessed "an impersonal objectivity." Here, again, the Church was an innovator: in place of the divinely inspired guidance which had previously led to unanimity, the naked scrimmage of interests was subjected to the authority of a leader elected by a simple majority of the relevant voting body.[3] This new technique of institutional governance—"the relevant voting body"—was to provide a thin edge for a wedge which eventually would be driven into the heart of the post-Gregorian *saeculum.*

When the worldly basis of papal dominion came to be questioned in the course of the thirteenth century, a particularly modern answer was anticipated because the pope had few divisions and no army. Sovereignty, it would be argued, derived from either profane violence (William of Occam) or the will of the popular majority (Marsilius of Padua).[4] But to consider these ideas here is to run ahead of the story of how the reconstitution of central, secular authority was given shape by the Papal Revolution. The post-Gregorian papacy grew in strength in part because of its ability to master the legal process.

The so-called second feudal age was characterized by both the centrifugal forces of decentralization and the centripetal forces of consolidation. The second half of the twelfth century witnessed the halting progress of secular initiatives. It is instructive to compare England and France in this regard.

In England, royal authority mobilized national resistance while fostering a new consciousness through its quasi-absolutist policies. The invaders at first successfully pushed forward the frontiers of the Danelaw so that by 878 only southwestern England was not conquered; it was from this base in Wessex that Alfred and his successors ousted the invaders and began a fundamentally novel process of state formation. The Anglo-Saxon war of national liberation was successful because the monarchy had created a new and efficient local administrative structure.

3. Peter Brown, "Society and the Supernatural: A Medieval Change," *Daedalus* 104 (1975): 143–44.

4. Georges Duby, *The Age of Cathedrals* (Chicago, 1981), 261–62.

National governing structures were also revolutionized as the Anglo-Saxons aggressively asserted their regality. In 943 King Edmund exacted an oath of fealty from all men; at almost exactly this time a feudal oath of homage was being substituted for this symbolic gesture of submission in the Frankish kingdom. In addition, the Anglo-Saxon kings laid claim to royal control over the maintenance of peace and created a machinery of justice and law enforcement. The processes of "outlawry" and the "ban" were enforced by a body of royal servants—-the sheriffs or shire-reeves. Monarchs kept control of the legal system in their own hands because their servants were unsuccessful in making their offices hereditary. Connecting the central authority with these local officers was "the writ—a short, concise, tersely formulated document, written in the vernacular, which was unique in Europe in its day."[5]

While it would most likely be a mistake to overemphasize the efficiency of Anglo-Saxon royal government, it nonetheless provides a striking contrast to the French experience, in which there was no effective counterweight to the dissolution of central authority. Students of the Anglo-Saxon period have emphasized the territorial shift in production and settlement patterns in the period bracketing the year 1000 as well as the precocious governmental modernization—"a 'national' state in the making."[6] Seen in this way, the Norman Conquest of 1066 was an overlay of continental feudalism on top of "the framework of the Old English State."[7] As territorial rulers, they governed all their subjects directly.

Significantly, the Anglo-Saxon oath of fealty was used in 1086 by William the Conqueror to exact obedience from "whose soever men they were" and repeated by his two successors. This pledge of fealty took precedence ahead of all other ties of vassalage. Anglo-Norman kingship, "the fruit of a double conquest," did not destroy the powers of the nobility so much as force this class to operate, even in opposition, within the framework of the state.[8] In this way, the English nobility "was defined not in

5. Geoffrey Barraclough, *The Crucible of Europe: The Ninth and Tenth Centuries in European History* (Berkeley and Los Angeles, 1976), 126–40.

6. V. H. Galbraith, *Domesday Book: Its Place in Administrative History* (Oxford, 1974), 27.

7. F. M. Stenton, *Anglo-Saxon England* (Oxford, 1943), 674; quoted in Barraclough, *The Crucible of Europe*, 142.

8. Marc Bloch, *Feudal Society* (Chicago, 1961), 431. For a consideration of the impact of this "double conquest" on the lives of the peasantry, see R. M. Smith, " 'Modernization' and the Corporate Medieval Village Community in England: Some Sceptical Reflections," in A. R. H. Baker and Derek Gregory (eds.), *Explorations in Historical Geography* (Cambridge, 1984), 140–79. I will return to this point below.

terms of blood and lineage, but tenurially and administratively."[9] In Marc Bloch's account, the contrast with France is striking: the Capetian "kings reassembled France rather than unified it" so that "the French monarchy, even when the State had been revived, continued permanently to bear the mark of that agglomeration of counties, castellanies and rights over churches which, in very 'feudal' fashion, it had made the foundation of its power."[10] This agglomerative inheritance would be revamped only after 1789.

After the year 1000 the diversity of political cultures which came to characterize early modern Europe began to take shape. The English nation-state was established in conditions of military occupation. France was "reassembled" by the Capetians. Germany was "disassembled" as a result of the Investiture Crisis, which pitted the papacy against the Holy Roman Emperors, who were also Germany's secular rulers. Spain was slowly reconquered in a crusade against the Moslems.[11] Italy was a coherent geographical space but not a sovereign political entity.

Some medieval monarchs stood alone atop a pyramid of contractual relationships and asserted their preeminence. Others were immersed in the welter of conflicting loyalties and could not break free. The contrast between England and the Empire makes this point concerning the diversity of politico-administrative transitions occurring around the year 1000. In England, the center not only held but also grew stronger when the Angevin kings of England created royal bureaucracies. The Salian and Hohenstaufen emperors could not do so.

English legal historians have long been concerned with the transition from a "very feudal society," cemented by obligations and duties whose highest value was loyalty, to a "modern society" in which rights and freedoms are regulated by the rule of law. To be sure, any civil polity with a

---

9. J. C. Holt, "Feudal Society and the Family in Early Medieval England: I. The Revolution of 1066," *Transactions of the Royal Historical Society*, 5th ser., 33 (1983): 200. In much the same way, the centrifugal tendencies of the Angevin nobility were constrained by the strong central authority of the local counts. Moreover, the Angevin state's domination of surplus extraction through taxation—as well as its control over both the local church and the military—was of crucial importance in the twelfth-century transformation of the Anglo-Norman state into an empire that stretched from Scotland to the Pyrenees with Angers at its center; Bernard J. Bachrach, "The Angevin Economy, 960–1060: Ancient or Feudal?," *Studies in Medieval and Renaissance History*, new ser., 10 (1998): 34–35.

10. Bloch, *Feudal Society*, 425–26.

11. The Christian forces received their second wind in 1034 when the Caliphate of Cordoba was replaced by a fractious array of independent Moslem kingdoms. This marked a sharp change in the trajectory of the *reconquista* which would eventually drive the Moslems from the mainland of Europe.

legal system is bound to regulate social life. What was novel about the English experience of early modernization is that a law of real property came
to form the institutional core of the state.

For almost a century the dominant interpretation of this development
followed the outline set forth by F. Pollock and F. W. Maitland, in which the
aggressive state-formation policies of the Angevin monarchs—notably the
clever and calculating Henry II (1154–89)—tamed overmighty subjects in
the interest of bolstering royal power.[12] This view held sway for nearly a
century; it now seems to be in the process of revision by S.F.C. Milsom and
Robert C. Palmer.[13] These revisionists are concerned with the contextual
circumstances which led to the novel organization of the English state; they
are not particularly concerned to dispute the long historiographical tradition which has stressed the peculiarity of the English. At the heart of their
analysis is a dramatic reinterpretation of Henry II's motivation: "Where
Maitland saw property rights to be protected, Milsom [and Palmer] sees
only contractual obligations. Where Maitland saw purposeful, far-sighted
innovation, Milsom [and Palmer] sees limited innovations magnified by
juristic accident."[14] In contrast to Maitland, who saw a Machiavellian in
Henry II, Milsom and Palmer see a feudal opportunist seeking to restore
order to a country which had been racked by civil war before his accession.[15]

Feudal social relations were thus the victim of their own success: driven
by the state-formation offensive of the second feudal age, royal authorities
turned their attention to domesticating the baronage, often replacing it
with mercenaries and/or civil servants, hiring special officials, extending

12. *The History of English Law before the Time of Edward I,* 2d ed. (Introduction by S. F. C. Milsom; Cambridge, 1968).

13. Milsom, *The Legal Framework of English Law* (Cambridge, 1976); Palmer,
"The Feudal Framework of English Law," *Michigan Law Review* 79 (1981):
1130–64.

14. Palmer, "Feudal Framework," 1130. Palmer, in particular, connects Henry's
feudal regality to his desire to find a peaceful accommodation between the opposing parties. The Compromise of 1153 drove a wedge into the feudal system by reducing lords' discretionary, disciplinary powers and subjecting them to adjudica-
tion by the newly formed royal system of bureaucratic justice which followed the
Assize of Northampton (1176).

15. The early centralization of the English state thus interacted with the creation of legal principles that were common throughout the whole realm. In this
way, the native evolution of the "common law" seems to have had the effect of pre-
cluding the later introduction of Roman Law principles that would have magnified
the privileges of the rulers at the expense of the rights of their subjects. This would
have immense implications in the development of new forms of private property
and wage labor in the later transition to full-scale capitalism. See C. H. McIlwain,
"Medieval Estates," in *The Cambridge Medieval History* (Cambridge, 1932), 7:
709–14.

the scope of the royal law, fostering the mercantile activities of towns, and expanding the role of the state in the collection of taxes. Feudal society was based on an exchange of services so that, in theory, it could have existed outside the money economy. However, theory does not always describe reality. Already, by the second half of the twelfth century, in the words of a contemporary, "The abundance of resources, or the lack of them, exalts or humbles the power of princes. For those who are lacking in them become prey to their enemies, whilst those who are well supplied with them despoil their foes. Money is necessary in time of war, but also in time of peace."[16]

By the end of Henry II's reign—unexpectedly and absolutely unintentionally—England possessed not only a bureaucratic system of full-time royal justices but also a revolutionary, new interpretation of rights which pried the tenant loose from his obligations to his lord by establishing a property relationship between a tenant and his tenement. The royal law had become "institutionalized royal authority." The royal law was to be the umpire governing disputes between lords and tenants. But who was to govern the umpire? The Magna Carta (1215), then, was a response to nobles' desires to "put the king under restrictions similar to those under which the king's court put them."[17]

The primacy of royal law was a precondition for the development of the theory of individual ownership by which "The tenurial system converted the villagers into tenants, and the theory of the law placed the freehold of most of the lands of the manor in the lord."[18] Henry III's attempts to exploit the ambiguities of the Great Charter's control over his regalian rights not only provoked resentment but also widened demands for admission to the political nation by the gentry of the shires.[19] Political struggles modified the arbitrary power of the Norman Conqueror by narrowing the English king's sphere of action. It became understood—the rules of the game—that when he needed money to carry out his military and diplomatic policies the king would be limited in his capacity to appropriate the

16. Richard FitzNigel, *The Dialogue of the Exchequer* (c. 1179); quoted in Carolyn Webber and Aaron Wildavsky, *A History of Taxation and Expenditure in the Western World* (New York, 1986), 187. See also Stephen D. B. Brown, "Military Service and Monetary Reward in the Eleventh and Twelfth Centuries," *History* 74 (1989): 20–38.

17. Robert C. Palmer, "The Economic and Cultural Impact of the Origins of Property," *Law and History Review* 3 (1985): 376, 394.

18. A. W. B. Simpson, *A History of the Land Law* (Oxford, 1986), 108. See also Smith, " 'Modernization' and the Corporate Medieval Village Community in England," *passim*.

19. J. R. Maddicott, "Magna Carta and the Local Community 1215–1259," *Past and Present* 102 (1984): 25–65.

assets of the members of the political nation. Indeed, it could be argued that the Norman Conquest was the high-water mark of absolutism because the subsequent trajectory of English history not only began to point constitutional affairs toward parliamentary rule under the law but also began to connect governance with new forms of consent.

English feudal monarchs used brute force and expected unquestioning loyalty from their subjects, but this expectation was contested. Contestation resulted in compromises, particularly in times of war when fiscal necessity resulted in political dialogue and institutional innovation.[20] These monarchs were frustrated in their quest for absolute authority, so they had to employ legal instruments to transform the bewildering melange of consensual arrangements—the subinfeudated undergrowth of feudal society—into a rough balance between their own centripetal policies and the centrifugal tendencies of their overmighty subjects. Royal justice acted as the midwife of constitutional government by providing "a normative and procedural grid" within which an almost infinite gradation of citizenship rights were contested and constructed.[21] To be sure, this was never intended to be a democratic polity. The advance of representative assemblies; participatory government at the national, regional, and local levels; and fiscal responsibility proceeded at a snail's pace. But they all moved.

A regard for legality pervaded the upper echelons of the political system by defining the rights and liberties of both governors and subjects, although, to be sure, this was honored more often in words than in actions. It is also germane to note that the construction of legal personality, which developed through the process of juridical accreditation, created a novel psychological category. A new kind of individual became possible: the legal subject. This is a rather different individual from Jacob Burckhardt's "Renaissance Man." It is a more public creature whose self is constructed in the act of repressing his willfulness in order to become both socially conscious and self-conscious.

It is not unfair to say that legality gave life to this fictive person by setting *him* within its force field. The creation of legal personality was deeply gendered. Acting together with the clerical vision of marriage and the lineage's descent through the male line, the legal grid denied women a public

---

20. Gerald L. Harriss, "War and the Emergence of the English Parliament, 1297–1360," *Journal of Medieval History* 2 (1976): 35–56.

21. Brian Downing, "Medieval Origins of Constitutional Government in the West," *Theory and Society* 18 (1989): 243.

personality.[22] Women were defined as wives and daughters whose essential purpose was biological reproduction and whose cultural character emphasized their virginal purity. This created three novel thrusts in the sacred culture of early modern Christianity distinguishing it from the self-abnegation of late antiquity: first, the massive enhancement of the image of the Virgin Mary; second, the emphasis on the Holy Family and particularly the Madonna and Child; and third, the transvaluation of motherhood itself.[23]

If the Norman Conquest of England created an absolutist, feudalized sovereignty, the failure of imperial conquest of Italy resulted in the development of Europe's most complex political system. There, in comparison with the practices of antiquity, power was shattered and recombined. For centuries it was given and sold in fragments by inventing new nuclei in imitation of those same fragments or as a new invention by landed lords, merchants, notaries, armed *consorterie*, communes—urban and rural—and even *villani*. The extreme elevation of power, so characteristic of the ancient world, was no longer possible. "The Middle Ages, the period which to many still represents the triumph of fertile and image-laden myths, had demythologized power."[24]

If the impulse of medieval politics was the creation of multiple acephalous federations, then the strategic project of early modernization was to channel these impulses into territorial units rather than to allow their proliferation and recombination to lead to a decentered vacuum of sovereignty. England—with its precociously centralized state—represented one end of a continuum; Italy—with its "chaos of interests"[25]—represented the other tendency: an interface between fragmentation and consolidation of stunning complexity and local particularity. In addition to the state, power

22.   For restrictions on bilateral descent in northern Europe, see Georges Duby, *The Knight, the Lady, and the Priest: The Making of Modern Marriage in Medieval France* (New York, 1983), *passim.*

23.   On this last point, see Clarissa W. Atkinson, " 'Precious Balsam in a Fragile Glass': The Ideology of Virginity in the Later Middle Ages," *Journal of Family History* 8 (1983): 131–43. See also Marina Warner, *Alone of All Her Sex* (London, 1976).

24.   Giovanni Tabacco, *The Struggle for Power in Medieval Italy: Structures of Political Rule* (Cambridge, 1989), 319–20. For the emergence of lineages/*consorteria/societates turrium* (tower societies) which dominated Italian towns after the year 1000, see David Herlihy, "Family Solidarity in Medieval Italian History," in D. Herlihy, R. S. Lopez, and V. Slessarev (eds.), *Economy, Society, and Government in Medieval Italy* (Kent, Ohio, 1969), 173–84.

25.   Tabacco, *The Struggle for Power*, 256.

was diffused through other networks including families, households, kin groups, parishes, villages, occupational associations, guilds, mercantile companies, religious fraternities, knightly fellowships, and armies.

These communities of power were established by loose, overlapping collectivities which were derived from voluntary cooperation in the pursuit of some limited goal and created their own traditions of rights and duties.[26] Marc Bloch writes that "The originality of the [western feudal] system consisted in the emphasis it placed on the idea of an agreement capable of binding the rulers; and in this way, oppressive as it may have been to the poor, it has in truth bequeathed to our Western civilization something with which we still desire to live."[27] As Michel Foucault has argued, power was everywhere, not because it embraced everything but because it came from everywhere. In deciphering power mechanisms on the basis of a strategy that is immanent in force relationships, we must be careful not to mistake it for "sovereignty"—the general design or institutional crystallization that is embodied in the state apparatus, in the formulation of the law, and in the various social hegemonies. By analyzing the mechanisms of power in the sphere of force relations we can "escape from the system of Law-and-Sovereign. . . . go one step further [and] do without the persona of the Prince."[28]

If the religious culture of early modernization was characterized by a Foucauldian *volonté de savoir* (will to knowledge), its material culture was driven by a will to power. If feudalism had begun as a military system activated by ties of dependence and loyalty—without resort to money—it maintained this character for only a short period around the year 1000. The early modern state was an actor in its own right, not simply the distillate of class forces or the social relations of production.

To make sense of the rise of the absolutist state we have to jettison the ideological framework of an ordered society—in which some prayed, some fought, and most worked—that was already becoming obsolete by the thirteenth century and replace it with a vision of an early modern society developing according to its own dynamic. Robert Fossier's comments give us a sense of heightened perspective in considering the these changes:

> The old framework, already out of date in the thirteenth century, of an ordered society, had burst asunder. Some clerics—theoreticians or im-

26. Susan Reynolds, *Kingdoms and Communities in Western Europe, 900–1300* (Oxford, 1984).

27. *Feudal Society,* 452.

28. Foucault, *The History of Sexuality,* vol. 1, *An Introduction* (New York, 1978), 92–97.

plicated agents of authority—still claimed there were three orders, the "estates," and indeed this went on being said until 1789, and can still be read in works which reek with nostalgia for sabre and incense; all demented notions which do not stand up to the impartial glance. . . . The idea of the State belongs to all ages, but it only matters when it takes over the armed forces, taxation, justice, gets involved with the guilds, controls the finances and the regulations of groups in which men thought they were safe; the communes, guilds, and fraternities. The emergence of this single ruling body necessarily annuls all the functions, which have devolved on one or another order of society.[29]

Money—the sinews of power according to Cicero—and negotiated consent were two sides of the same coin. Indeed, as Richard FitzNigel, a twelfth-century treasurer of the exchequer, wrote:

> We are, of course, aware that kingdoms are governed and laws maintained primarily by prudence, fortitude, temperance and justice, and the other virtues, for which reason the rulers of the world must practice them with all their might. But there are occasions on which sound and wise schemes take effect earlier through the agency of money, and apparent difficulties are smoothed away by it, as though by skillful negotiation.[30]

The process of early modernization moved Western society—slowly, hesitantly, and even reluctantly—away from the authoritarian governmental structures inherited from the ancient world. A sense of the distance traveled along this journey—away from the "otherness" of sacred power in antiquity—is conveyed in the following assessment of Roman social relations:

> Rome . . . was a state that obeyed not laws but orders from its governing class. . . . Roman public law itself becomes clearer as soon as one ceases to look for rules and accepts the fact that everything depended on the relative strength of the various parties in contention. What is even more curious is that Rome was in no sense a traditionalist state, governed in the English manner by respect for custom. Roman institutions were a jumble and remained remarkably fluid throughout Roman history. Rome was an authoritarian state unconstrained by rules. . . . Roman loyalty was to a man, not to a pact.[31]

29. Robert Fossier (ed.), "Europe's Second Wind," in *The Cambridge Illustrated History of the Middle Ages, 1250–1520* (Cambridge, 1987), 438.

30. Richard FitzNigel, *The Dialogue of the Exchequer*, quoted in Kathleen Biddick, "People and Things: Power in Early English Development," *Comparative Studies in Society and History* 32 (1990): 9.

31. Paul Veyne, "The Roman Empire," in Paul Veyne (ed.), *A History of Private Life*, vol. 1, *From Pagan Rome to Byzantium* (Cambridge, Mass., 1987), 175.

The "second age of feudalism" was the time when the modern state was born. To quote Fossier again, "let's bury the ordered society before 1500 without further argument, since it was then that the monster was born which took over the Divine Plan and arranged the social classes as it liked. This was the State."[32] The emergence of a "multiple acephalous federation" had created an evolutionary system deriving its energy from the competition between states. This occasioned the development of new military and fiscal technologies which territorialized the exercise of power—over people, over space, and over things—in specific locations.

2.

In the course of the eleventh and twelfth centuries, the older intellectual style was revolutionized: in place of Benedictine *scriptoria* where knowledge was copied, universities—which taught both systematic theology and legal science—were places where knowledge was created through the application of dialectical reasoning. The art of reasoning, the exercise of *ratio*, was now ranked highest among the faculties of the educated man. Reason, said Berengar of Tours (d. 1088), "was 'the honor of man' and his 'specific light,' that reflection of the celestial light which is man's prerogative." The "mystique of light" was celebrated in the cathedrals and abbey churches that sprang up across the landscape, most especially in the Parisian basin—the heartland of the kingdom of France.[33]

This new mode of reasoning was central to the twelfth-century cultural renaissance, when "Christian Europe absorbed Antiquity not in one great bite but in several nibbles interrupted by slow periods of silent digestion."[34] The book itself was "desacralized" in the making of a new intellectual technology of power: "the monastic book, even including its spiritual and intellectual functions, was first and foremost a treasure. The university book was chiefly a tool." Accompanying the changing function of the book was a more general development in which the use of the written word was diffused and recognized as binding proof. This was the thin edge of the wedge which would slowly prize legality from custom, to the detriment of the latter.[35]

Monopoly of learning gave the clergy both access to and control over the law, another crucial technology of power, sustained by a remarkable,

32. Fossier, "Europe's Second Wind," 518.

33. Duby, *The Age of Cathedrals*, 38–39, 15.

34. Hugh Trevor-Roper, *The Rise of Christian Europe* (London, 1965), 131. The classic study is Charles Homer Haskins, *The Renaissance of the Twelfth Century* (Cambridge, Mass., 1927).

35. Jacques Le Goff, *Medieval Civilization 400–1500* (Oxford, 1958), 345–46.

uniquely single-minded *esprit de corps.* In an age when leadership and lordship were intertwined, the Church's innovations in legal practice transformed the conduct of civil society. Not only did this provide "normative pacification, confirming property and market relations," but the growth of canon law also provided an alternative to violence as a technique for organizing secular life.[36] It was in conjunction with this innovation in the technology of knowledge that universities were founded to instruct clerks in the legal dialectic. Begun in 1087, the University of Bologna was the preeminent institution for legal training; it had thousands of students, as did a series of other great universities which were soon established across the length and breadth of western Europe.

A new kind of man—the intellectual—emerged in the West: "the cathedral schools were lists, the scene of intellectual exploits that were as thrilling as military exploits and, like them, prepared the combatants to take on the world. As a young man, Abelard had distinguished himself in such tournaments. His victories had brought him—as to a heroic knight—glory, money, and womanly love."[37] Interestingly, Abelard was himself the firstborn son of a knight, whose scholarly activity has been characterized as displaying the "persistent belligerence" of "the knightly life without the bloodshed."[38] Slowly, and almost imperceptibly, a new kind of society could be conceived: a society governed by the rule of law and administered by intellectuals.

In the course of the twelfth century another landmark was being achieved: both the accumulation of records and the establishment of routine began to congeal in new departments with fixed offices. Making documents for immediate administrative use, preserving them as a form of social memory, and using them again are three quite distinct processes which do not necessarily follow one another. The English state's accounting system—based on raw data notched onto wooden "tally sticks" and then assembled into formal registers called "Pipe Rolls"—provided a centralized method of overseeing its income flows and debt load. The exchequer provided a model of bureaucratic administration which was extended to other branches of the central government and then into every village and manor in the realm.

The extension of administrative literacy was intimately connected with a new technology of control. The first stages of this innovation took place

36. Michael Mann, *A History of Power from the Beginning to A.D. 1760*, vol. 2, *The Sources of Social Power* (Cambridge, 1986), 377.
37. Duby, *The Age of Cathedrals*, 114.
38. M. T. Clanchy, *Abelard: A Medieval Life* (Oxford, 1997), 141.

during the reign of Henry I (1100–35). The key figure in the early modernization of English bureaucratic government was Hubert Walter, who was not only Archbishop of Canterbury but also Richard I's chief justiciar (1193–98) and John's chancellor (1199–1205). His achievement—"the formal beginning of the era of artificial memory"—was recognized in statutes in 1275 and 1293 when the coronation of Richard I was fixed as the earliest point of recorded history.[39] Hubert Walter's period in high office was the time when documentary archives were organized and when written evidence began to gain priority over the spoken word.

The makeshift nature of this process meant that the documentary record ("artificial memory") became dominant even before the spread of literacy. Indeed, the spread of functional or practical literacy was demanded by the novel requirements of these state-formation initiatives, which were recognized and institutionalized in the practice of the law. This new administrative system grew by leaps and bounds. Its output of letters doubled every two or three decades. Accompanying the widespread familiarity with documentary records were two important innovations: cursive script made the production of documents faster while seals provided a shorthand template which enabled even the illiterate to take part in the new technology.

The use of written documents was promoted by the king's agents. It gradually made its way down the social scale, to barons by 1200 (William Marshal, for example, had a permanent staff of three clerks to assist him, which was all the more necessary since the great knight and latter-day baron was illiterate), to knights by 1250, and to peasants by 1300. In fact, the Statute of Exeter (1285), rather unrealistically, expected "bondsmen" (i.e., serfs) would have their own seals. This novel ability to concentrate a distinctively different kind of financial and legal power in the hands of those who administered the state's bureaucracy did not escape the notice of perspicacious contemporaries.[40] The mid-fourteenth-century writing offices of chancery, privy seal, and signet annually issued thirty to forty thousand letters a year, some open and formal, others closed and personal.[41]

---

39. Michael Clanchy, *From Memory to Written Record: England 1066–1307* (London, 1979), 138–47, 123. See also Brian Stock, *The Implications of Literacy* (Princeton, 1983).

40. Clanchy, *From Memory to Written Record*, 56, 43, 89, 38, 36; David Crouch, *William Marshal: Court, Career and Chivalry in the Angevin Empire 1147–1219* (London, 1990), 23, 135, 142–48.

41. Gerald Harriss, "Political Society and the Growth of Government in Late Medieval England," *Past and Present* 138 (1993): 35, quoting the estimate of A. L. Brown, *The Governance of Late Medieval England, 1272–1461* (London, 1989), 43.

The English state was not alone in this massive proliferation of administrative paper. In point of fact, it was following a path blazed by the papal government and, rather later, by its Inquisition. The foremost medieval state formation was the Roman Catholic Church. Christendom was "a polity in the West, not just a religious order." Indeed, "it was the most effective single force in western society."[42] The clergy became the first translocal, transtribal, transfeudal, transnational class in Europe to achieve political and legal unity.[43] In the late twelfth century the annual output of papal letters was 280; a century later it was 50,000. Similarly, though less spectacularly, the French monarchy's output rose sixfold in the same time period.[44] The slow reassemblage of the French state during the twelfth century, culminating in the spectacular advances made during the reign of Philip Augustus, was paralleled in the rather slower congealment of bureaucratic early modernization. These distinctive processes of development also had very significant implications for the structure of royal administration: kings amalgamated a system in which an ambulatory court was blended with a fixed governmental structure overlooking finances and the dispensation of royal justice.

In France, the royal archives were deposited in Paris from the reign of Philip Augustus, but the papers of the royal *bailliages* and *sénéchaussées* were the personal property of the officials, which meant that the central depository of official paperwork was seriously defective.[45] The French king's inner circle of *curiales* consisted of a small number of his dependent creatures, while the English monarch's entourage was composed of a representative body drawn from all his main followers.[46] For example, if we confine ourselves to the identification of royal scribes, it would seem that

42. Judith Herrin, *The Formation of Christendom* (Princeton, 1987), 480; R. W. Southern, *Western Society and the Church in the Middle Ages* (Harmondsworth, 1970), 39.

43. Berman, *Law and Revolution*, 108.

44. Clanchy, *From Memory to Written Record*, 45. These figures represent surviving documents, and it seems certain that the number of records for the earlier period is severely underestimated in the papal archive; on the other hand, the French monarchy's output was rather less than the English. Moreover, in England, Clanchy notes that the wax used for attaching royal seals to letters is another source for determining the changing tempo of administrative literacy. Between the 1220s and the 1271 the annual usage of sealing wax rose eightfold, from about three pounds per week to twenty-six pounds (58–59).

45. Robert Fawtier, *The Capetian Kings of France: Monarchy and Nation 987–1328* (London, 1960), 187, 179.

46. C. Warren Hollister and John W. Baldwin, "The Rise of Administrative Kingship: Henry I and Philip Augustus," *American Historical Review* 83 (1978): 867–905.

the five or six clerks working under Philip Augustus in France around 1200 were not many more than the four scribes operating under the *magister scriptorii* seventy years earlier under Henry I and many fewer than the number identified in the administrative heyday of Hubert Walter.[47]

Another difference between the novelty of English experience and the comparable lag in French administrative organization was the employment of educated personnel. English monarchs were far more likely to be employing university-trained *magisters* than were the French. The English administration used many times more of these educated clerics from top to bottom despite the fact that the University of Paris was the center of learning during this period.[48] The contrast with Germany is once again suggestive: the imperial government tried to consolidate its territories but was frustrated by a lack of skilled men whose loyalty could be taken for granted. The revolution in governmental administration was not absent in Germany; rather, it was displaced to a lower level—that of the imperial princes and ecclesiastics, whose courts became the real, effective centers of power.[49]

Jacob Burckhardt's classic history of the Renaissance notes that Florentines employed statistical concepts in their drive to analyze social life in a systematic manner. This view of things runs through their accounting practices, their historical writing, their manuals of conduct, and their social regulations.[50] The most singular text produced as a result of this quantitative mentality was the *catasto* of 1427, a spectacularly detailed tax register. This document remains as a testament to Florentine administrative efficiency. The preservation of this document makes it unique, but it was not without parallel elsewhere. Indeed, in the neighboring Tuscan town of Pistoia, a *Liber focorum* (Book of Hearths) survives from 1244. In Venice, furthermore, such censuslike enumerations are said to have been employed even before the year 1000. The Venetian Senate in 1411 had described another, similar taxation instrument on which the Florentine *catasto* appears

47.   Hollister and Baldwin, "Administrative Kingship," 873, 893. The authors are citing the results of expert analyses of scribal hands: for England, T. A. M. Bishop, *Scriptores Regis* (Oxford, 1961); and for France, Françoise Gasparri, *L'écriture des actes de Louis VI, Louis VII et Philippe Augustus* (Geneva, 1973).

48.   John W. Baldwin, "*Studium et Regnum:* The Penetration of University Personnel into French and English Administration at the Turn of the Twelfth and Thirteenth Centuries," *Revue des Études Islamiques* 44 (1976): 210.

49.   For an example of this process at work on the estates of the bishop of Eichstatt, see Benjamin Arnold, "German Bishops and Their Military Retinues in the Medieval Empire," *German History* 7 (1989): 176.

50.   *The Civilization of the Renaissance in Italy* (London, 1951), 51–52.

to have been modeled. No trace of these Venetian documents remains in the archives. This is not surprising in view of the fact that it was a policy in many Italian states that old taxation registers were to be destroyed whenever a new appraisal was undertaken.[51]

Other communities boast similar taxation registers whose provenance can be dated back to the early modern urge to create an infrastructure of "artificial memory." From the middle of the thirteenth century the system of direct taxation in most Tuscan towns was standardized and integrated, leading to "painstaking surveys."[52] This regulatory initiative—"the ever more systematic use of jurists and their subtle tools, to define relations between centres of power and to calculate roughly the state of play within the tight network of interests and ambitions"[53]—was a practical application of literacy to the imperatives of governance. Lawyers and notaries were kept busy keeping track of people, things, and power relationships between people and things—a grid of surveillance that was predicated on the widespread knowledge of, and familiarity with, written instruments.

Another way to chart the spread of this new technology is through the growth of administrative procedures and bureaucratic personnel. Again the best examples come from northern Italy, where, around 1050, notarized parchments were accorded legal recognition. In the following centuries a specialized body of notaries emerged in all the major commercial centers. In Pisa, there were 79 notaries among an adult male population of 4,271 as early as 1228. By 1293 the number of notaries enlisted in their guild was 232. By this later date there may have been 200 notaries practicing at Genoa, nearly 500 in Verona, 600 in Florence, more than 1000 in Bologna, and a staggering 1,500 in Milan. In Pisa alone, these scribes were producing something like 80,000 pieces of legal paper annually by the end of the thirteenth century.[54] Another remarkable example of the use of literacy comes from the archive of Francesco di Marco Datini, whose cache of five hundred ledgers and account books, three hundred deeds of partnership,

51. David Herlihy and Christiane Klapisch-Zuber, *Tuscans and Their Families: A Study of the Florentine Catasto of 1427* (New Haven, 1985), 9–10.

52. David Herlihy, "Direct and Indirect Taxation in Tuscan Urban Finance, ca. 1200–1400," reprinted in *Cities and Society in Medieval Italy* (London, 1980), 396.

53. Tabacco, *The Struggle for Power in Medieval Italy,* 208.

54. David Herlihy, *Pisa in the Early Renaissance* (New Haven, 1958), 36, 10–11, 20. The figures on notaries in Milan, Bologna, and Verona are found in Fernard Braudel, *The Perspective of the World* (New York, 1984), 547. He suggests that the reason why Florence had only 500 notaries was because "business was so well-organized there that bookkeeping methods often rendered the services of a notary unnecessary."

numerous insurance policies, bills of lading, bills of exchange, cheques, and a truly astonishing 140,000 letters was kept in his home in Prato, where it was discovered in 1870.[55]

In addition to such private-sector professionals, we need to consider the massive growth of the public bureaucracy in propelling the growth of "artificial memory." Pisa again supplies us with relevant statistics: there were 285 government officials of whom 115 (40 percent) were chancellors, notaries, and scribes. It would appear that public business absorbed almost one-half of notarial services even before the massive increase of bureaucracy that would come to characterize the Renaissance State. One has the sense that this particular *volonté de savoir* was imbricated in the marrow of early modern society in Italy, where "ink-stained fingers were not a sign of clerical bookishness, but of practical energy and patient dedication to trade."[56]

The optic provided by artificial memory also enables us to observe family life. In contrast to earlier forms of documentation, the products of early modern administrators survey a much wider range of the whole population. The history of the family, and in particular the outward dimensions of both production and reproduction, suddenly gains clarity, detail, and statistical shape. The 1427 *catasto* is the most remarkable surviving example of a massive social project. Inspired as they were by their classical republican arguments about equality, liberty, patriotism, and "enlightenment," fifteenth-century Florentines saw a direct analogy between the Roman census and their own.[57] Bearing this in mind, we can approach its detailed description of the Florentine population with a sense of admiration for early modern scribal regard for information that was widely disseminated among the population by its "notarial culture," abetted by a massive educational project.[58]

We must also keep in mind the fact that there was nothing unusual in the way that Florentines collected this kind of knowledge. By the thirteenth and fourteenth centuries, the use of literacy to survey the communal population seems to have been common practice throughout the penin-

---

55. For Datini, see Iris Origo, *The Merchant of Prato* (Harmondsworth, 1957), 7–8.

56. Mark Phillips, *The Memoir of Marco Parenti* (Princeton, 1987), 82.

57. Judith Brown, "Florence, Renaissance and Early Modern State: Reappraisals," *Journal of Modern History* 56 (1984): 285–300.

58. Peter Burke, "The Uses of Literacy in Early Modern Italy," in P. Burke and R. Porter (eds.), *The Social History of Language* (Cambridge, 1987), 21–42. See also Peter Denly, "Governments and Schools in Late Medieval Italy," in Trevor Dean and Christopher Wickham (eds.), *City and Countryside in Late Medieval and Renaissance Italy* (London, 1990), 93–107.

sula.[59] These new forms of artificial memory were also employed north of the Alps. We have to locate the Domesday Book of 1086, English manorial registers, and the 1279–80 Hundred Rolls, as well as the French Hearth Tax of 1328, in the same framework: a will to self-knowledge that took on a statistical shape.

New disciplinary technologies created regulatory grids within which the lives of all people would henceforth be framed—by money, the state, and the supervision of everyday life. This was a halting and slow process. One cannot overemphasize the novelty of these innovations, yet one cannot be too wary about emphasizing their limited and selective impact. New forms of legal documentation are like a lens through which we can see an image slowly coming into focus.

3.

If the Centaur/warrior had been the master of Europe at the height of the feudal age, the logic of early modernization would eventually replace him with a new type of aristocrat—the courtier/statesman. If the master's role had been predicated on direct involvement in warfare in the first feudal age, in the second feudal age it would be transmuted into the organizational skills of logistics and finance required to put a force of men into the field of battle when the ties of dependence were attenuated by subinfeudation and the corrosive effects of money. In these new circumstances, "simple personal prowess, replicated within knightly families across the generations, was no longer enough to win battles or maintain social domination."[60]

By 1200, most armies were made up of mercenaries, not just vassals. Indeed, the core of the magnate's fighting force was the military household, which was "remarkably heterogeneous in its composition, both socially and geographically." These men—"knights bachelor" in the language of the time—were, in reality, mercenaries who "supplied the standing professional element, capable of acting independently and, for major campaigns, of rapid expansion."[61]

59. Peter Burke, "Classifying the People: The Census as Collective Representation," in *The Historical Anthropology of Early Modern Italy* (Cambridge, 1987), 27–39.

60. William McNeill, *The Pursuit of Power: Technology, Armed Force, and Society since A.D. 1000* (Chicago, 1988), 68.

61. J. O. Prestwich, "The Military Household of the Norman Kings," *English Historical Review* 378 (1981): 26, 33. For a glimpse at the culture of these armed bachelors, see Duby, "Youth in Aristocratic Society," in *The Chivalrous Society* (Berkeley and Los Angeles, 1977), 112–22.

Nonresident vassals posed a problem for any military commander. They resisted their obligations. They restricted the size of their contingents. They reduced the duration of voluntary service. They regulated the area within which service was due. They willingly substituted money payments instead of military assistance. Nevertheless, state agents persisted in maintaining, if not reinforcing, a system of obligations so that feudal warfare did not simply change into free mercenary warfare overnight.

The older forms of obligation and service were valuable to monarchs and princes because they devolved capital expenses, educational training, and maintenance onto those who were responsible to royalty for feudal forms of service. This meant that while they often ended up paying these fighters wages, the wages were far below the cost of the services rendered. Keeping track of obligations discharged, services rendered, and money expended was a complex procedure which gave a major impetus to the development of administrative literacy. "Listing, summoning, revictualling and payment were all tasks henceforward entrusted to paid officials whose outstanding technical capacity rested on constant use of written records."[62]

It is also misleading to privilege the role of the Centaur/warrior because new weapons systems changed the balance of power in battle, to the detriment of the horsed fighter. Even at the very height of the knights' powers in the eleventh and twelfth centuries, armies were frequently divided equally between mounted cavalry, on one hand, and archers and infantry on the other.[63] Early modern warfare became a more complicated business than it had been before the year 1000, when impulsive onslaughts by armed horsemen ruled the battlefields of Europe. A contemporary wrote that "From one day to the next and larger and larger grow the machines devised by men which change the way in which things are done . . . and at present there may be found many things and clever devices which were neither known nor used in former times."[64]

Hybrid armed forces, which blended the qualities of the knight banneret with those of the foot soldier, proliferated. Crossbowmen, shooting from distances of one hundred yards, could unleash a bolt that could unseat a knight. Skilled archers were supplemented by pikemen and cavalry—for flank protection and the pursuit of a clumsy, downed horseman. In the thirteenth century, after their successful campaign to colonize Wales, the English enlisted troops of longbowmen who were superlatively trained

---

62. Philippe Contamine, *War in the Middle Ages* (Oxford, 1984), 85, 97, 115.
63. For example, the Battle of Hastings (October 14, 1066) was fought by this kind of composite force of 7,000 men; Contamine, *War in the Middle Ages,* 52.
64. Jean de Bueil, quoted in Contamine, *War in the Middle Ages,* 137–38.

archers. The longbow was a far more efficient weapon than the crossbow because its rate of fire was four times as fast. A skillful archer, shooting at long range, could keep two arrows in the air simultaneously. Because the longbow was the monopoly of the English and Welsh archers, the light infantry's battlefield superiority overcame huge odds against the French at both Crécy (1346) and Agincourt (1415).[65]

The Chinese initially discovered gunpowder in 1044, although they used it for firecrackers in their celebrations. It was only in 1326 that the Florentines used gunpowder as a military weapon, although Roger Bacon had produced the first Western recipe for it as early as 1267. Within twenty years of the Florentine adoption it had spread across the face of Europe. As Italian poet Petrarch noted in the 1350s, "these instruments which discharge balls of metal with most tremendous noise and slashes of fire . . . were a few years ago very rare and were viewed with the greatest astonishment and admiration, but now they are become as common and familiar as any other kind of arms. So quick and ingenious are the minds of men in learning the most pernicious arts."[66]

Explosive weaponry was used in siege warfare—forged-iron cannons, firing low-density stone projectiles aimed at fortified masonry walls, were deployed against the firepower of the besieged. Most artillery was huge and cumbersome. Its rate of fire was extraordinarily slow, and its accuracy was faulty.[67] The early handgun, called an *arquebus*, was imprecise and hard to fire until the matchlock was developed in the middle of the fif-

---

65. Archer Jones, *The Art of War in the Western World* (Oxford, 1989), 155–57. The English won these legendary victories, but they reaped meager strategic rewards because "The thousands of square miles and the millions of people of France swallowed up English armies of 10,000 or even 20,000 men. The English had an inadequate ratio of force to French space and population and had no solution to the defensive strength of fortifications" (173, 168). It is ironic to note that the three most celebrated English victories in the Hundred Years War (Crécy, Poitiers, and Agincourt) were all achieved by armies which were "not entering the French kingdom to attempt its conquest, but were actually leaving it, heading for the coast in search of transport to take them back to England, the main aim of the expedition already fulfilled"; Christopher Allmand, *The Hundred Years War* (Cambridge, 1989), 54.

66. Petrarch, quoted in C. Cipolla, *Guns, Sails, and Empires* (New York, 1965), 22.

67. The development of corned gunpowder, which replaced the mealed variety, greatly increased explosive force. The forged-iron cannons were simply unable to withstand this radical increase in pressure. Together with the development of cast-iron shot, it demanded new techniques of weapons manufacturing. The fifteenth-century discovery of methods of casting copper-tin bronzes resolved this technological bottleneck and issued in a new stage in the history of warfare; Bert Hall, "Metallurgy and the Military: Costs and Traditions in Renaissance Ordnance," unpublished paper presented to the Economic History Workshop, University of Toronto, January 18, 1993.

teenth century. These light guns were much cheaper to produce than the crossbow and required less skill to operate than the longbow. While the *arquebus* lacked accuracy, it could be shot and then reloaded quickly; its rate of fire was far superior to that of the crossbow.

Rather than immediately supplanting the older weapons, explosive-charged cannons and handguns seem to have coexisted with them until the end of the fifteenth century. The reason for this seeming failure to exploit new technology can be found in the social culture of warfare. Commanders were trained in older forms of combat and were enchanted by the chivalric code of individual courage, while serving men were usually a miscellaneous jumble of brigands, thugs, and lumpenproletarians whose training was nonexistent.[68] Aristocratic contempt for the foot soldiers was unbridled but myopic. When armed with long pikes and disciplined to maintain ranks, the infantry could withstand the charge of the heavy cavalry and inflict severe casualties on it and its valuable mounts.[69]

If new technical factors were slowly changing the character of battle, we must be careful not to telescope the process because one system did not simply supersede its predecessor; rather, elements of change blended with those of continuity to produce field armies of mixed constitution. This complexity also governed the motivation of the fighters. Of course, money was a valuable method of supplementing a feudal host, but there were many occasions when the flowers of chivalry were only too happy to put themselves in the service of God, the search for glory, and a contingency fee for success. The Norman Conquerors, the Templars, the Hospitallers, the Teutonic Knights, and the Crusaders (at least in their more romantic phases) all conform to this pattern. Garrison service and policing operations did not. Indeed, there was an ongoing tension between the search for glory and the demands of regular service. Territorial rulers were hardly likely to trust their bodily protection and the day-to-day reproduction of their authority to a band of knights errant.

What were the social origins of these knights? Many were the younger sons of noble and gentle houses—William Marshal's career again provides

---

68. The Swiss militia were the exception to this rule.

69. By the fourteenth century, the Swiss militia were recognized as the heavy infantry *par excellence;* they possessed the cohesion of ancient professional armies and the drilled restraint which was almost totally lacking in the disparate feudal hosts. Their *esprit de corps,* their mobility, and above all their ability to work together like the fingers of one hand made them a fighting force out of all proportion to their numbers or their technology. Indeed, the Swiss fighting forces, which shattered the armies—and ultimately the pretensions—of the dukes of Burgundy in

us with the paradigmatic figure, but his very success also makes him quite unrepresentative since few could attain his eminence. Most knights were altogether grubbier, more mendacious, and less masterful. Most knights lived in a netherworld of frustrated ambitions and the daily reality of declining status. They were hired thugs whose chivalric code should not obscure an altogether more nasty and brutish everyday reality. A not inconsiderable number of these paladins were criminals who were pardoned in order to have them serve military ends. In the English forces which fought alongside Edward III in France and Scotland they seem to have been present in the hundreds. In 1339–40 there is documentary record of 850 such pardons; "several hundred" were granted in 1346–47, 140 at Poitiers in 1356, and 260 a few years later (1360).[70] The division between these convicts/ soldiers of fortune and the regular army was blurred in other ways, too. Given the ramshackle finances of most political leaders, the oversupply of trained fighters, and the infrequent and unpredictable demand for their services, it was not surprising that rootless gangs of discharged fighters lived at interstitial points in the social structure.

Warfare was endemic, yet set-piece battles were rare. The strategic thrust of warfare was largely defensive, and the Centaur/warrior's field of action was usually defined by its orbit around a fortified stronghold. Most battle units lacked planning, subdivisions, chains of command, uniformity in organization, *esprit de corps*, common experience, and the internal articulation which could take advantage of their massed forces. They were usually rather less than the sum of their parts. Most pitched battles were fought without consulting land maps or any other kind of military intelligence. The pivotal moment in any confrontation was when order broke down, panic set in, and the rudimentary military organization that had been cobbled together in the hours preceding the confrontation lost its coherence. This was the instant when unexpected paralysis led to indiscriminate slaughter and large-scale capture of the defeated. Military strategy, therefore, was dominated by an open fear of both the pitched battle and the confrontation in open country. This resulted in a siege mentality and the war of attrition—what was called *"guerre guerroyante,* made up of losses and recaptures, surprises, incursions, ambushes and sallies." While full-scale battles were so infrequent that a professional soldier might be in-

---

the fifteenth century provided the key to the modern military machine in their regimen of self-control, preparation, organization, and internal articulation.

70. Contamine, *War in the Middle Ages,* 239, quoting H. J. Hewitt, *The Organization of War under Edward III, 1338–1362* (Manchester, 1966), 30.

volved in only one or two in the course of his long career, they were deadly: at Courtrai (1302) 40 percent of French knights were killed. About the same rate of loss occurred at both Poitiers (1356) and Agincourt (1415).[71] Foot soldiers were often slaughtered indiscriminately in the frenzied heat of battle.

Until the state was able to disarm its subjects, civil society could not be demilitarized. The monopolization of violence in the hands of the state was a long and arduous process. We can see its roots in the very structure and logic of early modernization. A landmark was reached in the fifteenth century when informed observers noted that "the king of France had disarmed his people in order to rule without resistance."[72] We might, for the sake of argument, suggest that this landmark was reached along two converging routes: first, the ability of states to pay for professional armies through the creation of routinely generated sources of revenue; and second, the spiraling cost of military affairs resulting from increasing technical complexity in both weapons and warfare.[73]

After the year 1000 the increasing scale of military operations slowly dovetailed with the centralization of power. Castle building and hiring mercenary armies for long sieges stretched lordly financial resources and limited the great game to the richest monarchs. Money was taxed from the subject population, granted by dependent vassals, and squeezed from merchant bankers. Rules were created to govern fiscal relations during "the twelfth century [which] marks the beginning of a conceptual distinction between public and private roles and prerogatives of rulers and ruled, [so that] it may be viewed as a distant beginning of the modern era."[74] The makeshift expedients of the monarchs of the second age of feudalism provided precedents which were followed by their successors. While it was generally believed that the feudal monarch was expected to use his own revenues to cover ordinary expenses, the soaring cost of war frequently invalidated such simple accounting procedures.

There was no single model for the feudal state. Each was created out of available historical materials, and all were influenced in their creation by their contingent relationship to the others. The linkage between the science

71. Contamine, *War in the Middle Ages,* 228–30, 219, 257–58.

72. Quoted in Contamine, *War in the Middle Ages,* 249.

73. Leonard Dudley, *The Word and the Sword: How Techniques of Information and Violence Have Shaped Our World* (Oxford, 1991), 101–37.

74. Webber and Wildavsky, *History of Taxation and Expenditure,* 151. Such "rules" were as frequently broken as they were observed, but the important point is that their observation led to the growth of routine procedures, spreading from precedent to precedent.

of violence and social regulation developed in an administrative culture in which literacy, "artificial memory," and state-formation initiatives were already well-known technologies of power. A new dynamic was being created in which "efficient tax collection, debt-funding, and skilled professional military management kept peace at home while exporting the uncertainties of organized violence to the realm of foreign affairs, diplomacy, and war."[75] To exploit the military potential of explosive weapons required an organizational revolution which would mold armies to the requirements of new modes of destruction. When this bond had matured, in the course of the fifteenth century, Leviathan was armed and dangerous.

SAILING ON THE TIDE OF HISTORY

The commercial society . . . has generally escaped recognition because it existed primarily in the linear dimension. Having no extended areas to administer, the commercial or linear societies normally had no need for government of the sort we take for granted in the state. Our modern preoccupation with territory makes it difficult for us to think in such terms, and we tend to see the state and society as two aspects of a single reality. Yet, looked at in a geographical context, the state is simply the normal government of an areal society. Today, for us to recognize the existence of a society without territory or political administration merely on the ground that it maintains itself by an active exchange of goods and messages, as well as a highly developed sense of common purpose, requires a very special effort.

Edward Whiting Fox,
History in Geographic Perspective

In the year 1000 there were few cities in Europe. The commercialization of social relations took place alongside—and not always in opposition to— feudalization. Like the feudalists, capitalists took advantage of the increasing circulation of money to increase their social power. For both, this was a crucial way of "Sailing on the Tide of History." Towns organized themselves in opposition to feudalism although they usually traced their origins to liberties sold to communes by feudal lords in their constant search for new sources of cash. Thereafter, urban life and feudalism existed symbiotically. Town governments were rarely reluctant to exploit their own hinterlands. Linking cities and their resident commodity traders together into a commercial trading system was the way to super-profits

75. McNeill, *The Pursuit of Power*, 79.

earned from the circulation of precious goods. Capitalists created new methods of self-organization—"In the name of God and profit." Below the level of the high fliers, fairs and markets proliferated as exchange relations permeated the social fabric. This infrastructure of urban functions created another layer in the organization and operation of social power.

1.

In surveying urban history of the year 1000 it is important to remember that "the Eurocentric view of the Dark Ages [is] ill-conceived. If the lights went out in Europe, they were certainly still shining brightly in the Middle East."[76] In the year 1000, London and Paris were small, muddy towns, but Islamic Cordoba had a huge population living in 260,377 houses, working in 80,455 shops, and trading in 4,300 markets.[77]

In the year 1000 there were few real cities in Europe. Moreover, there was little continuity with the earlier cities of antiquity. The Germanic invasions of the third, fourth, and fifth centuries—the *Völkerwanderung*—had destroyed almost all Roman cities. The invaders had no taste for urban life, so that while some Roman centers were continuously inhabited, this was not a continuation of ancient urban life except in the case of bishoprics which remained on the same sites even though their relationship with the hinterland came to be organized on a completely different basis. Furthermore, Roman towns had been situated on land routes with strategic importance, whereas the earliest medieval towns were located on the Italian sea coast or the inland waterways of the Rhine valley and its tributaries. It was only in the second phase of medieval urban renewal that road traffic again became significant.

76. Janet Abu-Lughod, *Before European Hegemony: The World System* A.D. *1250–1350* (Oxford, 1989), ix.

77. Henri Pirenne, *Medieval Cities: Their Origins and the Revival of Trade* (Princeton, 1925), 56; Richard Erdoes, AD *1000: Living on the Brink of Apocalypse* (New York, 1988), 46–47; Paul Boissonnade, *Life and Work in Medieval Europe* (New York, 1964), suggests (112–14) that the populations of London and Paris were probably 8,000 in the year 1000, while Paul Bairoch, *Cities and Economic Development* (Chicago, 1988), opts for a rather higher figure, between twenty and twenty-five thousand (119). In contrast, Georges Duby suggests that Paris was "tiny," only having rather more than 3,000 inhabitants in the mid-eleventh century. Duby further states that, around 1050, the Parisian population was confined to the Île-de-la-Cité (the island in the middle of the Seine); the right bank was a little port, while the West Bank was covered with vineyards and virtually unsettled; *France in the Middle Ages, 987–1460* (Oxford, 1991), 133.

The most important implication of the invasions of the Northmen and the Arabs was the impetus that they gave to creation of town walls, which gave the medieval city a unique physiognomy. Within these walls, the early medieval cities developed a unique system of social relations. As early as the eleventh century, Alain of Lille said that "Money, not Caesar, is everything now." Permanent resident settlements which were differentiated economically and topographically from the surrounding countryside prefigured eleventh- and twelfth-century juridical innovations, leading to emergence of communes that conceded personal liberties to the towns' bourgeois inhabitants.[78] In a very real sense, though, each town's transition from settlement to commune was *sui generis* even though all experienced a juridical transition that was the logical conclusion of their physical separation from the surrounding countryside and their successful struggle to escape from feudal domination.[79]

Italy was the most urbanized part of Europe. In the year 1000 its "mature" city system was found in the South. The Northern Italian urban system was, by way of contrast, "immature." Furthermore, the urban distribution of the main cities in the Italian space was quite unlike the formation that had come to exist in 1300. In the year 1000 the urban balance was displaced toward the South, which was then the most flourishing part of Italy while under Arab and Byzantine rule. The biggest Southern cities were Napoli, Amalfi, Roma, Bari, and especially Palermo, which has been estimated to have had as many as 350,000 people. In the North, Genoa, Pisa, Ravenna, Ancona, and above all Venice were the main maritime centers of consequence, while Florence, Pavia, Lucca, Milano, and Verona stood out in an underdeveloped rural landscape. These northern cities were still comparatively small in the year 1000. Three centuries later, the cities of northern Italy had caught up with—and even surpassed—their southern counterparts: Venice and Milan had both grown prodigiously to reach perhaps 200,000 residents, and Florence was reported to have 135,000 inhabitants in the 1330s. For the country as a whole, about one in five of its population lived in cities with more than 5,000 inhabitants. In contrast to the year

78. David M. Nicholas, "Medieval Urban Origins in Northern Continental Europe: State of Research and Some Tentative Conclusions," *Studies in Medieval and Renaissance History* 6 (1969), 55–114. Alain of Lille is quoted in Fernand Braudel, *The Structures of Everyday Life*, vol. 1, *Civilization and Capitalism, 15th–18th Century* (New York, 1981), 511. See also Edward Whiting Fox, *History in Geographic Perspective* (New York, 1971), chap. 3.

79. Sometimes this escape from feudal domination was aided and abetted by feudalists who had been only too willing to accept urban money in trade for political liberties.

1000, the Italian urban league-table in 1300 was dominated by large central and northern cities, many of which were not coastal but located inland in the midst of thriving regions.[80]

In the Low Countries, for example, the burgeoning trading community of Bruges was situated in the shadow of the Count of Flanders's castles, whose origins were described as follows:

> In order to satisfy the needs of the castle folk, there began to throng before his [i.e., the count's] gate near the castle bridge traders and merchants selling costly goods, then innkeepers to feed and house those doing business with the prince, who was often to be seen there; they built houses and set up inns where those who could not be put up at the castle were accommodated. . . . The houses increase to such an extent that there soon grew up a large town which in the common speech of the lower class is still called "Bridge."

By the early fourteenth century, Flanders was dotted with cloth-making towns—not only Bruges but also Aachen, Antwerp, Brussels, Ghent, Lille, Louvain, and Ypres, which all had populations in excess of twenty thousand. In addition, each of these stars was surrounded by its own constellation of smaller, urban moons. The countryside of Flanders was in this way enmeshed in a dense metropolitan network that was second only to that of northern Italy.[81]

To give the foregoing examples some perspective we need to keep in mind that in the early fourteenth century only about one European in ten lived in cities. Furthermore, while Flanders and Brabant may have been the most densely urbanized region in northern Europe, Paris was the biggest European city—the 1328 tax returns reported 61,098 hearths, which, using a multiplier of four persons per hearth, would yield a population of 244,392.[82] Early fourteenth-century Paris had spread far beyond Philip Augustus's five-kilometer walls that had been built to girdle his capital around 1200. Over the course of the thirteenth century fifty streets had

---

80. Paola Malamina, "Italian Cities 1300–1800: A Quantitative Approach," *Rivista di Storia Economica* 14 (1998): 191–216.

81. Annals of Saint-Bertin, quoted in N. J. G. Pounds, *An Historical Geography of Europe, 450 B.C.–A.D. 1330* (Cambridge, 1973), 267–70, 348–59. The description of the origins of Bruges is quoted on 268. See also Herman Van der Wee, "Structural Changes and Specialization in the Industry of the Southern Netherlands, 1100–1600," *Economic History Review*, 2d ser., 28 (1975): 203–21.

82. H. van Werverke, "The Rise of the Towns," in M. M. Postan, E. E. Rich, and Edward Miller (eds.), *Cambridge Economic History of Europe*, vol. 3 (Cambridge, 1963), 39. Jacques Le Goff disputes this "overestimate" of the Parisian population, which he puts at "no more than 80,000"; *Medieval Civilization*, 293.

sprouted beyond these ramparts.[83] London was the second-largest city north of the Alps; its population around 1300 is estimated to have been nearly 100,000.[84] Similar growth—evidenced by the rebuilding of defensive walls—took place everywhere.

Many cities were not much bigger than a large village, yet they nonetheless supplied the countryside with urban functions—marketing and trade. Underdevelopment of the Flemish countryside led to the development of towns in the context of rapid population growth after the year 1000. These towns were supplied with grain from nearby Picardy via the canal network. Mercantile enterprises provided the route by which Flemings broke out of their marshy homeland's restrictive environment. They adapted resources to population growth by colonizing new forms of activity.[85] In the corridor which stretched from Italy to the Netherlands, lines of communication and exchange connected distant communities. This ability to conquer the bottleneck of distance enabled the commercial city to extend its area of domination far beyond its immediate hinterland.

Towns were not simply peaceful oases in a desert of warring feudal factions. Cities were no less willing to engage in violence than feudalists, the only difference being that urban violence was frequently willful and not random. European towns "ruled their countrysides autocratically, regarding them exactly as later powers regarded their colonies, and treating them as such. They pursued an economic policy of their own via their satellites and the nervous system of urban relay points; they were capable of breaking down obstacles and creating or recreating protective privileges."[86] The ability of towns to dominate the surrounding countryside made it unusual for mere villages to possess their own market facilities. In the West, the town "swallowed everything, forced everything to submit to its laws, its demands and its controls." The market, which "sailed on the tide of history," became one of the mechanisms it employed in creating this hegemony.

---

83. Bronislaw Geremek, *The Margins of Society in Late Medieval Paris* (Cambridge, 1987), 67.

84. D. Keene, *Cheapside before the Great Fire* (London, 1985). Pamela Nightingale disputes Keene's figures and estimates that London's population, c. 1300, was on the order of 60,000; "The Growth of London in the Medieval English Economy," in Richard Britnell and John Hatcher (eds.), *Progress and Problems in Medieval England* (Cambridge, 1996), 89–106.

85. David Nicholas, "Of Poverty and Primacy: Demand, Liquidity, and the Flemish Economic Miracle, 1050–1200," *American Historical Review* 96 (1991): 17–41.

86. Braudel, *The Structures of Everyday Life*, 510.

Town and country were never separate like oil and water. An eleventh-century urban center of 3,000 inhabitants required the land and labor of ten villages to survive, approximately 85 square kilometers of arable land. But if its hinterland was a mixture of woodland, pasture, and arable land, then one would probably need to double this total to arrive at the "village territory" of a small canton. The bottleneck stemming from the low yield of agriculture in the surrounding region was frequently prized open by the intensive cultivation of suburban gardens and orchards as well as regional trading networks which spurred country-dwellers to more productive forms of husbandry.[87]

In the territories governed by centralizing monarchies, towns and cities grew up in response to the concentration of people organized by the following activities: ecclesiastical functions, governance and administration resulting from political centralization, and university and monastic training. Trading hubs, marketing sites, industrial communities, and pseudo-urban locations serving purely local needs also created concentrations of urban population even if some such places lacked the appropriate legal credentials.[88] Some trading centers grew up on the remains of older cities, others were created by the "charters" conferred by feudal lords who were eager to grab some cash in exchange for granting liberties, while some simply grew up in response to a natural market opportunity. In many places, lords not only fostered markets but also intervened to ensure that these local outlets for farm products stayed viable. It was also in the lord's interest to safeguard his peasants' ability to sell their farm and craft products. Local markets injected cash into circulation which could then be tapped by landlords if they decided it was in their interest to commute feudal obligations.[89]

A search for common origins of urban life in the feudal countryside is spurious because structures differed from place to place according to unique local balances between contending forces. This variety is not surprising because early modernization created a social formation that was

87. The quotations in the two previous paragraphs are taken from Fernand Braudel, *The Wheels of Commerce* (New York, 1982), 28, 59; Braudel, *The Structures of Everyday Life*, 486–87; Braudel, *The Perspective of the World*, 282. The "average" canton in France in 1969 was 160–170 square kilometers.

88. Pounds, *An Historical Geography of Europe*, 343–59; Bairoch, *Cities and Economic Development*, 137 (Table 8.2). For an example of the urban role of a very small community, see R. H. Hilton, "Small Town Society in England before the Black Death," in *Class Conflict and the Crisis of Feudalism* (London, 1990), 19–40.

89. Commutation of obligations into cash payments was sometimes negotiated on a year-by-year basis, and sometimes permanent freedom from such feudal burdens was purchased by the peasantry.

characterized by its combined and uneven development. When we stop the process and put it under the microscope, we see a hybrid species in the midst of its mutation. What is essential is the substance of the evolutionary process—after the year 1000, the early modernization of material life created a new kind of society.

2.

Like a pearl, urbanization began life as an irritant within the shell of another social formation. Incipient capitalist tendencies can be detected from the outset of early modernization.[90] The "discovery" of credit "worked as techniques of control that linked agrarian lords with financiers who monopolized the exchange of agricultural products from the point of production to distribution in the expanding centers."[91] In addition, these new methods of control were connected to the accumulation of administrative literacy. In contrast to the feudalists who "congeal historical thought and seem to stop historical time or at least assimilate it to the history of the Church," the merchants fractured time and freed it from biblical injunctions. As Jacques Le Goff writes, "Debts came inexorably to term, and yet time was pliable, and it was in this pliability that profit and loss resided. This was where the merchant's intelligence, experience, and cunning counted."[92]

The growth of an infrastructure of urban functions was, perhaps, of even greater importance than the emergence of cities in changing the character of social relations. The spread of urban functions acted as a very significant counterweight to the hegemony of the manorialists in four ways. First, autarky—the production of food for the lord's kitchen—gave way to the demand for money rents. Second, the egalitarian oaths which linked members of the town community stood in direct contrast to the feudal vassal's oath of homage and subordination. Third, *Stadtluft macht frei nach Jahr und Tag* (town air makes freedom after a year and a day): runaway serfs could gain citizenship by living within the city's walls for a year and a day.[93] Fourth, the urban trading classes were interested in stable, pre-

90. Jacques Heers, "The 'Feudal' Economy and Capitalism: Words, Ideas and Reality," *Journal of European Economic History* 3 (1974): 609–53.

91. Kathleen Biddick, "Power in Early English Development," *Comparative Studies in Society and History* 32 (1990): 9.

92. "Merchant's Time and Church's Time," in *Time, Work, and Culture in the Middle Ages* (Chicago, 1980), 33, 42, 37.

93. Le Goff, *Medieval Civilization*, 292–97. This was not a hard-and-fast rule, however; in Venice it took a foreigner twenty-five years' residence to qualify for

dictable social conditions in which to transact their business. An environment conducive to buying low and selling high simply could not be provided by warriors whose very *raison d'être* was based on plunder.

The largest and most successful of these towns were autonomous
worlds, linked to one another through the mechanisms of long-distance
trade and buttressed with liberties, which could be likened to juridical ramparts. As such, towns were the first focus for patriotism in the West.[94] This
nascent urban civilization acted as a solvent on feudal contracts by introducing commercial considerations into all arrangements. The commercialization of social relations favored the normalization of political authority
by effectively guaranteeing order, justice, and above all predictability. The
emergence of cities was thus associated with the introjection of legal norms
into quotidian political relations. "The unique feature of the law of western
Christendom was that the individual person lived under a plurality of legal
systems, each of which governed one of the overlapping subcommunities
of which he was a member."[95] For city folk, the commune was a guarantor
standing between each one individually and the secular warlords upon
whose favor urban freedom was contingent. For city folk, therefore, the
everyday experience of early modernization was refracted through living
in a "multiple acephalous federation," in contrast to rural dwellers who did
not have the benefit of this added layer of complexity in their social relations with the overbearing and overmighty men of arms.

In the words of John of Viterbo, c. 1250,

> "City" means "you dwell safe from violence." For residence is without
> violence, because the ruler of the city will protect the lowliest men lest
> they suffer injury from the more powerful, since "we cannot be equal
> with those more powerful." . . . [The city] is truly called a place of im-
> munity, because its inhabitants are guarded by its walls and towers and
> protected in it from their enemies and foes.[96]

The town rescued men and women from seigneurial oppression: "the communal movement itself was, for former serfs, a kind of Exodus." Of course,

---

citizenship, whereas in Genoa it appears that foreigners were immediately naturalized and granted the usual privileges—apprenticeship in the guild system, rights to
set up banks and business partnerships, and rights to work on the trading vessels
and in the trades and crafts of the town—if they agreed to the duties as well as the
privileges of citizenship.

94. Braudel, *The Structures of Everyday Life*, 512.

95. Berman, *Law and Revolution*, 395.

96. Quoted in Antony Black, *Guilds and Civil Society in European Political
Thought* (London, 1984), 38.

the commune was not itself immune to social and political divisions. Among the members of the urban population, patricians privileged property, security of person, legal equality, and individual diversity while the plebeian counterculture argued for redistribution of wealth, the abolition of private ownership, greater social conformity, and a tightly knit, warm, charismatic community. These two interrelated tendencies have been likened to "red and white corpuscles in the bloodstream of medieval and Renaissance political thought" because they transmitted the oxygen of communal freedom—counsel, consent, and election—throughout the body politic. In this way, they kept the organism alive when it was threatened with suffocation by the rediscovered classical models which would be used to glorify elites and to legitimate the centralization of power.[97]

The citizens' tendency to think about the urban community in sacramental terms of love and friendship meant that the discourse of urban freedom gained immeasurably from the disengagement of the sacred and profane which gave the whole process of early modernization its distinctive ethos. It is in this regard that constitutionalist principles were first elaborated by twelfth- and thirteenth-century canonists who challenged sacred monarchies and, quite unintentionally, ended up partially secularizing politics. Both clerics and citizens looked to the law as the categorical moral authority because, for them, sworn association, election, and consent played a larger role than simple coercion and ritual subordination—the feudalists' hallmarks.[98]

The Church, rather more than the secular powers, first legitimated the development of commerce and urban society in their accommodation with the system of "multiple acephalous federation." The growth of cities across the length and breadth of early modern Europe in this way worked in tandem with the Gregorian reforms to create a massive counterweight against the absolutist technologies of power that were being employed by the secular territorial magnates in the process of early modern state formation. Urban society and legal process together presented the state with a thousand tiny obstacles to achieving its goal of unified sovereignty.

Yet, curiously, with the exception of Marsilius of Padua, there were no political theorists who took seriously the role played by corporate organizations; rather, political philosophy was conceived in the womb of religious controversy. This startling absence has been accounted for by referring to the influence of Aristotle, which was so great among the clerical intelligentsia

---

97. Black, *Guilds and Civil Society in European Political Thought,* 64, 43, 44.
98. Black, *Guilds and Civil Society in European Political Thought,* 63, 81, 24.

that even though "Most people participated in public affairs through guilds and similar associations . . . philosophers saw social personality only in terms of family [i.e., *oeconomia*] and state, domesticity [i.e., *oikos*] and formal politics. A whole range of actual socio-political life vanishes into the air whenever we look at a work of political theory."[99] This gulf—it is surely more than just a lacuna—seems to have been the price paid for reclaiming the classical heritage in the twelfth-century Renaissance.

3.

Before the year 1000, the largest part of European economic life had been autarkic. In the space of a few generations following the year 1000, northwestern Europe went from being a society predominantly organized by and through gift exchange to become a money economy. The organizational changes in material life were perhaps the most lasting effect of this spectacular commercial adventure. Like other aspects of the experience of early modernization, the interaction of cause and effect was so tightly knotted that any attempt to assert primacy is doomed to failure.

The realm of international trade, the real home of capitalism's aggressive and expansionary impulses in Braudel's schema, has been characterized as "the zone of the anti-market, where the great predators roam and the law of the jungle operates."[100] Italy's geographical position between the luxury producers of the Orient and the luxury consumers of the Occident came to the fore around the year 1000. "Commerce was the frontier of the Italians."[101] Italy was at this time not much more than a geographical expression. Italians thought of themselves as Florentines, Genoese, Pisans, Venetians, and so on. At the heart of the matter was the emergence of independent mercantile communities whose prosperity was based on the provision of services to a far-flung marketplace. Linking Byzantium and the Levant with trans-Alpine Europe, Italians acted as middlemen, trading spices, perfumes, ivory, silks, and cotton textiles in exchange for woolen

---

99. Black, *Guilds and Civil Society in European Political Thought*, 86, 84.

100. *The Wheels of Commerce*, 229. Braudel's schema divides exchange—"an enclosing circle and a turning hinge" into three zones: the lowest stratum or the "non-economy, into which capitalism thrusts its roots but which it can never really penetrate"; the true market "economy" in which supply and demand are always subject to change but where prices had fluctuated in unison since the twelfth century in Europe; and the upper level of the large-scale predators who could corner markets, thereby making super-profits (224, 227–28, 229).

101. Robert Lopez, "The Trade of Medieval Europe: The South," in M. M. Postan and E. E. Rich (eds.), *The Cambridge Economic History of Europe*, vol. 3 (Cambridge, 1963), 304.

goods, slaves, timber, iron, and precious metals. Trade in luxury goods was very heavily capital intensive and fraught with risks, yet surprisingly large amounts of profit could be gained from seemingly small amounts of goods. At the high point of the economic cycle, at the very end of the thirteenth century, about 4,000 tons of luxury merchandise arrived in both Venice and Genoa in their annual trade with the Levant and Byzantium.[102] Of course, many ventures ended up as a total disaster as a result of piracy, pilferage, loss at sea, or robbery on land.

The Italian achievement was to do business more efficiently by developing commercial instruments which took advantage of techniques of artificial memory. These techniques were crucial in commerce as early modern merchants sought to diversify their product lines, to spread their risks, and to keep their capital liquid. To achieve these ends, commercial instruments were created which enabled a diversified group of individuals to pool their resources into a separate account for each venture. The most famous example of this strategy was the *commenda* contract which drew together the money of an investor and the practical skills of the merchant adventurer. Our first documented examples are drawn from the records of Genoese notaries which start in 1156. It seems likely that similar commercial instruments were available to members of the merchant communities in other Italian communes before this date. In fact, there is an isolated Venetian document (dated August 1073) which is essentially the same. Other risk-splitting partnership arrangements were called *societas maris* and *collegianta*. The sea loan and the *cambium maritimum* enabled borrowers to gain access to capital, the repayment of which was contingent upon the safe arrival of the ship or the successful completion of the voyage. These techniques—a sleeping partner who supplied the capital and a traveling merchant who conducted business abroad—were the way in which long-distance trade was accomplished by the Italian sea-republics that connected northwestern European consumers with the luxury goods from the Orient which they coveted.

Among Tuscans another form of business association prevailed; *compagnie* were made up of partners who supplied both capital and management while being liable to third parties for any debt contracted by any of the others. "The *compagnia* was originally a family partnership—men who lived in the same house, who broke the same bread (as the word *com-*

102. G. Luzzatto, *An Economic History of Italy from the Fall of the Roman Empire to the Beginning of the Sixteenth Century* (London, 1961), 73 ff. On the trade in iron from Europe to Asia Minor around the year 1000, see H. Pirenne, *Economic and Social History of Medieval Europe* (New York, 1937), 18.

pagno implies), whose interests were identical, and who therefore found it natural to accept unlimited liability for each other's actions. . . . A *compagnia* was as stable and secure as the family name it bore, and its credit rested, at least in part, on the solid landed property which that family owned."[103] While these partners received no salary, they were compensated by the company's profits, Such Tuscan partnerships—which relied most heavily on family, first, and then *paesani*—were generally short-lived because it was only at their dissolution that individuals could draw out their capital and profit.

Within each company there was usually a vertical, age-graded organization in the *fondaco* (overseas branch) leading from the teenaged *garzoni* (shop boy), to the older *fattori-scrivani* or *contabili* or *chiavi* (denoting their letter-writing, bookkeeping, and cashier's duties), and finally to the dependable *fattore* (manager) who oversaw operations and was usually a man who had already climbed the ladder for several decades in these trading businesses. Italian wandering merchants were thus tied together in a patriarchal web which demanded filial obedience, scrupulous honesty, and hard work from the underlings. The patriarch held his trading family together by the usual mixture of the stick—summary dismissal and beatings were not unusual—and the carrot—the prospect of sharing in profits and climbing the ladder. In Francesco di Marco Datini's company, all were expected to adhere to the vision of life summarized in these words at the top of the ledgers: "In the name of God and profit."[104]

A capital market developed in the Italian trading communities. At its base were pawnbrokers and petty moneylenders. Above these usurers there were respectable money changers who regulated currency and detected counterfeit coins. At the top of the financial world were the bankers, financiers, and insurance agents whose business was regulated by complex accounting procedures which can be dated to the heady times of the thirteenth century.[105] While the Genoese archives are the most complete, it is the impression of historians that they disclose common practices of a commercial culture of capital accumulation. Although our sources are silent, it seems likely that, from a very early date, a distinct class of lenders came to exist alongside the pioneering merchants who adventured across the seas

103. Origo, *The Merchant of Prato*, 109.
104. Origo, *The Merchant of Prato*, 114–18, 9.
105. European credit and banking activities were comparatively retarded compared to those prevailing in Islamic culture and Chinese society. For an illuminating discussion, see Abu-Lughod, *Before European Hegemony, passim*. For a detailed account of one capitalist's activities in the realm of exchange, see Origo, *The Merchant of Prato*, esp. 146 ff.

in search of profit. Instruments and the creation of a scribal literacy in notarial skills suggest that early modern capitalism created its own financial culture. There was, then, a drift toward both long-term partnerships and a crude form of investment banking. It may be somewhat anachronistic to use contemporary terms to describe the practices followed seven hundred years ago, but how else can we make sense of the financial innovations which led Italian merchants to maintain branch offices across the face of Europe? This would have been impossible without technical efficiency in bookkeeping, scribal literacy, delegation of authority, communication through the post, and the legal recognition of bills of exchange.

The riches of the Italian mercantile cities grew by leaps and bounds. Genoa might have been the second city of Italian commerce, but its tax revenues in 1292 were about seven times higher than those calculated for the French monarchy during the reign of Philip Augustus in the early thirteenth century.[106] In 1292, Paris had banking representatives from more than twenty major Italian merchant companies; they paid 10 percent of the tax which Philip the Fair collected in Paris although they numbered less than 1 percent of the taxpayers.[107] In the early fifteenth century, the Venetian state budget was, on a per capita basis, seven times that of the French monarchy.[108] These comparative statistics—shards of light in a sea of darkness—tend to overestimate wealth, but they do give us a sense of proportion. So, too, does a consideration of crude statistics of population densities: the territory of Florence was twice as densely populated as the Paris Basin in the early fourteenth century; Lombardy supported even greater numbers per unit of land; and Genoa, quite completely the creation of trade and commerce, based its operations from a coastal city with a tiny hinterland backed up against "a screen of barren mountains,"[109] while Venice, standing serenely on stilts in its lagoon, was the largest and richest city in thirteenth-century Europe.

Italians synchronized a huge trading system that stretched from the British Isles in the northeast to the Orient. Notarial accounts in the extensive Genoese archives suggest that between 1154 and 1205 cloth exports gradually displaced Sudanese gold imported from the Maghreb as the principal item of export to the Levant.[110] The northern terminal point on this

---

106. Lopez, "The Trade of Medieval Europe: The South," 314–15.
107. Lopez, "The Trade of Medieval Europe: The South," 71–72.
108. Braudel, *The Perspective of the World*, 119–21.
109. A French diplomatic report quoted in Braudel, *The Perspective of the World*, 157.
110. E. H. Byrne, "Genoese Trade with Syria in the Twelfth Century," *American Historical Review* 25 (1919): 191–219.

trade axis was the annual cycle of fairs and markets in the counties of Champagne and Flanders. These events were central to the international commercial activity of the Western world because they enabled the Italians to acquire northern cloths—the primary industrial product—which they then distributed throughout the Mediterranean world. The counts of Champagne and Flanders and, later, the kings of France benefited immensely from the expanding volume of trade in their domains. Their incomes reflected the advantages they could acquire by pacifying their territories to make them safe for business.

The earliest documentation relating to the Champagne Fairs dates from 1114, by which time these commercial sites were already in full bloom. Six major fairs were held over the course of the year in four towns: a summer and fall fair in Troyes, a May and autumn fair in Provins, another in Lagny near Paris, and one at Bar-sur-Aube. Other smaller towns had lesser trade meetings: Bar-sur-Seine, Châlons-sur-Marne, Château-Thierry, Nogent, Rheims, Vitry, Tonnerre, Sézanne, St. Florentin, La Ferté Gaucher, Ervy, Méry-sur-Seine, and Ramerput. In reorganizing the map of Europe, commercial routes cut across political boundaries. In the thirteenth century, the dominance of the French fairs was challenged and superseded by the Flemish rivals, another cycle of six meetings spread across the whole year, which offered Italian merchants closer contact with the source of cloth manufacturing.[111]

In both France and the Low Countries there is evidence of evolution from market trading at the fairs to merchant banking and consignment wholesaling in main centers such as Paris and Bruges. By the later thirteenth century, the fairs had become predominantly financial meetings where periodic settlements could be negotiated. This development cycle—from fairground buying and selling to an infinite variety of more complex arrangements—was a feature of these northwestern circuits of trade as well as the central European trading systems which were to concentrate in Frankfurt and Leipzig.[112] Further north, the Hanseatic merchants successfully banded together to keep the Italians out of the Baltic staple trade. Their success did not thwart the intrusion of oriental spices and luxury goods into this part of the continent so much as giving them the profits from acting as middlemen.

111. J. A. van Houtte, "The Rise and Decline of the Market of Bruges," *Economic History Review*, 2d ser., 19 (1966): 29–47; Herman Van der Wee, "Structural Changes and Specialization in the Industry of the Southern Netherlands."

112. O. Verlinden, "Markets and Fairs," in Postan, Rich, and Miller (eds.), *Cambridge Economic History of Europe*, vol. 3, 126–134, 142–44.

The Italians' trade hegemony during the first cycle of early modernization was dependent upon their ability to connect consumers spread across a vast expanse of land and sea. Costs rose abruptly in relation to land distances. Crossing the Alps remained labor intensive. Pack trains of mules strained alongside human porters. Wheeled transport was impossible. Convenience was the paramount consideration, so the higher passes (Mont Genèvre [1,825 meters], Great St. Bernard [2,433 meters], and Mont Cenis [2,068 meters]) were used most often before 1250. Later, the Septimer, St. Gotthard, and Brenner passes gained in popularity. Therefore, most of the trade along the Italian/Flemish corridor bears witness to an increase in the number of trips more than any improvements in efficiency. The control of space was at the heart of the issue. There would be commercial advantages to political centralization because long-distance trade involved the movement of luxury goods which were obviously attractive to robbers. Routes became safer, but in exchange, some were burdened with an amazing variety of tolls and customs: for example, the Rhine alone had nineteen tolls around 1200, thirty-five in 1300, fifty in 1400, and sixty in 1500.[113]

While mastering commercial transactions which spread across vast stretches of territory, the Italians also tried to conquer distance. The quickening pace of maritime trade led to the substitution of small, coast-hugging sailing ships with galleys, manned by large crews of oarsmen and improved with stern post rudders, lateen sails for beating into the wind, and more efficient construction techniques which went some way toward balancing these larger vessels in heavy seas. In 1277 the Italian merchants began to sail through Gibraltar, directly to their markets in the northwest. Waterborne transport was both more efficient and faster than overland routes, but even the Genoese, who pioneered open-ocean sailing, were careful to stay out of the North Atlantic during the stormy winter months. Early voyages were incremental steps forward in the conquest of space. They were evidence of the embryonic development of what would later develop into a revolution in maritime transportation.[114]

113. Gerald A. J. Hodgett, *A Social and Economic History of Medieval Europe* (London, 1972), 107–9.

114. By the fifteenth century, 8,000 tons of goods were being shipped annually through Gibraltar—three-quarters in Genoese ships and the rest in Venetian ones; P. Chaunu, *European Expansion in the Later Middle Ages* (Amsterdam, 1979), 82. For a discussion of the reasons for the Italian monopoly over the trade from the Mediterranean to the North Atlantic, see Archibald Lewis, "Northern European Sea Power and the Straits of Gibraltar, 1031–1350 A.D.," reprinted in *The Sea and Medieval Civilization* (London, 1978).

In yet another contrast with the ancient world, where the high cost of overland transport isolated inland areas, the early modern social organization crisscrossed the countryside with microlevel exchange networks. Roads—sometimes impassable in wet weather—connected producers with suppliers. Commodities were transported along these deeply rutted tracks with carts and wagons which were deceptively complex to build.[115] On the many slow-flowing rivers of northwestern Europe, barges were used to transport bulky commodities at a much lower cost than land transport offered.[116] The supply of grains to Flanders provides the preeminent example of waterborne transportation networks. As early as 1200 this region was crisscrossed with canals that brought grain from northern France, whose entire agrarian economy was geared to supplying the large, urban Flemish market.[117] In England, too, the rivers were used to transport bulk commodities, while roads and bridges were developed rather more for their governmental benefits to itinerant kings and their mobile agents than for their economic value in creating a transportation infrastructure.[118] Overland grain shipments fell to one-third of their fourth-century level by 1500, mostly as a result of exploiting the river networks of northwestern Europe.[119] It is of the greatest significance that there were few equivalents to this riverine trade available in the Mediterranean basin, which, with the notable exception of the Po Valley in Northern Italy, lacked navigable river

115. For a very evocative, albeit anachronistic, discussion of the activities involved in making farm wagons, carts, and implements, see George Sturt, *The Wheelwright's Shop* (Cambridge, 1963). One presumes that many of the procedures described by Sturt were themselves the product of slow technical evolution; nonetheless, his discussion of the attachment of spokes into felloes smacks of the timber framer's mortise and tenon joinery.

116. Even as late as 1800, a box of tools could be shipped across the Atlantic for significantly less than it cost to transport that box from New York to East Hampton, at the northern tip of Long Island. Or, as a United States Senate committee reported in 1816, "a ton of goods could be brought 3,000 miles from Europe to America for about nine dollars but . . . for the same sum it could be moved only about 30 miles overland in this country,"; quoted in Charles Hummel, *The Hammer in Hand* (Charlottesville, Va., 1968), 33.

117. Nicholas, "Of Poverty and Primacy," 27–28, 33.

118. F. M. Stenton, "The Road System of Medieval England,"*Economic History Review* 7 (1936): 1–21.

119. While national markets were still in the future, the grain trade became extralocal: "The extreme disparity between the price of corn in Poland and Sicily, or between the gold-silver ratio in Lisbon and Bohemia, was slowly reduced"; Fossier, "General Conclusions," in *The Cambridge Illustrated History of the Middle Ages*, 521. It is important to avoid telescoping developments; as late as 1500, there were fifteen separate regional systems in England and Wales; Robert Dodgshon, *The European Past: Spatial Evolution and Spatial Order* (London, 1987), 205, 219.

systems featuring tranquil currents and a predictable stream of water throughout the whole year.

Small-scale commerce was a matter of local staple exchange which reflected new methods of organizing space connected with the improved flexibility of transport technology. Local markets sprouted up in response to the profusion of small, wage-earning households and the developing division of labor that was mediated by monetary transactions.[120] If we look beyond the statutorily chartered markets and towns of this time, we see that commercial relations gave even small settlements (of under 2,000) urban characteristics and a complex division of labor. "Even the smallest places had food traders (bakers, butchers, fishmongers), craftsmen in textiles, clothing, leather, and metal, building workers, and those providing services such as innkeepers and musicians." Christopher Dyer suggests that this hidden dimension included towns and potential towns lacking burgage tenurial arrangement, trading centers on marginal sites, trading places at administrative centres, suburban villages, country inns, ports, and crossroads, as well as unregulated fairs and markets with their informal shops and stalls.[121]

4.

The Carolingian archipelago was transformed by marketing relations that resulted from the increasing velocity of circulation. Both at the Braudelian heights of international commerce and at the roadside marketplaces that proliferated to service local customers, exchange permeated the social fabric.[122] The growing network of towns, markets, manufactures, officials, and regulations combined to effect a qualitative transformation in social rela-

120. R. H. Britnell, "The Proliferation of Markets in England, 1200–1349," *Economic History Review,* 2d ser., 34 (1981): 213–21.

121. "The Hidden Trade of the Middle Ages: Evidence from the West Midlands of England," *Journal of Historical Geography* 18 (1992): 141–57.

122. Saying this, however, does not mean that trade was particularly important in the so-called Dark Ages. These centuries were dominated by the disintegration of the old system which was taking place before the reintegration of the new one after the year 1000. What is at issue, therefore, is not simply the velocity of circulating money but rather the role that monetary transactions—taxation, rental payments, and exchange relations—played in the lives of the mass of the population. Seen in this perspective, economic relations during the Dark Ages were *comparatively* autarkic and the population was spatially confined. Indeed, M. M. Postan long ago taught us that the notion of a "natural economy," making do without money, was quite unhelpful, see "The Rise of a Money Economy," in *Essays on Medieval Agriculture and General Problems of the Medieval Economy* (Cambridge, 1973), 28–40.

tions. It is anachronistic to speak of a "capitalist market economy" when a large part of the population was enmeshed in feudal social relations. When we turn our focus to the virtually uncharted domestic mode of production of the medieval peasant *oikos*, however, it becomes apparent that the household deployed its own labor in complex ways that corresponded to its particular interests and skills, sex ratio, and age structure. The household also was, in many places, interpenetrated by the supervening demands of the manorial economy.[123] We thus would be well advised to avoid the temptation of going overboard and describing early modern society in thirteenth-century England as a "capitalist market-economy without factories."[124]

POSITIVE FEEDBACKS

For the first ten generations who lived after the year 1000, the interplay between climatic trends, population growth, land clearance, novel forms of energy substitution, and the creation of new forms of production combined to create a virtuous circle of growth and development. A fourfold increase in population occurred between 1000 and 1300; at the same time, a higher percentage of these people were fed better, clothed better, and housed better. These "positive feedbacks" featured not only a radical expansion of settlement patterns in the northern and western parts of Europe but also a transformation in the relationship between the ancient Mediterranean core and the northwestern periphery. By the fourteenth century, this long secular boom had created a bipolar social system in Europe: the Mediterranean core was now balanced by a northwestern counterpart. This spatial reorganization had enormous implications for the internal structure of European society and set the stage for the globalism that took place when recovery from the Black Death got under way in the fifteenth century.

While the Roman Empire was declining and falling, population shrinkage and social instability accompanied a regression of the influence of both urban civilization and agricultural activity. "Much of the rural world . . . was successively abandoned or, more precisely, slowly emptied of its population: here more rapidly, there more slowly, each region following a rhythm determined by its soil, its climate, the routes of invaders, and the

123. M. Patricia Hogan, "The Labor of Their Days—Work in the Medieval Village," *Studies in Medieval and Renaissance History*, new ser., 8 (1989): 77–186.

124. Alan Macfarlane, *The Origins of English Individualism* (Oxford, 1978), 196.

vectors of bacteria." The end of antiquity coincided with "a thinning of the *rural* world."[125] As we have already seen, the urban civilization of Roman antiquity literally disintegrated, with catastrophic implications for these population centers. The Dark Ages saw a reduction in population from Roman levels to its nadir of about twenty-six million in A.D. 700 in the wake of the Justinian pandemic.[126]

Rather than wringing our hands over the loss of ancient civilization, however, it is vitally important to recognize that

> When the empire collapsed it released the tax-paying millions of western Europe from a paralyzing oppression. . . . What was loss to the empire and to those who served it was gain to everyone else. The resources now retained for personal consumption presumably enabled the ordinary peasants of western Europe to live better than they had done before, and by living better presumably to live longer. . . . Districts which had once been little more than military cantonments and colonial outposts, regions where sparse communities had once led a gypsy life of subsistence husbandry by making temporary clearances in the encircling forest and scrub and moving on when the soil was spent, had evolved by the early Middle Ages into centres of political power and cultural ascendancy.[127]

Much the same point is made by Chris Wickham, who argues that in any preindustrial society, "the richer the civilization, the greater the exploitation of the producer: the equation can be refined, but its base is as simple as that. The overall level and sophistication of material culture declined *because* the peasantry were better off."[128] Similarly, Klaus Randsborg writes: "The picture of the barbarian as the destroyer of civilization should rather be turned on its head. The classical societies set up divisions, between the peoples of Europe, and the developing strength of the advanced cultures thus had an inbuilt inertia" as well as having "negative consequences for the societies with which the classical world came into contact."[129] In other words, antiquity was a social dead end.

125. F. Cheyette, "The Origins of European Villages and the First European Expansion," *Journal of Economic History* 37 (1977): 197.

126. For a very general survey of population levels, see Colin McEvedy and Richard Jones, *Atlas of World Population History* (Harmondsworth, 1978), 19–26.

127. A. R. Bridbury, "The Dark Ages," *Economic History Review*, 2d ser., 22 (1969): 533.

128. Chris Wickham, "Italy and the Early Middle Ages," in *Land and Power* (London, 1994), esp. 114–15.

129. "Barbarians, Classical Antiquity and the Rise of Western Europe: An Archaeological Essay," *Past and Present* 137 (1992): 15.

After 700 the growth cycle slowly began to reassert itself. The most commonly believed estimates suggest that the Roman level was once more attained by the year 1000. It is thought that the European total was about eighty million in the early fourteenth century.[130] J. C. Russell suggests that there were rather lower levels for the total population in western and central Europe (not including the Mediterranean) at the seventh-century nadir, when the trans-Alpine population totaled 5.5 million, but then there were rather faster rates of growth. Russell further suggests that by the year 1000 there were 12 million in western and central Europe. This total trebled to 35.5 million in 1340.[131] In contrast to Russell's estimate of a northern and central European population of 5.5 million c. 700, Braudel suggests that the population of Gaul (i.e., France) was "between 7.5 and 9 million" at the time of Charlemagne, while the Carolingian Empire "may have contained between 15 and 18 million inhabitants." Braudel also claims that the long cycle of demographic growth began around 950, but he seems to discount the suggestion that there was a tripling by the early fourteenth century since he believes that the 1328 *État des paroisses et des feux* "reported the French population as about 20 million."[132] A very much more pessimistic view of population growth rates after the year 1000 is put forward by A. R. Bridbury, who claims that "We seem to be driven to the conclusion that the population of England, in the age of Domesday, far from preparing itself for a mighty surge forward, had in fact by then more or less stabilised its numbers. . . . Massive population growth was a phenomenon that belonged to an altogether earlier period."[133] Bridbury seems to be alone in this opinion, however; all other scholars I have consulted regard the growth of population after the year 1000—in England and continental Europe—as a matter of fact.

---

130. McEvedy and Jones, *Atlas of World Population History*, 19–26.

131. *Late Ancient and Medieval Population Control* (Philadelphia, 1985), 36. I concur with his sense of trend—slow growth from c. 700 to the year 1000 and then three centuries of much more substantial demographic expansion. My own guesstimate, however, is that Russell's totals are far too low, especially for the period from around the year 1000 to the decades leading up to the Black Death. Furthermore, Russell—like so many others—seems to be trapped by the "unthinkability" that the early modern population's growth rates after the year 1000 or its total size in 1300 could not have been greater than—or even as great as—what has been documented for the first phase of the classic Industrial Revolution.

132. Fernand Braudel, *The Identity of France*, vol. 2, *People and Production* (London, 1990), 123, 137

133. "The Domesday Valuation of Manorial Income," in *The English Economy from Bede to the Reformation*, 124.

1.

Most authorities agree that after the year 1000 there were three centuries of absolute growth to which the north and west of Europe contributed disproportionately. The center of gravity shifted because Mediterranean Europe does not seem to have been anything like as prolific as the population north of the Alps. One key reason for this geographical shift of population distribution was that the colonization of the trans-Alpine forests, wastelands, hillsides, marshes, fens, and polders radically *magnified* the usable land mass in northwestern Europe. Settled villages and cooperative systems of crop rotation gradually replaced an itinerant existence. Rural society in the period of transition from late antiquity to early modernization was located on the edge of the wilderness. Braudel provides a valuable corrective when he writes, "one should dismiss the image often suggested in the past of Gaul under the Carolingians as made up essentially of tiny territorial units, self-contained islands imprisoned within 'the massively expanding forests, all-invading wastelands, heaths, and moors.' " He goes overboard, however, when he then writes "it was actually thronged with itinerants, wandering preachers, monks whom the poorer abbeys had had to send away, rebellious serfs—for the peasant revolt was still rumbling—pilgrims, soldiers and traders."[134]

For contemporaries, "wasteland" denoted any region outside the surveillance of civilization, rather than unused or useless land. Men and women who lived in groups represented one social tendency; those who lived in solitude represented its antithesis. The ancient contrast between city and country (*urbs* and *rus* in Roman usage) was replaced by that between nature and culture. What was built, cultivated, and inhabited (city, castle, and village) stood opposed to what was essentially wild. The ocean and forest were the northwestern equivalents of the eastern desert.[135]

The word "forest" had its own peculiar juridical meaning, which began to be recorded in the three centuries after 650. "Forest" was land reserved

134. *Identity of France*, vol. 2, *People and Production*, 121–22. Note how Braudel employs his rhetorical flourish. One has only to ask, how many "itinerants, wandering preachers, monks whom the poorer abbeys had had to send away, rebellious serfs . . . pilgrims, soldiers and traders"? Obviously, these colorful characters could not—and did not—represent more than a fraction of the total population. Thus, is it not impossible for the older vision of population island—dismissed so backhandedly by Braudel—to have coexisted with the trading networks he seems to favor? It should also be noted that "rebellious serfs" means rebellious slaves and not, as might be thought, servile tenants, as would be the case in the later usage of this term.

135. Jacques Le Goff, "The Wilderness in the Medieval West," in Le Goff, *The Medieval Imagination* (Chicago, 1988), 47–59.

for the king's hunting privileges. The history of these hunting rights mirrors the development of powers over property. Furthermore, "forests" did not have to be woodland—in fact, most "forests" were only partly wooded.[136] Even before large-scale land clearances, the forests were an integral part of the rural economy. How much of Europe was covered in woodlands? The best guesses seem to be that perhaps two-thirds of what we now call Germany, c. 500, was wooded, but only only 15 percent of England in 1066; France seems to fallen somewhere in between these two figures, while Italy had perhaps more woodland than our contemporary perceptions would suggest.[137]

Woodlands provided resources that complemented the rural economy of the village. Their natural products were reprocessed in an organic economy. Wood-pasture districts, which had extensive rights of common (lands not yet defined by private property rights), attracted settlers because they provided the fuel and raw materials for industrial by-employments. The woodland population consisted of "huntsmen, charcoal-burners, blacksmiths, gatherers of wax and wild honey, . . . dealers in wood-ash, which was important in the manufacture of glass and soap, and barkstrippers, whose wares were used for tanning hides or could be plaited to make cords."[138] Huntsmen not only supplied animal protein—large animals like bears, deer, wild boars, wildcats, and wolves; smaller animals like beavers, foxes, hares, martens, otters, and squirrels; a wide variety of wildfowl such as species of bustards, cranes, curlews, ducks, finches, geese, gulls, herons, larks, partridges, pheasants, pigeon, plover, quail, snipe, swan, teal, thrush, and woodcocks; and crustaceans, eels, fish, and frogs from the streams—but also hides for use in tanneries and in the bookbinderies of monastic libraries.

Wood was the building material *par excellence*. Timber was also valuable for heating, lighting, and toolmaking. Twigs and shoots were harvested to supply sticks, wattles, fencing materials, vine poles, materials for weaving and knotting—baskets, crates, and all sorts of containers—tools, handles, and, of course, firewood. Charcoal was needed to forge iron implements. Clay deposits were vital for brickmaking and pottery. Peasants shod themselves in primitive footwear or clogs (*sabots*) fashioned from solid wood. The vegetation of the woodlands supplied mosses and dried leaves

136. Chris Wickham, "European Forests in the Early Middle Ages: Landscape and Land Clearance," in *Land and Power*, 158–62.

137. Wickham, "European Forests," 169, 173.

138. Jean Birrell, "Peasant Craftsmen in the Medieval Forest," *Agricultural History Review* 17 (1969): 91–107; quotation from p. 97.

for bedding. Ferns, fungi, herbs, plants, seeds, and wildflowers were employed as pharmaceuticals. Beechmast provided oil. Wild fruit trees—apple, pear, cherry, and plum—were often grafted onto orchard stocks to improve their genetic characteristics. Above all, the forests were the grazing ground for livestock. Indeed, "the commonest way of indicating the size of a stretch of forest was by reference to the number of pigs it could sustain." Fresh leaves, young shoots, grass in the undergrowth, wild mushrooms, herbs and truffles, chestnuts, acorns, and beechmast were all valuable resources in an economy which devoted almost all its efforts at cereal cultivation to feeding people.[139]

Communities without access to woods had great difficulty in feeding their domesticated animals. In contrast, villagers living next to woodlands benefited from their resources. The forest was only one frontier; watery marshes, barren heaths, and high rugged mountains were also beyond the pale of "civilized" human settlement during the Dark Ages in northwestern Europe. The Carolingian population huddled into islands of settlement in a sea of "wilderness." The ancient inheritance of Gallo-Roman, Celtic, and Germanic agriculture had prized thin, sandy soils that were easily drained and could be worked with scratch plows. Thus, the barbarian population concentrated on the higher ground and usually left the valleys untouched.

The barbarians' descendants were pioneers. They colonized the wilderness. Wastelands were encroached upon by a hungry population whose nibbling at the margins altered the ecology of the countryside. The largely undocumented introduction of the iron-flanged, moldboard plow was the key to the spatial transfer of agricultural production. This was accompanied by the Carolingian shift from the thin, sandy loess soils to the heavy clay lands of the river valleys.[140]

The rural landscape's layout became randomly ordered into asymmetrical blocks. Even the image of a kaleidoscope is misleading because it suggests too much spatial regularity. The rural landscape had the unpredictable appearance of a multidimensional crazy quilt. Natural factors interacted with social forces: some land was fertile, other land was acidic and barren; some land was flat, other land was mountainous; some land was easily worked, other land was not; some land was free-draining, other land was

---

139. Marc Bloch, *French Rural History* (Berkeley and Los Angeles, 1970), 5–8. See also Wickham, "European Forests," 184–87.

140. Walter Janssen, "Some Major Aspects of Frankish and Medieval Settlement," in P. H. Sawyer (ed.), *Medieval Settlement: Continuity and Change* (London, 1976), 49.

waterlogged; some land possessed several feet of topsoil, other land was sandy or rocky; some land received adequate rainfall, other land was arid; some land was encumbered with onerous feudal exactions, other land was essentially free; some land was worked plantation style, in large farms, other land was minutely subdivided into dwarf-holdings; some land was intensively cultivated for commercial exchanges, other land was worked extensively for use values; some land had supported human settlements for countless generations, other land was reclaimed from its primeval state; some land was devoted exclusively to cereal monoculture, other land was pastoral so that sheep and cattle outnumbered men and women; and some land was densely populated, other land was deserted. These layered images of synchronic variety must be set alongside a picture of diachronic change, change that was driven by the increase of human numbers and the growing complexity of economic activities.

The population archipelago of the Carolingian era gradually extended to form an almost complete overlay of humanity. In many places, mixed husbandry gave way to monoculture based on cereals. One line of explanation would privilege the introduction of new forms of technology which "pulled" the reluctant peasants into the world of harnesses and plows. Another interpretation would suggest that population growth in the little Carolingian islands forced desperate people to seek a calorie-maximizing strategy and, in so doing, "pushed" them into the hands of the lords as they experienced ever-greater dependence on cereals.[141] It would be wrong to equate social progress with cereal farming because the historical record seems to point in the opposite direction—cereal monoculture was usually the hallmark of a socially polarized system in which the overwhelming mass of the population was ruthlessly exploited for the benefit of a few secular and priestly rulers.

The grip of famine was tighter in the age of Charlemagne (768–814) than it would be in the forty-six years after the accession of Hugh Capet (987–1033). In Charlemagne's forty-six years there were eight years of *fames praevalida, maxima, horrida,* or *crudelissima*—great famines that were said to have been accompanied by starvation and even cannibalism—while in the period of early Capetian rule there were only three.[142] It would be misleading, however, to consider that some miraculous rescue occurred with the onset of the new millennium. In fact, the early-middle decades of

141. Wickham, "European Forests," 196.
142. P. Bonnassie, "From One Servitude to Another: The Peasantry of the Frankish Kingdom at the Time of Hugh Capet and Robert the Pious (987–1031)," in *From Slavery to Feudalism in South-western Europe* (Cambridge, 1991), 291–92.

the eleventh century were particularly horrific. The population of France suffered from ten general famines in the tenth century, whereas there were twenty-six in the eleventh century. The twelfth century, however, was markedly better; there were only two national dearths.[143] This line of argument suggests that there was a slow, incremental improvement in grain yields. Georges Duby reckons that there was an average return on seed of 2:1 for cereal crops around the year 1000. Average yields had been even lower in Carolingian France so that any shortfall would have meant that the rural population was almost immediately brought face to face with the dilemma of eating or saving its seed-corn.[144]

But people do not eat averages. The key point is not so much the average yield as the likelihood that in any particular year there will not be a crop failure. Thus, the first stages of the conquest of the material world involved the creation of a safety net which could support a growing population without springing the Malthusian trap. In part this was the product of new technologies, and in part it involved the shift from slavery to feudalism. The immense colonization movement which spread settled rural civilizations from the Carolingian population archipelagoes across the length and breadth of northwestern Europe was in large part the achievement of countless anonymous peasants who were responding to the carrot of frontier land as well as the stick of downward social mobility in the long-settled manorial centers.

This process largely took place outside the purview of the documentary record. Historians have identified it with the breakup of the large Carolingian estates and the initiatives of the free peasantry

> who, in their struggle against hunger, cleared forests, drained marshes, terraced hillsides, ploughed virgin lands and improved their tools and cultural practices. The peasant allod [i.e., freehold land carved from the waste] was even the site of the most complex technical innovations. . . . [T]hey were burdened with rents proportionate to the crop; the lords taxed the fruits of labour. . . . These processes of agrarian expansion were clearly in total contradiction to the slave system. They assumed a highly mobile labour force which had to be established far from the estate centres, where assarting was taking place. They implied that the initiative had in the main to be left to the actual cultivators, who were extremely difficult to control on holdings which retained only the most tenuous links with the *curtis* (or what remained of it). They required,

143. Braudel, *The Structures of Everyday Life,* 74.
144. Georges Duby, *Rural Economy and Country Life in the Medieval West* (London, 1968), 22–27.

in fact, a transformation of the servile labour force which could only be achieved through enfranchisement.[145]

Pierre Bonnassie suggests that there was a "privileged moment" around the year 1000 when

> society was free (juridically) from any form of servitude, where the tendency was towards a total emancipation of the peasant class. But this situation was intolerable for the ruling class, who reacted extremely violently by the imposition of the *seigneurie banale*, that is the imposition on this free peasantry (anciently or recently free) of radically new burdens which the documents call "exactions, new usages, new customs, bad usages, bad customs" . . . transforming the descendants of the free peasantry of the year 1000 into *manants*, villeins, or worse, into *hommes propres* and *hommes de corps*, in brief, into serfs.[146]

Our focus changes somewhat when we consider how local demographic growth took place *alongside* massive population movements after the year 1000 in eastern Germany and the East Elbian frontier peopled by Germans. The population of Saxony increased by a factor of ten between 1100 and 1300; outside Germany, perhaps 200,000 emigrants had moved to the Slav lands east of the Elbe by 1200; in the next century, an even larger number followed them in this eastward migration.[147] In Silesia, *ostsiedlung* (eastward migration) led to the creation of 120 towns and 1,200 villages; in Pomerania, the numbers were different but the overall thrust of German colonization produced a new society that replicated the institutions of the old core.[148]

The breakdown of central authority—in particular, the period of electoral "antikingship" in the first half of the twelfth century—was crucial for Germans. Colonization was often spurred by the intensive exploitation—and extension—of rights of lordship by nobles and clerical orders who struggled to break free from royal controls.[149] For the common people, the

---

145. Pierre Bonnassie, "The Survival and Extinction of the Slave System in the Early Medieval West (Fourth to Eleventh Centuries)," in *From Slavery to Feudalism in South-western Europe*, 45–46.

146. "The Survival and Extinction of the Slave System," 57–58.

147. Wilhelm Abel, *Agricultural Fluctuations in Europe from the Thirteenth to the Twentieth Centuries* (London, 1980), 28.

148. Robert Bartlett, *The Making of Europe* (Princeton, 1993), 297.

149. A relevant point is made by Frantisek Graus, who writes that

the ruler's retinue [was] the most important germ cell of the early medieval state. It was the prince's retinue that constituted his strength and formed the basis of his rule, not the mythical tribal contingent of free men on which nineteenth-century historians placed such stress. The allegiance owed by

colonization movements offered land without feudal ties or with only moderate forms of personal servitude, at the precise time when the burden of feudal exactions was increasing in the regions of old settlement. Peopling of the frontier went ahead with the aid of recruiting agents who acted as intermediaries between the landowning princes and the peasantry. Their role was crucial; without skilled agricultural labor the newly acquired lands were of little cash value because the native Slav population was not only thinly settled but also unfamiliar with early modern methods of cultivation.

Land settled, worked, and leased by Flemings, Hollanders, Frisians, Saxons, and other western migrants was governed by Germanic law which granted landlords a much higher rate of return than the Slavonic residents were expected to pay. Settling his lands with Germans enabled the Bishop of Gnesen to raise his rental income an astounding 800-fold. Another factor of no little importance was the discovery of rich ore deposits. By and large, Germans took the leading part in mining ventures, and the glitter of silver and other precious metals was one of the strongest attractions of the eastern frontier. From the discovery of silver just before the year 1000 at Rammelsberg in Saxony, the thickly wooded slopes and abundant streams in the valleys of the Eastern Alps, the Carpathians, the Erzgebirge, and the Sudeten Mountains provided a natural workshop for an industrial population. These people gained their livelihoods from digging into the earth, isolating the minerals from dirt, preparing ores for the smelters by purifying them, and then converting these ores into metals.[150]

German settlers "won" new land which was recovered from the waste. They brought with them not only new implements (such as the heavy felling axe and the iron-flanged, moldboard plow) but also new knowledge gained from the earlier colonization of their native lands. The cultivated area was massively extended, and its productivity was radically increased. New social relations were introduced. In place of the indigenous system of communal exploitation of the land based on serfdom and slavery, the Germans territorialized social relations, individualizing ownership and responsibility. Burdens were attached to a determinate piece of land, al-

the retainers to the ruler differed considerably according to circumstances, as did the forms of recompense of the vassals—but here again racial factors were not of fundamental significance. What was decisive was the way the retinue was organized and the way in which the vassals became members of the medieval aristocracy. ("Slavs and Germans," in Geoffrey Barraclough [ed.], *Eastern and Western Europe in the Middle Ages* [London, 1971], 38)

150. John U. Nef, "Mining and Metallurgy in Medieval Civilisation," in M. M. Poston and E. E. Rich (eds.), *The Cambridge Economic History of Europe*, vol. 2 (Cambridge, 1963), 435–38.

though at this time the immigrant German peasants as well as the Slav natives were personally free.[151]

The Germans' "colonizing fever" moved forward on a broad front although, to be sure, it proceeded irregularly. The southern frontier was settled first. By 1350 the movement was largely played out when its original source of labor was reduced by the plague. East Elbia had a primitive economy around the year 1000; as a result of the German colonizing movement it was crisscrossed with communications routes, commercial networks, and urban communities. Bulk commodities—furs, timber, pitch, tar, resin, grain, and metals—were floated down the rivers to the Baltic. German Hanseatic communities—Lübeck, Wismar, Rostock, Stettin, and Danzig—sprang up along the coast while smaller distributive centers emerged inland; both were studded with the warehouses and exchanges of a mercantile population who traded the staples of eastern and central Europe for the salt from the Bay of Biscay and finished cloth from Flanders and Brabant.[152] The hinterland, of course, was connected with these commercial centers that transmitted "economic Germanization" into the Slavic heartlands. In the first two centuries of colonization, Germans had created some 1,200 villages in Silesia and another 1,400 in east Prussia.

The Elbe had originally marked the eastern border of the old areas of Germanic settlement, the heartland of East Francia, between the Rhine and the Elbe. In these original areas of settlement the rights of farmers were firmly anchored in *Weistümer* (legal codes and customary rules). These agreements between the lord and "his" *Gemeinde* (village community) arose in the conditions of massive feudalization that developed from the later part of the eleventh century. If we look at this process only from the top down, from the point of view of the lords' extension of powers, we miss an essential element of it—namely, the opportunity for self-organization that it afforded to the local community within the confines of new techniques of political and material organization.[153]

151. H. Aubin, "Medieval Agrarian Society in Its Prime: The Lands East of the Elbe and German Colonization Eastwards," in M. M. Postan (ed.), *The Cambridge Economic History of Europe*, vol. 1 (Cambridge, 1966), 482.

152. Postan, "Economic Relations between Eastern and Western Europe," in G. Barraclough (ed.), *Eastern and Western Europe in the Middle Ages*, 144–47, 156–65; see also Postan, "The Trade of Medieval Europe: The North," in Postan and Rich (eds.), *The Cambridge Economic History of Europe*, vol. 2, 119–56. It is a remarkable fact that the bow-staves used by the English archers at the battle of Crécy in 1346 were fashioned from wood from the Carpathian mountains that had been shipped from eastern Hungary through Prussia and the Baltic ports (125).

153. Our understanding of the self-government of the peasant community is largely read backward from a later period; it is understood to have emerged from

2.

Human settlement patterns were also at the mercy of the weather. Especially in the north and west of Europe, the usable land mass itself was subject to a natural process of expansion (when it was warmer and drier) and contraction (when it became wetter and colder). During favorable times, grain was grown in Iceland and vines were planted in both England and Poland. Analysis of the Fernau glacier in the Tyrolian Alps indicates that from 750 until about 1215 the European climate became both warmer and drier. Then, from their high point in 1215, the Alpine glaciers began to advance back down the slopes, which seems to indicate a combination of longer winters, heavier snowfalls, and cooler summers.[154] The effect of this "Little Climatic Optimum" was to extend temporarily the usable land mass, whereas the climatic reversal would have had precisely the opposite effect. However, we must be careful to keep in mind that even if 1215 marks the turning point from a warming trend to a cooling one, the thirteenth century population was still largely living under the influence of the "Little Climatic Optimum."

It took a century or more for long-term changes in climate to have a perceptible impact on human lives. It was only after 1300 that climatic changes became significant. Then, in the space of a few generations, northern and western Europe was to become as much as four degrees colder. The frontier for cultivation moved southward. In hilly and mountainous regions, altitudinal limits for fruit, grains, and vine crops fell. Along the northwest coast, the North Sea encroached on the polders which had been reclaimed during the colonizing movements of the preceding two centuries. In the twelfth- and thirteenth-century boom times peasants were able to eke out a living on these marginal lands, but when the frontiers of cultivation receded this ground quite literally disappeared beneath them.

Climatic shifts increased the likelihood of two consecutive crop failures seventyfold, from once in seven hundred years to once in ten. A particularly telling example of the variable impact of climatic change on human ecology comes from the abandoned farms of the Lammermuir Hills in southern Scotland, where 4,890 hectares of land, 400 meters above sea

---

the disintegration of classic manorial modes of production and their replacement with indirect forms of exploitation. For a useful—though synchronic—discussion of the underside of fiscal feudalism, see Jerome Blum, "The Internal Structure and Polity of the European Village Community from the Fifteenth to the Nineteenth Century," *Journal of Modern History* 46 (1974): 541–76.

154. H. H. Lamb, "Climate in Historical Times," in *Climate: Past, Present and Future* (London, 1977), 455 n.2.

level, were opened up for cultivation after 1150. In the heyday of this colonization it is estimated that the oat crop would have failed about once in twenty years. By 1350 the rate of failure would have been one year in five, while by 1450 it would have been one year in three.[155]

While there were exceptionally wet summers in the second decade of the fourteenth century, which had disastrous short-term consequences that were evidenced by giant spikes in European mortality statistics,[156] the great mass of the population on the North European Plain was not as hard hit by the trend toward cooler weather and shorter growing seasons as would be the case in hilly regions. These northern alpine zones had been heavily colonized in the earlier period of warming climate. Populations that had colonized marginal agrarian areas, like the Lammermuir Hills, found themselves subverted by the changing ecological conditions. The long-term worsening of the climate interacted with the short-term unpredictability of the weather to undermine the material base of their daily lives.

The implications of population growth in the eleventh, twelfth, and thirteenth centuries had linked the fates of millions of people to the colonization of marginal and even submarginal land.[157] In England, the greatest population growth in the eleventh, twelfth, and thirteenth centuries had taken place in the highland zone where "expansion was enormous: settlements starting from a very small base developed into quite large villages in the two hundred years after DB [Domesday Book]. In Staffordshire the growth was nine and a third times, in Herefordshire five times, in the East Riding [of Yorkshire] nine or ten times, in the North Riding between eleven and a half and thirteen a half times and in the West Riding three and a half times."[158]

155. Mark Bailey, "*Per Impetuum Maris:* Natural Disaster and Economic Decline in Eastern England, 1275–1350," in B. M. S. Campbell (ed.), *Before the Black Death* (Manchester, 1991), 184–208; M. L. Parry, "Evaluating the Impact of Climatic Change," in C. D. Smith and M. L. Parry (eds.), *Consequences of Climatic Change* (Nottingham, 1981), 12.

156. William Chester Jordan, *The Great Famine: Northern Europe in the Early Fourteenth Century* (Princeton, 1996), esp. 7–39.

157. E. Le Roy Ladurie, *Times of Feast, Times of Famine: A History of Climate since the Year 1000* (New York, 1971), *passim*.

158. H. C. Hallam, "Population Movements in England, 1086–1350," in H. C. Hallam (ed.), *The Agrarian History of England and Wales*, vol. 2, *1086–1350* (Cambridge, 1988), 510–11. These estimates are very rough guesses based on counting tenant numbers enumerated in the Domesday Book and comparing them with later manorial documents. It is a method that is subject to criticism on the grounds that it neglects subtenants and the landless while it is too blunt to detect

These calamities played themself out not only within the microecology of individual villages but also between regional systems of agricultural production which had been flattened into a rough homogeneity by the press of human numbers. Benefits that might have been enjoyed by a system of comparative advantage—adjusting production to the peculiarities of the local ecology and exchanging products through the marketplace—were only partially realized.[159] Because large amounts of land were devoted to the replication of homologous units of subsistence farming, based on the exploitation of resources in ways that were both ecologically negligent and economically inept, the benefits of commercialization were largely thwarted.

The marginal populations were caught on the horns of a dilemma: on one hand, their growing numbers had forced them to colonize bogs, fens, heaths, woodlands, and other rugged terrain; on the other hand, most of this land was unable to support intensive cultivation and was likely to be quickly exhausted, thereby leaving them exposed on the downward slide of diminishing returns. Studies on "deserted villages," once thought to have been caused by the Black Death, show that this process was already in train by the end of the thirteenth century.[160] In some districts, like the West Midlands in England, the expansion of village settlements had been so vigorous in the preceding generations that late thirteenth- and early fourteenth-century desertions could be seen as the "thinning out" of a countryside overstocked with villages.[161]

The growth of the population after the year 1000 had a deleterious impact on the environment: forests were cut down, thin soils were worn out, some regions became desertified, some land unsuitable for grain production became waterlogged, and flood disasters became more common. One example of this changing ecology is the forest cover of the mountainous

---

changes in the organization of the manors, which were often divided and sometimes amalgamated. See John Hatcher, "New Settlement: South-western England," in Hallam (ed.), *The Agrarian History of England and Wales*, vol. 2, *1086–1350*, 236. See also Bruce M. S. Campbell, "Laying Foundations," *Agricultural History Review* 37 (1989): 188–92, H. S. A. Fox, "Land, Labour and People, 1042–1350," *Journal of Historical Geography* 17 (1991): 457–64. The thrust of these criticisms, however, suggests that Hallam's count represents minimal estimates.

159. Mark Bailey, "The Concept of the Margin in the Medieval English Economy," *Economic History Review*, 2d ser., 42 (1989): 1–17. See also Jan Titow, "Lost Rents, Vacant Holdings and the Contraction of Peasant Cultivation after the Black Death," *Agricultural History Review* 42 (1994): 97–114.

160. Christopher Dyer, "New Settlement: The West Midlands," in Hallam (ed.), *The Agrarian History of England and Wales*, vol. 2, *1086–1350*, 232–34.

161. Christopher Dyer, "Deserted Medieval Villages in the West Midlands," *Economic History Review*, 2d ser., 35 (1982): 33.

Hercynian region, where, over a period of centuries of human occupation, the original deciduous forest of oak and beech, and its rich undergrowths, were "replaced by the sterile carapace of bark and needles from resinous trees." In this region, animals were driven out of their traditional foraging grounds and forced to seek pasturage elsewhere. The needs of these animals called forth innovations in husbandry—permanent pasture, hay meadows, and various modes of stall feeding.[162] The heyday of the "Little Climate Optimum" thus provided a window of opportunity, a window that began to close in the later thirteenth century.[163] In the interim, ten generations enjoyed the fruits of their labor during the best of times.

3.

During the period of optimum climatic conditions, land colonization and complex crop rotations significantly increased both the output and quality of the food supply. In our image of the mythic peasant, we envisage a plowman driving his team of oxen. The diffusion of the heavy iron plow enabled farmers to work dense clay soils of the North European Plain. Yet, as has been discovered from a close analysis of the historical record, the dominance of the ox team was neither complete nor timeless. Plows were originally drawn by teams of oxen, but in some places they came to be pulled by horses whose harness collars nearly doubled the oxen's efficiency and whose iron shoes radically increased their endurance.

Once again, the year 1000 seems to mark a turning point: after this time the horse gradually began to replace the heavier, slower, and stronger ox. There were two aspects to this process. First, the fragmentation of farming duties and the need for greater flexibility made the horse the animal of choice among peasants. Second, the versatility of the horse—which could be used for harrowing, plowing, riding, pack carrying, and haulage—enhanced its value. Iron-shod horses also contributed to increasing the efficiency of transportation even if their potential was limited by the terrible state of the roads. Horses made it possible to carry goods twice as far in half the time "with the net result that [the peasant's] range of operations would quadruple."[164] Carts and wagons became a more common sight; so, too,

---

162. Jean Chapelot and Robert Fossier, *The Village and House in the Middle Ages* (Berkeley and Los Angeles, 1985), 169.

163. Teresa Dunin-Wasowicz, "Climate as a Factor Affecting the Human Environment in the Middle Ages,"*Journal of European Economic History* 4 (1975): 691–706.

164. John Langdon, "Horse Hauling,"*Past and Present* 103 (1984): 62. On the estates of the Abbey of Peterborough the two animals existed in a complementary

were wheelbarrows in the fields and barnyards. The switch from oxen to horses made it possible to deepen the market by including more people and more activities in commercialized exchange.

The feedback mechanism at work between these processes is worth noting. At the outset of the feudal revolution, horses were used mainly for warfare and thus had to be "fiery," so it was essential that they be fed with oats, which were grown in three-field rotations on special types of rich, loamy soil (i.e., the Paris and Thames valleys). More horses enhanced the demand for blacksmiths, which in turn led to a proliferation of iron tools as the village smithy became a reality. Then, the spread of better tools enhanced productivity, thereby making it possible to effect a qualitative change in the character of peasant existence. It became preferable to clear the land rather than exploiting it in an updated form of slash-and-burn agriculture. In sum, the implications of these changes marked a transition from a modified type of post-Paleolithic hunting and gathering toward modern farming.

In fact, "For most people [living in the tenth century], the Iron Age had not yet begun. . . . [U]ntil about 1060, for all of Europe, we have only five charters, two chronicles, and one income record giving evidence of iron production."[165] It was "about 1100 that the blacksmith's forge took root in what was to become the centre of the village." This was "a landmark in peasant history; . . . the peasants found a natural leader and communicator with their master in the man who could handle fire and repair the lord's sword."[166]

The village blacksmith also produced a wide variety of tools. The most important tools were those used by carpenters and wheelwrights. The massive supply of timber was a factor endowment of incalculable value in northern Europe, and wood was the premier building material. Wood was used for domestic fires, and charcoal was employed in the industrial production of iron, which inexorably infiltrated into a thousand nooks and crannies of the material world. Wood was fashioned into industrial equipment and household furniture, carts and wagons, containers and especially barrels of all sorts, boats and barges, and scaffolding for the construction of castles and cathedrals.

---

set of arrangements: oxen were used for plowing, and horses were employed in haulage. In this way, the economic strengths of each animal were optimized. See also Biddick, *The Other Economy: Pastoral Economy on a Medieval Estate* (Berkeley and Los Angeles, 1989), 131.

165. Fichtenau, *Living in the Tenth Century: Mentalities and Social Orders* (Chicago, 1991), 335, 339, 337.

166. Robert Fossier, *Peasant Life in the Medieval West* (Oxford, 1988), 57, 65–66.

The woodworkers' toolkit was somewhat surprising. Adzes and axes were their primary means of shaping and smoothing raw wood, augers and gimlets were used for drilling holes, chisels were employed for squaring the sides of mortises and the edges of tenons, drawknifes and gouges were used for carving and embellishing the squared timbers, and scribing tools and squares enabled the craftsman to produce plumb and true lines. It is something of a shock to realize that saws of all types as well as smoothing instruments like planes were used only for small, detail work rather than for construction. Given an almost limitless supply of forest, the choicest trees were those with straight grain. They were chopped down with felling axes, and their straight grain meant that they could be easily split into lengths using wedges before being squared and smoothed with broad axes and adzes. Pit sawing was unnecessary as long as easily split, straight-grained timber was readily available.[167]

The axe and the adz were both chopping tools which the skilled carpenter wielded to shape wood.[168] While sharp tools and rudimentary techniques had been available to earlier carpenters, it was only after about 1100 that they were integrated into common practice. Edge tools were integral in first transforming trees into lumber; this semiprocessed wood was then modified into timbers that were used to create a settled human landscape. Metallurgical advances seem to have been crucial in this development. It is

167. Until the advent of the process of rolling steel strip in water-powered mills in the middle of the seventeenth century, most saws were small bow saws which themselves had hardly changed since Roman times. They were used to cut shapes like a contemporary carpenter's bandsaw or jigsaw. See W. L. Goodman, *The History of Woodworking Tools* (London, 1964), 145. Aboriginal populations who lived along the northwest coast of North America built massive residential structures by splitting Douglas fir and Sitka spruce trees of immense proportions using nothing more than brute force, assisted by wooden wedges. Similarly, in Japan, giant *hinoki* (cypress) logs were also split with wedges when the great temples were first built (seventh and eighth centuries A.D.). More than half a millennium later, when the accessible supply of giant, straight-grained cypress was exhausted, saws became indispensable to the builders of temples and castles. Indeed, much of what is regarded as the traditional toolkit of the Japanese carpenter resulted from changes that occurred in the last few centuries. In historical perspective, the original tools (axe, adz, and *namozori* chisels) were only recently replaced by the now-familiar array of saws, chisels, and planes; William Coaldrake, *The Way of the Carpenter: Tools and Japanese Architecture* (New York, 1990), *passim*.

168. In the anonymous, fifteenth-century poem "The Debate of the Carpenter's Tools" we are given a direct insight into their importance. The axe and the adz are mentioned five times; no other tool is given comparable recognition. The complete poem (in both original and annotated versions) is reproduced in Roy Underhill, *The Woodwright's Shop* (Chapel Hill, 1981), 5–20, 241–43. Underhill's "original" is based on a manuscript in the Bodleian Library (Ashmole 61).

of great interest to note that in a cache of eleventh- and twelfth-century axes, seven had a steel tip welded over the iron base, seven others had a steel tip inserted between iron cheeks, and seven of the eight others were solid steel. The cutting edges were hardened and tempered just as would be the case with the very best tools available today.[169] Furthermore, the keenest edge could be ground using special stones and then honed using a leather strap or nothing more than a few lapping strokes across the carpenter's own hand. Skill transformed primitive practice into an art form, and the cutting edge on these tools was second to none.[170]

Even relying primarily on such seemingly clumsy tools as the axe and adz, skilled carpenters fashioned timbers with precision while joining them with great strength. Timber-framing techniques developed by leaps and bounds—they became both more complex and more intricate. The key transitional moment in carpentry occurred in the late twelfth century, at the same time as in masonry. In the space of a few generations, woodworkers mastered a bewildering assortment of pegged mortise and tenon joints to distribute pressure downward while learning how to use about two dozen different scarf joints to tie timbers together so that great heights could be reached while maintaining much of the strength of an unjointed length. They also devised methods of diagonal bracing which greatly enhanced the structural rigidity of their elaborate post-and-beam systems.[171]

Just as the flying buttress enabled masons to create a sense of light and airiness in the great stone cathedrals, so the carpenters' ability to span great spaces with complex trusses and intricate rafter systems derived from the mechanical efficiency of their joinery. Timbers in a properly constructed roof truss did not sag. Because skilled timber framers knew that wood is so much stronger along the grain than across the grain, they devised rafter systems employing triangles—king posts, queen posts, hammerbeams, and struts—to divert lateral strains across the beams to the vertical, long-grain posts. Posts were designed to resist crushing and buckling. Most were overengineered because it was a relatively simple matter to add in a margin of safety. Because horizontal beams were more likely to

169. Goodman, *The History of Woodworking Tools*, 9, 38. The axes were Russian.

170. Indeed, these high-carbon tools may have been sharper than their modern equivalents, which are forged with steel alloys that retard rust at the cost of making it difficult to obtain an easily sharpened and long-lasting edge. Much of the mystique surrounding Japanese tools is understandable when one realizes that they are produced from high-carbon steel which not only is harder than its modern Western equivalents but also sharpens to a finer cutting edge.

171. The best discussion of this subject is Cecil Alec Hewett, *English Historic Carpentry* (London, 1980).

break—as a result of fiber failure, bending or deflection, or shear failure—carpenters were again prone to overbuild them to avoid disaster. The matter was complicated by several other technical factors—wood species do not possess the same qualities or the same strength, wet and dry wood react differently, and, perhaps most significant, hidden knots, "checks," "shakes," and splits can seriously compromise mechanical performance, as would insect damage. The mathematical skills to determine the engineering requirements were hardly part of a timber framer's mental toolkit, yet it is probably safe to say that what the timber framers lacked in technical knowledge they made up for with an intimate understanding of their raw materials.[172]

As a result of patronage by wealthy lords and clerics, large timber-framed buildings—manor houses, colleges, chapter houses, churches, monastic granges, and tithe barns—began to sprout up. Stone-walled buildings usually had roof systems supplied by timber framers. The emergence of new pockets of wealth among the rural and urban populations in the more settled communities supplemented this elite demand for sophisticated timber-framed buildings. Furthermore, in a wooden world even the villagers' water was drawn by pumps constructed by carpenters.[173] In this positive feedback system, improved buildings were created by the spread of sharp tools and new joinery techniques while the availability of these consumer goods meant that it now became possible for those with money to invest in better houses and barns. This was a virtuous circle of growth—an autocatalytic system in which change took place faster and faster once it had started.

The causal arrows were reciprocal. The increase in demand for the blacksmiths' products was part and parcel of the improved supply of skilled woodworkers, not only carpenters but also coopers, who produced barrels and wooden containers of all sizes and descriptions, wheelwrights, and myriad others engaged in local trades and crafts. The end result was that money that might otherwise have been used for ritual purposes was transformed into capital stock. As the velocity of money increased and its distribution widened to create a larger body of consumers, the demand for—and supply of—more proficient woodworking increased. The increased availability of

172. Tedd Benson, *Building the Timber Frame House: The Revival of a Forgotten Craft* (New York, 1980), 154–72, 197–205; R. Bruce Hoadley, *Understanding Wood: A Craftsman's Guide to Wood Technology* (Newton, Conn., 1980), chap. 6 ("Strength of Wood"), 107–36.

173. For a very graphic example of this now-lost skill, see Walter Rose, *The Village Carpenter* (Cambridge, 1937), 77–93.

sharp tools manufactured by blacksmiths complemented the spreading knowledge of new systems of joinery so that improved methods of carpentry percolated downward and began to influence vernacular building. It would be wise, however, to acknowledge the limits to this kind of growth. Most people were unable to take advantage of these innovations because of their poverty. The majority lived in such miserable hovels that, for them, even a rudimentary cruck-framed building was something of a luxury.[174]

4.

Across the northwestern European countryside the ancient technique of harnessing the power of water, wind, and the tides through the use of mills greatly enhanced productivity and extended the division of labor. Deriving from a Roman invention, the waterwheel was the most important invention of the Middle Ages insofar as it replaced human energy with another power source. Tapping this source of inanimate energy meant that, for the first time in history, a complex civilization could be built on the foundation of something other than the sweating backs of slaves and/or dependent laborers.[175]

The ancient water mill was connected to complex systems of water transfer; most have been found in the immediate vicinity of aqueducts. The medieval waterwheels were, by way of contrast, located on streams of every size, and a few were even put to work on tidal inlets. Waterwheels were used primarily for flour milling, although by 1500 some were being applied to industrial processes, sometimes on a very substantial scale. Feudal-manorial societies in the northwest of Europe enthusiastically adopted water-powered milling as a means of fiscal extraction from dependent peasants. "If the ancient world gave birth to the vertical water wheel and nurtured the earliest stages of its growth, it was the medieval West that brought it through adolescence and into adulthood."[176]

The Anglo-Norman conquerors' Domesday Book of 1086 recorded 6,082 water mills[177] in the parts of southern England they surveyed—an

174. L. F. Salzman, *Building in England down to 1540* (Oxford, 1952); M. W. Barley, *The English Farmhouse and Cottage* (London, 1961); B. Bunker, *Cruck Building* (Sheffield, 1970); Trudy West, *The Timber-frame House in England* (Newton Abbott, 1970).

175. Lynn S. White, "Technology and Invention in the Middle Ages," *Speculum* 15 (1940): 141–59.

176. Terry Reynolds, *Stronger Than a Hundred Men: A History of the Vertical Water Wheel* (Baltimore, 1983), 48.

177. This number of mills is put forward by Sir Henry Darby, *Domesday England* (Cambridge, 1977), 361, based on his revision of the usually accepted num-

average of one per fifty households. By the third quarter of the thirteenth century the number of water mills in England had probably doubled, and in the fifty years after 1275, there was another increase in mill building.[178] In the northern French county of Picardy there were 40 mills in 1080, 80 in 1125, and 245 in 1175.[179] In all of France, there were 20,000 water mills by the early eleventh century; nearly two centuries later, the number had doubled.[180] It is estimated that there were 250,000 mills (of all types) in thirteenth-century Europe which combined to supply something on the order of one million horsepower.[181] One million horsepower would be equivalent to more than three million slaves.[182]

In places where the rivers flowed too slowly, the wind's energy was regulated to supply power. There is some difference of opinion regarding the recording of the first windmill—was it in 1137 or 1185?—but there is no disagreement that the windmill was an English invention and that an intense spate of windmill building occurred in England in the late twelfth and early thirteenth centuries.[183] In places where rivers flowed slowly, such as the fen country around Cambridge, windmills were common. There were thirty-nine of these seigneurial powerplants by 1279 in place of the two water mills recorded in 1086.[184]

---

ber of 5,624, which was reported by M. T. Hodgen, "Domesday Water Mills," *Antiquity* 13 (1939): 261–79. R. Lennard suggested that Hodgen's total is "almost certainly too low"; *Rural England 1086–1135* (London, 1959), 278.

178. Jean Gimpel, *The Medieval Machine* (Harmondsworth, 1976), 1–74. For the total number of mills in England in 1300, see Richard Holt, *The Mills of Medieval England* (Oxford, 1988), 116. Even Holt's total is probably something of an underestimate; research by Christopher Dyer and John Langdon suggests that peasants often held small mills by which they could harness the water that ran through their lands; "English Medieval Mills," *Bulletin of the University of Birmingham*, January 23, 1984, 1–2.

179. Duby, *The Early Growth of the European Economy* (Ithaca, 1974), 187.

180. In the labor-hungry period of the late fourteenth century and fifteenth century, these machines supplied an obvious demand. By the end of the fifteenth century there were 70,000 water mills as well as 20,000 windmills in France; Braudel, *The Identity of France*, vol. 2, *People and Production*, 145.

181. Braudel, *The Structures of Everyday Life*, 371, 353–58.

182. In a footnote, Braudel suggests that a man generates 0.3 hp; *The Identity of France*, vol. 2, *People and Production*, 692 n. 54.

183. The earlier date is championed by Edward J. Kealey (*Harvesting the Wind: Windmill Pioneers in Twelfth-Century England* [Berkeley and Los Angeles, 1987], 2, 69, 197 ff.), while the later date is put forward by Richard Holt (*The Mills of Medieval England*, 20 n. 8, Appendix 1, 171–75), who notes that the earliest examples of this invention were largely located along the North Sea coast. Holt relates this use of sail to a knowledge of seafaring that might have been shared with Dutchmen, Belgians, and Frenchmen from the other side of the North Sea.

184. Holt, *The Mills of Medieval England*, 86–87.

In addition to 12,000–15,000 water mills, there were probably 4,000 windmills in early fourteenth-century England.[185] Richard Holt makes the very useful point that while the number of mills may have only doubled since 1066, there was a constant process of reorganization so that smaller, less powerful mills were being phased out of service and larger, more powerful ones became the norm. Thus, a simple count is somewhat misleading since the number of mills is not a reliable guide to the changing volume of power derived from this source.[186] Inanimately powered mills supplied between two and ten horsepower, the variation being the result of bigger blades or faster wind and river currents. The average watermill was, at the very least, ten times as powerful as a two-man handmill operating at peak output. In some places, where the wind was unpredictable or river flows were seasonal, inanimate power was replaced (or supplemented) for short periods by human or animal muscle-power.

Mills were a wonder to contemporaries. In the words of an anonymous monk at the Cistercian monastery of Clairvaux:

> the river . . . throws itself first impetuously into the mill, where it is very busy and takes plenty of exercise, as much to grind the wheat under the weight of the mills as to shake the fine sieve which separates the flour from the bran. Behold it already in the next-door building. It fills the cauldron and gives itself up to the fire which cooks it to prepare drink for the monks, if, by chance, the vine has given the vine-grower's industry the evil answer of sterility, and if, the blood of the grapes being absent, it has been necessary to compensate for it with the daughter of the corn-ear [i.e., beer]. Yet the river does not consider itself to be discharged. The fullers, set up near the mill, call the river to them. In the mill it is busy preparing the brothers' food; it is therefore justifiable to demand that now it should think of their clothes. It does not contradict, and refuses to do nothing ordered of it. It raises and drops alternately those heavy pestles or mallets . . . and spares the fullers a great labour. Merciful God! What consolations you grant to your poor servants to prevent too great a sadness from overcoming them! How much you relieve the difficulties of your children who do penance, and how you take the extra burden of work away from them! How many horses would be exhausted, how many men would tire their arms in the labours which, without any work on our part, are done for us by this gracious river to which we owe our clothes and our food! It combines its efforts with our own, and after it has borne the heat and burden of the day, it expects only one reward for its work: this is per-

185. John Langdon, "Lordship and Peasant Consumerism in the Milling Industry of Early Fourteenth-Century England," *Past and Present* 145 (1994): 9.
186. *The Mills of Medieval England*, 112–13.

mission to go away free after having carefully performed all that it has been ordered to do.[187]

By 1135, this monastery had diverted water 2.2 miles (3.5 km) to power its mill. Water flow was controlled by building dams and diverting flows through canals and millraces. In Toulouse, helter-skelter development had created some sixty floating mills across the Garonne by the mid-twelfth century; then, in an act of almost unrivaled civil engineering, these were all replaced by a new system which featured three dams (the largest being 1,300 feet [400 m] long) and forty-three fixed mills. The largest of these dams, which lasted until 1709, was built by ramming thousands of twenty-foot oak piles into the river bed in two parallel palisades and filling the space in between with earth, wood, gravel, and boulders.[188] Elsewhere, rivers and streams were diverted to harness water power. Often, these modifications created havoc for both fishing and navigation, but as is so often the case, money talked—and the money that talked the loudest was connected to the mills.

Mills "represent a progressive step towards a more effective use of natural forces, animate or inanimate, and hence led to economies in human labour, or—what comes to much the same thing—a more productive return. Why was this? Perhaps because there were fewer men available, but most of all because the master had fewer slaves."[189] As Pierre Bonnassie notes, "Just how important this was becomes apparent when we call to mind what it replaced, that is the hand mill. This rotating drum, in almost universal use in the Roman world from the second century AD, was in practice almost exclusively worked by slaves (mostly female) and the work was long, tedious and exhausting—hour after hour, day and night. Its employment thus supposed the existence of a large labour force exclusively devoted to it. The diffusion of the water mill, therefore, for thousands and thousands of human beings, had a beneficial effect; it lightened their labour."[190]

This point is debated by Pierre Dockès, who believes that the time wives and daughters spent milling by hand could be accounted as "costless," while the manorial mill charged *multure* (a fee of between one-tenth and one-twentieth charged in kind, that is, taken by the lord from the flour the miller had ground) and the miller also regularly short-measured his tied

187. Quoted in Le Goff, *Medieval Civilization*, 221.
188. Reynolds, *Stronger than a Hundred Men*, 65.
189. Bloch, "Medieval Inventions," in *Land and Work in Medieval Europe* (New York, 1967), 181–82.
190. Bonnassie, "The Survival and Extinction of the Slave System," 38.

customers. In addition, the peasant (or his wife) had to travel to the mill with his or her grain and back with his or her flour, as well as spending time while the miller did his job. Adding these factors together, Dockès argues that it is not clear that the water mill liberated the peasantry from anything except its money.[191]

There was an underground persistence of hand mills—even though they were often confiscated and destroyed by feudalists—and a constant struggle against the lord's banal right of milling. Perhaps 20 percent of all grain was ground by hand mills in the fourteenth century, mostly for peasants' domestic use.[192] The stronger the seigneurial powers, the more likely it was that lords were implementing a straightforward monopoly over grain milling to enhance their power plants' profitability. The operation of this kind of seigneurial monopoly was most evident in intensively manorialized reaches of northern England rather than in other regions, where independent peasants and free mills—often associated with town boroughs—were common. Northern England was a peripheral border region only lightly touched by the currents of commercialization. Its political economy had been profoundly reconstructed after the Norman Conquest of 1066 to enhance the military powers of the border lords, who took advantage of their monopoly powers to enforce higher *multure* rates and were active in pursuing their right of suit of mill, thereby further enhancing returns on their investments.

The adoption of the water mill was based not only on the decline of slavery but also on the rise of the feudal *ban*, which enabled lords to force their dependent subordinates to make use of these capital investments. Marc Bloch claimed that top-down feudal relations were at the heart of the supersession of hand-milling. Those exercising lordship demanded that servile peasants bring their corn to the lord's mill and to pay *banalités* to the lord for that privilege.[193] In opposition to Marc Bloch's classic account, John Langdon suggests that coercive power, far from ensuring the spread of milling, actually retarded it.[194] As is the case in so many academic controversies, Langdon and Bloch (posthumously) seem to be arguing at cross-purposes: not all mills were owned by feudalists, and many that were owned by them were, in fact, subcontracted to intermediaries who most likely had a more commercial interest in their day-to-day operation.

191. Dockès, *Medieval Slavery and Liberation* (Chicago, 1982), 182–96.
192. Langdon, "Lordship and Peasant Consumerism," 30–31.
193. Bloch, "The Advent and Triumph of the Watermill," in *Land and Work in Medieval Europe*, esp. 143–47, 152 ff.
194. "Lordship and Peasant Consumerism," 38.

It seems reasonable to postulate that there was a two-stage process which saw mills first "discovered" in antiquity but proliferating only in the early ninth century, in connection with the disintegration of Frankish hegemony in the heartland of western Europe and the concomitant expansion of independent peasant holding.[195] In England, there is for all intents and purposes no information on the history of mills before the Domesday Book of 1086; at that time there were probably as many as 7,000 inanimate power plants throughout the country, which is a strong testimony to the Saxons' role. We should not forget that much of the Norman power system was built on Saxon antecedents. So, here again, the role of political economy cannot be divorced from an understanding of technology. After the year 1000, the feudal revolution made it possible for the lords to control their subjects and their subjects' property. Still, the awkward fact remains that not all mills were owned or controlled by feudalists.

In England, c. 1300, there were around 20,000 specialized craftsmen—carpenters, blacksmiths, masons, and weavers making sailcloth for windmills—who were engaged full time in the building and maintenance of mills.[196] The carpenters' skill was again crucial not only in building the mills but especially in constructing the wheels that transferred the energy of the rivers and winds to the millstones. The spur wheel, pit wheel, and crown wheel in a large mill would have had several hundred wooden cogs. Each cog was precisely fitted into a mortise tapered on both edges and both sides so tightly that it could resist immense strains without the mechanical assistance of any additional nails or spikes to hold it in place. If one cog was out of perfect alignment it would break, and the mill would be brought to a standstill until the necessary repairs were completed.

Windmills posed the additional problem of requiring that the whole mass of the mill be able to rotate on an axis—usually a gigantic timber as much as three feet in cross section—so as to catch the wind.[197] Using the skills and sharp tools that were available to master carpenters, windmills

195. Reynolds, *Stronger than a Hundred Men*, 50.
196. John Langdon, "The Mobilization of Labour in the Milling Industry of Thirteenth- and Early Fourteenth-Century England," *Canadian Journal of History* 31 (1996): 38–58.
197. Rose, *The Village Carpenter*, 104 ff. To be sure, this is a very late discussion, but it is indicative of the biases of most historians that the skill and intelligence of craftsmen are transparent and therefore taken for granted. The scholarly literature pays them almost no heed. The two books on English windmills I consulted, R. J. Brown's *Windmills of England* (London, 1976) and Stanley Freese's *Windmills and Millwrighting* (Cambridge, 1957), are both silent on the issue of building practices before 1600.

were erected on a pyramid of stout timbers. Some had foundations that were below grade, but the state of the art was a series of "cross trees" and sloping tie-beams supporting the main post above the ground so as to avoid the inevitable rot that accompanied buried foundations. The thirteenth-century windmills seem to have had a sailspan that was smaller than the 60 to 70 feet that was achieved by nineteenth-century millwrights, but the available evidence does not allow us to be much more specific than that.[198]

Inanimate power was employed not only for grinding corn and fulling cloth but also for forging and hammering iron, sawing wood and stone, and a wide set of other activities in which crushing, grinding, polishing, pulping, beating, pounding, and mashing all benefited immensely when new power sources and reciprocal actions were substituted for human muscle power. These technical advances would have been massively enhanced with the addition of a simple camshaft and gears, a crank and connecting rod system, and a flywheel.[199] Other rudimentary engines—trepans, capstans, pulleys, cranes, jacks, levers, pedals, cranks, and lathes—mostly employed human or animal muscle power, but these could be converted so that they were driven by wind and/or water power.[200]

> The house medieval man lived in might have been made of wood sawed at a hydropowered sawmill; the bowls he ate from, turned on a water-powered lathe; the pipes that his water flowed from, bored by water-power. The flour he ate was probably ground at a watermill; the oil he put on his bread could have been crushed from olives by water-wheel. The leather of the shoes he put on his feet and the textiles he wore on his back could have been produced, in part, by water-powered tanning and fulling mills. The iron of his tools could have been mined with the aid of water-powered drainage pumps, ventilating fans, and hoisting devices; was probably smelted in a furnace with wateractivated bellows; and was probably forged with hydraulic stamps and bellows. If he was a clerk, the paper he wrote on was, most likely, the product of a water-powered mill. If he was a soldier, his armour and weapons might have been polished and sharpened by stones turned by vertical water wheels. While no single individual in the Middle Ages was affected by water power in all these ways, most were affected in at least several. Water power had become, by the sixteenth century, and probably much earlier, an inescapable part of daily life in the West.[201]

198. Holt, *The Mills of Medieval England*, 140, 142–43.
199. M.-D. Chenu, *Nature, Man, and Society in the Twelfth Century* (Chicago, 1968), 43.
200. Braudel, *The Structures of Everyday Life*, 337.
201. Reynolds, *Stronger than a Hundred Men*, 96–97.

Notwithstanding this long and impressive list of innovations, there was no industrial revolution in the Middle Ages, nor even in the following centuries.[202] The commercial infrastructure only rarely made it profitable for water mills, windmills, or other engines to be widely employed in industrial production.[203] It was only in well-situated and/or state-of-the-art enterprises that water power could be economically justified. Fulling mills were the best example of an industrial application. Furthermore, most aristocratic mill owners were content to take advantage of their seigneurial rights of fiscal extraction and quite unwilling to dabble in revolutionizing production.

The first evidence for most of these technical innovations can be dated from the Carolingian period, when calendars not only "show a coercive attitude towards natural resources" but also an annual rhythm depicting distinctive northern activities. Widespread incorporation into daily practice took place much later.[204] "About A.D. 1000 God the Creator began to be depicted as a master craftsman holding scales and an architect's compass."[205] To some extent, this attitude was prevalent in Latin Christianity from its origins, as it placed a significantly greater emphasis on labor than did the pagan Greeks and Romans. Indeed, because Christians believed that their creator had given humans dominion over the beasts of the field, they were indifferent to the feelings of natural objects. In contrast to the animism of the pagans, Christians saw nature as being outside human society.[206] The key was that work itself acquired a spiritual value, and mastering the natural world was a form of collaboration with the Creator. There was, thus, an opening through which it would be possible to dignify labor in the form of good works in contrast to the contemplativeness of Byzantine Christianity.[207]

The Benedictine rhythms of communal prayer, which regulated the hours of the day for the monks, had been established at the end of the sixth

---

202. Indeed, the concept of a single "industrial revolution" is itself misleading since it tries to compress an unfolding, evolutionary process into a single event.

203. Holt, *The Mills of Medieval England*, 145–58.

204. Lynn White, Jr., *Medieval Technology and Social Change* (Oxford, 1962), 39–89.

205. Kealey, *Harvesting the Wind*, 84.

206. Jane Schneider, "Spirits and the Spirit of Capitalism," in Ellen Badone (ed.), *Religious Orthodoxy and Popular Faith in European Society* (Princeton, 1990), 24–53.

207. Lynn White, Jr., "Cultural Elements and Technological Advance in the Middle Ages," in *Technology and Innovation in the Middle Ages* (Berkeley and Los Angeles, 1978), 246 ff.

century in the belief that repetitive group prayer would free sinners from their otherworldly torments.[208] The monks believed that time belonged to God and therefore were willing to be organized and driven by the bells. Monastic discipline "helped to give human enterprise the regular collective beat and rhythm of the machine; for the clock is not merely a means of keeping track of the hours, but of synchronising the actions of men."[209] Bell-ringing *clepsydra* (water clocks) were part of the physical fabric of their monasteries, and the early twelfth-century Cistercian Rule explicitly provides for their maintenance.[210]

Benedictine monasteries led the way in the application of new technologies—not just clocks, which applied gravity to create regulated bursts of energy, but also water mills, cropping patterns, and animal husbandry. This was particularly important on those estates, like the Cistercians', which employed lay brothers to do the menial work. Perhaps their most significant innovation was the application of time-management techniques to productive routines.[211] Monasteries often served as the locations for fairs and were centers of conspicuous consumption; in addition, they stimulated economic development by acting as banking and credit institutions. In all these ways, they prefigured the urban centers. Monks sought to do away with unnecessary labor to have more time for study, meditation, and prayer.[212] So, if they were economic innovators, it was in spite of themselves.

In this vein, it is instructive to consider Roger Bacon's speculative remarks:

> Machines may be made by which the largest ships, with only one man steering them, will be moved faster than if they were filled with rowers; wagons may be built which will move with incredible speed and without the aid of beasts; flying machines can be constructed in which man may . . . beat the air with wings like a bird. . . . Machines will make it possible to go to the bottom of seas and rivers.[213]

---

208. Duby, *The Age of Cathedrals*, 61–66.

209. Lewis Mumford, *Technics and Civilization* (London, 1946), 13–14.

210. David Landes, *Revolution in Time: Clocks and the Making of the Modern World* (Cambridge, Mass., 1983), 68–70.

211. E. Zerubavel, "The Benedictine Ethic and the Modern Spirit of Scheduling: On Schedules and Social Organization," *Sociological Inquiry* 50 (1980): 157–69.

212. Lewis Mumford, *The City in History* (Harmondsworth, 1961), 299–300; see also Ilana Friedrich Silber, "Monasticism and the 'Protestant Ethic': Asceticism, Rationality and Wealth in the Medieval West," *British Journal of Sociology* 44 (1993): 103–24.

213. Quoted in Braudel, *The Perspective of the World*, 548. Roger Bacon, sometimes considered the inventor of gunpowder, was a thirteenth-century Leonardo da Vinci in the breadth of his imagination.

Today we may regard Roger Bacon's speculations as the keen insights of a technological visionary, but on a more mundane level, the rise of wage labor and the increasing penetration of monetary reckoning into social relations represented more fundamental changes in the relations of production. Particularly in urban economies, masters were able to enforce work rules and methods in their shops so that they could make their employees—mostly apprentices but also journeymen—adopt new techniques. The emergence of wage labor acted as a means whereby technological breakthroughs—largely the result of anonymous tinkering—were imbricated in the everyday production routines, thus transforming the labor process. The competitive character of marketing meant that those producers who were able to maintain standards while reducing costs were at an advantage. Most of this progress is invisible—we can see the results of a massive upgrading in both relative and absolute levels of urban wealth, but we must infer the means whereby they were achieved.[214]

These processes were of a piece. They were part and parcel of the massive energy thrown out in all directions by the social explosion which occurred after the year 1000. It is particularly important to note in this regard that after the year 1000 there was a boom in mining. It derived partly from the demand for lead for church roofs, bronze for church bells, and glass for church windows; partly from the massive demand for iron products fashioned at the blacksmith's forge; and partly from the widespread demand for precious metals (especially silver from eastern parts of Germany) for coinage.[215] Yet, until the use of inorganic energy derived from coal superseded the organic energy of humans, animals, water, wind, and tides harnessed in mills, its revolutionary potential to free production was hardly exploited. Even though the basic principles of energy substitution were known from an early date, the lag between invention and application stands as a testament to the massive complexity of early modernization.

5.

By the year 1000 the north of Europe had developed an agricultural system that was radically different from Mediterranean methods of farming which prevailed in antiquity: the scratch plow, square fields on light soils, biennial crop rotations, and cultivation of wheat and olives. In contrast, the

214. Steven A. Epstein, *Wage Labor and Guilds in Medieval Europe* (Chapel Hill, 1991), esp. 244–48. The "invisibility" of technical skill and its development are usually taken for granted, which is unfortunate but perhaps inevitable since we cannot argue much from silence.

215. Nef, "Mining and Metallurgy in Medieval Civilisation," 435–38.

agricultural regime of northwestern Europe came to be characterized by deep plowing with animal traction on the heavy soils of the river valleys, long strip fields, complex rotations with spring and summer crops, and the cultivation of cereals (principally rye) that could withstand the rigors of the climate while having a shorter growing season. In addition, the older Germanic and Celtic traditions of grazing were maintained so that the animal population (and, hence, the caloric value of animal proteins) was preserved. By slow, cumulative increments, the European miracle of mastering the physical world began to take form.

Maintaining soil productivity requires constant nitrogen replenishment. Employing legumes, manure from animals, and complex crop rotations, early modern farmers realized productivity benefits by increasing the soil's vital nutrients.[216] "In the middle of the [thirteenth] century there were five-fold yields of wheat in Lorraine and Languedoc, eight-fold in Picardy and the Île-de-France . . . even ten- or twelve-fold yields were achieved in good years."[217] While these figures represent state-of-the-art accomplishments achieved through intensive labor applications and substantial levels of nitrogen replenishment, it seems likely that the use of new techniques allied to the mastery of new iron plows, axes, and horseshoes (all of which were manufactured by village smithies) extended the carrying capacity of the land and made it possible to feed a much larger population. By the early fourteenth century there were on the order of four times as many people occupying a quite differently constituted land mass.

Along Europe's Mediterranean fringe, by way of a contrast, there was no break with antiquity in the year 1000. The ancient cropping system

216. Robert S. Shiel, "Improving Soil Productivity in the Prefertilizer Era," in Campbell and Overton (eds.), *Land, Labour, and Productivity,* 51–77. See also Mark Overton and Bruce M. S. Campbell, "Productivity Change in European Agricultural Development," in Bruce Campbell and Mark Overton (eds.), *Land, Labour, and Livestock* (Manchester, 1991), 1–50, and Bruce M. S. Campbell and Mark Overton, "A New Perspective on Medieval and Early Modern Agriculture: Six Centuries of Norfolk Farming *c.* 1250–*c.* 1850," *Past and Present* 141 (1993): 38–105.

217. Fossier, *Peasant Life in the Medieval West,* 115. The author notes that "the whole of southern Europe seems to have been unaffected by these agrarian improvements, with only three-fold yields in the Alps of Provence and five-fold in Tuscany." There were micro-ecologies in southern Europe (such as Santa Maria Impruneta near Florence) where similar improvements in productivity were created, but these were exceptional. In Norfolk, England, early fourteenth-century crop yields were higher than at any time before the "agricultural revolution" of the second quarter of the eighteenth century. They dipped during intervening periods and approached the medieval level only for a brief time in the 1630s, which was another period of population pressure; Campbell and Overton, "A New Perspective on Medieval and Early Modern Agriculture," 74.

based on wheat and barley survived intact from Castile to Greece as late as 1400. Thereafter the reliance on barley was broken only as a result of the "reverse Malthusianism" of the fifteenth century in southern France; it did not change in Spain, Greece, or the Maghreb.[218]

Human habitation had a significant impact on the ecosystem, altering the physical and chemical properties of the countryside.[219] The northern European landscape reflected the human assertion of physical mastery: forests, marshes, heaths, and fens were reclaimed from the wilderness and brought into civilization. The wealth of these forests "only existed when incorporated into the economy through intermediaries—shepherds tending their flocks (not only the pigs at acorn time), woodcutters, charcoal-burners, carters: a whole community whose profession it was to exploit, to utilize and to destroy. The forest was worth nothing unless it was used."[220] On closer inspection, the land itself was changed as a result of its reciprocal interaction with the press of humanity. This was not just a simple matter of soil exhaustion, as has often been claimed by those who deny the possibility that the spring to the Ricardian trap of diminishing returns could be delayed by the desperate strategy of massive labor inputs. It was also a rather more complex transformation of the ecological equilibrium between plant covers, soils, and inorganic nutrients. Land, like all other variables, was not immutable; it, too, could be modified in the give and take between humans and their environment in the historical process of early modernization after the year 1000.[221]

The interplay between economic growth and demographic change was thus dynamic. Causal arrows did not point in only one direction. Not only did economic growth lead to population growth, but in a number of places, the application of labor power made it possible to increase productivity per unit of land. Indeed, "keeping the land in good heart required labour as much as livestock—to supervise herds; pen flocks in movable folds; gather and spread manure; dig marl; cart night soil, sea sand, and any other extraneous sources of fertiliser that might be available; plough and harrow the

218. Emmanuel Le Roy Ladurie, *The Peasants of Languedoc* (Chicago, 1974), 45–48.

219. W. S. Cooter, "Ecological Dimensions of Medieval Agrarian Systems," *Agricultural History* 52 (1978): 458–77.

220. Braudel, *The Structures of Everyday Life*, 364. Braudel is, of course, being characteristically hyperbolic here: the unused forest was not "worth nothing" because its value was rather more symbolic (for aristocrats who hunted) than economic (for peasants who worked).

221. R. S. Loomis, "Ecological Dimensions of Medieval Agrarian Systems: A Reply," *Agricultural History* 52 (1978): 478–83.

land; eliminate weeds, and harvest with care—and it was consequently when labour was cheapest and most abundant that the most intensive arable farming systems attained their peak of productivity." Bruce Campbell argues that, in intensive systems of cultivation, productivity increases per acre reached a peak in the early fourteenth century, at the same time that productivity per hour of labor declined. There was thus an involutional response to the pressure of human numbers. The productivity levels of land attained at the beginning of the fourteenth century, by the application of virtually limitless inputs of human labor, would not be reached again until the eighteenth century's agricultural revolution.

On the extensive margin of cultivation, by way of contrast, yield per acre actually rose after the Black Death because "cropping was increasingly concentrated on to the better land, with corresponding benefits for individual crop yields, and associated with this went an improvement in the ratio of high-to-low value crops which constituted a source of aggregate productivity growth." On this extensive margin of cultivation, where the soils could not support intensive methods of production, yields were low during the early fourteenth century not because the soil was "exhausted" but rather because so much unsuitable land was under the plow. In the changed conditions after 1348, Campbell claims, the range of yields narrowed as population declined and labor inputs were reduced in the intensive systems of cultivation. On the extensive margin of cultivation there was marked improvement in yields resulting from specialization.[222]

Campbell's research is extremely important because it belies the theories which relate economic regression with the feudal mode of production. Campbell (as well as Herman Van der Wee for the Netherlands and Emmanuel Le Roy Ladurie for Northern France) makes it apparent that there was no inherent linkage between the social relations of production and technical aspects of farming which inexorably led to a crisis. Campbell's research proves that the seignorial demesnes were capable of being farmed in both flexible and adaptable ways. Feudal agriculture—rather like plantation slavery in the nineteenth-century United States—was a most peculiar institution; neither was doomed to die as a result of internal contradictions, and both ended as a result of civil war which led to the reorganization of the state and dramatic changes in the social relations of production.

222. Bruce M. S. Campbell, "Land, Labour, Livestock, and Productivity Trends in English Seignorial Agriculture, 1208–1450," in Campbell and Overton (eds.), *Land, Labour, and Productivity*, 182, 177. Herman Van der Wee and Emmanuel Le Roy Ladurie are both cited by Campbell.

Of course, there were limits to growth before the Black Death, but these limits were displaced so that for many of those who supplied labor power, the returns were harder labor and coarser fare. This fate was not so bad if you consider the alternative—slow death by starvation. Social differentiation within the peasantry became a deadly variant of the zero-sum game. Mortality rates shot up when the finely tuned equilibrium was upset by climatic variations which led to harvest failures.

Europe had become a hothouse demographic regime whose involutional characteristics have been described so trenchantly for another place at another time: "a marked tendency (and ability) to respond to a rising population through intensification; that is, through absorbing increased numbers of cultivators on a unit of cultivated land."[223] Population was so abundant that even if its marginal productivity was insignificant, the gains in productive power deriving from massive applications of labor power were seized by its surplus men and women who lived—subsisted—on that margin. This suggests such profound poverty that "the position of the rural population is that of a man standing permanently up to the neck in water, so that even a ripple is sufficient to drown him.[224] Or, as a contemporary said of the poorer peasantry, they have "nothing but a stomach and, what is worse, nothing to put in it."[225] But is this darkly pessimistic vision the whole picture?

The expansion and elaboration of economic activities created multiple linkages which reached all the way down to the diet of the common people. Nothing was left untouched by the massive changes which rippled throughout early modern society. Diet became more varied, and the food supply became more reliable. Famine became less dangerous when the common people were better fed in ordinary times. The contrast between the landlocked autarky of the year 1000 and the vigorous commercialization of the thirteenth century is a basic fact of life. That earlier world was "another universe, another economy, another society, another culture."[226]

Access to the luxury of animal protein was, of course, severely stratified. Much of the peasantry was forced to be vegetarian, and only festive fare

---

223. Clifford Geertz, *Agricultural Involution: The Processes of Ecological Change in Indonesia* (Berkeley and Los Angeles, 1963), 32.

224. R. H. Tawney, *Land and Labor in China* (Boston, 1966), 77. For a similar, if less graphically stated, discussion of rural immiseration in pre-plague England, see Ian Kershaw, "The Great Famine and Agrarian Crisis in England, 1315–1322," *Past and Present* 59 (1973): 3–50. See also Jordan, *The Great Famine*.

225. Quoted in Michel Mollat, *The Poor in the Middle Ages* (New Haven, 1986), 121.

226. Braudel, *The Wheels of Commerce*, 60.

would include poultry, meat, and/or dairy products. If there was an upward flow of animal protein from poor to rich, there was also a downward flow of taste which found expression in the butcher shops of every market town and in the poacher's bag. When official ordinances decreed meatfree days, this was an acknowledgment that, on the other days of the week, those who could afford it would eat meat. In a Christian society which forbade the eating of the flesh of terrestial quadrupeds on 150 days per year, fish protein was of great importance. The rivers, streams, and ponds (natural and humanmade) of northwestern Europe were the source of freshwater fish like perch and pike which were far more important components in the diet than saltwater fish like cod or herring. One of the little-known advances in economic activity after the year 1000 took place in aquaculture, or fish harvesting.[227]

The rich might eat venison while the poor, if they were lucky, would eat salt pork, but both belonged to a community of carnivores.[228] Twelfth-century lepers, for example, had a weekly ration of three loaves of bread, a pie, and a measure of peas; in 1325, the allotment was bread, oil, salt, onions, meat on three days, and eggs or herrings on the other four. Inmates of fourteenth-century leprosariums enjoyed protein and iron-rich diets which were a testimony to the agrarian transformation that took place after the year 1000. Laborers performing building works and even the poorest peasants doing harvest works were able to enjoy this kind of fare as a supplement to their cash wages. Another group for whom food was provided was soldiers; those who manned the garrisons for Edward I's army in Scotland in the early fourteenth century were provided with a diet which supplied them with 5,000 calories daily.[229]

The wealthier strata in village society ate in this way as a matter of right. Moreover, the increased complexity of economic life meant that mutton and beef could be purchased in small quantities to supplement the bacon and sausages made from the family pig.[230] So, the expansion of the

227. Richard C. Hoffman, "Economic Development and Aquatic Ecosystems in Medieval Europe," *American Historical Review* 101 (1996): 646–52. One wonders what the landlocked population of Southern Europe, living some distance from the Mediterranean, ate on the 150 days per year when meat was forbidden. For these people, freshwater fish was not an option.

228. Braudel, *The Structures of Everyday Life*, 187 ff.

229. M. Prestwich, "Victualling Estimates for English Garrisons in Scotland during the Early Fourteenth Century," *English Historical Review* 82 (1967): 538. Five thousand calories a day is a lot; only a person doing arduous physical labor needs anything like this amount. Most sedentary adults of the late twentieth century require less than half that amount of energy.

230. Duby, *Rural Economy and Country Life*, 65–67; Christopher Dyer, *Standards of Living in the Later Middle Ages* (Cambridge, 1989), 151–60.

agricultural economy lay behind a massive increase and diversification in the supply of calories for the population. But do the aggregate increases in *per capita* food energy give a fair indication of the distribution of this potential freedom from starvation? Or was this advance reserved for the more fortunate who could claim entitlement through their social or economic station?

The history of the biology of the human body provides a valuable entry into these reciprocal interactions. The end of the barbarian invasions, the feudal revolution, and the creation of ordered communities in the shadow of the castle all combined to explode the limits of the Carolingian archipelago of settlement and to create a new style of rural life. It was not necessarily a better way of life: the average height of the German populations declined by two inches as a consequence of the shift from a mixed agriculture to cereal monoculture.[231] Economic progress has always cut both ways. The extension of cereal farming enabled more people to live per acre of land even though these people often had worse diets than the modified hunters/gatherers who preceded them. Similarly, the increased density of population accompanying "civilization" has usually been achieved at the cost of declining life expectation as more diseases became endemic.

Bread, porridge-like *companaticum*, and ale were the "mainstay of existence."[232] Meat was only rarely available; it could, of course, be hunted, but it was not produced for human consumption among the mass of the population. Such a diet was low in protein and deficient in iron. Right through the year 1000, and well into the eleventh century, as we have seen, mass famines were still frequent.[233] On the other hand, the lower classes benefited from improvements in cooking utensils, especially the large, globular pot in which lentils could be simmered. It was a double benefit when these cooking vessels came to be produced from iron because these pots might have poisoned the population in the same way that fluoride in our water supply poisons us.

The meat component in the peasant diet seems to have declined with the process of sedentary manorialization. Eggs, chickens, and geese were raised but were often diverted to the lord's table in payment of seigneurial exactions. The intake of meat protein improved whenever the peasantry kept pigs. Pork would be the staple item in its carnivorous diet for centuries.[234]

---

231. Bartlett, *The Making of Europe*, 155.
232. Duby, *Rural Economy and Country Life in the Medieval West*, 8–9.
233. Duby, *The Early Growth of the European Economy*, 158–59.
234. The Abbey of Peterborough, for example, "collected the bulk of its chickens from its peasants," who also "contributed enough eggs annually to serve each

Rabbits, which would later become the poor person's chicken, were introduced into northern Europe (from Spain) around 800. Because these rabbits took a long time to adjust to living in a feral state in England's colder, wetter climate, they were at first raised in purpose-built seigneurial warrens. Rabbits began to live wild in large numbers from the end of the fourteenth century, and it was from this time that their meat was incorporated into popular recipes.[235] William Cobbett—the rural riding, Romantic radical—would claim that the best poor men's countries were those where the rabbit proliferated in the early nineteenth century. The meat component in the peasantry's diets was most frequently game that had been poached from the lords' forests.

In the period after the year 1000, the demand for meat—mostly coming from the upper classes, the clerics, and the towns—led to the specialized development of livestock herds. The general population profited from this pastoral economy indirectly, from the massive increase in the production of milk, butter, and cheese. Of course, the society which outlawed meat eating on Fridays (and Lent and other holidays) was able to do so because it came up with an alternative: salted herring from the Atlantic and, in particular, freshwater fish raised by aquaculturalists.

Changes in peasant diet are hard to detect, but caloric levels might have been raised during the massive growth in population after the year 1000 if large numbers of people switched from land-intensive grains and meats to labor-intensive peas and beans. The emergence of the three-field farming system after 1250 and the more specialized rotations which appeared in some regions are testimony to the increasing importance of nitrogen-fixing legumes which were planted every spring. On the much-studied estates of the bishop of Winchester, the area sown with legumes rose from less than 1 percent in 1206 to more than 8 percent in 1345. In eastern Norfolk and eastern Kent, where husbandry techniques were the most ad-

---

of the sixty monks of the monastic household three times weekly." It is not clear, however, if these were all the chickens and eggs produced by the peasantry; nevertheless, it is a clear sign of the upward flow of wealth that characterized this economy. Moreover, the fact that this wealth moved from peasant to lord in such a visible form underscores the personal nature of feudal exactions. Having to part with a chicken or a few eggs several times a week was a more immediate reminder of living in an empire of subjugation than paying money rent once a year. See Kathleen Biddick, *The Other Economy*, 125.

235. Lynn White, "Food and History," in Dwain N. Walcher, Norman Kretchmer, and Henry L. Barnett (eds.), *Food, Man, and Society* (New York, 1976), 12–30. See also E. M. Veale, "The Rabbit in England," *Agricultural History Review* 5 (1957): 85–90; Mark Bailey, "The Rabbit and the Medieval East Anglian Economy," *Agricultural History Review* 36 (1988): 1–20.

vanced, the proportion of the total demesne acreage sown with legumes was almost 25 percent.[236] Of the 65,606 bushels of cereals harvested in 1309–10 on the manors of the Abbey of Peterborough, 7.5 percent were legumes. Between one-quarter and one-half of the peas, beans, and vetches were fed to pigs; the rest was fed to the estate's workers.[237]

Vegetables and legumes "appear infrequently in the [manorial] records and only rarely were they listed amongst rents and tithes, probably because, being grown on the small private plots and gardens of the peasantry, they were not subject to such demands."[238] The poor ate a diet of coarse maislin bread and pease porridge.[239] John Hus, the Czech reformer who was executed as a heretic in 1415, claimed that "when I was a poor student I used to make a spoon out of a piece of bread till I had done eating my pease porridge, then I ate the spoon."[240] Quite literally, peasants had "pease porridge hot, pease porridge cold, pease porridge in the pot nine days old." Thus, while grains may have composed about 90 percent of all references to crops in the monastic documents, to which historians are usually limited in their study of the rural economy, they would appear to have been much less significant in the diet eaten by the great mass of the common people. Historians have misled themselves if they have only considered these demesne-focused manorial documents instead of taking into account the legume-intensive diet that was produced for personal use from the peasants' own croft or garden.[241]

236. B. M. S. Campbell and J. P. Power, "Mapping the Agricultural Geography of Medieval England," *Journal of Historical Geography* 15 (1989): 24–39. See also Campbell, "Arable Productivity in Medieval England: Some Evidence from Norfolk," *Journal of Economic History* 43 (1983): 379–404; "Agricultural Progress in Medieval England: Some Evidence from Eastern Norfolk," *Economic History Review,* 2d ser., 36 (1983): 26–46; "The Diffusion of Vetches in Medieval England," *Economic History Review,* 2d ser., 41 (1988): 193–208; as well as Campbell and Overton, "A New Perspective on Medieval and Early Modern Agriculture," *passim.*

237. Biddick, *The Other Economy,* 77 (Table 20).

238. Pounds, *An Historical Geography of Europe,* 374.

239. Edward Britton, *The Community of the Vill: A Study in the History of the Family and Village Life in Fourteenth Century England* (Toronto, 1977), 161–62; H. C. Hallam, *Rural Society, 1066–1348* (London, 1981), 65–67, 248–51. M. M. Postan notes the increase in leguminous crops in the pre-1348 period but gives short shrift to their use in the peasants' diet; *The Medieval Economy and Society* (Harmondsworth, 1975), 56–57. R. H. Hilton also suggests that the diet of the poor was largely composed of carbohydrates and discounts the value of second-class proteins supplied by legumes; *A Medieval Society: The West Midlands at the End of the Thirteenth Century* (London, 1966), 110–13.

240. Quoted in Michael Mullett, *Popular Culture and Popular Protest in Late Medieval and Early Modern Europe* (London, 1987), 115.

241. David Grigg, *Population Growth and Agrarian Change* (Cambridge, 1980), 73, 75. See also Duby, *Rural Economy,* 94–98; Fichtenau, *Living in the Tenth Century,* 342–45.

Analysis of the food served to lodging servants and wage laborers (*famuli*) provides some further insight into the social distribution of calories. Both bread and ale were divided into three qualities, for three different sorts of people. The typical servant or laborer was normally given large quantities of coarse, dark bread, an average of more than five pounds per day. Pottage made from oats and legumes was a secondary staple. Surprisingly, ale was rarely present in the manorial accounts because while they were at work, the poor drank water. Cheese and butter are seldom mentioned, and then in only minimal amounts; meat, eggs, and milk were wholly absent from their diets. In contrast, the food supplied during the harvest and at plowing time (as well as on holidays and other festival celebrations) was both substantial and replete with the first-class animal proteins so completely lacking during the rest of the year. Yet, these benefits were not shared equally; it is essential to bear in mind that this food was supplied to workers, not to their families. Wives and children obviously had to make do from the cottage garden and family plot. In addition, the peasants' ale came from their own source of supply and must have been paid for out of their own pockets.[242]

In general, the poor had restricted access to primary proteins. Fishing, for example, was subjected to private control so that it became "a twig in the bundle of remunerative rights being assembled into lordship." This was bitterly resented, and poaching was common.[243] Other nutrients were in all likelihood subjected to a similar socioeconomic bias which was cross-cut with a partriarchy of the table. Women and children were considered to have less entitlement.

The major increase in the sowing of peas and beans occurred in the time of rising population. It was a method of internal colonization by which a larger population could provide for its subsistence not only by extending the cultivated area but also by increasing caloric productivity per acre. Of course, survival would have been purchased at the cost of reducing the vital intake of first-class proteins and iron.

Dietary change may be one reason why the evidence of the early fourteenth century seems to suggest that demographic growth was slowing down. One might venture that the cause of this slowdown was only partly higher mortality; most probably, declining growth also resulted from lower fertility among the poorer elements in the population who were becoming subject, once more, to the stultifying effects of poor diet, which

242. H. C. Hallam, "The Life of the People: The Worker's Diet," in *The Agrarian History of England and Wales*, vol. 2, *1086–1350*, 825–45.
243. Hoffman, "Economic Development and Aquatic Ecosystems," 653–54.

caused iron-deficiency anemia among women of childbearing age. Adult women require twice as much iron as men because menstruation, pregnancy, childbirth, and lactation are all voracious consumers of this vital mineral. Moreover, it would seem reasonable that "the early medieval diet would have resulted in a high rate of female mortality due to iron-deficiency anemia." Perhaps this was also the case among the desperate, famished poor whose numbers mushroomed in the century after 1250.[244]

The fifteenth-century population surveys analyzed by David Herlihy all show a numerical preponderance of women, which was precisely the opposite state of affairs for similar evidence from the Carolingian period, when the sex ratio was skewed in favor of men.[245] This insightful research also goes some way to suggesting how we can connect long-term improvements in diet to variations in human fertility and, especially, female survival during the difficult childbearing years. Diet was the keystone which held together a biological arch: high mortality, a generally low level of female health, and quite probably a low rate of fertility caused by both early death and secondary sterility among those who could survive throughout their fecund period. One might plausibly reckon that even the surviving women would have had trouble carrying a fetus to term as a result of their high rates of spontaneous abortions, miscarriages, difficult deliveries, and stillbirths. Increasing the iron (and protein) in female diet would therefore have had dramatic effects since the improved food supply probably led to lower female mortality rates, indicated by the changing sex ratios, as well as higher fertility levels among the survivors.

If these improvements were not uniform, taking a bottom-up perspective on the long term makes it seem reasonable to suggest that there was a

244. Vern Bullough and Cameron Campbell, "Female Longevity and Diet in the Middle Ages," *Speculum* 55 (1980): 324. Anemic individuals are at substantially greater risk from diseases such as pneumonia, bronchitis, and emphysema because they further diminish the supply of oxygen to the blood. Cardiac problems compound the problem by reducing the efficacy of the oxyhemoglobin curve (322).

245. Herlihy, "Life Expectancies for Women in Medieval Society," in R. T. Morewedge (ed.), *The Role of Women in the Middle Ages* (Albany, N.Y., 1975), 1–22. It might also be relevant to note here that the godly women who were most likely to have embarked on a life of saintly self-abnegation and food abstinence were largely children of elite parents. For these young women, rejection of food might have been easier in the sense that they had not grown up with material privation. The connection between gluttony, lust, and privilege perhaps meant that self-denial appealed to such young women when they reached puberty and decided to reject the worldly roles assigned to them; Caroline Walker Bynum, "Fast, Feast, and Flesh: The Religious Significance of Food to Medieval Women," *Representations* (1985): 1–25.

very substantial upgrading of the diet of those least entitled as a result of their position at the bottom of society. It was surely of the greatest significance for these people that famine seems to have been held at bay during the two centuries of demographic advance after about 1050. Taking all the evidence together yields a composite picture in which agricultural expansion was able to keep pace with demographic advance and also reached down to the least privileged, whose diets were upgraded sufficiently to counteract their lack of entitlement to food. In this regard, colonization after the year 1000 was a success insofar as it enabled more people to live in Europe as well as enabling more of them to live better than their forebears.

6.

The medieval population/resources equation had three dimensions, none of which was fixed. First, land clearances (*assarts*) led to a significant massive increase in cultivated territory—especially pasture on which to feed the draft animals whose muscle power was harnessed to furrow through the heavy clay soils of the northwest. Second, not only did the population grow dramatically in the ten generations after the year 1000, but it also became spatially distributed in a radically new way. Economy and demography were engaged in a dynamic interplay.[246] Third, significant improvements in agrarian technique and labor productivity raised yields from a

---

246. Georges Duby seems to be of two minds concerning the driving force behind this colonization movement. He is unwilling to allow for an exclusive focus upon either lordly or peasant initiative. He first states that "the tide of demographic expansion was the main stimulus for the fragmentation and multiplication of agricultural holdings, and for the pronounced mobility of the rural population that was becoming more marked as the twelfth century progressed," but a few pages later he writes, "The peak period of intense activity appears to lie between the years 1075 and 1180. It is difficult to state precisely its relations to demographic growth, for its chronology is just as hazy"; *The Early Growth of the European Economy*, 184–85, 202–3. Robert Fossier is likewise ambivalent with regard to the mechanisms by which the French countryside was peopled, although his chronology is rather more clearly defined. Fossier, too, is impressed with "l'extraordinaire variété des contingencies locales qui characterise l'époque centrale du Moyen Age"; "La Démographie médiévale: Problèmes de méthode (Xᵉ–XIIIᵉ siècles)," *Annales de Démographie Historique* (1975): 143–65; "Peuplement de la France du Nord entre le Xᵉ et le XVIᵉ siècles," *Annales de Démographie Historique* (1979): 59–99. These two articles by Fossier provide an impressive survey of the massive effort by French historians to discover the social organization of rural society. They are, to some extent, transfixed by local variation, so that one comes away with the idea that the motive force of change can only have been sheer demographic vitality. Fossier declines to face the relationship between modes of production and modes of reproduction, so he gives us no idea about the nature of this interaction; "Peuplement de la France," 75.

fixed unit of land. Intensified land use could be accompanied by extremely high population densities that were, in turn, fed by the proactive deployment of human resources.[247]

247. Christopher Thornton, "The Determinants of Land Productivity on the Bishop of Winchester's Demesne of Rimpton, 1208–1403," in Bruce M. S. Campbell and Mark Overton (eds.), *Land, Labour, and Livestock*, 183–210.

3 Living in the Material World

THE SEIGNEURIAL MESH

Viewed from the bottom up, the feudal revolution captured the mass of the population in "The Seigneurial Mesh." Feudalism was not taken for granted; rather, it was violently imposed. The transformation of freemen and slaves into serfs occurred around the year 1000 under conditions of brutal subjugation. The subsistence economy of use and common rights of the mass of the population was thereafter pitted against the lords' seigneurial economy of exchange and fiscal extraction. The political economy of feudalism imposed a double rent on the servile population—they paid economic rent for the land they worked while being subjected to a bewildering variety of extra-economic charges on their bodies and their time. Particular attention is focused on the divergent routes followed in the aftermath of the feudal revolution. Commutation of extra-economic rent proceeded faster on the continent during la révolution censive, whereas, in contrast, thirteenth-century England was characterized by a feudal reaction. This, in turn, led to the creation of a massive inventory of manorial documents, making it possible to describe not only the range of extra-economic charges that feudalists levied upon the servile population but also the strategic implementation of feudal dues.

If the success of the Gregorian Reformation represented one aspect of the early modernization of Europe, then the feudal social revolution was the other side of this coin. In the period around the year 1000 the various grades of dependent cultivators found themselves being assimilated into a single class, although originally they and their landholdings had been arrayed in a continuum of juridical conditions, stretching from freedom to slavery. The fact that "innumerable peasants, by ancestral status free—in the primitive sense; not slaves—had got entangled in the meshes of the *seigneurie"* is "really the crucial problem" in the rise of dependent cultivation.[1]

The creation of rural seigneuries had its origins in the transformation of freemen and slaves into serfs and villeins. This was the dominant social process of the twelve generations who lived from the rise of the Carolingians through to the year 1000. After the year 1000, the specialized development of these manorial units evolved in response to the positive feedback system elaborated in the preceding chapters. The dramatic increase in the role of a money economy did not transform the manor into an exchange economy, but its autarkic character was shattered as commercial considerations permeated every transaction.[2]

In a large part of the old feudal heartland, *la révolution censive* obliterated the original role of the manorial system during the twelfth century. The analysis of manorial court rolls thus has been confined to England, where they have survived in abundance. This survival seems to be rather less a reflection of England's legendary, stable social evolution and rather more an indication of the distinctive characteristics of the English road to early modernization: renewed feudalism, legalism, and strong central government administration which backed the rights of feudal lords in national courts.[3] English manorial records, created for their own administrative rea-

1. Marc Bloch, "The Rise of Dependent Cultivation and Seigneurial Institutions," in M. M. Postan (ed.), *The Cambridge Economic History of Europe*, vol. 1 (Cambridge, 1966), 253, 255.

2. It is apposite to mention that a more optimistic view of market penetration is presented by Graeme Donald Snooks, although I remain unconvinced by his argument. Snooks suggests that 40 percent of the economy was involved in market activities and 60 percent in subsistence. Snooks further estimates that 30 percent of the GDP entered the market, of which three-quarters found its way into international trade. It is crucial to bear in mind that this "market sector" was dominated by manorialists—1,100 tenants-in-chief and 6,000 undertenants who controlled a rural workforce of 268,279—who were trading the surplus generated from their estates to get their hands on the cash necessary to purchase luxury goods. Snooks's econometric studies of the Domesday Book are mainly concerned with macroeconomic measures, viewed from the top down. His measurements are based on exchange values and not use values, which would be more relevant to those living in the subsistence sector. Most dependent peasants—Snooks's rural workforce of 268,279—lived at the subsistence level and had little involvement with marketing arrangements. See "The Dynamic Role of the Market in the Anglo-Norman Economy and Beyond, 1086–1300," in Richard H. Britnell and B. M. S. Campbell (eds.), *A Commercialising Economy: England 1086 to c. 1300* (Manchester, 1995), 27–54; see also J. McDonald and G. D. Snooks, *Domesday Economy: A New Approach to Anglo-Norman History* (Oxford, 1986).

3. The use of these documents for systematic social history was pioneered by a group of scholars at the Pontifical Institute for Medieval Studies at the University

sons as a regulatory tool to maintain the landlord's surveillance of the inhabitants of his empire of domination, are perhaps the most exceptional documentary survival from the feudal period.[4]

The survival of English manorial records thus appears to be a double exception: first, because they were kept in such large numbers when the manorial system was in decline elsewhere in the northwest heartland of the feudal system; and second, because, in the words of Jacques Le Goff, "From now on, the destruction of archives and inventories (later known as *terriers*) was to be one of the essential gestures in revolts."[5] The primary consideration in creating these documents was to involve villagers in a system which ended up diverting their resources to the lord's exchequer. These documents were the instrument of the servile classes' subjection within the new regulatory gaze of artificial memory.

---

of Toronto. The main works are J. A. Raftis, *Tenure and Mobility: Studies in the Social History of the Medieval English Village* (Toronto, 1964); J. A. Raftis, *Warboys: Two Hundred Years in the Life of a Medieval English Village* (Toronto, 1974); E. B. Dewindt, *Land and People in Holywell-cum-Needingworth: Structures of Tenure and Patterns of Social Organization in an East Midlands Village, 1252–1457* (Toronto, 1972); and Edward Britton, *The Community of the Vill: A Study in the History of the Family and Village Life in Fourteenth-Century England* (Toronto, 1977). For two evaluations of this work, see Keith Wrightson, "Medieval Villagers in Perspective," *Peasant Studies* 7 (1978): 203–17; and Zvi Razi, "The Toronto School's Reconstitution of Medieval Peasant Society," *Past and Present* 85 (1980): 141–57. French records are not so detailed. They are further removed from the observation of individuals, so that scholarly efforts have been devoted to recovering the aggregated, local relationships between "la conquête des sols" and "déplacement des hommes" in order to gain "le sens d'un mouvement, et non plus de le quantifier"; Robert Fossier, "La Démographie médiévale: Problèmes de méthode (Xe-XIIIe siècles)," *Annales de Démographie Historique* (1975): 145.

4. It is necessary to bear this in mind because any historical source—and particularly routinely generated sources—is liable to distort past realities. These products of artificial memory inform us about their own concerns. The historian's "science," as it were, is to evaluate this distortion. For a discussion of this problem of selective bias and the usefulness of English manorial documents for research in historical demography with particular reference to Zvi Razi's study of Halesowen, see L. R. Poos and R. M. Smith, " 'Legal Windows onto Historical Populations'? Recent Research on Demography and the Manor Court in Medieval England," *Law and History Review* 2 (1984): 128–52; Zvi Razi, "The Use of Manorial Court Rolls in Demographic Analysis: A Reconsideration," *Law and History Review* 3 (1985): 191–200; L. R. Poos and R. M. Smith, " 'Shades Still on the Window': A Reply to Zvi Razi," *Law and History Review* 3 (1985): 409–29; and Zvi Razi, "The Demographic Transparency of Manorial Court Rolls," *Law and History Review* 5 (1987): 523–35.

5. Jacques Le Goff, *Medieval Civilization 400–1500* (Oxford, 1988), 345–46.

1.

It was in relation to the orderly maintenance of stable domestic government among his dependent population that "the lord's interest in the supply of demesne labour induced him to interfere in the personal affairs of his servile dependents, extending regulation beyond the immediate tenant to include the peasant family as well."[6] It is not clear, however, to what extent this "interference" was conducted on a daily basis as opposed to the more generalized maintenance of frontiers and boundaries within the social formation. In considering this question it is perhaps useful to recall a relevant point made by Marc Bloch: "The slave had been an ox in the stable, always under his master's orders; the villein, even if he was a serf, was a worker who came on certain days and who left as soon as the job was finished."[7]

The creation of peasant tenements was "the result of a far-reaching innovation, a new method of utilizing dependent labour. In this period [i.e., from the end of the sixth century], great landowners seem to have been discovering that it was profitable to marry off some of their slaves, settle them on a manse, and make them responsible for cultivating its appurtenant lands and feeding their own families. The process would relieve the master by reducing costs of staff maintenance, generate enthusiasm for work on the part of the servile task-force, increase its productivity and ensure its replacement, since these slave couples would be entrusted with seeing to their childrens' upbringing themselves until they became of working age."[8] The transformation of slaves and freemen into serfs and villeins forms the baseline from which subsequent developments materialized.

In the Carolingian period the peasant tenement (*manse*) seems to have had three different meanings. Often it was an enclosure on which the house was built; sometimes it was the whole farmstead, including its landed properties; and the term was also used in a generic form to denote a measurement of land. This physical connotation was only one side of the coin; the other side was the fact that the manse was a kind of tenure, heritable in the family of the man who had cleared and worked that property. When the word appeared around A.D. 650 it already had a strong seigneurial stamp, since we learn about manses from the accounts of lords and kings who had adopted the single-family farm as the basic unit on which rents

6. Chris Middleton, "Peasants, Patriarchy and the Feudal Mode of Production in England: I," *Sociological Review* 29 (1981): 110.

7. Marc Bloch, "How and Why Ancient Slavery Came to an End," in Bloch, *Slavery and Serfdom in the Middle Ages* (Berkeley and Los Angeles, 1975), 23.

8. Georges Duby, *The Early Growth of the European Economy* (Ithaca, 1974), 40.

and dues were imposed. David Herlihy suggests that this was not a complete novelty. He connects the manse with the ancient "squatters' sovereignty" and argues that there was an element of continuity in the customs governing colonization in western Europe: "the work of settlement, it would seem, had to be organized on the basis of the small group of willing workers: small, able, at a time when capital, markets and transport were defective, to survive largely by foraging in the wilderness over those critical years until the land should fructify; willing, not driven like the slave to the sloppy performance of his *sordidum servitium*, but able through spontaneous effort to sustain the hard labours that colonization required."[9]

The manse thus arose out of settlement, was permanently in the possession of the man who worked it, was heritable in his family though burdened with service to the owner of the land, and was roughly equal in size across units. It meant a heritable tenement that was the colonizers' analogue to the landowners' property rights. The development of a similar set of interconnections between units of land, lineages, status hierarchies, and feudal dependency in Britain is suggested by T. M. Charles-Edwards. He notes that the possession of a hide distinguished a freeman from a man of dependent status. He further suggests that, in the later seventh century, many legally free peasants had been reduced to something less than independence. They had become the tenants of manorial lords in a system of patronage and dependence.[10]

Another top-down view of this early medieval reorganization has been proposed by Walter Goffart, who notes that the methods of control revealed in Carolingian *polyptych* can be located in the militarization of social relations in the fourth century. In Goffart's view, ownership and rents were transformed under the pressure of tax legislation in the late Roman state which dissolved earlier distinctions between "public" and "private" forms of revenue. He writes that "the distinction between tax and rent, which we take seriously but their vocabulary ignored, would have depended only upon the identity of the recipient." For Goffart, the key element is the transition from rents in money to rents in kind. Thus "the 'ordaining' of an estate was not a passive registry of the status quo but a positive reorganization, the sort of moment when, on a given vill, diversity

---

9. David Herlihy, "The Carolingian *Mansus*," *Economic History Review*, 2d ser., 13 (1960): 79–89. For a further discussion of the demographic implications of this pioneering form of family formation, see Monique Zerner-Chardavoine, "Enfants et jeunes au IXᵉ siècle: La démographie du polyptyque de Marseille 813–814," *Provence Historique* (1981): 355–84.

10. T. M. Charles-Edwards, "Kinship, Status and the Origins of the Hide," *Past and Present* 56 (1972): 3–33.

and incoherence in the size of peasant tenures and in the amount of their services were superseded by roughly uniform *coloniae* (or *mansi*) owning uniform services and dues." The Frankish seigneurie, which had an organic bond between peasant tenures and demesnal services, was a creative adaptation within a countryside whose economic life continued to be pervaded by Roman tax law. Those who drew up the *polyptych* in the act of appropriating wealth from the peasantry had become estate managers; they had drawn themselves nearer to the peasantry, proportioned the size of peasant manses to the *servitia* they owed, and not only maintained dues in kind but also provided for the productive use of labor services on the demesne. The seventh-century peasantry, for their part, were not taxed on their land, per se, but rather they continued to fulfill personal tax obligations by cultivating the soil.[11] The peasants' *retrait lignager*—the right to inherit villein holdings for customary tenants' families—was a crucial counterweight to the arbitrary power of seigneurs. In a sense this was a quid pro quo—it gave the lord a solid core of reliable tenants who had some interest in the vitality of the manor while it gave the peasant patriarchs the semblance of control over their property, thereby entrenching their power within the manse.[12]

In the two centuries bracketing the year 1000, the servile peasantry came to form the vast majority of the total population. By 1100 its conditions, obligations, and rights were fairly homogeneous, although the "assimilation of tenants into a common pattern of dependence did not mean the elimination of local and national variations; indeed, it is not surprising that such peculiarities should exist, but [rather] that there should be so many common features of dependence over a wide area."[13]

2.

The feudal social revolution also had a spatial dimension, a hierarchy of zones:

> The centre or core was in northern France, in the Parisian basin, distinct in every sense—densely populated, a rich agriculture, politically and intellectually preponderant. Beyond, a ring of brilliant secondary zones, from the Thames basin, to Flanders, to southern Germany, to the Po valley and to Northern Spain. Further afield begins a more backward periphery: late in development, backward in techniques, more sparsely

11. Walter Goffart, "From Roman Taxation to Mediaeval Seigneurie," *Speculum* 47 (1972): 165–87, 373–94.
12. Marc Bloch, "The Rise of Dependent Cultivation and Seignorial Institutions," 179–80.
13. R. H. Hilton, *Bond Men Made Free* (London, 1973), 56, 59.

populated, unfavourable terms of trade with the central zones and loose political structures.[14]

Seigneurial society in its prime was located on the lowland areas of northwest Europe where wealth was measured in abstracted units of labor—that is, in manors, which were themselves founded upon the replication of the peasant family, their primary unit of production. The supply of the manorial labor force cannot simply be seen as an automatic response to improvements in life chances. Population growth was thus both a cause and an effect of the colonization movement. The colonizing labor force was provided by the peasant cultivator and his family. Social relations of production fused bonded labor with the cellular reproduction of manorial institutions. The organic simplicity of manorial institutions was crucially linked to the processes of cellular division by which colonization was accomplished. In turn, the colonized land mass provided the ecological window of opportunity which removed the limits to growth inherent in the spatial organization of the Carolingian archipelago. As was to happen again in the future, after the pioneering generations passed through this window of opportunity, their descendants entered into a period of free-fall when the long secular boom ended and a new regime of negative feedbacks slammed it shut in their faces. In the interim, however, ten generations of peasants lived in a feudal world.

There was a symbiotic interaction between the political, military, and economic development of seigneurial power and the social organization of those who were kept within its empire of subjugation. While a distinct minority of the population remained free, the great majority were connected to their protectors by personal bondage. Manorial land was encumbered with both feudal rent and economic rent; together, these exactions skimmed off about half of the villein's gross output. The more stable feudal society which began to emerge after the year 1000 was accompanied by the earliest documented obligations of manorial service: the less well organized the seigneury, the less rapid and less productive its economic development.[15] England's developing state structure was unique in its entrenchment of

14. Guy Bois, "Author's Foreword to the English Edition," *The Crisis of Feudalism* (Cambridge: 1984), xi. See also Marc Bloch, *Feudal Society* (Chicago, 1961), 445–46.

15. Jean Chapelot and Robert Fossier, *The Village and House in the Middle Ages* (Berkeley and Los Angeles, 1985), 140–48. This argument turns Karl Marx's famous aphorism upside-down: "Social relations are closely bound up with productive forces. In acquiring new productive forces men change their mode of production; and in changing their mode of production, in changing their way of living, they change all their social relations. The hand-mill gives you society with the feu-

private property rights, while the Norman Conquest was of crucial importance in changing slaves and freemen into serfs and villeins. The English countryside was converted from a dispersed pattern of settlement to a regulated grid of planned communities which has provided the basis for that marvel of census enumeration—the Domesday Book of 1086.[16]

It was under conditions of murder and mayhem that seigneurialism came to dominate social relations in the northwest of Europe. Even before it addressed material needs, feudalism was a system of protection offered by the strong to the weak. Labor could be extracted by extra-economic compulsion because personal dependence had been "the only social adhesive that counted" in the early Middle Ages. Feudal relations began to develop in "the upheavals of the ninth and tenth centuries [when] the crying social need was for protection, which only the powerful could provide. To do so, they needed the labour of men to feed them and their fighting men, their vassals [and, of course, their horses]. The final breakdown of the state machine further threatened the small man with the fate of which, probably, human beings are most afraid, absence of legal and social identity."[17] The ties between vassal and chief—or between landlords and *their* villeins—only slowly subdued a turbulent countryside.

The triumph of the armed rider put a new form of social power into operation, but its application was conditioned by the particular structure of each different state formation. Thus, while the Paris Basin may have been the *locus classicus* of feudal society, it was in England where this social formation became most deeply rooted. The precocious centralization of the English state had generalized social relations to a far greater extent than was the case in France, where the Capetians had "reassembled" the state and, in so doing, had had to concede far more power to intermediaries than was the case across the Channel. This situation prevailed in the feudal heartland of southern England; on the margins (the marches), the central

---

dal lord; the steam-mill society with the industrial capitalist"; *The Poverty of Philosophy,* 122, quoted in G. A. Cohen, *Karl Marx's Theory of History: A Defence* (Princeton, 1978), 143–44. It is perhaps germane to remember that the transition from hunting and gathering to civilization was accompanied by, and interacted with, massive population growth and significant deterioration in the health and life expectation of the masses. Political economy is about both power and production; one is well advised to see the two interacting rather than giving primacy to one factor as if it were some sort of Newtonian "prime mover."

16. Kathleen A. Biddick, "Malthus in a Straitjacket? Analyzing Agrarian Change in Medieval England," *Journal of Interdisciplinary History* 20 (1990): 632–33.

17. Maurice Keen, *The Pelican History of Medieval Europe* (Harmondsworth, 1969), 51.

state granted local lords much greater independence. In their conquest of the "Celtic fringe" (i.e., Wales, Scotland, and Ireland) and even the upland regions of the north and west of England, they were motivated by much the same crusading ideals and imperialist discourse that drove forward the German colonization of the lands east of the Elbe.[18] The fact that these Celtic peoples were also Christian was disregarded by emphasizing their barbarism and lack of civilized behavior in economic, chivalric, and dynastic activities. Of particular significance in this regard is the fact that while the English had adopted the novel Christian ideas about monogamy and restrictions on consanguineous marriages, the Celts had not. Their marital customs were thereby branded as bestial because, according to the new theories of marriage, they thought nothing of committing incest and adultery.[19]

Christianization developed in tandem with feudalism and peasant society to form the classic framework for European rural life under the *ancien régime.* Until the year 1000 rural parishes were unusual because the common arena of Christian worship that had been inherited from antiquity was the urban diocese presided over by a bishop. In the following two centuries, paralleling the development of the seigneury, the countryside was organized into a system of parochial units.[20] New social relations connected the fighting classes and the laboring classes shortly after the year 1000. French medieval historians call this two-pronged process of local, spatial organization *encellulement:* "the church and the castle ["the seignorial cell"] are the twin anchors of settlement."[21]

The establishment of feudalism, with its grinding equality in servitude, has to be connected with the pervasive millenarianism sublimating political resistance into another sphere in which a classless society would be established among the children of God. The violence of the feudal status quo created a fertile soil for those who questioned its legitimacy. In making a

18. See James Given, *State and Society in Medieval Europe* (Ithaca, 1990); R. R. Davies, *Domination and Conquest: The Experience of Ireland, Scotland and Wales* (Cambridge, 1990).

19. John Gillingham, "The Beginnings of English Imperialism," *Journal of Historical Sociology* 5 (1992): 392–409; see also Richard Hoffman, "Outsiders by Birth and Blood: Racist Ideologies and Realities around the Periphery of Medieval European Culture," *Studies in Medieval and Renaissance History* 10 (1984): 3–34.

20. On the organization of the rural parochial system, see Susan Reynolds, *Kingdoms and Communities in Western Europe, 900–1300* (Oxford, 1984), 79–100.

21. Chapelot and Fossier, *The Village and House in the Middle Ages,* 148. Dietrich Gerhard suggests that alongside the castle and the church, we should also add the peasant community as one of the main rivets of rural life; *Old Europe: A Study in Continuity, 1000–1800* (New York, 1981), 19.

pact with the feudalists, the Church was quite literally making a pact with the devil of the popular imagination. It was a hard bargain, one which was to have profound consequences.

Since it has been so influential, it is worthwhile recapitulating Georges Duby's explication of the feudal revolution:

> The real arena of power was now the great domain; it was here that the warriors continued their rapine—the general population had become the sole object of their pillaging. This was a new mode of production, based on the seignory, the *potestas*, the right of confiscation within a zone of military occupation. What penetrated into the realm of customs [i.e., into law] was nothing other than the whole range of extortions that the populace had to bear whenever its rulers were not on campaign. The castellan and his band of retainers put on a terrifying show of force so that the villagers were thereby impelled to pay up their taxes without raising too much of a fuss. The knights were oppression incarnate. Taking with one hand, receiving with the other, the knights were the real hub of the seignorial economy, the driving wheel of the system of exploitation.
>
> The process of seignorialization bound to labor any layman who was not a man of arms. Those who labored are, like Adam after the Fall, condemned to sweat in forced labor, condemned to the servile condition. The incontestable growth of the rural economy accentuated the contrast between leisure and labor in this period; it made men aware—in a major upheaval in mental attitudes—of the part that production played in the social organism, of the role of that surplus product of peasant labor that fed the specialists in both kinds of combat, spiritual and temporal, a surplus consumed by the soldiers of both armies. The establishment of new relations of domination had shifted the locus of the food-producing function in social space. Previously, the obligation to toil in order to feed a master had been relegated outside the sphere of the "people": it had fallen upon slaves. Now, after the year 1000, with the increased weight of the power of the ban, this burden came to be borne by all "rustics." Toil was the common fate of all men who were neither warriors nor priests.
>
> The family's image dominated all modes of thought, obstinately superimposing itself on every representation of power, dichotomized on the basis of age, in virtue of which each individual was assigned his proper place in that other procession, biological and genetic, wherein the successive generations were made to follow one after the other in orderly sequence in households, in dynasties, in an eluctable order. . . .[22]

22. Georges Duby, *The Three Orders: Feudal Society Imagined* (Chicago, 1980), 151–65. I have taken the liberty of smoothing the flow of this lengthy quotation but have tried to keep the original's meaning and its flavor.

Lords needed the surplus which a stable peasantry could yield, and peasants needed the peace and protection which armed protectors could provide. Peasants paid through the nose in exchange for lordly protection, whether they liked it or not. They were subjected to a bewildering variety of taxes and fines on their economic activities. Their bodies were not free, and they were required to provide labor services which reflected the primitive technical conditions in which they were first demanded.

Freeholding peasants existed at all times and in all places, but for the mass of the population the essential social reality became the fact that landowners demanded (and received) labor services and myriad special taxes as their rental payment. In the words of English medievalist R. H. Hilton,

> the *seigneurie*, lordship or manor . . . was the institution that the two great classes met face to face—the landowners great and small and the peasants rich and poor, the first to receive, the second to give their labour or the fruits of their labour, in cash or in kind. It was the principal theatre of that act of coercion, sanctified by custom, legitimated juridically in the various forms of dependence, ranging from serfdom to villeinage, by which the infinitely scattered surpluses of the peasant economy were concentrated into the hands of the politically and socially dominant class.[23]

Labor services, in the continental heartland of feudalism north of the Loire, "were the principal dues owed by tenants of the *villa* to the lord, being far more important than quit-rents (*cens*) and . . . both industrial and agricultural *corvées* were extremely heavy." How heavy? From the later, English evidence discussed by M. M. Postan, it would appear that the average feudal levy was near or more than half of the villein's gross output. Of course, it has to be borne in mind that the evidence Postan cites blends two forms of expropriation: land-rent and seigneurial exactions. The feudal rent, insofar as it was collected in labor services, would be largely unmonetized. The importance of this factor is that there is no shorthand rule of thumb by which one can measure the lost opportunity costs squeezed from the peasantry by the landlord's ability to commandeer labor at will.[24] Indeed, from the bottom-up perspective of the servile population the key di-

---

23. R. H. Hilton, "Feudalism or *Féodalité and Seigneurie* in France and England," in *Class Conflict and the Crisis of Feudalism* (London, 1985), 157.

24. F. L. Ganshof and A. Verhulst, "Medieval Agrarian Society in Its Prime: France, the Low Countries, and Western Germany," 314; M. M. Postan, "Medieval Agrarian Society in Its Prime: England," 603; both in M. M. Postan (ed.), *The Cambridge Economic History of Europe*, vol. 1.

mension of feudalism was that it was a mode of labor appropriation which had been set in motion by the lords' military domination.

The vitality of the seigneurial empire of subjugation hinged upon retaining control of the dependent population while using its *force majeure* to collect something more than—and different from—a market rent for the use of its land. The political intent of this process is obvious—the manor was not necessarily a homogeneous territorial bloc: "Widely dispersed, the lord's rights were, moreover, very diverse, some being exercised over the land and some over people."[25] Seen from the perspective of the peasantry, the spatial organization of feudal society seemed like

> a chequerboard on which occupation was legitimized in some spaces but not others. Within the former, arable rights in land were assiduously regulated through the relations of lord and peasant. Outside these assessed areas, that is, over the surrounding waste, peasant communities had certain use-rights . . . but not the right to extend the arable since this would breach their assessment and, in the process, the conditions on which they held land. New arable or newly assessed land could only be created by the king or lord since, during the heyday of feudalism, it meant extending the feudal concept of land tenure, apportioning blocks of assessed land in return for a fixed levy of services, renders and dues.[26]

The Normans, like the Anglo-Saxons and Franks before them, enacted laws to protect their privileged access to the products of the woodlands. In the twelfth century, royal forests may have covered one-third of the landscape. In effect, these regulations *minified* the land mass of England by creating "no-go" zones which excluded the peasantry from the forest's natural economy.[27] In so doing, these laws firmly attached peasants into the political economy by crowding them onto those feudalized squares on the "chequerboard." Yet, as is always the case, there were countervailing tendencies at work in the heart of the political economy: peasants who colonized the woodlands frequently exchanged their labor power for a relaxation of feudal levies. In effect, these colonizers were able to bargain to commute their feudal obligations as a trade-off for assarting the wilderness and increasing its value for landlords who retained property rights over it.

25. Georges Duby, "The Manor and the Peasant Economy," in *The Chivalrous Society* (Berkeley and Los Angeles, 1977), 193.

26. Robert Dodgshon, *The European Past: Spatial Evolution and Spatial Order* (London, 1987), 192.

27. Della Hooke, "Pre-Conquest Woodland: Its Distribution and Usage," *Agricultural History Review* 37 (1989): 125–29; see also Frank Barlow, *The Feudal Kingdom of England* (London, 1961), 123.

The great lords frequently had estates distributed over a wide area.[28] Barons held many manors, castles, and villages, and exercised lordship over large numbers of dependents. The Beauchamp family, earls of Warwick in the late thirteenth century, for example, had a core of manors in the west Midlands—nine in Worcestershire, ten in Warwickshire, and three in Gloucestershire—but their holdings reached into five other counties across the length and breadth of the realm. Such men were national figures who were not always present locally. Furthermore, even properties on a single manor could be fragmented between villages or other institutional agencies as well as among tenants of differing legal status (not to mention subtenants and sub-subtenants and so on). For feudal landowners, the obstacles of geography were compounded by the micro-organization of their properties. Administration was therefore usually haphazard unless it was delegated to middlemen who skimmed off their share of the take.

Between the pinnacle of the aristocracy and the mass of the peasantry there was a small group of knights, men who were the active agents in the everyday administration of local society. They deferred to the grandees, who quite literally patronized them. In the 1,100 villages and hamlets of the west Midlands, there were some 200 of these intermediaries in the later thirteenth century. Some of these knights held a few manors of their own, and most of the others had enough land and the requisite breeding to distinguish them from the peasantry. These men, then, made up the secular ruling class that, on an everyday basis, imposed feudal controls on the peasantry and kept those controls in working order.

In many villages there was no resident gentleman, let alone a baron in his castle. In the English West Midlands, for example, "Out of 135 villages in Gloucestershire, in the Cotswolds, and the Avon Valley only thirteen had resident gentry." Local society was usually ruled through the agency of the lord's administrative infrastructure. His manorial court was run by the village reeve, assisted by his messors and beadles (franklins); it was overseen by the local bailiff, working with the various wardens, keepers, and parkers who had more specific duties. The central administration of the estate was the responsibility of the steward, whose work was aided by the specialized labors of the receiver and auditor.

Knights were accompanied at the top of local society by the massive presence of the Church, whose corporate holdings dwarfed even those of the greatest landlords. In the West Midlands, the bishop and priory of

---

28. The following paragraphs are based on R. H. Hilton, *A Medieval Society: The West Midlands at the End of the Thirteenth Century* (London, 1966), 23–64.

Worcester had lands in twenty-nine villages or hamlets, the abbots of Evesham and Pershore spread their tentacles into twelve and four communities respectively, and the priories of Great Malvern and Little Malvern had three and five separate establishments. Thus, the Church was able to exercise lordship in fifty-three localities; in contrast, the Beauchamps' main branch had eight seigneuries, while the other temporal feudalists together added up to a total that was roughly similar to that of the ecclesiastics.

Although a large proportion of the population of the West Midlands was free from feudal status, they could hardly escape the ever-present surveillance of the seigneurs. The feudal class dominated the political and social life of the countryside; one was free in relation to the unfreedom that came with this domination in much the same way that in late antiquity one was free in relation to the others who were enslaved. It was the role of ancient slavery (and not its numerical weight) that conditioned the social relations of production. Similarly, one might argue that in the feudal landscape the presence of servile tenants conditioned the social relations of production in areas that were partly free and partly servile. It was a contested relationship, not an emblem or badge.

Driven by their need for cash—the warrior class's military expenses were rising five times as fast as their rental incomes in the 1180–1260 period[29]—and squeezed by the efficiencies of the central government in tapping the money economy, seigneurial lords tried three strategies. They either worked their lands more profitably with better management techniques

29. The national standards in the English law were perhaps the foremost expression of the centralization of its state formation. There was a price to be paid for consolidation. The immense sums which the English Crown took from England to pay for its military activities in Normandy not only had an inflationary effect but also were crucially related to the development of administration and written records. While there was a general movement all over northern Europe on the part of feudal lords to monetize their social relations, the inflationary spiral was most acute in England. The quantity of silver that was being coined at this time was not surpassed until the nineteenth century. Indeed, "The volume of the English currency was rising like a rocket between 1180 and 1280"; D. M. Metcalf, "A Survey of Numismatic Research into the Pennies of the First Three Edwards (1279–1344) and Their Continental Imitations," in N. J. Mayhew (ed.), *Edwardian Monetary Affairs 1279–1344* (Oxford, 1977), 7 (cited in R. H. Britnell, "The Proliferation of Markets in England, 1200–1349," *Economic History Review*, 2d ser., 34 [1981]: 212). See also N. J. Mayhew, "Money and Prices in England from Henry II to Edward III," *Agricultural History Review* 35 (1987): 121–32; P. D. A. Harvey, "The English Inflation of 1180–1220," *Past and Present* 61 (1973): 3–30. For a revisionist argument which would seek to turn around the causality between economic change and legal innovation by giving priority to the royal state-formation initiative, see Robert C. Palmer, "The Economic and Cultural Impact of the Origins of Property," *Law and History Review* 3 (1985).

copied from ecclesiastical landlords, increased feudal exactions, or cashed out their seigneurial domination of the land (and their tenants) in exchange for monetary payments. Often, the same lord used all three methods on different parts of his estate.

The money economy of exchange and private property was pitted against the subsistence economy of use and common rights. The Statutes of Merton (1236) and Westminster (1285) threw the power of the state behind the encloser who planted hedgerows to separate his land from communal constraints. A capitalized pastoral economy split villages, increased polarization, hardened divisions, and undermined common rights.[30] It is crucial to recognize that these changes took place within a feudal social formation. Indeed, it could be argued that the mass of the English population received the worst of both worlds: they were still subjected to the indignities and constraints of personal servitude while being exposed, without resources, to the dirty end of the cash nexus.

English social history of the thirteenth century was exceptional in that lordship was itself rationalized into a money-making operation; in many other parts of Europe the older forms of feudalism were jettisoned and obligations were transformed into money payments. Marc Bloch called the massive commutation of feudal controls into monetary payments *la révolution censive.*[31] In reaction to the central government's novel claims for precedence, English nobles vigorously maintained that their relationship with their villeins was to be kept free from royal intervention, outside the scope of royal justice.[32] Frequently, the letter of the law was scoured to turn up new sources of seigneurial revenue. This seigneurial offensive—we might want to call it fiscal feudalism—was so successful that an estimated

30. On the incursion of marketing strategies into village communities, see Kathleen Biddick, "Missing Links: Taxable Wealth, Markets, and Stratification among Medieval English Peasants," *Journal of Interdisciplinary History* 18 (1987): 277–98.

31. Marc Bloch, *French Rural History* (Berkeley and Los Angeles, 1970), 77 ff. See also B. H. Slicher van Bath, *The Agrarian History of Western Europe: A.D. 500–1850* (London, 1963), 145–51; Georges Duby, *Rural Economy and Country Life in the Medieval West* (London, 1968), 203–20; Ganshof and Verhulst, "Medieval Agrarian Society in Its Prime: France, the Low Countries, and Western Germany," 305–39. Even on the Continent, the movement was not unidirectional. The late thirteenth century witnessed the reemergence of Roman Law concepts that enabled lawyers to detect a similarity between those who were still bound to the soil and the Imperial *colonus.* This was the thin edge of a terrible wedge; Ganshof and Verhulst, "Medieval Agrarian Society in Its Prime: France, the Low Countries, and Western Germany", 337.

32. Paul R. Hyams, *Kings, Lords and Peasants in Medieval England: The Common Law of Villeinage in the Twelfth and Thirteenth Centuries* (Oxford, 1980).

60 percent of the peasantry was legally unfree in the sense that its members were unable to seek legal action in the royal courts against their
lords.[33] Fiscal feudalism thus mutated from the earlier Domesday system
of strict manorialism. It was an adjustment to the increasing monetization
of social relations—the lords' need for money as much as the tenants' ability to pay.

In the thirteenth century the law of villeinage was applied with its
fullest vigor on large estates, at the expense of the servile population.[34]
Labor services came to be exploited more fully and were later found to be
fully operational on those large estates where manorial lords farmed their
own demesne; on other manors, where they were not immediately useful,
the lord turned a profit by making the peasant pay to free himself from
them. It would be a huge mistake, therefore, to contrast feudalism with the
money economy: the two existed in symbiosis.[35]

Feudal incidents were all the taxes and charges which the servile population was forced to pay for the dubious privilege of being protected by living within the lord's empire of subjugation. They provided lords—large
and small—with a political asset which was given as a barter payment to
contractual retainers in exchange for their services. The practice of subinfeudation "brought further entanglements into the cobweb of feudal connections."[36] If subinfeudation made matters more complicated, then that
was the price for rendering both territorial control and personal surveillance more effective. As the whole galaxy of feudal ties became complicated, intertwined, and even contradictory, lords tried to thin out the
subinfeudated undergrowth of hereditary vassals. The phenomenon of
contractual retaining—lifelong clientage—turned on the need to create
less ambiguous relations between lord and servant. It also involved a new

33. For a particularly telling example of this process of fiscal feudalism in
which legal rights were transformed into money income, see Richard Holt, "Whose
Were the Profits of Corn Milling?," *Past and Present* 116 (1987): 3–23. See also
R. H. Hilton, *The Decline of Serfdom in Medieval England* (London, 1983), 16;
Hilton, *Bond Men Made Free*, 127–28; John Hatcher, "English Serfdom and
Villeinage: Towards a Reassessment," *Past and Present* 90 (1981): 37.

34. R. H. Hilton, "Freedom and Villeinage in England," *Past and Present* 31
(1965): 13–14. In fact, during the twelfth century the actual condition of the villagers was much less servile and less burdened with heavy labor dues than it would
be a century later, after the seigneurial offensive to tighten the screws of "fiscal
feudalism"; M. M. Postan (ed.), *The Medieval Economy and Society* (Harmondsworth, 1975), 168.

35. This was much the same relationship as that in which slavery and capitalism existed together in the United States before the Civil War.

36. E. A. Kosminsky, *Studies in the Agrarian History of England in the Thirteenth Century* (Oxford, 1956), 274.

attitude toward legal forms of property and the economic valuation of that property as inflation pinched noble incomes. The cash value of land and feudal incidents came to the fore.

Agricultural treatises informed lords about the frauds perpetrated by the officials who governed their estates.[37] Monetary transfers and the perquisites of office replaced lands held in knights' fee. Alongside their bands of armed retainers, thirteenth-century lords were likely to staff their households with professional receivers, treasurers, auditors, and bailiffs who had specific jobs in an administrative hierarchy headed by the estate steward. By the end of the century, "nearly every large estate shows evidence of a staff of administrative personnel retained by pensions, robes, and long-term relationships and differentiated hierarchically according to their function and status."[38] This clerical professionalism extended to both large and small estates. Smaller manors were more likely to be farmed by noncustomary tenants whose cash rents were of more value than their labor services. Smaller manors were also more likely to be involved in market production, if only because the tenant was required to find money to pay rents.[39] We should allow for substantial variation in the methods by which large magnates sought to enhance and protect their private power. If their methods changed, the lords' goals were constant. The strategic continuity in the political relations of feudalism meant that the role of contractual mercenaries stretched across several centuries—across the whole feudal period.[40]

37. D. Oschinsky, *Walter of Henley and Other Treatises on Estate Management and Accounting* (Oxford, 1971).

38. Scott L. Waugh, "Tenure to Contract: Lordship and Clientage in Thirteenth-Century England," *English Historical Review* 401 (1986): 824. In fact, William Marshal's household seems to have had much of the administrative structure of retaining, as it was based on the great man's political clout. A generation earlier, in his father's day, lords would have drawn together their vassals through the distribution of contingent landed attachments; David Crouch, *William Marshal: Court, Career and Chivalry in the Angevin Empire, 1147–1219* (London, 1990), 133 ff.

39. R. H. Britnell, "Minor Landlords in England and Medieval Agrarian Capitalism," *Past and Present* 89 (1980): 4. It was probably also the case that the largest manors were connected with the provision of surplus consumption products for their super-rich aristocratic or clerical owners.

40. P. R. Coss, "Bastard Feudalism Revised," *Past and Present* 125 (1989): 27–64. For an elaboration of the argument emphasizing the strategic innovations of feudalism (and their connection with state-formation initiatives) see David Crouch, D. A. Carpenter, and P. R. Coss, "Debate: Bastard Feudalism Revised," *Past and Present* 131 (1991): 165–203. In making sense of the change from lord/vassal to patron/client, I also benefited from reading J. Russell Major, " 'Bastard Feudalism' and the Kiss: Changing Social Mores in Late Medieval and Early Modern France," *Journal of Interdisciplinary History* 17 (1987): 509–35.

The lords' cash flow was crucial in maintaining their primary role as fighting men. Feudal society was built for and, indeed, predicated upon warfare. For more than a century after the Battle of Lincoln in 1217— when the son of Philip Augustus was expelled from England and the hemorrhaging defeats of the previous generation of Angevin kings were staunched—the thrust of English policy was one of internal colonization of Wales, Scotland, and England itself. Huge sums of money were spent on building royal castles and, toward the end of the thirteenth century, a more aggressive military posture was adopted. This, too, required money. More taxes meant more local officials. Contemporaries complained about

> Escheators; sub-escheators; coroners; sheriffs; under-sheriffs; taxers; . . . keepers and constables of the peace and of castles and land on the coast; takers and receivers of wool; assessors and receivers of the ninth and other subsidies; . . . keepers of forests, verderers, clerks and other ministers of forests, chases and parks; collectors and controllers of customs; troners, butlers and their substitutes; keepers of the king's horses and their grooms; . . . purveyors of victuals; purveyors for the king's household and its subsidiary households; keepers of goals; electors, triers and arrayers of men-at-arms, hobelars and archers; bailiffs itinerant and other bailiffs and ministers.[41]

The frequency and weight of royal taxation were arbitrary and unpredictable, and tax collection was backed by the full force of the state. Tax collectors paid no heed to the conditions of the peasantry who bore their brunt: money was demanded and gathered during the famine of 1315–17 as well as during the traditionally lean seasons between harvests, the time of the best fighting weather.

Bullying, extortion, swindles, trickery, and the forced seizure of goods were commonplace. Crops in the barn were taken, seed-corn was sold, plow teams were broken up, sheep were plucked from their folds, horses were confiscated, and men were commandeered and impressed into service. English troops fighting against fellow Britons may not have practiced a scorched-earth policy, but their needs cut a deep swath into the peasant's domestic economy. The depth of these cuts was most noticeable in the eastern and northern regions. For a population already enduring squeezed living standards, the impact of military campaigning was an additional blow driving many into destitution. There is evidence that in some counties royal taxation was associated with land abandonment. Finally, "the oppressed narrator of the *Song of the Husbandman* [c. 1300] represents him-

41. Quoted in J. R. Maddicott, *The English Peasantry and the Demands of the Crown 1294–1341* (Oxford, 1975), 3.

self as being the victim not only of hundred bailiffs, tax-collectors and pur-veyors, but also of the lord and his officials, bailiff, hayward and wood-ward."[42] It was an immense relief for these people that the Hundred Years War was fought on the fields of France; the French peasantry obviously were not so fortunate.

3.

What is distinctive about the feudal period after the year 1000 was the co-incidence of two forms of exploitation. Many peasants were subjected to a "double rent," on both the land and their bodies. Although there was evi-dently wide variation, from manor to manor, in the daily operation of this system, its weight bore down on all who lived and worked in the country-side. Over time this relationship mutated and "was conceived less as a per-sonal tie and more as an inferiority of class which by a sort of contagion could pass from the soil to the man."[43] In this sense, servility in feudal so-ciety was reminiscent of slavery in antiquity since in both instances it be-came a fact of life into which one was born rather than a relationship into which one had contracted. In neither case was the laborer free to sell her or his labor in an open market. The political economy of the marketplace it-self was rigged in favor of those who bought this labor power. The servile classes were thus kept in a state of subjugation by the force of extra-economic compulsion—their ancestors had been forced to submit, and they were never allowed to forget it.[44]

The elemental fact of servility was that their personal lives and their "servile tenements [were] held in bondage at the will of the lord for cus-tomary services and obligations."[45] A particularly galling aspect of these

42. Maddicott, *The English Peasantry and the Demands of the Crown*, 75. On the economic impact of royal demands for "purveyance," see also Mavis Mate, "The Estates of Canterbury Cathedral Priory before the Black Death 1315–1348," *Studies in Medieval and Renaissance History*, new ser., 8 (1986): 20, 26.

43. Marc Bloch, *Feudal Society*, 279.

44. We find a modern marketplace only when the laborer gained property in his or her labor power and became formally free to bargain for its sale. This was a very long and drawn out process; while we can find the antecedents of proletarian-ization in the ancient world (after all, the very word is Roman in origin), it was only in the modern world that it became the cornerstone of a social system. In the vast stretch of time between antiquity and modernity, many combinations of part-free and part-servile labor were annealed together. This fusion was most usually based on the implication of the family in the wider system of production. It is not so much wrong to call this a transitional stage as beside the point—how many tran-sitions are *in process* for two thousand years?

45. J. A. Raftis, *Tenure and Mobility*, 201.

seigneurial rights was the way in which they dovetailed with the moral discipline urged on the feudal classes by the priesthood. When unfree villeins were indicted in the manorial court for having been convicted by the ecclesiastical court for moral lapses, they were subject to another fine for alienating the lord's property. This form of double jeopardy could be avoided only if the hapless peasant allowed himself or herself to be bodily whipped rather than paying the fine. Lords were less concerned with the moral discipline of their tenants than with watching them (and especially their coins) slip from seigneurial control.[46]

Yet the homogeneity of subjugation which occurred around 1100 was a chimera. It was a fleeting historical moment even though it was not without a lasting imprint. The creation of lordship and dependency embraced the separate holdings of family-based households as well as the village community. The lordship, specific to feudalism, was where "the two main classes of feudal society [met] for the transfer of the surplus . . . and its conversion into landowner income." Even more than brute force, the exercise of jurisdiction was the principal expression of social power in feudal society.[47] Feudalism, then, pivoted on this element of political control. If the anvil of peasant resistance was established by the enduring subsistence imperatives of the family economy, then the changing organization of the dominant classes hammered it again and again in the process of extracting its surplus product. Feudal relations were the product of historical experience, which is why, above all, their application was uneven.

Five factors of outstanding importance characterized this traffic in rights. First, the nature of the lord's demands changed as he was drawn into a cash nexus and consequently came to need money rather more than services. Second, the organization of production and, in particular, the profitability of farming of the demesne for marketable surpluses fluctuated and so exerted a variable influence on the lord's involvement in direct management of both the land and the servile population. Third, the dominant trends in state formation delimited the power of the individual seigneur at the cost of enhancing that of the whole class. Fourth, the character of the surplus was in flux as a result of both intensive and extensive modes of exploiting the material world. Fifth, feudal social organization was mapped

46. Tim North, "Legerwite in the Thirteenth and Fourteenth Centuries," *Past and Present* 111 (1986): 8. Of course, serfs could be sold, although this was an infrequent occurrence. For some examples, see Edward Miller, "Social Structure: Northern England," in H. C. Hallam (ed.), *The Agrarian History of England and Wales*, vol. 2, 1086–1350 (Cambridge, 1988), 695–96.

47. R. H. Hilton, "A Crisis of Feudalism," *Past and Present* 80 (1978): 7–8.

out spatially so that a feudalized core always stood in contrast to the periphery, where both lords and peasants could experiment with new modes of behavior.

If the old axiom "No lord without land" and its corollary "No land without a lord" are an incomplete description of social realities, nevertheless they contained more than a grain of truth. In all societies the political struggle over the disposition of surplus wealth "is the universal light with which all other colours are tinged and by whose peculiarity they are modified. It is a special ether which determines the specific gravity of everything that appears in it."[48] Thus, the islands of free land in feudal society were not exempt from the tidal influences of the sea in which they were located. Nor was free status of much value when available land or resources were made available only to those who would agree to forfeit that freedom in exchange for economic opportunity. In times of Malthusian crisis—high levels of population growth engendering first an increased demand for land and then its fragmentation—the peasantry was set against itself and its surplus was squeezed by the imposition of new taxes; in times of falling demand (or an inability to pay) the dependent peasantry was not free to bargain a new deal but rather was expected to buy itself out of its old obligations.

4.

If we make the false assumption that issues of political power and villeinage were more important in theory than in practice then we will misunderstand both the complexity of village society and the multifarious relationships that connected lords and peasants through the nexus of the manorial court.[49] On the Staffordshire estates of the bishop of Coventry and Wakefield, the exercise of lordship in 1291 produced 38 percent of the total income. On the neighboring Lancastrian Estate in 1313–14 these feudal exactions brought in almost exactly the same proportion. Even lesser lords extracted considerable profits from the exercise of lordship. At nearby Tutbury Priory in 1295, feudal exactions accounted for 21 percent of total revenues. On the adjacent Verdon estate in 1327, exactions were 19 percent of all income.[50]

---

48. Karl Marx, *The Grundrisse*, edited by David McLellan (New York, 1971), 41.

49. It must always be kept in mind that "lords were more concerned with the possibility of profit in the entire system than with coercive control over its several parts"; J. A. Raftis, "Social Change Versus Revolution," in *Peasant Economic Development within the English Manorial System* (Montreal, 1996), 7.

50. R. H. Hilton, "Lord and Peasant in Staffordshire in the Middle Ages," in *The English Peasantry in the Middle Ages* (Oxford, 1975), 232–33.

Similar figures for the profitability of feudal, extra-economic power come from the 1287–88 account roll of Henry le Cat, who was a direct tenant and subtenant of no less than five different individuals in the community of Hevingham in Norfolk. The le Cat account exemplifies both the subdivision of lordship and its re-amalgamation. From this extraordinary document we learn that "seignorial jurisdiction was the single most profitable source of income . . . yielding no less than 30 percent of gross manorial receipts." To this figure we need to add the additional income such minor lords derived from requiring the servile population to use their mill and the revenue they accrued from the sale of these same villeins' labor services, which combined to account for a further 10 percent of their revenue. The le Cat family was at the bottom of the seigneurial world. Its members never attained knighthood. Its land was spread over several contiguous townships, and its lordship was patched together from a number of different relationships. The family seemed to have practiced direct management of its demesne lands and to have been actively engaged in marketing the surplus. For these "comparatively low status lords," feudalism was lucrative.[51]

The court rolls of Ramsey Abbey provide unusually detailed information about the way that lords wielded their discretionary power over their tenants through the imposition of labor services. The villagers of Broughton, Huntingdonshire, owed the manor 4,302.5 "works" (workdays) for a thirty-eight-week period over the winter, spring, and summer of 1314–15. Of these, 37 percent were excused from performance, 43 percent were performed on a wide variety of jobs, and the remaining 20 percent were commuted (sold for cash payments). Among the works excused, 51.3 percent were remitted because they were owed by the manorial officials (reeve, beadle, woodward, four plowmen), 43.2 percent were forgiven on account of feast days, and the remaining 5 percent were pardoned because of sickness. The works rendered were extremely diverse: "69 works were expended upon cutting and collecting thatch; 623 works were expended for ploughing and related work; 147 works were expended on threshing, 63 works on building, 24 works on watching (at the fair of St. Ives), 40 works on gathering manure, 271 on

51. Bruce M. S. Campbell, "The Complexity of Manorial Structure in Medieval Norfolk: A Case Study," *Norfolk Archaeology* 39 (1986): 239–42. The land described in the account roll was not the whole of the le Cat estate; the family's holdings in other communities were not included. For other examples of the profitable nature of feudalism, see Christopher Dyer, "Social Structure: The East Midlands," in H. C. Hallam (ed.), *The Agrarian History of England and Wales*, vol. 2, 1086–1350, 667–68; and Edward Miller, "Social Structure: Northern England," 693–95.

gates and hedges, 94 on carpentry, 168 on cutting wood and thorns, 220 on cutting fen, 97 on weeding, and 60 on marling." What is so striking about these figures is the huge surplus that the manorial authorities could sell or trade back to their tenants in exchange for services in administering the manor. Indeed, thirteenth-century population growth emphasized the inherent flexibility of the feudal system, which could run this manor while tapping less than 50 percent of the works it was owed.[52] Wherever the seigneurial regime breathed life, lordship was a powerful force "siphoning off peasant wealth as it accumulated."[53]

These examples (and countless others which will always remain obscured from our view by the lack of appropriate documentation) underscore the crucial point that the exercise of feudal power took place locally and was everywhere unique. This unequal bargain meant that the particular application of customary rights and exactions was highly variable. In general, however, the establishment of an empire of feudal subjugation was accompanied by three forms of compensation over and above rental payments for land use. First were the confiscations on the dependent populations' bodies which confirmed their servile status, for example annual recognitions (*tallage*), death duties (*heriot*), marriages fees (*merchet*), fines for sexual misconduct (*leyrwite*) and annual exemptions from residing on the manor (*chevage*). Second were special payments exacted as a form of tribute: for grinding corn at the lord's mill, for selling animals in the lord's market, for baking bread in the lord's oven, for crushing grapes in the lord's winepress, for foraging animals in the lord's woods, or for digging peat or for collecting kindling. Third was a multiplicity of labor services—such as plowing, weeding, harvesting, mowing, haymaking, and carrying—as well as minor (but nonetheless valuable) predations on the peasant family's capital such as the requirement that their tenants' sheep be pastured on fallow demesne land because even their sheep's dung was to be the lord's property, commandeered for manuring the demesne.

Because the peasant's economic activities took place "at the will of the lord," chores were usually required at exactly the same time that the adult male, servile peasant farmer had the most need for his own labor and that of his family. Commuting labor services into money payments satisfied the

52. J. A. Raftis, "The Structure of Commutation in a Fourteenth-Century Village," in T. A. Sandquist and M. R. Powicke (eds.), *Essays in Medieval History Presented to Bertie Wilkinson* (Toronto, 1969), 282–300.
53. Mavis Mate, "The Agrarian Economy of South-east England before the Black Death: Depressed or Buoyant?," in Bruce M. S. Campbell (ed.), *Before the Black Death* (Manchester, 1991), 101.

lord's need for cash and the peasant's desire to reduce their arbitrariness; the haphazard character of these obligations rankled almost as much as their weight. They were an immediate and constant reminder of the political relations which had long ago been interposed between the lord and his peasants but which continued to make economic life of the unfree population something which could not be reduced to an axis of supply and demand. Similarly, peasants were forbidden from owning dovecotes or pigeon houses, among other things. Furthermore, even when the husbandman and his family were freed from the subjugation of serfdom, they were in no position to enjoy this newfound economic liberty since generations of subsistence farming and feudal exactions meant that they entered the marketplace without capital resources. As a rule of thumb, capitalism works best for those with capital.

The common rights of tenants were augmented by the emergence of the village community as both a political counterweight and a guarantor of collective values: it was "by closing their ranks [that] small husbandmen were better able to defend themselves against poverty and the excessive demands of their lords."[54] The inherent tensions between two divergent conceptions of freedom and liberty were intensified in the course of the thirteenth century when the land frontier available for colonization was closing and acute overpopulation led to land fragmentation. In this setting, the importance of both manorial and communal courts was enhanced. The landlords' demand for higher revenue thus combined with the peasants' need for security to bolster legal frameworks informing property arrangements. In essence, this created a quid pro quo: landowners gained from the formal recognition of property rights while tenants achieved common law respect for their *usufruct*, or use rights.

The definition of traditional rights and obligations was a particular bone of contention which slowly transmuted the naked oppression of enforced servitude into unequal access to legal redress. For example, it may well be true that "tallage, one of the hallmarks of serfdom, frequently became a fixed, often annual, payment,"[55] but custom did not protect the tenants of Crowland Abbey from having to fork over a "double tallage" in 1314 after their landlords had spent an unusually large sum entertaining the king, who was passing by on his way to war.[56] Another example of the capricious and situational character of feudal exactions can be quoted here. In 1342,

54. Duby, *Rural Economy and Country Life in the Medieval West*, 282.
55. Hatcher, "English Serfdom and Villeinage," 9.
56. F. M. Page, *The Estates of Crowland Abbey* (Cambridge, 1934), 59–60; cited in Maddicott, *The English Peasantry and the Demands of the Crown*, 20–21.

the lord of the manor of Goring in Sussex was unable to find tenants on his old terms, so he converted a tenement held in villeinage to free tenure and leased three others for money rents. Then, four years later, when the situation had changed, he called in two of these leases and regranted them to new tenants in villeinage.[57] The key point is not that every lord used his feudal rights in a vigorous manner but rather that "as long as serfdom lasted, they were always there—always in reserve." Without any right of appeal beyond the seigneurial court, dependent cultivators enjoyed neither freedom of tenure nor the economic freedom to benefit from fixed rents in a period of rising prices.[58]

Not all commoners were caught up in the feudal system. Even though it was the dominant system of surplus extraction, it was by no means the only mode of production nor the singular site of power.[59] While lordship was generally important as an instrument of control and domination in the late medieval countryside, "in many villages the lord was not present as part of the visible structure of local society."[60] In fact, the self-regulation of the village community was of profound importance:

> [T]he management of rural communities was not in the hands of these lord's representatives. A significant role in the reproduction of this structure of domination was played by members of the subjugated classes. This sort of contradiction is not surprising because it was the outcome of a hegemonic relationship which had adapted itself to the business of living. It enjoined an element of accommodation on all members of society. The manorial or seigneurial courts were largely in the hands of the well-to-do villagers, who declared custom, adjudicated in disputes, formulated communal regulations, promulgated bylaws, kept out strangers, and generally speaking provided the essential lines of communication between the estate officialdom, or the lord himself, and the community of peasant householders.[61]

57. Mate, "The Agrarian Economy of South-east England before the Black Death," 101.

58. Barbara F. Harvey, "Introduction: The 'crisis' of the Early Fourteenth Century," in Campbell (ed.), *Before the Black Death*, 17.

59. Indeed, "We are sure to go astray, if we try to conceive of peasant economies as exclusively 'subsistence' oriented and to suspect capitalism wherever the peasants show evidence of being 'market' oriented. It is much sounder to take it for granted, as a starting point, that for ages peasant economies have had a double orientation towards both. In this way, much fruitless discussion about the nature of so-called 'subsistence' economies can be avoided"; D. Thorner, "Peasant Economy as a Category in History," in T. Shanin (ed.), *Peasants and Peasant Societies* (Oxford, 1987), 65.

60. R. H. Hilton, *The English Peasantry*, 27.

61. Hilton, "A Crisis of Feudalism," 9.

Manorial officers—ale tasters, bailiffs, constables, jurymen, overseers, tithing-men, and woodwards—represented the landed elements in rural society; they decided the day-to-day policy having to do with cropping, gleaning, plowing, reaping, sowing, stinting animals on the fallow, and timing their release onto the arable fields after the harvest. This cooperation was aimed at creating a communal policy of resource allocation within the framework of manorial hegemony.[62] Furthermore, for the village "kulaks," feudalism was not without its benefits. The customary tenant's failure to accumulate land/capital was balanced by the seigneurial imperative which often strived to keep traditional holdings intact so as to preserve their vitality and, of course, their ability to generate a surplus that could be siphoned upward. In contrast, freeholdings were frequently split over and over again so that they became dwarf-holdings.

Lordship was extensive, not intensive. Its application may often have been draconian, ruthless, and brutal, but it was never totalitarian. Grudging consent was the order of the times. Nowhere, perhaps, was this distance between lords and peasants more prominent than in the organization of production. Apart from demesne lands, which were never as prominent as our documentary record would suggest,[63] most agricultural production took place on the family farms:

> [T]he peasant, with his usufruct of the land and control of the process
> of production, held a major trump, while the lord, excluded from this
> process, only took his rent by virtue of a political compulsion. In the
> long term, this resulted in an evolution in relative economic strength in
> favour of the peasant, and generated an erosion of the rate of levy.
> Thereafter, only a new definition of the non-economic constraints—a
> political rearrangement of relationship of exploitation—was capable of
> reversing this trend for a time.[64]

62. W. O. Ault, *Open-Field Farming in Medieval England* (London, 1972). See also Ault, *Open-Field Husbandry and the Village Community* (Philadelphia, 1965; Transactions of the American Philosophical Society, new series, 55); and Zvi Razi, "Family, Land and the Village Community in Later Medieval England," *Past and Present* 93 (1981): 10–16.

63. A vastly disproportionate share of the documentary record derives from ecclesiastical or collegiate institutions. In the Midland counties in 1279, for example, 68 percent of all arable land was held by nonseigneurial occupiers (i.e., peasant freeholders and tenants). Of the remaining land, which was farmed as manorial demesnes, only a fraction was held by nonnobles; R. H. Britnell, *The Commercialization of English Society 1000–1500* (Cambridge, 1993), 120; Bruce M. S. Campbell, "Measuring the Commercialization of Seigneurial Agriculture c. 1300," in Richard H. Britnell and Bruce M. S. Campbell (eds.), *A Commercializing Economy*, 135.

64. Bois, *The Crisis of Feudalism*, 397. This quotation refers to the crisis of the feudal mode of production in the fourteenth century, but it captures the essentially

Reinvestment in agriculture was a low priority among feudalists; these men were not nascent capitalists. It distorts their social reality to analyze their activities according to the political economy of our time. In most earlier, pre-modern economies, one acquired goods in order to benefit from their redistribution. Power relations were as much a manifestation of patronage and clientage as of exploitation and self-aggradizement.

A market economy for food, personal unfreedom, and economic constraints created a triple bind for those who were caught in the web of feudalism. Feudalism was predicated on the lack of a free market relationship between buyers and sellers of labor and land; it also presumed the solidarity of the seigneurial class. It did not mean that all land was encumbered with feudal rights—or that all feudal rights were applied with either the same force or the same pressure—but rather these privileges described the field of gravitational forces in this social formation, establishing the relations between landlords and their tenants. Saying this, it is important to note that feudal social relations bore down unequally so that there were some people who escaped them while other people were captured in this net. Most students of history are concerned to explicate both the continuities and the changes in social relations which are immanent at any particular moment. Like any set of social relationships, close inspection of feudal systems reveals not only inconsistencies but also an uneven operation of their central tendencies both over time and across space. Without such a contradictory state of affairs, entropy would ensue.

The political economy of the manorial empire of subjugation provided peasants with frequent opportunities for resistance to the everyday domination imposed upon them by warriors/clergy-cum-landlords. Defiance usually took the form of heel-dragging and the poor performance—or neglect—of duties. Fines and exactions were frequently left unpaid; their collection created significant extra costs for the seigneurial class, which first had to create and then had to sustain a disciplinary infrastructure of manorial officials which was often more trouble than it was worth. That said, the chasm that ran like a fault line through rural society was the one which separated the villagers from their masters.

---

political dimension of economic relations, which were an integral part of the social system and also the prime motor of its changing application between the year 1000 and the withering of feudalism in the wake of the Black Death. It should also be mentioned that Bois refers to the French experience of feudalism as a result of the much more generalized commutation of feudal exactions in the wake of *la révolution censive,* while in thirteenth-century England there was a seigneurial offensive.

Internal stratification within the peasantry was less significant than the external rules of social apartheid which separated the peasantry from its feudal masters. Yet, it is inaccurate to depict the seigneurial relationship in terms of an army of occupation even if this was its initial manifestation. Over time, it became imbricated within the skin of daily life. The manorial system was a hegemonic frontier of constant struggle, pitting the lords' strategic appropriation of the surplus against the dependents' claims to control over their economic, social, intellectual, and personal freedom.

> Virtually every instance of personal domination [was] intimately con-
> nected with the process of appropriation. Dominant elites extract[ed]
> material taxes in the form of labor, grain, cash, and service in addition
> to extracting symbolic taxes in the form of deference, demeanor, pos-
> ture, verbal formulas, and acts of humility. In actual practice, of course,
> the two are joined inasmuch as every public act of appropriation is, fig-
> uratively, a ritual of subordination.[65]

The lord created a "public transcript" of protection and institutionalized justice. This was one side of the coin of inequality; the other side was char-acterized by beatings, insults, sexual abuse, forced self-abasement, and a denial of dignity which was aimed at permeating the character of the sub-ordinates. In reply, subordinates created their own "hidden transcript" of anger, indignation, frustration, unspoken ripostes, stifled hatreds, bitten tongues, and swallowed bile that proclaimed itself publicly in the actions of runaways and occasional rebellions.

Those who stayed to face the music also resisted domination, but they had to rely on a wide range of down-to-earth tactics such as dissembling, feigning ignorance, and playing dumb. To minimize appropriation they also had recourse to low-profile stratagems: the dereliction of duties, care-less labor, shirking, foot-dragging, and the deliberate misreading of cus-toms which led to the delivery of inferior rents in kind and the late pay-ment of money rents. Higher-profile ploys included clearing clandestine fields and rearranging plots, squatting, illegal gleaning, poaching, pilfering, theft, arson, and sabotage of crops, water supplies, and livestock. The mano-rial court was the playhouse which staged the theater of domination at the heart of the feudal system. There, rehearsals went on constantly in every act, every speech, and every thought which proclaimed the legitimacy of power relations. Offstage, a recalcitrant countertheater disputed these claims in a chorus of disapproving anonymity—rumors, gossip, grumbles,

65. James C. Scott, *Domination and the Arts of Resistance* (New Haven, 1990), 186.

folktales, symbolic inversions, and rituals of reversal. The *ressentiment* of the powerless contested the command performances of consent taking place on the public stage.[66]

The preceding exegesis on the political culture of absolute power is too starkly drawn. Like a structured set of grammatical rules, it is only a beginner's guide to the language of control. The vernacular idiom was modified because neither power nor powerlessness was complete. In place of these dichotomous antinomies there was a continuum of accommodation—the slang, dialect, patois, and jargon of the colloquial, routine, and prosaic discourse of power. The application of absolute power was constrained by the multiple resistances it provoked as much as by its essential inutility. A serf had rights which differentiated his or her condition from that of a slave.[67] There was thus a contractual element in the relationship between a villein and a lord which was lacking between the ancient slaveholder and his *instrumentum vocale* (speaking tool). The serf/villein had property in him- or herself, although it has to be understood that such property was not absolute. Indeed, one of the key elements of feudal power was the lord's control over the serf's body.[68] "The tenants, like the ploughs and the pigs, were manorial assets; and in conjunction with the ploughs and the pigs were enumerated [in Domesday Book] and valued for what they could do for the manorial lord."[69]

Yet one does not want to go overboard in the direction of mitigating the violence and brutality of feudal social relations. Only the person who was not liable to being beaten could feel himself or herself to be free. As Pierre Bonnassie notes, it is unfortunate that the history of punishments has never been written.

66. Scott, *Domination and the Acts of Resistance*, 14 and *passim*.

67. For a very instructive discussion of the evolution of power relationships between lords and peasants over *la longue durée*, see Michael Toch, "Asking the Way and Telling the Law: Speech in Medieval Germany," *Journal of Interdisciplinary History* 16 (1986): 667–82. As he notes, the "assertion of collective peasants' speech seems a clear corollary to the social and economic processes which brought about the constitution of a peasantry organized in village communities and disassociated spatially, socially, and to some extent economically, but not legally, from the lord" (674).

68. It would appear, however, that the *jus primae noctae* (the lord's right of sexual access to peasant women on their marriage night) is a myth. See Alain Boureau, *The Lord's First Night: The Myth of the Droit de Cuissage* (Chicago, 1998). However, Georges Duby suggests that the sexuality of "youth" in feudal society was "meandering. They freely availed themselves of peasant women. . . . These bachelors were abductors by their very nature"; *Medieval Marriage: Two Models from Twelfth-Century France* (Baltimore, 1978), 13.

69. A. R. Bridbury, "Domesday Book: A Re-interpretation," in *The English Economy from Bede to the Reformation* (London, 1992), 96.

We will ... never know how many serfs were mutilated, tortured, burned or simply (if one can put it that way) hanged: such atrocities cannot, as a general rule, be known except when they concerned individuals who did not belong to the perpetrator of the violence. Only then was there complaint, hence traces in the archives. In almost every other case, silence reigned. It is, nevertheless, not unreasonable to assume that the gibbets adjacent to fortresses were there for more than purely decorative purposes. ... The image of the thrashed villein, indeed, permeates the whole of medieval literature, and should not be treated simply as a cliché lacking historical significance.

Peasant freedom was fiercely contested by those who believed that they could "seize, or kill, or upon whom they could make such judgement as they wished." This was the opinion of the Chapter of Paris toward its servile villeins in the middle of the thirteenth century. It encapsulates a belief in the "crushing 'burden of contempt' ... which the society of the well-born inflicted on those who enabled it to survive." To be sure, there were oscillations in its intensity, but the lords' class consciousness was keynoted by their refusal to accord human dignity to the peasantry. The narrative sources "almost invariably professed hostility and contempt. The peasant was the *animal brutum* of Bernard of Angers, the *rusticus piger, deformis et undique turpis* ["lazy, misshapen and in every respect vile peasant"] of Adelbero of Laon, a creature whose behaviour demonstrated *agrestis ferocitus* to William of Jumièges."[70]

If we read between the lines of early eleventh-century diatribes, the peasants' objectives emerge clearly. They wanted a return to the time of Adam, when there were neither masters, slaves, nor serfs. Egalitarian and libertarian tendencies are as ancient as the system that sought to deny them and attempted to base its social order on hierarchy and inequality. Since the great mass of the population was without voice, we are only able to make out their demands by reading the condescension of their betters against its grain.[71]

70. Pierre Bonnassie, "The Survival and Extinction of the Slave System in the Early Medieval West (Fourth to Eleventh Centuries)," 19 ff.; "From One Servitude to Another: The Peasantry of the Frankish Kingdom at the Time of Hugh Capet and Robert the Pious (987–1031)," 288; "Marc Bloch, Historian of Servitude: Reflections on the Concept of 'Servile Class,' " 331–35. These essays are collected in *From Slavery to Feudalism in South-western Europe* (Cambridge, 1991), to which the page references refer.

71. Jean-Pierre Poly and Eric Bournazel, *The Feudal Transformation 900–1200* (New York, 1991), 137. "Reading against the grain" is precisely the practice recommended by Walter Benjamin, whose "Seventh Thesis on the Philosophy of History" suggests that the "historical materialist ... regards it as his task to brush his-

The peasantry never accepted the lords' and clerics' negative stereotypes as anything other than ideological constructions; rather, they contested them. The Norman peasants who rebelled in 996 are said to have claimed:

> We are men like them
> We have the same limbs
> And just as big hearts
> And we can suffer just as much.

For the ideologues of the established order, this represented a grotesque inversion of normalcy. Another rustic song described what a world turned upside down would look like:

> The bishops, naked, have only for ever to follow the plough
> Singing, goad in hand, the song of our first parents.

This song, which, for Adalbero, served to characterize peasant mentality, was none other than that song which, faithfully transmitted from generation to generation, would again be heard during the insurrectional movements of the fourteenth century, in France and England:

> When Adam delved and Eve Span
> Who was then the gentleman?

This was, of course, a radically egalitarian image.[72]

The feudal system of domination was not established without a fight. The key event seems to have been the Norman Revolt of 996, when peasants who refused to perform labor services were met with draconian reprisals. Similarly, in Catalonia, a "true reign of terror was necessary to suppress the free peasants."[73] Head-on resistance proved futile, but one should not underestimate "the resistance of the tenants who hated sacrificing the cultivation of their holdings to work on the lord's fields. The struggle, carried on as it was by a sort of passive resistance, has left little trace in the documents, but that it took place appears to be beyond dispute."[74] It

---

tory against the grain"; see Hannah Arendt (ed.), *Illuminations: Essays and Reflections* (London, 1970), 259.

72. Bonnassie, "Marc Bloch, Historian of Servitude," 339; see also Sylvia Resnikow, "The Cultural Construction of a Democratic Proverb," *Studies in English and Germanic Philology* 36 (1937): 391–405.

73. Robert Fossier, *Peasant Life in the Medieval West* (Oxford, 1988), 172; Duby, *The Three Orders*, 161, 277, 327; Le Goff, *Medieval Civilization*, 301–5; Poly and Bournazel, *The Feudal Transformation*, 136.

74. Ganshof and Verhulst, "Medieval Agrarian Society in Its Prime: France, the Low Countries, and Western Germany," 314. Jean-Pierre Poly and Eric Bournazel

was met with savagery. Peasant rebels had their hands and feet cut off while "In Berry, the battle of Châteauneuf-sur-Cher ended in carnage; hundreds of peasants, driven back to the river, were trampled underfoot or drowned; the rest were put to the sword by the *milites* of Eudes of Déols. In fact, as early as the year 1000, the balance of power between an aristocracy exclusively devoted to war, and accordingly trained and equipped, and a peasantry increasingly unarmed, was too unequal for these attempts at resistance to have had any chance of success."[75] Full-scale peasant movements were few and far between; revolutionary class consciousness was not much more than a ghostly specter haunting the rich and powerful.

Given the seigneurial class's total monopolization of the means of violence, direct confrontation was suicidal. Mutiny was met by ferocious retribution. A serf who killed his lord was punished in an exemplary fashion—by drawing and quartering—just as if he had committed treason. Indeed, in the eyes of those who drew up the legal system, that is exactly what he had done. This treason was doubly dangerous because it also smacked of parricide, since the justification for social hierarchy was always discussed in terms of the Fourth Commandment.

5.

Feudalism was, therefore, rather more than a system of landownership and tenancy. For those who wielded power, the key issue was the extraction of the peasants' surplus wealth in order to finance their lifestyle. For those who were the object of this policy, the key issue was to define subsistence in such a way that their production was shielded from seigneurial extraction. This struggle was predicated on the extra-economic extraction of peasant wealth—by armed force in the first instance and then by legal administration once the system had been established and was fully operational.

The playing field was rarely level. Indeed, it is appropriate to mention that in periods of relative labor scarcity, such as the late eleventh and early twelfth centuries and the later fourteenth century after the Black Death, the primordial characteristics of enforced servitude came to the fore. At other times the peasantry—"harvest-sensitive" and enduring "slow, long-

---

write that the lords' desire to impose labor services "came up against those spontaneous tendencies that have always given life to the collective action or oppressed peasantries: the sabotage of forced work, flight, and incessant dealing in land or goods stolen from under the nose of the master and his stewards"; *The Feudal Transformation*, 259.

75. Bonnassie, "From One Servitude to Another," 309–12.

term starvation"—could be disciplined by hunger.[76] The feudalized peasantry was thus the product of its historical experience. It may have been the anvil beaten by the hammer of exploitation, but the density and strength of that anvil wore out many hammers in the course of drawing its historical mettle.

Reflecting the elemental diversity of local conditions, the class struggle in feudal society was splintered into several hundred thousand fragments, each of which was colored in a hue of its own. The feudal system had been laid over a framework of local communities. It was also extended to the new lands which were colonized during the first phase of early modernization. This fusion was first experienced as a social conquest but, over time, it settled into a process of accommodation.

DEGREES OF UNFREEDOM

After the feudal revolution, the common people may have been united in subjugation in the seigneurial empire, but subsequently the marginal population grew as the wilderness frontier was colonized by an expanding mass of surplus people. By the late thirteenth century, at the height of the feudal reaction, only one in three English people was living on a manor. In contrast to the mythical serf of our historical imagination—a cereal farmer working strips of manorial land encumbered with labor services and feudal dues—the historical record reveals a much less tidy picture. In this chapter, a series of synchronic and diachronic themes are discussed to delineate the contours of socioeconomic exploitation which generated "Degrees of Unfreedom." Special consideration is given to the organization of agricultural production in the peasant's economy because this was the keystone in a series of interlocking components—population size and demographic trends, land use, climate, technology, feudal incidents, and political relations, both within the peasant community and between the peasantry and the landlord class. Many of these factors are considered in this chapter, although their implications for peasants' family formations are discussed later. Finally, the range of differentiation between members of the peasantry as well as the ceiling to upward mobility are related to the experience of servile unfreedom.

Lordship only rarely extended to directing the methods and day-to-day tasks of peasant production. This point had important implications for two aspects of agrarian practice: first, the organization of capital formation and,

76. J. L. Bolton, *The Medieval English Economy, 1150–1500* (London, 1980), 115.

in particular, animal husbandry; and second, cropping patterns and their relationship to market production. On the farm itself, money was usually spent on expansion rather than intensification and improvement. Reinvesting profit for the purpose of increasing production was not the first choice.

Without closely supervised, enthusiastic labor it was not easy to keep the cropland free of weeds. Labor services were often commuted so that most demesne land could be worked by paid laborers whose work could be regulated more strictly than that of customary tenants.[77] The unlimited nature of this labor supply meant that the inefficiency of these unskilled workers wasn't particularly troubling; such an army of landless laborers—and their wives and children—would work for a pittance. This labor was so cheap that many landlords profited by grabbing cash from the commutation of customary labor obligations. These transactional terms of trade meant it was in the lords' interest to substitute extra unskilled workers by commuting compulsory labor services. The downside of this situation was that when lords pursued a quick profit strategy, they did so at the expense of making capital investments to their demesnes.[78]

Feudal labor services and wage work were therefore alternative, but it is crucial to keep in mind that it was the landlord who had the discretion to choose which would be employed on his estate. Seasonal, discontinuous operations requiring the simultaneous deployment of a large labor force were usually performed by the labor dues of the customary tenants. Operations which demanded either specialized skills or continuous application were the province of wage workers since it was impossible to depend on the intermittent and grudging services of the villeinage to carry them out. On

77. David Postles, "Cleaning the Medieval Arable," *Agricultural History Review* 37 (1989): 130–143. The key point to keep in mind, though, is that if the paid workers were more responsive to supervisory control than were customary tenants, they were nonetheless usually unskilled and rarely directed. The weakest link in the chain of command was what we would call overseers. This inadequacy in middle management would persist right into the late nineteenth century, not only in production but also in administration. Thus, both prisons and factories—as well as schools—were the subject of much managerial theory but little practical improvement until the modern period. Indeed, the creation of a fully functional chain of command is one of the hallmarks of modernity.

78. Christopher Thornton, "The Determinants of Land Productivity on the Bishop of Winchester's Demesne of Rimpton, 1208–1403," in Bruce M. S. Campbell and Mark Overton (eds.), *Land, Labour, and Livestock* (Manchester, 1991), 183–210. Of course, the ability of English lords to turn back the clock to demand, and to receive, labor services in place of money payments was a characteristic of fiscal feudalism of the thirteenth century. Elsewhere, the power of lords was less and *la révolution censive* resulted.

the Abbey of Wistow in thirteenth- and fourteenth-century Huntingdonshire, for example, major customary tenants employed servants, transient
wage laborers, and dependent members of their own households to perform demesne commitments while they concerned themselves with their
own holdings.[79] The nearby Abbey of Peterborough reorganized its estate
during the twelfth century to secure the regular supply of full-virgate
villeins who provided plow teams. The excess population of servile tenants
was driven downward, into the proletariat, to provide the manorial economy with a reserve army of cheap hired labor.[80]

Wage labor was not infrequently associated with a high level of manorialism and demesne farming for the market. On the Crowland Abbey
manor of Cottenham the total wage bill, including food, was more than
twice the value of customary services performed by villeins.[81] Yet, manorial documents are somewhat misleading since "it was in the peasant
households that labor freely hired was most generally employed."[82]
Seigneurial control over the labor of the unmarried servants and adult
agricultural laborers/dwarf-holders was thus not infrequently coincidental
with the interests of those villagers who also employed labor: both wanted
to inhibit the mobility of labor and fix it within a specified field of force, the
manor in the case of the landlord and the family in the case of the substantial peasant patriarch.[83]

There was also a spatial dimension to these contrasting agrarian
regimes. Proximity to the urban market would have been likely to rein-
force the predilection for wheat growing and also for strictly controlled
demesne production.[84] The most completely manorialized communities
were often closest to the centers of population and marketing opportunities. Labor services and demesne production survived together on land
which had been settled earliest and was frequently in the hands of great ec-

79. M. Patricia Hogan, "The Labor of Their Days—Work in the Medieval Village," *Studies in Medieval and Renaissance History*, new ser., 8 (1989): 87–88.

80. Kathleen Biddick, *The Other Economy: Pastoral Economy on a Medieval
Estate* (Berkeley and Los Angeles, 1989), 58–61.

81. M. M. Postan, *The Famulus: The Estate Labourer in the Twelfth and Thirteenth Centuries* (Cambridge, 1954), 2.

82. Postan, *The Famulus*, 2, 4–5, 35 n. 1.

83. L. R. Poos, "The Social Context of Statute of Labourers' Enforcement,"
Law and History Review 1 (1983): 27–52. Wealthy villagers actively intervened to
bring forward prosecutions against their laborers and servants who had become recalcitrant in supplying their labor at pre-plague wages in the new conditions of
labor scarcity during the 1350s and thereafter.

84. Stefano Fenoaltea, "Authority, Efficiency, and Agricultural Organization in
Medieval England and Beyond: A Hypothesis," *Journal of Economic History* 35
(1975): 703–5.

clesiastical landowners. To be sure, there was a microlevel, local dimension to this distinction since assarting had created an interstitial fringe of freedom within the broad belt of feudal control across the south and east of England.[85] But if the landlords were able to exercise some control over the use of their own demesne lands, they were "not able to determine the application of labour and other resources within the economy of the [peasant] holding; nor, on the whole, was there much attempt in terms of leases . . . to specify good husbandry practices."[86]

The lords' inability to penetrate the peasantry's farming practices to extract a higher marketable surplus was a crucial reason why so many landlords were willing to centralize production. With production under their own control they hoped to gain the lion's share of profits from the soil. This happened in England in the period of high farming which developed in time of rapid inflation after 1180. Surging inflation radically depreciated the value of rents and commuted labor services. It was therefore in the lord's interest to gather these disparate forms of property back into his own hands so that he could at least keep pace with the changing value of money.

1.

The archetypical peasant was a cereal cultivator, but many lived in communities whose social organization was founded on tending flocks. Animal husbandry is among the oldest human occupations. Transhumance, following the sheep from summer to winter pastures, meant that sheepherding was a relatively footloose life. In comparison with the stability demanded by the rhythms of planting, weeding, and harvesting food grains, the shepherd led an itinerant life. In southern France, for example, they orbited between the migrant world of the shepherd's *cabane* and the sedentary world of the villager's *domus*. There was a deep social division between the shepherds who grazed their own animals on other people's meadows (interflocked with sheep belonging to others) and the farmer-owners who had their own landed property as well as their sheep flock. The rural nomads formed a semiproletariat of "long-term bachelor shepherds" who subcontracted their labor in a bewildering variety of arrangements.

Pierre Maury of Montaillou was simultaneously a partner, an employee, and the foreman over his friends, the other employees. Such men crisscrossed the Pyrenees, shuttling back and forth between southern and

85. Dodgshon, *The European Past*, 270–74.
86. Hilton, "A Crisis of Feudalism," 9.

northern Catalonia in Spain, the principality of Andorra, the kingdom of France, and the upper Ariège in the Comté de Foix. Barter, "sheep share-cropping," employment networks, and camaraderie were linked with the life-cycle of their animals—winter and summer pasturing, lambing, milk-ing, cheesemaking, and shearing the fleeces. The sheep flocks at once con-nected the shepherd with the natural economy of transhumance and the market economy of meat, wool, dairy products, and meadow rentals. Mountain liberty gave such men the freedom to sleep under the stars, to freeze almost to death in the winter snows, and to be soaked to the skin by spring and autumn showers. But for the shepherd, sheep also meant liberty and freedom from feudal controls. For Pierre Maury, "goatskin philoso-pher," life seems to have been an idyll.[87]

Our detailed information concerning the happy shepherds of the Pyre-nees should not obscure the fact that there were many pastoral economies. Each one was the result of two intersecting forces: the ecological workshop of the natural world and the social demands of a carnivorous society. Ani-mals were an integral part of the rural economy; besides meat, they pro-vided traction, milk and cheese, hides and wool, tallow, and manure. Fur-thermore, in European rural history, draft animals were the key form of working capital whose presence made it possible to find substitutes for human labor. The energy produced by an ox is about 3.8 times that of a man working at maximum rate of physical exertion, while a horse pro-duces 5.7 units of peak manpower.[88] As we have seen, around the year 1000 there was an increase in the number of horses available to both knights and peasant farmers, but stocking densities would remain low because fodder was always in relatively short supply. Moreover, the growth of the Euro-pean population in the dozen generations after the year 1000 made it both necessary and profitable to give priority to human food needs.[89] Compared

87. The preceding two paragraphs (and quotations) are drawn from Emmanuel Le Roy Ladurie, *Montaillou: Cathars and Catholics in a French Village 1294–1324* (London, 1978), 69–135.

88. E. A. Wrigley, "Energy Availability and Agricultural Productivity," in Bruce M. S. Campbell and Mark Overton (eds.), *Land, Labour, and Livestock*, 326. Frederick Cottrell proposes a slightly lower estimate for the energy produced by horses as compared to men, noting that a horse consumes roughly ten times as much heat energy (in foodstuffs) as a man. Compared strictly on the basis of en-ergy, manpower is roughly 2.5 times as efficient. Furthermore, animals were not driven continuously at their maximum rate of energy expenditure, whereas, in many cases, men have been literally worked to death; *Energy and Society: The Re-lation between Energy, Social Change, and Economic Development* (New York, 1955), 21.

89. There are no data for the Middle Ages, but in England there were some 700,000 working horses in 1800, which preempted the output from 3.5 million

with Chinese, Europeans ate more meat and livestock products; compared with Indians, Europeans had more, stronger, and better-fed draft animals.[90]

The English county of Kent during the three centuries after the year 1000 provides an excellent example of this complex relationship. At the time of the Domesday Book (1086) it would appear that about 60,000–75,000 pigs were foraging on the acorns and beechmast in the woodlands of the Weald. As for Pierre Maury and his Pyrenean compatriots, transhumance was also important in the Kentish agrarian economy. As the population grew and demand for wood products rose, scarce resources had to be used efficiently. The Kentish forests were a haven for squatters' settlements whose assarts and encroachments amounted to a process of attrition that was fraying the woodland ecology. In reply, the twelfth- and early thirteenth-century lords staged a counteroffensive. They sold off some of their extraordinarily complex rights to the forest, thereby acknowledging that these squatters had established a foothold on the land. They concentrated their attention on protecting the remainder of their resources by creating enclosed parks and woodlots. The older practice of rough pasturage—pannaging—was superseded; woodlands were turned into coppices which were regularly harvested.

In the best-situated parts of the Weald of Kent, tenants were required to fell the trees, to fashion them on site according to strict specifications, and to deliver them to a convenient embarkation point. Transportation bottlenecks—it cost as much to move logs a mile or two overland as to float them dozens of miles along the coast to the metropolitan market—meant that the woodland nearest navigable waterways was most thoroughly exploited. So great was the demand for wood that the ecology of the forest was itself changed. In some areas of Kent, slow-growing, majestic oaks were supplanted by faster-growing species which could be harvested in a regular cycle, such as alder for wicker and wattling, or hawthorn, which was used as firewood or else in the making of dikes and sluices that were created to drain the nearby marshes. Oaks became more highly valued as timber than for the production of acorns. In fact, there is evidence that oak (and beech) trees were frequently cut even before they produced mast for pannage because the value of the wood itself rose precipitously. The value of woodland rose from less than a quarter of the value of the poorest arable land in the eleventh century to far beyond that of any other land by 1300.

---

acres to supply their fodder requirements; Wrigley, "Energy Availability and Agricultural Productivity," 332.

90. E. L. Jones, *The European Miracle* (Cambridge, 1981), 4.

In the northern part of the county, forest land rose in value fourfold by 1250 and continued its upward spiral in the following century, when it was supplying fuel to "very many merchants—as well of our Kingdom of England as of the parts of France, Flanders, Zealand and Eastland [Holland], and elsewhere." K. P. Witney, a historian of the Kentish woodlands, claims that "these woods were a source of wealth comparable to the coalfields of the nineteenth century and the oilfields today, with the added advantage of being constantly renewable." In these circumstances, rough foraging was transformed into a much more closely regulated system.[91]

A similar conflict between the needs of pigs for foraging and the requirements of coppicing took place on the estate of the Abbey of Peterborough, where preeminence was given to the woodland resources. Coppiced plots had to be herbivore-proof during their early stages of regeneration, when browsers could do great damage to new, tender shoots. The abbey's woodlands were managed as a renewable resource that was constantly being tended—the timber was grown to maturity on a thirty-year cycle while the underwood was harvested regularly and cropped: faggots for firewood and rods for weaving wattles, fences, and folds, as well as providing raw material for charcoal makers. What about the porkers? They were kept in pigstys and fed on legumes and stubble.[92]

Pastoral economies employed different herding systems for different animals. For mixed herds, complex strategies were created. For example, between 1100 and 1300, the organization of the Abbot of Peterborough's dispersed estate was not static. Its herds were reorganized so as to enhance the special characteristics of each animal: oxen were valued for traction, horses for haulage and the conspicuous display of lordship, sheep for their wool, and pigs for their meat and tallow. There was no hard and fast division between Peterborough's cereal and pastoral economies. Not only were grain yields improved, but this was accomplished in tandem with a very substantial increase in the size of the abbey's herds and flocks. Some of the cereals produced on the abbey estate were devoted to feeding its human population; the rest were used to feed and fatten the animals. The Peterborough estate's array of manorial units was specialized according to an interlocking system of comparative advantage so that the subsistence requirements of the feudal corporation could be preserved while it selectively engaged in the market-oriented production of wool. Agrarian production routines deployed the labor of the abbey's dependent peasants to

91. K. P. Witney, "The Woodland Economy of Kent, 1066–1348," *Agricultural History Review* 38 (1990):20–39.
92. Biddick, *The Other Economy*, 22–24, 121–25.

enhance the fruits of its landed endowment. The estate wielded its seigneurial powers to amplify those acts of ritual consumption that were a central element in the expression of lordship.

Most pastoral farms were nothing like the size of the Peterborough estate, so it is crucial to recognize the cumulative importance of these smaller units. An example referring to the Peterborough flocks helps to make this point. English wool exports totaled 17 million pounds at the beginning of the fourteenth century. This meant that approximately 8.5 million sheep had been shorn whose wool was exported. In 1309–10 there were 2,916 wethers counted among the 8,792 animals in the Peterborough flock. Thus, just one in three animals was a castrated, adult male wether—these sheep supplied most of the wool—and the rest of the abbey's flock were ewes, lambs, and yearlings. It is astounding to realize that while the Peterborough estate was one of the largest in the kingdom, its five tons of wool accounted for only 0.06 percent of the national yield.[93] Since there were not another 1,700 estates of this size—indeed, there were scarcely three dozen—it must follow that a substantial portion of the nation's wool-clip came from a great many, much smaller flocks.[94]

Peasants with a few dozen sheep were the key. It seems that in 1300 an average fleece weighed two pounds and that, therefore, a peasant with a flock of twenty-five sheep would produce fifty pounds[95]—it takes only a little arithmetic to reckon that 340,000 peasants with this size of flock would yield the whole wool-clip without any contribution from the noble landowners. Furthermore, if the English population—to take a very conservative estimate—was 5 million in 1300 then there would have been 1 million peasant households in total. To give a further sense of perspective to our quantitative simulation, we need to take account of the fact that there were probably 20,000 villages in England, c. 1300. Therefore, this seemingly gigantic number of peasant producers can be cut down to its proper size when we realize that there would have been an average of seventeen such peasant flocks per village. This exercise has assumed that only one-third of the peasant households were able to produce a significant

93. The example from Peterborough is drawn from Biddick, *The Other Economy,* 100–1 and *passim.* It is also necessary to point out that the numbers of sheep referred to in the preceding example refer only to those whose wool was destined for export. How many more were shorn for the local market?

94. It has been argued by A. R. Bridbury that big landowners supplied about one-third of the national wool exports; "Before the Black Death," *Economic History Review,* 2d ser., 30 (1977), 398.

95. J. P. Bischoff, "Fleece Weights and Sheep Breeds in Late Thirteenth- and Early Fourteenth-Century England," *Agricultural History* (1982): 143–60.

marketable surplus in woolen fleeces. Bruce Campbell and Mark Overton note that "sheep were much more a peasant than a demesne animal" because "before 1350 seigneurial foldcourse owners had been more interested in their grain harvest than their wool clip."[96]

The crucial point to be drawn from this little quantitative exercise is that animal husbandry was widespread. In some places, animal husbandry was thoroughly intertwined with cereal farming, but in others it squeezed out competition from grain growers. Land that was devoted solely to sheep grazing was unavailable for cereal farming and, given the huge size of the English flocks, this forced hungry men and women to scratch plow at very marginal lands. Furthermore, the Cistercian order's new techniques of sheep rearing on its extensive granges, which were composed of large, carefully assembled tracts, pushed the competition between sheep and humans further beyond the pale of the rich cereal-farming lands.

By 1300, then, a much larger human population meant that pasture and hay were in short supply and, in comparison with the peasant's few acres, only the lord's demesne was well supplied with recycled fertilizer. With its larger stock of animals, demesne land was more likely to be properly manured and could therefore be kept fertile, in good heart.[97] Ignorance of scientific breeding methods kept matters at a standstill. Manorial livestock herds, that Achilles' heel of the medieval agrarian economy, were regulated through the elimination of weaklings rather than building up the quality of herds through selective breeding. Animals were small, and their carcass weights were low, as were wool and milk yields, because the natural pasturage was very rarely supplemented through a regimen of stall feeding.[98] Institutional factors also undermined the creation of large herds. Episcopal landlords often found that their livestock assets were stripped when the crown administered their estates during vacancies.[99] Among the peasantry,

---

96. It was only after 1370 that this pattern began to change, so that by the sixteenth century the ownership pattern had been "inverted" and most sheep were in the hands of a few substantial "gentlemen flockmasters"; Bruce M.S. Campbell and Mark Overton, "A New Perspective on Medieval and Early Modern Agriculture," *Past and Present* 141 (1993): 77–78. See also Mark Bailey, "Sand into Gold: The Evolution of the Foldcourse System in West Suffolk, 1200–1600," *Agricultural History Review* 38 (1990): 40–57.

97. Postan, *The Medieval Economy and Society,* 74–76, 106–7, 108–16.

98. R. H. Hilton, "Rent and Capital Formation in Feudal Society," in *The English Peasantry,* 179–80. See also A. Grant, "Animal Resources," in A. Grant and G. Astill (eds.), *The Countryside of Medieval England* (Oxford, 1988), 149–87.

99. Kathleen Biddick (with Catrien C. J. H. Bijleveld), "Agrarian Productivity on the Estates of the Bishopric of Winchester in the Early Thirteenth Century: A

the accumulation of livestock was hamstrung by the arbitrary demand for *heriot*—the feudal fine which gave the lord the dead man's best beast (or some cash equivalent in the case of *inter-vivos* land transfers).

2.

After the year 1000, the rate of demographic advance was much faster in northwestern Europe. France, for instance, might have grown nearly four-fold while Italy only doubled. Moreover, within France itself, population growth was more intense in the north than in the south.[100] There was no such thing as a typical farm but rather a vast continuum stretching from the wage laborer with a garden and maybe a pig or a cow or several sheep to the integrated plantations of the feudal lords. Hundreds of thousands of different units of production and consumption constituted the agrarian economy. Some were specialized, but most were organized to look after subsistence needs first and only then to consider embarking on market-oriented activities.[101] Of course, the feudal demand for fines and rent as well as the royal taxes meant that "subsistence" incorporated these forays into the money economy.

In both our evidence and our stereotypes, it was the plowman (*laboureur*) and not the laborer (*manouvrier*) who was the archetypical medieval peasant. It was this social group which owned plow teams and therefore supplied the crucial labor to farm the lord's demesne. In fact, the myth of the archetypical medieval peasant hopelessly simplifies social relations by taking one part and identifying it with the whole of village society.[102] As early as the Domesday Book (1086), most villages were made up of several dif-

---

Managerial Perspective," in Campbell and Overton (eds.), *Land, Labour, and Productivity*, 98–104; see also Biddick, *The Other Economy*, 52–53.

100. Colin McEvedy and Richard Jones, *Atlas of World Population History* (Harmondsworth, 1978), 55–60, 106–9. In contrast to the 16 million suggested by McEvedy and Jones, French historical demographer Pierre Goubert suggests that the total for the French population in 1328 was just below 20 million; P. Goubert, in F. Braudel and E. Labrousse (eds.), *Histoire economique et sociale de la France*, vol. 2, quoted by E. Le Roy Ladurie, *The French Peasantry 1450–1660* (Berkeley and Los Angeles, 1987), 23.

101. This bottom-up argument contrasts with Graeme Snooks's view that 40 percent of the Domesday agricultural economy was geared to the market sector and was dominated by tenants-in-chief and undertenants who employed a servile rural workforce. The difference between Snooks's viewpoint and mine is that I am concerned with farmers, whereas he is concerned with production; see Snooks, "The Dynamic Role of the Market."

102. For a telling examination of the complicated subdivision of the labor process on one extremely well-documented manor, see Hogan, "The Labor of Their Days."

ferent strata, some of whom conformed to the stereotype of the plowman, others who were smallholders, and still others who were landless laborers. These different groups interacted in complementary, if unequal, ways: the plowman's family economy sometimes employed adult laborers and more frequently took the children from the lower strata into their households as living-in servants. The timing of this labor transfer was usually connected to the plowman's family cycle, taking in teenagers when his children were small and substituting his own family's labor as his sons and daughters matured. As the ratio between hands and mouths increased it was more likely that plowmen would enter the land market and increase the size of their holdings, through subletting odd strips, crofts, enclosures, or gardens or else through the outright purchase of free land. The compositional blend of social strata persisted throughout the whole feudal period and, indeed, well beyond.

In a money economy, the family farm was never a completely self-sufficient autarky because land would have been made available to peasants only in exchange for their recognition of, and submission to, the tributary demands of lordship and state formation. The increasing circulation of money after the year 1000 was a general, trans-European phenomenon. In England, for example, the taxation demands of the crown forced lords into cash cropping. Merchants advanced money and collected grain or wool. By the end of the twelfth century the Abbey of Peterborough was a "share-cropper of money," and the king was deflecting a growing share of that money crop into his treasury. Having to come up with ready cash meant that a good part of the abbey's income was burdened with debt surcharges owed to moneylenders. The impact of royal fiscal policies on the dependent tenants of the Peterborough manors was very substantial. Some were elevated into an intermediary position as plowmen who had tremendous security at the cost of heavy tributary payments; the rest were driven downward to form a reserve army of surplus labor. These rural proletarians found that some of their feudal dues were commuted into money payments while the abbey still retained discretionary control over this source of human energy in order to tap it during the labor-intensive periods of harvesting and haymaking.[103]

The opportunities afforded by the commercial economy did not break apart some natural community but, rather, these opportunities entered through preexisting fissures to disintegrate old arrangements and to reintegrate them in new social relations. These new social relations of produc-

103. Biddick, *The Other Economy,* 49–53, 57–61.

tion were associated with a major contrast in the cropping patterns on demesne lands and peasant holdings: the former was more likely to be used for producing wheat for sale in the marketplace while the latter was more likely to be growing rye or barley for subsistence.[104] The peasantry practiced "polyculture" on its land, in contrast to the cash-crop monoculture of the lord's demesne.[105] Open-field farming was a communal practice. Most land was worked in fragments scattered among the village fields. Considerable discussion, planning, and coordination were required so that the tendency to choose conservative—as opposed to risk-taking—action was almost inevitable. Yet, it is mistaken to consider these farming practices only insofar as they relate to productivity. There is a strong argument that these peasants were trading them off against other goals—stability, predictability, sustainability, and equitability—to reduce the risk of complete failure and starvation.[106] Of course, the peasantry was also under pressure to produce marketable grain (and other products that could be converted into ready cash) to pay their rents as well as their feudal dues.

There were built-in contradictions—a vicious cycle—in the feudal system biased against both capital formation and intensified productivity. To escape this low-level equilibrium trap it was necessary for the peasantry to accumulate capital—by increasing both their landholdings and their stocks of livestock—for labor-intensive cropping practices to be aided by massive increases in the application of fertilizer in the form of animal manure. Seigneurial exactions made it difficult—some would say impossible—for peasants to create or maintain large holdings because the thrust of feudal policy was to skim off whatever surplus the peasant family accumulated. Moreover, the demands of demesne farming thwarted peasant accumulation since it was in the lord's interest to have a complement of plowmen rather than just a few kulaks.

In manorialized zones, "the lord of the village controlled the land market which meant that the accumulation of properties by an alliance of lineages could not take place, except between free families holding in free tenure." This was not likely, however, because there was a tendency for concentrated, free holding to be split by partible forms of inheritance.[107]

104. Duby, *Rural Economy*, 90; Postan, "Medieval Agrarian Society in Its Prime: England," 600 ff.

105. Bois, *The Crisis of Feudalism*, 192 ff. See also Dyer, *Standards of Living in the Later Middle Ages* (Cambridge, 1989), 127 ff.

106. Jules N. Pretty, "Sustainable Agriculture in the Middle Ages: The English Manor," *Agricultural History Review* 38 (1990): 1–19.

107. R. H. Hilton, "Medieval Peasants: Any Lessons?" in *Class Conflict and the Crisis of Feudalism*, 43. With regard to the propensity for peasants to divide their

For this reason, it was even more likely that free land would be minutely subdivided than customary land. There is evidence that manorial tenants on the lands of the bishop of Worcester were deterred from dividing their holdings among their surviving children. Landlords had an interest in keeping customary holdings intact so that their feudal rent—in particular, labor services from the plowmen—could be collected and the lowest levels of the manorial administration could be staffed with recruits from this peasant elite.[108]

This vicious cycle led to an in-built tendency to favor an optimal plowman's holding—as against either the morcellization of standard plots into dwarf-holdings or the accretion of land into large concentrations. In other places, such as Norfolk, which was not manorialized, this contradiction may have been avoided and productivity may have been more responsive to market incentives. While Norfolk may not have been manorialized, there were huge tracts of the English countryside that were, and it was in these places that the social relations of production were perhaps more important than the material forces of productivity.[109]

To break out of this zero-sum game it was necessary to radically alter the power relations which enabled the landed class to exercise its lordship at the expense of peasant's entrepreneurial activities. Rather than pulling against each other, lord and peasant had to have similar sets of incentives. Capital accumulation could become possible only when the dependent classes had legal rights. Feudalism made this impossible by enabling arbitrary seigneurial exactions to intervene between the farm and the marketplace as well as between the peasant and his property.

3.

In contrast to the international culture of the seigneurial class, the hallmark of the peasantry was its internal differentiation resulting from the peculiarities of local circumstances—"a luxuriant diversity."[110] Historians are almost pathologically unwilling to generalize, and in this instance their caution is well founded. Indeed, as Karl Marx would later note with regard to the French peasantry of his own time:

---

goods among their children, see Hilton, "Reasons for Inequality among Medieval Peasants," in *Class Conflict and the Crisis of Feudalism*, 73.

108. Christopher Dyer, *Lords and Peasants in a Changing Society* (Cambridge, 1980), 107.

109. This point is mentioned only in passing in Bruce Campbell and Mark Overton's survey of Norfolk farming, "A New Perspective on Medieval and Early Modern Agriculture," 100.

110. John Hatcher, "English Serfdom and Villeinage," 9.

Each individual peasant family is almost self-sufficient; it itself directly produces the major part of its consumption and thus acquires the means of life more through exchange with nature than in intercourse with society. A small holding, a peasant and his family; alongside them another peasant and another family. . . . In so far as there is merely a local interconnection among these small-holding peasants and the identity of their interests begets no community, no national bond and no political organization among them, they do not form a class.

Primary producers may have shared a similar experience of subjugation vis-à-vis the seigneurial classes, but they were almost always divided among themselves by their inability to form associational linkages outside the locality in which they lived, worked, and died: they were a "simple addition of homologous magnitudes, much as potatoes in a sack form a sack of potatoes."[111]

At the risk of doing violence to the particularity of experience, there appears to have been a two-dimensional spectrum along which local society was arrayed. The axis of time and social change provided the horizontal dimension; the vertical one was the product of an intercorrelation between the local political economy of state formation and the ecological workshop supplied by the indigenous habitat. Paradoxically, one way to consider this complicated relationship is to create a model of the peasant economy which is abstracted in both time and space.

The deviation between this fiction and our documented social reality provides access to the interaction of forces framing the everyday life of the great mass of the rural population. So, let us start with that enduring stereotype—the classic feudal estate. The lord in his castle dominated a village of bondsmen's households. The lord's demesne was farmed with the labor of these dependent cultivators, each of whom had been given a similar amount of land in exchange for his services. "The household which was the centre of gravity of the social and economic life of the village—and very likely at the physical centre too—was that of the 'tiller' or 'ploughman' of the poets, the 'husbandman' of statute and legal process, the holder of the whole or half yardland in the manorial extents."[112] This was not a perfectly realized social class, but whatever antagonism they felt toward the cottagers and landless laborers "could be compared rather to a family quarrel than to the hostility arising from a social gulf."[113] In fact, the trans-

111. Karl Marx, *The Eighteenth Brumaire of Louis Bonaparte* (New York, 1963), 123–24.

112. R. H. Hilton, *The English Peasantry in the Middle Ages*, 28. See also Bois, *The Crisis of Feudalism*, 395.

113. Hilton, *The English Peasantry*, 51.

formation of this "antagonism" into a "social gulf" would mark a decisive cultural change in the class relations among the peasantry. When this happened, during the century after the Black Death in England, the "homologous magnitudes" underwent a profound mutation.

Class conflict within the village community was further inhibited by the comparative failure of wealthier elements to separate themselves from their fellows, many of whom were undergoing severe downward social mobility from the relative autonomy of the husbandman (i.e., housed bondman) to the abject destitution of wage laboring in conditions of severe underemployment. There were two brakes on upward mobility out of the peasantry: first, population growth expanded the social pyramid at the bottom; and, second, institutional forces—feudal control over landholding and inheritance practices—militated against accumulation.

Within the peasantry living in a single village the economic division between large- and smallholders was crosscut with another, complicating factor—the legal distinctions which separated villeinage from freedom. It has been suggested that "households holding by unfree tenure may well have constituted little more than a third of total households."[114] In highly manorialized regions, the unfree population seems to have been more like two-thirds of the peasantry. The landless were more likely to be free— often gaining this status by illegitimate birth or personal migration— mainly because they had little of worth which could be extracted from them through the imposition of seigneurial jurisdiction.[115]

Some peasants were villeins by birth; others were villeins by tenure. There was, thus, "a possible fourfold division between free or unfree land held by free or unfree tenants."[116] How important was the juxtaposition of tenants of very different juridical status and economic position? One might also want to know how much of the manorialized land was farmed by free tenants as opposed to servile tenants, but unfortunately I have not seen any attempt to address this crucial point by disaggregating the rough-and-ready distinction between demesne and customary land. The answer

114. Hatcher, "English Serfdom and Villeinage," 7. Hatcher's estimate includes the nonpeasant population; Edmund King suggests that 40 percent of the rural population was unfree; *England, 1115–1425* (London, 1979), 50.

115. This may be the reason for the discrepancy between Hatcher's one-third and King's 40 percent of households who were holding land by unfree tenure, on one hand, and the estimated 60 percent of the peasantry who were legally unfree in the sense that they were unable to seek legal action in the royal courts against their lords that was quoted earlier.

116. P. D. A. Harvey, "Conclusion," in *The Peasant Land Market in Medieval England* (Oxford, 1984), 331–32.

to this question would seem to be that the serfs farmed significantly more land than their numbers would suggest and also that this was even more true in the circumstances of high population growth and land scarcity which prevailed in the thirteenth and fourteenth centuries, when it was common for free men to take on land burdened with feudal tenure even though this meant that they were selling their freedom for a mess of pottage. Hungry, desperate people will do almost anything. As Bertholdt Brecht would later write, first comes food, then comes morality.

The combination of free land, fragmented holdings, partible inheritance, and lack of centralized supervision represented one tendency in the rural economy. Servile land, unbroken traditional holdings, impartible inheritance, and control by manorial authorities represented a contrasting polarity. Most agrarian systems were, in practice, strung out along a continuum stretching from one pole to the other. In each manor the actual pattern of landholding—as distinct from landownership—was the product of a complex balance of forces. Furthermore, and of immense importance, in the culture of the village there was a rough equality among the dependent family farmers, so that they were more-or-less "homologous magnitudes, much as potatoes in a sack [are] a sackful of potatoes." Smallholders and richer peasants were part of a shared social universe. Their cultural horizons were the same, too.[117] While their lifestyles were essentially similar, peasants may have differed from one another in accordance to the abundance rather than the quality of their possessions.

The peasant economy was the product of a series of diverse components— diet, population size and demographic trends, land use, climate, technology, feudal incidents, and political relations, both within the peasant community and between the peasantry and the landlord class.[118] Within the village, the individual peasant family was similarly differentiated by another set of variable factors: manorial size and organization, legal status (free or villein), rents and feudal taxes, size of holding, tenurial conditions, soil fertility and productivity, technology, marketing opportunities, alternative income sources (either in industry or service), inheritance customs, family size, life-cycle stage, and gender relations. Moreover, these characteristics were not static. Diversity was a result of the particular amalgam of individual factors (on either a village or a familial level) which was constantly in flux.

117. Hilton, *Bond Men Made Free*, 35.
118. K. Lunden, "Some Causes of Change in a Peasant Economy: Interactions between Cultivated Area, Farming Population, Climate, Taxation, and Technology," *Scandinavian Economic History Review* 22 (1974): 117–35. See also J. A. Raftis, "Social Structure: The East Midlands," in Hallam (ed.), *The Agrarian History of England and Wales*, vol. 2, *1086–1350*, 649.

Another dimension to the differentiation among the peasantry must be connected with the process of "territorializing the holdings of manorial tenants." P. D. A. Harvey writes that "in 1100 the lord of a manor was the lord of men who held lands of him; in 1200 he was the lord of lands that were occupied by tenants. The change is slight but significant. In 1100 the tenant's holding could be viewed simply as a standard share in the vill's resources; by 1200 it was far more likely to be viewed as precisely defined in its area and its other rights." The process of territorialization formed the "shared baseline" in the way in which manorial seigneuries led to the creation of standardized holdings "with uniform obligations and apparently of uniform sizes."[119] The written record was thus an attempt to fix social relations and to dislodge them from memory.

If there was any uniformity in the everyday reality described in the written record, it was the fortuitous product of diverse customs, local conditions, and historical evolution which followed in the wake of this process of territorializing servitude. These factors usually led to a disparity between the legal figment of standardization and the complex variety of lived experience. What is particularly notable about the documentation relating to the land market among English peasants is its strong regional bias: almost all the early materials come from East Anglia, where there was marked subdivision not only of manorial jurisdictions but also of peasant plots. Later evidence of the peasant land market largely relates to the lords' attempts to control it and thereby control their title to the land and the services owed by its occupants. It would seem that during the later thirteenth century, feudal lords in other parts of England used the law to regularize their peasants' traffic in land by forcing them to record their transactions in manorial courts. In this way, these other feudal lords were able to maintain more of their discretionary powers than their East Anglian counterparts.[120] Later seigneurial documents fossilized social relations because their main aim had been to establish the liability of estate officers and thereby control their peculation.[121]

The village community was thus not an undifferentiated mass with identical interests. The law, too, was a double-edged sword: recognized customs which were created for protection in a time of land shortage could be-

119. Harvey, "Introduction," in *The Peasant Land Market*, 12, 8.
120. Paul R. Hyams, "The Origins of a Peasant Land Market in England," *Economic History Review*, 2d ser., 23 (1970): 18–31. As we shall see later in the discussion of feudalism and family formation, this differential evolution had significant implications for the self-organization of the peasantry.
121. A. E. Levett, "The Financial Organization of the Manor," in *Studies in Manorial History* (Oxford, 1938), 44–45.

come exploitative in a time of surplus. Population changes by themselves are insufficient to explain the character of political struggle. Changes in the level of population or the supply of land could alter the supply and demand axes, but the lords' power was not concerned solely with economistic measures. Their customary powers were economic as well as social, political, and juridical. These powers were backed up by their monopoly on military force. Moreover, "Changes in the level of population or the supply of land could make labour or land more scarce or more abundant, but for tenants both in the power of their lords and protected by custom these changes alone did not determine the amount and type of rent they paid."[122]

While it is important to note the uneven chronology of exploitation deriving from the class relations of feudal society, it is nonetheless crucial to keep in mind that "Of all the limitations upon freedom the denial of the right to move, to seek new farms, new employments, new lords, was the most fundamental. All other incidents of unfreedom can be interpreted as stemming from, or accessory to, the bringing of men to the soil and to their lords and the denial of free will."[123] Even though it did not represent the majority of the rural population, the servile population of the thirteenth century had been peculiarly privileged by its access to land held in customary tenure.[124] In a period of acute overpopulation, land shortage, and diminishing prospects for internal colonization by assarting, the customary population was made to pay for the maintenance of its servility. Whatever small benefits it derived from being protected from market forces were countered by the intensification of the bonds of feudal relations.

4.

The early modernization of the agrarian sector had been accompanied by considerable demographic and social vitality. A new kind of society was emerging in northwestern Europe; this novelty is apparent when we contrast it with late Manchu China, where under 2 percent of the 400 million

122. Hatcher, "English Serfdom and Villeinage," 37.
123. Hatcher, "English Serfdom and Villeinage," 30.
124. It is important to make it clear that the preceding discussion has concentrated overmuch on the manorial sector of the feudalized rural economy. The reason for slanting in this direction is simple: there is almost no information concerning the nonmanorial rural economy. Almost all of our evidence comes from the records that documented the daily operation of feudalism, even though the best estimates suggest that the servile population made up one-third to two-fifths of the English rural population in the heartland of the thirteenth-century feudal reaction. Therefore, as much as two-thirds of the rural population is unrepresented in a history that gives primacy to these documents. But, again, how does one tell another story from silence?

(i.e., eight million) people were nonproducers. Perhaps 15 percent of the 40 million people in northwestern Europe were not peasants. These 6 million nonproducers were supported by the agricultural surplus.[125]

Thirteenth- and fourteenth-century English agriculture not only fed many times more people than in the year 1000, but large numbers of people enjoyed its "various and opulent" characteristics, such as the profits derived from the vast expansion of the wool-clip and almost two centuries of rising cereal prices. Urbanization, aristocratic largesse, and the wholly nonproductive monastic population of 70,000 adults are all evidence of its surplus wealth, which is still visible in the stone buildings which form such a major part of the country's "heritage."[126] Yet today's "heritage" is a laconic memorial of past oppression.

An indication of the wretchedness of the majority of the rural population in the generation or two before the Black Death is provided by rural histories of manorial farming. In eastern Norfolk, where there were 500 people per square mile, "it is the absolute smallness of even the largest holdings that most attracts attention." On the manor of Martham, where there had been 107 tenants working 1,066 statute acres in the twelfth century, there were 376 tenants by 1292. Whereas ten tenants had holdings of more than twenty acres in the first survey, only one did so at the later date. Correlatively, twenty-two had less than five acres in the twelfth century, but by 1292 the number of these smallholders had risen an astounding 1,409 percent. Not only did landholdings shrink, but the strips in the fields also seem to have been subdivided.[127] Moreover, since many of the poorest families might have been completely landless—perhaps possessing only a cottage and its garden—these people would have been omitted altogether from most surviving documents. They may have subcontracted land from the titular peasant holders. The very active land market which medievalists have uncovered is perhaps the apex at the tip of a very large iceberg of such arrangements.

125. Emmanuel Le Roy Ladurie, "Rural Civilization," in *The Territory of the Historian* (Chicago, 1979), 87. The figure for China is from Jones, *The European Miracle,* 4.

126. Bridbury, "Before the Black Death," 393–410. I calculated 70,000 preplague monasteries by doubling J. C. Russell's estimates for 1377 in "The Clerical Population of Medieval England," *Traditio* 2 (1944): 177–212.

127. B. M. S. Campbell, "Inheritance and the Land Market in a Peasant Community," in R. M. Smith (ed.), *Land, Kinship and Life-Cycle* (Cambridge, 1984), 92, 103; B. M. S. Campbell, "People and Land in the Middle Ages, 1066–1500," in R. A. Butlin and R. A. Dodgshon (eds.), *An Historical Geography of England and Wales,* 2d ed. (London, 1990), 94.

Occasional, unexpected sources give us tiny windows through which to see these social relations in action: "The scale of subletting on a free holding was exposed at Cleeve [a manor of the Bishop of Worcester] when, a generation before 1299, the lord bought out a tenant who had fallen into debt, and became the direct lord of his twenty-one subtenants." Similarly, on the Essex manor of Gressenhall, at least one-third of the tenancies recorded in a 1282 survey were held by more than one tenant. The nearby, royal manor of Havering, Essex, a couple of years after the purgative impact of the Black Death, was peopled by 187 tenants and 253 subtenants.[128] Thus it is important to recognize that

> the villein holding was much divided among various occupants and types of ownership, while preserving a [fictional] unity towards the lord; for we have seen that the widow, the aged and impotent, and the able-bodied men without an inheritance, were all the occupiers of dower land on the holding of another man, who was held responsible to the abbot for the rent and services of the entire area. Simple as the land system might seem from above, it was, therefore, from beneath a patchwork organization of private arrangements, protected by the custom of the manor.[129]

If such a wide variety of adaptations could exist within the shell of a powerful manorial structure, then it would hardly be surprising to find an even more vigorous growth of subtenanting in those places where land was not encumbered with an overmighty lord. Rarely does one encounter the maintenance of the traditional yardland or virgate; rather, we find a multiplication of dwarf-holdings. Most peasant holdings were too small for them to meet their subsistence needs except by recourse to new methods of land use and food consumption.[130]

Obscure landless or near-landless men and women are often "screened from our view," yet we catch fleeting glimpses of *anilepimen, anilepi-*

128. Dyer, *Standards of Living in the Later Middle Ages*, 120; Zvi Razi, "Manorial Court Rolls and Local Population: An East Anglian Case Study," *Economic History Review*, 2d ser., 49 (1996): 758–63; M. K. McIntosh, "Land, Tenure, and Population in the Royal Manor of Havering, Essex, 1251–1352/3," *Economic History Review*, 2d ser., 33 (1980): esp. 20–25.

129. Frances M. Page, "The Customary Poor-Law of Three Cambridgeshire Manors," *Cambridge Historical Journal* 3 (1930): 133. Later authorities have reiterated Page's point concerning the artificiality of the customary tenancy; see, for example, Ambrose Raftis, "Peasants and the Collapse of the Manorial Economy on Some Ramsey Abbey Estates," in Richard Britnell and John Hatcher (eds.), *Progress and Problems in Medieval England* (Cambridge, 1996), 199.

130. E. Miller and J. Hatcher, *Medieval England: Rural Society and Economic Change 1086–1348* (London, 1978), 141–42.

wymen, undersetles, or *coterelli.*[131] Around 1300, rural society seems to have been populated by a "submerged and pullulating throng . . . like the stars that are visible to astronomers only in their effects upon the orbits of neighbouring bodies." These people can be perceived only in the influence they exerted upon other factors at times of crisis. Living in extended families or as unmarried domestic servants, they were numerous enough to account for the feeding, clothing, and employment of a very substantial proportion of the population without reference to the market. Extended families, indeed, were so organized, if that is the word, that members who were kept alive in this way were chronically underemployed. These people were a reserve, adding nothing to the wealth of the community as the market measured such things. What they subtracted from it in order to survive, they subtracted from their families and neighbors in ways which the market was not sensitive enough to register. When famines and the plague struck, they took the places of those who had perished, in an orderly succession that left the world of markets and land tenure virtually undisturbed by the losses the community had sustained.[132]

Our historical record of rural population densities is very patchy, but "In parts of the English Fenlands densities reached 114 per square kilometre in the thirteenth century; the same parishes had an average density in 1951 of only 80 per square kilometre." It would appear that the French population in 1328 numbered just below 20 million, which is roughly the same as it would be in 1700. If we consider only the rural population, then the early fourteenth-century French countryside was rather fuller than it was to be nearly five hundred years later, on the eve of the 1789 Revolution.[133] If English rural densities were as high as they were in the French countryside before the Black Death, then the population would have ex-

131. Miller and Hatcher, *Medieval England,* 55, H. C. Hallam, "Social Structure, Eastern England," in *The Agrarian History of England and Wales,* vol. 2, *1086–1350,* 619–20; and Hogan, "The Labor of Their Days," 87–88.

132. A. R. Bridbury, "The Black Death," *Economic History Review,* 2d ser., 26 (1973): 590; Zvi Razi, *Life, Marriage and Death in a Medieval Parish* (Cambridge, 1980). In this regard it is, I think, relevant to mention that in the contemporary Third World "the number of smallholders and landless households will increase by about 50 million, to nearly 220 million, by the year 2000. Together, these groups represent three-quarters of the agricultural households in developing countries"; World Commission on Environment and Development, *Our Common Future* (Oxford, 1987), 142. The growth of such landless households is nonlinear, in contrast to that of the population in general. The importance of this point will be developed further in chapter 4, "Reproducing Feudalism."

133. David Grigg, *Population Growth and Agrarian Change* (Cambridge, 1980), 67. For another useful analysis of the relative impact of overpopulation, see N. J. G. Pounds, "Overpopulation in France and the Low Countries in the Later

ceeded the levels attained in Thomas Malthus's time, when the rural population's size and growth so exercised the parson. But were rural densities uniformly high? I think so. Not only did the land mass devoted to cereal production in England decline after the mid-fourteenth century, but it never again reached this high-water mark—neither during the Napoleonic Wars nor during the parlous days of the Second World War. Furthermore, after the mid-fourteenth century plagues, the land was farmed in much larger units. Deserted villages, settled by pioneering assarters during the Little Climatic Optimum after the year 1000, would forever remain deserted.

The population of northwest Europe was possibly declining even before the Black Death. The colonizing thrust was played out; replication ran into a dead end. In some places, the frontier of settlement even seems to have been receding. Poorer lands which had been cultivated in the expansionary tide after the year 1000 were being deserted, particularly those which were the last to have been colonized because they were in marginal ecological zones. In other places, soils were quickly exhausted, while elsewhere, crops could not be sustained on them when the climate became colder, wetter, and more prone to violent storms. These problems were particularly acute in zones of high altitude and below sea level.[134] The estates of Canterbury Cathedral Priory have been intensively studied by Mavis Mate, who points out that one of the ways these feudal landlords managed to keep their enterprises afloat was by strictly controlling costs while switching from labor-intensive crops to pastoralism, thereby reducing their wage rolls.[135] Those who kept their jobs had to cope with declining purchasing power as their real wages fell.

The worst of these crises occurred in the second decade of the fourteenth century, when a succession of long hard winters were followed by wet weather in the spring and summer which destroyed the crops, leaving the population destitute. Various estimates of mortality seem to agree that

Middle Ages," *Journal of Social History* 3 (1970): 225–48. The total for the French population in 1328 is provided by P. Goubert, in F. Braudel and E. Labrousse (eds.), *Histoire economique et sociale de la France*, vol. 2, quoted by Le Roy Ladurie, *The French Peasantry 1450–1660*, 23. For another suggestion that much of Europe did not regain pre-plague population totals until the nineteenth century, see David Herlihy, *Medieval Households* (Cambridge, Mass., 1985), 80, 144.

134. Duby, *Rural Economy*, 87. See also A. R. H. Baker, "Evidence in 'Nonarum Inquisitions' of Contracting Arable Land in England during the Early Fourteenth Century," *Economic History Review*, 2d ser., 19 (1966/7): 518–32.

135. Mate, "The Estates of Canterbury Cathedral Priory before the Black Death," 25–26.

as many as one person in six died. On the manor of Halesowen, Worcestershire, 13 percent of 320 manorial tenants' deaths recorded in the seventy-eight years before the Black Death occurred in the three-year period following the harvest of 1315.[136] In Languedoc, in southern France, there was famine and dearth in twenty of the forty-six years before the Black Death.[137] In the Norfolk village of Coltishall during the fourteenth century, "the population was losing its ability to weather periodic food shortages. . . . [A] growing proportion of the population faced the prospect of having to sell land if harvests failed."[138]

What happened to those people—the vast majority of the rural population—who lost their already tenuous connection with the land? For this submerged and pullulating throng, life itself was in jeopardy. Those who were beyond the pale of landholding were the hardest hit by recurrent famines. The study of *heriots*, or fines payable at death to the manorial lord, suggests that "poorer sections of the population were the ones to succumb most frequently to privations following the failures of crops. . . . [They] could keep body and soul together only in years of moderately good harvests."[139] The population/resources equation radically changed around the beginning of the fourteenth century. Land hunger became prevalent in the face of a vanished frontier. An increasing portion of the peasantry now suffered harrowing poverty as it sought to eke a livelihood from marginal land. Peasants overworked the more fertile soils into exhaustion. Furthermore, this squeeze took place in the conditions of a deteriorating climate. The classic *crise de subsistence*—in which burials skyrocketed and, for a while at least, births plummeted—tightened its grip. The long secular boom had ground to a halt. The positive feedbacks that had buoyed the ten generations living after the year 1000 were reversed, and in place of its virtuous circle of benefits, the new system of negative feedbacks created a vicious circle of disadvantages.

136. Henry S. Lucas, "The Great European Famine of 1315, 1316, and 1317," in E. M. Carus-Wilson (ed.), *Essays in Economic History*, vol. 2 (London, 1962), 49–72; I. Kershaw, "The Great Famine and Agrarian Crisis in England, 1315–1322," *Past and Present* 59 (1973): 3–50; Razi, *Life, Marriage and Death*, 42 (Table 6); William Chester Jordan, *The Great Famine: Northern Europe in the Early Fourteenth Century* (Princeton, 1996).
137. Emmanuel Le Roy Ladurie, *The Peasants of Languedoc* (Chicago, 1974), 13.
138. Campbell, "Inheritance and the Land Market," 118.
139. Postan, *The Medieval Economy and Society*, 38.

4 Reproducing Feudalism

THINKING WITH DEMOGRAPHY

Ambitious projects and dramatic actions of the past make more interesting reading than the everyday life of the past with its limitations and its mundane existence in the framework of imperfect systems. More substantial than the high points, however, when we take a global view, are the terrain and the roots from which our modern history has sprung.

Heinrich Fichtenau, *Living in the Tenth Century:
Mentalities and Social Orders*

The crucial development in the study of family history has been the discovery that there was a decade-long gap between puberty and marriage which distinguished northwestern Europe's culture of family formation from all others. But how and when did this difference emerge? "Thinking with Demography" sets out to delineate this difference and then to consider its origins. We are on firm ground only for the period after about 1550, when Renaissance states began to create a database of vital events. Therefore, much of this chapter is conjectural in that it connects possibilities to chart the probable historical changes whereby Christianity, feudalism, and distinctive demographic processes that long existed in northwestern Europe were fused to create the early modern culture of family formation. This system of deferred marriage and nuclear-family residences probably existed before the year 1000.

A new kind of society emerged in the centuries after the year 1000. Many novel processes—religious and spiritual, legal and constitutional, social and economic, technological and demographic—recombined to create a social mutation. The historical emergence of the northwestern European marriage system was a helical construction in which Christian culture and barbarian demography wrapped themselves around one another. Manorialized feudal society at first formed another strand in what was to become a triple helix combining the biological, cultural, and material modes to form a finely adjusted system of social reproduction.

Changes in population composition and vital rates identify pivotal transformations in social life. But these experiences can be understood only by placing them in context and by finding nondemographic explanations for them. By reconstituting demographic statistics from their biological, cultural, and material elements, we can comprehend the quantitative implications of immense social movements. The transformation of reproductive patterns was part of a massive shift in the nature of social relations because social change was experienced by thinking people who reflected on it and changed their behavior with regard to it. Of course, causal arrows also flowed in the other direction: changing forms of behavior modified social systems.

How do people without access to modern contraceptive technology restrict their numbers? Almost all anthropological investigations reveal a welter of cultural adaptations to the basic biological fact that human fertility is never close to the physiological maximum. According to Henri Leridon, "First, the biological maximum for women who remain fecund and exposed to risk from their fifteenth to their forty-fifth birthdays, and who do not breast-feed their children, would be 17 to 18 children." In any population there would be some women who would be sterile, but most of the difference between Leridon's "biological maximum" and observed total fertility rates could be accounted for only by referring to cultural and historical factors such as the age and incidence of nuptiality, breast-feeding practices, abortions (both spontaneous and calculated), starvation-induced amenorrhea, coital frequency, rates of widowhood, remarriage, separation or desertion, and so forth.[1]

1. Henri Leridon, *Human Fertility* (Chicago, 1977), 147; see also F. Lorimer, *Culture and Human Fertility* (New York, 1954), esp. 51–54. Leridon's point regarding the cultural construction of human fertility is recognized in the pioneering article on the subject by Louis Henry, "Some Data on Natural Fertility," *Eugenics Quarterly* 8 (1961): 81–91, but its importance is often lost on his followers. For another useful discussion of this point, see John Bongaarts, "Why High Birth Rates Are So Low," *Population and Development Review* 1 (1975): 289–96.

Uniquely, northwest Europeans married late. To be more precise, the link between puberty and marriage was dramatically more attentuated in northwestern Europe than elsewhere. The identification of this austere "Malthusian" regime has been the greatest achievement of early modern historical demography. Basing his conclusions on fifty-four published studies describing age at first marriage for women in northwest Europe, Michael Flinn shows that the average age at marriage fluctuated around twenty-five. Flinn does not provide us with measurements to assess the spread of the distribution around this midpoint, but other studies have determined the standard deviation to be about six years, meaning that about two-thirds of all northwest European women married for the first time between twenty-two and twenty-eight.[2] A few teenage brides were counterbalanced, as it were, by a similar number of women who married in their thirties. Perhaps one woman in ten never married. In the demographer's jargon, that tenth woman was permanently celibate.

These statistics provide us with a single measure which distinguishes the creation of new families in northwestern Europe from that in other societies.[3] This unique marriage strategy was vitally important for two reasons: first, it provided a "safety valve"—or margin for error—in the ongoing adjustment between population and resources that characterized the reproduction of generations and social formations; and second, it meant that the role of women was less dependent and vulnerable insofar as they were marrying as young adults, not older children.

2. Michael Flinn, *The European Demographic System, 1500–1820* (Baltimore, 1981). See also Daniel Scott Smith, "A Homeostatic Demographic Regime: Patterns in West European Family Reconstitution Studies," in R. D. Lee (ed.), *Population Patterns in the Past* (New York, 1977), 19–51.

3. Perhaps the closest analogy with the European experience is nineteenth-century Japan, where a fault line divided the early-marrying eastern half of the country from the later-marrying western parts. In eastern Japan women married in their late teens and early twenties, while in the west brides were more likely to be in their early to middle twenties; Akira Hayami, "Another *Fossa Magna:* Proportion Marrying and Age at Marriage in Late Nineteenth-Century Japan," *Journal of Family History* 12 (1987): 57–72. The control of fertility in early modern Japan was, however, only partly the result of this smaller gap between puberty and marriage—it was also partly the result of deliberate infanticide; T. C. Smith, *Nakahara: Family Farming and Population in a Japanese Village, 1717–1830* (Stanford, 1977). Taken together, slightly later ages at marriage and stringent controls within marriage kept population from overwhelming a slow incremental gain in per capita income per head. A larger proportion of the Japanese population was released from primary food production and worked in rural, domestic industries than in any preindustrial social formation outside northwestern Europe; Susan B. Hanley and Kozo Yamamura, *Economic and Demographic Change in Preindustrial Japan, 1600–1868* (Princeton, 1977).

1.

In looking for the roots of the western European system of "Malthusian" marriage, we might consider the mesh between the Christianization of northern and western Europe and the aboriginal demographic structures. If we ask not when or why but how the northwest European system of deferred or "Malthusian" marriage came into being, a plausible answer could be set forth within the limits of a strictly demographic analysis. Consider two extreme examples.

First, one might argue that with the exceptions of such pestilential holocausts as the Justinian pandemic or the Black Death, the preindustrial level of background mortality in the northwest European biota was likely to have resulted in a life expectation at birth of about forty years. Given low rates of growth, the puberty/marriage nexus would have been definitively severed, or else some programmatic restrictions on births—through either infanticide or contraception—would have been rigorously pursued.

Second, in contrast, one might argue that before 1500 the frequency of severe and debilitating mortality crises was endemic in northwest Europe so that over the long term, life expectation at birth was closer to twenty-five years, with the result that fertility was unrestricted and first marriage for women was close to puberty. Neither of our scenarios can be proved with any degree of certainty by recourse to empirical evidence, but they are "good to think with."

We might argue that the social system that Tacitus was told existed in Germany was in fact a world of high marriage ages and low mortality, while the one into which he was born was one of low marriage ages—for women, of course, because that is the real point at issue—and high mortality.[4] A low mortality regime would have meant, *ceteris paribus*, a functional accommodation—late ages at first marriage for women. Moreover, Tacitus is quite clear that among the Germans "to restrict the number of children, or to kill any of those born after the heir, is considered wicked." The usual arrangement among tribal peoples of regulating population through postnatal measures was therefore ruled out, and one would certainly like to know why this was so. If low mortality had been accompanied by early marriage, without benefit of infanticide as it were, then the German population would have grown exponentially. It did not, so we have to assume that a quite different strategy was employed to balance population

4. Tacitus, *The Agricola and The Germania*, edited by H. Mattingly (Harmondsworth, 1970), sec. 20, 118.

and resources, a quite different strategy that was, in effect, congruent with a system of later marriage ages and spousal equality.

What do we have to support an incursion into the deeper recesses of barbarian demography? Not much. Our evidence is limited to scattered contemporary comments (which are suspect sources because they usually deride contemporary social arrangements in terms of their own prescriptive conventions) and paleodemographic analysis of human burial sites. For the period of late antiquity and the early Middle Ages, the best information that has come to my attention was unearthed in Frénouville (Calvados), lower Normandy, where there were two discrete burial sites—one dating from the end of the third century and another from the end of the seventh century. Most of the skeletal remains are those of adults, so it only makes sense to confine ourselves to the adult mortality experience. It would appear that the median age at death for those who had survived to adulthood was in the late forties, that the modal age of death for all adults was in their fifties, and that fully 26 percent of those who had survived until age eighteen could have expected to have lived into their sixties. For women there was a notable double mortality peak—many died young, often when they gave birth for the first time. Those women who survived this gauntlet were able to live as long as males. In the most pessimistic reading, these statistics regarding adult mortality suggest a life expectation at birth of 31.2 years.[5]

For Britain, about half of all "Dark Age" and "medieval" skeletal remains could be attributed to persons under twenty.[6] This age distribution of deaths would be expected in a population with a life expectation at birth of just under thirty years.[7] The demographic statistics from these two excavations appear to fit almost exactly with those reported for Hungarian burial sites of the ninth through twelfth centuries.[8] However, unlike his British and Hungarian colleagues, whose information on infant mortality has been based on skeletal remains, Luc Buchet presumes a high level of infant and child mortality but cannot provide any evidence to substantiate

5. Luc Buchet, "La Nécropole gallo-romaine et mérovingienne de Frénouville (Calvados)," *Archéologie Médiévale* 8 (1978): 5–53.

6. Don Brothwell, "Paleodemography and Earlier British Populations," *World Archaeology* 4 (1972): 82 (Table 24).

7. S. Ledermann, *Nouvelles tables-types de mortalité* (Paris, 1969), 136.

8. G. Acsadi and J. Nemeskeri, "Paleodemographische Probleme," *Homo* 8 (1957): 132–48.

this assumption.[9] For this reason, I consider Buchet's estimate of life expectation at birth to be pessimistic.[10]

We might be able to reconcile Buchet's pessimistic model of infant mortality with the rather more optimistic information regarding adult mortality experience by connecting both to the age-specific impact of epidemics and famines. If those most at risk were infants, then the recurrence of plague, in particular, would have transformed the age profile of this population by repeatedly winnowing its surviving youngsters. After a period of time—and we should not forget that the evidence of the Justinian pandemic stretches from its first appearance in Europe in 542 right through until the early eighth century[11]—the demography of a plague-riddled population would have a peculiar age structure: there would be a comparatively large number of surviving adults who had an immunity to the disease and a comparatively small number of children, since only those with an immunity would be likely to survive. Thus, high levels of infant mortality and a small ratio of children in the whole population would reflect this biological conjuncture, not the background level of infant mortality that might be presumed to have resulted from neglectful or positively harmful childcare practices. Comparatively low levels of adult mortality could have reflected the background level of medical care in hard conditions of life when there was no epidemic disease as well as the "disease experience" which gave survivors a kind of immunity later in life. Addition-

9. For a similar suggestion, without hard evidence, of high levels of infant mortality during this period, see P. Riché, "Problèmes de démographie historique du haut moyen âge (Ve-VIIIe siècles)," *Annales de Démographie Historique* (1966): 45.

10. Before the nineteenth-century revolution in hygiene, there were vast local differences in infant mortality levels. Moreover, since almost all women delivered their babies without scientific obstetrical assistance before the very end of the nineteenth century—and since that scientific obstetrical assistance was often likely to be deleterious to the health of both mother and child—it is mistaken to assume that there was any significant improvement in either birthing or neonatal care over the long term. Indeed, to presume an upward curve of medical science denotes the unthinking belief in progress as much as the all-too-familiar ethnocentric view that earlier nonscientific cultures were helpless in the face of medical trauma. While there can be no doubt that aggregate measures provide substantial evidence of massive progress in the last four or five generations, the record before the last part of the nineteenth century is much less sanguine. Indeed, it seems to me that before that time there is at least as much evidence for the damaging effects of scientific medicine as for its benefits.

11. J.-N. Biraben and Jacques Le Goff, "The Plague in the Early Middle Ages," in R. Forster and O. Ranum (eds.), *Biology of Man in History* (Baltimore, 1975), 48–80.

ally, a population with this age structure would have an in-built bias against growth since the second generation would, *ceteris paribus*, be no larger than the first. Thus, the slow growth of the European population from the later eighth century to the tenth century could have been, in part, a reflection of this inherent, structural propensity against growth. In part, of course, this bias against population growth had other causes: the destructive impact of continuous invasions by Vikings and Magyars, settlement in a comparatively small number of densely populated islands in a sea of wilderness, backward agricultural techniques, primitive marketing of agricultural surpluses, the violence of early feudalism, and so on. I do not wish to separate these phenomena but rather to suggest that while the demographic factors operated in an economic environment, the economic factors functioned likewise within demographic constraints. Growth, as well as the lack of growth or even decline, cannot be understood apart from the dynamic interplay of interrelated factors.[12]

We have another line of argument regarding the human biology of the Mediterranean world that might make an argument from silence somewhat more palatable. William McNeill has suggested that about two thousand years ago the world—or at least the so-called civilized world—had become part of a unified disease system as a result of the confluence of disease pools. Since trade, military expansion, population density, and administrative routine made contacts more frequent within the Mediterranean world, the triumph of Rome was very much the culmination of this process. Diseases such as measles, smallpox, and plague, as well as tuberculosis, diphtheria, influenza, and malaria, became part of a human biota. Yet it is important to bear in mind that these diseases were part of a civilized biota and, what is more, part of a biota that was then centered—as was Western civilization itself—on the Mediterranean. Many, but by no means all, of the civilized diseases were also warm-weather diseases that required substantial population densities and systematic forms of social interchange to establish a symbiotic relationship with humans.

The issue, then, is not that these diseases could not attack the less sedentary populations north of the Alps with occasional—yet devastating—results, but rather that it was only in the Mediterranean basin that they were

---

12. It is unclear whether the British medieval skeletons, from the deserted village of Wharram Percy, Yorkshire, date from before or after the Black Death. Such information would be helpful in clarifying the relationship between the age distribution of the dead and the particular biological conditions in which they died. Thus, if the Wharram Percy skeletons were mostly post-1348, an argument concerning the age specificity of mortality could be advanced similar to the one I have proposed in relation to Buchet's study.

to become endemic. The cost of civilization was intensified exploitation, by the state apparatus and the labor process as well as by the biological environment that was in the process of being created by this very civilizing process. It would be hard to imagine that this new biota could effectively penetrate the Alpine barrier and attach itself among a sparse population living in a quite different ecological system. I suggest that in the process of civilization, a process of the last millennium before the Common Era, the Mediterranean developed a system of background and crisis mortality that was unlike the accommodation then in existence among the Germanic tribes, who may well have suffered even more acutely from the same crises but were not subject to the devastating regime of background mortality that was the price being exacted by the civilizing process. What I am proposing, therefore, is that one of the roots of the Western European marriage system is to be found in the historical accommodation between humans and their biological space, and that that accommodation took on a peculiar form north of the Alps.[13]

If the argument about biological accommodation has any strength, then Christianity proved to be a particularly felicitous partner in legitimating this state of affairs. Jack Goody has argued that the fourth-century emergence of new family forms was the direct result of the transition from sect to church which was paralleled by the enactment of ecclesiastical bans on incest. The Church thus reconfigured "strategies of heirship, and in particular the control over close marriages, those between consanguineal, affinal and spiritual kin." These novel restrictions on the ancient practices of endogamy, adoption, and concubinage made it more difficult for the propertied classes in the Empire to transfer property within the family over generations because it closed the option of creating tight, endogamous knots of restricted elementary families within which wealth could be secured in the face of demographic uncertainties.

In effect, the new institutional Church thrust itself into the process of inheritance by making it both possible and attractive for the dying to divert wealth from family and kin to its coffers. Not surprisingly, this created tensions between the interests of the senior generation using its earthly possessions to secure heavenly benefits and those of the junior generation

13. Don Brothwell, for example, thinks that the "disease load" should not be assumed to have been higher in the past in comparison with "so many of the underdeveloped countries today, which tend to be thought of as displaying a similar demographic picture to some earlier societies." He notes that we should approach this problem with a sensitivity to the differential constitution of mortality as well as its historical disposition; "Paleodemography and Earlier British Populations," 86.

more concerned with the production of material goods. As Goody notes, "It does not seem accidental that the Church appears to have condemned the very practices that would have deprived it of property." The great buildup in Church wealth ensued rapidly, so that by the seventh century about one-third of the productive land in France, for example, was in ecclesiastical hands. Thus, it became possible for the Church to accumulate wealth—to create an endowment of property for itself—and to establish places of worship as well as funding its charitable, ecclesiastical, and residential activities.[14]

Given the importance of Goody's controversial argument, it is hardly surprising that much debate has followed its publication. In essence, there have been three thrusts to this criticism. The first point has been that Goody has oversimplified the organization of family life in the pre-Christian Mediterranean by overemphasizing the importance of endogamy and paternal power.[15] The second criticism has been that Goody has confused motivation for creating new rules regarding both spirituality and sexuality with the implementation and results of these rules, which were created for their own reasons.[16] The third line of dissent has suggested that Goody's argument makes the mistake of conflating the Church's ability to legislate in matters of family formation with its ability to enforce these laws.[17] Goody has obviously drawn our attention to an extremely complex historical development, although for our present purposes it is probably worthwhile to worry less about the veracity of Goody's account than to point to his emphasis on the end product's distinctive character. The early modern Western family—and most particularly its northwestern manifestations—was novel, and it is clear that we have to relate this novelty to the unique Christian emphasis on rebirth in Christ. This religious concept wrapped both family life and sexuality in the institutional structure of the Church.

From its inheritance of intertestamentary Judaism, more particularly from the radical fringes which had a fanatical devotion to self-abnegation and ritual purity, Christianity possessed a profoundly ambivalent attitude

---

14. Jack Goody, *The Development of Marriage and the Family in Europe* (Cambridge, 1983), 84, 98–99, 94, 105.

15. Michael Mitterauer, "Christianity and Endogamy," *Continuity and Change* 6 (1991): 295–333; Richard Saller, "European Family History and Roman Law," *Continuity and Change* 6 (1991): 335–46.

16. Joseph Lynch, *Godparents and Kinship in Early Medieval Europe* (Princeton, 1986), 259–60; Michael M. Sheehan, "The European Family and Canon Law," *Continuity and Change* 6 (1991): 347–60.

17. Lloyd Bonfield, "Canon Law and Family Law in Medieval Western Christendom," *Continuity and Change* 6 (1991): 361–74.

toward the body and sexuality.[18] As Saint Paul told the Corinthians, it was better to marry than to burn with desire (I Cor. 7:33). Marital sexual relations were given a grudging acceptance, although it was made clear that holy activity was incompatible with them: "Do not refuse each other except by mutual consent, and then only for an agreed time, to leave yourselves free for prayer" (I Cor. 7:5). This ambivalence toward sexuality was emphasized in Saint Paul's message to fathers: "He that giveth his daughter in marriage doeth well, but he that giveth her not doeth better" (I Cor. 7:38). The Pauline ideology of sexual austerity was later confirmed within the newly established, fourth-century Church by such powerful prince-bishops as Ambrose of Milan, who was Augustine's patron and mentor. He observed "Marriage is honourable but celibacy is more honourable; that which is good need not be avoided, but that which is better should be chosen."[19] Augustine himself infused the policing of families with an uncompromising moral severity, so that formal supervision was buttressed by internalized modes of submission. His primordial influence was crucial in the formation of Western Christianity.[20]

Although the continuities with its original religious milieu are striking, so too were the changes. Christianity radically broke away from its Judaic and pagan inheritance in separating descent from reproduction. Christianity was from its beginnings a religion of revelation which believers joined by being reborn in Christ's grace. For Christians, therefore, expectations of salvation were not linked with lineage, nor were the achievements of ancestors passed on to descendants. For this reason—because charisma was not transmitted through priestly dynasties—Christians were not enjoined to maintain the patriline as a religious task, nor were they expected to continue the cult of the dead through physical or fictitious descendants.[21] Formal marriage rules were an indicator of deeper, more important changes in the way in which the world was understood.

The negative view of human sexuality was constructed in terms of Christian revelation. It developed into a set of taboos regarding marriage—

18. John Allegro, *The Dead Sea Scrolls* (Harmondsworth, 1964), esp. 110–19; Edmund Wilson, *The Scrolls from the Dead Sea* (London, 1955), 34–35. With regard to a somewhat different set of forces which drove elite culture in the same direction, see Michel Foucault, *The Care of the Self* (New York, 1986).

19. Quoted in Paul Johnson, *A History of Christianity* (Harmondsworth, 1976), 109.

20. For a recent restatement of this position with an emphasis on the Augustinian linkage of original sin and human sexuality, see Elaine Pagels, *Adam, Eve, and the Serpent* (New York, 1988), esp. chap. 5.

21. Mitterauer, "Christianity and Endogamy," 325. See also John Bossy, "Vile Bodies," *Past and Present* 124 (1989), esp. 182–83.

what Goody would call "strategies of heirship"—as a result of the incompatability of inherited traditions with novel expectations regarding individual salvation. Spiritual kinship was unknown in Judaism but it made "cultural sense [for Christians] when it is seen as flowing out of the confrontation between a pessimistic view of sexual activity and a conviction that baptism created a spiritual family, which had to be kept free from the taint inherent in sexuality."[22] Indeed, sexual pollution was incompatible with anything holy. Carnal birth was contrasted with spiritual birth, which, at baptism, created "a web of kinship, a family that was the mirror image of the natural family."

Relations between spiritual kin were significantly restricted because they had been joined in the religious vision of rebirth in Christ that took place when a believer (or the child of a believer) was baptized. This spiritual family was pure and therefore had to be shielded from contact with sexual relations, which were understood to be inherently sinful and defiling. Because ties of grace bound together the spiritual family, it could not be connected by ties of sex without profanation. As Joseph Lynch writes, "the taboo on sexual contact among spiritual kin has a compelling logic to it; it makes cultural sense."

As the role of spiritual kinship grew, and as its sacred character flourished, sponsorship by natural parents waned. "By the early ninth century, the view that baptismal sponsorship was incompatible with natural parenthood of the same child had triumphed, spelling the end of the seven-hundred-year tradition of parental sponsorship. . . . These attitudes and the behavior patterns they encouraged were exported as part of Christianity to northern and northwestern Europe by the Latin church and to Slavic lands by the Orthodox church." The central position of baptism in Christian society was driven by the logic of its theology that every Christian was born carnally and in sin but was then reborn spiritually in Christ's grace. Baptism was a second birth that provided a rite of entry into the Church and full citizenship in the secular world.

This holy relationship and the accompanying incest taboos found fertile soil north of the Alps, where they were grafted onto Frankish kinship systems. In the Carolingian period "the combined impact of papal decretals, royal capitularies, episcopal statutes, canonical collections, penitentials, and sermons eventually remade the popular perception of spiritual kinsmen and put them sexually off limits to one another." In so doing, the north-

22. The quotations in the following four paragraphs are taken from Lynch, *Godparents and Kinship in Early Medieval Europe*, 261, 275, 277, 279, 334, 256–57.

west European system of family formation had decisively turned its back on inherited traditions of endogamy.

Historical demographers have provided further evidence that the early modern, northwestern European practice of deferred marriage among women was not common in earlier periods among Mediterranean populations, in which few girls seem to have delayed their marriage much beyond puberty. This might be the place to consider some further historical material and to ponder its implications. In Mesopotamia, teenaged girls were married to adult men in their thirties, as was the case among the Jews whose intimate lives have been chronicled in the remnants of the Cairo geniza.[23] One gains some appreciation of the rabbinical injunction to early marriage for women from the following extract from the Mesopotamian Talmud: "Concerning the man who loves his wife as himself, who honors her more than himself, who guides his sons and daughters in the right path, and arranges for them to be married around the period of puberty, of him it is written: *Thou shalt know that thy tent is at peace.*"[24] One wonders if *both* daughters and sons were to be married at puberty; certainly, other evidence would suggest that we should not read this extract in that way.

Among the Romans, or at least the elite, there was a pronounced inequality in spousal marriage ages. Girls who had just reached menarche were frequently married to men in their mid-twenties.[25] Analyzing ancient funerary inscriptions, Brent D. Shaw has argued that, in contrast to their pagan ancestors, Christians experienced "a rise in the average age at marriage of women . . . from the mode of 12–15 attested epigraphically for

23. On Mesopotamia, see Martha Roth, "Age at Marriage and the Household: A Study of Neo-Babylonian and Neo-Assyrian Forms," *Comparative Studies in Society and History* 29 (1987): 737; for the Jews of medieval Cairo, see S. D. Goitein, *A Mediterranean Society*, vol. 3, *The Family* (Berkeley and Los Angeles, 1978), 163 ff.

24. Quoted in Peter Brown, *The Body and Society: Men, Women, and Sexual Renunciation in Early Christianity* (New York, 1988), 63.

25. Keith Hopkins, "The Age of Roman Girls at Marriage," *Population Studies* 18 (1965): 309–27. Brent D. Shaw has recently presented an upward revision of Hopkins's ages at first marriage, although he still would agree that even plebeian women were usually teenagers when they were first married; "The Age of Roman Girls at Marriage: Some Reconsiderations" (unpublished manuscript). In a personal communication, Shaw acknowledged that it would be a big help in resolving the differences between Hopkins's findings and his own if we had *any* idea of when these Roman girls reached menarche. Indeed, if the kind of systematic starvation depicted in the Pompeii servile skeletons is any indication, then there was likely to have been a rather significant difference in this aspect of class-specific biology. In any event, the age gap between spouses does not seem to be greatly diminished by the point at which Roman girls were married: whether girls were in their early or late teens, their husbands were still at least a decade older.

the pagan era ... [to] modes in the range 14–21, with a concentration in the years 15–18 (the age at marriage of men remaining at about 25)."[26] Similar findings—based on Inquisition registers,[27] Renaissance taxation records,[28] marriage contracts from the Toulouse area,[29] and fourteenth-century Macedonian documents[30]—have all described a situation in which teenaged girls were married to men ten years their senior. Early ages at first marriage for women continued to be a characteristic of eastern Europe as late as 1900: "by age 20–24 some three-quarters of women are still single in the [western] European pattern, while in Eastern Europe three-quarters are married in this age group."[31]

Alan Macfarlane has suggested that "it is impossible to explain the differences between demographic zones in Europe before the nineteenth century by physical geography, by political boundaries, or by technology." In rejecting a materialist explanation of the relationship between family formation and household organization—or modes of reproduction and modes of production—Macfarlane suggests that we might concentrate instead on the role of broad cultural/ethnic regions which coincided with the spatial distribution of distinctive family systems.[32] Macfarlane's explanation was

26. Brent D. Shaw, "Funerary Epigraphy and Family Life in the Later Roman Empire," *Historia* 33 (1984): 473 n. 36. However, it is unclear whether this apparent rise in the age at first marriage for Christian women signifies a cultural change or whether it reflects the lower-class origins of Christians, who would be less well nourished than the aristocrats. Thus, both Christian and pagan young girls could have been married at puberty if menarche would have occurred several years later in the former group.

27. In the Languedoc mountain village of Montaillou, "not one woman was left a spinster" in the 1294–1324 period; "fully adult" men married "young innocents," many of whom were teenagers not far removed from puberty; Emmanuel Le Roy Ladurie, *Montaillou: Cathars and Catholics in a French Village 1294–1324,* (London, 1978), 191.

28. The average age at first marriage for rural women was 18.4, while their husbands were 25.6. Florentine men were even older, 29.9, and they married younger brides, 17.9. The most common age at which both rural and urban Tuscan women married was 16; David Herlihy and Christiane Klapisch-Zuber, *Tuscans and Their Families: A Study of the Florentine Catasto of 1427* (New Haven, 1985), 210.

29. G. Laribière, "Le Mariage à Toulouse aux XIVe et XVe siècles," *Annales du Midi* 79 (1967): 334–61.

30. A. E. Laiou-Thomadakis, *Peasant Society in the Late Byzantine Empire: A Social and Demographic Study* (Princeton, 1977), 273.

31. H. J. Hajnal, "European Marriage Patterns in Perspective," in D. V. Glass and D. E. C. Eversley (eds.), *Population in History* (London, 1965), 101–43. See also H. J. Hajnal, "Two Kinds of Pre-Industrial Household Formation System," in R. Wall (ed.), *Family Forms in Historic Europe* (Cambridge, 1983), 1–64.

32. Alan Macfarlane, "Demographic Structures and Cultural Regions in Europe," *Cambridge Anthropology* 6 (1981): 9.

derived by grafting John Hajnal's pacesetting studies of household forma-tion—which stressed an east-west division: "a line running roughly from Leningrad to Trieste"—onto Jean-Louis Flandrin's findings about a similar north-south "fault line" which split France in two.[33] Macfarlane's argu-ment benefited enormously from his clever recognition that this tripartite cultural division seems to find a deep resonance in Peter Burke's sketch of the geography of popular cultural regions in early modern Europe.[34] At about the same time, Peter Laslett summarized his pioneering work on household structure by suggesting yet another partition by adding a fourth, "central," region.[35]

These divisions—Hajnal's two, Macfarlane's three, or Laslett's four—have a heuristic benefit by making it clear that the age at first marriage for women is the keystone in the arch of family formation strategies.[36] Where the age at first marriage for women is high—in both the "northwestern" and "central" regions—it is found to be correlated with a "very low" and "low" proclivity for complexity. In contrast, where the age at first marriage for women was low—the "Mediterranean" and "eastern" zones—there was a "high" or "very high" tendency for complex, multiple-family house-holds. What happened to the young women who did not marry at puberty? Adolescent and young adult "life-cycle servants" were "very common" in both the later-marrying "northwest" and "central" regions, while being "not uncommon" in the "Mediterranean" and "irrelevant" in the "east."[37] The age at first marriage of women, therefore, not only had profound de-

33. J.-L. Flandring, *Families in Former Times: Kinship, Household, and Sexu-ality* (Cambridge, 1979), 72.

34. Peter Burke, *Popular Culture in Early Modern Europe* (London, 1978), 51–58.

35. Peter Laslett, "Family and Household as Work Group and Kin Group: Areas of Traditional Europe Compared," in Wall (ed.), *Family Forms in Historic Eu-rope*, 513–63.

36. To reach a little further, it would appear from archaeological evidence that at the "natural dividing line between an early and a middle phase in barbarian Eu-rope" agricultural communities were made up of "individual houses . . . that mark a complete break from Oriental tradition [so that] we are dealing with dwellings no larger than would house a natural or nuclear family averaging, say, five persons." These sites "show a remarkable degree of uniformity in house type and layout, as does the material culture from Belgrade to Brussels. . . . This should argue for a rapid spread of the peoples who brought this culture into central and northern Eu-rope." Grahame Clark and Stuart Piggott go on to argue that "it may not be ex-travagant to see an origin for much of medieval Europe in the prehistoric societies which developed in the second millennium B.C."; *Prehistoric Societies* (Har-mondsworth, 1970), 222–23, 227, 235, 249, 255, 302–5.

37. Laslett, "Family and Household," 526–27 (Table 17.5).

mographic implications but was also a cornerstone in the reproduction of different cultural systems.[38]

The historical evidence regarding age at first marriage for women in ancient and early medieval northwest Europe is more ambivalent. Perhaps the best, early hard evidence comes from the monastic survey of the lands and population of St. Germain des Prés at the beginning of the ninth century. This *polyptych* has been analyzed to suggest that marriage ages were "comparatively late for both men and women." Indeed, the key to understanding the organization of marriage and household formation was the surprising concentration of people into small "population islands," surrounded by the vastness of the forests. These communities experienced the paradox of high population pressure in the midst of a vast virgin wilderness; they also possessed the capacity for expansion when the marriage age dropped and the colonization of the surrounding virgin lands began in earnest.[39] But these late marriages were not the result of the formation of independent, nuclear family households. Another Carolingian estate survey, that of St. Victor of Marseilles, suggests that "both men and women, were postponing marriage until their late twenties." David Herlihy comments that the evidence from St. Victor implies that "Marriages in the early Middle Ages thus seem closely to resemble the barbarian model described by Tacitus." The St. Victor evidence therefore suggests that this Carolingian population's late marriages might have been the reflection of a barbarian incursion into the Mediterranean basin.[40]

Herlihy's analysis of this latter case has not been without its critics, however. Summarizing recent French studies of the St. Victor *polyptych*, Pierre Toubert has written that among these peasants there was "un âge au mariage plus précoce pour les filles que pour les garçons" (a more precocious age at marriage for girls than for boys). The specialists are thus divided as to whether this precocious age at first marriage for women was mid-teen or, as some assert, as young as ten or twelve. This revision in the age at first marriage makes it appear that the peasants of St. Victor of Mar-

---

38. Gross divisions of this sort may be so broad that whatever one gains from them in descriptive coherence, one loses as a result of their insensitivity to local conditions. This point was made by André Burguière, "Pour une typologie des formes d'organisation domestique de l'Europe moderne (XVI–XIX siècles)." *Annales: Économies, societés, civilisations* 41 (1986): 639–55. For a valuable summary of the state of play in these discussions, see L. R. Poos, "The Pre-History of Demographic Regions in Traditional Europe," *Sociologia Ruralis* 26 (1986): 228–48.

39. David Herlihy, *Medieval Households* (Cambridge, Mass., 1985), 72.

40. Herlihy, *Medieval Households*, 77, 78. See also Stephen Weinberg, "Peasant Households in Provence: ca. 800–1100," *Speculum* 48 (1973): 247–57.

seilles conformed to the Mediterranean system of reproduction in which marriage coincided with puberty for women, which was followed by elevated fertility between about fifteen and thirty, after which age women ceased childbearing.[41] We might also wonder about the differential impact external pressures had upon family life.

While the Church may have developed an ideological monopoly, it was north of the Alps that the Christian message seems to have found its most fertile seedbed. With the papal coronation of Charlemagne as anointed king-emperor in 800, it seemed that the Germanization of Christian society in the west had become complete.[42]

> Through the Church, the Carolingian age legislated in enormous detail on every aspect of conduct, especially on economic, family and sexual relationships. A huge, determined and continuous effort was made to bring the actual behaviour of individuals into line with Christian teachings. Bishops set up courts, which increasingly covered the whole field of marriage and inheritance. They went on visitations to ensure that the law was obeyed. A great deal of legislation covered the discipline and conduct of the clergy, in an attempt to ensure that, at the parish level where it really mattered, the right teaching was given and enforced.[43]

What does this intertwined development of political and religious cultures mean in relation to family formation? We might again refer back to Tacitus's *Germania;* he suggests that, rather more than in Rome, a woman "enters her husband's home to be the partner of his toils and perils, [so] that both in peace and in war she is to share his sufferings and adventures."[44] We must bear in mind this author's desire to use these barbarians as a foil with which to ridicule the more civilized behavior of his Roman counterparts. Nonetheless we cannot but be attentive to the fact that he underscores their expectation of partnership in marriage, which was at odds with the ancient system in which men monopolized both power and respect. Ancient marriages did not require—or expect—that the conjugal pair be

41. Pierre Toubert, "Le moment carolingien (VIIIᵉ–Xᵉ siècle)," in A. Burguière, C. Klapisch-Zuber, and M. Segalen (eds.), *Mondes Lointains, Mondes Anciens: Histoire de la Famille*, vol. 1 (Paris, 1986), 340–41.

42. Ulrich Stutz, "The Proprietary Church as an Element of Medieval Germanic Ecclesiastical Law," in Geoffrey Barraclough (ed.), *Medieval Germany, 911–1250: Essays by German Historians* (Oxford, 1961), 35–70.

43. Johnson, *A History of Christianity,* 174–75. See also Lester K. Little, "Romanesque Christianity in Germanic Europe," *Journal of Interdisciplinary History* 23 (1992): 453–74.

44. Tacitus, *The Agricola and The Germania*, sec. 18, 117.

emotionally compatible. Yet we must also keep sight of the fact that among these barbarians, informal marriages in which women were transferred without dowry were common, as was divorce. Moreover, men could easily divorce their wives, but women could not divorce their husbands.[45]

In part this system of family formation was a reflection of a simpler division of labor that had existed in Germanic society. Men were expected to be warriors, while women had a large element of control over the domestic mode of production. If by Tacitus's time these people were no longer engaged in a wandering pastoralism, plow agriculture only slowly became the dominant form of arable husbandry. Semi-permanent settlements in which tracts of land were periodically brought into and out of production seem to have been common. The land itself was allocated according to "rank" within kindred groups. Private ownership was becoming acceptable.[46] How did these changes emerge?

Through an obscure process of interpenetration, Germanic traditions of partible inheritance combined with Christianization to give aristocratic women freedom from both marriage-by-purchase and easy divorce, as well as providing them with an estate and the political power that went with it. It is important to avoid the temptation to reduce this complex interplay into orderly sequences since, for those living through it, there was no evident pattern or directionality. Indeed, as late as "829 the Frankish bishops, while remaining intransigent on monogamy, declaring that a man might have only one partner, were prepared to tolerate concubinage as a poor substitute for full marriage. They could hardly do otherwise if they did not want to destroy society."[47] It is also important to note that theology was at this time essentially concerned with holy dying and so had a lot to say on the subjects of baptism, the Eucharist, and penance, but it was largely silent on the subject of marriage because there was no liturgy connected with it. For churchmen, the exchange of vows was indistinguishable from the physical union. In these turbulent times, many "holy widows refused remarriage and insisted on taking the veil and entering monastic life." Their families seem to have been powerless to prevent them from alienating property by "impulsive or excessively generous donations, at odds with family strategies and at the expense of the patrimony." In the Carolingian

45. Herlihy, *Medieval Households*, 50–51.
46. Malcolm Todd, *Everyday Life of the Barbarians* (London, 1972), 38. See also Chris Wickham, "Pastoralism and Underdevelopment in the Early Middle Ages," in *Land and Power* (London, 1994), esp. 122–23.
47. Georges Duby, *The Knight, the Lady, and the Priest: The Making of Modern Marriage in Medieval France* (New York, 1983), 41.

kingdom, for example, "The private rights of women to the control of property had been established giving them, as daughters, sisters, mothers, and wives, a position of economic equality within the family."[48]

The disintegration of the Carolingian empire saw power slip from the central monarchy in the west and into the hands of the great nobles. Feudal families were constructed differently from their barbarian predecessors in that primogeniture and the indivisibility of the patrimony became the keys to their lineage strategy. "The success of the aristocracy as a class in adjusting itself to this broad political change was accomplished largely at the expense of aristocratic women."[49] It should be noted that younger sons were also disempowered. Georges Duby has written widely on these matters, so in the following paragraphs I will quote him extensively:

> the man responsible for a family's honor would try to preserve its prestige by exercising stricter control over the marriages of the young men and women subject to his authority. He would hand over the women quite willingly but would allow only *some* of the men to contract lawful marriages, thus forcing most of the knights to remain bachelors, which only increased their resentment and unruliness.

This new organization of family life was a major characteristic of the feudal revolution. It marked "the fundamental transformation that . . . turned the ruling class into small rival dynasties rooted in their estates and clinging to the memory of the male ancestors." Of particular importance in this process was the shift from horizontal to vertical modes of reckoning kinship. The male "line stretched back to cover more and more of the past, and thus of the dead, so it gradually reached to a single ancestor." Kings and great feudal princes "tightened the bond of vassalic friendship by using marriage as a means of making alliances and of providing their most faithful followers with wives. But, above all, marriage was a way of striking out on one's own: some knights, by taking or stealing a wife or receiving one at the hands of their lord, managed to escape from another man's house and to found one of their own."[50]

It was in these conditions of political disintegration—which were mirrored in the sexual and dynastic tensions that circulated through the great

48. Jane Tibbetts Schulenburg, "Female Sanctity: Public and Private Roles, ca. 500–1100," in M. Erler and M. Kowaleski (eds.), *Women and Power in the Middle Ages* (Athens, Ga., 1988), 102–25.

49. JoAnn McNamara and Suzanne Wemple, "The Power of Women through the Family in Medieval Europe, 500–1100," in Erler and Kowaleski (eds.), *Women and Power in the Middle Ages*, 83–101.

50. Duby, *The Knight, the Lady, and the Priest*, 93–94.

houses—that ecclesiastical reformers sought to enhance the social role of the Church as an arbiter of legitimation. "Marriage is plainly seen here as a remedy against sexual desire, bringing order, discipline, and peace, and removing men and women from the sphere where unions are free, unregulated, disorderly."[51] It introduced policies that tried to limit women's public involvement and leadership roles through the prescription of a feminine sphere which was defined by the delineation of female nature, abilities, rights, and responsibilities.

This gendering program argued for sexual segregation while encouraging ritual purity. Fear of female sexuality was behind clerical demands that women be kept out of the public sphere. In compensation for this drastic diminution of their social roles, the Church began to promote a new image—domesticated and privatized—for females. In contrast with the decentralized organization of the ancient Church, from the ninth century we can identify a new strategy as a strong, assertive ecclesiastical structure slowly emerged. This would lead to a changed religious atmosphere whose concerns for ritual purity "fostered an exaggerated fear of women that often led to a full-blown misogyny."[52] This new gendered division between the public and the private, and between the sacred and the profane, stands in stark contrast to the earlier situation, when the missionary Church had been able to coexist with Germanic traditions that provided women with an independent power base derived from their control over their own share of the inheritance.

The Church's concern to draw marriage into its sphere of control by insisting on the consent of both partners in the eyes of God, therefore, would have made more of an impact on the upper classes than on the lower. It seems that Tacitus's image of Germanic marital equality is a useful guide to the family formations of the lowest strata in the population since it was within this group that the status of women vis-à-vis their husbands was least influenced by dynastic factors. It was this group of freemen and -women who would bear the brunt of change as Germanic tribal societies evolved into feudal systems. Perhaps it was the strength of their nuclear family ties that gave them the ability to accommodate themselves to the radical downward social mobility they experienced during the formation of manorial regimes. For the vast majority of the population, "The Christianization of marriage practices seems to have been effected easily enough in the lower strata of society, among people with few possessions and above all among those with none—the serfs, who did not even own their own bodies.

51. Duby, *The Knight, the Lady, and the Priest,* 62.
52. Schulenburg, "Female Sanctity," 117–20.

Among the masses, about whom we know very little, the Church's version of marriage easily replaced the secular forms of union, i.e. concubinage."[53]

Georges Duby's suggestion that "concubinage" was the dominant form of marriage among the masses has been contested by Alexander C. Murray, who suggests that concubinage and polygamy were not Germanic marriage customs and that these "relatively rare" practices seem to have been confined to the upper class.[54] We can easily overestimate the power of the upper strata to control peasant marriages. We can just as easily underestimate the internal dynamics of family life, as opposed to its legal obligations and prescriptive images.[55]

The Germanization of Christian culture provided a context in which freewomen could maintain an element of control over their bodies and their life choices. Processes of social reproduction look rather different if we consider them from the bottom up and if we ask: how successful were the nobles and the Church in controlling peasant marriages and peasant family life? It would seem that Roman influence was negligible and that technical change was minimal, so that the intensification of agricultural routines seems to have reflected a steady rate of population growth.[56] The differentiation of social formations north of the Alps led to the increasing powerlessness of freemen. It is important to note that downward pressures on the status of women also seem to have intensified as Germanic society became organized around plow agriculture, with the concomitant emergence of fixed-field systems and decline of pastoralism and plant gathering. In effect, the domestic mode of production was becoming masculinized. Women's changing powers within marriage reflected both increasing social stratification and changing material organization. Poorer women had more say in choosing a mate. For them, the older cultural traditions described by Tacitus still breathed life, if only because they were rarely pawns in dynastic marriage strategies. They were also more likely to be in a stable monogamous union, if only because they were less frequently divorced.[57]

53. Duby, *The Knight, the Lady, and the Priest*, 48.

54. Alexander C. Murray, *Germanic Kinship Structure: Studies in Law and Society in Antiquity and the Early Middle Ages* (Toronto, 1983), 62. Murray's view of Germanic marriage practices is supported by Malcolm Todd in *Everyday Life of the Barbarians*, 30.

55. For a similar willingness to consider the evidence of prescriptive literature without weighing it against information derived from other sources, see Riché, "Problèmes de démographie historique du haut moyen âge," 41.

56. Malcolm Todd, *The Northern Barbarians: 100 BC–AD 300* (Oxford, 1987), 114, 100.

57. Suzanne Fonay Wemple, *Women in Frankish Society* (Philadelphia, 1981), 70–71.

Distinguishing the region of late ages of first marriage for women from the rest focuses our attention on the interplay between family formation and household organization—or modes of reproduction and modes of production. In this regard, it is germane to note that Duby writes: "Ninth-century inventories show peasants on large [ecclesiastical] estates firmly paired off. The tightening of the marriage bond served the interests of the masters: it helped to pin their dependents down on their tenures and, by encouraging the lower orders to have children, increased the value of the lords' domains."[58] Evidence from all the Carolingian *polyptychs* seems to agree that family structure was founded on the simple conjugal family, normally constituted by the father, the mother, and their unmarried children. These nuclear families were not large: most were grouped around a modal size of five. Only eight of the 2,600 families counted on the estates of St. Germain des Prés had nine or more co-residents.[59]

A Bavarian manorial survey from the early ninth century suggests that the seigneurial manipulation of family groups may have been of real significance in structuring households. Peasant families were often socially complete but seigneurially divided. Administrative confusion resulting from intermarriage between different lordships were periodically resolved by deeds of exchange. Combined with a "relatively low incidence of nuptiality . . . there is scarcely a hint of complexity or extension" in household structure. Even more interesting is the fact that the fragmented household environment was interlocked with the dependent peasantry's four life-cycle stages. First, during childhood, from birth to fifteen, they were kept on their parents' holding; second, at fifteen they were circulated off the holding and transferred either to the demesne or to another household which was deficient in its supply of labor; and third, marriage and the assumption of a tenancy seem to have been coincident, although it is not clear if this involved the inheritance of a family holding or their assumption of another tenement when aged tenants were ejected. The last phase of the peasant's life-cycle involved a form of enforced retirement. There was thus an optimal allocation of human and agricultural resources taking

---

58. Duby, *The Knight, the Lady and the Priest*, 48.

59. Toubert, "Le moment carolingien," 337–39. In contrast to this northwestern pattern, Richard Ring's study of the contemporaneous survey of the monastery of Santa Maria di Farfa in central Italy provides evidence of a system that was much more stereotypical, in that joint- and stem-families were predominant among the wealthier tenants; "Early Medieval Peasant Households in Central Italy," *Journal of Family History* 2 (1979): 2–25. My own preference is to see the Farfa lists as exemplifying the differences between the Mediterranean and northwest Europe rather than seeing them as a specifically medieval family system.

place in an integrated social system in which "the pre-eminent meaning of *'familia'* in the early Middle Ages did not refer to 'family' in our modern sense but rather to the totality of the lord's dependents."

It is worthwhile noting that Carl I. Hammer, the author of this Bavarian study, speculates that the modern family type (relatively mature partners and simple residential structures) would later be "most evident in northern and western Europe, precisely in the areas of the classical manorial regime. The social arrangements and cultural patterns imposed by the aristocracy (including the church) on its plantation slaves for administrative efficiency may have been so deeply implanted and pervasive that they survived the decline after the eleventh century of the institutional environment which had nurtured them. The lords planned and tended, but it was amongst the enslaved masses of early-medieval Europe that the modern family emerged."[60] The northwestern European family may thus trace its roots to an unexpected by-product of another aspect of our Western heritage, slavery, or to be more precise, to the transition from slavery to servility. There "was no action or belief or institution in Greco-Roman antiquity that was not one way or other affected by the possibility that some one individual *might* be a slave."[61]

The most significant social change in the Late Empire was the homogenization of the rural population that derived from the superimposition of tax and rent. This leveling was the product of the the fiscal measures the Romans adopted to finance their expanding state structure and in particular their armed forces. It led to the "intensification of the forms of exploitation, among which the introduction of widespread serfdom was perhaps, in the long run, the most important element."[62] We can gain a sense of this profound change by comparing the quite divergent ways in which ancient and early medieval societies represented themselves in analyzing domestic units. Ancient enumerations were undertaken by "inveterate census takers," but they only counted some individuals—those free men who were fit for war and/or liable for taxes. They did not consider household units. Indeed, ancient concepts of the family and the household reflected the social realities of a slaveholding society that was also funda-

---

60. Carl I. Hammer, Jr., "Family and *Familia* in Early-Medieval Bavaria," in Wall (ed.), *Family Forms in Historic Europe*, 217–48. It is interesting to note that the four-stage life cycle identified by Hammer corresponds very closely to that discovered in local studies of rural and urban society in northwestern Europe from the sixteenth through nineteenth centuries.

61. Moses Finley, *Ancient Slavery and Modern Ideology* (Harmondsworth, 1983), 65.

62. G. E. M. de Ste. Croix, *The Class Struggle in the Ancient Greek World* (Ithaca, 1981), 251.

mentally sexist. From their inception, the archaic state formations compensated male family heads for being dependent on the king or the state bureaucracy by guaranteeing their domestic dominance. "Male family heads allocated the resources of society to their families the way the state allocated the resources of society to them. The control of male family heads over their female kin and minor sons was as important to the existence of the state as was the control of the king over his soldiers." Therefore, control over the sexual behavior of citizens was a major means of social control because class hierarchy was "constantly reconstituted in the family through sexual dominance."[63]

These ancient patriarchal families did not simply mirror the order of the state—they created and constantly reinforced that order. In a large part, this hegemonic state of affairs was buttressed by the unthinkability of other, possible worlds. Ideology and material life were inextricably intertwined in a world in which "The patriarchal family is the cell out of which the larger body of patriarchal dominance arises." It is also critical to recognize that the system of patriarchy can function only with the cooperation of women which is secured by gender indoctrination; educational indoctrination; the denial to women of knowledge of their history; and the dividing of women, one from the other, by defining respectability and deviance according to women's sexual activities, by restraints and outright coercion, by discrimination in access to economic resources and political power, and, finally, by awarding class privileges to conforming women.[64]

Patriarchial dominance found its most characteristic expression in Aristotle, for whom "the female is, as it were, a multilated male."[65] The Aristotelian tradition was to be immensely influential. It envisaged a hierarchically ordered body whose higher form was male: "a biological chiarascuro drawn in blood." Biological inferiority was, as it were, the physical display of a woman's subordinate moral qualities. Control of the sexual body was an aspect of corporeal self-discipline by which those men who were natural rulers first learned to rule themselves in order to rule all others—women and children as well as slaves and inferior males. Therefore, "sperma, for Aristotle, makes the man *and* serves as synedoche for citizen."[66] It is for this reason, then, that the male who was penetrated was something less

63. Gerda Lerner, *The Creation of Patriarchy* (New York, 1986), 216–17.

64. Lerner, *The Creation of Patriarchy*, 209, 217.

65. Lerner, *The Creation of Patriarchy*, 216–17, 209. Aristotle is quoted by Lerner (207).

66. Thomas Laqueur, *Making Sex: Body and Gender from the Greeks to Freud*, (Cambridge, Mass., 1990), 42, 55. See also Vern L. Bullough, "Medieval Medical and Scientific Views of Women," *Viator* 4 (1974): 485–501.

than a man, whereas the man who penetrated another male (or a female) did not place himself in an ambivalent position.[67]

In the world of antiquity there was an ingrained belief in the inherent and intrinsic inequality of persons which expressed itself in a *timocratic* political system in which those men with wealth and power were granted public recognition in relation to their wealth and power. Households, therefore, were naturally regarded as being assymetrical, incommensurable moral entities, and so in their census enumerations the ancients did not consider domestic units to be comparable. "Households differed so widely from each other that they could not be encompassed in a single system of social analysis, or utilized as a useful unit of social measurement."[68]

The rise of Christian society reached into and changed domestic life, although the break with antiquity was not complete in terms of the moral economy of patriarchy since "In the New Testament, the father of the house is the *oikosdespotes*, the despot or absolute lord over the house in a sense entirely lacking the humorous overtones of 'domestic tyrant.' "[69] Paul, in particular, was outspoken in his misogyny. In I Corinthians 11:9 he states: "Neither was the man created for the woman; but the woman for the man"; while in Ephesians 5:22 he declares: "Wives, submit yourselves unto your own husbands, as unto the Lord. . . ."

Christianity made the correspondence between social harmony and sexual order problematic. "It radically restructured the meanings of sexual heat; in its campaigns against infanticide, it diminished the powers of fathers; in its reorganization of religious life, it altered dramatically what it was to be male and female; in its advocacy of virginity, it proclaimed the possibility of a relationship to society and the body that most ancient doctors . . . would have found injurious to the health."[70] Nonetheless, in contrast to the ancient models of self-representation, Christians believed in the equality of all sinners and the necessity of conjugality for those who could not devote themselves to a monastic existence.

In combination with the demise of slavery, this Christian model of marriage created a social mutation of the most profound importance. It was an explosive mixture that radically transformed the way in which the educated classes represented social reality. "Medieval surveyors . . . made the

67. See Michel Foucault, *The Uses of Pleasure* (New York, 1985) and *The Care of the Self.*

68. David Herlihy, "The Making of the Medieval Family: Symmetry, Structure, and Sentiment," *Journal of Family History* 8 (1983): 116–30.

69. Heinrich Fichtenau, *Living in the Tenth Century: Mentalities and Social Orders* (Chicago, 1991), 100.

70. Laqueur, *Making Sex*, 59.

humble peasant hearth and farm the [standardized] units by which the entire community should be measured." Ancient censuses had not used the household in counting subjects or in assessing their wealth, but by the eighth and ninth centuries the family farm, "called variously *mansus, focus, familia, casata, casa massaricia* (in Italy), *hufe* (in Germany), *hide* (in England)," had become the basic component of manorial and fiscal assessment.[71] Vast differences in wealth and power did not break the bonds of comparability; this uniformity indicated the emergence of a single ethic of marriage from which there could be no variant standards of behavior— or morality—within the Christian community.[72]

2.

It might be useful to connect these speculations: seigneurial interference in the life-cycle of the dependent population and the lower levels of background mortality in trans-Alpine, northwestern Europe combined with the successful missionary work of the Christian penitentials in making sexual asceticism a central element in conjugal family life. The emergence of the family as a moral unit was linked to the Christian concern with *ordo caritatis* (ordered love). The love of God and salvation of one's soul outstripped all other forms of love; it was followed by the elevation of conjugal relationships. In elevating the conjugal family, Christian ideologists beginning with Thomas Aquinas noted that its affective relationships were "natural" and therefore stable and durable as opposed to the unstable and shifting love one felt for those who were unrelated. In the disturbed conditions after the Black Death, this theological opposition slowly developed into a defensive perimeter that was drawn up between the family's inner circle and the surrounding society that was pervaded by the cash nexus and the contract.[73]

The northwestern European system of relatively late ages at first marriage seems to have become an integral part of the architecture of production and reproduction even before we are first able to witness it through the empirical filter of parish register demography. In other parts of Europe the various strands do not form the same articulated structure, which seems to me to prove the point that what is at issue is not the existence of

71. David Herlihy, "Households in the Early Middle Ages: Symmetry and Sainthood," in Robert McC. Netting, Richard R. Wilk, and Eric J. Arnould (eds.), *Households: Comparative and Historical Studies of the Domestic Group* (Berkeley and Los Angeles, 1984), 383–406.

72. Herlihy, "The Making of the Medieval Family," 121.

73. David Herlihy, "Family," *American Historical Review* 96 (1991): 1–16.

"Christian marriage ideology" or "a homeostatic demographic system" or "a feudal mode of production" but the interconnection of these elements within a quite distinctive ecological environment. The contingent historical bonds that linked cultural, biological, and material modes of reproduction kept the parts in proper orientation to each other while giving them a wholly new identity together. These three strands—the political, biological, and cultural—formed the triple helix of family life. They were recombined in the passage from antiquity to early modernization. The strands of the family helix were historically bonded in time and space. Contingencies shaped the evolution of the Western family, whose past structures have no explanation other than the shadow of their past.[74] The contrast with the ancient world, then, provides us with a point of departure.

STRONG STEMS/WEAK BRANCHES

"Strong Stems/Weak Branches" discusses the ways that economic and social forces inherent in the feudal relations of production differentiated experience, across generations and also within families. Processes of downward social mobility, together with the nonlinear impact of demographic growth, created very different life chances for any noninheriting sons and daughters who were over and above replacement. The individual peasant family was differentiated by a contingent and variable combination of factors: manorial size and organization, legal status (free or villein), rents and feudal taxes, size of holding, tenurial conditions, soil fertility and productivity, technology, marketing opportunities, alternative income sources (in either industry or service), inheritance customs, family size, life-cycle stage, and gender relations. Moreover, these characteristics were not static. Diversity was a result of the particular amalgam of individual factors (on either a village or a familial level), which was constantly in flux.

The disappearance of slavery was one of the great landmarks in European social history. There is a strong scholarly consensus that this contributed to demographic growth, agrarian expansion, and increased economic production.[75] The emergent network of peasant villages was

74. In this last sentence I am quite consciously paraphrasing Stephen Jay Gould's defense of Charles Darwin's model of evolution while also extending his argument to suggest its relevance for understanding human social history; Gould, *Wonderful Life: The Burgess Shale and the Meaning of Life* (New York, 1989), 301.

75. Georges Duby, *The Early Growth of the European Economy* (Ithaca, 1974), 40. See also Adriaan Verhulst, "The Decline of Slavery and the Economic Expansion of the Early Middle Ages," *Past and Present* 133 (1991): 195–203.

something new, unlike anything Europe had seen before. The creation of peasant villages was also a technical innovation which unleashed the productive powers of more intensive forms of agriculture.[76] To quote George Duby once again:

> The most profound repercussions on the growth of population and productivity arose from the development of unfree status. As long as young men and women remained members of a gang of household slaves in a master's dwelling, without legal possession of goods, homes or even their own bodies (. . . such gangs might well have been maintained at full strength on big seventh-century estates in Gaul), a whole section of the rural population languished in conditions most unfavourable for human reproduction. Children exposed to the dangers of childbirth and infancy in slave gangs had least chance of survival. When masters gradually allowed such gangs to disperse and decided to settle their slaves as couples on farms managed by themselves, not only did they stimulate the productive capacities of these workers, they placed them in a much better position to beget children and bring them into the adult world. From this progeny they continued to recruit the servants necessary for running their households, but many sons and daughters of slave tenants were still available for setting up new homes. And when the establishment of banal lordship came to smooth over distinctions between free and unfree peasants, making peasant status more uniform, mixed marriages became more usual, joining together, with the master's consent, children of slaves with those of other villagers, now subject to the same customs. Such marriages had already been common among tenants of the abbey of St. Germain-des-Prés in the early ninth century. Matrimonial segregation soon disappeared between two groups within the peasantry who, until recently, were kept apart by the legal criteria of ancient slavery, and this fusion was precipitated by the mobility of the rural population promoted in turn by demographic expansion.[77]

Since status passed through mothers, male slaves who married female serfs would have had children whose juridical position improved. Upward movement on the status ladder, from slave to serf, might have been accomplished by selective marital strategies. If this selective process of calculating marriage on the basis of heritable status was carried through over a number of generations, then there would have been a gradual but persist-

---

76. F. Cheyette, "The Origins of European Villages and the First European Expansion," *Journal of Economic History* 37 (1977): 203–05.

77. Duby, *The Early Growth of the European Economy*, 183–84.

ent decline of slavery.[78] Whether this strategy was as consciously imple-
mented as Emily Coleman suggests is, however, another matter.

Evidence from Bavarian documents seems to imply that the "handmaid's"
strategy of shifting personal identity from slave to serf was fraught with
many obstacles. Moreover, legal unfreedom was not always synonymous
with lowly economic or social status. Furthermore, marriage across the
free/unfree divide called many other, external actors into family formation
strategies which would make the individualized mobility described by
Coleman much harder to achieve by one's own efforts. As Duby notes,
from the late tenth century onward the intermediate status of *censualis*
captured people who earlier would have been on both sides of the juridical
divide. These people paid yearly fines to their overlords—*chevage* or head
taxes—but were not held to any other kind of service. For some individuals this was an improvement; for all members of the subordinate classes it
was an everyday experience of the imbrication of feudal powers into their
personal lives.[79]

The feudal synthesis of Roman law, Germanic custom, and Christian
sexual economy created an interface along which the peasantry's family
formation practices would be arrayed. Considered from the viewpoint of
the peasantry, the desire for independence from this system of domination
sparked resistance which had material, political, and cultural dimensions:
meeting their subsistence needs, frustrating demands for tribute, and controlling the supply of their labor. The goal of autarky for the peasant family household exerted a constant centripetal force which drew its members
together and kept them separate from their kin and neighbors. While the
way in which any single peasant family balanced its material, political, and
cultural functions was to some extent unique, the historical pressures
which flattened the peasantry into rough homogeneity around the year
1000 also served to draw disparate families together into collectivities that
could be employed to protect their interests over and against those of their
lords. Village communities, then, were another centripetal force holding
families together.

If we could look inside these peasants' huts, we would uncover a quite
different system of classification. The apparent unanimity of the manse

78. Emily R. Coleman, "Medieval Marriage Characteristics: A Neglected Factor in the History of Medieval Serfdom," *Journal of Interdisciplinary History* 2
(1971): 205–17.

79. Carl I. Hammer, "The Handmaid's Tale: Morganatic Relationships in
Early-Medieval Bavaria," *Continuity and Change* 10 (1995): 345–68.

would be revealed to be the unsteady product of its own centrifugal tendencies—set in motion by the family cycle and, in particular, by the gender and age differences between its members—that were kept from flying apart by the political economy of family formation. The politics of these peasant families was patriarchal in the sense that they institutionalized an upward flow of wealth, from women and children to husbands/fathers who were privileged to represent the public face of the household.[80] Women were excluded from public systems of mutual dependence; they could not serve on the institutions that constituted the self-management of communal life.[81] A picture of diachronic change of family formation and reformation over time would further undermine the easy generalizations concerning the centripetal ordering of family life in the age of feudalism.

The feudal synthesis marked a fundamental transformation, yet it represented a series of tendencies rather more than a concrete mechanism. We might consider its influence from a variety of angles. In particular, we should concern ourselves with its impact on the reproduction of family life among the mass of the population who were now somewhat more free to take control of themselves and their bodies. This essential point marks the passage from antiquity to early modernization in the history of the family.

History was itself a significant variable, so I will try to describe the helical construction of family life by blending the synchronic analysis of its structural dynamics into a discussion that will emphasize the diachronic changes which resulted from the inherent contradictions built into these family formation processes. In this way I hope to be able to show why it has been necessary to locate the roots of early modernization in the deep past, around "the year 1000 [when] things became serious."[82]

1.

The rough homogeneity among the peasantry was more evident in legal status and prescriptive ideology than in the experience of daily life.

> Since the tenth and the eleventh centuries, when this doctrine was formulated, until the fifteenth, when its demolition was apparent to all, the Middle Ages—certainly the clergy and the dominant element and perhaps the rest of them (by force of hearing it constantly promul-

---

80. The theory of "wealth flows" comes from the work of John C. Caldwell. See, in particular, *Theory of Fertility Decline* (New York, 1982).

81. Judith M. Bennett, "Public Power and Authority in the Medieval English Countryside," in Erler and Kowaleski (eds.), *Women and Power in the Middle Ages*, 18–36.

82. Jacques Le Goff, *Medieval Civilization 400–1500* (Oxford, 1988), 55.

gated)—voluntarily erased the idea of classes in favour of that of God-given social orders. Theirs was of course an imaginary society, which could not prevent collisions, rivalries and conflict, but one which assigned to each member his [her] role in a harmony, which was presumed to exist by a general consent.[83]

Robert Fossier may be correct on this point, but let's not forget that "When Adam delved/ and Eve span,/ Who was then/ the Gentleman?" These contradictions were always immanent in what could be called the feudal mode of reproduction.

The 1279–80 Hundred Rolls and the contemporaneous *Inquisitiones Post Mortem* of landed wards of the Crown illustrate immense diversity in the social relations of a very feudal society. Vills were often divided into several manors, some tenants were free while others were servile, some land was subjected to servile tenancy while other land was not, the same tenant could hold land—in different tenurial relationships—from several different landlords, and labor rents and money rents were almost random in their application. The one tendency that seems to hold is that the larger the estate and the more powerful the landowner, the more likely it was that the classic conditions of servile manorialism would be present at this time of feudal reaction in England.

Labor rents were not always collected but were often sold off on a piecemeal basis.[84] The complexity of this ground-level reality speaks to the evolution of feudal power over time, which led to its kaleidoscopic application in everyday life. Absolute powers could be exercised by the mighty over their dependents, but what usually happened is that the exercise of this power was left to the discretion of the overmighty. The situational character of feudal exactions did not make them any less painful for the servile. Indeed, it probably made them considerably more repugnant because the dependent condition of the undermighty was thereby underscored.

So, we might begin to set the stage for the discussion of peasant family formations by looking at the social tensions which could be obscured by an excessive concern with the self-representation of a society of three orders in which peasant equality was prescribed, not experienced. Our concern with locating the roots of early modernization in the feudal period leads us to consider the forces that would ultimately undermine it. Three contra-

83. Robert Fossier (ed.), *The Cambridge Illustrated History of the Middle Ages, 1250–1520* (Cambridge, 1987), 516–17.

84. E. A. Kosminsky, "Services and Money Rents in the Thirteenth Century," in E. M. Carus-Wilson (ed.), *Essays in Economic History*, vol. 2 (London, 1962), 31–48.

dictions at the heart of feudal society provided motors of social change: first, the motion supplied by seigneurial demands for money; second, the destabilizing implications of demographic changes; and third, the social divisions within the peasantry.

The social power of the feudal classes came from their discretionary control over land, the iron lung of material life in the feudal mode of production. Control over access to land—its quality, its quantity, and the speed of supply—was like an oxygen valve which regulated the respiration of the social system. As much as their juridical powers, the feudalists' disposition of land gave them a prime influence in the family formation of the dependent classes. This regulative control was predicated on the fact that "The 'villeinage' were regarded as part of the demesne; villeins' goods were the lord's goods, and peasant income, extracted through rent, labour tallage and fines, a major source of seigneurial income [which means that] . . . as far as the lord was concerned, villeins were property."[85] This point regarding feudal property rights in another human being is elemental, but it is too often so qualified that its brutality is inadvertently downplayed.

Important as these powers were, we must avoid totalizing them. The manor was not the Gulag Archipelago of an earlier age. It was not the place in which totalitarian coercion allowed the dominant classes to work their bond servants to death. We cannot overlook the elements of negotiation and reciprocity in everyday life on the manor. "Seigneurial control may have played some role, but only to the extent necessary to *protect their interests*. . . . [I]t is as unrealistic to assume that pronouncements of law control behaviour as it is to dismiss lordship and the greater or lesser degree of collectivist interaction which characterized medieval English village society."[86] In theory, rents were fixed and the recognition of patriarchal powers was an essential quid pro quo in the creation of the manse so that, in theory again, peasant holdings were standardized and supplied with a garden and dwelling, individual landholdings were organized in communal fields, and inheritance rights were recognized. In its very origin "this society was strongly attached not only to the organic bond making a single entity of the family, but also to the fixed abode where its members would huddle together round the hearth and store their stocks of food, and to the *appendicia*, the various scattered parcels in the surrounding fields providing food for the household."[87]

85. Rosamond Faith, "Debate: Seigneurial Control of Women's Marriage," *Past and Present* 99 (1983): 140.
86. L. R. Poos and Lloyd Bonfield, "Law and Individualism in Medieval England," *Social History* 11 (1986): 300–1 (emphasis added).
87. Duby, *The Early Growth of the European Economy*, 35.

Rather than exhibiting an unvarying homogeneity, the peasants' households were always stratified. Our earliest censuslike enumeration of the peasant families in northwestern Europe, which comes from the ninth-century *polyptych* (survey) of the abbot Irminon of the lands of the monastery of St. Germain des Prés (on the Left Bank in Paris), is particularly revealing with regard to the size and structure of peasant manses. Rich peasants had large households. They imported older children from their poorer neighbors to supplement their family's labor force in order to work their lands. Correlatively, the lower tier of the peasantry not only supplied labor to the upper tier but was doubly disadvantaged because it lost the labor power of its adolescent and unmarried children even though it had already absorbed the costs of their physical and social development.[88]

This evidence begs a series of interrelated questions: Was there ever a standardized size for the manse? If the manse was not a standardized unit, was it an indivisible one? What was the role of seigneurial pressure in creating systems of impartible inheritance? In the upper ranks of feudal society, as we have seen, the Carolingians acceded to their vassal's right to secure patrimonies in the course of the ninth century with the capitulary of Quierzy-sur-Oise (877) although it was not until the eleventh century that aristocratic lineages switched their strategic course and began to limit inheritance to the eldest son.

So, we might well ask, does our evidence of family heritability among the peasants also imply primogeniture among the peasantry? This complex of issues is difficult to answer, not only because the evidence is so sparse but also because demographic conditions meant that undivided patrimonies, passed down generation after generation, were not automatic. Given optimum demographic conditions, three families in five would be survived by a male heir, one in five by a female heiress, and the final one in five by no heir at all. Of course, perhaps a quarter of all families would produce an excessive number of male heirs who would survive to adulthood. Many of these young men would, *ceteris paribus*, be paired with heiresses, while others would mate with widows.[89]

88. Herlihy, *Medieval Households*, 69–72. Other analysts, particularly those working on English manorial documents, suggest a tripartite division within the peasantry. The essential point is that the third order in feudal society was never a homogeneous, interchangeable mass.

89. E. A. Wrigley, "Fertility Strategy for the Individual and the Group," in Charles Tilly (ed.), *Historical Studies of Changing Fertility* (Princeton, 1978), 135–54. See also R. M. Smith, "Some Issues Concerning Families and Their Property in Rural England 1250–1800," in *Land, Kinship and Life-Cycle* (Cambridge, 1984), esp. 38–62.

In this demographic lottery, inheritance was conducted at both the individual and the social levels. To the extent that it concerned the transmission of niches in a relatively stable structure, some landholdings passed along the male line, others went down the female line, and still others reverted to collateral descendents when the couple had no direct heirs. In addressing these matters, we need to keep a balance between the real and the ideal in considering the probability of fully extended families existing in significant numbers.

The evidence from St. Germain des Prés seems to suggest that in the early ninth century there was not a demographically stable population, nor was the manse indivisible. There appears to have been a "surpeuplement et fractionnement du manse" (overpopulation and morcellization of the manse) which was provoked by demographic pressures of a population that was capable of rapid replacement. Pierre Toubert also suggests that the Carolingian manse was periodically redistributed between its coholders, implying that primogeniture was not practiced and that a surplus of heirs led to a rough-and-ready solution. The Carolingian manse might have been a fiscal unit or obligation—thereby linking it with ancient modes of appropriation—not a discrete landed parcel.

This complex interplay between peasant families and their landed endowment congealed into a more stable and regulated system as seigneurial pressure led to the passage from the Carolingian domain to the rural manor of the year 1000. The political pressure of the seigneurial class adapted strategies of domainal exploitation to the reality of the simple, conjugal family by creating legally fixed tenurial units that facilitated the collection of taxes and labor services. The spatially fixed tenurial unit was a later development which emerged with the consolidation of the manorial system. Toubert also reaffirms the connection between the feudal revolution, *encellulement*, and the Gregorian reform of marriage in the imposition of the Christian doctrine of indissoluble marriage.[90]

The combined effects of demographic expansion, changing taxation methods, and the quadrupled productivity of human labor enabled seigneurial officers to reduce the size of standard holdings. Alongside the traditional circle of heads of households, "cabins, *bordes*, and cottages" multiplied outside the old enclosures. Georges Duby suggests that the ancient manses kept their vestigial integrity until the last half of the twelfth cen-

---

90. Toubert, "Le moment carolingien," 339, 344–45. For a discussion of the transformation of freemen into the tenants of manorial lords in the Anglo-Saxon mode of tribute, see T. H. Aston, "The Origins of the Manor in England," *Transactions of the Royal Historical Society*, 5th ser., 8 (1958): 59–83.

tury, when *la révolution censive* dissolved the complex organization of the manor in favor of money rents.[91] The cultivation of new land meant that the fictive integrity of the manse and its appurtenant lands is misleading. Lords had unwittingly driven the surplus sons and daughters of the manse outward.[92]

Centrifugal motion was crucial in magnifying the land mass, and it was also crucial in underscoring the different systems of family formation in the old-settled core and the frontier settlements. This divergence took place not only on the marches of colonization but also within the interstices of the old feudal core. Thus, it is difficult to create a strong linkage between patterns of feudal landholding, undivided tenements, and extended family structures. Only a minority within the peasantry was in a position to enact a strong patriarchal policy of complex household formation. For the majority, available resources were not sufficient, or else there were too many claimants to satisfy them all. Furthermore, for the younger generation there were strong inducements to escape the thralldom of the patriarch, while the availability of land provided them with plenty of opportunity to do so. Therefore, the most that can be suggested is that on a minority of peasant holdings—those of the upper tier in the old-settled core—some members of the younger generation would be held in a subservient position while they waited to inherit. This group of primary heirs constituted itself into peasant patriarchs. Those who were outside the direct line of inheritance were much more likely either to migrate or to falter in creating lineal descent groups in their natal village.[93]

Isolating the question in this way underscores the *bimodal* distribution of peasant families that was reinforced by the outward, centrifugal motion of surplus sons and daughters. In contrast to the classic manse with its strong stem, extended vertically across several generations, in which age-graded and gendered patriarchal control was directed downward, we should also expect to find another type of family whose internal structure would be more open in the sense that paternal control was weaker and, therefore,

---

91. Georges Duby, *Rural Economy and Country Life in the Medieval West,* (London, 1968), 116–19, 239–40.

92. David Herlihy, "Three Patterns of Social Mobility in Medieval Society," *Journal of Interdisciplinary History* 3 (1973): 623–47.

93. The difference between the stable core of the peasantry and the rest has been an abiding theme of the scholars working at the Pontifical Institute in Toronto. For a useful summary of the argument that focuses on the social life of the peasantry rather than tenurial obligations, see Anne DeWindt, "Peasant Power Structures in Fourteenth-Century King's Ripton," *Mediaeval Studies* 38 (1976): 236–67.

age and birth rank would be less important. It would be nuclear, fragile, and free from connections with the seigneurial economy. Its sons would have little to inherit, and its daughters would have no expectation of being dowered.[94] The sons of these families would be footloose colonizers and wanderers; the daughters would have to sell their labor, to move out of the family home and to work as domestic servants in order to dower themselves. Without their own strong centripetal field of force, the fortunes of these weak branches would be especially subject to the larger rhythms of expansion and contraction.[95]

94. This point is drawn from Robert Wheaton's cross-cultural discussion of the relationship between joint family household structures and patrilineal kinship systems. Noting that matrilineality was not part of the European tradition, he distinguishes two alternative systems of family formation—one favoring the older generation, the other the younger insofar as it did not feature the same robust, upward flows of wealth that reflected the patriarch's control over a common economic project. Wheaton thus draws our attention to the tendency of the former to recruit its labor force from its kin as opposed to wage laborers; "Family and Kinship in Western Europe: The Problem of the Joint Family Household," *Journal of Interdisciplinary History* 5 (1975): 601–28.

95. If, however, the strong central stem was able to dominate the weaker branches, then a rather different outcome could ensue. This is evident from Emmanuel Le Roy Ladurie's research into the family formation practices in the Cévennes region of Languedoc. There, after the peasant purgatory of the Black Death, legal records list dramatic rates of family attrition—eight of ten families disappeared from the tax rolls. During the next six generations, or 150 years, many of the surviving families also departed. In reaction to this terrible hemorrhage, the survivors closed ranks and reconstituted themselves by magnifying their subjugation to the patriarch and emphasizing their solidarity with each other through their paternal lineages. Extended domestic patriarchies and fraternities—*frérèches*—were substituted for the nuclear family households which seemed to have been normal before 1350. Young couples were integrated into the preexisting residence by promising to live under the patriarch's roof and to eat from the communal pot—*à feu et à pot*—while granting total obedience to the husband's father. Dowries were passed from father to father. A community of goods encompassed the hearth, homestead, bread, wine, cooking pot, table, purse, and debts, a community of goods that was managed by the patriarch. In Languedoc—and in the Auvergne, the Bourbonnais, and the Nivernais—families with multiple nuclei were four times as prevalent as in northern France. These domestic production and consumption units supplied their own work force "in a context of absurdly high wages." But with the revival of population in the sixteenth century, these extended families became less common in southern France. They persisted into the nineteenth century in isolated pockets in the mountain regions, where self-sufficiency was a virtue and the market would long remain distant from everyday life. In explaining the fourteenth-century revival and subsequent survival of "the old bedrock of customary law . . . and family structures inherited from the distant past," Le Roy Ladurie connects these domestic strategies to the fourteenth-century crisis when the collapse of political and social hierarchies engendered an "urgent emotional need for security [in

We can further consider this point by discussing it in relation to the nonlinear impact of demographic change along with the divergence between ideals and social reality.[96] In conditions of demographic expansion, married couples remained intact as units of demographic reproduction for longer periods of time, while a higher proportion of children were likely to reach adulthood and themselves marry. As we know from simple Malthusian arithmetic, even small changes, when aggregated and allowed to multiply over several generations, would have had profound implications. Viewing the impact of the process on different fragments of the whole population is important because it makes the expansion of the lower tier of cottagers problematic from the perspective of homeostatic demographic theories.

Why did these people increase their fertility in the face of declining mortality? Why, in other words, when rising life expectation yielded more survivors, did they produce children over and above replacement? How were these additional children to find their way in a world that was already overcrowded? Marginal groups—such as noninheriting children of cottagers—were dramatically more influenced by population growth and harvest failure than the core group in the upper tier of householders. Increasing population produced a disproportionate rise in their numbers, which can be demonstrated in the following way.

First, imagine a population of cottagers in which about 10 percent are marginal in the sense that they will not ultimately inherit a niche, either directly or indirectly.

Second, let us suppose that in the course of three generations the total population doubles but the number of niche places remains stable at 90.

Third, the marginal population will increase eleven times, to 110, and will rise from 10 percent of the first population to 55 percent of the second, larger community.

---

which] neither the dislocated monarchy nor the weakened feudality was capable of providing the individual with the moral and material protection he needed. . . . social order, the right to work in peace, security, and the mutual advantages that come from a respect for legality. And so the individual reappraised—in his ties of affection as in his legal arrangements—his natural protector, the father-patriarch, or his substitute, the older brother"; *The Peasants of Languedoc* (Princeton, 1996), 29–36; *The French Peasantry 1450–1660* (Berkeley and Los Angeles, 1987), 83–88. For a later period, see John W. Shaffer, *Family and Farm: Agrarian Change and Household Organization in the Loire Valley, 1500–1900* (Albany, N.Y., 1982), esp. 20–37.

96. Andrew Abbott, "Transcending General Linear Reality," *Sociological Theory* 6 (1988): 169–86.

This enlarged body of marginal people would create pressures on food and land which were nonlinear in their response. Moreover, there would be other effects resulting from a shift in the mortality schedule. Not the least would be the changing configuration of the age pyramid, which would rapidly broaden at its base. Better chances of child survival would combine with the diminishing chance of marital breakup to swell the lower age groups. Generations would follow one another more quickly.[97]

2.

Basic features of family formation—household structure, inheritance, age and gender stratification, and the marriage process—were all influenced by the context in which they took place. The key element in defining that context which provides an element of coherence to the period was the role of extrafamilial political power. The range of motion available to peasant families in feudal society was demarcated by its exercise. A particularly telling example of this point comes from a consideration of peasant family formation around 1200—the time when *la révolution censive* was taking place on the continent while in parts of England the feudal counteroffensive was under way.

Georges Duby claims that at this time increasing numbers of peasants were engaged in leasehold arrangements, subdivision, and partible inheritance strategies—which favored the fluidity of the peasant patrimony, the relaxation of family ties, the development of individual enterprise, and social agility—in exchange for the payment of monetary fines. He implies that the family was nuclearized in the densely populated rural areas of the continent, like the Paris Basin which had been the heartland of feudalism.[98] Much the same forces were at work in eastern parts of England, most notably East Anglia, which was manorially divided, densely populated, and economically diversified. It was in this part of England that the land market was very active and the peasantry was very mobile. It would appear that the family-land bond was rather weak, kin density was quite low, and nuclear families were predominant.[99]

97. In the preceding examples of nonlinear implications of population growth on marginal populations, I am drawing upon Jack Goldstone's insightful commentary in *Revolution and Rebellion in the Early Modern World* (Berkeley and Los Angeles, 1991), 32 ff.

98. Georges Duby, "Medieval Agriculture 900–1500," in C. M. Cipolla (ed.), *The Fontana Economic History of Europe: The Middle Ages* (Glasgow, 1972), 184. We should assume that the family which was becoming nuclearized refers to the patriarchal stem, not the marginal branches.

99. R. M. Smith, "Kin and Neighbours in a Thirteenth-Century Suffolk Community," *Journal of Family History* 4 (1979): 219–56; "Families and Their Land in

It is crucial to recognize that manorial organization was quite different in East Anglia from other parts of England, where there was an identity between the village and the manor. Zvi Razi suggests that in the heavily feudalized regions, the manor court and the upper strata of the peasantry were interdependent. In such communities many tenements were occupied by a main residence and surrounding cottages, housing subaltern branches of the functionally extended peasant lineages. The manorial authorities and the peasant patriarchs used their powers to ensure that kin ties were the main organ of welfare for the poor, the infirm, and the aged. In the Midlands village of Halesowen "the bulk of the land was distributed through blood and marriage, despite the existence of a brisk land market. . . . [I]t is plausible to assume that kin density in these villages was high and the functionally extended family predominated."[100]

Razi's study of family formation in Halesowen delineates the complementarity of the centrifugal forces of downward social mobility and the centripetal forces of peasant patriarchy on the classic feudal manor. Using model populations to construct a series of probabilistic measurements, Razi's study underscores the highly stratified life chances of these villagers. The bimodal family system was paralleled by differential reproduction rates among the two tiers of the peasantry. The strong stem's control over its precious niche simultaneously connected it upward to the lord's demand for services and connected it downward in its control over the women and children (of all ages) within its sway. These elite peasant families produced a bumper crop of children, overinsuring the patrimony with a surfeit of heirs. The landed wealth accumulated in the course of a rich peasant's lifetime was redistributed (albeit unequally) at his death. Overpopulation was endemic in the sense that those who were outside the charmed circle of inheritance were flung outward to form a perpetual underclass on the margins of village society. Social differentiation thus took place within the peasant family.

Razi's study of the distinctive reproduction of peasant families makes sense when it is placed in its temporal and spatial context. It is therefore crucial to understand that Razi's study concerns the reproduction of the Halesowen peasantry in the period after 1280, when the population had reached its zenith and the colonization of the margin had stretched beyond

---

an Area of Partible Inheritance: Redgrave, Suffolk, 1260–1320," in *Land, Kinship and Life-Cycle*, 135–96.

100. Zvi Razi, "The Myth of the Immutable English Family," *Past and Present* 140 (1993): 19.

the point of diminishing returns. The process of generational recycling which had previously coped with the overreplacement demography of the peasant patriarchs, via the outward mobility of their excess sons and daughters, ran into a dead end. This was a time of land hunger and severely declining living standards for the teeming mass of smallholders, cottagers, and landless laborers who crowded onto the land. The world of the Halesowen dwarf-holders was terrible. They did not reproduce themselves, but rather they were harvest sensitive, dying in large numbers whenever the crop failed.[101]

Halesowen was located in the heartland of the revived feudalism, so its villagers' experience was quite unlike that of the dwarf-holders living in East Anglian communities like Redgrave, Suffolk, or Coltishall, Norfolk, studied by R. M. Smith and B. M. S. Campbell. Yet, it is not clear that we can read their differences back in time to some common point of departure—that is, back to a time when peasant patriarchs governed their separate manses. It is more likely that the different settlement histories of these two regions, and their different traditions of inheritance, interacted with the historical evolution of feudal society to produce different outcomes.[102] It seems that we are on firmer ground in comparing the results of Zvi Razi's study of the perpetuation of the feudal control over Halesowen's families with Georges Duby's description of the nuclearization of family life on the continent. We might posit a fourfold division between free and unfree tenants holding land by feudal or commuted forms of rent: Halesowen was located in that part of the quadrant in which unfree tenants held their land from feudal landlords who were interested in maintaining the integrity of their peasant patrimony in order to perpetuate their supply of labor services.[103]

101. Zvi Razi, *Life, Marriage and Death in a Medieval Parish* (Cambridge, 1980), *passim*.

102. However, we might not want to push this point too far, since in East Anglia there were also heavily manorialized communities in which feudal services were onerous and where there is evidence of strong ties between peasant lineages and the land, such as the Lincolnshire fen villages of Weston, Spalding, Pinchbeck, and Sutton as well as the Essex manor of Havering and the Norfolk manor of Sedgeford; Razi, "The Myth of the Immutable English Peasant Family," 20–22. Thus, it may be the case that Smith's Redgrave and Campbell's Coltishall were no more representative of East Anglia than Razi's Halesowen was typical of the East Midlands. Perhaps the most that we can say is that these intensively studied communities represented polar opposites along a broad continuum.

103. Joan Thirsk has suggested that primogeniture developed among the peasantry as a result of strong seigneurial pressure that connected it with demesne agriculture's heavy demand for labor services; "The Common Fields," *Past and Present* 29 (1964): 12. Similarly, Rosamond Faith has argued that "there is obvi-

The keystone in this arch of family formation was the landowner's competence to act as a feudalist, that is, to value his tenants' services more highly than money rents. As long as this policy was maintained, there was a strong centripetal pressure preserving the peasant patriarch's patrimony. Evidence of this authority comes from two sources: first, the lord's regulation of widow remarriage in the interest of maintaining a competently tenanted manse; and second, the lord's supervision of an orderly transmission of land between generations. It is in relation to the lord's demand for income that we can understand that *merchet* was not a fixed-price fine but rather was determined by variables such as family wealth, status, and endogamy (i.e., intra- or extramanorial). It was also a tax on a girl's dowry: "Is not merchet the means of taxing, and at a variable rate, the girl's share of the chattels at her own entry into her inheritance [i.e., her dowry], her marriage?"[104]

Women who paid their own *merchet* bought this marriage license for less money than women whose fine was paid by their father or husband.[105] While it is obvious that the lords held the whip hand in these negotiations, there is little evidence that they forced their tenants to pair and to breed. Such intimate details were left to the discretion of the concerned individuals (and their families). On just this point, Marc Bloch has written that "Juridically, as well as almost always practically, the marriage of a serf was free within a prescribed group, but within that group only. It was this limitation that figured among the primordial and quasi-universal characteristics of his [*sic*] status."[106] If the stem family was a patriarchal ideal, it was not an experiential reality; or, to be more precise, even when this ideal was attained, it was short-lived because comparatively late ages at first marriage would have made it unlikely that surviving parents shared a household with married children.[107]

---

ously a connection between strong lordship and weak kinship" in the sense that farming cooperation in heavily manorialized communities involved the whole village rather the extended family network; "Peasant Families and Inheritance Customs in Medieval England," *Agricultural History Review* 14 (1966): 84.

104. Elinor Searle, "Freedom and Marriage in Medieval England: An Alternative Hypothesis," *Economic History Review*, 2d ser., 29 (1976): 484.

105. Judith M. Bennett, "Medieval Peasant Marriage: An Examination of Marriage License Fines in *Liber Gersumarum*," in J. A. Raftis (ed.), *Pathways to Medieval Peasants* (Toronto, 1981), 208–11.

106. Marc Bloch, "Personal Liberty and Servitude in the Middle Ages, Particularly in France: Contribution to a Class Study," in *Slavery and Serfdom in the Middle Ages* (Berkeley and Los Angeles, 1975), 39. It should be mentioned here that Bloch is referring to the early Middle Ages, when personal servitude replaced slavery as the characteristic form of bondage. As we have seen, there were mutations in the serf's condition over time and between places.

107. Herlihy, *Medieval Households*, 70–78.

If the patrimony was hereditary, was the designated heir (and his family) likely to be living with his parents while they were still alive? Perhaps more to the point, was the designated heir allowed the same freedom as his noninheriting brothers and sisters? In proposing these questions we can see how the peasantry's relationship with the landowner provided a distinctive coloration to the question of family formation. After all, feudalists rented their land to their tenants in the expectation that they would receive not only rent but also services. Lords demanded that their land be occupied and expected that their tenants had the responsibility to provide for an orderly succession. If there was no standard holding in terms of acreage, there was still an expectation on the part of seigneurial lords that holdings would supply services so that their manorial demesnes could function. As long as, and wherever, this demand for service was a vital part of the everyday life of the manor, it buttressed the centripetal manse and the authority of the peasant patriarch. Yet we must be careful in advancing this argument because it will not do to create false distinctions or to consider that patriarchy was an imposition from above. Let me expand on this point.

The social reality of family formation was much more complex than can be suggested by a dichotomous antinomy which would link feudalism and extended, patriarchal families over and against postfeudal social systems and nuclear families. It is important to recognize that peasant patriarchs had their own reasons for supporting a family formation system in which patriarchy, primogeniture, and extended households were conjoined. Not the least of their reasons was that this system provided for an upward flow of wealth from women and children (of all ages) to the husband/father. In this way there was an identity of interests between the feudal system and peasant patriarchy. This point obscures rather more than it illuminates if we make the false presumption that the feudal system was systematic in a mechanical sense, whereas social systems are systematic in a quite different way. We must be careful here because social systems are balances of probabilities, each of which is open to negotiation and human agency. Seen in this way, the relationship between land and family formation is rather more contingent than a structural analysis of the feudal system might suggest. "Rather than seeing the family structure of the early medieval peasantry as uniform and unvarying, it would be more fruitful to view it as complex and changeable. . . . Quite simply, it seems much more likely that where it was preferable to them and practical, the peasants maintained an extended family situation. And where it was not, they did not."[108]

108. Emily R. Coleman, "People and Property: The Structure of a Medieval Seigneury," *Journal of European Economic History* 6 (1977): 693.

Lords looked to their tenants for a steady source of rents and services that would be easy to collect. Changes in either the demand for land or its supply modified the character of the bargain. For the lords, inflation created novel imperatives: a context in which new alternatives could be considered even if they contradicted the logic of the feudal system. Peasants, for their part, entered the bargain looking for the basic resources with which to form and to maintain a household. Over time, demographic expansion and economic development posed two quite, different alternative strategies: subdivision and intensification of production on smaller units of land, or else impartibility and the out-migration of all noninheritors. As can be readily imagined, the way in which these different factors came into play was not predetermined but rather subject to bargaining and negotiation. The reproduction of the peasant family's structure was thus colored by the way in which these options were played out, against the backdrop of an unequal distribution of power between lords and peasants.

In a schematic way we might suggest that peasants who were over and above replacement were presented with two stark alternatives: they could either wait in the hopes of marrying into a niche, or else these extra, noninheriting sons and daughters of the village could emigrate.[109] For these people, colonization of new land had been a godsend. The luckiest ones could even find a way to subsidize the formation of a new household without having to leave their native hearth. The less fortunate ones could move away where they could set up on their own and support themselves with income derived from their labor as well as with common rights to keep a cow, a pig, and perhaps even a vegetable garden. This scenario was played out as the population in the countryside thickened. If boom times were like a siphon sucking people out of their native cottages, then frontier communities were like sponges in their ability to soak up these footloose extras.

What about those who stayed behind? In what ways were their lives altered by the existence of this outlet? We have already had a glimpse of the rising reproduction levels in rural areas that provided some of the migrants. It would seem obvious that the opportunity to export noninheriting children relaxed the pressure on resources that the exporting regions would have experienced. Parents with additional, noninheriting children would have had the knowledge that their offspring could relocate. It would seem not unreasonable, therefore, to suggest that colonization acted not

109. E. A. Wrigley estimates that about three-fifths of all families were likely to have an inheriting son; another fifth would have had an inheriting daughter; and one-fifth of all niches would become vacant in the course of each generation; Wrigley, "Fertility Strategy for the Individual and the Group," 135–54.

only as a magnet attracting migrants but also as an insurance policy in per-petuating the reproduction of those who would become migrants. In addi-tion to absorbing the excess claimants, colonization also provided an alter-native for children who might inherit in the course of time but were in the meantime required to wait for a niche to open. If only one of the children would eventually inherit the family farm/household, that does not mean that he or she was unavailable as a source of income while waiting. Indeed, many would often spend some time as living-in servants in husbandry during the long wait between puberty and marriage/inheritance.

3.

This chapter has provided a framework for understanding the reproduction of the peasant family in feudal society by identifying two conflicting ten-dencies at work within this social formation. I have argued that the swelling growth of the peasantry was both a response to and a prompt of above-replacement fertility among the rural population. Colonization pro-vided both an outlet for and a stimulus to this demographic dynamic in those villages which were the source of migrants. To make sense of this mi-gration system I have stressed these reciprocating linkages because in this way we can conceptualize the complementarity of population growth pro-cesses in both the freer receiving zones and the feudalized sending regions.

Among a privileged minority, the centripetal forces radiating from the manse created a hierarchical, ordered patriarchy; among the rest, the cen-trifugal forces of landlessness threw out surplus sons and daughters, who formed an underclass which was continuously being re-created—genera-tion after generation—by the capillary processes of downward social mo-bility. While the creation of the manorial system would appear to have been based on the formation of peasant tenements, it is reasonably clear that it was never the case that all peasant households conformed to type. From the outset there was always a broad continuum, stretching from the landless to those with a superfluity of land who imported others into their households to work their land. Over time, demographic growth and eco-nomic development rendered social reality more, not less, complex.

One way we can made this stark picture somewhat more nuanced is by adding both a temporal and a spatial dimension to it. The substantial pop-ulation growth that took place was possible because after the year 1000 there were new frontiers to conquer where there were new niches for downwardly mobile people to fill. Colonization took place in favorable cli-matic conditions. Villages and hamlets, cities and markets sprung up every-where. If a late marriage system was being practiced after the year 1000, then the opportunities for flexible interpretations were substantial because frontier conditions and the creation of new settlements relaxed the pressures of homeostatic regulation. In particular, we need to keep in mind the sheer length of time during which social and economic life was dominated by a massive secular boom. After the year 1000, this *longue durée* was like a rising tide which lifted all boats. During these ten generations the implications of downward social mobility were, in effect, displaced outward. Even if most women were first married as much as ten years after puberty, they did so in such favorable climatic and economic conditions that, *ceteris paribus*, mortality was not likely to respond directly to rising numbers. The sparse evidence we possess does, in fact, suggest that life expectations may have risen during the long secular boom. There is thus no contradiction between the existence of a system of prudential marriage after the year 1000 and the contemporaneous existence of a long, long period of growth.[110] Furthermore, it was—and still is—entirely possible for most people to enjoy some of the benefits of this secular boom and yet for most of them also to be experiencing exploitation as a result of new modes of social stratification. Exploitation—poverty, destitution, and disentitlement— is a concept that speaks to the nuance of social relations, and understanding it benefits from seeing these social relations in their own context.[111] It was—and still is—entirely possible for more people to live in a worse way as capital flows upward in conditions of hardening social stratification because it was—and still is—possible for these people to be experiencing economic amelioration *and* social deterioration.

The accumulation of population after the year 1000 took place in conditions that became involutional only when the secular boom ran out of steam. By 1300, the first cycle of early modernization, which had originated with the positive feedback mechanisms that congealed after the year 1000, was over. Rural Europe had become a low-level equilibrium trap in which demographic pressure seemed to forestall economic advance. Circumstances had now swung violently against both growth and expansion.

110. Furthermore, it would be misleadingly simpleminded to lift explanations based on Malthusian "positive checks" or "prudential checks" from a social-scientific boilerplate without paying attention to the contingencies of their context. Recourse to homeostatic models that have been developed for explaining the course of population history from the sixteenth through nineteenth centuries is unhelpful because these homeostatic models of stable population dynamics do not, in point of fact, have much explanatory power for that period. For an extended discussion of the weakness of the application of these social-scientific models in explaining English population history, see David Levine, *Reproducing Families: The Political Economy of English Population History* (Cambridge, 1987), *passim*.

111. I shall return to this point in my concluding remarks.

The most characteristic aspect of rural society before the Black Death was the massive proliferation of subtenancies, squatting, farming marginal soils, and sheer desperation, which together add up to a form of life on the margin resulting in standards of living "so modest as to be in many cases indistinguishable from the bread-line."[112]

The rural economy had entered an involutionary phase by the end of the thirteenth century. New forms of intensive cultivation were being practiced on dwarf-holdings as the traditional yardlands and oxgangs of the husbandmen were encroached on by all sorts of subcontracting arrangements. Fourteenth-century English rural society was characterized by massive land subdivision and the comcomitant marginalization of the majority of the population, giving one an eery sense of déjà vu: in effect, by 1300 the countryside had come to resemble nothing so much as the mushrooming rural population of today's Third World.[113]

THE LIMITS OF PATRIARCHY

While the ideology of both Christianity and feudalism was profoundly misogynistic, "The Limits of Patriarchy" suggests that this is not the only way to understand domestic power relations. The Christian emphasis on the equality of all believers had to be awkwardly accommodated with ancient traditions of patria potestas. The inner dynamics of family formation resulted in stresses and strains which were particularly evident in the lives of younger, noninheriting children. The landless, for whom feudal controls over marriage were of less significance than economic opportunities, were especially likely to have taken individual control over their personal lives. In theory, the downward flow of obligations was usually much stronger than the upward flow of rights, but in everyday life, there was a continuous dialogue between men and women and between adults and children, with the inevitable result that socially understood ideals of patriarchal domination clashed with the reality of individual choice. Intergenerational relations, in particular the timing of marriage and choice of partner,

112. Barbara F. Harvey, "Introduction: The 'Crisis' of the Early Fourteenth Century," in B. M. S. Campbell (ed.), *Before the Black Death: Studies in the "Crisis" of the Early Fourteenth Century* (Manchester, 1991), 15.

113. This is not to say that the involutional circumstances of the year 1300 were permanent or that the demographic forces were so strong that further economic growth was impossible. What I am arguing is that at this time the rising tide of the previous 300 years was ebbing. When would the tide rise again? We'll never know because the Black Death introduced a radically new set of gravitational forces so powerful that the long-term tidal flows were altered.

were fraught with tension. The emergence of the single-family household and the Church's insistence on consensual unions interacted with the organization of peasants' domestic space as well as their public behavior. Spousal relations and sexuality cannot be understood apart from the violent temper of daily life. For young women this was an especially dangerous situation because all women were expected to subordinate themselves to the demands of reproduction and family life. Most did exactly that, by taking inspiration from the cult of the Virgin Mary.

Even if the extended family was a minority experience during the feudal period, it is important to keep in mind that this minority represented an ideal for many peasants, lords, and contemporary social commentators. The power of this ideal is thought to have held the family together and kept many on (or near) ancestral lands. But when we ask whether there is strong evidence that extended families were common among the upper tier of the peasantry, we are again thrown back upon the Carolingian surveys. These unique documents suggest that most households were nuclear in structure; among the minority of complex households, horizontal extension was more common than vertical forms.

We have little choice other than posing our discussion in these stylized terms because for almost half a millennium, after the illuminating shaft of light from the Carolingian *polyptychs*, our sources are virtually silent. It is only with the advent of the English manorial records that we are again privileged to see the peasantry making their own families. While it is true that there are other sources surviving from the intervening centuries— they peer down at its external shape from above and outside—none of them look inside the process of family formation.

1.

We might start with peasant housing, evidence for which comes from excavation and archaeological reconstruction. Few extant examples survive, and most of these come from the fourteenth and fifteenth centuries. Prior to the feudal revolution of the year 1000 there had been little stability in the spatial organization of peasant society. Thus, churchyards were not the focal point of a stable community but rather the meeting place of several neighboring clearings: "In the tenth century this settlement of uncertain, temporary and insubstantial character can most frequently be connected with the place where its inhabitants' remains are still to be found." In the tenth century, the process of *encellulement* had not yet begun. During the next two hundred years peasant buildings became what we would consider single-family residences with a central hearth for cooking and warmth.[114] It is not coincidental that the emergence of *focagium* (a hearth tax), which counted not heads nor houses nor even heads of households, also dates from around 1100.[115]

As we have seen, the feudal revolution established new obligations which accorded a low priority to ties of blood and substituted the manor and the parish church for the extended clan structure and family group. This was accompanied by a spatial component which circumscribed humans "with collective obligations, whether religious or judicial, economic or moral." A process of congealment took place by 1100 so that stable communities were beginning to form around the blacksmith's forge, the mill, the wash-house, the marketplace, the seigneurial workshops, the parish church, and the graveyard.[116]

The most common house type among the peasantry was the *longa domus* (long house) that provided shelter for both humans and their animals. In some of these buildings space was compartmentalized under the same roof. Even the simplest buildings often provided separate entries for humans and animals. Some were complex, subdivided into several rooms, and quite large. "The warmth of the animals which had hitherto been indispensable for heating the human inhabitants in the great communal halls [and smaller byre-houses] of the early Middle Ages became less essential; so the entry of the hearth coincided with the departure of livestock; or at least with its isolation in an area specifically allocated when the house was built."[117]

In the deserted village of Wharram Percy, Yorkshire, for example, the biggest of these peasant houses was ninety-five feet long and twenty feet wide. But if the peasants' houses were big, they weren't very solid. The archaeologists' reconstruction of this Yorkshire village suggests that few of these houses lasted for more than a couple of generations. On one tenement site, nine slightly different houses were erected in the space of three centuries. Even the upper tier's one-story homes (with loft or *solar*) were dirty and smoky because the central hearths were not converted into wall

114. Robert Fossier, *Peasant Life in the Medieval West* (Oxford, 1988), 49, 51, 57.

115. Philippe Contamine, "Peasant Hearths to Papal Palace," in Georges Duby (ed.), *A History of Private Life*, vol. 2, *Revelations of the Medieval World* (Cambridge, Mass., 1988), 425.

116. Jean Chapelot and Robert Fossier, *The Village and House in the Middle Ages* (Berkeley and Los Angeles, 1985), 139, 150.

117. Fossier, *Peasant Life in the Medieval West*, 69.

fireplaces or stoves until the fifteenth century.[118] "In broad outline we witness the transition from rudimentary huts built with whatever materials happened to be at hand (earth, wood, branches, leaves) to more solid structures, designed to last, requiring sophisticated construction techniques and a considerable investment of time and money. . . . More substantial homes became increasingly common from the twelfth century on: Here the family could feel more at home, both materially and psychologically. The new housing provided better protection against cold, rain, and wind and permitted better care of work and household implements and stores."[119]

Some of these buildings were constructed by manorial lords, although this was more common after the Black Death, when lords were eager to increase the attractiveness of their holdings. Before 1350, on the other hand, there was less reason for them to do so.[120] Few of these examples were, strictly speaking, cottages. They were usually the homes and outbuildings of the wealthiest strata of the peasantry. In addition, it is important to keep in mind the glacial slowness of change: for most of the period in question, most houses were small and minimally furnished with a trestle table and a bench or two. Their floors were covered with straw, and almost all people slept on straw pallets, only rarely in a bed. No matter how carefully these houses were cleaned—and they were "swept frequently enough that brooms left U-shaped depressions on house sites"[121]—randomly dropped excrement and food wastes, both inside and outside the house, provided a paradise for microorganisms and other parasites. The roof thatch, the cob or daub-and-wattle walls, and the floors provided homes for fleas, mice, and rats. Even the richest peasants must have lived with dirt and smells which would overpower us.

It is important to bear in mind that the little evidence we possess relates to the stable core of the peasant elite; we know almost nothing about the conditions of the cottager's shack. It seems not unreasonable, though, to presume that these small huts were flimsier than the long houses about

118. Chapelot and Fossier, *The Village and House in the Middle Ages*, 219–20. See also J. G. Hurst, "The Changing Medieval Village in England," in Raftis (ed.), *Pathways to Medieval Peasants*, 27–62; Sarah M. McKinnon, "The Peasant House: The Evidence of Manuscript Illumination," in Raftis (ed.), *Pathways to Medieval Peasants*, 301–9.

119. Philippe Contamine, "Peasant Hearths to Papal Palace," 446–47, 458–59. See also M. W. Barley, *The English Farmhouse and Cottage* (London, 1961), 3–37.

120. H. E. J. Le Patourel, "Rural Building in England," in Edward Miller (ed.), *The Agrarian History of England and Wales*, vol. 3, (1348–1350) (Cambridge, 1991), 844–46.

121. Barbara Hanawalt, *The Ties That Bound* (Oxford, 1986), 147.

which we do have some evidence. No doubt, too, they had no internal differentiation, no rooms, and no privacy. We should also expect that for the majority of the population the appearance of a hearth did not automatically mean the exile of the animals, for the simple reason that their livestock had nowhere to go. The crude simplicity of these cottages meant that they could be built quickly, from ready-to-hand materials, without any site preparation or foundations. In this sense, the formation of a new family did not present any significant material obstacles.[122]

2.

The emergence of the discrete, single-family household was a landmark which coincided with the Church's insistence on consensual unions. It separated the couple from its wider networks of clan and lineage, thereby making the reproduction of families into an affair of two individuals, although for most propertied peasants this was more a matter of ideology than of everyday life. Indeed, when we look into the quality of domestic life, the first issue which confronts us is the relationship between the patriarchal power of the househead and his control over his property or his *usufruct*. Looking at feudalism as an unequal bargain between a male propertyholder and a male househead highlights the critical role played by the access to land. It also underscores that the importance of women was largely confined to their role in the biological transmission of the family line and the daily reproduction of the family's labor power.

The political organization of the village was dominated by the wealthy (male) elements in the peasantry. "Norms of female and male behavior in the medieval countryside drew heavily upon the private subordination of wives to their husbands. Femaleness was defined by the submissiveness of wives who were expected to defer to their husbands in both private and public.... Maleness was defined by the private authority of husbands who, as householders, controlled most domestic and community matters." In relation to this vision of gendered roles, the conjugal household, "and its ideal dichotomy of public men and private women," was a pivot of village life.[123] Public authority—with its manifold expressions in the royal and

122. Even as late as the nineteenth century, "one night houses" were a common residence for young married couples in the proto-industrial villages of northwestern England; John R. Gillis, "Peasant, Plebeian and Proletarian Marriage," in David Levine (ed.), *Proletarianization and Family History* (Orlando, 1984), 147–48.

123. Judith M. Bennett, "Public Power and Authority in the Medieval English Countryside," 18–36; Bennett, *Women in the Medieval Countryside: Gender and Household in Brigstock Before the Plague* (Oxford, 1987), 188. Sexual equality

manorial courts, juries, and tithings—involved adult, male househeads in a whole orbit of official relationships—reeves, bailiffs, and pledges (overseeing manorial operations and acting as sureties); affeerors (assessing fines); messors (overseeing practices with regard to planting, harvesting, grazing, and common rights); and aletasters (supervising sales and monitoring the quality of brewers)—in which they acted together and from which women were completely excluded. This public-private distinction had three dimensions. First, it distinguished married, male househeads from other men; second, it differentiated the old from the young; and third, it separated these peasant patriarchs from all women.

For the upper tier of the peasantry, marriage, inheritance, and generational transitions were all geared to maintaining solidarity with both generations dead and those still unborn. In Halesowen, for example, Zvi Razi discovered peasant "lineages." But because the vast majority of the peasantry was neither sufficiently well endowed with land nor likely to be subject to the same manorial controls, we must balance our treatment of the solid core of the customary tenants with an evenhanded consideration of those who were marginal, downwardly mobile, and often free.

It is useful to consider the available material within the matrix suggested by the split within the peasant community between the manse and the cottage. The benefit of this procedure is twofold: first, it provides us with a heightened sense of the endemic contradictions in this social formation; and second, it underscores some continuities in popular family life that persisted after the demise of feudalism. Because the health of the manorial system depended upon a regular payment—of both money and labor services—there was an inherent tendency for landlords to favor impartible inheritance to prop up the kind of patriarchal peasant households that would be able to pay their double rent.

The alternative, subdivision, would inevitably lead to a morcellization of holdings. Whatever benefits lords might have gained from higher rates of return per unit of land would have been offset by the likelihood of nonpayment and the cost of collection. While it would seem that subdivision would favor the supply of labor rents at the expense of money rents, just

---

was, perhaps, more attainable in the religious sphere; Peter Biller, "The Common Woman in the Western Church in the Thirteenth and Early Fourteenth Centuries," in W. J. Sheils and Diana Wood (eds.), *Women in the Church* (Oxford, 1990), 127–57. Spiritual equality was a particular demand of those deemed heretical, stemming from their radical critique of the intermediary role of a caste of celibate males in the celebration of the eucharist; Margaret Aston, "Lollard Women Priests?," in *Lollards and Reformers* (London, 1984), 49–70.

the opposite was the case. It was very difficult for lords to keep track of these kaleidoscopic obligations, and peasants, for their part, were unlikely to provide much assistance in this matter. For this reason, in the second wave of English feudalism in the thirteenth century, one of the lords' primary concerns was to establish their tenants' legally binding and uncontestable responsibilities.

The social relations of production in feudal society were thus indirectly responsible for connecting marriage with intergenerational transfers.[124] Superficially, at least, such transfers would appear to have been timed according to the life-expectation of the older generation because the court rolls tell us more about the post mortem transition from the older to younger generation at the death of the primary tenant than they do about inter vivos transfers. Vigorous population growth was characteristic of the countryside between c. 1000 and 1250–1300, the time of optimum climatic conditions. Life expectation was most likely to have been rather better in the twelfth and thirteenth centuries than in the half-century preceding the Black Death. Most empirical analysis of manorial documents is based on the later period, after 1250, when epidemics, famines, and high death rates became an ever more important characteristic of the peasantry's life chances in an age of overpopulation.

It would be valuable if we had reliable data with which to pin down the preceding point; however, the best that we have relates to the twelfth-century nobility of Picardy, for whom genealogical research has suggested a life expectation at birth greater than forty years for males. While the aristocratic males were better fed, they were also exposed to unusual military risks. Both nobles and commoners were similarly exposed to infectious diseases; blood lines were no guarantee of immunity. Thus the aristocratic rate of mortality was probably shared by others.[125]

An earlier generation of scholarship suggested that among the mass of the rural population in the manorialized regions of thirteenth-century England, landholding and marriage were closely linked: those without land did not marry. Recent commentators have repeated this argument as well: "Late marriage and the abstention of the unmarried from 'careless' heterosexual relations were thus the main factors serving to limit increases in

---

124. Of course, in some areas inheritance was not determined by primogeniture, but for the sake of presenting a reasonably coherent argument, these further elements of diversity will be sacrificed in the following account. It should nevertheless be borne in mind that inheritance customs are another force which rendered family life more, not less, complex.

125. Duby, *Rural Economy and Country Life*, 123–24, 182.

the population."[126] Studies of the peasant land market, and especially Zvi Razi's pathbreaking analysis of the customary tenants of Halesowen, counsel us to revise this overly schematic model. Razi discovered that the primary heir's or heiress's marital behavior was significantly different from that of younger siblings who married later and were only rarely able to inherit any land at the patriarch's death or retirement but were sometimes looked after in his lifetime.

In contrast to a simulated peasant population in which fathers might expect to live for some thirty years after the birth of their first son, institutional factors created a quite different marriage system in Halesowen. Demographic mechanisms would have raised the age at first marriage for men, if they could not marry until their father's death or retirement, but in Halesowen there was a system of reproduction based on the peasant lineage and its tenement which was particularly important for firstborn sons and daughters. Razi suggests that this section of the peasantry lived in functionally extended households, marrying earlier than their siblings.[127] "If sons [in the wealthiest strata] in Halesowen did not have to wait until their father's death to obtain land, and if they were prepared to start their independent life with a part of the family lands and sometimes even with quite a small holding, it is likely that many of them did so as soon as they reached the age of 20, the minimum legal age for holding land."[128] Thus, it appears from the example of Halesowen that the stratified distribution of the peasantry into land-rich and land-poor families worked through their inheritance practices to create a multitiered process of marriage and family formation.[129]

Children from landed families were either more advantaged or less advantaged than average according to their position in the birth order. The life chances of the younger generation of small peasants were similarly

---

126. George C. Homans, *English Villagers of the Thirteenth Century* (Boston, 1941), 158–59; Chris Middleton, "Peasants, Patriarchy and the Feudal Mode of Production in England: I," *Sociological Review* 29 (1981): 116.

127. This point regarding the functionally extended family is made more forcefully in Razi's "The Myth of the Immutable English Family" (8–15) than in *Life, Marriage and Death in a Medieval Parish* (55–64). In his monograph Razi was less concerned with the organization of households and more concerned with the dynamics of generational transition.

128. Razi, *Life, Marriage and Death in a Medieval Parish*, 60–61.

129. While Poos is elsewhere critical of Razi's arguments, on this point he is in complete agreement: "manorial court records, the primary source of greatest importance for reconstituting village society for the period, demonstrably tend to overemphasise the land and marital transactions of middling and upper ranks in village society, and are much less illustrative of landless labourers' activities"; *A Rural Society after the Black Death* (Cambridge, 1991), 146.

stratified, with the notable proviso that even the eldest sons (and daughters) were probably no better off than the younger children of the richer peasants. The inheritance prospects of the younger children of these small peasants were probably not much different from those of the children of landless cottagers. Those without a landed inheritance were not rigidly excluded from marriage, but rather they married later, had fewer children, and lived in comparative poverty while being much more likely to move away from the natal manor, to die in famines, and to be unable to continue the family line down through another generation.

For younger sons and daughters—especially those from the middling and lower strata of the peasantry—downward mobility and landlessness urged a more prudent marriage strategy. Their lack of capital caused them to seek employment in either domestic service, colonization, or industrial by-employments so that they often spent years accumulating the equivalent of an inheritance/dowry with which they could marry and found their own household. In some cases the designated heir died prematurely and the family's patrimony descended to them. A few would be lucky enough to be the collateral heirs of more distant kin dying without progeny. Some others, who were either luckier or more cunning, married upward into landed families.

3.

While there has been heated debate concerning the age at first marriage among the peasantry in feudal England—Was it about twenty-two for men and a couple of years younger for women? Or was it rather later?—there seems to be little consideration for the argument that English peasants married women who were pubescent teenagers.[130]

130. For an extended discussion about the techniques used in Razi's study, see the debate in *Law and History Review* (cited in chap. 3, note 4). I am unconvinced by Razi's appropriation of the technique of family reconstitution in linking individuals between generations. He himself acknowledges that the analysis of the manorial court rolls was bedeviled by the complexity of distinguishing separate individuals of the same name from one another. This task of identification was made more difficult by the fluidity of surnames, which was a particular problem among the village elite, who were densely internamed, both between and across generations. For this reason, as well as because there is so much more evidence about the rich peasants, there is a much greater likelihood that two rich individuals have been conjoined more often than their poorer kin and neighbors. It thus seems that Razi is on uncertain ground when he seeks to chart marriage ages, although this problem is rather less of a liability when he considers the interclass and intrafamiliar dynamics of this marriage system. Indeed, the very complexity of these rich peasants' lineages speaks to his point.

The question of women's age at first marriage, which was initiated by H. J. Hajnal,[131] has been the subject of some searching hypotheses. Briefly put, the revisionist argument goes something like this: in the northwest of Europe, and in particular in England, marriage was tied to household formation, which was, in turn, connected to the young couple's ability to find an available "niche" in the local economy. Because of deep-seated cultural conditioning, households in this part of Europe were nuclear. Youthful marriage on the Tuscan model (via the creation of joint households) was not an option. Therefore, English women's ages at first marriage were dependent upon the socioeconomic climate. Yet it is only with the 1377, 1378, and 1381 poll taxes that we have a source that yields the kind of quantitative information necessary to determine proportions married and (by inference) age at first marriage. Hajnal used this source, but it is claimed by more recent, revisionist historians—Richard Smith and P. J. P Goldberg— that he miscalculated it. These revisionists argue that by assuming that the poll tax listings of young women were reasonably complete there was a major bias introduced into Hajnal's estimates. A level of evasion on the order of 25 percent would have meant that, in all likelihood, those escaping detection were unmarried. In simple arithmetic terms, the revisionists argue that the numerator is essentially correct but the denominator is too small, which results in an inaccurate conclusion. By inflating the denominator, Smith and Goldberg provide estimates of female marriage ages that are significantly later than those proposed by Hajnal.[132]

131. H. J. Hajnal's "European Marriage Patterns in Perspective" and, more especially, "Two Kinds of Pre-Industrial Household Formation Systems" are the key texts from which this hypothesis spinning takes flight.

132. The relevant articles by Smith are "Some Reflections on the Evidence for the Origins of the 'European Marriage Pattern' in England," in C. Harris (ed.), *The Sociology of the Family* (Keele, 1979), 74–112; "Fertility, Economy and Household Formation in England over Three Centuries," *Population and Development Review* 7 (1981): 595–622; "The People of Tuscany and Their Families in the Fifteenth Century: Medieval or Mediterranean," *Journal of Family History* 6 (1981): 107–28; "Hypothèses sur la nuptialité en Angleterre aus XIII–XIV siècles," *Annales, E.S.C.* 39 (1983): 107–36; "Some Issues Concerning Families and Their Property in Rural England 1250–1800," in Smith (ed.), *Land, Kinship and Life-Cycle*, 1–86; "Marriage Processes in the English Past: Some Continuities," in Lloyd Bonfield, Richard M. Smith, and Keith Wrightson (eds.), *The World We Have Gained: Histories of Population and Social Structure* (Oxford, 1986), 43–99; "Human Resources," in G. Astill and A. Grant (eds.), *The Countryside of Medieval England* (Oxford, 1988), 188–212; "Demographic Developments in Rural England, 1300–1348: A Survey," in B. M. S. Campbell (ed.), *Before the Black Death*, 25–78; "Geographical Diversity in the Resort to Marriage in Late Medieval Europe," in P. J. P. Goldberg (ed.), *Woman Is a Worthy Wight: Women in English Society, c. 1200–1500* (Stroud, 1992), 16–59. The main works by Goldberg are "Marriage, Migration, Servanthood

The new estimates lead Smith and Goldberg to conjure up a social world of autonomy and independent agency that gave these women the ability to choose when—and to whom—they would marry. This, in turn, is connected to later ages at first marriage and high incidences of permanent celibacy. The revised social world of marriage in the wake of the Black Death that Smith and Goldberg have constructed is part and parcel of a "low pressure" demographic regime that would continue for centuries to follow.[133] It should also be noted that the evidential base on which Smith and Goldberg base their hypotheses is small, their scholarly apparatus is self-referential, and their inferences from it are tendentious.[134] To me, it seems that these emperors are indeed scantily clad—but not stark naked. Smith and Goldberg consistently overreach their evidence. Their evidence primarily suggests that, in fact, the poll tax denominator is too small and, therefore, the incidence of unmarried postpubescent women was higher than appears to be the case at first glance. As Bailey remarks, "Hajnal's speculative assumptions about [poll tax] reliability appear to have been too generous and optimistic, but a rejection of Hajnal does not imply an acceptance of very pessimistic assumptions. In the absence of any independent verification of the information contained in the poll taxes, historians

---

and Life-Cycle in Yorkshire Towns of the Later Middle Ages: Some York Cause Paper Evidence," *Continuity and Change* 1 (1986): 141–69; "Female Labour Service and Marriage in the Late Medieval Urban North," *Northern History* 22 (1986): 18–38; "Urban Identity and the Poll Taxes of 1377, 1379, and 1381," *Economic History Review*, 2d ser., 43 (1990): 194–216; *Women, Work, and Life Cycle in a Medieval Economy* (Oxford, 1992); "Introduction" and " 'For Better, For Worse': Marriage and Economic Opportunity for Women in Town and Country," in Goldberg (ed.), *Woman Is a Worthy Wight*, 1–15, 108–25.

133. In addition to studding their articles with references to their own work, R. H. Smith and P. J. P. Goldberg rely heavily on the E. A. Wrigley and R. S. Schofield study of later population trends in England; *Population History of England and Wales, 1541–1871* (London, 1981). They fail to acknowledge that this work has itself been the subject of controversy with regard to its arguments concerning "dilatory homeostasis," the theoretical way in which Wrigley and Schofield have tried to connect real wage trends and demographic statistics even though these two statistical series are out of synch by as much as sixty-five years. For my opinions regarding this aspect of the Wrigley and Schofield analysis of population statistics and the social history of work and wages, see David Levine, *Reproducing Families*, esp. 115–26.

134. Smith's and Goldberg's arguments have been subjected to withering criticisms by Mark Bailey, "Demographic Decline in Late Medieval England: Some Thoughts on Recent Research." *Economic History Review*, 2d ser., 49 (1966): 1–19. It should be noted, however, that Bailey does not question their reliance on Wrigley's and Schofield's reconstruction of later population history and, in particular, its questionable arguments regarding "dilatory homeostasis."

can only speculate about the extent of the evasions and under-recording of women, thus *any* reconstructions of marriage patterns from them remain conjectural."[135]

To jump from their basic statistical point regarding evasion (or under-counting of young women) to a discussion of motivation seems unwarranted because this evidence, by itself, tells us nothing about why these young women were less likely to have been married than had hitherto been thought. Goldberg's arguments about urban sex ratios are interesting, but almost all women lived in the countryside and, what is more, there is nothing to suggest that the urban sex ratios and servanthood rates that his evidence unearths are different from the situation which would have prevailed in these same small towns and cities before the Black Death. Finally, Goldberg's discussion of female autonomy and economic independence is truly misleading—these medieval women were independent in the same way that a Victorian laborer was free to starve or a Georgian pauper was free to sleep at the side of the road. Women did the meanest, lowest paying jobs—mostly small-scale market sales, some proto-industrial subcontracting, and prostitution. There is almost nothing to suggest that the labor shortage after the Black Death did much to change this state of affairs and absolutely nothing to suggest that such independent women could make a living wage from their own labors.[136]

Nevertheless, I would be unfair not to acknowledge that Smith and Goldberg do revise our understanding of the fourteenth-century statistical record in pointing out that the incidence of married women was incompatible with an age at first marriage for women at puberty. Why should peasant men have married women who were well past puberty, often in their mid-twenties? Why wouldn't they marry teenagers, as was the case in

---

135. Bailey, "Demographic Decline in Late Medieval England," 8.

136. For a quite different study of urban women's work, see Maryanne Kowaleski, "Women's Work in a Market Town: Exeter in the Late Fourteenth Century," in B. Hanawalt (ed.), *Women and Work in Pre-Industrial Europe* (Bloomington, 1986), 145–64. As Kowaleski writes, "since the work activities of women were so frequently linked to those of their husbands or fathers, women had a weak work identity and failed to participate in existing guilds or to organize themselves" (158). The political economy of urban society—women lacked the independent right to civic freedom and even widows rarely had access to capital, while none had formal training as apprentices—marginalized them from the power structure and thereby relegated them to working in the interstices of the formal economy. This was indeed a vicious circle that kept all women and many men out of the charmed inner sanctum of power. See Heather Swanson, "The Illusion of Economic Structure: Craft Guilds in Late Medieval English Towns," *Past and Present* 121 (1988): 29–48.

Mediterranean Europe? Answering these questions requires us to consider not only the characteristics of a good wife but also the role and responsibilities of a housewife. Most of the rural population in the feudalized northwest of Europe were peasant farmers who lived in nucleated families: "marriage joined together two individuals, not their families. It created a conjugal family, not a family alliance."[137] These nuclear families were by no means a homogenous social group and, at any point in time, they differed among themselves in the amount of land to which they had access.[138] An equality of wealth and status was usually a prerequisite for a marriage since the marriage was most often initiated by the matchmaking efforts of the senior generation. A woman's property as well as her personal abilities would count for as much as—and most probably rather more than—the affection the two partners felt for each other.

The English peasant family was, thus, quite different in its internal dynamics and self-organization from the Tuscan elite, in which early marriage of women was part of a distinctive gendering process. Tuscans infantilized women and focused attention on their role as chaste mothers. Yet, at the same time, most affective ties between these same mothers and their children were sundered when, in an attempt to "control their seed," males wrested control of wet-nursing from their wives.[139] This situation is in stark contrast with peasant mothers, for whom nursing was a very lengthy process, between eighteen and twenty-two months.[140] In part, of course,

137. Judith Bennett, "The Tie That Binds: Peasant Marriages and Families in Late Medieval England," *Journal of Interdisciplinary History* 15 (1984): 127.

138. Over the course of their lives, their households changed according to the rhythms of their family cycle. It would seem that when there were too many mouths, extra hands would be brought into the household in the form of servants. Part of the force of Hajnal's analysis of spatial variation in household formation systems is based on his insight that it was characteristic of the northwest European household to have a large number of co-resident servants.

139. Christiane Klapisch-Zuber, "Blood Parents and Milk Parents: Wet Nursing in Florence 1300–1530," in *Women, Family, and Ritual in Renaissance Italy* (Chicago, 1985), 132–64. What about the situation among the lower classes in Renaissance Florence and its countryside? These women were the wet nurses who suckled the children of the urban patricians. They married at just about the same age as their wealthier counterparts and, one might surmise, their commitment to nursing their own children (and those who were farmed out to them) would have lengthened their postpartum anovulatory period. It is not clear whether the children born to these wet nurses ("milk mothers") suffered rates of infant mortality that were higher than those of the urban aristocrats. Infant mortality had more to do with infectious disease and epidemics than social class. Money could not provide much of a barrier against contagion except by removing urban children to the countryside.

140. Fossier, *Peasant Life*, 22. I would be remiss not to point out that Fossier suggests that peasant women were teenagers when they married (21). He presents

this was simply a reflection of the vast disparity in wealth and power separating servile villagers from the aristocratic Florentines of the early Renaissance. In part, however, it was a reflection of something deeper: the expectation that a peasant woman would be more than a "breeder." It may be the case that "a married woman's fecundity [was] her most valuable asset," but it is rather a different matter to then suggest that her fecundity was "more valuable . . . [than] the labour she might contribute herself or the property she brought into the marriage."[141] But this line of argument is not only tendentious but also based on mere supposition, without any evidence to substantiate either the main point or the additional gloss made upon it. Indeed, a compelling case against this point of view has been made by Alan Macfarlane.[142] It is in opposition to this mythical notion of "breeders" that we need to note that a large (and growing) segment of the population was both landless and free from seigneurial control; hence, they were unlikely to have been "breeders." Among this group, the pressure of subsistence replaced patriarchy as the main impediment to the marital freedom of young women and the men they might marry. Therefore, not only was the affective life of the northwestern European peasant woman utterly different from that of Tuscan noble woman, so too was her responsibility for the domestic reproduction of her family's labor power.

What can we say about peasant sexuality? Can we learn anything about the texture of intimate relationships? The best evidence that we possess about the subject of interpersonal relations comes from the register of Jacques Fournier, bishop of Pamiers from 1318 to 1325 and later Pope Benedict XII at Avignon, who investigated the beliefs and behavior of the population of the Languedoc village of Montaillou.[143] It should hardly need emphasizing that this document is the product of the quest for mastery on the part of the early modern state-formation offensive and its tech-

---

no evidence to support this assertion. Gregory of Tours, in his quasi-anthropological *Histoire des Francs*, suggests that women in the late sixth century would have nursed their children for as long as three years. Contemporary aristocratic women would have arranged for their children to be breast-fed and raised by wet nurses; Riché, "Problèmes de démographie," 44. This split between the upper- and lower-class modes of child rearing seems to have been nearly universal. Quite clearly, among those strata of the population who could afford it, wives were expected to be sex objects and vessels rather more than they were allowed to be mothers.

141. C. Middleton, "Peasants, Patriarchy and the Feudal Mode of Production in England: 2," *Sociological Review* 29 (1981): 148.

142. Alan Macfarlane, *Marriage and Love in England 1300–1840* (Oxford, 1986).

143. The following paragraphs gloss Le Roy Ladurie's text, and I will not therefore supply separate references to each citation.

nology of artificial memory. It should also be mentioned that Languedoc does not seem to have been part of the northwestern European system of deferred marriage. On the other hand, even though this evidence is compromised—at least, it is compromised in terms of the argument I am advancing—there is nothing else quite like it. In addition, it provides a framework within which we can address the other surviving snippets on this subject.

Located high in the Pyrenees, Montaillou was a small community with a population of more than two hundred people organized into "an archipelago" of forty households which were moral entities more notable for their material and emotional investments than for their market value. This *domus* linked neighborhood, marriage, cousinship, and domestic service in a mutually reinforcing set of bonds. The worldly goods of a *domus* were indivisible. Familial solidarity was thus the highest social value. Marriage was the centerpiece of this demographic and social edifice. Thus the state of marriage was ranked at the top of the scale of moral value. To what extent did Montaillou's system of public respectability construct the experience of sexuality? Local endogamy was high, but there seems to have been a reluctance to permit incestuous unions, which would explain the strength of the ban on sexual and marital relations between first cousins. Thus the villagers of Montaillou grasped the spirit—but not the letter—of Lateran IV's injunctions against consanguineity.

Being a part of the Mediterranean cultural system, marriage in Montaillou was often arranged between an older man and a younger woman who was thereafter subjected to her husband's absolute authority. Montaillou's was a deeply misogynous society, with a highly ritualized code of honor. Le Roy Ladurie suggests that Montaillou's women were commonly beaten, sometimes raped, and usually feared as long as they were regarded as sexual objects. They were subjected to a system of regulation similar to the Andalusian *vergüenza*, which combines a sense of shame and modesty with concern for feminine reputation and public honor.

For women, sexual permissiveness—but not promiscuity—often stopped on the steps of the altar but returned after the husband's funeral. Of particular interest is Le Roy Ladurie's argument that "Many people were of the opinion that pleasure in itself was without sin, and if it was agreeable to the couples concerned it was not disagreeable to God either."[144] Moreover, some Cathars believed that pleasure alone guaranteed

144. Similar sentiments were expressed elsewhere. The heretical Lollard evangelist, John Becket, was absolved after abjuring his "errors," among which one learns was the belief that "sexual intercourse outside ecclesiastically sanctioned

the innocence of a liaison, so that it was only when one no longer felt desire that any carnal act would be consummated sinfully.

Purity for the Cathars was a matter not of outer cleanliness but of inner godliness. In this sense, they had unwittingly grasped the essential point of Abelard's ethics. Perhaps the most important point which needs to be made about this evidence is that the misogyny and violence reported in Montaillou were not exceptional. It is therefore hardly surprising that women were less attracted to Catharism than were men. As Peter Biller notes, "Catharism was *the* heresy of the Central Middle Ages, and in the case of this heresy the statistics point to the possibility that the Common Woman was voting with her feet—but voting *against* it: against hatred of woman, female flesh, human love, and marriage."[145]

The historical record from fifteenth-century Burgundy—which is located in the northwestern European zone of deferred marriage—substantiates Le Roy Ladurie's account of woman-hating violence. Here, too, there was a male youth culture which featured fighting, drinking, gambling, and sexual violence. Rape was common, gang rape directed against young women of the lower classes being the usual form of aggression.[146] In fifteenth-century Dijon, with a population under 10,000, it would seem that one of every 240 unmarried, lower-class women would have had an annual expectation of being raped. For lower-class women who lived continuously in this city between the ages of fifteen and twenty-four, the likelihood of being raped at least one time would have been much greater, since they were constantly at risk of sexual violence for a ten-year period.[147]

---

matrimony is permissable and sinless"; Poos, *A Rural Society after the Black Death*, 264.

145. Biller, "The Common Woman in the Western Church," 157. For a thorough analysis of the court records in this regard, see also Richard Abels and Ellen Harrison, "The Participation of Women in Languedocian Catharism," *Mediaeval Studies* 41 (1979): 215–51.

146. Jacques Rossiaud, *Medieval Prostitution* (Oxford, 1988). It should be noted that, according to contemporary French law, the rape of a prostitute was not a crime; Bronislaw Geremek, *The Margins of Society in Late Medieval Paris* (Cambridge, 1987), 225 n 79. English court records from the thirteenth century do not substantiate this horrific picture of sexual predation, although they; too, reveal a world of violence and gendered inequality before the law; John M. Carter, "Rape and Medieval English Society," *Comitatus* 13 (1982): 33–63; Ruth Kittel, "Rape in Thirteenth-Century England," in D. Kelly Weisberg (ed.), *Women and the Law*, vol. 2 (Cambridge, Mass., 1982), 101–15.

147. I arrived at this "annual expectation of rape" in the following manner: In a population of 10,000 there would have been 5,000 women, of whom 17 percent would have been in the 15–24 age group. Of these 850 women, I estimated that two-thirds (600) were members of the lower class and that they were all unmar-

Emmanuel Le Roy Ladurie and Jacques Rossiaud have studied young men of the lower and middling classes—both rural and urban—so it is instructive to set their accounts alongside Georges Duby's discussion of aristocratic young men, which considers an earlier period and a very much more exalted social group. Among these young men—who, like William Marshal, would be "youths" until marriage—there was a chivalrous culture of courtly love and a rather less polite "game": "For the triangle 'husband-wife-married lover,' the poets of the 'youthful band' wanted to substitute another triangle 'husband-lady-young courtly servant.' They wanted to break into the erotic circle to the advantage of 'youth.' " For these men, too, women were female prey: "Courtly love was consequently something more than sexual divagation. . . . [The male] followed a minutely wrought strategy which had every appearance of being a ritualized transposition of hunting techniques, tournaments, and laying siege to a fortress."[148]

This emphasis on a culture of violence demands further discussion, for it is important to situate the brutality of sexual relations within it. The preponderant view of historians is that "violence was deep-rooted in the social structure and in the mentality of the age." Impulsive behavior was common, and insensitivity to pain and a small regard for human life were primordial elements in the manners of feudal society around the year 1000.[149] In the following centuries, the growth of the state apparatus was keyed to limiting public violence—vendettas, blood feuds, homicide, blackmail, kidnapping, and extortion. The switch from personalized vendettas to a more abstract concept of crime and punishment was a long, arduous process that was completed only in the nineteenth century. Indeed, the monopolization of violence in the hands of the state is one of the hallmarks of modern society.

There is no statistical baseline with which to measure violence in the feudal world.[150] The evidence is nonetheless harrowing: in fourteenth-

---

ried. Jacques Rossiaud reports that 125 cases of rape came before the civil authorities, which would suggest an annual average of 2.5 cases. So, 2.5 cases per 600 women at risk would yield an annual expectation of being raped of 1:240. Of course, it should be pointed out that Rossiaud's statistics are no doubt wildly inaccurate, since he refers to *reported* cases, not all cases, of rape.

148. Georges Duby, "Youth in Aristocratic Society: Northwestern France in the Twelfth Century," in *The Chivalrous Society* (Berkeley and Los Angeles, 1977), 112–22; see also Duby, *The Age of Cathedrals* (Chicago, 1981), 255.

149. Marc Bloch, *Feudal Society* (Chicago, 1961), 411.

150. James B. Given, *Society and Homicide in Thirteenth-Century England* (Stanford, 1977), 35. I must point out that Given's Warwick homicide rate is the highest of the ones he has collected and that his rates are highly sensitive to his

century England, 23 percent of all felony indictments were for homicide. In the English county of Warwick, in 1232, the homicide rate was 64/100,000; in Florence in 1352–1355 it was 152/100,000.[151] Moreover, these statistics are likely to massively undercount the murder rate. There is no way of knowing the proportion of crimes that were subjected to judicial proceedings, and there is an almost complete lack of prosecution for violence directed downward, against the lower classes. Intrafamily violence is also remarkable for its absence from the court records. All students of the subject are in agreement that males composed the overwhelming majority of both victims and perpetrators. If, indeed, violence was a tool reserved largely for men, then it is equally relevant to note that we have no idea of the level of violence aimed at women, which was not considered to be worth the courts' time. Significantly, women who murdered men were more likely to be convicted and executed than men who murdered women. Women who murdered their husbands were regarded as treasonous, whereas husbands who killed their wives were treated as mere murderers.

This society was far less forgiving to the traitor than the killer whose violence was the result of passion. The whole ceremony of ritual punishment was dragged out to make spectacle of the traitor. The killer simply sloughed off his mortal coil.[152] Criminal statistics may not be representative, yet they still tell a terrible story of swift and deadly escalation from argument to murder. There were few restraints on interpersonal violence. Most killing occurred between acquaintances, often in the midst of drinking bouts. Because knives were carried by all, little provocation apparently was needed for their use in settling matters.

---

population estimates. M. Patricia Hogan's analysis gives a rather low estimate of homicide—one occurrence between 1290 and 1350—in the local society covered by the manorial court rolls of Warboys. This single instance of murder is thought to reflect local undercounting as a result of the royal courts' takeover of capital crimes; "Medieval Villainy: A Study in the Meaning and Control of Crime in an English Village," *Studies in Medieval and Renaissance History*, new ser., 2 (1979): 123–215, esp. 149–50). See also Marvin B. Becker, "Changing Patterns of Violence and Justice in Fourteenth- and Fifteenth-Century Florence," *Comparative Studies in Society and History* 18 (1976): 287; S. R. Blanshei, "Crime and Law Enforcement in Medieval Bologna," *Journal of Social History* 16 (1982): 121–38; and Barbara Hanawalt, "Violent Death in Fourteenth- and Early Fifteenth-Century England," *Comparative Studies in Society and History* 18 (1976): 302.

151. What do these numbers mean? In Canada in 1988, for example, the murder rate was 2.5/100,000. Britain's rate was one-third of Canada's, whereas in the United States, the murder rate was about three times the Canadian rate.

152. Given, *Society and Homicide*, 149. See also Hanawalt, "Violent Death," 306; Andrew Finch, "Women and Violence in the Later Middle Ages: The Evidence of the Officiality of Cerisy," *Continuity and Change* 7 (1992): 23–45.

4.

It would be shortsighted, however, to consider only the public and physical manifestations of brutality. Violence was also a social act which both reflected and reinforced the disadvantages of those without power. One way of considering this structural inequality is by setting it in the framework suggested by Amartya Sen's argument that famines are as much the product of socially constructed exchange "entitlements" as they are the result of deficient harvests. In Sen's analysis, access to the marketplace and informal arrangements between producers and consumers are at least as important as productivity itself.[153] In the public economy, then, those without power were obviously disadvantaged and, equally obviously, suffered as a result of their lack of entitlement to the social product.

The political economy of feudalism pivoted on the flow of wealth from primary producers upward to those who controlled the social construction of entitlements. In crude terms, the manor and the market were the primary channels through which wealth flowed, while the legal system acted to regulate that flow. The peasant family was also socially constructed to endow "the old and the male" and thereby to provide them with superior entitlements by virtue of their position atop upward flows of wealth which "include consumption: the kind and amount of food eaten, precedence in feeding, the clothing customarily worn, use of house space and facilities, and access to transport. They include power and access to services: who can tell who to do what; the right to be pampered and have the little services performed that make life graceful; the guarantee of support in argument, danger, or a bid for social and political power; and the right to make unchallenged decisions. They include labour: the amount of work done, the kind of work done, the right to control one's own working time, and access to leisure or to activities (such as bargaining) that give real pleasure."[154]

Because of their age and their experience, old men and women claimed to have greater knowledge of everyday affairs than younger ones. Authority might be delegated, although it ultimately depended on control over the means of production—and the concomitant threat of disinheritance. One of the key strategies for its implementation was the differential duties demanded from, and the differential rights given to, the young and the female. The violence of the status quo was wrapped in these gendered, intergenerational wealth flows. This was the crucial infraculture of the patriarchal family. It buttressed the entitlements of the old and the male while

153. Amartya Sen, *Poverty and Famines* (Oxford, 1981).
154. Caldwell, *Theory of Fertility Decline*, 165.

providing the cultural code within which those of the young and the female were downgraded. Not only were they to suffer and to be still, they were also advised to wait for their turn to lord it over their underlings.[155]

Our best evidence of the operation of differential entitlements leading to an upward wealth flow comes from the mechanisms that were developed to ensure an orderly transmission of land between generations. It needs to be emphasized that this evidence is from the workings of the seigneurial administration, whose primary interest was the maintenance of a competently run peasant tenement that could supply both rent and labor services. For this reason, these sources tell us more about the patriarchal upper tier of the servile population than either the customary smallholders or the landless or the free peasantry. In addition, these sources tend to tell us rather more about the prescriptive expectations of seigneurs (and their administrators) than the everyday reality of peasant families, since we know about their experiences from their relationship to these courts. Finally, these sources are concentrated in the century before the Black Death when the colonizing thrust of expansion was ending and the rural world was entering a period of involutional entropy. This was a zero-sum game in which the maintenance of the peasant patriarchy was one side of a coin whose other side was the inexorable downward mobility of those who were neither peasants nor patriarchs. So, we might first consider these expectations with regard to the reproduction of the normative family cycle: marriage, intergenerational transmission, and aging. Simple paradigms splinter on close inspection.

Marriage was a complex process. The two consenting partners must often have seen themselves as objects to be manipulated, not the emotional subjects of a sacramental union. For the children of peasant patriarchs, marriage was hardly a matter of free choice—servile status created limited horizons in the sense that it segregated the population they were at risk of marrying. Within the customary tenantry, another limitation restricted

155. On an everyday basis, however, the politics of entitlement frequently came into conflict with the discourse of honor. Evidence from the exceptionally well-documented Ramsey Abbey manors suggests that while men were the more frequent slanderers, women were brought to court for bold words almost as often. In terms of class differences, it appears that the poor were more likely to be brought to court for their slanders against their social superiors than the other way around. Yet there was a critical difference in this legal transcript since men spoke ill of one another in ways that were connected to their public activities, whereas women cast doubt on each other's private honor by casting aspersions on another's sexual fidelity; Patricia Hogan, "The Slight to Honor—Slander and Wrongful Prosecution in Five Medieval Villages," *Medieval and Renaissance Studies*, new ser., 12 (1991): 3–42.

the pool of eligibles still further—marriage off the manor, or outside the multimanorial empire of domination, posed further problems. The lord's property in the peasant would be devalued when marriage occurred outside seigneurial control; it meant the loss "without hope of recall, [of] the breeders plus all cultivators and other revenue-producers the couple would produce."[156] The use of the term "breeders" in the previous sentence is tendentious but also revealing.

There is little evidence to suggest that seigneurial authorities arranged the peasantry's marriages or constantly intervened in their family formations. If anything, in fact, the opposite appears closer to the mark. The peasantry may have been valued because of their ability to breed, but the choice of partner seems to have usually been their own concern. The lord's concern was to make sure that such marriages did not deplete his landed estate by draining it of present and future labor power and revenue sources. In this way, the marital horizons for the customary tenantry were limited by the political framework of feudalism, which bore down with unequal pressure on sons and daughters, and much more heavily on the firstborn than on his younger siblings. For these most privileged of children, there was a strong element of both class and manorial endogamy because, in a sense, the firstborn son paid for his inheritance by narrowing his marital choice to the daughters of other peasant patriarchs. Additionally, it is probably the case that the firstborn son's freedom of choice was further impeded by the actions of the wider family and kin network in the courtship and marriage process.

There were two aspects to this familial control of marriage. The first relates to the timing of such marriages, since a firstborn son often could not marry without his living father's permission to enter the marriage market; and the second concerns the actual choice of spouse, because even after the son had become eligible, he had still to receive his father's agreement to the betrothal. It was at this point in the proceedings that the interplay between the younger and older generations came to the fore. It was not enough to discover an attractive match; it was also necessary to find a suitable match. This was the product of a four-sided decision-making process—two individuals and two sets of parents—in which no one player had veto power. It was probably as difficult for a young woman to resist the imprecations of her parents as it was for a young man to sway his. If all these conditions were met, then courtship would lead to marriage, and marriage would lead to the creation of a new family unit.

156. Paul A. Brand and Paul R. Hyams, "Debate: Seigneurial Control of Women's Marriage," *Past and Present* 99 (1983): 130–31.

Let us pause now to consider courtship behavior leading up to the marriage of these peasants. What is most striking about the scholarly discussion of these matters is their small evidentiary base. A reasonably coherent picture can be developed from it, although we know more about the stages in the marriage process than about the methods of courtship.[157] Once freed to enter the marriage market, the first son of a peasant patriarch must have known that only a minority of the village women were likely to be considered a suitable match, so whether his (or her) choice was free is somewhat beside the point. Rather, both must have known each other since childhood. The key to initiating courtship would have been the agreement between both sets of parents and their children that a new life-cycle stage had been reached, signaling to the younger generation that the very character of their relationship was now fraught with new possibilities. What triggered this new phase in the life-cycle? A couple of factors were at work: the aging (or death) of the older generation and the maturation of the younger one would have been necessary causes, but not sufficient in themselves. What was probably of more significance in daily life was the relationship between the heir or heiress and his or her peer group. If we consider that the sons and daughters of the peasant patriarchs were members of a villagewide youth culture, then it would be almost impossible for their behavior to have been uninfluenced by it.

Oddly, the personal, sexual, and marital freedom of noninheriting younger siblings would have acted as a solvent on the restrictive powers of the older generation. Their sociability, seemingly characterized by flirtatious behavior and a casual attitude to premarital sex and illegitimacy, was the concern of moralists and the fear of parents. The generational battle in the homes of the peasant patriarchs could not have been uninfluenced by this social milieu—sons and daughters had in their disposition over themselves a card of their own to play. Moreover, this youthful card was enhanced by the Church's rules of consensual marriage, which sanctioned clandestine unions. Because a troth (promise) made a binding marriage in the eyes of the Church, the best-laid plans of a peasant patriarch could come unstuck if he was blind to the urges of his son or his daughter. This suggests that the culture of maypoles, youth guilds, dancing, festivals, games, and even the solemnities of the Church's ritual calendar all gave a measure of bargaining power to those who had reached puberty. It further suggests that parental power was not absolute, even if it was backed by the

157. What follows in the next paragraphs is based on my reading of Homans, *English Villagers of the Thirteenth Century* (160–76) and Hanawalt, *The Ties That Bound* (188–204).

threat of disinheritance. Those who married for love against the will of their parents must have faced a bleak future, but parents who too readily exercised their veto also ran risks, since much of their status and authority derived from their role in presiding over a peasant lineage. If it ran into a dead end, they would be empty-handed.

These schematic points describe the intrinsic complexity of the bargaining process and its kaleidoscopic potential for splintering individual experience. Recognizing that it is impossible to recover the motivations which triggered particular marriages, historians have sought to understand the marital strategies of the peasantry by creating a stylized description of the sum of these individual acts and decisions, which took place within a general set of social, economic, political, and personal factors. Given our sparse evidence, it is not possible to probe further into these matters. Having entered the marriage market and picked an appropriate partner, the courtship process slid into a familiar sequence of customary conventions.

> After the hand fasting & makyng of the contracte, the church goyng & weddyng shulde not be deffered to long, lest the wicked sowe hys vngracious sede in the mene season. . . . For in some places ther is such a maner, wel worthy to be rebuked, that at the hand fastynge there is made a great feast & superfluous bancket, & even the same night are the two hand fasted persones brought & layd together, yea certayne wekes afore they go to the church.[158]

In cases where property was a paramount concern, marriage contracts were drawn up and earnest money was exchanged. These details were often recorded in the full publicity of the manor court. Occasionally, eager peasant patriarchs enlisted the court's services while their children were still infants. But such instances are exceptional—the Church forbade child marriage, since it was considered impossible for a minor to give his or her informed consent.

The couple's marriage covenant had several dimensions. First, there was the settlement of material goods and landed property. Second, there was the public *trothplight* by which the couple announced their intentions. Third, there was the wedding in the Church and the ring ceremony. In

158. Miles Coverdale, *The Christen State of Matrimonye* (c. 1541); quoted in Homans, *English Villagers of the Thirteenth Century,* 164. Homans suggests that Coverdale's words carry conviction as a description of the behavior of countryfolk throughout the Middle Ages although nothing comparable has been discovered for that period. Coverdale's description is compatible with what is known. The reader will note the strong tone of prescriptive contempt that runs through this account.

most cases, these three stages followed one another in an orderly succession. However, there was no need for a settlement, a *public* trothplight, or a clerically sanctioned wedding. In terms of both the common law and the Church, a *private* agreement between the two partners was sufficient to constitute a legal, Christian marriage.

Why, then, did publicity surround each and every one of the three stages? In the first place, marriage was a rite of passage—from dependency to adulthood in the eyes of the couple's family and the wider community. Second, publicity sanctioned the match and was a means of granting approval to it. Third, publicity eliminated hidden impediments to a successful marriage, such as previous agreements and duplicitous scheming, by bringing the agreement into full view. Fourth, publicity and approval gave the match both legal and moral standing before the law and the Church. Fifth, publicity legitimated all subsequent children of the union. Sixth, publicity and communal approval enabled the servile population to enlist the Church on its side in the event that seigneurial authorities tried to thwart the choice of marriage partners.

Marriage was the key moment in the reproduction of the social system. It created a new unit, although it did not necessarily create a fully independent one. Among the peasant patriarchy it would seem that the first-born son's marriage often took place before the tenement had been transferred. As we have seen in Halesowen, inter vivos property transfers were common. The land market was another way in which a young couple could be settled while the peasant patriarch continued to enjoy the status of househead. The element of demographic lottery is relevant here, too, since it was likely to have been the case that only a minority of men who married still had living fathers. Other men married into the headship of another tenement, while some were lucky enough to inherit collaterally from a deceased relative without children. Furthermore, for the son who married while still in a dependent position vis-à-vis his father, there was a strong possibility that the marriage agreement contained a formal recognition of the older man's retirement and the younger man's responsibilities. And, of course, even surviving fathers did not live forever, so that the period of overlap when a tenement was organized as a functionally extended unit was most probably quite short. In addition, the new couple was connected to both its paternal and maternal families, which gave them more room to maneuver insofar as the new couple's kinship network was not simply a direct clone of that provided by the husband's father.

For the young married man, the wife's family connections supplied a range of options which could be called on to modify his father's control over the landed patrimony.[159] The peasant credit market, too, could supply bridging loans to smooth the transition from youth to adulthood via marriage and househeadship. Some youngsters, most probably junior members of the village elite, purchased a tenancy by taking on a vacant holding if they could raise the money to pay an entry fine.[160] Marriage and the assumption of househeadship were loosely coordinated so that close inspection privileges the individual parts at the expense of the whole process of social reproduction.

5.

In the foregoing discussion, young women have been both mute and passive. What was their role in the courtship process? What were their expectations from marriage? Again, silence speaks volumes with regard to their disenfranchisment but it does not tell us much about their sufferings and satisfactions. If we are unable to capture women's voices, we can nonetheless situate their experiences in the process of courtship and the institution of marriage. Our point of departure should be the elemental fact that all women, except only daughters, departed from their parental home at marriage while many men did not. For a woman, then, marriage was a double passage—from child to adult and from her father's home to her husband's. This often meant transferring completely out of her natal community, which was thick with kin ties, into another in which her only bonds passed through her husband and her husband's family. If she brought wealth with her—and most daughters of the peasant patriarchs were dowered—then this also passed from her father into her husband's control until his death. Moreover, her dowry was usually a final payment from her natal family's fund of wealth so that when her parents died she was unlikely to receive anything more.

In terms of their entitlements, then, daughters were doubly disadvantaged: first, because they received less than an equal or fair share even if they were the firstborn child, and second, because bargaining with regard to the dowry was characterized by the patriarch's desire to keep this outlay to a minimum. If eldest daughters' life chances were relatively impaired, then those of their younger sisters were much worse. If younger sons al-

---

159. Bennett, "The Tie That Binds," 123–25.

160. For a discussion of the peasant credit market, see M. M. Postan, *The Medieval Economy and Society* (Harmondsworth, 1975), 137; and Elaine Clark, "Debt Litigation in a Late Medieval English Vill," in Raftis (ed.), *Pathways to Medieval Peasants*, 263–64, 253–54.

most inevitably experienced downward social mobility, then younger sisters descended the social scale faster and more precipitously.

Women were socialized from infancy to conform to a traditional position of relative powerlessness. They had this message reinforced by a panoply of ideological structures, feudal and clerical as well as those of the popular culture of village society and the family itself. It seems that children as young as two or three were already modeling themselves after their same-sex parent. As they grew older this patterning was reinforced by the gendered organization of work.[161] Once again, we might ask "When Adam delved / and Eve spun / Who was then / the Gentleman?" It is not surprising that John Ball's egalitarianism was confined to the horizons of class; he simply could not conceive that the sexual division of labor could be altered. He was not alone in this view, and it would be surprising if many of his contemporaries were able to break free to imagine a quite different reality. The structures of gender domination must have seemed inevitable, so that most women acquiesced in their subordination. Their acquiescence was a reflection of their lack of entitlement—a clear example of the situation about which Amartya Sen writes "persistent inequality and exploitation often thrive by making passive allies out of the mistreated and the exploited."[162]

Women's aspirations—and also their socially constructed entitlements—were therefore encapsulated in a "female consciousness" which accepted the relative deprivation of gendered inequality and the sexual division of labor.[163] Their self-image derived from their social role as wives and their biological role as mothers. These roles gave them the responsibility of nurturing and perpetuating life itself. It should not be surprising to find women upholding the sexual division of labor because it defined what women do and therefore provided them with a sense of who they were in society, popular culture, and the family. The public face of a woman's work involved gathering and distributing the community's social resources—

161. Hanawalt, *The Ties That Bound*, 146, 157–61. She notes that young boys' identification with their fathers' work was somewhat more muted than that of young girls since sons were expected to help their mothers with housework and yardwork whereas daughters were not normally engaged in fieldwork (160–61).

162. Amartya Sen, "Individual Freedom as a Social Commitment," *New York Review of Books*, June 14, 1990, 51. He also writes that "The absence of present discontent or felt radical desires cannot wipe out the moral significance of this inequality if individual freedom—including the freedom to assess one's situation and the possibilities of changing it—is accepted as a major value."

163. Temma Kaplan, "Female Consciousness and Collective Action: The Case of Barcelona, 1910–1918," *Signs* 7 (1982): 545–46, 565–66. The next sentences are drawn from this illuminating discussion.

she judged herself by her ability to perform tasks and duties that were associated with being female. The private face of her work involved parenting and the daily preservation and reproduction of her family's labor power. Female consciousness was intimately connected with a woman's role as wife and mother. Female consciousness was also concerned with the way in which these activities were valued by the wider community. In this way, women's work had a definite place underpinning the hierarchy of daily life.

Female consciousness was not a privatizing vision; indeed, quite the opposite. Accepting the sexual division of labor was no doubt a means of survival, but it also provided women with a strong sense of collective rights, which they used to sustain the reproduction of their families. Insofar as they were involved in collective behavior, this meant that they demanded the rights their domestic and reproductive obligations entailed. It enables us to make sense of peasant women's concurrence that their biology explained their destiny.[164] It also provides us with the framework within which they worked. Barbara Hanawalt writes that because there was little available work for women outside the home, a peasant "woman's contribution was made within the context of her family. Women's work was more often directed toward the private household economy than the public one of the manor."[165] Peasant women infrequently found work outside the household—usually women worked outside the private sphere only during the harvest, although in the context of the general labor shortage after the Black Death this occurred rather more often—while her husband's work site was in the fields or forests: Adam delved (dug) . . . Eve span (spun).

Spinning was only one activity from among a vast repertoire with which a woman maintained her family. She collected kindling and made the fire; she foraged for nuts, berries, and herbs; she milked and pastured cows; she made cheese and butter; she fed the poultry and collected eggs; she had charge of the family pig; she tended the garden and orchard; she baked bread and brewed ale; and she was involved in cottage crafts which might involve both making the cloth and sewing the clothing her family wore. For most, this was a subsistence economy. While many medieval villages had a large service sector, it was by no means within the reach of all women to pay others to do this work because most women simply did not

164. On the other hand, the *beguines* were an urban group, and women who rejected their biological destiny, like Mary of Oignies, were overwhelmingly from bourgeois backgrounds.

165. Hanawalt, *The Ties That Bound*, 141.

have the ready cash with which to pay specialists.[166] Moreover, most artisans did not replicate the work which a housewife was expected to perform on a daily basis. Cooking, cleaning, and the unremitting burden of fetching water from the well were part of her daily cycle of domestic reproduction. In terms of the biological reproduction of the family, women, of course, got pregnant and bore babies, suckled them in infancy, instructed them—particularly their daughters—as they matured, and nursed them in their sicknesses.

Was the peasant woman's double day of labor regarded as more demanding than her husband's? The contemporary "Ballad of the Tyrannical Husband" suggests that while there was a keen awareness of the differences in the nature of men's and women's work, a concern with inequality was not mobilized toward social criticism but rather against individual men who were abusive, brutal, uncaring, thoughtless, neglectful, and/or too demanding of their spouses.[167] Gendered roles within the peasant family were expected to be unequal. Even though they were based on the ideal of reciprocity, the daily reality was one of dissimilar workloads. Despite—or maybe even because of—this disability, women's contribution was more valuable.

Peasant women held up more than half the sky. Remarriage rates for men were very high because, for a peasant farmer, the only thing worse than a lazy wife was a dead one. For the peasant widow, remarriage rates were high only when her property *usufruct* gave her an uncommon attraction to a man seeking to gain or to extend his standing in the village community. Widows were sometimes forced into a second (or third) marriage because lords were concerned to have their land tenanted by male househeads. Lords considered these unmarried women to be unprofitable tenants who were economically vulnerable and therefore likely to fail in paying their dues. In addition, there is evidence that among the customary population of the manor such widows were fined for remaining single and some were designated spouses by the manorial administration although many chose to pay the fine and thus to preserve their consent in the choice of a mate.[168] It is germane to note that the second husbands of these wid-

166. For a useful discussion of the situational character of much household production, see Judith M. Bennett, "The Village Ale-Wife: Women and Brewing in Fourteenth-Century England," in B. Hanawalt (ed.), *Women and Work in Pre-Industrial Europe*, 20–36.

167. Quoted in Hanawalt, *The Ties That Bound*, 146–47.

168. E. Clark, "The Decision to Marry," *Mediaeval Studies* 49 (1987): 500–2, 508–9; M. Mate, "The Agrarian Economy of South-east England before the Black Death: Depressed or Buoyant?," in Campbell (ed.), *Before the Black Death*, 96.

ows were often young, landless men whose value to the widowed, peasant matriarch was precisely their youth and their vigor. In addition, it speaks to the way in which even seigneurs valued legitimate marriage that they made it impossible for such a woman to keep an unmarried male servant in her household.[169] Conversely, remarriage rates were low for landless widows because they were doubly disabled: without economic compensation, they were already burdened with another man's children.

It is stretching matters to suggest that this marriage was one of "rough equality."[170] The peasants' marital economy was a "partnership in which each person contribute[d] a specialized skill that complements the other."[171] These women were expected to do a double day of labor and were without independent civil rights within the peasant community. It was, for all intents and purposes, impossible for women to act in the public sphere. If this was a "partnership," then it was an unequal one. The expectation of "partnership" played a significant role in joining together men and women of roughly similar ages. Most likely, this expectation was a crucial ingredient in making consent on the part of the prospective husband and wife something more than lip service. Bad as it was, gendered inequality in feudal society was still an improvement for women compared to the earlier situation in late antiquity, when monogamy was uncommon, adultery was frequent, divorce was routine, marital breakup was subject to the impulse of their masters, and the servile population surrendered humiliating payments for "wife-rent" to their lord.[172]

6.

Women were totally responsible for nurturing infants and largely responsible for protecting and instructing toddlers. While little boys may have fashioned themselves after their fathers, they spent most of their time with their mothers until they were about eight years old. What was the character of parent-child relations? The prescriptive literature—often written by

169. Peter Franklin, "Peasant Widows' 'Liberation' and Remarriage before the Black Death," *Economic History Review*, 2d ser., 39 (1986): 199, 200, 203.

170. Eileen Power, *Medieval Women* (Cambridge, 1975), 75.

171. Barbara Hanawalt, "Peasant Women's Contribution to the Home Economy," in *Women and Work in Pre-Industrial Europe*, 17. For the way in which married women's economic activities outside the household were connected to the internal, class-specific political economy of the domestic sphere, see also Helena Graham, " 'A woman's work . . .': Labour and Gender in the Late Medieval Countryside," in Goldberg (ed.), *Woman Is a Worthy Wight*, 126–48.

172. Jean Scammell, "Freedom and Marriage in Medieval England," *Economic History Review*, 2d ser., 27 (1974): 532–35.

celibates—tended toward stern discipline. Was this a reflection of social reality or a model that was to be imposed upon it in the hope of changing it?
Barbara Hanawalt has devised a very clever way to address this question
through the use of coroners' inquests, which read like "a very succinct
snapshot of life. The intimate detail of scenes comes through in rich texture
as neighbours and witnesses reconstructed" the event leading up to a death
by misadventure.[173] Her most striking finding is that the motor skills and
behavior patterns of medieval peasants' children matured according to
stages that are familiar to modern observations of child development.[174]

The birth of a child was a significant event that was surrounded by ritual
actions welcoming it into the community of its family and the wider community of Christian believers. Through the institution of godparenthood,
the social effect of baptism was to create a unique kinship network for each
particular child.[175] After baptism, the baby was kept tightly wrapped in
swaddling clothes for most of its first year, so that they were usually wet
and/or dirty. The baby thus probably suffered from a variety of skin infec-
tions. The medical/prescriptive literature was not unaware that the baby's
general health would benefit from regular bathing, but the likelihood that
such suggestions would be followed in detail seems remote. The infant's
needs were only one among many demands for its mother's attention.

173. Hanawalt, *The Ties That Bound*, vii. The following paragraphs are based
on chap. 11, "Childhood" (171–87). I have also benefited from reading Shulamith
Shahar's *Childhood in the Middle Ages* (London, 1990), which I will footnote
where appropriate.

174. Jean Piaget suggests that childhood can be divided as follows: "infancy" =
birth to about two years, "early childhood" = two to seven, "middle childhood" =
seven to twelve, and "adolescence" = after twelve; *Six Psychological Studies* (New
York, 1967), 5–6. Erik Erikson offers a slightly different timing sequence: "infancy"
= birth to fifteen months, "early childhood" = fifteen to thirty months, "the age of
play" = thirty months to six years, "school age" = six to puberty, and "youth" =
puberty to twenty; "Eight Ages of Man," in *Childhood and Society* (New York,
1963), 247–74. The medievals themselves followed classical prescriptions and divided childhood into three stages: *infantia* = birth to seven years, *pueritia* = seven
to twelve for girls and seven to fourteen for boys, and *adolescentia* = twelve/
fourteen to adulthood. However, they also had another category for postadoles-
cents, which they called *juventus*, that seemed to be concerned with unmarried
young men. Some medieval writers who accepted these conventional categories
nonetheless subdivided them so that they ended up with a description rather like
Piaget's or Erikson's; Shahar, *Childhood in the Middle Ages*, 22–31.

175. John Bossy, "Blood and Baptism: Kinship, Community and Christianity in
Western Europe from the Fourteenth to the Seventeenth Centuries," in Derek
Baker (ed.), *Sanctity and Secularity: The Church and the World* (Oxford, 1973),
129–43; see also Lynch, *Godparents and Kinship, passim*.

The swaddled child was normally confined to her or his cradle, near the fire. This bodily confinement was necessary, first, because peasant homes were impossible to childproof, and second, because their mothers had to get on with their daily routine of housework, baking, brewing, gardening, and minding the animals and fowl. So, babies were left unattended for periods of time and were most liable to have fatal accidents during the busiest hours of the day and the most demanding seasons of the year, May through August. These peasants' infants were nursed for two or three years, although they were not fed on demand, since their mothers were not always present. Peasant women sometimes also acted as wet nurses, suckling the children of townswomen or aristocrats. Such women had often already lost their own child, but sometimes poor wet nurses sacrificed their baby's health to perform this fiscally rewarding undertaking. It was generally unknown for peasant women to nurse the children of their kin and neighbors as an obligation, without payment.

If this mode of child care was the product of "neglect," as has sometimes been suggested, then it is necessary to show that realistic alternatives were available and were ignored. There is some suggestion that parents tried to arrange for child care—often by children or old women but never their fathers or grandfathers. There seems to be little evidence that peasant mothers shared this task among themselves. It is in the nature of the coroners' inquests that there is little evidence that parents were distraught over these accidental deaths but quite a lot to show that they were willing to risk their own lives to save their children by running into burning buildings and by jumping into rivers or ponds.

The evidence from coroners' inquests suggests that as soon as babies could creep and crawl they were allowed to do so when a child-minder was present. Infantile curiosity led them to play with fire, to get themselves scalded in hot liquids, and to fall into deep water. Indeed, the most dangerous years for children were those when they were able to take a lively interest in the environment and to explore it. Between the ages of one and three, about two-thirds of accidental deaths were related to child's play and occurred at home or just outside the front door of the cottage. For unswaddled toddlers, the peasant's world was fraught with hazards. Many died accidentally from falling into a body of water—a well, a pond, a pool, a deep puddle, a ditch, a river, or a stream.

By the age of three the incidence of accidental death began to diminish, which testifies to children's greater motor skills as well as their enhanced knowledge of their environment's dangers. Children surviving to four began a long, slow process of integration into their parents' world of work as they could begin to move about freely, without close supervision. They seem to have been given lots of latitude but, for transgressors, corporal punishment was normal. There is not one jot of evidence that outsiders intervened in parental discipline, no matter how brutal or abusive.

Between the ages of eight and twelve, boys slowly changed into little men and girls became little women. Most still lived at home. What was the emotional climate of the home? Evidence is unfortunately skimpy. The most that we can discern is that, from infancy, children were instructed in their lullabies to be grateful to their mothers for rearing them. A strong sense of solidarity with the common worries of survival of both individual and family was inculcated in them. The massive proliferation of images and stories relating to the Virgin Mary made motherhood a sentimental ideal of such charismatic energy that even misogynistic literature gave women respect in fulfilling this role. Fatherhood was identified with mastery; children were expected to obey.

Were parents emotionally distant? This is a very difficult question to answer since the sources never seem to have considered interpersonal relations in these terms. Perhaps the most that we can say is that while parents were demanding in their expectation that children render them obedience, there is a great deal of other evidence that parents for their part were willing to sacrifice for their children's present health and future well-being. When a teenager, St. Anselm of Canterbury had been distraught at his mother's death: "the ship of his heart had, as it were, lost its anchor and drifted almost entirely among the waves of the world."[176] It seems that this bond was weaker when children were given up at birth. Thus, for example, Héloïse never mentions their child in her letters to Abelard.[177]

Many children were orphaned, but they were not ignored as long as they were property holders. Lords made it their business to see that these youthful tenants rendered the services to which they were liable in much the same way that a widow's marital condition was a matter of seigneurial concern. As Elaine Clark notes, "the custom of guardianship assured both the lord and the community that productive lands would be in the hands of productive workers." Thus, for the orphans of customary tenants, the demands of lordship were an ever-present influence which shaped the per-

---

176. Quoted in Shahar, *Childhood in the Middle Ages*, 158.
177. We only know of their child's destiny because Abelard noted that it was entrusted to his sister in Brittany; Shahar, *Childhood in the Middle Ages*, 154.

ception and experience of childhood in the interest of the efficient functioning of the seigneurial estate.[178]

So, the family unit was not usually defined as a biological lineage but rather was a co-residential community. Beyond generalities, we are rarely able to discern answers to our questions about interpersonal relationships within these households. Were fathers given first priority at the table when food was in short supply? Were boys given more food than girls? One would probably venture to give affirmative answers to the two preceding questions if only because that would seem to follow from the patriarchal organization of wealth flows. Were shoes and clothes distributed so that all children had an equal opportunity to keep warm and dry? And what about the inevitable demands for fair treatment by those who felt hard done by? Answering these two questions is more difficult because we cannot witness these people talking with one another in order to judge the texture of their exchanges. Efforts to pierce this darkness are futile. A few scattered examples are probably as misleading as they are unrepresentative. We have reached a penumbral region of uncertainty. It is best, therefore, to satisfy ourselves with an image of childhood dominated by the struggle for survival in which a substantial identification with their family's common destiny was inculcated into children as a central part of their socialization.

7.

Directing the peasant family toward its common destiny was the uncontested province of the patriarch, although the application of patriarchal power was modified by the complexity of everyday life. If the peasant patriarch was the dominant member of this family unit, his domination was closely tied to the forms of power and his ability to mediate between his family and the wider social universe. For the living peasant patriarch, a vital restriction to his power was built into the role he played in mediating between the seigneur and his own family. Lords were apparently reluctant to permit significant accumulations of property in the hands of their dependent tenants. Indeed, the variable nature of feudal exactions bore down most heavily on those peasants who had the temerity to try and raise themselves above their station. In practice, this meant that very rich peasants who were able to transmit their wealth from generation to generation were still part of the village community, being neither culturally nor socially distanced from their poorer kin and neighbors. Feudalism defined the

178. Elaine Clark, "The Custody of Children in English Manor Courts," *Law and History Review* 3 (1985): 333–47. It hardly seems likely that the landless orphans were granted the same solicitude from communal authorities.

ceiling of upward social mobility for the peasantry in much the same way that marginalization and, ultimately, death marked the lower limit of downward social mobility.

The demographic reality of the period provided another limitation on the power of peasant patriarchs, since only a bare minority could expect to live long enough to lord it over all their children. Given a life expectation at birth of about forty years, one-half of all adult men could expect to live from about twenty-five until their early sixties, when their youngest children would be over twenty.[179] With rather worse prospects, of course, the median age of survival would plummet, and the number of adult men who were cut down in their prime further reduced this capacity for domination. Furthermore, we should also expect that there was a certain bias in the aggregated figures since those men from the harvest-sensitive part of the population probably died earlier than the peasant patriarchs who were both better fed and better housed and so less susceptible to wasting diseases such as tuberculosis or pneumonia.

The father who was generous toward his children probably had more hope of gentle treatment in his old age than the cottage tyrant. Thus we find evidence of patriarchs who arranged for an orderly, inter vivos transmission of the landed patrimony so that he and his wife could retire with a separate room or small hut, a garden, and something approaching pension rights.[180] These land-transfer agreements were always conditional on the heir's performance of his obligations. To the extent that the land market enabled peasant patriarchs to provide smallholdings for their younger sons, these children were under the control of their father and stood in the shadow of the firstborn son. Obviously, the value of a smallholding to a younger son was highly dependent upon context, so that the patriarch's power was restricted by his ability to offer his younger sons a suitable carrot to tolerate the use of his stick.

The ability of these old men to lord it over their children was provisional. Their control over an endowment gave them power, while the availability of positions beyond the manse would have militated against its deployment. As we have seen, these opportunities—colonization and townward migration would have been preeminent—were not fixed but

179. Based on Ledermann, *Nouvelles tables-types de mortalité*, 153.

180. Elaine Clark, "Some Aspects of Social Security in Medieval England," *Journal of Family History* 7 (1982): 307–20. In the conditions of family discontinuity that prevailed after the ravages of the Black Death, surviving old people often had to arrange maintenance agreements with nonfamily, but these documents record the same concern with contractual obligations and the conditional character of the bequest.

fluctuated over time as well as from place to place.[181] The patriarch may have been the lord and master in his cottage or hut, although, in reality, many decisions must have been reached after discussion between husband and wife. Certainly, this seems to be the only way to make sense of the vast body of evidence from wills in which the majority of men made their wives executors of their estates.[182]

Because the peasant family was in the process of continuously transforming itself, it is something of a mistake to regard the peasant patriarch's power as a commodity. Rather than being a fixed agglomeration of entitlements, this power was constantly being augmented and modified by the exigencies of the family cycle. The way in which external forces intruded upon the process of family formation also played a role in conditioning the upward flows of both wealth and power. No unit of production was self-sufficient, nor could it be in this complex society. Familial independence was organized through the formation of coalitions constructed out of social networks. The peasant patriarch's organizing initiative brought him personal power and enabled him, through the agency of friends and friends of friends, to arrange debts and credits in more or less symmetrical terms even though these people were not always of a similar social status. The most effective coalitions were those constructed by the most strategically placed, who usually acted as brokers between the villagers and the larger structures of power.[183]

Yet no matter how conditional the peasant patriarch's power may have been, it is critical to bear in mind that he had the support of the institutional power structure in using it. This meant that as long as the peasant patriarch's actions were not held to be intolerable—and the common recourse to violence would suggest that the "intolerable" was, in fact, horrific—those under his sway had little option but to put up with him unless they left his household with nothing.

The downward flow of obligations was thus much stronger than the upward flow of rights. In fact, even considering this relationship in terms of

181. The destination of these surplus children, who were thrown out of their natal home and village by the centrifugal forces of family formation, is not a matter of concern for us at this point. The creation of alternative niches was a crucial ingredient in the supersession of the early modern system of production and reproduction.

182. Hanawalt, *The Ties That Bound*, 153.

183. While a great deal of the social history of the medieval English village—and especially the works of those affiliated with the Pontifical Institute in Toronto—seems to conform to this description, I am actually paraphrasing Jane Schneider's discussion of "Family Patrimonies and Economic Behavior in Western Sicily," *Anthropological Quarterly* 42 (1969): 109–29.

rights and obligations lends it a contractual element which could be misleading unless we balance it with the recognition that the essence of patriarchal power was its authority, tempered by acts of kindness that were given by the patriarch out of generosity as a gift. This, then, speaks directly to the point that our predilection for considering the relations within the family as negotiation between equals does violence to the strictly authoritarian technique of patriarchal power. Yet, as must be apparent from the tenor of the previous discussion, overreliance on a model stressing the *patria potestas* (paternal power/authority) is equally deceptive because it overlooks the ways in which the reproduction of family life must be situated in the context of the daily interaction of its members. The point of historical study is not to approve (or disapprove) of social relationships but rather to understand how they were established, why they functioned in particular ways, whose interests they served, and in what circumstances they evolved—or mutated—into new forms. In answering how the character of a historical period impinged on the formation of families and the construction of individual identities, it is critical to consider the interplay between the multiple trajectories of social change and the panoply of existential realities.

8.

It is now time to take stock of how the early modernization of family life took root in European society after the year 1000. Seeing matters in a long-term perspective shows the ways in which the peasant family under feudalism was different from its predecessors while creating new degrees of freedom which would be more fully exploited by its successors.

The culture of the family was transformed in the process of early modernization. Building on the wreckage of antiquity, Christianity and feudalism grew up within the remains of this older social formation. In the ancient world power was exercised by a small number of adult men over most other men, all women, and all young people.

The two most dynamic mutations to emerge in the Christian centuries were the belief in the equality of all believers and the ordered liberties they all enjoyed while living in the *saeculum*, on earth. Freedom was contextual—the freedom of an adult male aristocrat was utterly different from that of a servile woman—but nonetheless, the freedom of all was understood to exist within a Christian framework, so that interpersonal relations henceforward took place between people of equal spiritual worth. This, then, underscores one of the inherent contradictions in the early modernization of social life. Christianity provided the vision of a more democratic society, but feudalism restricted access to it. Even though feudalism provided the contractual elements which promised social inclusion, it was a social system predicated on the exploitation of most of society for the liberation of the few.

We can see these contradictions at work in the operation of discrimination based on class, age, and gender in the realm of the family. At the most personal level, then, social liberation may have been uneven, but it seems obvious to me that these halting steps away from the ancient structures of human servitude were a better thing for those who lived and died in the long middle passage between slavery and freedom—a far, far better thing, in point of fact, than the continuation of ancient society.

5   Negative Feedbacks

THE BACTERIOLOGICAL HOLOCAUST

The Black Death arrived in Europe in 1348; its first visitation killed roughly half the population. The subsequent recurrences of "The Bacteriological Holocaust" kept attacking the remnant, so that by the mid-fifteenth century there was an overall reduction of the population to only one-third its earlier level. This chapter describes the impact of the plague and explains why recovery was so slow.

The pre-plague period is often cited for the "Malthusian" dynamic of "relative overpopulation [which] was so great as to push the death-rates to a punishing height." In the terse words of another authority, "What a 'magnificent' field of action for the Black Death of 1348, that holocaust of the undernourished."[1] While both M. M. Postan and Emmanuel Le Roy Ladurie suggest that there was some connection between poverty, malnutrition, and mortality from plague, neither is able to explain what that linkage might have been. The richer members of the peasantry did not live in more hygienic surroundings, nor were their bodies kept cleaner. The very nature of the plague was that it did not respect persons. There was, in point of fact, no connection between malnutrition, poverty, and death from disease. The Black Death carried off rich and poor, noble and commoner, prelates and parishioners. There is little evidence to suggest that anyone—rich or poor—was especially knowledgeable concerning the nature of the plague or the mode of its transmission. In the culture of the times, it was seen as a sign of divine warning or even judgment on a sinful people.

1. M. M. Postan, *The Medieval Economy and Society* (Harmondsworth, 1995), 38; Emmanuel Le Roy Ladurie, *The Peasants of Languedoc* (Princeton, 1996), 13.

1.

The noxious bacteriological concoction we know as the Black Death had·developed its deadly form among the bacillus, *Yersina pestis*, living in the, stomachs of the fleas, *Xenopsylla cheopsis*, which lived on rodents who were native to the central Asian steppes. The key historical mutation in the bacillus most likely took place as the result of an incorrect genetic replication in the ongoing cycle of reproduction.[2] Then, the interaction between *Yersina pestis* and humans turned deadly.

It would seem that the plague flea breeds most freely and lives longest in the debris of cereals. William McNeill has hypothesized that the rats and

2. There have been recurrent attempts to question the plague's role in the Black Death. Most recently, Graham Twigg has argued that comparisons with the modern versions of the plague create some significant problems in identifying the earlier disease. Twigg argues that the rat flea, which is the primary carrier of the modern plague bacillus, *Yersina pestis*, needs average temperatures above twenty-five degrees centigrade for hatching. The modern plague is thus a warm-weather disease, whereas the Black Death spread across Europe, even reaching polar regions. Furthermore, its impact was not limited to the summer months. Second, the spread of modern plague is comparatively slow—"one epizootic in India took six weeks to travel three hundred feet." In contrast, the Black Death moved at a rate approximating the speed of human foot travel; "The Black Death in England: An Epidemiological Dilemma," in N. Bulst and R. Delort (eds.), *Maldies et société (XIIᵉ–XVIIIᵉ siècles)* (Paris, 1989), 75–98; see also Twigg, *The Black Death: A Biological Appraisal* (London, 1984). Three objections can be made to Twigg's arguments. First, recent DNA testing of sixteenth-century plague victims' remains in southern France have provided new evidence that the infectious agent in the Black Death was, indeed, *Yersina pestis*; cited in Joel E. Cohen, "The Bright Side of the Black Death," *New York Review of Books*, March 4, 1999, 26. Second, Twigg's attempt to compare modern experience of the plague with the Black Death might be misleading because bacilli, like other organisms, can mutate, resulting in a massive increase in their virulence; R. E. Lenski, "Evolution of Plague Virulence," *Nature*, August 11, 1988, 473–74 (cited in Rosemary Horrox, *The Black Death* [Manchester, 1994], 8 n. 8). It is only fair to mention that Twigg has considered and rejected this second point. He notes that *Yersina pestis* is a stable organism, with "still only one stereotype" despite the fact that it now can be found in more than 200 rodent species and 100 flea species; "The Black Death in England: An Epidemiological Dilemma," 93. It would seem, therefore, that this argument will be resolved only when further, refined DNA testing on fourteenth-century victims provides conclusive evidence. Third, most studies of modern plague focus on its bubonic manifestation, whereas there would seem to be a good argument to suggest that the Black Death was, in fact, a deadly combination of bubonic and pneumonic varieties which was active in different places. This would account for the evidence that not all victims had the same symptoms. In this regard, it is crucial to keep in mind that the plague bacillus, *Yersina pestis*, and rat fleas can survive for as long as ten or even twelve weeks away from their rodent hosts. Thus, if there was a new, mutant form of the bacillus which spread from rats to humans *and back again* as the fleas jumped from host to host, this would account for the Black Death's speed of transmission as well as its movement along trade routes.

and newly infected rats' fleas hitched a ride in the grain-stuffed saddlebags of Mongol horsemen who had conquered Eurasia in the thirteenth century. Ironically, in this way, the staff of life became the scepter of death. The Mongols' speed and mobility therefore transferred *Yersina pestis* across the Eurasian steppelands from its earlier enzootic focus in the Himalayan foothills. After its hitchhiking travels, the infection apparently moved from one rodent community to another across the vast expanse of Eurasia. Each *caravanseri* seems to have provided a fertile breeding ground for the new combination of bacillus, fleas, and rodents.

There was no effective method of protection, which made the plague so frightening. It destroyed all bonds of community in a maelstrom of fear and loathing. The primary evidence of contemporary witnesses leaves the reader in no doubt that the Black Death shook European society to its foundations. Three forms of the bacillus were likely to be at work during any eruption of the plague. Most graphic, contemporary evidence probably relates to people who were infected by the *bubonic* mode, which attacked the lymphatic gland system and usually caused death within a few days, although it was not always fatal. The *septicemic* strain attacked the blood stream directly and caused almost immediate death, as did the *pneumonic* variety, which was located in the lungs and could be passed between people. The impact of plague mortality was electrifying, bewildering, and terrifying. Yet, while many died, others survived. Our historical record is inadequate to discover the reasons for resistance to infection and mortality—or both. The sources are, however, in agreement about the character of the disease. Most, but not all, victims would be covered in swellings (buboes) that occurred at the regional lymph node nearest the site of the original infection. For three or four days the victim would vomit blood, and his or her body would be shaken by convulsions as the disease was carried by the bloodstream to other organs. Death usually occurred within seventy-two hours of this external evidence of infection.[3]

Much of this bacteriological history will always remain mysterious, so it is to McNeill's credit—and for our benefit—that he has been willing to speculate about these linkages by pushing his historical evidence against

3. L. F. Hirst, *The Conquest of Plague: A Study of the Evolution of Epidemiology* (Oxford, 1953), 28–30. Larry Poos states that the plague was "enzootic" (i.e., "established in permanent cycles of infection among rodents with further vector spread to humans"), not "endemic," which is the usual term misused by medieval historians; *A Rural Society after the Black Death* (Cambridge, 1991), 112 n. 4. See also J.-N. Biraben, "Current Medical and Epidemiological Views on Plague," *Local Population Studies,* Suppl. (1977): 25–36; L. Bradley, "Some Medical Aspects of Plague," *Local Population Studies,* Suppl. (1977): 11–24.

the grain of epidemiology. While there is a suggestion that, as early as 1331, an epidemic killed nine-tenths of the population of the province of Hopei, in southern China, there is little evidence of its impact on human populations until later. The first really firm proof of its interaction with humans comes from 1346, when the disease broke out in the Mongol armies besieging the Crimean trading town of Caffa.[4] The plague reached southern Europe from the Levant in two separate stages in the fall of 1347. The disease first spread throughout Italy in Genoese ships which had unloaded cargo in Messina in October. The second path of infection radiated from Marseilles following the arrival of ships there in December, 1347. Over the next two years, the disease reached almost every nook and cranny in the European landscape, although there were a few places—such as Bohemia—which, mysteriously, did not seem to have been affected by the first epidemic.

English local historians have tried to gain an insight into the deadly effects of the plague by analyzing the mortality of customary tenants whose deaths were the occasion for transactions in the manorial court. Diversity of experience was a distinguishing hallmark of these documents: while two-thirds died on some manors, in other sources the death rate was "just" one-third. On four manors of the bishop of Winchester, death duties were collected from an annual average of eighty tenants per year in the decade before the Black Death, but in 1348–49 a total of 1,205 heriots were collected, which would suggest that mortality in the first year of the plague was fifteen times more severe than average. On twenty-eight manors of the bishop of Durham, the mortality of tenants ranged from 21 to 78 percent. So, it would not be far off the mark to suggest a 50 percent death rate among adult male peasants. Among ecclesiastics, variability in experience again characterizes the historical record: the deaths of 45 percent of inmates in ten monastic houses were recorded, but "only" 18 percent of bishops. Finally, randomness seems to have been spatially constructed, too: in one English village 747 people died in 1349, while in a similar, neighboring village only five lost their lives.[5] The Black Death was "the most funda-

---

4. William McNeill, Plagues and Peoples (New York, 1976), 140–46. Janet Abu-Lughod notes that, from the 1330s, there is a decline of documentation concerning European traders and missionaries in the Mongol empire. She speculates that this was connected to a decrease in overland trade; she further suggests that the contemporaneous contraction of Flemish textile production and the bankruptcies in Italian banking circles may have been related to the faraway troubles in the trading system; Before European Hegemony: The World System A. D. 1250–1350 (Oxford, 1989), 174–75.

5. John Hatcher, Plague, Population and the English Economy 1348–1530 (London, 1977), 22–23; Edward Miller, "The Occupation of the Land: Southern

mental reality . . . [so that] renewed attacks of the plague undermined the traditional customary-tenant population" of the villages of Ramsey Abbey. Large families were decimated; small families simply vanished.[6]

Among the secular elite in towns and among the landed upper class, the plague's impact was also devastating: they could run, but they couldn't hide. In the Pyrenean town of Perpignan, it seems that about two-thirds of the scribes and legists died during the plague epidemic in 1348.[7] In German Hanseatic towns, for example, about 50 percent of the master artisans, craftsmen, and town governors died in the years 1349–51.[8]

The immediate response to the massive vacancies was a surge of marriages. This testifies to the reserve army of unmarrieds—quite apart from the newly widowed—whose personal desires had been held in check by the land hunger of the pre-plague epoch. It would seem that there was also a baby boom in the immediate post-plague period—"there were pregnant women wherever you looked" in the words of one contemporary—largely as a result of these new marriages.[9] In the Burgundian village of Givry, there were 750 deaths in a population of 1,800 in 1349 as well as eighty-six marriages, whereas in the decade preceding the plague there was an average of ten or twelve marriages.[10]

The historiography of plague mortality is littered with controversy, not infrequently the result of comparing results from different sources. It is crucial to always keep in mind the fact that the people whose deaths were recorded were mostly adult males in the prime of their lives. The historical

---

Counties," in Miller (ed.), *The Agrarian History of England and Wales,* vol. 3, *1348–1500* (Cambridge, 1991), 139; R. A. Lomas, "The Black Death in County Durham," *Journal of Medieval History* 15 (1989): 129; Georges Duby, *Rural Economy and Country Life in the Medieval West* (London, 1968), 298; Robert Gottfried, *The Black Death: Natural and Human Disaster in Medieval Europe* (New York, 1983), 54–76; L. R. Poos, "The Rural Population of Essex in the Later Middle Ages," *Economic History Review,* 2d ser., 38 (1985): 515–30.

6. Ambrose Raftis, *Peasant Economic Development within the English Manorial System* (Montreal, 1996), 68.

7. Richard W. Emery, "The Black Death of 1348 in Perpignan," *Speculum* 42 (1967): 611–21.

8. Wilhelm Abel, *Agricultural Fluctuations in Europe from the Thirteenth to the Twentieth Centuries* (London, 1980), 44–45.

9. Jean de Venette; quoted in Horrox, *The Black Death,* 57. See also Postan, *The Medieval Economy and Society,* 43. On this point regarding the quick response of the surviving population to the openings created by the recurrent bouts of mortality, see David Herlihy and Christiane Klapisch-Zuber, *Tuscans and Their Families: A Study of the Florentine Catasto of 1427* (New Haven, 1985), 81–88.

10. Robert Fossier, "The Great Trial," in *The Cambridge Illustrated History of the Middle Ages,* vol. 3, *1250–1520* (Cambridge, 1986), 55–56.

record is largely silent about the death rate from plague for women, children, and the elderly. Contemporary chroniclers often suggested that the plague's impact was selective, so that adult males' death rates—drawn from "hard" documentary sources—were unlikely to have been representative of all these others. Thus, the second major eruption of bubonic plague in 1361—the so-called *pestis puerorum* (children's plague)—was particularly deadly for those who had had no prior experience of the disease. Similarly, in Languedoc, the first outbreak of the plague in 1348 took its terrible toll in the lowlands spreading along the Gulf of Lion, whereas the next visitation in 1363—known as the "mountain plague"—equalized the casualty count. In northern and central France, the most severe death rates in 1348 occurred among children and the poor, and the death rate was considerably lower there than it was in Languedoc. Those most able to pay taxes were least affected; the number of taxable hearths did not decline sharply until the missing children of the next generation would have become heads of their own households, around 1360.[11] In such places, the recurrence of the plague in 1361 would have been a kind of double jeopardy. Not only was the inheriting generation already diminished by its first experience with the deadly virus in 1348, but the "virgin population" made up of the dead successors' siblings were liable to a similar death toll when they were infected. Overall rates of replacement cannot, therefore, be read off a template constructed from the experience of adult male tenants.[12] Those who survived one epidemic were less likely to be struck down thereafter; perhaps some people had a natural (or acquired) immunity to the disease.[13]

The Black Death attacked the northern and central Italian communes with a spectacular ferocity. The best evidence comes from Tuscany. Flo-

11. Raymond Cazelles, "La peste de 1348–1349 en langue d'oil, epidemie proletarienne et enfantine," *Bulletin philologique et historique* (1962), esp. 298–99, 303–6. For the spatial impact of the first and second visitations of the plague in Languedoc, see Le Roy Ladurie, *The Peasants of Languedoc*, 14.

12. J. C. Russell seems to be unusual in the attention he has given to the age and sex specificity of plague mortality, yet he still determines overall population trends from adult male mortality; *British Medieval Population* (Albuquerque, 1948).

13. Hirst, *The Conquest of Plague*, 440. Certainly, successive outbreaks do not appear to have been as deadly (to adult males) as the initial outbreak; however, there is a huge area of uncertainty about the bacteriology of the Black Death. We know, for instance, that the impact of the bubonic strain was rather less deadly than the pneumonic, but we have no way of knowing which strain was in evidence at different times and in different places. If, as was the case of smallpox in the eighteenth century, there were several competing strains of the disease, then we are simply powerless to provide much more than generalizations.

rence's population fell from roughly 135,000 in 1338 to under 50,000 in 1351. By the time of the 1427 *Catasto*, the city's population was enumerated at 44,068—an overall decline of 68 percent. In the rural area surrounding Florence, losses were only marginally less. The population of Prato, a mid-sized Tuscan commune thirty kilometers northwest of Florence, seems to have begun a slow decline in the generation before mid-century, but thereafter the fall was precipitous. If its enumerated population in 1427 is taken as an index of 100, then Prato's total in 1298–1305 was 424.3. In the countryside of Prato the overall decline was rather less dramatic, from an index figure of 266.6 at the beginning of the fourteenth century down to 100 at the time of the 1427 *Catasto*. In the smaller Tuscan towns of Pistoia, Pisa, Arezzo, Volterra, and San Gimignano, where there was also an initial halving of the taxable hearths, the later fourteenth century was a period of prolonged decline. Later figures suggest a population as little as one-quarter the size of its pre-plague levels. The historians of these demographic relations note that "In the thirteenth century, these secondary Tuscan towns had competed vigorously against one another; and also against Florence. Their subsequent steep demographic decline allowed Florence to consolidate its economic and political hegemony and to assume the status of a regional metropolis."[14]

Siena, Florence's prime rival for power in Tuscany, seems to have been the most grievously wounded Tuscan city if we are to lend credence to the chronicle of an employee in the *Biccherna* (the city's accounting office) who suggests an urban death rate of 84 percent. His own experience was profoundly searing:

> Father abandoned child, wife husband, one brother another; for this illness seemed to strike through the breath and sight. And so they died. And none could be found to bury the dead for money or friendship. Members of a household brought their dead to a ditch as best they could, without priest, without divine offices. Nor did the [death] bell sound. And in many places in Siena great pits were dug and piled deep with the multitude of dead. . . . And I, Agnolo di Tura, called the Fat, buried my five children with my own hands.

I would be remiss if I didn't point out that W. M. Bowsky believes that Agnolo's estimate is "high," but this scepticism is peculiar in that he quotes another, anonymous chronicler to the effect that the plague (in the three months of June, July, and August of 1348) killed three out of every four in the Sienese population. Across the Sienese *contado*, the governing council

---

14. Herlihy and Klapisch-Zuber, *Tuscans and Their Families*, 60–72.

recognized that "decrease is unequal. Some have decreased moderately, others immensely, still others have been completely wiped out."[15] In 1353, for example, the male population of the commune of Sassoforte had fallen to 31 percent of its pre-plague level; the neighboring commune of Montemassi suffered at least a 73 percent death rate among adult males.[16]

Petrarch, who lived through the first fury of the pandemic and lost his lover and many friends, asked the basic question 550 years ago:

> When will posterity believe that there was a time when, without combustion on heaven or earth, without war or other visible calamity, not just this or that country but almost the whole earth was left uninhabited . . . empty houses, deserted cities, unkempt fields, ground crowded with corpses, everywhere a vast and dreadful silence?[17]

A full world was emptied.

In the 1420s plague mortality in Tuscany could still account for nearly twenty per cent reductions in population levels in a single visitation.[18] Even at the end of the fifteenth century, the Florentine demagogue, Savonarola, could frighten the masses who lived in fear of their seemingly inevitable rendezvous with the grim reaper:

> There will not be enough men left to bury the dead; nor means to dig enough graves. So many will lie dead in the houses, that men will go through the streets crying, "Send forth your dead!" And the dead will be heaped in carts and on horses; they will be piled up and burnt. Men will pass through the streets crying aloud, "Are there any dead? Are there any dead?"[19]

Savonarola's audience had good reason to be frightened. The plague did not go away. It returned, again and again, generation after generation.

---

15. W. M. Bowsky, "The Impact of the Black Death upon Sienese Government and Society," *Speculum* 39 (1964): 17–25.

16. The counts of adult male deaths in both Sassoforte and Montemassi are likely to underestimate the actual death toll of the plague since no allowance is made by these numbers for the immigration of replacements from neighboring communities whose experience of the Black Death in 1348 was less horrific. These kind of figures are shards of light in a dark, dark zone of uncertainty; they must be treated with both respect and caution. Incidentally, Sassoforte and Montemassi are the two towns depicted in the background of Simone Martini's famous painting (1328) of the *condottiere* Guidoriccio da Fogliano, which is sometimes held to be the first entirely secular artwork of the Renaissance.

17. Quoted in Hugh Trevor-Roper, *The Rise of Christian Europe* (London, 1965), 165.

18. Herlihy and Klapisch-Zuber, *Tuscans and Their Families*, 60–92.

19. Quoted in Margaret Aston, *The Fifteenth Century* (London, 1968), 15.

There was no effective method of protection, which made the plague so much more frightening. It destroyed all bonds of community in a maelstrom of fear and loathing. As Giovanni Boccaccio wrote in the *Decameron* about the first visitation of plague in Florence, as a result of which "it is reliably thought that over a hundred thousand human lives were extinguished within the walls of the city":

> this scourge had implanted so great a terror in the hearts of men and women that brothers abandoned brothers, and in many cases wives deserted their husbands. But even worse, and almost incredible, was the fact that fathers and mothers refused to nurse and assist their own children, as though they did not belong to them.[20]

2.

This new mortality regime—a recurring cycle of pestilential fury—had become the specter haunting Europe. The primary evidence of contemporary witnesses leaves the reader in no doubt that the Black Death shook European society to its foundations. The impact of plague mortality was so bewildering that the religious art of Florence and Siena became more intense, suggesting "a greater piety or a mystical rapture." In the fresco cycle in Pisa, the image of Christ is given "an angry mien" in his address to the damned. In many paintings "devils, the embodiments of guilt, become more prominent, more aggressive and more vengeful." The effect of the plague, acting in combination with other forces of social disintegration, "tended in fact to polarize society towards strenuous religiosity on the one hand and religious dissidence on the other. The culture of the time is characterized by a heightened tension between the two."[21]

---

20. Giovanni Boccaccio, *Decameron*, ed. G. H. McWilliams (Harmondsworth, 1972), 54. In view of the persistent claim of parents' indifference to their own children's welfare, it is interesting to note that it was "almost incredible" to Boccaccio that parents would abandon their children "as though they did not belong to them." I should also point out that most commentators seem to believe that passive indifference to the suffering of the victims and, especially, disregard for their dead bodies—which was so shocking as to be mentioned by all witnesses of the 1348 visitation—came to be counterbalanced both by attempts at medical intervention (quarantine was slowly introduced in the Venetian territories) and a heroic, penitential willingness to nurse the afflicted and to bury the dead.

21. Millard Meiss, *Painting in Florence and Siena after the Black Death* (Princeton, 1951), 73, 76, 84, 93. After the wrenching shock which resulted from the failures of a number of prominent bankers and the dalliance with a dictatorship in the early 1340s, Tuscans were hard hit by a general crop failure in 1346 and then another dearth in 1347 caused by exceptionally heavy hailstorms. The Black Death, then, was hardly alone in its devastating impact on the social fabric of the Arno city.

This tension may not have been the result of the plague's first visitation but its recurrent outbreaks—in fourteenth-century Italy, for example, in 1362–63, 1373–74, 1383–84, 1389, 1390, and 1399–1400. In terms of cultural practices, the first outbreak of the plague made hardly a ripple, but after the second visitation in the early 1360s there was a transformation in testamentary bequests. In particular, there was a increased interest in preserving testators' individual memories by focusing inheritance on specific forms of remembrance often linked with the name of the founder—social charities, dowry funds for poor respectable girls, gifts to hospitals, chapel foundations, perpetual masses, memorial feasts, monumental plaques, and commissioned artworks—as opposed to the earlier, mendicant model of indiscriminate charity. This change was accompanied by attempts to control property beyond the grave, which also restricted its free disposition. Precisely because the fear of death was widely shared, the psychological impact of recurrent plague epidemics created a more uniform, more democratic mentality which turned on individualism and the cult of memory in the Renaissance.[22]

Sometimes the impact of plague was national, but often it was local and even more virulent. This unpredictability was a variation on a common, recurrent theme which dominated the life of all who lived through this terrible period. In Paris, between 1348 and 1500, there were more than forty separate outbreaks of the plague.[23] In the Netherlands, 45 of the 135 years between 1360 and 1494 suffered national epidemics.[24] In England, there were national epidemics in 30 of the 109 years between 1377 and 1485. John Hatcher argues that the fifteenth-century English outbreaks were harrowingly severe. In northern England, the epidemic struck with particular harshness in the 1430s and then again in the last ten years of the Wars

22. Samuel K. Cohn, Jr., *The Cult of Remembrance and the Black Death* (Baltimore, 1992), *passim*. In making this argument Cohn is setting himself against other historians who argue that the impact of the Black Death did not change cultural practices because, they argue, the experience of death had already been incorporated into their mental landscape. Iris Origo's detailed discussion of Francesco di Marco Datini's response to the somewhat later plague outbreaks largely supports Cohn's hypotheses; see *The Merchant of Prato* (Harmondsworth, 1957), esp. 311–29.

23. J.-N. Biraben, *Les hommes et la peste en France et dans le pays européen et méditerranéens* (Paris, 1976), I:155–90.

24. W. P. Blockmans, "Effects of Plague in the Low Countries," *Revue Belgie de Philologie et Histoire* 58 (1980); cited in Robert Gottfried, *The Black Death*, 133.

of the Roses, 1475–1485.[25] In German territory, there was a recorded plague outbreak in every single year between 1472 and 1545.[26]

The Black Death halved the population as a whole, and in many places it was cut even more drastically. In Languedoc, for example, there was a precipitous decline from 210,000 hearths counted in 1328 to 75,000 in 1382.[27] Further eastward, in the diocese of Geneva, the population in 1339 was almost two and one-half times as large as it would be a century later.[28] The French population was halved. The English population may have declined to as little as one-third of its pre-plague level by the middle of the fifteenth century.[29]

In considering the social implications of the Black Death, it is crucial to emphasize the point that it was a recurrent pandemic. Its real devastation was not just the result of its initial encounter with a virgin population but, rather, the way in which its repeated attacks precluded a quick recovery. These repetitive attacks turned the demography of the next five or six generations inside out. In each decade during the five or six generations after the Black Death there were seven years of normal mortality and three years of crisis mortality. The implications of the recurrent plague visitations translated into making the average annual death rate 2.2 times the normal background level (i.e., seven years of background, normal mortality plus three years of five times that level equals 22 units of mortality divided by 10 to yield an annual average of 2.2). If these crisis deaths were randomly distributed across the life span, then this massive increase in mortality would have radically diminished this population's fertility pro-

---

25. Hatcher, *Plague, Population and the English Economy 1348–1530*, 57. See also "The Great Slump of the Mid-Fifteenth Century," in Richard Britnell and John Hatcher (eds.), *Progress and Problems in Medieval England* (Cambridge, 1996), 245. The mention of northern England refers to A. J. Pollard, *North-eastern England during the Wars of the Roses* (Oxford, 1990), 46–48.

26. Biraben, *Les hommes et la peste*, I:408–9.

27. Fossier, "The Great Trial," 55.

28. E. Le Roy Ladurie, *The French Peasantry, 1450–1660* (Berkeley and Los Angeles, 1987), 27.

29. Le Roy Ladurie, *The French Peasantry, 1450–1660*, 21–94; T. H. Hollingsworth, *Historical Demography* (London, 1969), 380–88. The Essex tithing data analyzed by L. R. Poos "imply that at the beginning of the sixteenth century local population stood at well under one-half the level it had achieved two centuries earlier"; Poos, "The Rural Population of Essex," 529. My own impression, based on comparison of census-based population densities from the nineteenth century with manorial studies I have read, is that the pre-plague countryside was most likely more densely populated than its historians are willing to consider.

file because of the disproportionate numbers of men and women who had died during their prime years of childbearing; if, on the other hand, the age-specific mortality impact was different and the plague largely killed children and infants, then age-specific fertility rates might even have been higher because so many women would have lost the contraceptive effect of nursing. Whatever the case may have been, one reason why demographic recovery was so slow was that after repeated bouts of crisis mortality, it was not simply a matter of filling newly vacated niches but also of overcoming an inherent structural bias against growth itself.[30]

The Black Death reconstructed the age profile of the European population, from a broadly based pyramid toward a more jagged and vertically extended one. The plague pandemic set new demographic mechanisms in train so that for more than one hundred years a negative rate of population growth prevailed. For what it is worth, my own conjecture about English population history would be as follows.

First, the mortality from the first visitation of the Black Death killed off about 50 percent of the population. This initial loss was being made up in the next dozen years because niches had opened up and youthful, fertile marriages speedily ensued.

Second, the recurrence of the plague (which thereafter became "enzootic," established in permanent cycles of infection) had a significant age-specific component, so that the young died more frequently, which meant, in turn, that age-specific fertility rates were bumped upward because a sig-

30. Another possible explanation of the structural bias against growth has been floated in recent years: the plague may have had a sex-selective impact, so that there were more deaths among young men than among young women. In a series of English cities studied by P. J. P. Goldberg, the sex ratio was roughly nine males for every ten females; "Urban Identity and the Poll Taxes of 1377, 1379, and 1381," *Economic History Review*, 2d ser., 43 (1990): esp. 198–201. The upshot of this relationship would have been an oversupply of young women. *Ceteris paribus*, an imbalanced sex ratio would result in higher rates of female celibacy and later ages at marriage. This seems to have been what happened during the first wave of English colonization, 1650–1750, when women married less often and later than in the preceding or following periods; David Levine, *Reproducing Families: The Political Economy of English Population History* (Cambridge, 1987), 82–86. However, Goldberg's argument seems to be severely compromised because the sex ratio of the rural population examined from the same source (1377 Poll Tax registers) seems to have been precisely opposite to the urban ones: eleven males for every ten females. Of course, most women lived in rural areas, so that there would be an overall undersupply of women which would, *ceteris paribus*, have depressed marriage ages. Are we to believe that these sex ratios can be linked with later ages at first marriage for women in the small provincial towns—none of which had a population of more than about 5,000—but had no impact on women's marriage ages in the rural fastnesses? I remain unconvinced.

nificant proportion of fecund women lost the prophylactic effect of nursing (which lasted up to two years) when their infants died.

Third, in the plague-dominated circumstances of c. 1363–1480, entry into marriage was made easier because of the recurrent loss of life among niche holders while fertility within marriage was rather higher, as explained above. The average married couple thus lived together for a shorter time, which meant that a greater proportion of time was spent in the early period of marriage, when fertility was higher. The global import of this combination was that fertility rates per year of marriage were higher.

Fourth, when the positive check of the plague began to moderate, at the turn of the fifteenth and sixteenth centuries, these high rates of marital fertility persisted in conditions of declining mortality. Thus, the age pyramid quickly widened at its base when there was no countervailing prudential check. This created a structural bias toward growth—high fertility acting in concert with larger generations following more closely on one another's heels—which accounts for the sixteenth-century boom in population.[31]

My conjectures are influenced by what I perceive to be parallels between the European Black Death and the holocaust wreaked among the "virgin populations" in the New World. Within a century after European contact, only 10 percent of the aboriginal population remained in both Peru and Mexico. Ninety percent had died! If epidemic disease could be so deadly in the New World, is it not then imaginable that similar devastation could occur in the Old World in response to a new (and more virulent) strain of bubonic plague in the fourteenth and fifteenth centuries?

The reader should be informed that my conjectures would be classified as "extravagant claims" by Richard Britnell and B. M. S. Campbell because they would be "difficult to reconcile with the available evidence, for on known patterns of land use and crop yields it is unclear how a population in excess of 5 million could have been fed."[32] Yet Campbell's own research seems to me to be one of the principal reasons to support the "extravagant claims" I am advancing: apparently there were population densities as high as 500 per square mile on the Norfolk manor of Hakeford Hall.[33] Another

31. It will be noted that this compensatory fertility response was not immediately discarded when the mortality conditions began to change (c. 1480–1500), but rather the now-old behavior continued in a new context. The parish registers of Elizabethan England provide evidence of high levels of marital fertility.

32. Richard H. Britnell and B. M. S. Campbell, "Introduction," in *A Commercialising Economy: England 1086 to c. 1300* (Manchester, 1995), 3.

33. This figure is reported in R. M. Smith, "Demographic Developments in Rural England, 1300–1348: A Survey," in B. M. S. Campbell (ed.), *Before the Black*

reason why I disagree with Britnell and Campbell—and most other historians for whom it is simply unthinkable (or "extravagant") to posit very large numbers for the pre-plague population—is that I simply do not believe that manorial documents provide an accurate guide to social conditions. Knowing their limitations and deficiencies, I have tried to expand the framework of discussion beyond "available evidence . . . on known patterns of land use and crop yields." As I have argued in earlier parts of this book, downward social mobility, centuries of colonizing marginal lands, complex subtenanting arrangements, different cropping patterns, and intensive forms of cottage gardening had most likely resulted in a peasant economy that was radically different from the one that is visible from manorial records.

LUXURIANT DESPAIR

The five generations living in the wake of the Black Death reworked the earlier discourse on holiness by redirecting their focus on sinfulness toward their uncertainty of salvation in conditions of unpredictable death. These forces led to a radical increase in inner-directed anxiety and outer-directed searches for traitors in their midst. Joan of Arc's trial and execution put the tensions between naive belief and inquisitional interrogation into the historical context of an age of scapegoating. The profound uncertainty about, and quest for, salvation is personalized by paying special attention to the spiritual revelations of the last great medieval, Martin Luther.

The generations living in the wake of the Black Death reworked the discourse on holiness. The experience of living in the shadow of the plague led to total social and moral breakdown, as people were seized by terror. A common response to this terror found expression in the massive increase in the cultural fascination with Hell and Satan.[34] It seemed to many that predictions calling for the end of the world were coming true, or, at the very least, divine retribution was being called down on a sinful people. Across a long stretch of time, the coming of the plague stretched social relations beyond their normal tolerance.

Death: Studies in the "Crisis" of the Early Fourteenth Century (Manchester, 1991), 44. In point of fact, the page Smith cites from Campbell's article does not provide information about population densities, nor, I should add, do many other manorial court roll researchers ever report this statistic.

34. Jean Delumeau, *La Peur en Occident* (Paris, 1978), 108–42, 323–26.

It would be a profound mistake to imagine that Europeans became habituated to recurrent visitations of swingeing mortality. If anything, quite the opposite seems to be the case. One of the best statements of this combination of terror and anomie comes from the *Buch der Vergift des Pestilenz*, written by Hieronymous Brunschwig:

> In the year 1473, I was in a city where plague began, the likes of which I had never seen before. All love and friendship among the population disappeared. All mercy vanished. Everyone abandoned his neighbor; brother left brother behind; wives left their husbands; parents left their children behind and fled. For people died not of plague alone, but from abandonment, with no one to hold their hands. Even worse, the priests and the mendicant friars would neither hear confessions nor bring the sacrament to the sick, nor would they allow the dead to be buried in the graves their relatives had purchased for them. City officials showed no mercy; the angry police dragged the bodies of the dead out or locked up houses with people in them.[35]

This disoriented response to the plague was of profound significance because it turned Western culture inward by deepening anxiety, guilt, and introspection. In so doing, it led to novel forms of religious experience and generalized some psychological characteristics that hitherto had been confined behind the monastic walls and that came into contact with secular society only through the agency of the mendicant orders. The experience of living in the shadow of the plague radically changed the reception of the friars' message.[36] Indeed, fascination with death was a major cultural motif in the individuated forms of devotion and mysticism which flourished in this environment of luxuriant despair.

1.

The mendicants' popular preaching had always driven men and women into the most profound existential doubt in order to provide them with a

---

35. Quoted in Paul A. Russell, "Syphilis, God's Scourge or Nature's Vengeance?," *Archive for Reformation History* 80 (1989): 287. The fact that plague visitations recurred kept the terror fresh in everyone's mind. In the small southwestern town of Freiburg, for example, there were eight plague visitations between 1474 and 1527; Tom Scott, *Freiburg and the Breisgau: Town-Country Relations in the Age of Reformation and Peasants' War* (Oxford, 1986) 118. In the Saxon town of Zwickau, on the other hand, there were no recorded plague visitations between 1472 and 1552; Susan Karant-Nunn, *Zwickau in Transition, 1500–1547: The Reformation as an Agent of Change* (Columbus, Ohio, 1987), 218.

36. Jean Delumeau, *Sin and Fear: The Emergence of the Western Guilt Culture, 13th–18th Centuries* (New York, 1990). See also Philippe Ariès, *The Hour of Our Death* (London, 1981).

sheltering refuge within the certainties of the Church's controlled access to the afterlife. Its formulae, concepts, dogmas, sacraments, and ritual magic seemed to be of little use in these new and terrifying circumstances. The pervasive presence of death led to a contempt for the world and material life as well as an obsessive preoccupation with death itself. The inherent putrefaction of the body was connected with the sense that decay and sin were the inevitable accompaniment of life on earth. This was regularly contrasted with the possibility of salvation. Cultural historians have drawn our attention to the bodily rot, the swarming corruption of worms, the living skeletons, the withered and decomposing corpses, and the "skulls and bones [that] were heaped up in charnel houses along the cloisters enclosing the ground [of the Holy Innocents Church in Paris] on three sides, and lay there open to the eye by thousands, preaching to all the lesson of equality."[37]

Because the moment of one's death was unpredictable, it was freighted with the existential baggage of divine judgment. Death was placed at the center of each individual's life, just as the village cemetery was the center of communal life. "The cemetery served as a forum, public square, and mall, where all members of the parish could stroll, socialize, and assemble. Here they conducted their spiritual and temporal business, played their games, and carried on their love affairs." Whereas the Church had previously emphasized the resurrection of those who had lived their earthly lives within its cultic community and who had celebrated their rites of passage with the various sacraments, there was now a massive shift in emphasis that made the judgment of each individual soul more immediate. Masses for the dead became more frequent, and the sale of indulgences skyrocketed. Individual judgment coexisted with the preoccupation about the Last Judgment. "The one does not exclude the other. There is no reason to diametrically oppose them . . . [because] Europeans painted, sculpted, described, and announced the end of the world (and hence the general resurrection)" with a relentless energy that externalized their inner doubts and fears.[38]

---

37. Johan Huizinga, *The Waning of the Middle Ages* (Harmondsworth, 1965), 144.

38. Delumeau, *Sin and Fear*, 64, 90–91; Ariès, *The Hour of Our Death*, 64. I would be remiss not to point out that these two authors disagree about the role of the Black Death. Delumeau gives it a centrality which Ariès does not. In effect, Ariès argues that there were considerable continuities before and after 1348, whereas Delumeau is more impressed with the discontinuities. To be sure, Delumeau recognizes these earlier, embryonic developments, but he argues that they would come to flower only in the atmosphere of grim despair that reached out beyond the cloister to embrace Christendom itself.

Under the omnipresent image of death, demented and crazed people performed the *danse macabre* (dance of death). In Bavaria and South Germany, a similar cultic practice emerged in the period after 1350: the belief in *Armseelen*, poor souls in purgatory who danced and performed rites in village graveyards.[39] In the fifteenth century, the meditation on death was drawn into the intellectual culture of the *devotio moderna*, largely through the massive proliferation of what are known as block books—a crude form of woodcut that preceded the invention of movable type by about thirty years. Even before the advent of printing, the distribution of "picture catechisms" acted upon the popular imagination to enlarge the area of self-scrutiny by referring Christians to the moral guidelines provided by the Ten Commandments.[40]

The most popular early printed books were manuals of devotion. These works were part of a spiritual revival that took mystical religion out of the cloister and spread it far and wide among the burghers of the German towns. What arose was a lay monastic movement, exemplified by the Brethren of the Common Life.[41] Its more intellectual adherents were attracted to Christian humanism. The most outstanding advocate of a return to apostolic simplicity was Erasmus, who, like Luther, grew up in this world. The best-sellers were *Ars moriendi* (The Art of Dying) and Thomas à Kempis's *Imitation of Christ*, which crystallized this form of popular spirituality even before the Gutenberg press made it possible to radically increase production. Together, and reinforced by public preaching, these literary works that spoke to the manic preoccupation with the protocols of death have been described as "a major weapon of mass pedagogy."[42]

The Augustinian emphasis on original sin "gained both its strongest colouring and widest audience" so that an entire civilization constantly had its face rubbed in this macabre anthropology. Augustine's influence was

39. Lionel Rothkrug, "German Holiness and Western Sanctity," *Historical Reflexions/Reflexions Historiques* 15 (1988): 203.

40. Steven E. Ozment, *The Reformation in the Cities* (New Haven, 1975), 16–32.

41. William M. Landeen, "The Beginnings of the *Devotio Moderna* in Germany (Part I)," *Washington State University Research Studies* 19 (1951): 162–202; "The Beginnings of the *Devotio Moderna* in Germany (Part II)," *Washington State University Research Studies* 19 (1951): 221–53; "The Devotio Moderna in Germany (Part III)," *Washington State University Research Studies* 21 (1953): 275–309; "The Devotio Moderna in Germany (Part IV)," *Washington State University Research Studies* 22 (1954): 57–75.

42. Delumeau, *Sin and Fear*, 57–58. The author is quoting Roger Chartier concerning "mass pedagogy"; "Les Arts de Mourir, 1450–1600," *Annales. E.S.C.*, 31 (1976): 55.

connected with a spirituality that spoke more of the Passion than of the Resurrection of the Savior, more of sin than of pardon, more of Hell than of Paradise. Augustinians saw God as a stern Judge, not a loving Father. This pessimism represented a turning away from both Abelard's morality of intention and Thomas Aquinas's fusion of Aristotelianism and Christianity. "Sin, ignorance, and weakness: These three negative conditions are inseparable in early modern religious discourse."[43]

What went on in the believer's confession? It is important to rid ourselves of an anachronism—the individual, private confessional was developed only in the later sixteenth century by the intellectual and spiritual leader of the Counter-Reformation, Cardinal Borromeo of Milan. To a significant extent, pre-Reformation confession was an annual, often-public activity.[44] Second, while sins were confessed and contrition could reconcile the sinner to God, the indulgence was the Church's fundamental penitential instrument. It enabled the sinner to shorten her or his time in purgatory by balancing the scales of godly justice with a credit from the Church's treasury of merits.[45]

At the heart of the sacramental confession system was its reliance on internalized feelings of guilt. Only by working on inner beliefs could the penitent be reformed, reconciled, and reintegrated into Christian society. In theory, then, social control and the cure of anxiety could be accommodated in a single system that provided absolution to the Christian sinner. In reality, formulaic absolution acted like legalized magic—pictorial Trees of Sin portrayed the bewildering variety of transgressions. The machinery of clerical justice—featuring a complex administrative apparatus of excommunications, restitutions, reservations, jurisdictions, irregularities, impediments, and casuistic distinctions—was manned by male celibates. Needless to say, human sexuality was identified with sin and a fear of pollution, stemming from contamination from semen, menstrual blood, and the blood of childbirth. It appears that in the fourteenth and fifteenth centuries clerics relaxed their obdurate misogyny as they tried to accommodate themselves to a society that would not and could not approximate monastic ideals. Furthermore, the rising influence of the Cult of the Virgin created unimagined complications. In popular imagery it was common to

43. Delumeau, *Sin and Fear*, 248, 260, 557, 262, 269.
44. John Bossy, "The Social History of Confession in the Age of the Reformation," *Transactions of the Royal Historical Society*, 5th ser., 25 (1975): 29–32.
45. Lawrence G. Duggan, "Fear and Confession on the Eve of the Reformation," *Archive for Reformation History* 75 (1984): 160–61. Duggan disputes Bossy's emphasis on public confession (162–63).

show Mary nursing the Christ child, so she must have lactated. Did she also menstruate?[46] Yet however much they blurred the older hatreds, the overwhelming message to the laity—and particularly to the female half of the laity—was negative and pejorative. "Sexuality—even unintentional and unavoidable—always threatened to be incompatible with the holy."[47]

Confession was intimately connected with this theology of self-hatred, although it "was as much an expression as a cause of anxiety. Men [and women] submitted to its scrutiny because they were in desperate fear of appearing before God with a single sin left unrecognized and unabsolved. Even confessors sometimes shrank from so dreadful a responsibility, itself a source of unbearable anxiety. . . . Europeans of the fourteenth century, and for some time thereafter, were thus profoundly anxious and at the same time frightened by almost every aspect of experience."[48] Jean Delumeau suggests that the obsession with absolute purity transformed the examination of conscience into a psychotic refusal to accept one's own body and desires. In this way, scrupulous personalities experienced a spiritualized version of the "washing mania" described by twentieth-century psychiatrists. An entire cultural environment devoted itself to ritual procedures that served as security blankets for those generations which were living in terror. It was also a joyless fear. In contrast to the ecstasy of St. Francis, the terrible God of Judgment did not laugh.[49]

2.

In the shadow of the Black Death, the Roman Catholic Church had become a reactive force. This reaction stands in stark contrast to its proactive stance around the year 1000. Delumeau's encyclopedic study of the collective culture of guilt is largely based on an analysis of the discourse of elite culture. So, we should ask about the extent to which this guilt complex penetrated the whole society living in the shadow of the plague. The facets of the religious crisis were interrelated because they drew their energy from

46. Charles T. Wood, "The Doctors' Dilemma: Sin, Salvation, and the Menstrual Cycle in Medieval Thought," *Speculum* 56 (1981): 710–27.

47. Thomas Tentler, *Sin and Confession on the Eve of the Reformation* (Princeton, 1977), 228.

48. William J. Bouwsma, "Anxiety and the Formation of Early Modern Culture," in Barbara C. Malament (ed.), *After the Reformation* (Philadelphia, 1980), 221–22. John Carroll has attempted to relate social history and psychological mentalities, but I find his argument, while challenging, to be schematic as well as displaying some surprising unfamiliarity with the texture of historical developments; "The Role of Guilt in the Formation of Modern Society: England 1350–1800," *British Journal of Sociology* 32 (1981): 459–503.

49. Delumeau, *Sin and Fear*, 298, 316, 296.

the way in which people tried to make sense of their world, a world that was out of joint. By seeing the ways in which the popular dimensions of the religious crisis derived from a common inspiration, we can better understand the whirlwind that the Church was riding.

The character of popular religion was syncretic, that is to say, it was an amalgam composed of a variety of dissimilar elements. Therefore we need to look at the interaction between intensified piety and heightened consciousness of sin from other angles. The religious life of the thirteenth-century villager was less influenced by sermons, treatises, and official promulgations than by an inherited tradition of rites, rituals, cults, and customs that gave meaning to the everyday workings of local society.[50] Most of this little tradition has been irretrievably lost. Much of it was irreducibly local.

The practices of popular religion in the fifteenth century have been intensively studied by German Reformation historians who have sought to understand the spiritual continuities that stretched across this theological rift. In part, such work has been given impetus by the recognition that, even during the nineteenth century when amateur folklorists scoured the countryside, Christianization was often superficial in the sense that the popular classes were able to juggle both theoretical and practical appreciations of religious magic while appropriating whatever seemed to serve their own needs.[51] By looking at matters from this vantage point, we can recognize that popular religion was quite probably very unstable. Set at the interface between literacy and orality, but looking away from schematic constructions and toward the *bricolage* of local knowledge, popular religion was continuously being made and remade. What, then, can we understand of the situation prevailing for the six generations who lived in the period between the Black Death and the Reformation in Germany?

Religion ordered daily life. The Church's magic was thus employed to arrange the material and spiritual worlds into proper alignment. Sacred manifestations—in persons, places, or events—also entailed the possibility of access to sacred power. The Church developed a system of sacraments which were ritual actions symbolizing the Church's role as a supernatural mediator. The actions of the sacraments offered multiple powers which

50. Joseph W. Goering, "The Changing Face of the Village Parish II: The Thirteenth Century," in J. A. Raftis (ed.), *Pathways to Medieval Peasants* (Toronto, 1981), 323–33.

51. Hermann Hörger, "Organizational Forms of Popular Piety in Rural Old Bavaria (Sixteenth to Nineteenth Centuries)," in Kaspar von Greyerz (ed.), *Religion and Society in Early Modern Europe* (London, 1984), 212–22.

provided a means to salvation, offering protection to the body, soul, and spirit while providing a form of resistance to the imprecations of the Devil. Sacraments targeted the whole person so that they had both inner-worldly as well as transcendental efficacy. The seven sacraments were ritual practices that cleansed the inner self. The accompanying seven acts of mercy—feeding the hungry, housing the wayfarer, dressing the naked, quenching the thirsty, visiting the sick, dowering the orphan, and burying the dead—purified social life through good works. Alongside these protocols of official piety there was a murkier set of practices called sacramentals. These were ritual blessings; they employed persons or objects that had been consecrated by their role in liturgical actions. For example, the water or salt from the baptismal ceremony could be used to bless animals or crops, and in this way popular religion crossed the border between theology and spiritualism. The use of these sacramentals was "apotropaic," which means that their use suggests an element of healing and exorcism directed toward this-worldly applications.

This twilight zone beyond the official economy of the sacred was concerned with the social reproduction of the household and the community as well as the biological reproduction of the plant and animal world. Sacred meaning was imparted by ritual cycles in order to invoke divine power and blessing in the ongoing reconstitution of social and biological life. Time was structured according to the individual life-cycle of each believer as well as the annual calendrical cycle. The variety of local amalgams remains bewildering, although certain general themes point toward popular reworkings of the Church's magic for their own reasons. In addition, it was ordinary people—not a professional caste—who invoked sacred power and thereby created order in their daily life. To some extent, this involved mimicking the Christian liturgy, but it was also a form of animism which could be called a pre-Christian survival. This way of looking at things is unhelpful, though, because it suggests that popular religion was both timeless and unchanging, whereas what seems most striking was the way in which official and customary usages were blended.

Rural people welcomed Christian grace, but they redirected it to protect themselves and to defend their crops and animals from the actions of the uncontrollable forces of the natural world. The clergy were welcomed into this world insofar as they made their thaumaturgic powers available for popular use. The clergy were kept at arm's length insofar as they seemed to reserve these special faculties and to dole them out by retail. Moreover, it should also be mentioned that much of this popular religion was able to co-exist with the theology of the Roman Catholic Church since it was largely concerned with investing daily life with order. The Church seems to have been ambivalent about these forms of popular religion and, while no official theological support was provided for them, they were largely tolerated. Popular religious beliefs were considered to be heretical only if they reached out to explain and to administer sacred contacts between the living and the dead, who were of course not considered to be spiritually dead but rather living in the afterlife or in purgatory.[52]

In a certain sense, doctrinal hardening had a logic of its own. But, when we stand back from the particularity of these intellectual currents, it is impossible not to be impressed by the fact that a society in crisis found its outlet in readily accessible building blocks of intolerance. The mendicant orders led this bloodthirsty campaign. Since their inception at the beginning of the thirteenth century they had tried to co-opt popular religious culture and guide it along orthodox channels. It was, indeed, their guiding belief that the crooked timber of humanity could be reformed so that something entirely straight would be built from these raw materials.[53] In directing this sedulous quest for conformity, the friars—who were missionaries, polemicists, preachers, and inquisitors—had created a stack of kindling which was waiting to be ignited.[54] These fires of rage were sparked by the pestilential fury of the Black Death. "Conspiracy theories prosper best in the soil of the imagination."[55] The sedulous quest for conformity was perverted in the course of the fourteenth century into something altogether more frightening—first, the scapegoating of identifiable groups like

---

52. The preceding paragraphs are based on Robert Scribner's insightful articles. The most germane ones for this subject are "Cosmic Order and Daily Life: Sacred and Secular in Pre-Industrial German Society," in von Greyerz (ed.), *Religion and Society in Early Modern Europe*, 17–32; "Ritual and Popular Religion in Catholic Germany at the Time of the Reformation," in *Popular Culture and Popular Movements in Reformation Germany* (London, 1987), 17–47; "The Impact of the Reformation on Daily Life," in *Mensch und Objekt im Mittlealter und in der frühen Neuzeit: Leben-Alltag-Kultur* (Vienna, 1990), 316–43 (Österreichische Akademie der Wissenschaften, 568); "Symbolising Boundaries: Defining Social Space in the Daily Life of Early Modern Germany," in G. Blaschitz, H. Hundsbichler, and G. Jaritz (eds.), *Symboles des Alltags* (Graz, 1992), 821–41; and "The Reformation, Popular Magic, and the 'Disenchantment of the World,' " *Journal of Interdisciplinary History* 23 (1993): esp. 475–94.

53. This phrase intentionally echoes Immanuel Kant: "As so krummen Holze, als woraus der Mensch gemacht ist, kann nichts ganz Gerades dizimmert werden" (Out of timber so crooked as that from which man is made nothing entirely straight can be built), quoted in Conor Cruise O'Brien, "Paradise Lost," *New York Review of Books*, April 25, 1991, 53.

54. Jeremy Cohen, *The Friars and the Jews* (Ithaca, 1982).

55. Carlo Ginzburg, *Ecstasies* (New York, 1991), 65.

lepers and Jews, and then, second, the displacement of these hatreds onto a much less obviously identifiable group of witches.

The development of mass frenzies that led to the killing of communities seems to have begun in the Languedoc, a recently conquered frontier region centering on Carcassonne, which had been the heartland of the Cathar heresy. Of great interest to readers of Emmanuel Le Roy Ladurie's great book on *Montaillou*, the driving force of the Inquisition was personified by none other than Jacques Fournier, then-bishop of Pamiers, who would climb the greasy pole of heretic-finding to become Pope Benedict XII in Avignon. At first, the inquisitors' primary targets were heretics like the Languedocian Cathars, but by the 1320s, lepers and Jews came within the purview of their courts, and within a few years they, too, were killed or else driven out of the kingdom of France. At the time of the Black Death, many of these communities had relocated in the borderlands just outside the kingdom of France— in Dauphiné, Savoy, and Provence.[56] From these western Alpine regions, the exterminating furies moved eastward and northward.

The most spectacular victims were Western society's most marginalized and least protected group—the Jews.[57] In Germany, even before 1348, local crusaders, led by *Judenschläger* (Jew killers), had channeled popular rage against Jews; in the later 1330s, fanatic hordes known as *Armleders* destroyed life and property in hundreds of south German communities. In the southern swath of country—stretching from Württemberg, across Bavaria, and into Austria—it was widely believed that Jews desecrated the Host. Having burned down all traces of Jewish settlement, it was common to rebuild churches dedicated to the Virgin Mary on the ruins.[58]

Massive disorientation followed the first visitation of the plague. Western society was crisscrossed by millenarian bands of flagellants who blended with its flotsam of vagabonds, outlaws, bankrupts, and criminals.[59]

56. Ginzburg, *Ecstasies* 33 ff.

57. The Moslem world, by way of contrast, reacted to the Black Death very differently. Its communal response does not seem to have been tinged with fear, guilt, millenarianism, and militancy directed against scapegoats. Among Moslems, plague was considered to be a mercy from God which provided the faithful with the opportunity to enjoy a martyr's death. In view of their opinion that the plague came directly from God, it was enjoined that the faithful should not flee; Michael Dols, "The Comparative Communal Responses to the Black Death in Muslim and Christian Societies," *Viator* 5 (1974): 269–87.

58. Lionel Rothkrug, "Religious Practices and Collective Perceptions," *Historical Reflections/Reflexions Historiques* 7 (1980): 63–65; "German Holiness and Western Sanctity," 175, 179.

59. N. Cohn, *Pursuit of the Millennium* (Oxford, 1970), 137–41; Robert E. Lerner, "The Black Death and Western European Eschatological Mentalities," *American Historical Review* 86 (1981): 533–52.

Pope Clement VI tried to outlaw both the flagellant manifestations and anti-Semitic pogroms in October, 1349, but he was powerless in the face of popular belief that the plague was a sign of the coming rule of the Antichrist. Apocalyptic panic held a terrified people in its grip. Southwestern Germany, the Rhineland in particular, was a hotbed of these impulses. The political confusion that was endemic in this region impeded clerical control over such deviant groups.[60] Flagellants were described by a contemporary in vivid terms:

> While the plague was still active and spreading from town to town, men in Germany, Flanders, Hainault, and Lorraine uprose and began a new sect on their own authority. Stripped to the waist, they gathered in large groups and bands and marched in procession through the crossroads and squares of cities and good towns. They formed circles and beat upon their backs with weighted scourges, rejoicing as they did so in loud voices and singing hymns suitable to their rite and newly composed for it.

These flagellants were men who were forbidden to engage in sexual or social intercourse with women; not for the last time, this concern with pollution found another outlet in anti-Semitism. To quote the same author again:

> the Jews were suddenly and violently charged with infecting the wells and water, and corrupting the air. The whole world rose up against them cruelly on this account. In Germany . . . they were massacred and slaughtered by Christians, and many thousands were burned every-where, indiscriminately. The unshaken if fatuous constancy of the [Jewish] men and their wives was remarkable. For mothers hurled their children first into the fire that they might not be baptized, and then leapt in after them to burn with their husbands and children. It is said that many bad Christians were burned who in a like manner put poison into wells. But in truth, such poisonings, granted that they actually were perpetrated, could not have caused so great a plague nor infected so many people.[61]

Horrific pogroms took place all over Germany. All two thousand Jews in Strasbourg were burned in February, 1349. A few months later, all three thousand were killed in Mainz. Large communities in Frankfurt and Cologne were similarly destroyed. In other centers—for example Baden, Burren, Dresden, Eisenach, Erfurt, Freiburg, Gotha, Landsberg, Memmin-

---

60. Richard Kieckhefer, "Radical Tendencies in the Flagellant Movement of the Mid-Fourteenth Century," *Journal of Medieval and Renaissance Studies* 4 (1974): 157–76.

61. Jean de Venette, quoted in Gottfried, *The Black Death*, 69, 73.

gen, Solothurn, Speyer, Stuttgart, Ulm, Worms, and Zofingen—the Christians' fury was let loose on the "king's Jews," although, of course, there was no king to protect them. In all, 350 separate massacres took place in Germany between 1348 and 1351.[62] Pogroms, which had before this time been largely directed from above for the fiscal benefit of secular authorities, had now taken on a nasty twist when popular images of demonization and pollution were given free reign.

Tens of thousands of Jews were massacred. Survivors were mostly driven eastward or else confined to segregated districts and restricted in their activities. Organized expulsions took place later. Jews were banished from Vienna (1421), Cologne (1424), Dresden (1430), Augsburg (1440), Erfurt (1458), Mainz (1470), Bamberg (1478), Heilbronn (1490), Magdeburg (1493), Nuremberg (1499), and Ulm (1499), as well as being excluded from Upper and Lower Bavaria, Mecklenburg, Pomerania, Styria, Carinthia, and Lower Austria before 1500. If the emperor, some princes, and most princebishops did provide Jews with a refuge, they did so for a steep price.[63]

In the popular culture of European Christendom, Jews had already been linked with ritual murders and blood sacrifices, the desecration of the Host, and the poisoning of wells, in addition to being agents of sexual pollution. In Bavaria, legends of *Hostienfrevel* (crimes against the host) were accompanied by recurrent pogroms.[64] The link between Satan and the Jews was, of course, far older. It permeates the descriptions and accounts of Jesus life in the chapters of the New Testament attributed to his apostles Matthew, Luke, and John.[65] The point I want to make here is not that popular antiSemitism was new but rather that the intensity of violence became both quantitatively and qualitatively different in the wake of the Black Death. It was qualitatively different in the sense that the Jews were attacked as a people, not as individual practitioners of the demonic arts. In quantitative terms, Jews were the primary victims of this popular search for scapegoats. Inquisitors were aided and abetted by an increasingly dogmatic vision of the black magic arts.

The doctrine of witchcraft which emerged in the century following the Black Death amalgamated five separate elements into a coherent system:

62. Gottfried, *The Black Death*, 74.

63. Ironically, this fiscal screw proved to be the German Jews' most significant negotiating tool when they expanded their numbers in the disarray of the second quarter of the seventeenth century; Jonathan I. Israel, "Central European Jewry during the Thirty Years War," *Central European History* 16 (1983): 3–30.

64. Joshua Trachtenberg, *The Devil and the Jews* (New Haven, 1943), 102–8.

65. Elaine Pagels, *The Origin of Satan* (New York, 1995).

an interest in magic and sorcery was transmuted into the legal concept of black magic through which harm was inflicted on others; the witch sold her or his soul to the Devil in order to gain extraordinary earthly powers; for witches, copulation with the Devil was a rite of initiation and was most frequently linked to females; individual witches were joined together in secret societies; and these leagues were assembled over large distances because, it was argued, the witch's magical powers included the ability to fly. There seems to be little doubt that this coherent doctrine was knit together from both popular fantasies and the fabrications of deluded scholars.[66]

Carlo Ginzburg has given Norman Cohn's argument about intellectual convergence a geographic component. He has noted that the image of the witches' Sabbath emerged in the Western Alps. Furthermore, he has argued that this took place in the wake of the Black Death:

> The arrival, half way through the fourteenth century, of the plague bacillae . . . set off a series of chain reactions. Obsession with conspiracy, anti-heretical stereotypes and shamanistic traits fused, inducing the emergence of the image of the witch sect. But the transformation of the old beliefs in a diabolical direction occurred over decades along the entire Alpine arc. . . . For a long time the society of witches continued to be associated with the regions in which it had been first discovered.

Ginzburg goes on to give the activities of San Bernardino of Siena pride of place in explaining the trajectory of witchcraft theory. When San Bernardino was called to Rome in 1427, "he had repeatedly attacked witches and sorcerers, arousing utter astonishment in his auditors." Yet he was able to turn their utter astonishment into his own particular triumph: the devotion to the name of Jesus propagated by Bernardino entailed an exchange between symbol and the reality symbolized. "He fought sorcerers and enchanters on their own ground, with weapons not too dissimilar from theirs." Moreover, Bernardino's sermons suggested a series of questions to judges that they were to ask those accused of witchcraft in the future.[67]

The theory of witchcraft had begun to take root in the thirteenth century, when Aquinas rejected the traditional view that evil superstitions were "illusions of the devil" by imputing diabolical acts to real women who gathered at night. In Aquinas's view, they brought innocent people into disrepute while arrogating to themselves—by means of a distinct pact with the devil himself—powers that were properly God's own. It was only a short step for other theorists of the diabolical to link together the wood-

66. Norman Cohn, *Europe's Inner Demons* (London, 1975).
67. Ginzburg, *Ecstasies*, 63–86, 296 ff.

land spirits and fauns of ancient paganism with the horned demons with goat's feet that were present at the devil's sabbath. In the thirteenth century, "diminutive *vetule* (little old ladies!) . . . were treated mercifully" because they were considered to be both poor and simpleminded, so that they were therefore understood to be victims who had been led astray by superstitious temptations. "In the fifteenth century, on the other hand, the *malefica* is burned without hesitation, for she can be convicted of harming her neighbours—threatening their lives, the sexual potency or the health of their cattle—with the aid of the devil."[68]

3.

For a besieged Church whose secular powers had become profoundly insecure in the wake of the Black Death, witchcraft came to be seen as a competing source of magical power. In this regard, it is interesting to quote Peter Brown's observation that accusations of witchcraft often occur when

> *two systems of power* are sensed to clash within the one society. On the one hand, there is *articulate* power, power defined and agreed upon by every one (and especially by its holders!): authority rested in precise persons; admiration and success gained by recognised channels. Running counter to this there may be other forms of influence less easy to pin down: *inarticulate* power: the disturbing tangibles of social life; the imponderable advantages of certain groups; personal skills that succeed in a way that is unacceptable or difficult to understand. Where these two systems overlap, we may expect to find the sorcerer.[69]

The most famous example of late medieval witchfinding is provided by the case of Joan of Arc. It will be useful, therefore, to dwell on it to draw out how these forces interacted with contemporary anxieties about sensuality, original sin, and spiritual pollution.[70]

The kingdom of France was in chaos in the 1420s. French disarray was so complete that wolf packs frequently entered Paris, through either a breach in the ramparts or an unguarded gate.[71] The reign of the mad King

68. Jean-Claude Schmitt, *The Holy Greyhound: Guinefort, Healer of Children since the Thirteenth Century* (Cambridge, 1984), 14–24, 34–35.

69. Peter Brown, "Sorcery, Demons and the Rise of Christianity," in *Religion and Society in the Age of St. Augustine* (London, 1972), 119.

70. I am following the account in Marina Warner's *Joan of Arc* (London, 1981), and all quotations are from this excellent text unless otherwise stated.

71. Fernand Braudel, *The Structures of Everyday Life*, vol. 1, *Civilization and Capitalism 15th–18th Century* (New York, 1981), 66. In September, 1438, the wolves were again at the city's walls, but they had to content themselves with attacking people in the surrounding suburbs.

Charles VI (1380–1422) had witnessed the disintegration of social authority. This dislocation was given a vicious twist by internecine feuds and factional murders among the ruling elite. England's triumphant victory at Agincourt and subsequent alliance with the Burgundians resulted in a puppet regime which occupied Paris and most of northern France. France was beset by factional fighting, financial collapse, military defeat, English scorched-earth warfare, pillaging and looting on the part of unemployed soldiers who joined forces in freebooting bands of *routiers* and *écoucheurs*, and seething peasant discontent. Ground rents in the heartland of the Île de France were only 10 percent of their level a century earlier—before the wars and the plague. The French countryside was quadruply oppressed from "the genocide that had been perpetrated . . . by bacilli, economic crisis, brigandage, and the English."[72]

The great breadbasket of the Île de France had been almost deserted, as chronicled around 1461 by Thomas Basin:

> From the Loire to the Seine, and from there to the Somme, nearly all the fields were left for many years, not merely untended but without people capable of cultivating them, except for rare patches of soil, for the peasants had been killed or put to flight. . . . We ourselves have seen the vast plains of Champagne, Beauce, Brie, Gâtinais, Chartres, Berry, Maine, Perche, Vexin, Norman and French, Caux, Senlis, Soissonais, Valois, as far as Laon and beyond, as far as Hainault, absolutely deserted, uncultivated, abandoned, devoid of all inhabitants, overgrown with brushwood and brambles.[73]

Joan of Arc emerged in the late winter of 1429 as France's unlikely savior. The Maid of Orléans's intervention was critical. She rallied a flagging cause, and this intervention ultimately helped the Valois kings to turn the tide of the Hundred Years' War.

Joan was born in about 1412 in the village of Domremy. She was the fifth child (and second daughter) of Jacques of Arc (or Dars)[74] and Isabella Romée.[75] Her native village is situated on the border between Champagne and Lorraine, on the Meuse. This area felt the full force of the Anglo/Burgundian offensive, which is not surprising since the Meuse formed a

---

72. Le Roy Ladurie, *The French Peasantry*, 62, 56.

73. Quoted in Warner, *Joan of Arc*, 34. For a scholarly discussion of the impact of fighting in Northern France, see Le Roy Ladurie, *The French Peasantry*, 37–43.

74. Or "Darc," as in the contemporary documentation. "D'Arc" is a seventeenth-century addition that was set forth by her collateral descendants, who wanted to affirm their long-standing claims to nobility by tracing their titles back to her.

75. Jan van Herwaarden, "The Appearance of Joan of Arc," in van Herwaarden (ed.), *Joan of Arc: Reality and Myth* (Hilversum, 1994), 32–34.

natural border between the kingdom of France and the duchy of Burgundy, which traditionally had been a part of the Holy Roman Empire. Joan's father was a village dignitary in a loyalist Valois community that, like so many other communities in the late feudal world, normally acknowledged two competing feudal overlords and multiple ecclesiastical allegiances. Her own family was studded with male ecclesiastics—Simon d'Arc was chaplain of Our Lady at the Royal Palace of Chaumont, Pierre d'Arc was a canon of Troyes, and, closer to home, Michel d'Arc was the curé of Bar-sur-Seine. Joan thus spent her early years in an atmosphere of bloody fights and interminable warfare as well as a family committed to the orthodox religion. Insecurity haunted her childhood, and she responded to it by developing an inclination for clear-cut situations with identifiable centers of authority.[76] So it is again not surprising that she was devoted to the legitimacy of the Valois and dedicated her life to returning them to the throne of a united France, freed from foreign interlopers.

Joan's childhood was of great interest to her inquisitors since they located her two primary heretical traits in her earliest activities—her voices and her cross-dressing. Joan's voices were of critical importance since they provided her inquisitors with the information that they would use to convict her of heresy. As Marina Warner writes:

> Thus it was altogether possible for Joan's voices to be demonic, however heavenly their appearance. This was the ambiguity at the heart of the society that tried Joan of Arc, the crevasse that opened at its feet. It was wedded to an ancient dualism, seeing an eternal contest between absolute good and absolute evil taking place perpetually in the world and in the microcosm of each person's soul; but such a cosy surface of absolutism was cracked by a deep relativism in the diagnosis and location of evil. The society was pain-wracked and haunted; it sought to pinpoint the nature and the place of evil, to find the person embodying it, because in an age when the patterns of thought have become anthromorphic, it must be embodied. This attempt was like trapping mercury, for what seemed evil slipped away from the analyst's finger and thumb with maddening agility. The location most feared for evil's thriving was in the heart of heresy and of heresy's handmaid, witchcraft.[77]

Recent scholars have suggested that we can understand Joan's voices in terms of the composite, syncretic system of belief that characterized popular religiosity. It is also suggested that she was not convicted of witchcraft

---

76. Warner, *Joan of Arc,* 39–42. For the cousins or uncles who were ecclesiastics, see Lucien Fabre, *Joan of Arc* (London, 1925), 22.
77. Warner, *Joan of Arc,* 101–2.

because she was, as it were, just slightly ahead of her time—a century later the evidence she provided to her inquisitors would have been used to convict her of witchcraft, but in her own lifetime the "theory" of witchcraft was still inchoate. That may be one reason why her interrogators never put Joan to the question—she was never tortured. They could catch her up as a heretic, but the other charges concerning witchcraft were less easily resolved. Nevertheless, they were fascinated—and horrified—by what Joan told them about her intimate visions of the archangel Michael and Saints Catherine and Margaret.

> Her enemies . . . were obsessed with determining the extent of Joan's sensual experience of her voices, the extent of her bodily contact with them, the nature of their physical manifestation. . . . Joan was their plaything, she was lured into a gin she did not even understand to be there, which bit into her deeper and deeper as she struggled to express her truth in a language that she could not fully master and would yet be intelligible to her questioners. As they were adept in branches of learning she hardly knew by name, she took their lead from them, borrowed their images to render explicit the ineffable. The trap into which they prodded her closed inexorably.[78]

Joan first spoke to the inquisitors about her voices at the second public session of her interrogation at Rouen on February 22, 1430. They were told that she was thirteen the first time she had heard a voice in her father's garden in the summer of 1426. In the double-think of witchfinding, the witch-hunters were among her most committed believers, and they seized on her openness to strike at the heterodox implications of her beliefs. Thus, the fact that she had never told anyone else about her visions or voices but had kept them private was, in the eyes of her interrogators, an absolute signal since she had had no right to trust in them without formal permission.

In the course of her interrogation Joan told her examiners about the fairies which were said to visit her village on Laetare Sunday—in the middle of Lent on the fourth Sunday after Shrove Tuesday. Every spring, on the Sunday of the Fountains, Domremy's village youngsters took a picnic to a large tree and ate, drank, sang, and danced while making garlands to hang on the tree's branches. This large tree was known locally as *L'Arbre des Fées* (the fairy tree). The youngsters' activities revealed the survival of ancient pagan spring festivals. Joan was artful enough to tell the inquisitors "Whether this was true, she does not know. She said that she herself had never seen a fairy, as far as she knew, either at the tree or anywhere else."

78. Warner, *Joan of Arc*, 121.

But if she was able to wriggle away from that trap by insisting that she did not see a fairy in the *bois chesnu* (dark wood) of Domremy, she was steadfast in maintaining that she had been visited by Saints Catherine and Margaret and the archangel Michael.

Since Joan's trial was undertaken for political effect—to discredit her in popular eyes and thereby to undermine the aura that attached to the anti-English/Burgundian crusade that she had launched for the Valois king of France—the main point was to pin her down in terms of the Church's definition of heretical belief. This was easily accomplished by the interrogators, who were all well versed in inquisitorial double-think. Since she was not a man of the Church, she could not legitimately receive a message from God via his saints and angels, nor was she a nobleman, nor was she an adult, nor, indeed, even a man. She had "transgressed against class, sex, social boundaries and feudal expectations: the transgression lent her charisma and earned her immense influence for a while. . . . For Joan's enemies, her witchcraft lay—not in the spells or charms or wonders she had accomplished—but in the phenomenon of articulate power itself exercised from a source that due order would require to remain inarticulate."[79]

If the peasant girl's naive audacity dismayed her male inquisitors, the content of her visions shocked them. Her visions "were too special and, at the same time, too mundane. Her contact with the supernatural was too intimate and too regular . . . [so that] she was all unknowingly, deeply embroiled in a fundamental quarrel in Christian theology, and her innocent replies testifying to the reality of her voices were immuring her on the wrong side." Joan's voices had bodies, spoke French, wore clothes, and could be held and touched. Her simple piety trespassed against the axiom of the holy in Christian thought that abstractions should remain abstract and not take on material shape. She was trapped. "Joan was buried in the body. She used what she knew to express the unknown; her saints' reality was clothed in familiar robes and familiar images. More than her defiance of the Church's authority, more than her claims to know the future, more than her perhaps heterodox enthusiasm for the host, she was condemned for experiencing the other world as simply and as concretely as she experienced this world every day."[80] In this, Joan does not seem to have been all that unusual. Her crime was getting caught up in the toils of the inquisition.

Joan was unusual. In particular, her commitment to male dress disconcerted her examiners. It was doubly distressing to her inquisitors because

79. These two paragraphs are taken from Marina Warner, "Joan of Arc: A Gender Myth," in van Herwaarden (ed.), *Joan of Arc*, 97–117 (quotation from 110).

80. Warner, *Joan of Arc*, 121, 128, 136, 130.

she was a virgin. Apart from the obvious parallels with the Virgin Mary, whose cult was growing in the fourteenth and early fifteenth centuries, Joan's virginity had deep symbolic resonance among her contemporaries. As Marina Warner writes:

> The concept of virginity which she embodied—literally—had enormous power in her culture. Juxtaposed to the vivisected and dismembered body of the kingdom, her virginity provided an urgent symbol of integrity. By synecdoche, Joan's intact sexuality stood for the whole of her and, in the ambitions of her supporters, for the whole of France.[81]

Joan confounded the social expectations of articulate power by her refusal to wear garments that properly reflected her social station. Her sumptuary transgression was compounded because her hair was worn in an improper manner. This was another act of insubordination.[82]

> The said Jeanne put off and entirely abandoned woman's clothes, with her hair cropped short and round in the fashion of young men, she wore shirt, breeches, doublet, with hose joined together, long and fastened to the said doublet by twenty points, long leggings laced on the outside, a short mantle reaching to the knee, or thereabouts, a close-cut cap, tight-fitting boots or buskins, long spurs, sword, dagger, breastplate, lance and other arms in the style of a man-at-arms.[83]

Her inappropriate costume was trebly dangerous: first, because she was immodest; second, because she was dressed like a man; and, third, because she was dressed above her station "in the style of a man-at-arms." Moreover, luxury "stained her reputation in the same way as calling her a harlot. For the female, fettered by carnality, lust and luxury were synonymous."[84] For the Virgin Maid—whose virginity had been carefully examined by both her Valois patrons and her Anglo/Burgundian enemies—these imputations of carnality suggested that appearance and reality were out of whack. Was her intact hymen yet another sign that she was not only bewitched but also in league with the forces of darkness which sought to confound mere mortals?

Joan's self-representation—her costume, her appearance, and her bearing—thus denied her ordained role as a subordinate procreator. Joan threatened to transcend her appointed earthly station and, in so doing, she

81. Warner, *Joan of Arc*, 32.
82. Warner notes that "*shamans*, in the rituals of many cultures, cross-dress in order to deepen their power"; "Joan of Arc: A Gender Myth," 116.
83. This description comes from the charges against Joan, quoted in Warner, *Joan of Arc*, 141.
84. Warner, *Joan of Arc*, 173.

called into question the accepted framework of virtue. To her inquisitors, Joan was the bodily incarnation of *inarticulate power*: her sumptuary transgressions seemed to put Joan in a liminal state. She had taken on the ancient virtue of reason and the feudal armature of courage, which were supposed to be characteristic of the opposite sex, while denying the meekness and humility that were thought to be her biological destiny.

Christian theology was deeply troubled by gender ambivalence even though its most basic tenet—the equality of all sinners before the grace of God—was itself hardly even an equivocal endorsement of patriarchy. Nonetheless, Christian society was deeply patriarchal, and its leaders usually tended to look right past this knot of contradictions. In Joan's case, transvestism provided her inquisitors with a wedge with which they could prise open the deeper secrets that were located in the darkness of her heart. The Anglo/Burgundian inquisitors wanted to prove her to be a hoax as well as a witch or, at the very least, a heretic. The crucial thing for them was that "If proved a hoax, Joan tainted with falsehood the whole French [i.e., Valois] argument of legitimate rights to the French crown."[85]

The central historical issue surrounding Joan's remarkable story is that for a short time in the spring and summer of 1429 she was believed—or else used in desperation—by the king of France. The corollary to this central issue is that she was persecuted and extirpated. In fact, she was probably believed more profoundly by her persecutors than by her patron, since there was never any attempt to rescue or ransom her after she was captured. For the Valois king of France, she had served her purpose and seemed to promise more trouble: the Virgin Maid, who was controlled by her voices, was impossible for any man to control. Her execution is a fact of singular historical moment since she is the only saint in the Roman Catholic cosmography who was killed by the secular authorities at the behest of the Church Inquisition. For nineteenth-century French Romantics, "Joan of Arc is the Christ of France" who "redeemed the crimes of the monarchy, as Jesus redeemed the sins of the world: [and] like Jesus, she redeemed her passion; like Jesus, she had her Golgotha and her Calvary."[86] Yet she was, in fact, burned at the stake by her contemporaries. The most important thing for her enemies was that she was exterminated. Legal niceties were subordinated to political necessity. So, she may have been regarded as a witch but they were satisfied with convicting her as an heretical transvestite.

85. Warner, *Joan of Arc*, 140.
86. Alexandre Dumas, *Jeanne d'Arc (1429–1431)*, quoted in Warner, *Joan of Arc*, 268.

4.

Joan's remarkable story provides a perspective on the changing character of popular religion in the period after the year 1000. The Gregorian Reformation had been successful because it controlled the fervor and energy of popular religion in the eleventh century by channeling it in approved directions. The fact that huge numbers of clerics died from the plague while many others deserted their cures went some way toward undermining faith in the institutional Church. The challenge that emerged for the Church in the wake of the Black Death was likewise addressed within its ritual framework. But its success was not so clear-cut as it had been earlier, which probably has something to do with the size and complexity of the task as well as the institutional rigidity of the Church itself.

These misgivings coalesced into a series of contradictions that had been immanent in the very structure of the thirteenth-century imperial Church. The thirteenth century—the century of friars, cathedrals, and doctrinal *summae*—is generally held to be the culmination of the Gregorian Reform movement. The assertion of papal power reached its ultimate high-water mark in 1302 when Pope Boniface published *Unam Sanctum,* in which he affirmed the sacramental role of clerical intervention between Christians and their God in the secular construction of peace and justice. The papacy, according to this argument, was also able to call on its "treasury of merits" to grant indulgences to sinners in order to lessen their time in purgatory. This theological novelty was soon followed in 1343 by Clement VI's edict *Unigenitus,* which officially proclaimed that the treasury of merits derived from the redeeming blood of the crucified Christ was an infinite reservoir. The next step in this process of theological aggrandizement was the claim that there would be individual judgment of souls in purgatory. This idea was first advanced in 1336 by Benedict XII, the erstwhile hunter of Cathars in Montaillou. It was only a century later, in the reign of Sixtus IV (1471–84), that it was given official sanction.

These novelties were advanced by papal allies to extend the jurisdiction of the church into the afterlife. Together, these ecclesiopolitical decrees signaled both the Church's waning concern for universal judgment and its rising interest in its own cash flows. Through the *summa confessorum,* the abstruse reasoning of Thomas Aquinas that lay behind these doctrinal innovations passed into the common pastoral theology. Theologians were split on this issue. By and large, this massive extension of papal powers was supported by Dominicans. The Franciscans opposed this power grab. The

Spiritual Franciscans were simultaneously feuding with the papacy over the question of mendicant poverty.[87]

The institutional Church experienced a massive plunge in the esteem and respect that ordinary Christians held for it. No action was so significant in this regard as the French king's removal of the papacy from Rome to Avignon. The emergence of rival claimants for the throne of St. Peter further emphasized the disparity between the worldly Church and the spiritual message it was thought to embody. The Church had always feared the excesses of contemplative rapture, and its intellectuals had economized mystic energy. "Instead of the solitary ecstasy of the blessed moment comes a constant and collective habit of earnestness and fervour, cultivated by simple townspeople. . . . [This] was mysticism by retail."[88] These retailers were also spiritual democrats. If the mendicant orders were the most characteristic element in this clerical order, they were not the last radicals to discover that revolutionary movements often eat their own offspring.

The mendicant orders and their theories concerning property, poverty, and the worldly role of possessions were challenged from two sides. One line of attack came from members of the regular clergy who had been led by Secular Masters of the Sorbonne from the middle of the thirteenth century. This group was intent on glorifying the worldly lordship of the ecclesiastical project and also the primacy of its spiritual mission. For them, the voluntary rejection of property seemed hopelessly naïve when *nouveaux riches*—businessmen, traders, manufacturers, lawyers, notaries, and moneylenders—were literally showering money and lands into the coffers of the Church. The secular-mendicant controversy pivoted on an obscure philosophical issue of dogma: did Christ own or merely possess his moneybag? The way in which this question was answered shaped radically divergent visions of the clerical mission. In particular, these answers led directly to questions about the legitimacy of both property rights and ecclesiastical hierarchy.

The second line of reproach was more radical because it questioned why the Church was endowed with any wealth since its aim was spiritual.[89]

87. Robert W. Shaffern, "Learned Discussions of Indulgences for the Dead in the Middle Ages," *Church History* 61 (1992): 367–81.

88. Huizinga, *The Waning of the Middle Ages*, 144, 215–16.

89. James Doyne Dawson, "Richard FitzRalph and the Fourteenth-Century Poverty Controversies," *Journal of Ecclesiastical History* 34 (1983): 343; see also Dawson, "William of Saint-Amour and the Apostolic Tradition," *Mediaeval Studies* 40 (1978): 223–38.

John Wyclif would later revive these theories of lordship dependent on grace and the concept of natural possession without civil ownership. Like Marsilius of Padua before him and the Protestant reformers afterward, Wyclif would use these doctrines to call for the compulsory disendowment of the Church so that it could be compelled to return to the apostolic simplicity of its original state. What these two criticisms had in common was the view that friars, like the able-bodied poor, were consuming alms which would otherwise be better directed to the genuinely deserving.[90] For some, this rebuke dovetailed with the contemporary demonization of idleness.

What made these reproaches so potent was that the very nature of poverty had changed during the long cycle of population growth after the year 1000. In contrast to the ancient model, it was no longer just the incompetent and the infirm who were counted as objects of charity. The working poor had become more significant. Blaming the poor for their poverty stood in stark opposition to the early Christians' suspicion of wealth. In that older view, riches were distrusted, and unconditional charity to the poor was seen as a means by which the rich man could gain salvation. Thus, Paul told the Corinthians (2:8–9): "though he [Christ] was rich, yet for your sakes he became poor, that ye through his poverty might be rich." As everyone knew, it is more difficult for a rich man to enter the kingdom of heaven than for a camel to pass through the eye of a needle.

To many, the voluntary poverty of the friars began to represent a way of life that was growing old. They took issue not with the friars' voluntary poverty but rather with its institutionalization. A formalized dialectic of happiness and suffering was far removed from the immediacy which shook Christendom to its roots in the explosion following "Francis of Assisi's proclamation of the dignity of the poor and of the duty to restore that dignity."[91] The urgency of the mendicants' pseudo-apostolic imitation of Christ's poverty gave way to the commodification of penance through the sale of indulgences. For many, the friars were symptomatic of the way religion was being absorbed into the cash nexus. Moreover, charges of hypocrisy were commonplace, and the apostasy of individual mendicants reflected very badly on their project. The orders' immense wealth resulted in glorious buildings funded by donations from both rich and poor. Curry-

90. Maria Moisa, "Fourteenth-Century Preachers' Views of the Poor: Class or Status Group," in G. S. Jones and R. Samuel (eds.), *Class, Ideology, and Politics* (London, 1982), 160–75.

91. Michel Mollat, *The Poor in the Middle Ages* (New Haven, 1986), 11, 119 ff.

ing favor with the elites stuck in the craw of the regular clergy who were among their most vociferous critics.[92]

Questioning the Church's arrogation of authority—and the inevitable abuses it entailed—was not limited to spiritual matters. The Spiritual Franciscans Marsilius of Padua and John of Jandun had already introduced political theorists to a vision of a pastoral cure whose secular powers were to be exercised by the state in *Defensor Pacis* (1324). Written in a period of factionalism and civic strife, this work promised not only to secularize power but also to rob it of magical authority. Denying the papacy's temporal powers meant that, correlatively, those of secular rulers were enhanced at its expense.[93] At the same time, William of Occam came to much the same conclusions, although he began from a theological starting point, as opposed to the political science of Marsilius. It is noteworthy that this challenge to the plenitude of papal power came from the Spiritual wing of the Franciscan order, because it was at exactly this time that Pope John XXII was driving them out of the fold for their radical views about poverty and the apostolic mission.[94] Marsilius's attachment to the imperial cause was a political marriage of convenience: his papal enemy's enemy was Louis the Bavarian, the emperor, for whom he worked as a publicist. This was one of the first instances of the intellectual paladin selling his talents to what he apprehended to be the lesser of two evils.

In stark contrast to the Gregorian policy of co-opting the forces of reform, the Avignon papacy and its counterpart in Rome had utterly failed to come to grips with the spirit of their time. The fourteenth-century papacy put off its day of reckoning with the forces of reform. It succeeded by turning its back on the demands of the present in the vain hope that reassertions of magic, mystery, and authority could preserve its powers. This was a stopgap measure. Henceforth, the justification of power would be accomplished not only by armed men but also by claims for legitimacy which would acknowledge the consent of the governed.[95] Within the Church itself, the splits and schisms of the fourteenth century suggested a conciliar form of governance, which smacked of representative government, in place

92. C. Erickson, "The Fourteenth-Century Franciscans and Their Critics," *Franciscan Studies* 35 (1975): 107–35; A. Williams, "Chaucer and the Friars," *Speculum* 28 (1953): 499–513.

93. N. Rubinstein, "Marsilius of Padua and Italian Political Thought of His Time," in J. R. Hale, J. R. L. Highfield, and B. Smalley (eds.), *Europe in the Late Middle Ages* (London, 1965), 44–75.

94. M. D. Lambert, "The Franciscan Crisis under John XXII," *Franciscan Studies* 32 (1972): 123–43.

95. Georges Duby, *The Age of Cathedrals* (Chicago, 1981), 261–63.

of the unreformed imperial papacy. Although the Conciliar Movement ultimately failed, it provoked the conservative defenders of the papacy into action by appealing to their horror that "Whatever this raging mob decrees is ascribed to the holy spirit." These words were papalist Ambrogio Traversari's comments about the Council of Basel (1436), in which only 20 of more than 500 participants were bishops.[96]

Jan Hus, the Bohemian prophet, suggested an alternative organization of the spiritual powers on this earth when he wrote that

> every faithful disciple of Christ ought to consider when the pope issues an order whether this is expressly the order of any apostle or the law of Christ, or has any foundation in the law of Christ, and recognizing this to be the case he ought reverently and humbly to obey such an order. But if he truly recognizes that the order of the pope goes counter to the order and counsel of Christ, or turns to any harm of the church, then he ought boldly to resist, lest he should become a partner in crime by reason of consent.[97]

Quite clearly, this recipe for decentralized modes of interpretation stood foursquare against the whole project of the Roman Catholic Church, which had, for a thousand years, insisted on the primacy of its interpretation of Christian doctrine.[98] Given the small role the clerical elite played at Basel, it is not altogether surprising that this council had recognized the Bible as the final authority in religious matters. In Germany, too, antipapalism and anticlericalism gave a particular color to emergent national feelings that were strongly felt among the intelligentsia. These anti-Roman sentiments were also pronounced among the official classes of the empire—the princes, the higher nobility who largely manned the estates, and the city governors who all resented ecclesiastical interference in local affairs.[99]

The apostolic urge was being transformed: Abelard's philosophy—with its focus on intention, self-analysis, and contrition—was taken out of the textbooks and imbricated into the piety of the common life. The *devotio moderna* was inspired by a widespread desire to incorporate the monastic ideal with a life of spiritual development within society. The spread of internalized forms of devotion among the laity made the role of the clergy—and in particular the mendicant orders who controlled the business of selling indulgences—seem to many to be both objectionable and

---

96. Quoted in Aston, *The Fifteenth Century,* 138.
97. Quoted in Aston, *The Fifteenth Century,* 129.
98. On this last point see Elaine Pagels, *The Gnostic Gospels* (New York, 1979).
99. W. D. J. Cargill Thompson, "Seeing the Reformation in Medieval Perspective," *Journal of Ecclesiastical History* 25 (1974): 297–308.

anachronistic. In part, of course, this was a continuation of the processes which had been inaugurated with the onset of early modernization. In part, it was also a divergence—another social mutation underscoring and amplifying the novelties wrought by early modernization in the ever-present context of pestilential fury. Spiritual liberation was only the most visible tip of an iceberg of submerged demands for a devolution of interpretative power. Even before the advent of printing and easy access to scriptural authority, the politics of interpretation were becoming increasingly problematic.

5.

The Black Death intensified the contradictions of early modernization by pointedly emphasizing the ambiguous relationship between the clergy and the *saeculum*. Indeed, it modified the the Gregorian distinction between the clergy and the laity by insisting on a renewed Augustinianism which emphasized the difference between the saved and the damned. The path to salvation may have been prepared by Christ's Passion and the suffering of the Virgin Mary, but the massive fact of death—so unpredictable and sweeping in its impact that no one was secure—gave it a personal immediacy and provided the context in which this interpretative search for meaning took place. This drift toward "atomization" was part of a privatization of piety in which the "basic Christian unit tended to become the individual or the family, the privileged place of initiation to elementary religion, to the essential sacraments and daily observance (prayers and fasts)."[100] This shift toward the privacy of the introspective self was part of a more general movement in spatial organization as specialized functions, more rigidly defined, replaced undifferentiated areas. This ideal was "not without parallels to the authorities' vision of the ideal society: more hierarchy, more segregation, stricter regimentation, and closer monitoring of individual behavior."[101]

There is a danger of making an anachronistic assessment of the pre-Reformation Church's vitality from the way in which its public in Germany melted like an April snow in the wake of Luther's stand at the Diet of Worms in 1521. Fifteenth-century Germany was pervaded by a "mood of restlessness, of expectancy, of indefinable anxiety."[102] In fact, evidence

100. Jacques Verger, "Different Values and Authorities," in Robert Fossier (ed.), *The Cambridge Illustrated History of the Middle Ages, 1250–1520* (Cambridge, 1987), 3:150.

101. Philippe Contamine, "Peasant Hearth to Papal Palace: The Fourteenth and Fifteenth Centuries," in Georges Duby (ed.), *A History of Private Life*, vol. 2, *Revelations of the Medieval World* (Cambridge, Mass., 1985), 504.

102. A. G. Dickens, *The German Nation and Martin Luther* (London, 1974), 12.

suggests its continuing popularity: ritual brotherhoods, male *corpus christi* guilds, female rosary cults, the practice of *Augenkommunion* (communion of the eyes), the booming trade in indulgences, innumerable and repetitious masses, pilgrimages, shrines, authorized processions, veneration of saints, mystical writings, the spread of spiritual literature after Gutenberg's presses were put into mass production, predictions, prophecies, hallucinations, dreams, fantasies, visions, hysteria, and an immense funneling of wealth into building new or revamped ecclesiastical edifices. This turbulent, anxious, and often violent piety has been called *Frömmigkeit*.[103]

Frömmigkeit was focused upon the massive uncertainty concerning the appropriate measures to ensure salvation that flourished in the post-plague period. As Bernd Moeller writes, "These were the anxious gestures of people in distress and in need of help. Earlier times had not known their like in such cumulative intensity. . . . [T]hey show that people took the church's competence and effectiveness in matters of salvation just as much for granted as they did the efficacy of good works. . . . [T]he greatest hopes of strength and consolation continued to be the Mass and the eucharist, the central mystery of the church."[104] Indeed, because the eucharist seemed to assure religiosity that could be kept within clerical control, its powers were promoted and fostered by the clerical church as a useful tool in bridging the gulf between their doctrinal knowledge and popular religious behavior.[105] If psychological frenzy was the discourse of these times, then the elevation of the host provided its grammar. The eucharist was the hinge on which a priest-centered religiosity swung. The eucharist was of crucial importance in bringing thaumaturgic magic rituals within clerical surveillance while continuously drawing these syncretic beliefs back into the force-field controlled by the Roman Catholic hierarchy.

This intensified piety was profoundly conformist and nonheretical. If popular piety c. 1500 was conformist, this had not been the case in the first half of the fifteenth century, when heretical movements flourished and "if the church had not suppressed the danger with fire and sword at just the right time, there would have been acute danger of an uprising comparable

103. Bernd Moeller, "Religious Life in Germany on the Eve of the Reformation," in G. Strauss (ed.), *Pre-Reformation Germany* (London, 1977), 13–42. See also Lawrence G. Duggan, "The Unresponsiveness of the Late Medieval Church: A Reconsideration," *Sixteenth Century Journal* 9 (1978): 3–26.

104. Moeller, "Religious Life in Germany on the Eve of the Reformation," 19–20.

105. Charles Zika, "Hosts, Processions and Pilgrimages: Controlling the Sacred in Fifteenth-Century Germany," *Past and Present* 118 (1988): 25–60.

to the Albigensian wars."[106] At the same time, however, eschatological pressures were very high. Heresy seems to have decreased in late medieval Germany, but dissenting prophecy did not. The incidence of these chiliastic visions gives a more valuable index of popular attitudes than counting the prosecutions for heterodoxy. Deep dissatisfactions with the state of Christian order warned of coming chastisement of corrupt clergy while giving hope that a millennial reform was in the not too distant future.[107] The turbulent piety of the laity was pressuring the clergy to keep pace. The clergy failed to do so.

> The church had reached the point where it was unable to do anything more than react to stimuli given by others. Its theology and spiritual life lacked the genuine inner impulse to find its way out of the maze into which its own historical development had brought it. It produced no relevant, helpful response to the yearnings and explosive passions of men [and women] who submitted themselves to the church for guidance. The most characteristic symptom of this lack of response is the fatal importance given in this age to indulgence preaching, with its vulgar materialism and its preaching which was of its very nature so open to misunderstanding.[108]

The expectations of the laity were rising so fast that the performance of the clergy could not keep pace. An indication of how fast the piety of the laity was rising is suggested by the ninety-five confraternities that existed in Hamburg c. 1500. These rosary cults, centering upon the repetitive incantation of the Marian Psalter, proliferated under the ægis of the Dominicans as a similar form of spiritual expression that was especially designed for women.[109]

Intensified lay piety developed hand in hand with skepticism concerning the prestige arrogated by the clerical caste. The six generations living in the conditions of enzootic plague became increasingly anticlerical. In part, this can be explained by clerical abuses such as concubinage, pluralism, absenteeism, and the mechancial performance of routine duties which was particularly evident among the clerical proletariat who were given the task of

---

106. Gerhard Ritter, "Romantic and Revolutionary Elements in German Theology on the Eve of the Reformation," in Steven E. Ozment (ed.), *The Reformation in Medieval Perspective* (Chicago, 1971), 28.

107. Robert E. Lerner, "Medieval Prophecy and Religious Dissent," *Past and Present* 72 (1976): 3–24.

108. Moeller, "Religious Life in Germany on the Eve of the Reformation," 29.

109. Moeller, "Religious Life in Germany on the Eve of the Reformation," 16; Rothkrug, "Religious Practices and Collective Perceptions," 95–99.

performing masses for the donor's and his or her family's souls. In part, it can be related to the resentment that was felt about the clergy's special economic status. Clerics—especially canons in cathedral chapters, who were often younger sons from wealthy, noble families, and the upper levels of the episcopate, who were drawn from the same group—were well educated, well fed, well housed, free from taxation, and beyond the reach of secular justice, yet nonetheless indolent.[110] In part, too, this anticlericalism should be explained by the churchmen's double bind, whereby they could not meet the expectations of the laity even if their own performance was actually improving. Thus it is irrelevant to point out that not all clerics were lax, uneducated, and careless. Indeed, many were not.[111] Moreover, it is very important to keep in mind the massive numerical presence of the clergy, which meant that, in the nature of things, those who looked for sluggards and deadbeats could always find examples. As many as 10 percent of the people in a cathedral town like Worms, and 8 percent in Mainz in 1477 (even before the creation of its university), were members of religious orders. In a very ordinary place like Göttingen, 3 percent were clerics, while in the west Bavarian small town of Nördlingen, religious males constituted about half that level in 1459. These figures should be multiplied fourfold to yield a more realistic estimate of the proportion of the total adult male population who were able-bodied ecclesiastics.[112]

Apprehensive and impatient spirituality was symptomatic of the fears that haunted those who lived in the shadow of the Black Death. Martin Luther was a child of these times, but he rose above them by giving the

110. D. A. Eltis, "Tensions between Clergy and Laity in Some Western German Cities in the Later Middle Ages," *Journal of Ecclesiastical History* 43 (1992): 231–48.

111. Evidence from the small town of Duderstadt in the Eichsfeld district of Saxony (near where Luther spent almost all of his life) suggests that a significant improvement in the educational credentials of clerics continued unabated from the mid-fifteenth century until the Reformation. Many even studied at Erfurt and must have rubbed shoulders with Luther himself, during his student days there. See Reinhold Keirmayr, "On the Education of the Pre-Reformation Clergy," *Church History* 53 (1984): 7–16.

112. Moeller, "Religious Life in Germany on the Eve of the Reformation," 29; Eltis, "Tensions between Clergy and Laity," 233; and Christopher R. Friedrichs, *Urban Society in an Age of War: Nördlingen, 1580–1720* (Princeton, 1979), 35. Obviously there were differences in the numbers of clergy to be found from place to place, but it is worthwhile noting that the Nördlingen figure might be only half that for Göttingen because it was noted for an earlier period. This discrepancy in dating is significant because the number of clerical proletarians (such as chantry priests like the young Thomas Müntzer) exploded upward at the end of the fifteenth century and continued to rise thereafter; see Tom Scott, *Thomas Müntzer: Theology and Revolution in the German Revolution* (New York, 1989), 6.

characteristic *Frömmigkeit* a radically new theological answer to the quest for salvation. Few men have had as big an impact on their contemporaries as Luther, yet ironically, no public man has ever been more contemptuous of this world than Luther. There is a paradox here. Luther was contemptuous of the world but, at the same time, considerate and friendly to his vast circle of acolytes as well as being devotedly loving toward his family. He was gratified by carnal pleasures: his sexual appetite seems to me to be confirmed in his own words, while his passion for music was immense. I am convinced by Marjorie O'Rourke Boyle that we can reconcile these apparent contradictions by understanding that Luther had deeply imbibed the Stoic "binary perspectival system."[113] Looking at social reality through "bifocal lenses" enabled him to distinguish between humankind, about whose depravity he was scornful, and individual men and women, for whom he felt warmth, in whose company he felt joy, and to whom he was often deeply respectful. This intellectual dualism also characterized the way that Luther responded to the influence of Occamist philosophy by squaring reason and revelation in a unique way to overturn a thousand-year tradition of sacramentalizing society.[114]

For Luther, *Herrschaft* took place within the inherited Gelasian framework of Caesar's and Christ's swords. But Luther was derisively contemptuous of worldly power and, indeed, worldly experience. I want to dwell on his life story because, like that of William Marshal or Joan of Arc, Luther's experience acted like a prism through which we can refract the historical palette into its brilliant primary colors. Having done this, I will then reassemble these light waves into an image of my own making, an image that is less concerned with Martin Luther as an individual and more concerned with the lightning rod who collected the social energy of his times and redirected it. This is, I think, a reasonable strategy because it was Luther who gave the early modern language of *Herrschaft* a novel twist by reforming the re-formed Christendom of the year 1000.

Luther, like many others born in this period, experienced its horrors directly: two of his siblings died of the plague. In fact, only four of the nine children born to his parents survived the other terrors of the age to reach adulthood.[115] Martin Luther was born in 1484 in the small town of Mans-

113. Marjorie O'Rourke Boyle, "Stoic Luther: Paradoxical Sin and Necessity," *Archive for Reformation History* 73 (1982): 69–93.

114. Dickens, *The German Nation and Martin Luther*, 80. See also John M. Headley, "The Reformation as a Crisis in the Understanding of Tradition," *Archive for Reformation History* 78 (1987): 5–22.

115. Much of the following discussion is shaped by Heiko Oberman's biography, *Luther: Man between God and the Devil* (New Haven, 1989). I will note other

feld, sixty miles northeast of Erfurt. He was the second son of Hans Luder, a former peasant who had become a *hüttenmeister* (copper-mine foreman). His paternal grandfather, Heine Luder, had been a wealthy peasant in the village of Möhra in Saxony. Hans Luder married up. Martin's mother, Margarethe Lindemann, was the daughter of a well-established family of Eisenach burghers. His mother had married down. Luther's maternal kin were solidly bourgeois and well placed in contemporary Saxony—two pastors, two lawyers, a physician, two schoolmasters, a university docent, two ducal councillors, and three mayors. The Lindemanns were very well educated: three had doctorates, and three had master's degrees. These marital connections seem to have been highly valuable to the struggling entrepreneur Hans Luder and may even have provided some capital for his business ventures. Ian D. K. Siggins suggests that the maternal side of Martin's family was also crucial in forming his personality through the influence of their intense, urban piety. In addition, his mother was probably literate, while his father was probably not. The role of education in shaping the careers of his maternal kin probably made it easier for Martin Luther to stay in school, and it is more than a little significant that there seems to be no evidence of Martin's involvement in Hans Luder's mining activities.[116]

While it may have been the case that Martin Luther was born into the modern world—he had probably heard the story of the budding mining industry at the family table and so became aware of the problems of the entrepreneur—these social forces seem to have made little impact on his development. He was formed by the educational opportunities that his father's hard-won wealth had made possible. Hans Luder was the product of the bimodal system of family formation that threw out its excess children. In his case he was able to leave the family farm with some credit, connections, and an iron will to succeed. There has been a huge controversy over Martin's relationship with his father, sparked by Erik Erikson's *Young Man Luther*. In my opinion this is an anachronistic work. Erikson is remarkably insensitive to cultural difference and historical distance.[117] But

---

works where applicable, but I will not present all page references to Oberman's study except where I quote from it directly. Until its appearance, the standard English-language biography was Roland Bainton, *Here I Stand: A Life of Martin Luther* (New York, 1950).

116. Ian D. K. Siggins, "Luther's Mother Margarethe," *Harvard Theological Review* 71 (1978): 125–50.

117. See Rudolf M. Dekker and Herman W. Roodenburg, "A Suitable Case for Treatment? A Reappraisal of Erikson's *Young Man Luther*," *Theory and Society* 12 (1983): 775–800; see also R. H. Bainton, "Psychohistory and History: An Examina-

Erikson has done us a signal service in emphasizing the struggle within Martin Luther. Rather than being about disobedience to his earthly father, this struggle pivoted on the question of the proper mode of obedience to his divine father. This is a crucial distinction which underscores the difference between the mental world of Martin Luther and ours. Seeing matters in this way enables us to locate Martin Luther's aspirations within their own historical context, a context that was dominated by uncertainty, fear, and the quest for salvation.

Luther's Saxony was a young, vigorous, colonial society in which the strength of princely government was combined with the weakness of local institutions of self-government. Hans Luder frequently relocated his family along this frontier. Martin Luther's boyhood was spent in the small towns of Saxony and Thuringia—Eisleben, Mansfeld, Magdeburg, and Eisenach. His youth was spent in Erfurt, where he went to university and then entered the monastic life. His adult years were mostly lived out in Wittenberg, a tiny town of 2,500 which was thoroughly dominated by the ducal palace and its own university.[118] Luther's genius developed in quiet places. It would be only later, after he became a historical figure in 1517, that his character would mature in the full currents of human life.[119]

Martin Luther's social roots were dominated by his father's quest for earthly riches, which he would, quite literally, dig from the ground. Evidence suggests not only that there was tension between Martin Luther and Hans Luder—a tension made manifest when Luther enrolled himself in a monastic order in opposition to his father's desire that he become a lawyer—but also that Hans Luder came to respect his son's independence. There is rich irony in Luther's choice: not only did he reject his father's career planning, but he also rejected his father's earthly vision in choosing the monastic order which most emphatically distinguished between earthly and spiritual riches. On July 17, 1505, Martin Luther entered the

---

tion of Erikson's *Young Man Luther*," in R. A. Johnson (ed.), *Psychohistory and Religion: The Case of Young Man Luther* (Philadelphia, 1977), 19–56; and L. W. Spitz, "Psychohistory and History: The Case of *Young Man Luther*," in Johnson (ed.), *Psychohistory and Religion*, 57–87. Siggins sensibly points out that it might be more helpful to compare Luther's relationship with his mother—rather like Monica's impact on young Augustine or Susannah's influence on John Wesley—than to focus on the father/son dyad; "Luther's Mother Margarethe," 125–26, 146–50.

118. Thomas A. Brady, "Luther's Social Teaching and the Social Order of His Age," *Michigan Germanic Studies* 10 (1984): 276.

119. This sentence consciously paraphrases Johann Wolfgang von Goethe: "Es bildet ein Talent sich in der Stille, Sich ein Charakter in dem Strom der Welt."

monastery of the Augustinian Hermits in Erfurt. He had turned his back on his father's great expectations; "conversion meant turning away from the world and turning ascetically toward God . . . killing off one's own will, meager meals, coarse clothing, hard work during the day, keeping vigil during the night, chastising the flesh, self-mortification by begging, extensive fasting, and an uneventful monastic life in one place."[120] Martin Luther took his vows to heart.

While Luther's momentous decision to make a lifelong commitment to the monastery came in 1507, after he had served for a couple of years as a novice, the historian can locate it in the "psychogram" of the age. Martin Luther had already spent an adolescent year with the Brethren of Common Life in Magdeburg, where he had been enthralled by both the *devotio moderna* and patristic literature, especially St. Augustine. He then spent four more of his teenage years in Eisenach, where his maternal kin were solidly entrenched, lodging with the town mayor and again connected with a circle of pious laymen that was patronized by Johannes Braun, vicar at the local church of St. Mary. When he went to university at Erfurt, where he became of master of the liberal arts in 1502, he was introduced to the Occamite critique of Aristotelianism that separated God's word from human reason. His academic training was of immense importance in directing Luther away from the scholastic traditions which dominated orthodox theology. When Luther came to study theology, he approached that subject from the nominalists' position.[121]

To a young man of this time, this seemed to be the way to get closer to God and, thereby, to get closer to the assurance of salvation. In an age of *Frömmigkeit*, this was not an unreasonable thing to do. Indeed, Luther was hardly unique in seeking this route to salvation. What was extraordinary about his choice, a choice which his father came to celebrate by finding reflected glory in it, was that he entered the "Black Monastery" of the Observant Augustinians. Here again, we find the "psychogram" of the age being fixed in Luther's own experience. It was in this monastery that

---

120. Oberman, *Luther*, 127. See also George Yule, "Luther and the Ascetic Life," in W. J. Sheils (ed.), *Monks, Hermits, and the Ascetic Tradition* (Oxford, 1985), 229–39.

121. Steven Ozment, "Mysticism, Nominalism and Dissent," in C. Trinkhaus and H. Oberman (eds.), *The Pursuit of Holiness in Late Medieval and Renaissance Religion* (Leiden, 1974), 67–92; Ozment, *The Age of Reform 1250–1550* (New Haven, 1980), esp. chap. 6; Heiko A. Oberman, "The Shape of Late Medieval Thought: The Birthpangs of the Modern Era," *Archive for Reformation History* 64 (1973): 13–33.

Luther began to study Augustine's writings in earnest as early as 1509. Thus began Luther's fusion of Augustinian anthropology with nominalism that would later bear fruit in his "Reformation breakthrough." Luther found a paternal substitute in Father Johannes Von Staupitz, who was the head of the German Augustinian Observants. The Erfurt monastery was a central bastion of radical monastic reform. His connections with Staupitz led Luther up the ladder. Four years after his ordination, Luther was transferred to Wittenberg to rejoin his patron, who had gone there in 1509 to be vicar-general of the order in Germany. Once at Wittenberg, Luther became involved in administration—in 1515 he was elected district vicar in charge of ten monasteries—while also lecturing on the New Testament. Preparing these lectures was perhaps the crucial event in Luther's intellectual voyage of discovery, which led him to question the received doctrine and to formulate a new one.

With the benefit of hindsight which a historian takes for granted, we can see that the building blocks for this novel interpretation had already been set. Martin was the child of an odd couple, a restless entrepreneur and a determined *Hausfrau* who seems to have invested her aspirations to regain lost status in her son—status she lost with her marriage to an uneducated, disinherited peasant. Endowed with immense inner discipline, as a young man Luther had been educated in the most advanced schools of the day. Young man Luther grew up in a world that was in despair about salvation, and everything in his upbringing drew him more deeply into the vortex of despair engendered by these common concerns. Young Luther achieved success in his chosen calling, yet he was unsatisfied. Indeed, so far as we can tell, he lived most of these years in a state of existential uncertainty. Hans Luder, his father, had judged Martin Luther to be disobedient but had later accepted his son's career choice—but this was a small matter compared to the sure and certain knowledge that God the Father judged Martin Luther to be unworthy of his saving grace. This, in a nutshell, was the predicament that Martin Luther—son and sinner, professor and theologian, believer and churchman—faced squarely. It was a predicament that Luther shared with his contemporaries, one that could not be resolved by recourse to accepted practices and received doctrines.

Between his entry into the monastery in 1505 and the fateful day when he posted the Ninety-Five Theses on the door of the Castle Church in Wittenberg, Martin Luther found himself in a double bind. On one hand he tried, with all his might and extraordinary intellectual powers, to understand how he could make himself worthy of God's saving grace, while on the other hand knowing that the decision was not his to make.[122] Like others, the harder he tried, the less success he met in resolving this Sisyphean task. As he said, "My own situation was this: however blameless my life as a monk, I felt myself standing before God as a sinner with a most uneasy conscience; and I could not believe God would be appeased by any satisfaction I could offer. I did not love but hated this just God, who punishes sinners."[123] Luther's genius, then, was to propose a wholly new problematic— or, more correctly, he proposed that the original human anthropology found in the Pauline Epistles of the New Testament was the only guide for humans groping for salvation. In place of the scholastic goal of the monk, the mystic, and the pilgrim, who all endeavored to become like God through their wholesale identification with the divine, Luther's reinvented anthropology removed the possibility that humans could earn their own salvation through the traditional combination of good works, contrition, penance, and indulgences. For this reason, there was no need to endlessly inquire into one's motivations or to minutely subdivide sins, because simple faith in Christ's grace was the answer to the problems of sin, death, and salvation that vexed contemporaries. Thus, Luther argued, humans had to trust absolutely and unconditionally in the goodwill bestowed upon them by Christ's crucifixion. They had to have faith because they could be saved only by faith, and by faith alone. Justification by faith alone, justification through the unearned imputation of Christ's merits to the sinner, formed the flywheel of Luther's theology. Everything else was irrelevant; everything else was just obfuscation. With that, the entire sacramental edifice that had been built up by the Roman Catholic Church was denied legitimacy.

In effect, Luther substituted the claim that the righteous in faith based their hope for salvation on the promise: "For therein [in the Gospel] is the righteousness of God revealed" (Romans 1:17). As he is reported to have written:

> Then I began to understand the righteousness of God as a righteousness by which a just man lives *as by a gift of God, that means by faith.* I realized that it was to be understood this way: the righteousness of God is revealed through the Gospel, namely the so-called "passive" righteousness we receive, *through which God justifies us by faith through grace and mercy.* . . . Now I felt as if I had been born again: the gates had been opened and I had entered Paradise itself.

122. John von Rohr, "Medieval Consolation and the Young Luther's Despair," in Franklin H. Littell (ed.), *Reformation Studies* (Richmond, Virginia, 1962), 61–74.

123. Quoted in Dickens, *The German Nation and Martin Luther,* 86.

It should be noted that Luther's statement occurs almost thirty years after the fact and is somewhat misleading. There was no single moment of transformation but rather "Between 1513 and 1519 he experienced a series of breakthroughs of this kind, although none as significant as that of the understanding of God's righteousness and justification by faith."[124] Because he was devoted to the stark, uncompromising version of original sin that was derived from Augustinian anthropology, Luther had to summon the courage to sweep away the accumulated traditions of Roman Catholicism which claimed that the Church was the appointed channel through which salvation was granted.[125] This was no easy thing to do. In fact, Luther did it in a series of small, incremental steps.

The interaction between Luther's theological maturation and the rush of events inevitably obscures any definitive chronology. Suffice it to say, just two weeks after the Ninety-Five Theses were made public on October 31, 1517, they were translated into German and circulated throughout the country. From their date of publication, Luther became something more than a monk; he became a man of destiny. Luther was a radical and a revolutionary because he trumpeted the unthinkable—the common man had as much right to Christ's mercy as any other, while that mercy was freely given to those who had faith in it. Popular demand was unquenchable. Both in Germany and throughout Europe, the Roman Catholic system of salvation by observances, indulgences, and good works had worked upon popular obsessions like an addiction. Luther's intervention also stimulated an outpouring of popular piety while satisfying this appetite for certainty.

The key role in slaking this popular thirst was played by the printing press, which transmitted Luther's novel theology far and wide. The press turned Lutheranism into the "first mass movement of religious change backed by a new technology . . . of mechanical standardization and reproduction."[126] This is, I think, a point of immense importance since it is one of the main factors which gave Luther's critique of salvationist religion a mass audience. This leads us onto another point: that is, much of what Luther claimed was not particularly new—indeed, he was himself struck

124. Quoted in Oberman, *Luther*, 165 (my emphases), 165–66. See also W. D. J. Cargill Thompson, "The Problems of Luther's 'Tower Experience' and Its Place in His Intellectual Development," in D. Baker (ed.), *Religious Motivation: Biographical and Sociological Problems for the Church Historian* (Oxford, 1978), 187–211.

125. George Yule, "Late Medieval Piety, Humanism and Luther's Theology," in Keith Robbins (ed.), *Religion and Humanism* (Oxford, 1981), 167–79. See also Gerhard Ritter, "Lutheranism, Catholicism, and the Humanistic View of Life," *Archive for Reformation History* 44 (1953): 145–159.

126. Dickens, *The German Nation and Martin Luther*, 103.

by the similarities between his ideas and those of the Bohemian martyr Jan Hus. In fact, he was immediately accused of repeating the Hussite error by his opponents at the Leipzig debates in 1519.[127] Yet there was a difference between Luther and Hus. Both attacked the ecclesiological explanation for the institutional structure of the community of Christian believers, but Luther was able to attract a mass audience in the heartland of the northern Renaissance, whereas the Hussite message became caught up in the confused and fragmented politics of a nascent national liberation movement of a marginal land.[128]

There were many critics of the fifteenth-century church, but none was able to gain the public hearing that accompanied Luther's censures. The reason for his unique powers must be connected to his tremendous skill as a polemicist, skills that were aided and abetted by the radical enlargement in the information technology of the times. Luther was an accomplished philosopher and a revolutionary theologian, but what his audience saw—and identified with—was an anguished, pious, suffering Christian. Like all great historical figures, Luther was immensely complex; the more we delve into this complexity, the greater it becomes. However, his enormous prestige resulted from the grudging admiration that developed for this quarrelling monk.

Martin Luther grasped the existential confusion of living in the wake of the Black Death and rendered an intelligible response to his contemporaries' shared sense of *Frömmigkeit*. As one of Luther's young students wrote to his mother, faith in the pure light of the Gospel superseded the "*fantasey, zauwberey, Teüffels gespennszt,* and *Aberglawben*" (fantasy, magic, Devil's ghosts, and superstition) of her protective charms, fasts, pilgrimages, confession, festivals, vigils, rosary prayers, and endowed masses. For such people, the Reformation was a form of enlightenment that not only drove the old religion's burdensome superstitions out of the mind's eye but also dispelled them from their streets and away from their homes.[129] When Reformation Protestants wrote their autobiographies, it is

---

127. Scott H. Hendrix, " 'We Are All Hussites?,' " *Archive for Reformation History* 65 (1974): 134–60; S. Harrison Thompson, "Luther and Bohemia," *Archive for Reformation History* 44 (1953): 160–80.

128. Frederick G. Heymann, "The Hussite Revolution and the German Peasants' War: An Historical Comparison," *Medievalia et Humanistica*, new ser., 1 (1970): 141–59. See also Frantisek Graus, "The Crisis of the Middle Ages and the Hussites," in Ozment (ed.), *The Reformation in Medieval Perspective,* 76–103; John Klassen, "The Disadvantaged and the Hussite Revolution," *European Studies Review* 35 (1990): 249–72.

129. Ozment, *The Reformation in the Cities,* 83, 82.

clear that they had come to regard the plague as a punishment instituted directly by God, which inspired widespread fear and temporarily dissolved religiously sanctioned social order.[130] The Black Death was domesticated.

THE SOCIAL EARTHQUAKE

"The Social Earthquake" discusses the end of the feudal system in England, which was the result of a political conjuncture, sparked by a demographic disaster. Those who benefited from the old order did not give up their privileges—they lost them. This was not simply a matter of replacing one class with another but, rather, something more subtle: the mutation of both the privileged and subordinate classes into quite differently constituted species. Driving this massive social dislocation was the atrophy of the lords' institutional controls over the bodies of their dependent population and the emergence of a free market in both land and labor. In the midst of these transformations, the pivotal factor was the disintegrating political clout of the seigneurial class in the feudal heartlands. The changing relationship between lords and peasants—the virtual decomposition of lordship—was part and parcel of a wider series of changes which shifted the course of early modernization and changed the character of European society.

The centuries of commercial prosperity that began around the year 1000 have been described as a positive feedback system; equally, the regression that began around 1300, abetted by the massive social catastrophe that came with the recurrent visitations of the Black Death, might be conceived of as a negative feedback system in which declines in one part of the structure acted synergistically to contribute to declines elsewhere.[131] Social and economic linkages unraveled.

The Black Death acted like a trigger in producing a social earthquake. By broadening our sight lines to include these biological and cultural indicators of social change alongside the material ones, we can begin to connect the end of the feudal period with something more than changing population levels. There was nothing predictable about what happened. The Black

---

130. Kaspar von Greyerz, "Religion in the Life of German and Swiss Autobiographers (Sixteenth and Early Seventeenth Centuries)," in *Religion and Society in Early Modern Europe 1500–1800*, 226.

131. Outside Europe, this devolution of the preexisting system of power facilitated Europe's "easy conquest" in Asia during the sixteenth century. In this way, the "Fall of the East" preceded the "Rise of the West"; Abu-Lughod, *Before European Hegemony*, 356–64.

Death was a contingent event—an extraordinary chain connecting the biological mutations of bacilli with the fleas and rats which transmitted the disease to humans. In so doing, the Black Death transformed human history.[132]

1.

There have been two schools of thought on the reasons for the decline of feudalism. Some would argue for a neoclassical set of market relations; others would argue that because the system was established to create a form of sustenance for a warrior class, the key issue was the ability of that class to enforce its will by means of "extra-economic compulsion." The former argument is labeled "neo-Malthusian" because of its emphasis on the dynamic role of population movements; the latter explanation is "Marxist" because it locates the motor of social change in the struggle between classes over the distribution of the surplus product.[133] What is at issue for us is the definition of a *mode of production*—is it an economic struggle connected to the balance between supply and demand curves (of land and labor), or is it the totality of the struggle for subsistence? This debate is frequently muddied by a confusion regarding the distinction between the productive relations of "manorialism" and the political relations of "feudalism," so it is important to distinguish them from one another. Feudal oppression disappeared, but landlords did not.[134] The salience of this point emerges clearly when we look at the social experience of feudalism in the aftermath of the Black Death in England. Because the Peasant's Revolt of 1381 is so inti-

132. This line of argument begs a fundamental question to which I will turn in my concluding remarks: did the Black Death break apart a Malthusian stalemate which, all things being equal, would have precluded growth and development?

133. As is so often the case, structuring the debate in terms of polar opposition is decidedly unhelpful. Rather than looking for an "either/or" form of explanation, we might be better advised to consider one which contemplates "both/and" alternatives set in a historical narrative. But even if population change exerted a necessary, but not sufficient, role in explaining the demise of feudalism, we cannot therefore turn our problem on its head and argue that the class struggle would have succeeded in the absence of significant demographic transformations: that advice would be like Solomon cutting the disputed baby in two in order to satisfy both parties. In addition, it is one thing to note evidence that the contradictions in the feudal system of production were intensifying by the end of the thirteenth century, but it is altogether something else to suggest that, *ceteris paribus*, these difficulties would have brought down the house. We'll never know about that. What we do know is that there was an interaction between the various elements of the social system which went toward reproducing its structure and that that interaction experienced a profound mutation in the fourteenth century.

134. Andrew Jones, "The Rise and Fall of the Manorial System: A Critical Comment," *Journal of Economic History* 33 (1975): 941.

mately linked with the death rattle of feudalism that followed the Black Death, it provides a good point of entry for this discussion.[135]

The Peasant's Revolt was of short duration, and most of the action was localized in the home counties, around London. It was provoked by the king's third poll tax in four years. Its lesson "so far as contemporaries were concerned . . . [was] that taxation did not have to be onerous to be thought intolerable."[136] The Great Revolt of 1381 stopped the "fiscal experiments" (i.e., poll taxes) and "put an end to large expenditures on war. Effective war with France practically ceased" for a generation. The 1381 revolt reversed the drift of fiscal policies, which had, since the reign of Edward I (1271–1307), enabled the crown to wage war by extracting ever-higher taxes from the population.[137]

The boy king's June 14 Charter of Emancipation, issued hurriedly in response to Wat Tyler's demands for the immediate abolition of serfdom and all feudal services, was a dead letter. Parliament revoked Richard II's deal with the peasants the next year, and there is no evidence that it was ever considered to be anything other than a device to forestall events so that the forces of law and order could gain time to respond to the indignities that the peasants had heaped upon them. The rebels' leadership—the millenarian hedge-priest John Ball, the radical populist Wat Tyler, the East Anglian "King of the Commons" Geoffrey Litster, and the St. Albans townsman William Grindecobbe—were all either killed or executed while the eponymous man of the people, Jack Straw, was most likely no more than the figment of the chroniclers' imagination.[138]

135. This was by no means the only social struggle that took place at this time; it is, however, the best documented and the one that is the most subject to sustained historiographical debate on the transition from feudalism to capitalism.

136. A. R. Bridbury, "English Provincial Towns in the Later Middle Ages," *Economic History Review*, 2d ser., 34 (1981): 17.

137. E. Fryde, "Royal Fiscal Systems and State Formation," in Edward Miller (ed.), *The Agrarian History of England and Wales*, vol. 3, *1348–1500* (Cambridge, 1991), 237, 252, 259–60.

138. In regard to this last reference to "Jack Straw," it is, I think, permissible to anachronistically digress. Writing about the *Croquants* in sixteenth- and seventeenth-century southwestern France, Yves-Marie Bercé tells us that "Straw was a symbol of the daily life of the people." A twist of straw took on many different forms, and the words which referred to it were legion. Simultaneously, it was used for the decoration, delimitation, demarcation, and designation of both jurisdictions and social terrain. It stood for the torch or staff of justice while also identifying the lords' property rights. The straw twist additionally signified the communal bakehouse and mill as well as the commons, where people were at liberty to let their livestock forage. The specific meaning of the twist of straw depended upon its usage and the context in which that usage was deployed. Moreover, not only had

The Peasant's Revolt was a brief flash point, but it is of particular importance for three reason. First, it gives us a privileged entry into the minds of both lords and peasants. Second, it provides a reference with which we can chart their political relationship in the wake of the Black Death. Third, it furnishes us with a perspective with which to discern the changes in the relative value of land and labor occurring in the following century, when the foundations were laid for a wholly new social formation in the countryside. The fusion of state and seigneurial powers gave the English Rising its historical importance. It was, above all, a revolt against feudalism. In the words of one contemporary, "the supreme and overriding purpose of the revolt was the abolition of villeinage and all that went with it. This was the heart of the matter."[139]

Even before the Black Death landlords had petitioned seeking aid from the royal courts in improving their legal position against fugitive villeins. Thus, feudal lords were relying on the state to enforce class solidarity among themselves. Confronted with the imminent collapse of their familiar world, the governing elite—king, magnates, and gentry—coalesced under the umbrella of state authority, compelling individuals to stand by their obligations. After the Black Death, legal reforms that were largely oriented toward disciplining the working classes provided an overt and explicit governmental tool for the constitutional exercise of upper-class solidarity.[140] The English state's involvement in the direct enforcement of labor discipline "had the effect of unifying the discontent, because the target of resentment was no longer the individual lord alone but also the local officials of the government."[141]

"the twist of straw acquired this complex of uses . . . [but it also] had become something more than a mere sign. It was also a symbol. It stood for the right of the populace to enjoy a certain *freedom*, either by asserting the existence of a rustic language of that freedom or by marking out its limits. It formed part of a rustic language that was instantly understandable, and constituted a typical piece of peasant imagery. The step from symbol to myth was only a short one. It was natural that straw should become a recognised Croquant emblem." In so doing it identified "a way of life and mode of conduct peculiar to the peasant rebels . . . a kind of 'People's Power' "; *History of Peasant Revolts* (Ithaca, New York, 1990), 286–87.

139. Quoted in E. B. Fryde and Nathalie Fryde, "Peasant Rebellion and Peasant Discontents," in Miller (ed.), *The Agrarian History of England and Wales*, vol. 3, *1348–1500*, 760.

140. Robert C. Palmer, *English Law in the Age of the Black Death, 1348–1381* (Chapel Hill, 1993), 12, 141, 213. See also Fryde and Fryde, "Peasant Rebellion and Peasant Discontents," 754–55.

141. R. H. Hilton, "Peasant Movements in England before 1381," in *Class Conflict and the Crisis of Feudalism* (London, 1985), 62. See also Fryde and Fryde, "Peasant Rebellion and Peasant Discontents," 753–60.

The state apparatus and the feudal system of landholding had joined forces in the wake of the Black Death, when it seemed that a dearth of labor might send its cost skyrocketing.[142] Almost as soon as the plague reached England's shores, the 1349 Ordinance of Labourers was proclaimed. Less than two years later, the next Parliament enacted the 1351 Statute of Labourers because

> a great part of the people, and especially of workmen and servants, lately died of the pestilence, many—seeing the necessity of masters and great scarcity of servants—will not serve unless they may receive excessive wages, and some rather willing to beg in idleness than by labour to get their living.[143]

The sudden opportunity that the plague mortality gave to surviving laborers—to secure higher wages or to demand personal and tenurial freedom—catalyzed the political nation.[144] To the landowners who sat in Parliament, the population collapse had already transformed supply and demand to make labor scarce, but they were not going to permit these market forces to make it expensive, too.[145] "Almost overnight the Commons became the allies of the Crown and the Lords and their necessary agents for the enforcement of this policy [of legislative suppression of commoners' aspirations] in the shires."[146] This labor legislation was aimed at keeping wages

142. Everywhere, across Europe, "From Spain to Norway, princes, parliaments and city magistrates vied with each other to regulate wages"; Léopold Genicot, "Crisis: From the Middle Ages to Modern Times," in M. M. Postan (ed.), *The Cambridge Economic History of Europe*, vol. 1 (Cambridge, 1966), 706. The Castilian Cortes of 1351, for example, fixed wages of workers in response to allegations that "those who went to work in the fields demanded such high wages that the owners of the farms could not comply"; R. E. F. Smith, "Medieval Agrarian Society in Its Prime: Spain," in Postan (ed.), *The Cambridge Economic History of Europe*, vol. 1, 438. See also Philip Jones, "Medieval Agrarian Society in Its Prime: Italy," in Postan (ed.), *The Cambridge Economic History of Europe*, vol. 1, 362.

143. Quoted in E. Lipson, *The Economic History of England* (London, 1956), I:114.

144. Robert Palmer suggests that the landlords' need to reassert their control in the wake of the Black Death created the conditions in which the gentry emerged as local magistrates. Indeed, the need for officers of the Crown to staff these intermediate roles gave the gentry one of its defining characteristics as justices of the peace; *English Law in the Age of the Black Death, 1348–1381*, esp. 14–27.

145. John Hatcher, "England in the Aftermath of the Black Death," *Past and Present* 144 (1994): 10.

146. Gerald L. Harriss, "War and the Emergence of the English Parliament, 1297–1360," *Journal of Medieval History* 2 (1976): 53–55. In this article Harriss suggests that the ultimate congealment of the English early modern system of fiscal/constitutional order was provoked by the conditions developing after the Black Death which led the Crown, the Lords, and the Commons to redeploy sover-

down, and some local justices enforced its provisions, but many other members of their class simply ignored the law of the land in their rush to look after their own business.[147]

Similar laws were enacted in other countries, but what distinguished the Ordinance and Statute of Labourers was that they were enforced. Money collected from laborers was used to reduce property owners' tax burdens. The special standing committees made up of gentlemen property owners, who were charged with the enforcement of these antilabor laws, were given a share of the profits.[148] Recourse to these new laws was significant. In Lincolnshire, for example, nearly two cases in five were connected with breaking its compulsory services clauses, demanding and taking higher wages, or charging excessive prices. Most of those charged were laborers; few employers were prosecuted.[149] In 1352, for example, almost 10 percent of government revenues—more than £10,000 (out of a total of £114,767)— was raised by the yield from these penalties.[150] If these statutes were legislated by—and for—the feudal landowners, they were not without support from the wealthier elements in the village community, who also employed the labor of commoners.[151]

In the changed conditions which developed after the massive depletions caused by the Black Death, landlords had thus tried to use the political relationship inherent in feudal tenures to protect themselves from the new realities of the marketplace. The implementation of labor legislation reflected the constellation of political forces centered in Parliament, describ-

---

eignty to the Crown-in-Parliament. "By the second half of the fourteenth century there had formed a political society whose community of interest and common assumptions were to ensure the stability of English political life until the seventeenth century." Ironically, Harriss's argument lends greater weight to the impact of the Black Death than to war financing in explaining the development of the Crown-in-Parliament system of governance.

147. Mavis Mate, "Labour and Labour Services on the Estates of Canterbury Cathedral Priory in the Fourteenth Century," *Southern History* 7 (1985): 55–67.

148. W. M. Ormrod, "The Politics of Pestilence: Government in England after the Black Death," in W. M. Ormrod and P. G. Lindley (eds.), *The Black Death in England* (Stamford, 1996), 156.

149. Barbara Hanawalt, "Peasant Resistance to Royal and Seignorial Impositions," in F. X. Newman (ed.), *Social Unrest in the Late Middle Ages* (Binghamton, N.Y., 1986), 38 (citing the unpublished doctoral research of Madonna Hettinger).

150. Money derived from enforcing this legislation was used to defray taxes that were granted to prosecute the war with France; B. H. Putnam, *The Enforcement of the Statute of Labourers* (New York, 1908), 128–29.

151. L. R. Poos, "The Social Context of the Statute of Labourers' Enforcement," *Law and History Review* 1 (1983): 27–52.

ing the gravitational orbit of social relations in the fields and forests of the countryside. From a bottom-up perspective, there was little evidence that the landlords were willing to give up their extralegal powers conferred by the laws of villeinage; indeed, "the real significance of the labour laws lies not so much in their actual application as in the threat they posed to the interests and rights of all those—about a third of the total population—that made their livelihood by selling their services on the open market."[152]

The wage regulations of 1349–51 were "the most zealously enforced ordinance in medieval English history."[153] In Essex, which would be the flash point of the Peasant's Revolt, a generation later, "In 1352 alone, 7,556 persons (about 20 per cent of them women) were fined for Statute of Labourers violations . . ., and the estreat roll recording these fines does not cover seven of the county's eighteen hundreds. Thus it is likely that, at a crude estimate, roughly one in seven Essex people older than their mid-teens, or nearly one in four Essex males in the same age-range, were fined for violating the labour legislation in a single year."[154] Since about 50 percent of all Essex adult males were laborers, it would seem that one in two of them were charged with violating the law of the land and, one suspects, most of the rest were probably getting higher wages than allowed for in the Statute of Labourers but were not charged.

The immensely heavy mortality caused by the Black Death may have been "more purgative than toxic"[155] because the surplus population had been so great before 1348. The recurrent visitations of the pestilence created unprecedented contradictions between the interests of feudal landowners and the dependent population. These contradictions were not resolved immediately. The trickle of feudal rents and incidental payments demanded from villeins did not immediately cease, as might be expected in a situation in which labor became scarce. The first appearance of the plague was followed by a long series of poor harvests, leading to high prices which provided employers some flexibility in dealing with their laborers' demands for higher wages. If seigneurial incomes seemed to maintain themselves, it was largely because wages were traditionally "sticky." Or, to look

152. Ormrod, "The Politics of Pestilence," 158. Ormrod's assertion that one-third of the total population was proletarians is very interesting; unfortunately, it is unclear how he came to this figure. It is also unclear if they were full- or part-time proletarians. Of course, it is also unclear how much higher their numbers had been before the onset of the plague.

153. Fryde and Fryde, "Peasant Rebellion and Peasant Discontents," 755.

154. Poos, *A Rural Society after the Black Death*, 241.

155. A. R. Bridbury, "The Black Death," *Economic History Review*, 2d ser., 26 (1973): 584–85.

at this matter from another perspective, as R. H. Hilton suggests, "there was a general seigneurial reaction between the first plague [1348] and the 1370s, showing itself in the successful depression of wages below their natural level and in a relative increase in revenues from land."[156] Rising prices also masked the changing terms of trade between land and labor. Indeed, "in the generation after the Black Death, many a lord may have come nearer to taking the surplus product of his servile tenants than his predecessors in title had ever done."[157] The post–Black Death generation had been, in the words of another historian, "the Indian summer of demesne farming."[158] The harvest of 1375 was the best in twenty-five years and ushered in a new age in price history, but the 40 to 50 percent drop in prices did not bring wages down. In fact, these new circumstances drove employers to their "first unwaveringly resolute attempt ever made to get the [labor] legislation of 1351 enforced."[159]

If the "seigneurial reaction" after the Black Death was not completely successful, it was not for want of trying on the part of the upper classes. In the century after the Black Death, eight pieces of labor legislation were passed by the English Parliament, all with the aim of fixing rates of pay, enforcing contracts of employment, making work compulsory when offered (at fixed rates of pay), and even trying to require migrant workers to carry a kind of internal passport.[160] These severe demands proved to be unenforceable because it was impossible to create and to sustain the kind of surveillance network that would carry out the letter of the law. The feudalists' failure reflected both their reluctance to buck the economic currents of the time

156. R. H. Hilton, *The Decline of Serfdom in Medieval England* (London, 1983), 40–41. For a more skeptical assessment of the effectiveness of the post-plague "seigneurial reaction," see R. H. Britnell, "Feudal Reaction after the Black Death in the Palatinate of Durham," *Past and Present* 128 (1990): 28–47, as well as John Hatcher, who goes on at some length about the nonmonetary equivalents which landlords had to use to bribe their laborers to work and their tenants and *famuli* to stay; "England in the Aftermath of the Black Death," esp. 20 ff.

157. Barbara F. Harvey, "Introduction: The 'Crisis' of the Early Fourteenth Century," in Campbell (ed.), *Before the Black Death*, 23.

158. Bridbury, "The Black Death," 583–84.

159. Bridbury, "The Black Death," 590–91. Bridbury seems to connect the new regime of low grain prices with the demise of demesne farming. This argument is given a further twist by Mavis Mate, who suggests that the key turning point took place at the end of the 1380s, since there had been a brief hiatus in the downward drift of prices in the early part of that decade; "Agrarian Economy after the Black Death: The Manors of Canterbury Cathedral Priory, 1348–1391," *Economic History Review*, 2d ser., 30 (1984): esp. 352–54.

160. Elaine Clark, "Medieval Labor Law and English Local Courts," *American Journal of Legal History* 27 (1983): 330–53.

and the plebeians' ability to move with them. It has been estimated that wage levels rose three- or fourfold in the century after the Black Death.[161]

The Indian summer of demesne farming was quickly followed by the winter of the feudalists' discontent. The Peasant's Revolt must be situated in this transition:

> the root cause of the Revolt . . . is to be found in the persistent attempts made by manorial lords and employers of all degrees to halt changes which no power on earth could check or halt, still less reverse. If there had been no attempt to interfere with these changes there would have been no Revolt. . . . [W]hen everyone in authority, wherever one turned for work, seemed to be in a conspiracy to snatch back all the advantages and opportunities that surviving the pestilence afforded to even the humblest labourer, then the king's foreign gambles, his everlasting proddings and probings for money, and his newfangled taxes, proved to be more than ordinary men and women were prepared to put up with.[162]

Something had had to give. In the event, seigneurialism withered away as the social relations of production were de-feudalized across the length and breadth of the English countryside.

A century ago, J. Thorold Rogers wrote that the "solid Fruits of victory rested with the insurgents of June 1381 . . . the perils had been so great and the success of the insurrection was so near that wise men saw that it was better silently to grant that which they had stoutly refused in Parliament to concede."[163] Eight years later, in fact, the parliamentary regulations of 1389 recognized that the new conditions of peasant mobility and labor shortage had put an end to the reign of custom. This statute enacted that wages were to be promulgated locally, twice a year. Such flexibility was previously unknown. It was a frank acknowledgment that market relations and seigneurial controls could no longer continue to coexist.[164]

---

161. Christopher Dyer, "Were There Any Capitalists in Fifteenth-Century England?," in Jennifer Kermode (ed.), Enterprise and Individuality in Fifteenth-Century England (Stroud, Gloucestershire, 1991), 12.

162. A. R. Bridbury, "Introduction," in The English Economy from Bede to the Reformation (London, 1992), 37.

163. J. Thorold Rogers, Six Centuries of Work and Wages (London, 1903), 265; quoted in R. H. Hilton and T. S. Aston (eds.), "Introduction," The English Rising of 1381 (London, 1984), 2. Rogers's point seems to have escaped R. B. Dobson, who believes that "the results of the great revolt seem to have been negative where they were not negligible," so that it was "a historically unnecessary catastrophe"; The Peasants' Revolt of 1381 (London, 1970), 27–28.

164. Fryde and Fryde, "Peasant Rebellion and Peasant Discontents," 788–97. It is surely of capital importance that when the parliament of 1445 tried to abrogate

2.

Even though they had not constituted a majority of the rural population, the servile tenants of the thirteenth century had been peculiarly privileged by their access to land held in customary tenure. In that period of acute overpopulation, land shortage, and vanishing prospects for internal colonization, the customary population was made to pay for the maintenance of its servility. Whatever small benefits it derived from being protected from market forces was countered by the intensification of the bonds of feudal relations. Taken together, these factors had provided the gravitational field of English feudalism in the period when *la révolution censive* was in full swing elsewhere in Europe.[165]

At the time of the Black Death, the village community was not an undifferentiated mass with identical interests. Recognized customs from a time of land shortage could become exploitative in a time of surplus land. Changes in the level of population or the supply of land could alter supply and demand but by themselves are insufficient to explain the character of political struggle. This is because the power of feudal lords was not solely related to such economistic measures. Their powers were economic as well as social, political, and juridical. These powers were backed up by their monopoly on military force, which was cloaked in a mantle of parliamentary legislation. This point provides a framework for understanding the three-pronged, popular response to the seigneurial offensive after the Black Death: first, some negotiated favorable terms in exchange for accepting the continuation of feudal relations; second, many simply walked away from their obligations and negotiated new contracts as free men; and third, there were continuous uprisings and revolts, the most famous of which occurred in 1381. The second tactic proved to be the most successful because it

the local setting of wages, it provoked popular revolts and widespread noncompliance by masters and workers.

165. Marc Bloch, "The Rise of Dependent Cultivation and Seigneurial Institutions," in Postan (ed.), *The Cambridge Economic History of Europe*, vol. 1, 265–69. In this context, it does not seem to matter much whether the feudalists' various labor services were all used to farm the demesne or if they were simply an instrument of fiscality to wedge money from the peasant population. The main point is that English feudal landlords kept their customary populations within their immediate control and so were able to siphon off a much greater portion of their peasants' surplus than their continental counterparts who had sold off (i.e., commuted) much of the fiscal benefit deriving from extra-economic compulsion. For this reason, I find Father Raftis's analysis of variations within the peasant community to be somewhat beside the main point, no matter how interesting his research may be. In this respect, see his recent work *Peasant Economic Development*, *passim*.

probed the upper class at its weakest point, whereas armed resistance provoked terrible repression. The second tactic made the most sense to a laboring population whose work experiences were varied, flexible, discontinuous, mobile, and situational.

Workers wanted to be paid in cash, and they resisted seigneurial attempts to fix them with yearly contracts not only because they preferred to determine when, where, and how much of their labor was to be supplied but also because "Full-time service smacked of servility."[166] In contrast to the conditions of underemployment and outright unemployment which characterized the pre-plague era, laborers living in the third quarter of the fourteenth century were thrust into the novel circumstances of belonging to "a workforce which was simultaneously demanding high wages and refusing to accept work. . . . Refusal to work was apparently endemic. The compulsory service and the maximum wage clauses of the legislation were, of course, intimately linked, and some of the refusal to work was undoubtedly due to an unwillingness to accept employment for wages pegged at statutory levels. But it is also clear that the opposite was true: work was being refused because high wages had already been earned."[167]

For employers, the ability to control servants in their household—as opposed to masterless wage laborers who lived elsewhere and whose freedom was not limited by the patriarchal authority of househol50heads—was paralleled by another incentive, to substitute cheaper female workers for their more expensive male counterparts where this was feasible.[168] The economistic logic of resistance by wage workers is clearly evident from historical statistics which show that the real wages of *famuli* (servile estate laborers) rose more slowly and never reached the final levels of laborers, craftsmen, and others who were paid at a daily rate and who could find their own food—or get it provided under the table, as it were.[169]

---

166. Simon A. C. Penn and Christopher Dyer, "Wages and Earnings in Late Medieval England: Evidence from the Enforcement of the Labour Laws," *Economic History Review*, 2d ser., 43 (1990): 356–76; Nora Ritchie (née Kenyon), "Labour Conditions in Essex in the Reign of Richard II," in E. M. Carus-Wilson (ed.), *Essays in Economic History*, vol. 2 (London, 1962), 91–111.

167. Hatcher, "England in the Aftermath of the Black Death," 27.

168. Poos, *A Rural Society after the Black Death*, 182.

169. D. L. Farmer, "Prices and Wages," in Miller (ed.), *The Agrarian History of England and Wales*, vol. 3, 1348–1500, 467–83. Farmer does not make much of this point regarding nonmonetary supplements, whereas John Hatcher gives it great prominence in his critical survey of this article and other works which favor statistical evidence; "England in the Aftermath of the Black Death," 23–25. In a posthumously published article, Farmer contradictorily asserted that, on one hand, "The amount and content of the grain livery given to *famuli* was more important

There is also evidence that it became more common for women—both single and married—to work outside the family household for wages. There is even some evidence that such women were sometimes paid the same wage (for the same task) that men were paid, although they were unlikely to be engaged in hay mowing, the highest-paid work.[170] If employers made tactical decisions in balancing their payments to female servants and male laborers, these tactics were absolutely local actions—global thinking was quite different, as is evident from the preamble to the 1388 Statute of Cambridge: "Servants and labourers will not serve and labour, and have not for a long time, without outrageous and excessive pay, much more than has been given to such servants and labourers in any past time."[171]

While we must consider the prescriptive contempt that is evident from the source of this remark, it is also crucial evidence of the local, strategic power that servants and laborers possessed in withholding their labor from the rural economy when they chose to do so. They could withhold their labor because they were now being paid a lot more for each unit of labor they supplied and because prices were plummeting in the last quarter of the fourteenth century. In addition, the reduction in population pressure made it possible for each one of them to benefit more from their common rights—even in areas like Essex, where early enclosure had restricted their access to chases, fens, forests, marshes, and woodlands.

Because villagers in the thirteenth century had, in effect, been punished by manorial lords for their freedom, it is not surprising that peasants had attached surprisingly little value to it. When labor was plentiful and land was scarce, villeins had been rewarded by manorial lords for their servility. They, not freemen, had access to manorial land because they, not freemen,

---

to their condition than the money payments most received," but on the other hand, "It was, however, very rare in the fourteenth and fifteenth centuries for lords to provide substantial quantities of food outside these [festive] seasons for those who still held [land] in serjeanty"; "The *Famuli* in the Later Middle Ages," in Britnell and Hatcher (eds.), *Progress and Problems in Medieval England,* 233, 234.

170. Simon A. C. Penn, "Female Wage-Earners in Late Fourteenth-Century England," *Agricultural History Review* 35 (1987): 1–14. It is unclear if the exclusion of women from mowing was a matter of muscle power or simple sex discrimination. For a discussion of this point, for a later period, see Michael Roberts, "Sickles and Scythes: Women's and Men's Work at Harvest Time," *History Workshop* 7 (1979): 7–9. If it could be shown that *most* women were paid at an equal rate to most men, then my earlier criticisms of Smith and Goldberg's explanation of late ages at first marriage for women would be undermined. Penn's research does suggest that their argument might be illustrated with a few local examples, but the weight of most other evidence I have seen would seem to suggest otherwise.

171. Quoted in Poos, *A Rural Society after the Black Death,* 209.

could be subject to feudal exactions. This is why free men (and, occasionally, free women) were willing to take on the feudal responsibilities and villein status in order to farm manorial land before the Black Death.[172] Seen in the perspective of this long-standing experience of feudal exactions and their newly acquired knowledge regarding the economic benefits of freedom, the competition for labor gave the unfree population an unparalleled opportunity to seek out a better life elsewhere. In the words of a 1376 Commons petition:

> above all and a grater mischief is the receiving of such vagrant labourers and servants when they have fled from their master's service; for they are taken into service immediately in new places, at such dear wages that example and encouragement is afforded to all servants to depart into fresh places, and go from master to master as soon as they are displeased about any matter. For fear of such flights, the commons now dare not challenge or offend their servants, but give them whatever they wish to ask, in spite of the statutes and ordinances of the realm.[173]

In the later fourteenth century the changing terms of trade between now-scarce labor and now-plentiful land made a mockery of the earlier state of affairs, so that the cost, as it were, of villeinage would have become painfully obvious. Moreover, it should not be forgotten that the manorial lords' immediate response to their declining incomes had been to turn the feudal screw ever tighter. Thus it is appropriate to note that there was a spatial dimension to the Peasant's Revolt and the attempted reimposition of strict seigneurial controls which raised tensions in the highly manorialized south and east, where demesne production for the market was most firmly entrenched and where labor services were least likely to have been commuted. In these fluid circumstances the indignity of villeinage would have been exacerbated by the increasingly heavy economic penalties attached to it.[174]

Villeins struck out against their servitude and resisted feudal exactions. The quantitative extent of such flight is not really crucial, because if some fled, then the others bargained from a much stronger position. Furthermore, such mobility was probably more characteristic of the smallholders

---

172. M. M. Postan, "Legal Status and Economic Conditions in Medieval Villages," in *Essays on Medieval Agriculture and General Problems of the Medieval Economy* (Cambridge, 1973), 283–84.

173. Quoted in Hatcher, "England in the Aftermath of the Black Death," 19–20.

174. For an especially good overview of these forces, see Fryde and Fryde, "Peasant Rebellion and Peasant Discontents," 745–68, 784–97.

and cottagers than the substantial villeins who were the central core of the manorial tenantry. In the Huntingdonshire manor of Broughton, for example, fifty-six of ninety-six tenements had acquired new tenants between 1380 and 1400.[175] Obviously, this was a matter not only of old tenant families dying out and/or migrating but also of new ones taking up vacant holdings. It would thus appear that before 1400 the population had not dwindled to such an extent that there was no longer a demand for manorial holdings. But, in contrast to earlier periods, what is unusual about the end of the fourteenth century is that it had now become the tenants—most often the smaller ones—who were exercising choice by switching masters. The feudal lords of Broughton were no longer able to use their monopsony control over land to regulate the mass of the population. This state of affairs was acceptable to the lords because what they now had come to prize—even above their feudal rights, which were vanishing before their very eyes—was their need to maintain an income flow and their capital base, by whatever means necessary.[176]

Zvi Razi's analysis of the manor of Halesowen suggests that if outmigration had been a trickle before the Black Death, it was a constant stream in the next three generations, and it became a flood after about 1430. Razi also discovered that there was a sharp fall in the amount of land transferred within families and a correlative doubling in the land which the lord was leasing in an almost–free marketplace setting. Three-fifths of the landholding peasants identified in the 1310s had been still resident in the 1390s. In contrast, just one-quarter of the Halesowen families in 1410 survived to the 1490s. Thus, the fourth decade of the fifteenth century seems to have been a turning point in the local history of seigneurial control in Halesowen.[177] The fourth decade of the fifteenth century was precisely the moment when English fortunes in France were dramatically reversed and the landlord class switched from external predation to the internecine feud. Is it merely a coincidence that this decade should witness the dismantling of both the feudal state and the feudal manor?

The success of their ancestors' actions in keeping legal surveillance over their peasants to themselves rebounded against landowners in the changed

175. Raftis, *Peasant Economic Development*, 110.

176. Raftis writes directly to this point: "the nub of the matter was the [tenants'] financial capacity to enter and maintain valuable holdings. The lords of Ramsay, as no doubt lords elsewhere, gave priority to prospective tenants who could furnish the entry fines and maintain well-capitalized properties"; *Peasant Economic Development*, 19.

177. Zvi Razi, "The Myth of the Immutable English Family," *Past and Present* 140 (1993): 26–33.

conditions after the Black Death. Lawless gangsterism, virulent anticlericalism, popular fear and loathing of incompetent, self-serving authorities were all indications that the center was not holding.[178] Another indication of the declining powers of the feudal lords was the servile peasantry's temerity in petitioning Parliament for freedom in 1373 and then again in 1377. This second time it had the audacity to tell the collection of landlords sitting in Westminster about withdrawals of labor, confederacies, threatening behavior, the collection of fighting funds to defray legal costs, and even the purchase of exemplifications of the Domesday Book to provide evidence of freedoms subsequently lost after the Norman Conquest.[179]

Furthermore, England was not completely free from peasant *jacquerie* which burned administrative paper. During the 1381 Peasant's Revolt, for instance, many instances of this kind of retribution took place.[180] However, even during the Peasant's Revolt there appears to have been a fine discrimination among administrative materials on the part of the insurgents. Thus, for the most part they seem to have destroyed documents sealed with green wax because this was the color used for documents issued by the exchequer.[181] Indeed, this discriminating destruction points to the fact that most of the violence during the Peasant's Revolt was concerned with attacking the persons and property of the state; in particular, specific and selective assaults were confined to the fiscal and judicial establishment involved with the collection of the hated poll taxes.[182] The destruction of En-

178. Fryde and Fryde, "Peasant Rebellion and Peasant Discontents," 797–813.
179. Bridbury, "Introduction," *The English Economy from Bede to the Reformation*, 33.
180. L. R. Poos, "Peasant 'Biographies' from Medieval England," in N. Bulst and J.-P. Genet (eds.), *Medieval Lives and the Historian* (Kalamazoo, 1986), 201–2. See also Christopher Dyer, "Social and Economic Background to the Revolt of 1381," in Hilton and Aston (eds.), *The English Rising of 1381*, 12–13.
181. It is interesting to learn that "The uniquely complete and voluminous resources that survive today in the Public Record Office indicate that the rebels in 1381 can have created very few significant lacunae in the principal archives of the central government"; W. M. Ormrod, "The Peasants' Revolt and the Government of England," *Journal of British Studies* 29 (1991): 7. Why was this so? Ormrod suggests that one reason why the rebels did not wreak more havoc on these administrative materials was that comparatively few members of the government were actually to be found in the capital on the days in question. In the countryside, it was another question, and attacks on shire officials were more widespread and indiscriminate than those on their colleagues in the capital. While few officeholders in the shires were actually killed, they were hated as both officers of the state and local landlords (8–14), and this may account for why, in Essex for example, two-thirds of the series of manorial rolls now extant were damaged during the Peasant's Revolt (19).
182. Nicholas Brooks, "The Organization and Achievements of the Peasants of Kent and Essex in 1381," in H. Mayr-Harting and R. I. Moore (eds.), *Studies in Me-*

glish manorial records would become a common feature of the English social scene after 1381.[183]

Another significant subtext which ran through the English Rising was the way in which resistance to state authority was fueled by the spread of virulent anticlericalism and heresy. John Wyclif's heterodox interpretation of the Eucharist was perhaps the most visible factor undermining the hold that the Church had on its flock. Anticlericalism and eschatological visions of social retribution and judgment were also being spread by disenchanted members of the lesser clergy before and during the events of 1381. We should not forget that it was the hedge-priest John Ball who told the rebellious insurgents that "things cannot go well in England nor ever shall until all things are in common and there is neither villein nor noble, but all of us are of one condition." In saying this, Ball echoed the Joachite prophecies that seem to have found great resonance in England. He was also repeating, for popular consumption, the academic theological points concerning clerical riches and spiritual poverty which John Wyclif raised in his Oxford lectures.[184] High-ranking clerics were the targets of popular anger. Nor should we underestimate the significance of the fact that the Peasant's Revolt reached its climax on Corpus Christi Day (Thursday, June 13, 1381): "A day appropriated to celebrating the supreme sacrifice of Christ on the cross was thus a supremely appropriate day to celebrate the freedom thereby purchased equally for all men."[185]

We are able to catch an exceptional understanding of this process of disaffection within the village community from William Langland's *Piers the Ploughman*, the great vernacular poem of the period. Written in the late 1370s by an unbeneficed clergyman, a member of the clerical proletariat, the poem's poetic power is a reflection of Langland's openness to the diverse, contradictory, and even opposed ideological tendencies of the time.[186]

---

dieval History (London, 1985), 247–70; Margaret Aston, "Corpus Christi and Corpus Regni: Heresy and the Peasants' Revolt," *Past and Present* 143 (1994): 11.

183. R. B. Dobson, *The Peasants' Revolt of 1381*, 334; cited by Fryde and Fryde, "Peasant Rebellion and Peasant Discontents," 784.

184. Guy Fourquin, *The Anatomy of Popular Rebellion* (New York, 1978), 72–73, 101; N. Cohn, *The Pursuit of the Millennium*, 198–204.

185. Margaret Aston, "Corpus Christi and Corpus Regni," 19.

186. W. A. Pantin, *The English Church in the Fourteenth Century* (Cambridge, 1955); cited in J. F. Goodridge, "Introduction," *Piers the Ploughman* (Harmondsworth, 1966), 9. All further references to the poem are to this edition. I am following the reading suggested by David Aers in "*Piers Plowman* and Problems in the Perception of Poverty: A Culture in Transition," *Leeds Studies in English* 14 (1983): 5–25.

While mainly concerned with the plowman's spiritual pilgrimage, Langland gives us unique insight into contemporary social relations from the bottom up in recounting Piers's quest. At the beginning of his way, the protagonist is confronted with "wasters" and "beggars"—work-shy shirkers whose oppositional culture is centered on the tavern. There, Gluttony and his motley plebeian horde—shoemakers, tinkers, gamekeepers, hackneymen, haberdashers, whores and wenches, and parish clerks, ditchers, fiddlers, rat catchers, scavengers, rope makers, troopers—blasphemously parody the discourse of the official culture and reject its work ethos.[187]

Having reserved to himself the discretionary power to determine "a fair wage" and "food as he could spare," the plowman's world is turned right side up. Social relations are squared with biblical injunction:

> The sluggard will not plow by reason of the cold:
> therefore shall he beg in the harvest, and have nothing.[188]

Charity has thus been transformed into a discriminatory instrument so that Piers, and the other employers like him, would be able to use the threat of starvation to create a disciplined and docile labor force. The disciplinary employer and his subordinated hirelings foreshadowed a diabolical new moral order—the world of market relations that would utterly destroy a millennium of Christian charity. Langland, however, was something more than an apologist for the contemporary social order. He was deeply troubled by the emergent ethos of productive labor and the regimentation of workers.[189]

The post–Black Death landlord class was itself in a state of flux. "Of the 136 barons who attended the house of lords at the end of the thirteenth

187. *Piers the Ploughman*, 70–71.
188. *Piers the Ploughman*, 87.
189. We find in *Piers the Ploughman* a strong sense of contradictory currents of his time. Langland's response was pregnant with meaning. He valued labor and absolute, voluntary poverty—the internalization of work discipline and the imitation of Christ—in the worldly pursuit of holiness. His genius shows us how these divided social images could be held together—and even resolved—in one man's vision. Others must have wondered about the need for elaborate and expensive ecclesiastical institutions. They must also have been troubled by the ways in which the age-old question of poverty was being redefined to justify the Church's vast worldly wealth, diverted from assisting the truly needy. This money grab was justified by arguing that the poor would be disciplined and regulated as the object of social control and not the subject of spiritual concern. It would be enormously condescending to the intelligence of Langland's contemporaries if we were to allow his vision to be exceptional. Indeed, the poet's genius derives from his ability to explicate, generalize, and imaginatively reconstruct the dilemmas which they were all experiencing in everyday life.

century, the direct descendants of only 16 still survived in 1500, and only about a fifth of the gentry in 1500 can be traced back to landed families of their counties in 1300."[190] Furthermore, the income tax returns of 1412 show that the peerage had on average no more than a quarter of the land held by the whole armigerous class (i.e., the gentry and the nobility combined). Magnates, "engulfed in a sea of gentry families," had to run with the grain of political society. The growth of an intermediate class of gentlemen changed the social organization of the shires and thus created not only a political society but also something that could be equated with a nascent public opinion.[191]

The feudal class had been successful in the early Middle Ages because of its "extraordinary intra-class cohesiveness . . . manifested simultaneously in its formidable military strength, in its ability to regulate intra-lord conflict, and in its capacity to dominate the peasantry."[192] Now, pressed hard by rising expenditures and driven to the wall by declining manorial revenues resulting from their inability to dominate the peasantry and lord it over their dependents, the great feudal lords resorted to simple plunder in which it was each man for himself while the devil took the hindmost. The ecclesiastical landowners, who had previously relied on crown authority to back their manorial powers, were the most likely to see their assets stripped and their estates devalued.

It is impossible, therefore, to overemphasize the political significance of the aristocracy's intraclass solidarity. As William Shakespeare later wrote:

> O, when degree is shak'd,
> Which is the ladder of all high designs,
> The enterprise is sick! How could communities, . . .
> The primogenity and due of birth,
> Prerogative of age, crowns, sceptres, laurels,
> But by degree, stand in authentic place?
> Take but degree away, untune that string,
> And hark what discord follows! Each thing melts
> In mere oppugnancy.
>
> Troilus and Cressida, I, iii, 101–11

190. Christopher Dyer, Standards of Living in the Later Middle Ages (Cambridge, 1989), 47.
191. Gerald Harriss, "Political Society and the Growth of Government in Late Medieval England," Past and Present 138 (1993): 53–55. See also P. R. Coss, "The Formation of the English Gentry," Past and Present 147 (1995): 38–64.
192. Robert Brenner, "The Agrarian Roots of European Capitalism," Past and Present 97 (1982): 55.

Many individual members of the feudal nobility had been immensely enriched by the wars with France.[193] Seeing this lucrative source of revenue collapse as it could no longer be financed by poll taxes, the greater aristocrats found little alternative to attacking the architect of wartime failure: "Civil war was the retribution visited upon the medieval king whose foreign policy did not fix the gaze of his aristocratic feudal host on objectives which discharged the frictions generated by life and politics elsewhere than at home."[194] The monarchy's inability to lead his barons in war created dissension among the great magnates. Indeed, it was precisely for this reason that an under-mighty king like Richard II needed to fear his over-mighty subjects.[195]

By the the middle of the fifteenth century the feudal kingdom had disintegrated. This "war state" had first lost its territories in France and then settled into its long winter of discontent during the internecine Wars of the Roses. By focusing its energy on prizes and looting—the spoils of warfare in the Middle Ages—the nobility evaded the implications of its loss of power over its English tenants. Of course, it is equally true to say that by choosing warfare over estate administration the English ruling class was simply showing its true colors:

> it is hardly going too far to claim that engaging in warfare was one of
> the purposes for which feudal society existed. For a majority of the
> members of the military aristocracies that ruled the societies of western
> Europe, if not for all, war was what life was all about. How else were
> these armoured knights with their embattled residences to spend their
> time and money if not in exercising the skills which they had devoted
> so much thought and energy to developing and training?[196]

They were caught up in the contradiction of their social situation. Furthermore, and crucially, it is most probably the case that if the later medieval feudalists had prosecuted the social war against their tenants with the

193. K. B. McFarlane, "War and Society 1300–1600," in *England in the Fifteenth Century* (London, 1981), 143–49.

194. A. R. Bridbury, "The Hundred Years' War: Costs and Profits," in D. C. Coleman and A. H. John (eds.), *Trade, Government and Economy in Pre-Industrial England* (London, 1976), 85.

195. K. B. McFarlane, "The Wars of the Roses," in *England in the Fifteenth Century*, 238.

196. Bridbury, "Introduction," *The English Economy from Bede to the Reformation*, 41.

vigor, energy, and ruthlessness of their French campaigns, then villeinage might not have simply withered away.[197]

The real point, therefore, is not why the peasantry resisted feudalism but why the landlords were unable to maintain it—after all, flight had, for centuries, been the most common form of popular resistance to feudalism. While it is important to note the uneven nature of servile exploitation deriving from the class relations of feudal society, it is nonetheless crucial to keep in mind that "Of all the limitations upon freedom the denial of the right to move, to seek new farms, new employments, new lords, was the most fundamental. All other incidents of unfreedom can be interpreted as stemming from, or accessory to, the bringing of men to the soil and to their lords and the denial of free will."[198]

The decline in population resulting from the recurrent visitations of the plague thus should not be allowed to obscure the main point that if the seigneurial offensive had been successful—and it was in many other countries at this time—then feudalism would have persisted in England. The struggle against feudal exactions was enormously facilitated by the circumstances in which land became plentiful and labor scarce. But it only confuses the issue to insist that demographic decline undermined the feudal mode of extraction: falling population set the stage for this struggle, but it was not in itself sufficient to determine the outcome.

Dilatory rental payments blended with a threat to migrate so that prolonged refusals to meet "customary rents" were common.[199] The manorial court rolls of Hollywell-cum-Needingworth provides a useful index of resistance to labor services: 1288–1339, four per year; 1353–1403, fourteen per year. If we allow for the fact that the manorial population was probably halved, the number of acts of resistance rose ninefold. Of course, this count

197. The bald statements in this paragraph should be more nuanced to take account of the "great creativity" of the period in which Parliament developed a representative role, the council became a bureaucratic adjunct to royal governance, and mechanisms for taxation and expenditure were regularized, while the local justices and assizes were dovetailed in the jurisdiction of law, equity, and arbitration. See Harriss, "Political Society and the Growth of Government in Late Medieval England," 28–57.

198. John Hatcher, "English Serfdom and Villeinage: Towards a Reassessment," *Past and Present* 90 (1981): 30.

199. On this point regarding tenants' refusal (or inability) to make payments, see Ambrose Raftis, "Peasants and the Collapse of the Manorial Economy on Some Ramsey Abbey Estates," in Britnell and Hatcher (eds.), *Progress and Problems in Medieval England*, 191–206; for an interesting discussion of the widespread nature of this form of tenant resistance in mid-fifteenth century England, see Colin Richmond, "Landlord and Tenant: The Paston Evidence," in Kermode (ed.), *Enterprise and Individuality in Fifteenth-Century England*, 25–42.

considers only those tenants who had stayed around in conditions of increasing mobility.[200]

The response of manorial officers was muted. Their silence speaks volumes. They were happy to get anything from the tenantry. As one estate steward wrote in 1461, "The londe is so uot of tylthe that a-nedes any wol geve any thyng for it."[201] When manorial authorities decided to lease their demesnes and so reduce their dependence upon labor services, the keystone was removed from the seigneurial arch. In the demographic conditions following the Black Death, some peasant lineages died out, but many just vanished, as happened on the Norfolk manor of Forncett. Some of these migrants continued to pay the lord *chevage*, but most serfs simply disappeared into the local neighborhood. Those who left first were the ones holding land with the heaviest labor services attached. Lords who kept dossiers on their bondsmen living off the manor were increasingly impotent in exercising power over them. The most that they could do was to register their claims in the artificial memory of their court rolls. Economic opportunity slowly dissolved the remnants of the manorial empire of subjugation.[202]

On the bishop of Worcester's estates studied by Christopher Dyer, we can see the way that peasant resistance undermined the feudal system of "extra-economic compulsion." The bishop was a feudal landowner, and "the threat of a mass exodus" sufficiently frightened him (because of its danger to his estate) that his recourse to "unpopular exactions" (i.e., feudal rents) was curtailed. He had to be content with a depleted tenant population paying part of their rents, rather than having no tenants at all. Writing about this predicament on the Paston family's Norfolk estates, Colin Richmond notes: "so precious could a 'gret fermour' be that something close to pampering him might have to be recommended; such consideration for the tenant reveals how unusually, how uniquely disadvantaged

200. E. B. Dewindt, *Land and People in Holywell-cum-Needingworth: Structures of Tenure and Patterns of Social Organization in an East Midlands Village, 1252–1457* (Toronto, 1972), 268–69.

201. Richard Calle, steward of the Paston estate, quoted in Colin Richmond, *The Paston Family in the Fifteenth Century: The First Phase* (Cambridge, 1990), 25 n. 10. Richmond immediately goes on to make the point that "Land getting out of tilth brings us to the heart of the rent problem for landlords in a period when tenants could and did pick and choose: in the fifteenth century arable must very quickly have got out of tilth."

202. Frances G. Davenport, "The Decay of Villeinage in East Anglia," in E. M. Carus-Wilson (ed.), *Essays in Economic History*, vol. 2, 112–24; R. K. Field, "Migration in the Later Middle Ages: The Case of the Hampton Lovett Villeins," *Midland History* 8 (1983): 29–48.

mid-fifteenth century landowners were."[203] In a very real sense, then, the fourteenth century had seen a radical reversal in the terms of trade between labor and capital of such a magnitude that the whip hand of the feudal lord was restrained because he was lucky to even get a market rent for his property. Even then, collecting that market rent was by no means a sure thing because many tenants simply refused to pay. Landowners had to choose between demanding uncollectable rents or else letting their land go ·out of tilth. Demanding uncollectable rents was, therefore, rather like cutting off your nose to spite your face.

Gradually, not overnight, landlords had to adjust to the new reality in which they could no longer control their villeins through feudal methods of extra-economic compulsion. They lost control because their land, access to which was their ultimate economic sanction against the peasants, lost its value in a dramatic fashion and the villein could, as it were, substitute one lord for another at far better terms. In feudal England the peasantry had been effectively bound to the soil—"a villein was no villein save to his own lord"[204]—because the landlords had been supported by both a strong central police authority and the seigneurial control of *banal* justice. These factors vanished in the social turmoil of the Black Death, the Peasant's Revolt, and intraclass jostling that led to the agitation against Richard II and culminated in his dethronement in 1399 and his mysterious death a few months later while he was imprisoned.

A privileged glimpse into the complex forces at work is afforded by the court rolls of the Ramsey Abbey manor, which suggest a process working like a centrifuge to increase the separation of the village community into two distinctive polarities: on one hand, a solid core of customary tenants, who owed *ad opus* rents (labor services), were granted consolidated holdings, and dominated the administrative positions such as reeve, beadle, and plowman; and on the other hand, a transient group of tenants who were given smaller holdings, which were held at money rents *(ad censum)*. On this manor there was an apparent "increase of serfdom" among the village elite of yeoman families alongside an absolute decline in the total number of serfs who were connected to the manor.

The spread of *ad censum* market rents among the lesser peasantry indicates that its bonds to the feudal system were broken. The shortage of peasants to man the administration of the manorial regime meant that qualified villeins could negotiate with the manorial authorities for large,

203. Richmond, *The Paston Family,* 29.
204. L. C. Latham, "The Manor and the Village," in G. Barraclough (ed.), *Social Life in Early England* (London, 1960), 49.

compact farms, whereas the small tenants could bargain for individual parcels of land at money rents, freed from feudal obligations. The continuation of manorialism on the Ramsey Abbey lands after the Black Death depended upon the bargain struck between the owners of the land and the small group of villeins who could keep the system running.[205] That system was, however, a shadow of its former self.

It would be mistaken, however, to suggest that successful confrontation could be mediated only through the nexus of monetary payments. Mavis Mate's discussion of Cade's Rebellion (1450–51) illustrates that it is impossible to disentangle the strands of antiseigneurial discontent from political disenchantment and economic resistance. According to the legal documents the forces of order later used to settle the countryside, there was a strong element of leveling in mid-fifteenth century Sussex. Not only was the king said to be "a natell fool . . . [who] would ofte tymes hold a staff in his hands with a brid on the end playing therewith as a fooll and that another kyng must be ordeyned to rule the land," but there was also the more ominous claim that the rebels "wolde leve no gentilman alyve but such as thym [i.e., the rebels] list to have."[206]

In the midst of Cade's Rebellion, the tenants of Battle Abbey monastery refused to pay their feudal dues. This was the tip of a larger iceberg of insubordination that had united inhabitants in all parts of Sussex against the burden of seigneurial exactions. Disobedience affected not only serfs but also those who rented land from feudal landowners. In the two decades before Cade's Rebellion, on a large number of manors, local officials faced resistance to their expectation that tenants pay rent as well as provide customary services for carrying, plowing, weeding, reaping, and stacking at the will of the lord. Recalcitrance stemmed as much from their resentment of seigneurial control over their time as from the intrinsic burden of the services themselves. Many other serfs simply left the manorial economy without permission. In the context of widespread insubordination, then, the political events surrounding Cade's Rebellion were the visible culmination of two decades of persistent, but uncoordinated, resistance to the

205. J. A. Raftis, "The Structure of Commutation in a Fourteenth-Century Village," in T. A. Sandquist (ed.), *Essays in Medieval History* (Toronto, 1969), 289–90, 297–98.

206. Mavis Mate, "The Economic and Social Roots of Medieval Popular Rebellion: Sussex in 1450–1451," *Economic History Review*, 2d ser., 45 (1992): 661–76. For an analysis of conditions in a neighboring county which also stresses the role of wartime reverses, demobilization, and economic retrenchment, see J. N. Hare, "The Wiltshire Risings of 1450: Political and Economic Discontent in Mid-Fifteenth Century England," *Southern History* 4 (1982): 13–31.

seigneurial economy. As was the case during the Peasant's Revolt in 1381, the local context of resistance took on more serious overtones when it was imbricated within the national framework of humiliating defeats in France that characterized the end of of the Hundred Years' War.

One of Wat Tyler's programmatic aims in his meeting with young King Richard II at Mile End on June 14, 1381, had been to reduce all rent to a single payment of 4 pence. He had been killed for his temerity. Two or three generations later, landlords were only too willing to take what they could get. The political impotence of the bishop of Worcester, the monks of Battle Abbey, and even the archbishop of Canterbury[207] was evident in their deteriorating powers over their tenants. In Essex, for instance, "there remained an undercurrent of conflict between seigneurs and villagers, sometimes collective but more often individual, and by that very fact less likely to have left much trace in the records. It was an undercurrent in the process of being very slowly transformed from a more lord-villein to a more landlord-tenant pattern of confrontation."[208]

Christopher Dyer's findings on the fifteenth-century "rent strikes" on the bishop of Worcester's estates are germane precisely because they have led him to make the following point: "Collective refusals of recognitions, tallage, commuted labour services and similar dues, together with individual denials of servility and a general lack of respect for the demands of the manor court are valuable pointers towards peasant attitudes to [feudal elements in] rent." Interestingly, and of the very greatest importance, resistance to feudal elements in rent was coordinated, while resistance to "economic" rent on the land itself tended to be individual and sporadic.[209] The lord's ability to demand "non-economic" exactions from his tenants became a dead letter.

The feudal system was melting down "in mere oppugnancy." Lords' impotence in the face of this resistance points to the sufficient precondition for ending feudal landholding practices—a failure of will, resolve, and solidarity on the part of the feudal landlords. The old regime did not simply evaporate at a single point in time; rather, "Villeinage was never abolished; it withered away."[210] It withered away because the nature of the political

207. Mavis Mate, "Tenant Farming and Tenant Farmers: Sussex and Kent," in Miller (ed.), *The Agrarian History of England and Wales*, vol. 3, 1348–1500, 684–87.

208. Poos, *A Rural Society after the Black Death*, 252.

209. Christopher Dyer, "A Redistribution of Incomes in Fifteenth-Century England?," *Past and Present* 39 (1968): 20, 26. See also Christopher Dyer, *Lords and Peasants in a Changing Society* (Cambridge, 1980), 271–75.

210. Hilton, *The Decline of Serfdom*, 33.

struggle was its diffuseness as a result of the need for the same battle to be fought over and over again, in different localities, and against different landlords.

It would appear that landlords and their administrators were very well aware of the fact that the commutation of services for money payments gave the customary tenant a new kind of bargaining chip. It was thus crucial for landowners to distinguish freeholders' rights from those of copyholders who held their land as a disintegrating form of villein tenure. Estate administrators in the later Middle Ages were concerned to verify title to land, much of which had lost its characteristic "feudal tenure." For this reason there was gradual change in the terminology and nomenclature of landholding. It was a mutation in which elements of the old system were recombined into something quite new.[211]

Landowners were concerned to verify title so as to distinguish peasant occupation from peasant ownership. As a kind of quid pro quo, customary occupants gained substantial security in the land during their lifetime and that of their children. The land, which was not simply transformed into leasehold but remained copyhold, was kept from full peasant control because most of it was subject to discretionary entry fines. These "often appear to have provided the landlords with the lever they needed to dispose of customary peasant tenants, for in the long run fines could be substituted for competitive commercial rents." The upshot of this late medieval struggle paved the way to the future:

> With the peasants' failure to establish essentially freehold control over the land, the landlords were able to engross, consolidate and enclose, to create large farms and to lease them to capitalist tenants who could afford to make capitalist investments. This was the indispensable precondition for significant agrarian advance, since agricultural development was predicated upon significant inputs of capital, involving the introduction of new technologies and a larger scale of operation.[212]

---

211. Fryde and Fryde, "Peasant Rebellion and Peasant Discontent," 814–19. Allowing for his very different perspective on these matters, Raftis's analysis of the Abbey of Ramsey's manor of Warboys provides an excellent picture of this change; *Peasant Economic Development, passim.*

212. Robert Brenner, "Agrarian Class Structure and Economic Development in Pre-Industrial Europe," *Past and Present* 70 (1976): 62, 63. For two analyses which make much the same point—in rather different language—see B. M. S. Campbell, "A Fair Field Once Full of Folk: Agrarian Change in an Era of Population Decline, 1348–1500," *Agricultural History Review* 41 (1993): 60–70; and Dyer, "Were There Any Capitalists in Fifteenth-Century England," esp. 16 ff.

The feudal regime broke down over its inability to control the persons of the villeins. Yet, the landowners maintained discretionary control over their property, which would be, in the final analysis, of even greater importance to their survival, albeit in a metamorphosed condition.

The withering of feudal exactions was a process, not an event. One finds these extra-economic forms of domination, manifesting themselves vestigially, throughout the early modern period.[213] The significant fact is that they no longer controlled the respiration of the social structure but, rather, they were like foggy breath on a frosty morning—they proved that it still breathed life. Wat Tyler's call for peasant emancipation had not demanded the end of private property, although John Ball's millenarian vision had questioned its legitimacy. Both would have been keenly disappointed to learn that the bonds of feudalism were to be replaced with the thousand tiny chains shackling future generations to the cash nexus.

213. Thus, for example, Diarmid MacCulloch found evidence of "serfs" on 104 manors in twenty-one counties as late as 1560. But the customary naming of tenants as "serfs" is something less than the imposition of a whole, interrelated set of customary demands "at the will of the lord." Moreover, MacCulloch never tells us what proportion of tenants on each manor were labeled as "serfs." His evidence speaks to the last remnants of a dying world; "Bondmen under the Tudors," in C. Cross, D. Loades, and J. J. Scarisbrick (eds.), *Law and Government under the Tudors* (Cambridge, 1988), 91–111.

6   Recombinant Mutations

After the year 1000, during the first phase of early modernization, there had been a coincidental congealment of new state formations, new class relations, new modes of spatial and temporal organization, new technologies of power, new productive forces, new representations of the self, new demographic relations, and new family formations. What I have been describing is the operation of a positive feedback system in which the whole became rather more than the sum of its parts. It led to a "release of energy and creativity [that was] analogous to a process of nuclear fission."[1] Much of this energy resulted in extensive gains. I have also taken pains to indicate the intensive character of advance, pointing the way to a future wholly different from the human past in terms of mastery over the material world.

1.

The population density of Europe—especially the northwestern region—in 1300 was very substantially higher than it had been ten generations earlier, when the long cycle of growth began to take its first halting steps. Indeed, after the year 1000 the traditional social order of early modern Europe took shape as a complex, articulated network of towns, villages, and parishes. However much we want to draw attention to its organizational innovations, it is crucial to keep in mind the fact that early modern society, in common with its ancient predecessor, was based on an organic energy economy which created limits to growth. The division of social power developed on the model of a zero-sum game so that rapid population always

---

1. Peter Brown, "Society and the Supernatural: A Medieval Change," *Daedalus* 104 (1975): 134. For an appreciation of this specific point, see Anthony Black, *Guilds and Civil Society in European Political Thought* (London, 1984), 62.

pushed the marginal elements in the population downward. There were two ways in which this inexorable process of social descent could be forestalled: either colonization could extend the landed endowment, or subdivision and a more efficient division of labor could lead to higher productivity. Both of these strategies were deployed after the year 1000.

The massive energy generated by these forces was only partially encapsulated within the strong stem family presided over by the peasant patriarch. It is crucial to recognize that these centrifugal forces were socially creative. Not the least important aspect of this creative power was the nonlinear demographic response to marginalization and downward social mobility that continuously pushed the frontiers of material life outward—both quantitatively in the form of magnifying the land mass and qualitatively in terms of more intensive modes of production and exchange. The early modernization of material life was accompanied by three centuries of population growth and radical changes in economic life. This major reorganization of social life provided the essential context within which ten generations of Europeans would be born, marry, form families, and die.

The peasant family's reproduction provided the driving force of this expansion. At the heart of this process was the growth of the peasant labor force, which, freed from the institutional constraints of slavery and liberated from the ecological harness of late antiquity, reproduced itself vigorously. But rather than having recourse to the image of the unimodal peasant family, I have chosen to stress the contradictions emerging from the interplay between the patriarchal system's centripetal forces of upward wealth flows and the centrifugal forces of marginalization that involved all those who were not older, propertied males.

Although most of the population lived on the land, lateral growth was leaving its mark as a new infrastructure of economic life—cities, markets, roads, exchange networks, and production routines—developed. Social relations and cultural identities, too, were changing; perhaps the most remarkable aspect was in the creation of an infraculture of internalized discipline which had developed alongside the clerics' sedulous quest for uniformity. The Church's monopoly rights to moral legitimacy were not granted; they were won. Its claims were challenged whenever and wherever the clergy's own technologies of power were turned against them. The success of the Gregorian Reformation created its own contradictions, the foremost of which was the tension between the professional clergy's will to power and the laity's popular demand for moral legitimacy.

The pestilential fury unleashed by the Black Death created a different environment in which novel forms of social organization flourished. Its impact was like a determination event, which, in natural processes, brings about a change in a cell that would not show up in that cell's progeny until many generations later: like "all major economic, social, and . . . cultural changes determining the course of history" it was "obvious only to people living five centuries afterwards."[2]

The second phase of early modernization started in earnest in the new realms of freedom made possible by the Black Death. In every sense, the economic and cultural seeds of a new world order were germinating. Its growth was abetted by the demographic resurgence which began at this time, so that for every visible landmark in our traditional history there was a subterranean mass of human energy driving it outward. In the 1450s Hans Luder and Margaret Ziegler—he was a peasant's son and she was a small-town councillor's daughter—were born in provincial obscurity on the northeastern frontier of the Old Reich. Twenty or so years later, Hans and Margaret married and began their family in that same provincial obscurity. Their son, Martin Luther, would emerge from that provincial obscurity in 1517 to pull down Christendom's house of cards. Reading the experience of social history demands both a top-down and a bottom-up perspective.

2.

It is a moot point whether the release of energy and creativity after the year 1000 had played itself out around 1300, but it is clear that the evolutionary continuity of early modernization was stopped in its tracks—and redirected—by the Black Death. Recently, David Herlihy and Barbara Harvey have suggested that not only was late medieval society heading for a Malthusian disaster but also that, without the exogenous stimulus afforded by the Black Death, Europe's development may have been stalemated in a low-level equilibrium trap.[3] Thus, Harvey writes that

> left to its own devices, the early fourteenth-century economy would not have proved capable of fundamental long-term changes, comparable to those which actually took place in the very different circumstances created by the Black Death. *Such changes surely would have been impossible without a long-term and large-scale decline in population, going far beyond the decline which we glimpse in the first half of the century.* If, in the absence of plague, the positive check of rising mortal-

2. Robert Fossier (ed.), *The Cambridge Illustrated History of the Middle Ages,* vol. 3, *1250–1520* (Cambridge, 1987), 51.

3. For David Herlihy's posthumous view on this subject, see *The Black Death and the Transformation of the West* (Cambridge, Mass., 1997), esp. 38–39.

ity was not to bring about such a fall, the preventative check of falling fertility had to operate, and on a quite dramatic scale. But why should fertility have fallen on such a scale, if not to secure for those who practised the new restraint a higher standard of living than would otherwise have been available? This kind of economic ambition is precisely the vital ingredient of improvement that seems to have been, in general, absent from the agrarian base of society in the critical period.[4]

I disagree with this argument's demographic determinism, which smacks of Burke's suggestion, quoted in my opening remarks, that "The labouring people are only poor because they are numerous. Numbers in their nature imply poverty. In a fair distribution among a vast multitude, none can have much."

In the preceding chapters, we have seen that the vital ingredients for a transformation of the material world were at hand before 1300. To give a few examples, labor-intensive forms of agriculture based on nitrogen-fixing legumes were already being widely practiced; first- and second-class proteins were available to feed a lot more people—and to feed them better—than had been the case in the year 1000; the substitution of inanimate energy for human sweat and muscle power was well known and widely dispersed; new techniques were widely incorporated into building practices and production routines; marketing relations and commercialization had been both broadened and deepened in the ten generations living after the year 1000; and, finally, radically new techniques of state formation, business, and finance, allied to the spread of artificial memory, were commonplace.

I do not see why long-term economic and social change was unimaginable if the Black Death had not occurred. What is surely the issue here is that long-term economic and social change of the sort that occurred between 1350 and 1850 was only one option. It is misleading to be so transfixed by this model of development as to exclude all other options—alternative routes to modernization—from consideration. The stagnation in economy and society at the time of the Black Death was part and parcel of a short-term conjuncture, but this does not mean that that conjuncture was likely to remain a permanent state of affairs. Rather, if we rewind the tape of history and replay it again and again, there is little likelihood that the ensuing results will conform to the pattern we already know.[5]

4. Barbara F. Harvey, "Introduction: The 'Crisis' of the Early Fourteenth Century," in B. M. S. Campbell (ed.), *Before the Black Death: Studies in the "Crisis" of the Early Fourteenth Century* (Manchester, 1991), 24 (my emphasis).

5. On this point regarding the role of contingency in evolutionary dynamics and replaying the tape of history, see Stephen Jay Gould, *Wonderful Life: The Burgess Shale and the Meaning of Life* (New York, 1989), *passim*.

The problem with Harvey's and Herlihy's demographic-driven argument is that it neglects the political economy of social change, as if there was nothing more to feudalism than tournaments and castles. But if we go down to the farm, as it were, then, as we have seen, the ability of English lords to demand—and to collect—extra-economic forms of rent from their tenants made it impossible for "economic ambition" to lodge itself in the culture of the village.[6] This is really the heart of the matter. As long as the richest segment of the peasantry was kept in thrall to the surplus-siphoning techniques of feudalism, economic growth and social change for the mass of the population were straitjacketed. Profits that could have been invested to enhance productivity were systematically and ruthlessly diverted into the lords' cash boxes. Furthermore, the potential for other kinds of growth was kept at bay simply because the growth of the above-subsistence portion of the rural population was throttled. This, of course, begs a significant question: how many rich peasants could be considered to be kulaks? The only source I have ever seen which directs attention to answering this question is the English 1436 land tax, which counted 14,000 households—40,000 people, or something less than 2 percent of the total population—who fit this description. Moreover, few were able to establish enduring "peasant dynasties"; most of these proto-yeomen, kulak families rose and fell in the space of a couple of generations.[7]

In this regard, the contrast that Harvey makes between the positive and preventive checks is a clever rhetorical argument, but it is essentially beside the main point at issue. It is based on her prior expectation that economic growth was not possible unless there was a fall in the overall size of population from its peak in the early fourteenth century. Again, to my way of thinking, this line of argument is not tenable. It is, in point of fact, controverted by both historical example and contemporary experience. In early industrializing England, between 1760 and 1850, there was a rising population and a decline in plebeian living standards at the same time that

6. This is not an issue solely for historians of England's fourteenth century. The French peasantry before the Revolution was subordinated in precisely this way. See David Parker, *Class and State in* Ancien Regime *France: The Road to Modernity* (London, 1996); John Markoff, *The Abolition of Feudalism: Peasants, Lords, and Legislators in the French Revolution* (University Park, Penn., 1996). In northeastern Europe, where the settlement of the frontier had initially been accompanied by relatively free forms of landholding, the labor shortages accompanying the Black Death led the lords to impose the second wave of feudalism.

7. Jim Bolton, " 'The World Upside Down': Plague as an Agent of Economic and Social Change," in W. M. Ormrod and P. G. Lindley (eds.), *The Black Death in England* (Stamford, 1996), 53.

there was a very significant absolute rise in the "middling sorts"—who were not practicing systematic fertility control before the second half of the nineteenth century—as well as a truly massive increase in the amounts of wealth that flowed upward to all those who were able to keep their heads above subsistence. This upward flow of wealth funded a spectacular broadening and deepening of the market.

Similarly, in much of today's developing world there is a massive increase in the absolute size of the middle classes, whose lifestyles are modern and Western, in contrast to the deepening poverty of the rest of the population.[8] This is not to say that the rise of the developing world's middle class is keeping pace with the overall rise of the population; rather, it is to point out that there was another side to the nonlinear equation I proffered earlier in describing the role of downward mobility in explaining the overall growth of the population after the year 1000. By 1300, there were as many as six times more people living in northwestern. Europe than ten generations earlier. These extra people were living in new ways, in new places. Lots of them were town-dwellers, but even more were freeholding peasants. By no means all these extra people were living above subsistence: their numbers increased in absolute terms over three centuries and, no doubt, swelled as the short-term conjuncture worsened in the two generations before 1348. Yet, in comparison to the conditions of the mass of the population in the year 1000, there had been a very substantial increase in diversity, disparity, and differentiation. The middling sorts of their day and age were not only economically ambitious but also upwardly mobile.

Some—most?—had their aspirations thwarted by the surplus-siphoning techniques of feudalism, although others were able to realize their ambitions because they lived beyond the reach of the empire of subjugation and expropriation.[9] Their existence makes it awkward to label the whole social

8. For twentieth-century Brazil, by way of an example, this same phenomenon of sociodemographic differentiation led H. E. Daly to suggest that a "Marxian-Malthusian" analysis of population processes and economic development is worthwhile considering; "A Marxian-Malthusian View of Poverty and Development," *Population Studies* 25 (1971): 25–38; "Marx and Malthus in North-east Brazil: A Note on the World's Largest Class Difference in Fertility and Its Recent Trends," *Population Studies* 39 (1985): 329–38.

9. Remember, in the conditions of the early fourteenth century, it was peasant patriarchs on feudal manors who were most likely to be working large tenancies, whereas freeholding was almost always associated with subdivision and morcellization. A few freeholders may have risen above subsistence, but institutional factors and, especially, divided patrimonies made it unlikely that such peasant dynasties could stay above subsistence for many generations. Centripetal forces led to entropy. Being "beyond the reach of the feudalists" was, of course, the primary rea-

formation as "feudal," but on the other hand, it will not do to overlook the centrality of feudal relations of production in generating the wealth that kept the rulers afloat while giving the rest of society its distinctive coloration. Indeed, the period after the year 1000 was "feudal" in the same way that the American South in 1860 was a "slaveholding" society. The point is not that all the population conformed to this typology but rather that the typology captures the overarching importance of feudalism in Europe 1000 years ago and slavery in the southern United States 150 years ago. The ambitions and mobility the middling sorts displayed were hardly reconciled with the dominant models alive in the social imagination.[10] Still, these ambitions and mobility alert us to the fact that another social paradigm was already at work long before 1348, living and growing in the interstices of the older one. Who would expect anything else? The very nature of historical experience is change and continuity; it is a recipe that works itself out in time.

3.

After the Black Death's recurrent visitations, the social world was irrevocably changed in much the same way that meteorite showers terminated the reign of the dinosaurs. In pushing our metaphor, I would like to argue that the Black Death was akin to a "biological die-off" in which an ecological space was cleared, enabling mutations to develop in relative freedom. In the wake of the massive dislocation occasioned by the Black Death, we can identify a series of social mutations that would synthesize old characteristics into new combinations.[11] In this way, continuities were recom-

son for urban denizens to organize themselves in communes and for those communes to negotiate "liberties"—town air made them free from the feudalists' surplus-siphoning grasp.

10. Georges Duby, *The Three Orders: Feudal Society Imagined* (Chicago, 1980), *passim*.

11. Looking farther afield, it is crucial to keep in mind that the plague pandemic took place across Eurasia. In China, the population was halved by 1393. William McNeill credits the plague epidemics with breaking the power of the Mongol dynasty; *Plagues and Peoples* (New York, 1976), 132–75. In the Middle East, one-third seem to have died during the first outbreak, and repeated occurrences set in motion a long-term decline which extended into the nineteenth century in Egypt. In the Mamluk Empire there was no recovery from the Black Death but rather continuous, cumulative losses. The population of Egypt, for example, dropped from a height of perhaps 8 million in the early fourteenth century to 2.6 million in the 1780s, while Cairo's population was halved, from its total of more than 500,000 in 1300 to about a quarter-million in the later eighteenth century; Michael Dols, "The General Mortality of the Black Death in the Mamluk Empire,"

bined in the process of social change by which early modern social formations evolved in a new dynamic. I would identify four principal themes:
first, the new realms of social and cultural freedom that presaged representative, democratic institutions; second, the intensified division of labor that
pushed against the technological boundaries of the pre-industrial world;
third, the massive growth in state structures which emerged together with
a revolution in military tactics and organization; and fourth, the extension
of European hegemony across the face of the earth, about which Carlo
Cipolla has written that "Religion supplied the pretext and gold the motive."[12] In every sense, the economic and cultural roots of a new world
order pivoted on the redirection of these processes of vertical integration,
internal colonization, and lateral expansion that were at the heart of the
second phase of early modernization.

The second cycle of early modernization began in the social wreckage
that followed the Black Death. In the aftermath of this social cataclysm the
helical strands of social life were recombined. What is of particular interest
to us is that the implications of the struggle for mastery taking place in
these new arenas had two completely unexpected results. First, the demise
of feudal controls removed the ceiling to upward social mobility within the
peasantry so that, in the future, differentiation occurred within the village
community itself by enhancing cultural distancing to give the normal divisions within the peasantry a wholly new dynamic of cultural distancing.[13] Second, not only was private life sacramentalized, but it also became
worthwhile in its own right. The devaluation of the family—in contrast to

---

in A. L. Udovitch, (ed.), *The Islamic Middle East, 700–1900* (Princeton, 1981),
397–428.

12. C. Cipolla, *Guns, Sails, and Empires* (New York, 1965), 136.

13. Social differentiation was not accompanied by cultural distancing in the
medieval village. As we have seen, most communities were polarized; nevertheless,
"Poor smallholders and richer peasants were, in spite of the differences in their incomes, still part of the same social group, with a similar style of life, and differed
from one to the other in the abundance rather than the quality of their possessions"; R. H. Hilton, *Bond Men Made Free* (London, 1973), 35. In most places, at
most times, the landless were numerous but not self-reproducing. For these reasons, moves into the proletariat usually took place in the course of a single lifetime,
while most "proletarian action consisted of efforts to retain or recapture individual
control over the means of production"—that is, they tried to re-establish themselves as peasant patriarchs, albeit on a limited scale; Charles Tilly, "Demographic
Origins of the European Proletariat," in David Levine (ed.), *Proletarianization and
Family History* (Orlando, 1984), 11. Thus there was no independent, class-based
plebeian culture opposed to that of the peasant patriarchy, although there was a significant age stratification which articulated some of the contradictions immanent in
this social formation.

the spiritual life—was reconsidered. This transformation marked a fundamental divergence from the traditions which early modern society had inherited from ancient Christianity. It was part and parcel of a massive change in public life that led away from the ancient model of male domination and toward a new vision that was inherently more democratic, if only because it was based on acquired, not inherited, characteristics.

The evolutionary dynamic of early modernization was transformed by the generations whose lives were dominated by the pestilential fury of the Black Death. The *Annales* school of social history has taught us to look at both the sea foam and the submarine drift to understand the contradictory tides of historical change. As is so often the case in the writing of history, we have had to step backward in order to move forward.

After-words

If you want a generalization I would have to say that the historian has got to be listening all the time. He should not set up a book or a research project with a totally clear sense of exactly what he is going to be able to do. The material has got to speak through him.[1]

It is a journey that requires unlimited curiosity, and endless search for detail that may at first seem trivial, and an appreciation of the strangeness of objects oddly assorted, picked up as it were off a vast rubbish heap, rather like a historian's visit to a still unfashionable, and totally unselfconscious *marché aux puces* before bric-à-brac became modish.[2]

1.

Historians usually read the past by working through to its documented remains. *At the Dawn of Modernity* is not a work of primary research that took place in the archival flea markets. Yet, it is important to keep in mind the obvious fact that, as Greg Dening has noted, "These relics of experience—always interpretations of the experience, never the experience itself—are all that there is of the Past. Historians never confront the Past,

---

1. "Interview with E. P. Thompson," *Radical History Review* 3 (1976): 15. No matter how much we might want to "listen," however, there are many times when we hear no more than the sounds of silence. Adequate documentation is often lacking; only empathy can fill this gap.
2. Richard Cobb, *Death in Paris* (Oxford, 1978), 37.

only the inscriptions that the Past has left. History is always interpretation of interpretation, always a reading of a given text."[3] In my case, the writings of other historians have been employed as if each was a residue of the past and not just a secondhand account of it. Making sense of the chaotic dynamic of past contingencies demands a vision that inevitably outstrips anyone's ability to consult historical sources. I have tried, therefore, to comply with Marc Bloch's advice and to "follow the smell of burning flesh" as one reference led me on to others.

As the historians' products have piled up in the barnyard of history, they seem to create a veritable biomass of local studies. The mass ferments, but it is rarely the professional historian who seeks to recycle this composted material and to draw upon the stored energy of these products to increase oxidization and thereby enhance the fertility of our historical understanding. Each historian's case study is written in the belief that it is a unique rendering. In contrast, historical sociologists seek to connect individual entities into an organized whole. When historians attempt to do this, their efforts are usually labeled *haute vulgarization*. There are few kudos—and many stinging darts—for the historian who wants to generalize.

In a general sort of way, I have followed the investigative methods of Bob Woodward and Carl Bernstein, who unraveled the Watergate cover-up. They took information to be substantiated when it was confirmed by two separate sources. Similarly, I took an article or book to be important when it was referenced by two independent authorities. Sometimes this drew me to a new library within the Toronto system, sometimes this led me to a new section of the main library, sometimes this led to a new journal whose back issues were ransacked for promising materials, and sometimes this led back to the main catalog to see if the author had published anything else. It was part serendipity, part experience, part intuition, and part persistence. In this way I found myself breaking into new intellectual networks within which the most important works were frequently cited.[4] A lot of this secondary material exists; I have recycled it in my account. *At the Dawn of Modernity* is very much my own idiosyncratic attempt at historical sociology, or maybe sociological history.

---

3. Greg Dening, *The Death of William Gooch: A History's Anthropology* (Honolulu, 1995), 54.

4. Many of these publications were not always accessible for me in Toronto; I could not have gone very far along this path without the cheerful assistance—and detached bemusement—of Isabelle Gibb, who responded to my mad requests by connecting me with the Inter-Library Loan system.

For the historical *bricoleur*, the bulging library shelves are tools—an archival *marché aux puces*—which it is "good to think with."[5] It is in this sense that I have engaged in intellectual tinkering, using handed-down materials. Obviously, I have not accepted what I have read uncritically. Indeed, I have also tried to "think with" them and, in so doing, I have recast them in my own way and for my own reasons. Leaving the comfortable pigeonhole of specialism is a risk. One treads warily into contested terrain. I may not always have been surefooted in following traditional scholarship, but I have confronted this work by asking questions that are relevant to my concerns and to the prosecution of my argument. When there have been gaps in basic knowledge, resulting from either a lack of primary research or a lack of primary evidence, I have not shrunk from advancing conjectures about other ways of considering the subject. Some of the authorities cited in the following pages might shrink from acknowledging the use to which their findings have been put, and specialists in the field may find the generalizations to be at worst tendentious or at best just wide enough of their mark to be frustrating.[6] But this is again inevitable because the intellectual coherence of the whole has been established at the expense of properly recognizing the intractability of some of its parts.

2.

Most historians would probably agree with Abbé Galiani (1773) that "The science of details is the only useful one."[7] But most of them would probably be rather less happy to agree that the meaning of this detail lies in its generalization. The nominalism of social history, with its penchant for the case study, is often paraded as a kind of neutral objectivity, whereas, in fact, it is often the product of a depoliticized vision of the relations between past and present. Here, yet again, I agree wholeheartedly with Edward Thompson, who wrote:

5. Claude Lévi-Strauss, *The Savage Mind* (Chicago, 1966), 16 ff.
6. Consider, here, the comments of Norman Hampson in his "Introduction" to Alexis de Tocqueville's *The Ancien Regime* (London, 1988) when he states that "Concern for accuracy is a very proper preoccupation of the historian. When he neglects it he becomes a mere propagandist, a peddler of quack medicines. *But there is more to truth than the avoidance of error, and accuracy alone never made great history*" (xvi–xvii, my emphasis). There is, I think, a lot of insight in these italicized words; sometimes, it seems to me, history is too important to be left to empirical historians, who too frequently want to empty their subject of its larger relevance in pursuing "accuracy."
7. Quoted in Steven L. Kaplan, *Bread, Politics and Political Economy in the Reign of Louis XV* (The Hague, 1976), 596.

The new social history is becoming a series of prints, snapshots, stasis upon stasis. As a gain is registered, in the new dimension of social history, at the same time whole territories of established economic and political history are evacuated. The central concern of history, as a relevant humane study—to generalize and integrate and to attain a comprehension of the full social and cultural process—becomes lost.[8]

Clio is a demanding muse. Those who pay scant heed to the discipline of context, taking no cognizance of the contingency of that context and separating structure and process, find themselves in the dark when the owl of Minerva spreads its wings with the falling dusk. When we paint the past "gray in gray, then has a shape of life grown old."[9] Emmanuel Le Roy Ladurie makes a similar point while distancing himself from that kind of Hegelianism that makes "sacred what actually happened . . . [and declares] that whatever is real is rational and that whatever was the case necessarily was to be so from all eternity":

> that is not to say that social experience can be confined to a lineal schemata that would petrify living history nor must it be corseted within a rigourous unfolding of a single sequence, privileged in relation to others. For it would be absurd in the case of events and not structures to evacuate the force of contingency.[10]

In his jewel-like meditation upon *History's Anthropology*, Greg Dening seeks to show us that not only was the impact of Natives upon Strangers, and vice versa, profoundly contingent but so, too, is our recuperation of it. Let me quote him at some length:

> It is the irony of our History that we see what they could never see, the consequences of every accident and option that drove them to their meeting. For us even chance makes sense because it evolved into something that happened in a particular way at a particular time. And while we cannot count the structural conditions of culture and society that limit the play of chance, we make sense of personality, of class, of mythic perceptions and weave our understanding of their inevitability to our hindsighted sureness that something happened very particularly. By that we have a story. By that we have a History.
>
> . . . .

8. E. P. Thompson, quoted in Bryan D. Palmer, *E. P. Thompson: Objections and Oppositions* (London, 1994), 95. In the two decades since these words were written there has been a scholarly stampede away from generalization.

9. G. W. F. Hegel, *Philosophy of Right*, trans. T. M. Knox (Oxford, 1942), 12–13.

10. Emmanuel Le Roy Ladurie, *The French Peasantry 1450–1660* (Berkeley and Los Angeles, 1987), 398.

I want to say that since the only Past that remains is an after-medi-tation, the structures we see are always History, always meanings made. We never have the assurance that these meanings were predictive deter-minants of events still to come. We only have interpretation of what has gone before. But we know that these constructed meanings belong to public systems and, because of that, are out of time. They wrap particular events around.

. . . .

The true privilege of all histories, disciplined and undisciplined, is that they each offer a liminal moment. They offer a "retreat." In-be-tween Past and Present, in-between simulation and intervention, in-be-tween conserving and creating, histories are always metonymies of cul-ture in process. In histories we know ourselves as limited by our given experience and liberated by our contrivance. Ultimately, I think that is History's Anthropology.[11]

Social historians navigate between the Scylla of teleology and the Charyb-dis of historicism by keeping a clear eye on the rigors of chronological or-ganization. The cunning of history uneasily conforms to the statistician's model. The great mystery of human destinies is an essential objective to keep in our mind's eye if we are not to resign ourselves to prosaic descrip-tion of a disembodied, mutilated, incomplete, and artificial society, a mere caricature of its complexity.[12] So, it might be instructive to contrast the his-torian's narrative with the social-scientific mode of explanation in which experience is chopped up into little parts and each one is considered in its own right. To be sure, something is gained in precision, but much more is lost as complexity (or what social statisticians like to call intercollinearity) is reduced to a series of disconnected parts. Or, as Talleyrand quipped: "if we go on explaining, we shall cease to understand one another."

For the historian, it is the very act of connection that sets the parts in motion—an act of connection that takes place in time and space. For this reason, above all, when something happens and how it happens and in what context it happens are central in explaining what has happened in a way that is not prejudicial to the seamlessness of historical experience. There is, thus, a very deep methodological gulf between the method of ex-planation employed by the social statistician and that of the historian. Fer-nand Braudel made this point rather uncharitably when he wrote that "So-ciologists and economists in the past and anthropologists today have

11. Dening, *The Death of William Gooch*, 146, 147, 158.
12. Louis Chevalier, *Labouring Classes and Dangerous Classes in Paris during the First Half of the Nineteenth Century* (London, 1973), 40–41.

unfortunately accustomed us to their almost total indifference to history. It does of course simplify their task."[13]

The relationship between production and reproduction must be considered in reciprocal terms: social formations and state formations reproduce themselves in family formations, and vice versa. Cultural norms and material forces are thus in constant tension; innovations in the organization of reproduction pivot on the changing relations of production, which influence not only social classes but also men and women, as individuals and members of families. Because most people live their lives within families—as well as within states, markets, and communities—the chronology of demographic change needs to be understood as determined by changing relationships within families as well as between families and other, more public institutions.

The social historian, therefore, locates events and processes in context. This is not an unfair description of my goals of historicizing demography and making that historicized demography serve the purposes of historical narrative. Changes in population composition and vital rates have been used to identify pivotal transformations in social life. But these experiences can be understood only by placing them in context and by finding nondemographic explanations for them. While they may consider the same issues to be problematic, social scientists privilege persuasive simplification while historians are attracted to elegant complexities. This difference pivots on divergent understandings of causality in historical time. It is perhaps germane to quote E. P. Thompson once again:

> History is not a factory for the manufacture of Grand Theory, like some Concorde of the global air; nor is it an assembly-line for the production of midget theories of the state. Nor yet is it some gigantic experimental station in which theory of foreign manufacture can be "applied," "tested," and "confirmed." That is not its business at all. Its business is to recover, to "explain" and to "understand" its object: real history. The theories which historians adduce are directed to this objective, within the terms of historical logic, and there is no necessary surgery which can transplant foreign theories, like unchanged organs, into other, static, conceptual logics, or *vice versa*. Our objective is historical

13. Fernand Braudel, *The Wheels of Commerce* (New York, 1982), 227. Braudel not only is uncharitable, but his statement is also rather dated, since one may not unreasonably claim that interdisciplinary study—particularly, the interchange between history and anthropology—is one of the striking features of contemporary historiography.

knowledge; our hypotheses are advanced to explain this particular social formation in the past, this particular sequence of causation.[14]

Indeed, historians dwell on complexity in order to understand the limits of
possibility within which undetermined outcomes were resolved by the
bargaining between social agents, social structures, and social processes
that were experienced as a continuum of individual product-moments.
Historians allow complexities to surface because they believe that linear or
monolithic interpretations impart a leaden inevitability that obscures the
ambiguities and ambivalences of those who chose their course of action
from a confusing set of alternatives and in so choosing came to make their
own history. How, then, do we hold both change and continuity—unity
and diversity—within a single field of vision? Perhaps the most satisfactory method of analyzing historical time derives from the concept of uneven development:

> To reduce . . . history to a series of "stages" or to the successive appear-
> ance of "categories" is to make it excessively mechanical, to the point of
> rendering it unrecognizable. But to eliminate from historical study any
> allusion to successive stages of economic organization and any refer-
> ence to the progressive appearance of these "categories" is to make it
> merely incomprehensible.[15]

By jettisoning a literal-minded belief in revolutionary change, we are led
to substitute a more complex evolutionary pattern of social development.
And, if we are going to jettison a literal-minded belief in revolutionary
change, then we should also abandon a similar understanding of customary
practices and traditional populations—they are not a giant primordial mass
or even "a huge force, but . . . inert and neutralized."[16] Social modernization leads to curious hybridizations in which modern features are found to
be combined unevenly with traditional ones.

How do these modern and traditional characteristics interact? The optic
provided by the concept of uneven development draws us back to the ways
that apparently unpredictable outcomes emerge from unstable systems,
which will themselves provide the starting points for further development:

---

14. E. P. Thompson, "The Poverty of Theory: Or an Orrery of Errors," in *The
Poverty of Theory and Other Essays* (London, 1978), 238–39.

15. Ernest Mandel, *Marxist Economic Theory* (London, 1962), I:91.

16. Fernand Braudel, *The Perspective of the World* (New York, 1984), 44. In the
earlier, companion volume in his series "Civilization and Capitalism 15th-18th
Centuries," Braudel speaks of the silent majorities in history as being "forces which
were enormous but inert"; *The Wheels of Commerce*, 404.

this sensitivity of events to the details of their past cripples covering-law explanations of even modest temporal reach, [but] it imposes no real burden on narrative explanations. For if puny and unknowable details do in fact play an essential role in some particular history, narrative accounts can still describe and employ events and the effects of that detail even though the detail itself and its causal power is not recognized. As a causal explanation the resulting narrative would appear, from some ideal vantage, to be incomplete or incorrect. But at least it would remain parallel and in step with events that actually occurred.[17]

Michael Shermer has pushed this point a little further: "The actions of the individual elements of any historical sequence are generally postdictable but not specifically predictable." Furthermore, "A series of contingencies constructs necessities to produce a limited range of future possibilities. The more similar the contingent series, the more likely the distant necessities will resemble each other."[18] But we cannot chop up the past into so many small pieces that it will conform to our needs; rather, we need to explain historical change in terms of its own chronology.

The social-scientific mechanism of standardization is itself no more than a series of images which must be surveyed whole. Freeze-frames significantly enhance our visualization of moments in time, but those moments exist serially, in historical time. Or, as Thompson writes,

> In investigating history we are not flicking through a series of "stills," each of which shows us a moment of social time transfixed into a single eternal pose: for each one of these "stills" is not only a moment of being but also a moment of becoming: and even within each seemingly-static section there will be found contradictions and liaisons, dominant

17. George A. Reisch, "Chaos, History, and Narrative," *History and Theory* 30 (1991): 18. Reisch has been criticized by Paul A. Roth and Thomas A. Ryckman, "Chaos, Clio, and Scientistic Illusions of Understanding," *History and Theory* 34 (1995): 30–44, and defended by Michael Shermer, "Exorcising Laplace's Demon: Chaos and Antichaos, History and Metahistory," *History and Theory* 34 (1995): 59–83. In addition to these direct engagements with Reisch's 1991 article, I have also benefited from reading Charles Dyke, "Strange Attraction, Curious Liaison: Clio Meets Chaos," *Philosophical Forum* 21 (1990): 369–92; and Donald McCloskey, "History, Differential Equations, and the Problem of Narration," *History and Theory* 30 (1991): 21–36. For a fascinating and informative introduction to the ways in which some scientists have begun to deal with contingency in physical and biological systems, see James Gleicke, *Chaos: Making a New Science* (New York, 1987). While I find all these writings refreshing and challenging, they do not—in the end—go very far toward resolving the kinds of empirical issues on which writing history actually turns. They are rather better to think "about" than to think "with."

18. Shermer, "Exorcising Laplace's Demon," 71, 63.

and subordinate elements, declining or ascending energies. Any historical moment is both a result of prior process and an index towards the
direction of its future flow.[19]

For the social historian, the issue is not the hierarchical ordering of relationships but, rather, their concatenation.

A historically contingent blend of multiple levels of decision making is
akin to Anthony Giddens's double hermeneutic, which encompasses both
structural change and subjective agency.

> Sociology, unlike natural sciences, stands in a subject-subject relation
> to its field of study, not a subject-object relation; it deals with a pre-
> interpreted world, in which the meanings developed by active subjects
> actually enter into the actual constitution or production of that world.[20]

It is in the process of reproduction that history transforms order and is itself reordered. We can connect the aggregate and the individual by reference to Giddens's concept of "reflexive monitoring" in which "agency and
structure *presuppose one another.*"[21] Marshall Sahlins has written that

> The great challenge to an historical anthropology is not merely to
> know how events are ordered by culture, but how, in the process, the
> culture is reordered. How does the reproduction of a structure become
> its transformation?[22]

Similarly, Pierre Bourdieu writes:

> What we need . . . is a form of structural history that is rarely prac-
> ticed, which finds in each successive state of the structure under exami-
> nation both the product of previous struggles to maintain or to trans-
> form this structure and the principle, via the contradictions, the
> tensions, and the relations of force which constitute it, of subsequent
> transformations.[23]

19. Thompson, "The Poverty of Theory," 239.
20. Anthony Giddens, *New Rules of Sociological Method: A Positive Critique
of Interpretive Sociologies* (London, 1976), 146. See also *Central Problems in Social Theory: Action, Structure and Contradiction in Social Analysis* (Berkeley and
Los Angeles, 1979); *A Contemporary Critique of Historical Materialism* (London,
1981); and *The Constitution of Society: Outline of the Theory of Structuration*
(Berkeley and Los Angeles, 1984). I have also benefited from reading Ivan Karp,
"Agency and Social Theory: A Review of Anthony Giddens," *American Ethnolo-
gist* 13 (1986): 131–37.
21. Giddens, *Central Problems in Social Theory,* 53.
22. Marshall Sahlins, *Historical Metaphors and Mythical Realities; Structure
in the Early History of the Sandwich Islands Kingdom,* ASAO Special Publication
no. 1 (Ann Arbor, 1981), 5.
23. Quoted in Loïc J. D. Wacquant, "Towards a Reflexive Sociology: A Work
Shop with Pierre Bourdieu," *Sociological Theory* 7 (1989): 37.

By rendering "the reproduction of a structure" problematic, Sahlins and Bourdieu emphasize another point made by Anthony Giddens: "the seed of change is present . . . in every act which contributes toward the reproduction of any 'ordered' form of social life."[24]

Models of historical change cannot be predicated on the simple reproduction of social systems; they must be flexible enough to comprehend both replication and mutation within the same frame of reference. Change and continuity are not rigid categories so much as interacting polarities in the same field of force. Thus we might extend the points concerning social reproduction made by Giddins, Sahlins, and Bourdieu as follows: Social transformation can be understood as a continuum of product-moments resulting from the constant recombination of the triple helix of historical forces—biological, cultural, and material. Moreover, the contingent nature of these evolutionary processes underscores the uneven tempo of change, its combined effects, and the spatial variations in social upheaval.[25]

24. Giddens, *New Rules of Sociological Method*, 102. Social actors are positioned within networks as well as by systems of power. This double location allows them strategic possibilities for adopting subject positions including those of reversal or refusal; Ann Game, *Undoing the Social: Towards a Deconstructive Sociology* (Toronto, 1991), 45.

25. The paradigmatic metaphor which has suggested itself to me in conceptualizing this book on the history of early modernization is drawn from molecular biology. The biological clock is attuned to its system of information coding, which proceeds through time as the story of continuous division and recombination—reproduction and mutation. Cell divisions recombine inherited characteristics, while mutations emerge on those rare occasions when this coding system goes amiss. The evolutionary process is unpredictable; many mutations are called, but few are chosen. The internal dynamic of molecular reproduction interacts with the variability of external circumstances to create the context in which mutations fight for success. Indeed, as W. G. Runciman writes:

> once it is all over, evolution from one type or mode of society to another will always be seen to have come about through a process initiated by a mutation or recombination of practices and consummated by the transformation of existing roles and institutions that the carriers of those practices have brought into effect. A process of this nature will not and cannot generate a unilinear evolutionary sequence from one type or mode to the next. . . . [T]he advantage conferred by a practice on its carriers in the competition for power . . . may initially be so slight as to be hardly perceptible. There is not in sociology, as there is in biology, any special problem about accounting for very rapid evolution from one variety to the next because of the enormously greater speed of cultural transmission. . . . But this does not mean that the less favoured are bound to become extinct. On the contrary, . . . there should be cases of symbiotic equilibrium and . . . societies, like species, should sometimes find a niche in which they will reproduce their roles and institutions more or less unchanged for successive generations in the absence of outside interference.

("On the Tendency of Human Societies to Form Varieties," *Proceedings of the British Academy* 72 [1986]: 160, 163, 162.) For a somewhat different appreciation

Social change is both structured and contingent because ordered relationships take place within an unpredictable framework. At the beginning of this century, Henry Adams observed that "Chaos was the law of Nature; Order was the dream of man."[26] Indeed, Jean-Paul Sartre would later write that "History is not order. It is disorder: a rational disorder. At the very moment when it maintains order, i.e. structure, history is already on the way to undoing it."[27]

In a competitive social world there is a constant tension between customary traditions and the advantages gained from experimentation. Addressing these contradictions creates novel demands, and resolving them yields unexpected results. Yesterday's experience is only sometimes the guide for today's problems or tomorrow's solutions. Therefore, we should not be surprised to discover that the character of social change was uneven because development resulted from the unexpected recombination of inherited characteristics. The same set of social forces does not necessarily produce the same set of responses because historical conjunctures are profoundly differentiated due to their sensitivity to initial conditions. The precise impact between individual motivation and social determination is necessarily unpredictable and unique, so that timing is central to any historical description.

3.

In writing history, the multiplex processes of the past must be condensed, compressed, and simplified in the service of making them meaningful to the present. This produces an awkward writing against the grain of the historical narrative. In coming to terms with this dilemma I have had to develop a method of presentation which combines both structures and narrative in a single field of vision. In doing so it has seemed to me that the overall execution of the argument has proceeded in a way that is reminiscent of a CAT scan, recursively slicing through a body to provide a series of images which, when viewed together, provide a representation.

In thinking about the manner in which I have organized this text, another analogy has suggested itself to me: *cloisonism*. This artistic style characterized the work of Vincent van Gogh, Paul Gauguin, Anquetin,

---

of value in appropriating evolutionary models for social analysis, see Amartya Sen, "On the Darwinian View of Progress," *London Review of Books* 14 (November 5, 1992): 15–19.

26. Quoted in Shermer, "Exorcising Laplace's Demon," 62.

27. Jean-Paul Sartre; quoted in E. P. Thompson, "The Poverty of Theory," 230.

Henri-Marie-Raymond Toulouse-Lautrec, and others who rebelled against contemporary academic precepts but were unattracted to the pointillism of Georges Seurat. Indeed, what held this diverse group together was the magnetic attraction of color contrasts. *Cloisonism* was itself derived from a type of inlaid enamel work which had been widely used in Byzantine and medieval forms of religious art, particularly stained-glass images. This style was characterized by fields of intense colors, strong figural outlines, and little, if any, modeling in the round.[28]

Another way of writing this history would have been to stop this process in order to identify some crucial moments and/or individuals who lived between the year 1000 and the Reformation that would lend narrative perspective to the constant, profound mutations that characterize historical development. These events and people would be the visible tips of the proverbial icebergs. We might look at them so as to provide the process of social change with a series of landmarks indicating the currents along which social evolution was coursing. But, to my way of thinking, merely listing privileged moments has a tendency to fragment our comprehension. It is very unusual for a single person's life or a particular event to refract the complexities of any historical moment.[29] Excessive concern with such lists are an act of violence done to the complexity of the whole. We have to simplify to comprehend, in much the same way that we have to organize our understanding to make it intelligible.

Understanding this point is essential not only for the Thompsonian project of rescuing disadvantaged people from "the enormous condescension of posterity" but also for situating them alongside their contemporaries—and apart from us. No two people experienced the past in the same way precisely because each and every person was the bearer of a particular, unique bundle of choices and constraints, yet these multiple trajectories were conditioned and experienced in relation to their location in history. In reassembling fragments into strong figural outlines, I have tried to avoid

28. Bogomila Welsh-Ovcharov, *Vincent van Gogh and the Birth of Cloisonism* (Toronto, 1981), 41–42. Is it not appropriate to suggest here that the infinite multiplicity of historical facts stands in comparison to pointillism in much the same way that problematizing the past by highlighting its contrasting elements is related to *cloisonism?*

29. That is not to say that historical writing needs to be emptied of the biographical element; rather, I would argue that such individualized modes of commentary and analysis should be employed with cautious selectivity. Furthermore, historical studies *without* any individuals or events lose a grip on the essential contingencies needed to be explained in studying the past. The historian's dilemma is to strike a balance between these two alternatives.

the sybil's call to construct a piecemeal processional in which the context of social relations is obscured. Harvest failures, plagues, wars, and technological change as well as demographic and social structures were all worked out in particular networks, in human relationships, both in public life and in private life, so that law, ownership, and power all inflected the direction of history.[30]

In practicing "historical cloisonism," I have highlighted historical forces which I consider to be most significant, even though individual parts have been subordinated to the coherence of the larger picture. In reference to the social history of early modernization, there were several key points on which I focused in the preceding chapters: the ordering of political and religio-magical power, which provided the lineages of early modernization; the shards of modernity that were visible in the deployment of new techniques of human organization; the social experience of living in the material world; the reproduction of feudalism (via marriage and family formation) and its many connections to the tissues of social life; and the negative feedbacks that were connected with the sociobiological implications of an epidemiological holocaust.

Understanding the biological, cultural, and material economies which took place at the dawn of modernity enables us to locate the world we are now making in the disintegation of the earlier worlds we have lost.

4.

When I began work on this book in the late 1980s I hoped to contribute to the contemporary debate on "family values." The remarkable modernization of the family became a matter of nineteenth-century convergence around a certain normative standard which had deep roots in European social history.[31] It was acknowledged by all even though it was interpreted in quite distinctive ways according to one's nationality, ethnicity, class, gender, and age. Today, the loss of that prescriptive unanimity is a matter of fact. Those who mourn that loss cannot forget the sentimental family.[32] The cost exacted by modern memory is that socially nostalgic conservatives have mistaken the appearance of the sentimental family for the con-

---

30. E. P. Thompson, *The Making of the English Working Class* (Harmondsworth, 1968), 223–24. The quotation in the first sentence of this paragraph is from page 12 of this magnificent book.

31. John Gillis, *A World of Their Own Making: Myth, Ritual, and the Quest for Family Values* (New York, 1996).

32. Stephanie Coontz, *The Way We Never Were: American Families and the Nostalgia Trap* (New York, 1992).

tinuity and contradictions of past realities. The modern sentimental family is now widely perceived to be in crisis. In the last generation, a period one might call the age of late modernity, we seem to be in the process of making a different social system in a global world, one whose ripples can be felt in the most personal organization of private experience. Even though both males and females regard the nuclear family as the sentimental site for parenting, one in four births now takes place out of wedlock. Single-parent households (usually headed by women) have become so prevalent that as many as one in two children may live apart from their fathers at some time in their lives. More marriages are now terminated by divorce than by death. These conditions have led one influential commentator to suggest that in contemporary societies "Basic conjugal and parental sentiments" are no longer being inculcated in "the young," who lack "inward self-regulation of conduct."[33]

In the world we have lost, pluralism was the product of uncontrollable demography abetted by the rigidity of social hierarchies; in the world we are making, by way of contrast, familial pluralism would appear to be the product of centrifugal forces of individualism which castigate the family as being both repressive and antisocial. Within these fields of forces, social experience is widely variable. We therefore encounter a continuum of individual product-moments resulting from contending historical forces—political, cultural, and biological. The divisions and recombinations of the family cell, after all, go on during each generation. Mutations are continuous, neither new nor special; their effects are visible in statistics of fertility as well as in the ongoing reconstruction of gender and the life-cycle which hinges on a sequence of age-graded roles and activities. Social modernization—even our own age of late modernity—is not a developmental terminal point but rather a stage which is now in the process of being superseded. All that is solid melts into air.

If, as Jean-Louis Flandrin suggests, the early modern state pivoted on the "government of families," and if, as Jacques Donzelot informs us, the modern state practices "government through the family," then it can be argued that in our contemporary world of late modernity we have been evolving toward another configuration—government in spite of the family.[34] While this late modern system is still in its early stages, one can dis-

---

33. Ronald Fletcher, *The Shaking of the Foundations, Family and Society* (London, 1988), 203.

34. Jean-Louis Flandrin, *Families in Former Times: Kinship, Household and Sexuality* (Cambridge, 1979), 118 ff; Jacques Donzelot, *The Policing of Families* (New York, 1979), 48 ff.

cern its advent in the way in which individuals are being freed from the constraints of the sentimental family. Instead of presenting a benign picture of this process, or a Whiggish view of historical change, I would emphasize that I regard acculturation and assimilation as a forcing house of change, a social discipline. Without a political economy of social change it is impossible to avoid the shallow and simplistic arguments in which the history of the family is inevitably boiled down to an *histoire sentimentale*. Sociological theorists misunderstand this process of historical change. They have only the faintest idea what it was and no concept how it had occurred, or the context in which it was occurring. In particular, their dichotomy between traditional and modern—that is before and after about 1870—serves to flatten the past and, thereby, to obscure the lineages of these revolutionary changes.

As a historian, I have been appalled by the lack of depth in these discussions. That lack of depth was appalling because, for a historian, it is difficult to believe in static Pasts as opposed to Presents which have the benefit of change. Social historians have a sense that the culture they study is both invention and prescription.[35] In the last two decades the history of the family has enjoyed a remarkable popularity, partly, I think, because of the titillation derived from seeing others as we see ourselves. So much of the writing in this field has been concerned with emotions and sentiments that one cannot help believing that the writers are themselves concerned about their own feelings—or, perhaps, about the "authenticity" of their own feelings.[36] Or, to consider this issue from a quite different point of view, we might refer to one of Karl Marx's mighty insights:

> Men [*sic*] make their own history, but they do not make it just as they
> please; they do not make it under circumstances chosen by themselves,
> but under circumstances directly encountered, given and transmitted
> from the past. The tradition of all dead generations weighs like a night-
> mare on the brain of the living. And just when they seem engaged in
> revolutionising themselves and things, in creating something that has
> never yet existed, precisely in such periods of revolutionary crisis they
> anxiously conjure up the spirits of the past to their service and borrow
> from them names, battle cries and costumes in order to present the new

35. Here I am paraphrasing Dening, *A History's Anthropology* (Honolulu, 1988), 94.

36. By "authenticity" I mean that sense of sentimental ambivalence—certainty/uncertainty—which is so brilliantly explicated in Susan Sontag's *On Photography* (New York, 1977).

scene of world history in this time-honored disguise and this borrowed language.[37]

This means that we must understand that the sentimental family has been like an immense cosmos into which we have all been born, and which has presented itself to us as the unalterable order of things in which we must live and die. Its hegemony forces the individual to conform to its prescriptive rules. But this manner of life, so well adapted to the exigencies of modern life, was selected and came to dominate all others only in recent history. It had to originate as a social process, not in isolated individuals. It became a way of life common to whole groups, gaining supremacy over and against an earlier world of alien forces. Or, rather, the sentimental family was alien and became naturalized only in the making of the modern world.[38]

Historians have studied the family as both structure and process. Its patterns have been analyzed in terms of demographic characteristics of both individuals and the married couple, residential arrangements in the household, and kinship relations reaching beyond the walls of the primary residence; the family's changing configuration over time—its process—has been examined in relation to both the centripetal pull of collective strategies and the centrifugal force exerted by individual interests, principally those of gender and age. In addition, the family has been studied as a prescriptive image which was regulated by the exercise of power that was generated for sustaining religious and political order. Finally, it has been recognized that individual identities were created within the orbit of family life. Disaggregating private life into separate parts may have a heuristic value, but these separate parts must be reconstituted to appreciate the family's capacity which enables it to mediate between individual lives and the experience of larger communities.[39]

37. Karl Marx, *The Eighteenth Brumaire of Louis Bonaparte*, in Lewis S. Feuer (ed.), *Marx and Engels: Basic Writings on Politics and Philosophy* (New York, 1959), 320.

38. Quite intentionally, the preceding sentences have been written in language borrowed from Max Weber, *The Protestant Ethic and the Spirit of Capitalism* (New York, 1968), 54–56.

39. Katherine Lynch, "The Family and the History of Public Life," *Journal of Interdisciplinary History* 24 (1994): 665–84. See also Lawrence Stone, "Family History in the 1980s," *Journal of Interdisciplinary History* 12 (1981): 51–87; Louise Tilly, "Women's History and Family History: Fruitful Collaboration or Missed Connection?," *Journal of Family History* 12 (1987): 303–5; and Tamara Hareven, "The History of the Family and the Complexity of Social Change," *American Historical Review* 96 (1991): 95–124.

Unfortunately, far too much writing on the organization of family life has been written in the grammar of the "borrowed language" of the sentimental family, which reached its apotheosis in the immediate postwar world. This image is now in tatters around us. A recent sociological discussion has estimated that there are as many as 200 different "family" arrangements recognized by contemporary Americans and Europeans.[40] Too much of our historical vision has reflected that "time-honored disguise," bereft of a foundation in the exigencies of daily life. It is not too much to say that if this image was first repeated tragically in the 1950s, it has since been repeated farcically in more recent times.

Again and again, in listening to the debate on family values and its regurgitated clichés, I had an eerie remembrance of Marcel Proust's thoughts of things past: "In theory, one is aware that the Earth revolves, but in practice one does not perceive it; the ground upon which one treads seems not to move, and one can live undisturbed. So it is with time in one's life."

So, instead of writing a snappy text called *Forget the Family*, I found myself being driven backward to locate the making of modernity at the advent of a previous millennium. I also moved away from writing a short history of the modern family, since the search for origins grew out of control and the manuscript became a rather longer—and quite different—story about the roots of the world we have made.

40. Jan Bernardes, "Do We Really Know What 'The Family' Is?," in P. Close and R. Collins (eds.), *Family and Economy in Modern Society* (London, 1985), 192–95.

Index

Designer: Nola Burger
Compositor: Impressions
Text: 10/13 Aldus
Display: Aldus
Printer: Haddon Craftsmen
Binder: Haddon Craftsmen